Praise Pages

From "Fade In" to "Fade Out", from "Action" to reaction, Bryan Stoller gives us a comprehensive understanding of the arts and sciences of making movies. Filmmaking For Dummies, 2nd Edition, is the smartest book I've read on the subject.

> — Peter Saphier, Producer of Scarface and executive at Paramount Pictures

Bryan is an extraordinary filmmaker. He writes, produces, directs, and is fearless in raising money for the projects he believes in. He is wise beyond his years and an independent force to be reckoned with.

> — George W. Perkins, Executive Producer of Desperate Housewives

Amazing . . . that's a one word description for Bryan Michael Stoller's book.

> — Diana Y. Holliday, aspiring filmmaker (Amazon review)

Filmmaking

FOR

DUMMIES®

2ND EDITION

by Bryan Michael Stoller

Foreword by Jerry Lewis

WILEY

Wiley Publishing, Inc.

Filmmaking For Dummies® 2nd Edition
Published by
Wiley Publishing, Inc.
111 River St.
Hoboken, NJ 07030-5774
www.wiley.com

WILEY

About the Author

Bryan Michael Stoller is an international-award-winning filmmaker who has produced, written, and directed over 80 productions that include short comedy films, half-hour television shows, music videos, commercials, and feature films. Bryan and his films have been featured on *Entertainment Tonight* and Access Hollywood, as well as in many newspapers and periodicals, including *The Los Angeles Times, Premiere Magazine, The Hollywood Reporter,* and *People Magazine*. The first edition of *Filmmaking For Dummies* was featured along with Bryan in interviews on *CNN, E! Entertainment, NBC Dateline*, and with Katie Couric.

Bryan's film career began at the early age of 10, when he hosted the network series *Film Fun* with his little sister Nancy on *The Canadian Broadcasting Corporation*. In 1981, Bryan moved to Los Angeles to attend the American Film Institute.

His comedy shorts entitled *Undershorts* have appeared on ABC's *Foul-Ups, Bleeps & Blunders* hosted by Don Rickles and Steve Lawrence, and NBC's *TV's Bloopers & Practical Jokes* with Dick Clark and Ed McMahon. Bryan's parody, *The Linda Blair Witch Project*, starring Linda Blair possessed by famous comedians, streamed on Steven Spielberg's *CountingDown.com* Web site. Bryan's *Light Years Away* trailer streamed on Spielberg's *OnTheLot.com* Web site.

Bryan's work has appeared on major U.S. networks including NBC, ABC, HBO, and DirecTV. His top-rated episode of George Romero's *Tales from the Darkside* continues to run as a late-night favorite in syndication. His films have screened at MIFED in Italy, the Cannes Film Festival in France, and the American Film Market in Santa Monica, California. His screenplays have also won acclaimed awards at the Burbank Film Festival and the Santa Clarita International Film Festival.

You can find Bryan's award-winning film *Undercover Angel,* which stars Yasmine Bleeth *(Baywatch, Nash Bridges),* Dean Winters (HBO's *OZ, 30 Rock*), James Earl Jones, Casey Kasem, and Emily Mae Young (of Welch's Juice commercials) at any Blockbuster video or Wal-Mart store. The film has aired on UPN, Lifetime, Showtime, Bravo, and PAX TV.

In his 2001 mockumentary *Hollywood Goes to Las Vegas* (winner of the Telly Award), Bryan's dream of meeting actress Sandra Bullock finally came true. The program includes appearances by Haley Joel Osment, Nicolas Cage, John Travolta, Chris Rock, Sylvester Stallone, and Academy Award-winner Russell Crowe. In various other productions, Bryan has also directed George Carlin, Howie Mandel, Gilbert Gottfried, Barbra Streisand, Drew Barrymore, Jerry Lewis, and Dan Aykroyd. Dolly Parton wrote and recorded four original songs for one of Bryan's films.

King of Pop Michael Jackson, after making an appearance in Bryan's feature film, *Miss Castaway & the Island Girls* (also known as *Silly Movie 2*) developed with Bryan the big-screen adaptation of Jennings Michael Burch's book *They Cage the Animals at Night*. Bryan wrote the screenplay for Mel Gibson's Icon Productions.

Bryan continues to teach filmmaking seminars for The Learning Annex in the United States, as well as the Summer Film Institute and Alan Morissette's "What Do I Do Now?" seminars in Canada. He also teaches film and screen-writing at various venues including the Screenwriting Expo in Los Angeles, and acting techniques at various industry schools in the Los Angeles area, including Action in Acting, APS, The Casting Break, and the Creative Actor's Alliance, as well as internationally in Canada's capitol for the Ottawa School of Speech and Drama.

For more information on Bryan, check out his official Web site at `brian michalstoller.com`.

Dedication

To my Mom, who claims the film credit "Producer of the Director" on all my movies. To my Dad (who played the ambassador in my movie *The Random Factor*) — I miss you. And to my dog, Little Bear, who can't wait to get a copy of this book — he'll just eat it up, literally.

Author's Acknowledgments

The undertaking of this book has been very much like that of producing a movie. And of course, like the production of a film, this book wouldn't have been possible without all the help and support of such wonderful individuals.

I'd like to thank again Natasha Graf, the acquisitions editor for the first edition of this book, for her kindness and understanding and for believing in me; and Alissa D. Schwipps, my original editor, who made the writing of this book such an enjoyable experience. I'd also like to thank Michael Lewis and Tracy Barr for their help with the second edition.

Additional thanks goes out to family and friends who were there for support and feedback, including my sisters, Nancy and Marlene, and my friends, Gary Bosloy, Russel Molot, Tim Peyton, Peter Emslie, Tina and Alan Fleishman, Noah Golden, and Kamilla Bjorlin. To my friends Frank Tyson and Michael Jackson — thank you for allowing me to spend some writing time up at Neverland Ranch. Thanks to Alan Samuels, Philip Silver, and Jeremy Grody for reviewing some of the technical aspects in the sound chapters; Gloria Everett for being a sounding board on the budget and scheduling chapters; Cara Shapiro for reviewing the accuracy of the chapter on distribution; and my attorney, Michael E. Morales. And last but not least, thanks to Robert Caspari for being a true friend and a genius in his own right, and for his expertise on the technical review of this book.

And a special thanks to Jerry Lewis. It shows that life *is* magical when one of your favorite actor/filmmakers writes a foreword to your book!

My Cine-cere thanks to you all.

Publisher's Acknowledgments

We're proud of this book; please send us your comments through our Dummies online registration form located at www.dummies.com/register/.

Some of the people who helped bring this book to market include the following:

Acquisitions, Editorial, and Media Development

Project Editor: Tracy L. Barr

(Previous Edition: Alissa D. Schwipps)

Acquisitions Editor: Michael Lewis

Assistant Editor: Erin Calligan Mooney

Technical Editor: Robert Caspari

Senior Editorial Manager: Jennifer Ehrlich

Editorial Supervisor and Reprint Editor: Carmen Krikorian

Editorial Assistant: Joe Niesen

Cover Photos: © Creatas Images

Cartoons: Rich Tennant (www.the5thwave.com)

Composition Services

Project Coordinator: Erin Smith

Layout and Graphics: Reuben W. Davis, Melissa K. Jester, S.D. Jumper, Christin Swinford

Special Art:

Proofreaders: Joni Heredia, Caitie Kelly

Indexer: Potomac Indexing, LLC

Publishing and Editorial for Consumer Dummies

    Diane Graves Steele, Vice President and Publisher, Consumer Dummies

    Kristin Ferguson-Wagstaffe, Product Development Director, Consumer Dummies

    Ensley Eikenburg, Associate Publisher, Travel

    Kelly Regan, Editorial Director, Travel

Publishing for Technology Dummies

    Andy Cummings, Vice President and Publisher, Dummies Technology/General User

Composition Services

    Gerry Fahey, Vice President of Production Services

    Debbie Stailey, Director of Composition Services

Contents at a Glance

Table of Contents

Foreword

. . . .

Gertrude Stein said, "A rose, is a rose, is a rose," and Jerry Lewis says, *Filmmaking For Dummies* is a kind of book, a kind of book, a kind of book that all new and old film students can learn from.

It's the brainchild of Bryan Michael Stoller, whose company is Stellar Entertainment, and from the looks of this book, he's consistent.

He began in Canada at the age of 10 and knew then that he had to do it all, and he does — writes, produces, directs, and keeps away from acting because that's Jack Nicholson country, and no one ever wants to be there.

I met Bryan on the set of a film I was making at the time called *Slapstick*. It should have been called *Helter Skelter*. . . . Never have so many been killed by one bad idea.

But this kid Bryan worked his little heart out filming behind-the-scenes footage of *Slapstick,* and if the studio had been smart, it would have released what he shot! We might have had a winner.

Although our meeting was over 20 years ago, I still recall watching one of his early films in my trailer dressing room between shots and I can remember how impressed I was. And I knew he was good. . . . And I am never wrong when *I'm jealous*. So read on, you fledglings, and see if his book can help you fly to stardom.

—Jerry Lewis
Actor, comedian, and author of *The Total Film-Maker*

Introduction

Welcome to the wonderful world of filmmaking. Whether you love the escape of watching movies or the excitement, challenge, and magic of making a film yourself, this book is an informative, entertaining guide to help you realize your dream. For the beginning filmmaker, this book is your primer and reference guide to making a movie. For the seasoned professional, it's a perfect refresher course (with many new ideas) before starting your next big flick.

This book is not only for the professional filmmaker, but for anyone interested in making a film, whether you're an actor, a factory worker, or an office employee, and whether you're unemployed, retired, or independently wealthy. This book will inspire you to reach for your filmmaking goals — and it will be a great adventure along the way! *Filmmaking For Dummies,* 2nd Edition, comes out of my filmmaking experiences — both my successes and my mistakes — and is bursting with helpful information and secret tips to assist you in making your own successful movie.

In 1987, I directed an episode of *Tales from the Darkside* entitled "The Bitterest Pill." The show was about a crazy inventor who created a pill that gave him total recall. The premise of the episode was that knowledge is power. A little innocent-looking pill allowed you to remember everything you ever saw, ever heard — right back to the day the doctor pulled you from the womb and slapped you on the behind! With *Filmmaking For Dummies,* 2nd Edition, you gain the knowledge and thus the power to be a filmmaker. Whether you're a great filmmaker depends on how you apply this knowledge. Like the pill in my *Tales from the Darkside* episode, this book gives you all the knowledge you need to get started (it's up to you to recall it) and is your prescription for filmmaking — so read it and call your distributor in the morning!

About This Book

I've written this book with over 30 years of hands-on experience (I started young and naïve at the age of 10), so I know everything I talk about in this book through trial and error. I can save you a lot of time, trouble, and money because I've been there before — this book helps make your first time on the set seem more like you've been there before, too.

This book contains valuable information on:

- Writing or finding a screenplay
- Raising financing for your film
- Budgeting and scheduling your movie
- Hiring the right actors and crew
- Choosing the right camera and medium (digital, video, or motion picture film)
- Planning, shooting, and directing your film
- Putting your movie together in the editing room
- Finding a distributor to get your film in front of an audience
- Entering (and maybe even winning) film festivals

The new age of filmmaking includes the advent of digital technology (including high definition), so throughout this book, all creative elements apply, whether you're shooting with film stock or with a camcorder that records onto either videotape or digital files. Technically, shooting on film or recording to videotape or digital files is different, as I address in each particular example — but you soon realize that the similarities beat out the differences.

Conventions Used in This Book

To help you pick out information from a page, I use the following conventions throughout the text to make elements consistent and easy to understand:

- Web addresses appear in a special font (like `www.bryanmichael stoller.com`), so you can easily pick them out.
- New terms appear in *italics* and are closely followed by an easy-to-understand definition. Movie titles and the names of TV shows also appear in italics.
- **Bold** highlights the action parts of numbered steps or keywords in bulleted lists.

What You're Not to Read

Everything in this book is worth reading: It's all interesting and relevant to filmmaking, but not all of it is essential. You can safely skip the following bits of information without missing any need-to-know information:

- ✔ Text with a Technical Stuff icon beside it goes into behind-the-scenes or technical aspects of a topic. While riveting to those who like the back story, this information isn't strictly necessary.

- ✔ Sidebars, which look like text enclosed in a shaded gray box, consist of information that's interesting to know but not necessarily critical to your understanding of the chapter or section topic. If you do stop to read a sidebar, you'll either gain something you'll appreciate or at the very least be entertained.

Foolish Assumptions

In writing this book, I made some assumptions about you:

- ✔ You have some knowledge of the Internet and have access to the Web sites I list. I direct you to some pretty nifty sites to get free downloads, special software deals, and fun stuff to look at. Keep in mind, however, that Web addresses can change or become obsolete, so be prepared to find a few that may lead to a black hole in cyberspace.

- ✔ You also like to watch movies and are interested in how they're made so that you can make some of your own.

- ✔ You may be a beginner with a consumer camcorder or a seasoned professional who wants to make an independent film.

- ✔ If you don't want to actually make movies, you're a film buff who wants to know what goes on behind the scenes.

This book can't possibly cover every aspect of running a camera and putting together a film. So if you don't know the difference between a camera's eyepiece and the lens, and which end to look through, pick up other books that are more specific to the technical aspects of filmmaking. You may also want to pick up other *For Dummies* books that complement this one, such as *Digital Video For Dummies,* by Keith Underdahl; *Screenwriting For Dummies,* by Laura Schellhardt; and *Breaking into Acting For Dummies,* by Larry Garrison and Wallace Wang (all published by Wiley). After you start making your own films, you may need to read these books: *Stress Management For Dummies* (Elkin) and *High Blood Pressure For Dummies* (Rubin).

How This Book Is Organized

This book is divided into six parts — from the screenplay, all the way to the distribution — and of course the ever popular Part of Tens. These six parts are each self-contained, so they help you understand the filmmaking experience regardless of what order you read them in. If you're more interested in finding material or writing a screenplay, Part I will be of interest to you. If you want to know more about distribution before you decide to make a film, then you'll want to look at Part V first.

Part 1: Filmmaking and Storytelling

This part introduces you to the world of filmmaking and the excitement behind it. You see all the different genres to choose from to help you decide which one works best for your movie. This part also helps guide you to the right material, whether a short story, a news article, a true biographical story, or a completed screenplay.

Part II: Gearing Up to Make Your Film

This part shows you where to find financing for your film so that you can schedule and budget accurately. The preproduction process also includes finding the perfect location for the setting of your film, and finding the perfect crew. You audition actors and choose performers who will bring life to the characters in your screenplay. While you're gearing up for the actual shoot, you're also organizing your ideas for your shots on paper in the form of sketched images called *storyboards*.

Part III: Ready to Roll: Starting Production on Your Film

In this part, I introduce you to the magical box that captures your story on film stock, videotape, or digital files — it's called the camera. In a non-technical style, I explain how the camera and lens work. You see how lighting is more a science than just pointing some lamps in a particular direction. Sound is an important element to your production, and after reading this part, you may notice your hearing has become more acute.

This part also helps you work with your actors to get the best and most believable performances in front of the camera. I also cover the multifaceted job of the director — from a technical and creative sense. Now with the new age of digital technology (including high definition), anyone with a camcorder can go out and make a modest movie (with virtually no budget).

Part IV: Finishing Your Film in Post

In this part, you discover the magic of non-linear editing and how you can even possibly salvage bad scenes and make them work in postproduction. With computer software and editing technology, you can turn your home computer into a powerful postproduction editing system — and affordably, too! In this part, you also begin working with a composer to set your film to music, enhancing the visuals with sound effects, and employing other post-production sound techniques that make your movie sound great. Special visual effects don't have to be expensive, and you see how you can do many effects with the camera without exploding your budget. This stage in production is also the time to thank everyone who worked on the production by giving them the appropriate recognition in the opening or ending credit roll of your film.

Part V: Finding a Distributor for Your Film

This part deals with one of the most important aspects of the filmmaking process because, without distribution, no one will ever see your masterpiece, and your investors will never make their investment back — or any chance of a profit. You may want to read this part first so that you're aware of the commercial elements your film needs in order to get a distributor who can sell it successfully in the domestic markets (the U.S. and Canada), as well as the international territories. Along with finding the right distributor, you may also want to enter your film in film festivals to try to garner some award attention. (Film festivals can help attract a distributor if you haven't found one at this point.)

Part VI: The Part of Tens

For Dummies books are famous for The Part of Tens. Here, I share ten great tips on how to find talent for your film, along with how to raise attention through proper publicizing after your movie is finished. I talk from experience about ten ways to save you time, trouble, and money — maybe even save your production. I also list the ten best magazines and periodicals to keep you informed on the entertainment industry and to help you find some great material for your film.

Icons Used in This Book

This book uses icons to bring attention to things that you may find helpful or important.

This icon shares tips that can save you a lot of time and trouble.

This icon is a friendly reminder of things that you don't want to forget about when making a film.

This icon reveals secrets you'll know only from reading this book. These secrets lead you to helpful filmmaking information not known by the masses. But don't tell anyone — it's a secret!

This icon makes you aware of things that can negatively impact your film, so be sure to heed the advice here.

Information that appears beside this icon is interesting, but nonessential. It shares filmmaking esoterica that, as a budding filmmaker or film buff, you'll find interesting but don't need to know. Consider these fun-but-skippable nuggets.

Where to Go from Here

Unlike watching a film from beginning to end, you can open this book in the middle and dive right in to making your film. *Filmmaking For Dummies*, 2nd Edition, is written in a non-linear format, meaning you can start anywhere and read what you want to know in the order you want to know it. This means that you can start on any chapter in this book and move around from chapter to chapter in no particular order — and still understand how to make a film. You can even read from back to front if you're so inclined.

Part I
Filmmaking and Storytelling

The 5th Wave   By Rich Tennant

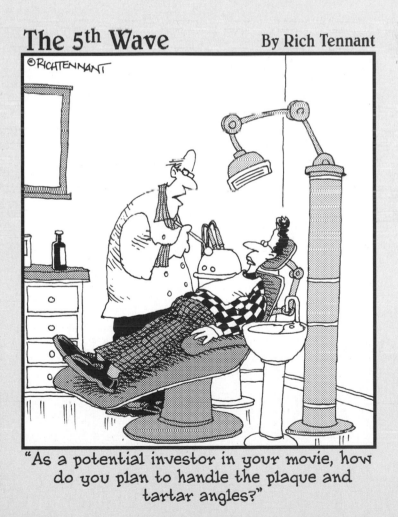

"As a potential investor in your movie, how do you plan to handle the plaque and tartar angles?"

In this part . . .

You're reading this book because either you want to be a movie mogul or you already are one. You've chosen an exciting career or hobby, and this part puts the world of filmmaking into perspective for you and sets you on track for a cinematic adventure.

In this part, I introduce you to the different film genres so you can decide what kind of story you want to share with an audience. I also guide you through a crash course on the process of writing an original screenplay — or finding a commercial script and getting the rights to produce it.

Chapter 1

So You Want to Be a Filmmaker

In This Chapter

▶ Recognizing how independent films differ from studio pictures

▶ Getting an overview of the filmmaking process

ilm is a powerful medium. With the right script under your arm and a staff of eager team players, you're about to begin an exciting ride. The single most important thing that goes into making a successful film is the passion to tell a story. And the best way to tell your stories is with pictures. Filmmaking is visual storytelling in the form of shots that make up scenes and scenes that eventually make up a complete film.

As a filmmaker, you have the power to affect people's emotions, make them see things differently, help them discover new ideas, or just create an escape for them. In a darkened theater, you have an audience's undivided attention. They're yours — entertain them, move them, make them laugh, make them cry. You can't find a more powerful medium to express yourself.

Independents Day versus the Hollywood Way

There are three types of full length films made to be distributed (hopefully) for a paying audience:

- ✔ **Studio films:** A studio film is usually green lit by the head of a major studio, has a healthy budget averaging $60 million and up (some go as high as $150 million or more), has major star names intended to guarantee some kind of box office success (as if such a guarantee were possible). Nowadays many studio films are based on comic book super-heroes (*Hulk, Batman, Spiderman*), popular TV shows (*Get Smart, Sex in the City*), best selling books (the *Harry Potter* series), high concept (unique ideas that have commercial appeal like *Jurassic Park*, or *Journey to the Center of the Earth*), and/or big name stars (*Brad Pitt, Tom Hanks,*

Angelina Jolie). If a major film studio puts up the money for a film, the studio — not the filmmaker — ultimately ends up calling the shots.

✔ **Independent films:** A true independent film is often a low-budget film (costing anywhere from $5,000 to $1 million) because the filmmaker has to raise money to make the film on his or her own, independent of a studio for the financing. Many films circulating the film-festival circuit are independent films, produced independently of the studios.

✔ **Independent studio films:** A studio's independent division is really a smaller "boutique" division of the big company, with smaller budgets and possibly fewer black suits deciding how to make and distribute the films that come from these divisions. *Sideways, Little Miss Sunshine,* and *Juno* are perfect examples of independent studio films — they were all distributed by Twentieth Century Fox' independent division, Fox Searchlight — but all received the exposure that a big studio picture expects, including studio marketing dollars when they are nominated during the major awards season.

The term "independent studio films" is actually oxymoronic because a film produced by a studio is not truly independent. A film made by a studio's "independent" division is a studio film, in disguise.

You can find both advantages and disadvantages to making a studio picture or an independent film. On an independent production, your film ends up on the screen the way you envisioned it, but you don't have much of a budget. A studio picture has larger financial backing and can afford to pay the astronomical salaries that actors demand, as well as pay for seamless special effects and longer shooting schedules, but the film ends up the way the studio envisions it — and in the most commercial way. The studio looks at dollars first and creativity second. Many independent filmmakers discover that, although having and making money is nice, being independent allows them to tell a story in the most creative way.

An independent film doesn't always have to be a low-budget or no-budget film, however. George Lucas is the ultimate independent filmmaker. He's independent of the studios and makes his own decisions on his films without the politics or red tape of a studio looking over his shoulder. *Star Wars* may not seem like an independent film, but that's exactly what it is — even though you may have difficulty seeing yourself as one of Lucas's peers.

Filmmaking: Traditional or Digital?

Today, you can shoot your movie in several different formats. You can choose *analog* video or *digital* video, high definition (HD) digital files, or a traditional film camera using super-8 or 16mm film, or — the choice of studio productions — 35mm motion-picture film stock.

The medium on which you set your story — whether it be actual film celluloid on which the images are developed, videotape, or digital (standard or high definition) with a film-style look — engender specific feelings and reactions from your audience. A movie shot on film stock tends to have a nostalgic feeling, like you're watching something that has already happened. Something shot on video elicits the feeling that it's happening right now — unfolding before your eyes, like the evening news. You can use this knowledge to enhance the emotional response your audience has to your film. Steven Spielberg, for example, made *Schindler's List* in black and white to help convey both the film as a past event and the dreariness of the era.

Traditional: Super-8, 16mm, or 35mm

Super-8 is an affordable introductory format for the beginning filmmaker, allowing the user to use celluloid film stock, develop it, and even physically cut it. Super-8 is half the width of 16mm, and less than $1/5$ the width of 35mm and thus is grainier and not a professional medium — unless you're going for this type of picture quality. Gritty music videos, documentaries, and home movies are suitable for Super-8.

16mm can produce adequate picture quality if your final product is going to television. If projected in a theater, 16mm produces a grainier image. Some TV shows like *Tales from the Darkside* were shot on 16mm; TV series like *Monk* (starring Tony Shalhoub) shoot on Super 16mm, a format that exposes a larger frame on existing 16mm film stock to create an even better image, with more detail and less grain.

The professional format of choice for most television shows and feature films is 35mm, which projects extremely well when blown up onto a theatre screen and exhibits pristine picture quality when transferred to the smaller television screen.

Going digital: Standard or high-def

In this age of digital technology, almost anyone with a computer and video camera can make a film. You can purchase (for around $2,600) or rent a 24-frame progressive digital camcorder (like the Panasonic AG-DVX-100B) that emulates the look of motion picture film, without incurring the cost of expensive film stock and an expensive motion-picture camera. For a little more money, you can shoot your movie using an HD (high definition) digital camera (like the Panasonic AG-HVX200, or Sony's PMW-EX1) that uses memory cards to store your footage.

If you can't afford one of these digital cameras, you can purchase computer software called Magic Bullet Frames (www.redgiantsoftware.com) that takes a harsh video image shot with an inexpensive home camcorder and transforms it to look more like it was shot with a motion-picture film camera. Many new computers come preloaded with free editing software. In Chapter 16, I give you tips on starting your very own digital-editing studio. You can also find out more information on the technical aspects of capturing digital footage to your computer, then editing and sharing your work in *Digital Video For Dummies* by Keith Underdahl (published by Wiley). You can uncover more camera information in Chapter 10.

High definition (HD) is the new-age technology that takes the camera image one step farther. The picture is much sharper, richer, and closer to what the human eye sees as opposed to what a standard definition (SD) video camera shows you. Watching HD is like looking through a window — the picture seems to breathe. The new HD digital cinema cameras combine HD technology with the 24-frame progressive technology to emulate a unique film-like picture quality in an electronic file format, without the use of physical film.

Developing Your Sense of Story

Because you can't possibly make a great film without having a great story, choosing the right material is more important than anything else. Great film careers have been built on making the right decisions about a story more than having the right talent and skills. So where do you find the good ideas to turn into films? An idea starts in your head like a tiny seed, and then it sprouts and begins to grow, eventually blossoming into an original screenplay. Don't have that tiny seed of an idea just yet?

Turn to Chapter 3, where I tell you how to find ideas and give you tips on turning your idea into a feature-length script. In that chapter, I also show you how to *option* (have temporary ownership of) existing material, whether it's someone's personal story or a published novel.

Financing Your Film: Where's the Money?

To get your film made, you have to have financing. Raising money isn't as difficult as it sounds if you have a great story and an organized business plan. You can find investors who are looking to put their money into a movie for the excitement of being involved with a film and/or the possibility of making a profit. Even friends and family are potential investors for your film — especially if your budget is in the low-numbers range.

In Chapter 5, I give you some great tips on how to find investors and how to put together a *prospectus* to attract them to fund your film. You also find out about other money-saving ideas like bartering and product placement. I even show you how to set up your own Web site to help raise awareness for your film, attract investors, and eventually serve as a promotional site for your completed film.

On a Budget: Scheduling Your Shoot

Budgeting your film is a delicate process. Often, you budget your film first (this is usually the case with independent low-budget films) by breaking down elements into categories, such as crew, props, equipment, and so on — the total amount you have to spend. Your costs are determined by how long you need to shoot your film (scheduling determines how many shoot days you have) because the length of your shoot tells you how long you need to have people on salary, how long you need to rent equipment and locations, and so on.

When you know you can only afford to pay salaries for a three-week shoot, you then have to schedule your film so that it can be shot in three weeks. You schedule your film's shoot by breaking down the script into separate elements (see Chapter 4) and deciding how many scenes and shots you can shoot each day, so that everything is completed in the three weeks you have to work with. An independent filmmaker doesn't usually have the luxury of scheduling the film first (breaking it down into how many days it will take to shoot) and then seeing how much it will cost.

Have a budget (and even a possible schedule) ready when you talk to a potential investor. It serves as ammunition to show that you didn't just draw a number out of a hat and that you did your homework and know where every dollar will go and to which category.

Planning Your Shoot, Shooting Your Plan

Planning your film includes envisioning your shots through *storyboarding,* the technique of sketching out rough diagrams of what your shots and angles will look like (see Chapter 9). You can storyboard your films even if you don't consider yourself an artist: Draw stick characters or use storyboard software, like Storyboard Quick (www.storyboardartist.com) or Frame Forge 3D (www.frameforge3d.com). Each comes with an eclectic cast of characters along with libraries of props and locations.

Surfing sites for filmmakers

Becoming a filmmaker includes plugging yourself into informative outlets that help you be more aware of the filmmaker's world. Here I list websites that may be helpful to you as a low-budget filmmaker:

✔ **The Internet Movie Database (www. imdb.com and www.imdbPro.com)** lists the credits of film and TV professionals and anyone who has made any type of mark in the entertainment industry. It's helpful for doing research or a background check on an actor, writer, or filmmaker. The difference between the two? Imdb.com is free, and imdbPro.com costs $12.95 but lists contact information and pertinent details not found on the free version.

✔ **The Independent Feature Project (www.ifp.org)** is an effective way to get connected right away to the world of independent filmmaking.

✔ **Storylink (www.storylink.com)** is a great site to network with other filmmakers and writers. You'll find discussion boards,

blogs, upcoming events, and profiles. It's jam-packed with great resources.

✔ **Film Independent (www.filminde pendent.org)** offers assistance to its members in helping get their movies made and seen. They also produce the Los Angeles Film Festival and the Independent Spirit Awards.

✔ **The Independent (www.aivf.org)** is an organization that supports independent filmmakers. At the Web site, you can find festival updates, along with what's happening in the Independent scene.

✔ **IndieTalk (www.indietalk.com)** is a discussion forum for filmmakers where you can post and read messages about screenwriting, finding distribution, financing, and lots of other topics. It's a great site for communicating with other independent filmmakers.

✔ **Hollywood Wiretap (www.hollywood wiretap.com)** offers up to the minute news on the Hollywood scene and the independent film world.

You also need to plan where you to shoot your film. You research where you're going to film much as you would plan a trip and then you make all the appropriate arrangements, like figuring out how you're going to get there and the type of accommodations, if your shoot is out of town. As you plan where to shoot your film, keep these points in mind (and head to Chapter 6 for more detailed information):

✔ You have to choose whether to film at a real location, on a sound stage, or in a virtual location that you conjure up inside your computer.

✔ Regardless of where you're shooting, you need to sign an agreement with the location owner to make sure you have it reserved for your shoot dates.

Hiring Your Cast and Crewing Up

Your film crew becomes your extended family (although maybe a dysfunctional one). You spend many days and nights together — through good and bad times — so hiring people who are passionate about your project and willing to put their all into it is important. You may have to defer salary to your crew if you're working on a tight budget. (Find out how to do that and more in Chapter 7.)

Acting is not as difficult as you may think. People are born natural actors and play many parts on the stage of life. Everyone is constantly in front of an audience — or performing monologues when alone. In Chapter 8, I lead you step by step through the process of finding a great cast to bring your screenplay to life. I also fill you in on acting secrets so that you can direct your actors and get the best performances.

Shooting in the Right Direction

Making a film requires special equipment, like *cranes* (tall apparatuses on which you place the camera for high shots), *dollies* (which are like giant skateboards that you put the camera on for movement), camera systems, and so on. It also involves lighting, sound, performances and more, all explained in the following sections.

Seeing the light

Lighting, which can set a mood and enhance the entire look of your film, is important. Without it, you'll leave your actors in the dark — literally.

The eye of the camera needs adequate light to "see" a proper image. What's adequate light? Whatever produces appropriate exposure for a film camera or gives enough light to get a proper light reading for a video or digital camera. Chapter 11 gives you the lowdown on lighting.

Lighting can be very powerful and can affect the mood and tone of every scene in your film. A great cinematographer combined with an efficient gaffer (see Chapter 7) will ensure that your film has a great look.

Being heard and scene

In addition to seeing your actors, you need to be able to hear them. This is where the art of sound comes in. You need to place microphones close enough to the actor to get a good sound recording, but not so close that the microphone creeps into the shot. The skill of recording great sound comes from the production sound mixer.

Production sound is extremely important because your actors must be heard correctly. Your sound mixer, who's primarily in charge of recording your actors dialogue on set, needs to know which microphones and sound-mixing equipment to use. Chapter 12 shares all the necessary details.

Actors taking your direction

If you're taking on the task of directing, you'll become a leader to your actors and crew. You'll need to know how to give your actors direction because it's the director's job to help the actors create believable performances that lure the audience into your story and make them care about your characters. Directing also involves guiding your actors to move effectively within the confines of the camera frame. Chapter 13 guides you in the right direction with some great secrets on how to warm up your actors and prepare them to give their best on the set.

Directing through the camera

In terms of telling your story visually, you'll need to understand a little about the camera (whether a film camera or a digital one). Much like driving a car, you don't need to understand how it works, but you need to know how to drive it (your cinematographer should be the expert with the camera and its internal operations).

Directing the camera requires some technical knowledge of how the camera works (film, video, or digital, including high definition) and what each lens and filter does, which I explain in Chapter 10. Chapter 14 addresses how to frame your shots and when to move the camera. In that chapter, you also discover the skills that make a successful director and how to run a smooth, organized set.

Cut It Out! Editing Your Film

During the editing phase, the film is finally assembled. Editing your film gives you a chance to step back and look at the sequence of events and all the available shot angles in order to shape and mold them into the most effective production. You can even repair a bad film (or at least make it better) during the editing process. During editing, you really see your film coming together.

Nonlinear editing software is now available for virtually any computer at affordable prices (many computers come with free editing software). With it, you can edit anything from a home movie to a professional theatrical-length piece (90 to 120 minutes). The technology of nonlinear editing allows you to cut your shots together in virtually any order. You can easily see different variations of cutting different shots together, rearrange them, and move or delete in between scenes in a concise and easy-to-understand manner. Chapter 15 tells you what the new-age digital technology makes available to you for editing your film on your desktop.

Listening to your film

Contrary to what most people think — that the sound they hear in the movie is the natural sound — the entire soundtrack must be built just as the visual elements of the film are built. At the editing stage, you add and create the audio, dialogue, sound effects, and music (Chapter 16 has the details). Titles and credits are important, too, and I discuss them in Chapter 18.

Simulating film with software

If you can't afford to shoot your movie on film or buy a digital 24 frame camera (standard or high definition), there are software programs that can make your video footage look more like film. These programs emulate grain, softness, subtle flutter, and so on. Magic Bullet Frames software, available at www.redgiantsoftware.com, can convert your harsh video footage and soften it to look like it was shot on film. The video-to-film software converts 30-frame video to a 24-frame pulldown, adding elements to create the illusion that your images were photographed on film as opposed to being shot on video.

The natural frame rate of video is equivalent to 30 frames per second (technically 29.97). Motion picture film operates at 24 frames or images per second. Converting video to mimic 24 frames (technically 23.97 in video) makes the image to look more film-like.

Gearing up for Cine Gear

Cine Gear is one of my favorite expos. Every June in Los Angeles, thousands of people flock to the outdoor Cine Gear expo to schmooze with fellow filmmakers, network, and see the latest developments in equipment technology (and in some cases, even experiment with the technology, hands-on). It's like a giant toy store for filmmakers. The expo runs for two days of exhibits and seminars, and you can get a free pass by pre-registering at the expo Web site (or pay $20 at the door). For information, go to www.cinegearexpo.com.

If you can't afford to shoot in high definition, Red Giant Software (www.red giantsoftware.com) makes a product called *Instant HD*. The software converts your standard definition image to look more like it was shot in high definition.

Distributing Your Film and Finding an Audience

The final, and probably most important, stage of making a film is distribution. Without the proper distribution, your film may sit on a shelf and never be experienced by an audience. Distribution can make the difference between your film making $10 (the ticket your mother buys) or $100 million at the box office. *The Blair Witch Project* may never have generated a dime if it hadn't been discovered at the Sundance Film Festival by a distributor. Even mediocre films have done well commercially because of successful distribution tactics. And great films have flopped at the box office because the distributor didn't carry out a successful distribution plan. Chapter 19 offers a slew of tips and secrets for finding a distributor.

Chapter 2

Genres in General

In This Chapter

▶ Finding your genres

▶ Fitting into categories

In the mood for a quiet romantic comedy or an action-packed adventure? Feel like a good scare with a suspense or horror movie? How about a sci-fi epic to take you to new worlds? Next time you walk into a video store, think about what genre interests you — not only to watch, but also what film genre you want to make. If you want to make people laugh and feel good, obviously a comedy is the way to go. If you want the audience to escape from everyday troubles and tribulations, a magical fantasy makes a great getaway. If you just want to excite your audience and take them on a whirlwind ride, then produce an action picture that plays like a never-ending roller coaster. Pick a genre that you enjoy watching, or combine genres as many films do.

In this chapter, I introduce you to the various film genres and tell you which ones are the most popular at the box office and which ones are best to avoid. Understanding the various genres and what characteristics make up each one helps you decide on the best story for you as a filmmaker to produce. I also introduce you to the *media categories* of filmmaking — commercials, music videos, shorts, industrials, documentaries, and feature-length films — and address the benefits of each. After all, not everyone can start out successfully by making feature films; these other categories give you a chance to get your feet wet before you make the leap to full-length features.

Exploring Film Genres

A *genre* is a category characterized by a particular style or form of content. In filmmaking, each genre has its own set of rules and characteristics. Commonly recognized genres include comedy, drama, horror, romance, action, and several others, all explained in the following sections.

Genres can be combined to create a variation in genres. A romance can be crossed with a comedy to become a romantic comedy, like *You've Got Mail.* A comedy crossed with a crime genre gives you *Who Framed Roger Rabbit* (combining animation techniques). *Minority Report,* which crosses multiple genre categories, is a science-fiction/suspense/thriller/crime drama.

The time period of your story is not a genre but a setting that can fit with virtually any genre. A *period piece* is a story set in the days of yesterday (a story set in the future is considered fantasy or science fiction). *Road to Perdition,* for example, is film noir but also a period piece. *The Green Mile* (in the fantasy, horror, and suspense genres) is a period piece, too, as is *Catch Me If You Can.* Unless you're doing a studio-financed picture with a healthy budget, avoid period pieces, period. They require special art direction, wardrobe, and props dealing with that specific time period.

John Truby, a prominent screenwriting consultant, developed a unique writers' software called Truby's Blockbuster. You can also purchase additional software packages for Blockbuster that guide you through specific tips and examples that help make up each separate genre (www.truby.com).

Making 'em laugh with comedy

Comedy can be dry humor, slapstick, or just plain silly fun. Comedy works with other genres, including romance, science fiction, fantasy, Western, and even drama. Many comedies branch out into a series of films based on the success of the original concept, such as *Airplane, The Naked Gun,* and the *Austin Powers* films. Here are some other comedies to laugh about:

- *Evan Almighty*
- *There's Something about Mary*
- *Wedding Crashers*
- *Scary Movie*

Scary Movie is a perfect example of a film *parody* — a subgenre that pokes fun at other movies. My parody film *Miss Cast Away & the Island Girls* (aka *Silly Movie 2*) crosses *Cast Away* with *Miss Congeniality* — what happens when a planeload of beauty contestants crash-land on a deserted island? Other popular parodies include *Loaded Weapon* (spoofing *Lethal Weapon* movies), *Meet the Spartans* (spoofing *300*), and many of Mel Brooks's movies including *Young Frankenstein* (parodying horror films) and *Blazing Saddles* (parodying Westerns).

Booking comic heroes

From the colorful pages of comic books, superheroes have claimed their own type of story. Not traditionally classified as a genre, the comic-book-hero film can be classified as an adaptation from comic book to film. These stories usually fall into the fantasy and science-fiction genres, and almost always the action genre as well. That's why the toy replicas you buy of your favorite superheroes are called *action figures. The Incredible Hulk* is classified as a science fiction character because the film explains how scientist Bruce Banner becomes the Hulk (as extraordinary as it may be). *Batman* is more of a fantasy because his history doesn't include a scientific explanation. Other popular comic-book heroes successfully pulled from the pages of comics and placed on the silver screen include *Spiderman, Superman, X-Men,* and *The Fantastic Four.*

Dark subject matter mixed with comedy is known as *black comedy.* A black comedy includes dark elements, combining pathos, pain, sickness, and death with comedic undertones. Often a black comedy has twisted humor in the characters and situations, as exemplified in films like *Fargo, Adaptation,* and *An American Werewolf in London.*

 Comedy is difficult for some filmmakers to conceptualize and comes naturally to others. Comedy requires proper structure, comedic timing, gimmicks, and unique setup and situations. Choose this genre only if comedy is something that is natural for you. You don't want the audience laughing *at* you; you want them laughing *with* you.

 If your film is a comedy, make sure that you set it up as one so the audience knows right away that it's okay to laugh. Don't wait until the film has rolled for five or ten minutes before introducing a comic gag or a humorous piece.

Getting dramatic about it

Drama is one of the broadest genres. A dramatic story has serious issues that usually deal with a character's struggle that could put him or her into a life-or-death situation. Drama is often combined with other genres: horror, crime, thriller, science fiction, Western, and even fantasy genres. Many dramas successfully include romance, such as *Titanic* and *A Beautiful Mind.* Examples of dramatic films include

- *The American President*
- *Gangs of New York*
- *There Will Be Blood*
- *Schindler's List*

Drama combined with comedy becomes a *dramedy*. Dramedy is different from black comedy in that it is much lighter, and the characters are more logical in their actions. The movie (and the TV show) *The Odd Couple* made for a great dramedy by contrasting two individuals with opposite personalities. *MASH* also made for a great dramedy with the underlying story of war combined with characters who kept their sense of humor to survive. *The Truman Show* and *Big* are other prime examples.

Even in times of tragedy, dramas need humor. No audience would sit through a drama and come out of the theater unscathed unless the film provided some comic relief. Audiences want that relief; they need to breathe between the tragic moments. The movie *Rainman* had a touch of comic relief in Dustin Hoffman's character, Raymond; the comic relief broke the tension at times when the story became too serious.

Horrifying horror films

Alfred Hitchcock pulled out all the stops in horror with his film *Psycho*. Steven Spielberg scared people out of the water for years with *Jaws*. M. Night Shamaylan successfully spooked audiences in *The Sixth Sense*. Audiences love being terrified and on the edge of their seats — in the safety of a movie theater. Horror uses the element of shock value that works by surprising the audience. When I was a kid, I hid under my little sister Nancy's bed and waited until she was tucked in for the night; then I jumped out and scared her — she was horrified. Here are a few titles that'll bring some chills to your bones:

- *The Exorcist*
- *Saw*
- *Scream*
- *The Shining*

A *slasher* film is a subcategory of the horror genre that often includes shots showing the killer's point of view, vulnerable teenage girls (usually virgins at the beginning of the picture who get murdered as soon as they lose their virginity), and very naïve victims. Slasher films also tend to be very graphic. *Friday the Thirteenth* and *Nightmare on Elm Street* are great examples of slasher films.

Horror films do well overseas, mainly because their graphic images translate visually in any language. Many domestic audiences like the sight of blood, too, as long as it's not their own.

Less is more when it comes to shooting horror films. The robot shark that kept breaking down during production of the film *Jaws* worked to Steven Spielberg's advantage, because the less we saw of the shark, the more suspenseful and frightening the threat became. If you want your horror film to be more effective, don't over-expose the villain.

Romancing the romantic

For the sensitive (myself included), a good romance makes for a great date movie and fills the bill when you're in the mood to be romanced. Romance stories focus on the love story and how it develops, regardless of whether it ends happily ever after or not. Romance mixes well with comedy, too, as in *When Harry Met Sally* and *My Big Fat Greek Wedding.* Others meld romance with fantasy to create fantasy romances, like *Ghost, Somewhere in Time,* and *The Princess Bride.* You'll be swept away by these titles:

- *An Affair to Remember*
- *The Bridges of Madison County*
- *Moonstruck*
- *Sleepless in Seattle*

There's always an audience for a good romance. If you cry at the movies when the guy finally gets the girl, that means you're sensitive, and a romance may be the perfect genre for you to undertake.

Getting physical: No talk and all action

Action movies like *Indiana Jones and the Kingdom of the Crystal Skull* are a treat for the eyes with the energy of a sporting event. With a good action picture, you can turn off the sound and enjoy the visuals without having to follow the dialogue. Audiences with a competitive nature enjoy action films with a lot of physical conflict. Action-packed examples include

- *Die Hard*
- *Bourne Identity*
- *Mission Impossible*
- *Speed*

Action does extremely well internationally. Everyone likes a good action piece, especially when it doesn't rely on a detailed story with heavy dialogue that can get lost in translation.

Shooting action scenes can be dangerous. Always have a trained stunt coordinator and a pyrotechnician on set if your film involves any explosions or gunfire.

Separating fact from (science) fiction

Audiences appreciate an escape and the opportunity to ask, "What if . . . ?" So science fiction has always been popular at the box office. If a film's subject stems from a scientific explanation (even if it's a rather fantastic explanation), it falls into this genre. Science fiction also includes interplanetary worlds with aliens and monsters and plays on the idea that we may not be alone in the universe. Here are some titles that are considered science fiction, even though you probably didn't study them in science class:

- *Close Encounters of the Third Kind*
- *Jurassic Park*
- *Men in Black*
- *Star Wars*

Science fiction stories can be very expensive to produce and are normally out of reach for a low-budget independent film. However, computer-generated creatures and effects are making it easier.

Indulging your fantasy

The fantasy genre combines fantasy worlds and magical elements that could never exist in today's world (this is what separates this genre from science fiction). Comic-book characters like Superman in the fictional city of Metropolis are part of the fantasy genre. For a fantastical adventure, take a look at these titles:

- *The Wizard of Oz*
- *Harry Potter: Order of the Phoenix*
- *The Chronicles of Narnia*
- *Lord of the Rings*

Although a fantasy story doesn't always require special effects — consider *It's a Wonderful Life,* which sets up a fantastical situation without visuals weighed down with special effects — making a film in the fantasy genre can be expensive if you have to create worlds that don't exist. Some effects (with some ingenuity) can be done inexpensively, as I show you in Chapter 17.

Go West, young man: Westerns

Westerns were popular years ago (they even ruled at the box office) but seem to have gone West over the years. Clint Eastwood can still make a Western that audiences will flock to see, though, and John Wayne Westerns will always be popular on TV, especially late at night and on rainy Sunday afternoons. Find a ghost town, some horses, and a couple of cowboy hats, grab a sarsaparilla, and you've got yourself a Western, like

- ✔ *The Good, the Bad, and the Ugly*
- ✔ *The Magnificent Seven*
- ✔ *Unforgiven*
- ✔ *The Wild Bunch*

A Western may be inexpensive to shoot if you have a couple of horses and a ghost town at your disposal, but Westerns aren't the most commercial of film genres today and are considered more of a risk. And for that reason, many distributors steer away from acquiring them.

Going to war

War movies have always been popular. It's the good team versus the bad team with lots of gunfire and explosions (which can be expensive for an independent filmmaker). War is a global theme; no matter what country or language, everyone can relate and get caught up in a good war movie. For this reason, war films do well internationally as well as at home.

War movies are categorized as action films in video stores. Mel Gibson's films *We Were Soldiers* and *Braveheart* are classified under the war/action genre. Here are some other films worth fighting for:

- ✔ *Apocalypse Now*
- ✔ *Saving Private Ryan*
- ✔ *Black Hawk Down*
- ✔ *Platoon*

War films seem to do better at the box office when the world isn't dealing with an actual war or with pending war issues. When there's talk of war, the studios tend to saturate the market, which makes the films less successful at the box office. Plus, these films come too close to reality; people dealing with war in the real world typically don't want to see more of it in the theater.

Thrilling audiences with suspense

Suspense thrillers keep you on the edge of your seat. A good suspense film is like a ball rolling downhill, picking up speed — the audience doesn't know where and when it's going to stop. Alfred Hitchcock was the master of suspense with such films as *North by Northwest*. Horror and crime films incorporate the suspense genre effectively as well. A suspense/thriller can also mix in science fiction, as in *Signs* and *Minority Report*. Other titles that'll keep you in suspense include

- *Fatal Attraction*
- *Rear Window*
- *The Fugitive*
- *Vertigo*

A good suspense thriller relies on a great script, not on special effects or even fast-paced action. This genre can be done on a low budget — you just need to intrigue your audience with a story that they'd love to see unfold.

Stealing the audience's attention: Crime pays

Audiences have always been intrigued by police dramas, detective tales, and mobster stories because an audience likes to piece the clues together and doesn't want to know all the answers right away. Many crime dramas fall into a subgenre known as *film noir* (which conjures up images of darkness and shadows in the 1940s, along with exaggerated high and low angles and often unique composition of shots to tell the story). The film *Dick Tracy* is a prime example of the crime genre and film noir. *Batman* (the series of theatrical films) is a science-fiction comic-book action story in the film-noir style. Other crime drama titles include

- *China Town*
- *The Godfather*
- *The Untouchables*
- *L.A. Confidential*

As an independent filmmaker on a limited budget avoid this genre, especially if it's a film-noir period piece. Crime genres usually contain visual elements — guns, explosions, expensive wardrobe, and blood effects (which ruin the expensive wardrobe) — that can contribute to a higher-cost production.

Making music with musicals

A musical film is like a real stage show combined with the magic of movie-making — without the intermission. Classic musicals include *The Sound of Music, My Fair Lady,* and *The Wizard of Oz* (which is also a great film in the family genre). Many of Disney's animated films, like *Beauty and the Beast,* are also considered musicals.

Musicals seem to be making a comeback, with *Moulin Rouge* and the Academy Award-winning *Chicago* earning high praise and doing well at the box office. Here are some other full length musicals that will have you shouting, "Bravo!":

- ✔ *Sweeney Todd: The Demon Barber of Fleet Street*
- ✔ *Grease*
- ✔ *Dreamgirls*
- ✔ *West Side Story*

A full-length musical film would be difficult and expensive for an independent film but could work more effectively as a short film (twenty minutes or less). A short three-minute musical film is what helped filmmaker Adam Stein move to the next round on the Steven Spielberg TV series, *On the Lot.*

Film soundtracks are big business. Sometimes the soundtrack does better financially than the film from which it came. Eminem broke records with his soundtrack from the film *8 Mile.* Selecting the right music for your film, including original songs, can make your film sing. Check out Chapter 16 for more information on movie music, songs, and soundtracks.

Kidding around: Family friendly films

A family picture often contains positive family values that both children and adults can enjoy. Family films encompass many genres, except for war, crime, and graphic horror. The *Harry Potter* films are classified as family entertainment but also fall into the fantasy genre. Jim Henson's Muppet films are examples of the family genre at its best. Other great movies to watch with your family include

- ✔ *Monsters, Inc.*
- ✔ *Ratatouille*
- ✔ *Enchanted*
- ✔ *The Wizard of Oz*

The family genre lends itself well to the technical category of animation (drawings, stop motion, or computer generated). Animation is a style that young people immediately accept as friendly, safe, and inviting.

Categorizing Your Genres

Your production not only is part of a particular genre or combination of genres, as explained in the preceding sections, but also falls under one of several media categories: feature film, documentary, short film, television program, TV commercial, and more. Read on for details of the different media categories.

Featuring films

Most filmmakers dream of making a feature film that will be projected in a movie theater to a captive audience. Getting your film into the theatres is much more difficult than getting your film onto DVD and TV. In addition to the actual cost to produce the picture, a major studio spends millions of dollars to get a movie into theatres. The costs include 35mm prints that have to be delivered to up to 3,000 theatres, along with the expense of advertising on television, radio, newspapers, and the Internet. Without a major advertising campaign, a theatrical film has a hard time recouping its picture cost plus the marketing and distribution expenses.

A major distributor such as Paramount Pictures or Warner Bros. tends to distribute big movies with big stars. A theatrically released picture often has to have an event feel to it to get the wide theatrical release, along with name stars that an audience is familiar with; otherwise, it's considered a risk, and few studios nowadays are willing to take that risk.

Animating animation

Animation is a technique that works with most genres (and combinations of genres), especially family films. Often, though, animation is more fitting for comedy or light humor. Fantasy and science fiction stories are also good candidates for animation, because drawing fantastic worlds or outer-space environments is easier (and cheaper) than creating them in a convincing setting. Filmmakers have the following animation techniques to choose from:

- **Traditional cel animation:** Individual drawings (up to 24 images for 24 frames a second — or 12 drawings shot two frames at a time) are inked onto clear acetate cels and photographed against painted backgrounds. Animated flipbooks use the same principles as cel animation. Disney's films in this style, from *Snow White and the Seven Dwarfs* to *The Lion King,* are popular examples of traditional cel animation.

- **Stop-motion animation:** Gumby, shown in the figure below, and Pokey are two of my favorite stop-motion characters. I started my filmmaking career emulating Gumby movies on super-8 film when I was 10 years old. *Tim Burton's Corpse Bride* and *Wallace*

& Gromit in *The Curse of the Were-rabbit* are stop-motion feature films that use three dimensional models often molded in clay and placed in miniature hand built sets. An animator moves the characters slightly into different positions between single frames taken by the motion-picture camera. Stop motion is a fairly inexpensive technique and a good way to learn about animation. An affordable and fun software program called *iStopMotion* lets you make your own stop motion films using your computer or digital camera (`www.iStopMotion.com`).

✔ **Computer animation:** Computer animation has become more the norm than the traditional three-dimensional stop-motion techniques used in the past years. Computer animation creates virtual three-dimensional characters in a digital environment. These images can then be articulated within the computer as if they were actual three-dimensional creations outside the computer. Successful computer-generated image (CGI) films include *Shrek, Toy Story, Ice Age, Beowulf, Ratatouille,* and *WALL-E*.

✔ **Flash animation:** Flash animation is a new technique that uses limited animation over the Internet. Flash animation has a staccato and sometimes jerky motion and uses simplified drawings with solid, clean lines and prime colors (as Dodo the bird, below, illustrates). It's an inexpensive and fun way to animate a short film and have it viewed by a large audience via the Internet.

courtesy Arthur Clokey

©Mr.Dodo, courtesy B.M.Stoller

The hardest thing about making a feature film is that it has to be feature-film length (meaning at least 90 minutes long), and you may not have enough money to pull it off, especially if you hope to shoot on 35mm film. You have to afford raw film stock and lab costs, which include developing, color timing, along with a negative cutter, and answer print (see Chapter 15). Also be prepared to spend a lot more time making a feature film than you would if you were making a TV commercial, short film, or documentary.

If you're planning on theatrical distribution for your film (see Chapter 19), you may want to shoot on 16mm or 35mm motion-picture stock. You can also shoot your film with the new 24p digital HD cameras, but you'll have to blow up the footage to a 35mm print later, which can be quite expensive.

Made-for-TV movie

A made-for-TV movie is a cross between a feature film and a television production. It is usually shot on a tight television schedule (two to three weeks, as opposed to a feature schedule of several weeks to several months) and casts recognized television names from popular TV series, as opposed to big screen actors. Budgets are much smaller and on scale with a TV series budget (between $1.5 and $3 million).

A made-for-TV movie is often developed in-house by the TV networks, and hiring is usually internal, using producers, directors, and crew that have worked with the network before. Sometimes, though, an independent film can find its way onto a network schedule — I was fortunate to license my independent film *Undercover Angel* starring Yasmine Bleeth, James Earl Jones, Dean Winters, Casey Kasem and Emily Mae Young to Lifetime Television, PAX, UPN and The Bravo Channel — but this is becoming less common.

Documenting documentaries

Documentaries feature actual people and events, as opposed to the fictional characters and stories used in feature filmmaking. In rare situations, a documentary may receive a theatrical release, such as *Roger and Me* and *Sicko* by filmmaker Michael Moore. The feature documentary by Al Gore, *An Inconvenient Truth,* received rave reviews from many film critics in addition to two Academy Awards.

If a documentary puts a fictional, humorous spin on its subjects, it can be categorized as a *mockumentary,* like *This Is Spinal Tap* and *Best in Show.* I did a mockumentary called *Hollywood Goes to Las Vegas* about a filmmaker (I hired myself) who wants to meet Sandra Bullock at a film convention and who encounters Russell Crowe, George Carlin, Haley Joel Osment, and John Travolta along the way.

Shooting short films: Keep it brief!

Producing a short film is a good way to get your foot in the door. A short film lasts, on average, 3–20 minutes, during which time it has to include an entire story arc, from beginning to end. Because of the short time in which to tell a story, the filmmaker often tells a controversial, funny or unique story that would normally not work as well in a feature length production. I've made over 50 short films called *Undershorts* that have appeared on *TV's Bloopers and Practical Jokes* with Dick Clark and Ed McMahon and *Foul-ups, Bleeps, and Blunders* with Don Rickles and Steve Lawrence. You can check out my *Undershorts* at www.bryanmichaelstoller.com. Most short films are more of a calling card and are difficult to sell but are ideal for garnering awards and exposure at film festivals.

Shorts can also be used as interstitials on television. *Interstitials* are short films that fill in the gaps between regular programming — usually on cable channels that don't run commercials. My comedy shorts have appeared as interstitials on HBO and various other pay and cable channels.

Short films that are between 1–4 minutes lend themselves well to the new technology of streaming over the Internet, using such sites as www.youtube.com and www.myspace.com. These short films can be quickly streamed or downloaded for immediate viewing. You can see my short parody film *The Linda Blair Witch Project,* at www.youtube.com/watch?v=ftqEhTpZtQs. Uploading your own film is free at youtube.com — hurry up, the world is waiting!

Directing television programs

Television directing consists of working under tight schedules (which means less time to do numerous takes, as compared to a feature film) and working under the pressure of a network and many television executives looking over your shoulder and making the final decisions. Directing a television series also consists of studying and emulating the style of the show, knowing the characters and their idiosyncrasies, and keeping the direction consistent with past episodes. Breaking into producing or directing television shows is a lot harder than making an independent feature film. With television, you have network executives and a lot of red tape to deal with. Developing a new concept for a TV show is the best way to get in the door.

Directing commercials

A 30-second commercial is quick to produce, and the pay can be very lucrative. Many big-time feature directors have come from a commercial background, such as Michael Bay, who directed *Bad Boys, Armageddon,* and *Transformers.* When I was 16, I was producing, directing, and writing several TV commercials a month out of my basement studio. Check with the TV stations and advertising agencies in your city to see whether you can produce some local commercials for them.

Minding your PSAs: Public service announcements

TV networks have an obligation to air *public service announcements,* also referred to as *PSAs,* for campaigns dealing with health and safety issues. PSAs include antismoking and antidrug commercials, don't-drink-and-drive campaigns, and environmental messages. The FCC requires TV stations to run public service announcements that are usually commissioned by various government agencies. Try making an inexpensive PSA on a subject that you're passionate about — this is your chance to make a statement. If it's well made, your local TV station may air it.

Feel like dancing? Music videos

Music videos are another great way to break into filmmaking. Find a local band and offer to shoot their first music video. Music videos can be shot inexpensively and are a fun way to experiment and play with visuals — and they're a great way to tell a story without dialogue.

Industrials: Industrial strength

An *industrial* is usually a film commissioned by a corporation showing how its products are manufactured. Industrial films can also be shot as training films for employees to find out more about the company and the products they represent. Industrials are often very technical and instructional in nature. Check out local corporations in your area to see whether they may be interested in having you produce an industrial video for them.

Chapter 3

Penning and Pitching a Great Story

In This Chapter

▶ Discovering where to find ideas

▶ Acquiring a story or screenplay

▶ Writing tips and secrets to a great story

In order to make a film, you must first find an interesting *screenplay* (a properly formatted manuscript that follows industry guidelines) or at least a great story idea. And where do screenplays come from, you ask? Well, anywhere actually. You can put out feelers in the industry to let writers know you're in the market for a screenplay, or you can write one of your own. You can find fascinating articles in your local newspaper, funny stories in magazines, and intriguing biographies that are just begging to be made into screenplays.

In this chapter, I show you the secrets to structuring the elements of your screenplay and developing characters that your audience will care about. You also see how easy it is to acquire stories or even the rights to a published book, if that's the route you want to take. Finally, you discover how to pitch your story ideas to a studio executive or potential investor in the hopes of getting your story made into a film.

Screening for the Perfect Screenplay

Finding a screenplay isn't difficult, but finding a good one is. If you look carefully, you can find many talented, up-and-coming writers who have good or maybe even great scripts under their arms just waiting to be made into films. Or, if you find a great story from a published book, you can adapt it into a screenplay.

If you're a beginning filmmaker, you should select or write a story that is realistic to shoot as a first-time movie. Don't choose material that's too ambitious. Keep the locations and characters to a minimum and keep away from special effects (they can be costly and time consuming).

The "write" way to find a writer

How do you find screenplay writers? Here are some ideas:

- ✔ **Put an ad in one of the entertainment trade papers** such as *Backstage West* (www.backstage.com) or *The Hollywood Reporter* (www.the hollywoodreporter.com) to let writers know that you're seeking an original screenplay for production.

- ✔ **Read screenplay magazines** such as *Creative Screenwriting* (www.creativescreenwriting.com) and *Script Magazine* (www.script magazine.com) and look for articles on writers. Check the classified sections and request available screenplays being advertised by writers.

  TIP Screenplay magazines usually list writers' newsletters and writers groups that you can join in order to find writers who have a screenplay ready to turn into a film. Also check out www.writerswrite.com for a one stop website with resources on writers for writers, including a place to post your job listing looking for a writer.

- ✔ **Attend writing seminars.** You can find these advertised in the various writers' magazines or in the classified sections of trade papers like *The Hollywood Reporter*. You can also find out about seminars from a writers' group; then network with the people in attendance, in addition to the speaker. Many attendees probably have a script they're peddling. Check out www.Storylink.com and www.scriptwritersnetwork.org to network with writers through blogs and discussions.

- ✔ **Send an e-mail to everyone you know.** We all have a screenplay in us. Tell friends, family, anyone you can that you're looking for a great screenplay or idea for a great film. After the word spreads, especially on the Internet, you'll start getting submissions.

- ✔ **Contact agencies that represent writers.** Send a query letter or call, and tell the agency that you're looking for scripts. Be sure to give them an idea of your budget range — how much money you have to make your film (a little or a lot); go to Chapter 4 for budgeting your film. You can request a list of agencies from the Writer's Guild of America at www.wga.org.

Adapting: A novel idea

One of the best ways to get a studio deal in Hollywood is to find a great book and option the rights to it. When you *option* a book, you're temporarily leasing the rights to it, giving you exclusive permission to adapt it to a screenplay and to shop it around as if you owned it. In a sense, you do own it — for a limited amount of time. An option can be as short as four months or as long as two years or more.

Inking for a script

InkTip.com is a great Web site that brings new and even seasoned writers (and their unproduced screenplays) together with filmmakers and producers. Searching for a script doesn't cost the producer or filmmaker anything, but you do have to qualify for free membership. You can apply for membership at its Web site (www.Inktip.com). You can also subscribe to InkTip.com's free e-mail newsletter and its bi-monthly *InkTip* magazine.

As a member, you gain access to writers' contact information and can contact writers directly with no agent or middleman. You can even download screenplays (as PDF files, a format that most computers accept — if yours doesn't, go to www.adobe.com/acrobat to download Adobe Acrobat Reader, free of charge). The InkTip network has a robust search engine that can find very specific types of screenplays. If you're looking for a sci-fi genre with a female lead that takes place on another planet and has some comedy undertones, but you want it to be a low to medium budget, click a few buttons, and away the search goes. The site also has listings of short screenplays available for production if you don't have the funds to do a full-length film.

Literally hundreds of thousands of books are out there. Go to the library or a secondhand bookstore. You're sure to stumble across a little gem that somebody has missed. Scan the racks for something that could work as a film. You could even take a short story and adapt it into a full-length feature film. *Brokeback Mountain* came from the short story by Annie Proulx. Many of Stephen King's short stories were adapted into full-length films: His short story "Rita Hayworth and the Shawshank Redemption" became the feature film *The Shawshank Redemption,* and his novella *The Body* was released as the theatrical film *Stand by Me.*

The popularity of the book will determine whether you can get an inexpensive option. The chances of getting an inexpensive option are very good for an older book — especially if you can contact the author directly.

When you option the rights to a novel, you draw up an agreement (preferably have an attorney do it) and you name a purchase price to be paid if and when you sell the novel to a studio or produce it yourself. You can often option for $1 and set a purchase price that is paid only when the film is produced. Often the purchase price of a script is 10 to 15 percent of the budget on an independent production, plus any agreed upon royalties on the picture's profits. You're probably saying to yourself, "Why even pay a dollar?" Any monetary amount makes it a legal agreement. Plus, I once optioned a story from a writer for $1, and he was able to treat himself to a fast-food hamburger — I felt good that I helped a starving artist.

Writing Your Own Original Screenplay

If you can't seem to find the perfect screenplay, then why not try writing your own? "Because I'm not a writer," you say. To that I say, "Just try." In Los Angeles, everyone, no matter what they do for a living, seems to be writing a screenplay. When you pass people on the street, you don't say "Hello." You say, "How's your screenplay going?" Usually people answer, "Great! Thanks for asking. How's yours?"

If you can converse with people and relate incidents and stories verbally, you can probably put your words on paper, so give it a try. I highly recommend the book *Screenwriting For Dummies* (for which I was technical editor) by Laura Schellhardt (published by Wiley). Start by perusing newspapers and magazines to trigger ideas for your story, or think about subjects that interest you and that you want to see on the big screen. Choose a story that keeps the reader glued to the page because they need to know what happens next.

Before you start writing your screenplay, familiarize yourself with the basics of what makes up good story structure. You also need to decide if you're ready to tackle a feature-length screenplay or ease your way in by doing a short story first (go to Chapter 2 for a discussion of media categories). Regardless of whether your screenplay is a short story or a feature-length one, similar story principals apply with regards to structuring your screenplay.

Note: A *spec script* is a speculative screenplay that a writer has written without being commissioned by someone to write it in the hopes of it being considered for production. It's usually a story the writer is extremely passionate about.

Structuring your screenplay

Feature films are usually structured into three acts. Each act is characterized by certain elements that moves the story forward. In a nutshell, Act One introduces the characters and starts the problem or conflict in motion. In Act Two the adventure begins and the conflict intensifies. In Act Three the problem comes to a head and is finally resolved. Here's a very simple example: In Act One the dog chases the cat up the tree. In Act Two, the cat is stuck in the tree, and an attempt is made to get it down safely. In Act Three the cat gets rescued. The following sections go into more detail.

Act One

Act One is the beginning of your story — you've got one chance to grab your audience and pull them in. In Act One you introduce your main character (the *protagonist)*. You also introduce the *inciting incident* — the element that sets your story into motion. In my movie *Teddy: First Dog,* the story is set into motion when an attempt on the President's life is diverted by the First Dog Teddy trying to warn him — and when the shots ring out, the President is protectively thrown into the Presidential limo by the Secret Service and whisked away. In the pandemonium, Teddy is left behind. After sneaking into the back of a truck and being transported a thousand miles away, Teddy meets a lonely foster boy, Danny Milbright (the protagonist). Danny, realizing the dog belongs to the President of the United States, vows to return the dog to the White House. So begins the journey that leads into Act Two.

Act Two

In Act Two the conflict intensifies and the enemy (the *antagonist)* is introduced, if not introduced by the end of Act One. The antagonist can be things like

- ✔ **A person:** Terrorists in *Air Force One,* vampire-like zombies in *I Am Legend,* or the Joker in *Batman: The Dark Knight*

- ✔ **Nature:** Any of the elements thrown out by Mother Nature: tornadoes in *Tornado!,* earthquakes in *Earthquake,* and a meteor racing toward Earth in *Armageddon.*

- ✔ **A disaster:** The sinking ship in *Titanic,* or the mechanical failure in *Apollo 13.*

The antagonist can also be any combination of these and other challenges.

In *Teddy: First Dog,* as Danny and Teddy venture across the country determined to make it to the White House, the two create a lot of conflict and encounter challenges and adventures. There are several antagonists in this film: the Secret Service who are after the pair, Animal Control workers who try to separate them, and more. By the end of Act Two, Danny is taken to a detention center as a runaway, awaiting his transport back to the foster home, and Teddy ends up at an animal shelter. It looks like the end for both Danny and Teddy.

Act Three

In Act Three the conflict comes to a climax and the problems are finally (hopefully) resolved. In *Teddy: First Dog,* for example, Teddy's life is spared when the scanning of his chip (imbedded in his shoulder) identifies his home address as 1600 Pennsylvania Avenue, and Danny goes to the White House to meet the President and to be reunited with Teddy. The story's resolution continues when Danny finds out that he is to be adopted by the President and First Lady, and Teddy, First Dog, is now his dog too!

Creating conflict

Conflict is what propels a story into motion. Without conflict, you have no action. Every day you deal with conflict, good or bad. Paying bills, getting stuck in traffic, having an argument with your spouse, missing your plane, getting a flat tire, being too rich — these are conflicts. Conflict usually starts when your protagonist, the lead character, encounters friction, a problem. Your character then deals with and tries to solve this problem. If the story is a good one, the protagonist grows from her experiences, whether she eventually solves this problem or not. A good story has your protagonist a changed person at the end of the film.

Conflict can also be an opposing character, the *antagonist,* like Patrick Swayze's coworker in *Ghost,* whose greed leads him to have his friend murdered. Or it can be the elements of nature, such as storm that strands Tom Hanks's character in *Cast Away* on a desert island or the island itself, or the deadly tornado that Helen Hunt's character faces in *Twister.* In *Titanic,* a historic and tragic event that was a natural disaster took the lives of many innocent passengers; the film also had a human antagonist in the form of Rose's fiancé. Conflict can also occur when the antagonist and protagonist want the same thing — money, custody of their child, the same woman, and so on.

When creating conflict in your screenplay, keep the following ideas in mind:

- ✔ **You don't want your story to be predictable.** What fun would that be for your audience?

- ✔ **Your story should be believable.** A story loses credibility if the answer to the hero's problem conveniently falls out of the sky. (This is called *deus ex machina,* a convention from Greek stage plays where a god is lowered in a chair from above, conveniently solves the situation, and then is cranked back up to the heavens. It works in cartoons and silly comedies, but not in most genres, especially dramatic pieces.) You don't want people saying your story was contrived.

- ✔ **Think outside the box.** Once a truck got stuck under a low bridge. The whole town came out to push and pull, but to no avail. The truck seemed permanently wedged under the bridge. Then a little girl, who was watching the firemen and townspeople pushing and pulling, stepped forward and said, "Why not let the air out of the tires?" She was thinking outside the box. People want to be surprised. I loved the twist in *The Sixth Sense* when Bruce Willis turns out to be a ghost. (I hope you've seen the film. If not, I apologize now for ruining it for you.)

- ✔ **Studios like high-concept ideas.** *High concept* means something out of the ordinary. *Jurassic Park* with dinosaurs being brought back to life in a theme park is a high-concept idea. *Spider-Man* is a high concept — a man is bitten by a scientifically altered spider and becomes a human spider. Another high concept is when Jeff Goldblum in *The Fly* accidentally merges with a fly to become a 6-foot insect with horrifying results. Hey, what a great idea for a sequel, *The Fly Meets Spider-Man* — and it's high concept!

Developing characters

You're taking a drive out to the country. Whom do you want to ride with you? Call up some of your favorite people and have them go along for the drive. Make it an enjoyable journey, not just a destination. The same is true with the characters in your film. Make them interesting enough that the reader will want to go with them on a ride, no matter what the destination is. Make them good company! Give your characters personality.

Your characters should be real and well rounded outside the scope of your screenplay as well. Does the audience care about these characters? The audience can then see them as no one else in the story sees them — their true selves are revealed by what they do when they're alone. Follow them around in your head and see what they do.

Follow the Law of Threes. If you want to establish a developing relationship in your story, you need at least three situations where your characters interact. If a relationship builds too fast, your audience will think it's contrived (too convenient). A great example of the Law of Threes is the three brief encounters between Elliott and E.T. in *E.T. the Extra-Terrestrial* before they befriend each other. First, Elliott hears something in the shed; then Elliott goes to the forest; and, finally, Elliott sits outside on a lawn chair in front of the shed and is approached by E.T. This gradual lead-up to their bond makes it more acceptable, believable, and effective for the audience.

Drafting your screenplay: Scene by scene

The process of writing a screenplay includes writing a first draft. You need to remember that it's only a first writing session, and there will be changes. Writing is rewriting. Knowing this helps your ideas flow from your thoughts to the page, and you won't be concerned about editing your words. You're free to put any and all of your ideas on paper at this first-draft stage.

If you have trouble getting a first draft down on paper, pick up some index cards. Cards are an excellent way to put your film together, and they can make writing a first draft much easier. Here's how it works:

1. **Write on an index card a scene that you envision in your film.**

   You only have to write the location and a brief summary of what the scene is about. If it takes place at the exterior of the diner, you would write: *Ext. Diner — Tim finds out that Sheila works at the diner outside of town.*

2. **After you've written all the scenes you've thought of, lay the cards out on the floor.**

Spreading out the cards helps you stand back and look at the whole picture, much like a traffic helicopter — you can see where your story moves and where it gets stuck.

3. **Fill in the missing pieces.**

   This part of the process is like doing a jigsaw puzzle — you have to find the perfect pieces to fill in the holes. When you get a brilliant idea for a missing scene, write it on an index card and slip it in where it belongs.

4. **Translate the final order of the scenes into a screenplay format.**

The advantage of using index cards is that they create a non-linear environment for experimenting with your story and the order of events. You can rearrange each scene in any order until the story begins to fall into place.

Using cards can also be useful in adapting a book into a screenplay. When I adapted Jennings Michael Burch's book for Mel Gibson's Icon Productions, the task of turning a 293-page book into a 100-page screenplay was overwhelming. I broke the book down into separate incidents or events and turned them into individual scenes on over 400 index cards. I arranged the cards and then decided which scenes to keep and which scenes to discard. I rearranged the order of some cards and saw which scenes needed to be consolidated. It helped organize the adapting process and made it much easier to end up with a completed screenplay.

When you're finished with your first draft of your new screenplay, put it down and walk away. That's right — just walk away. You're too close to it when you've just finished it to start considering rewrites. You need a break: Get away from your screenplay, take a vacation for a few days, or even a few weeks, before you begin rewriting. When you return, you have fresh eyes and can see things more objectively. If you revise too soon, you won't want to change a word — and odds are, you probably need to.

Keeping focused

Writing is fun, but it also requires discipline if you want to turn out a commercial screenplay to produce yourself or sell to a studio. In order to accomplish your dream of writing a screenplay, certain things will help you reach your goals:

   ✔ **Set a deadline and stick to it.** Tell everyone that you're writing a screenplay, and tell them the date you plan on finishing it. Give yourself a reasonable time (at least a couple months, if not more) to write a solid first draft. If you beat your deadline, people will be more impressed. Broadcasting your deadline forces you to sit down and write because everyone will be asking you how your screenplay is going, and you don't want to let everyone down now, do you?

✔ **Force yourself to sit down and write within a reasonable schedule.** If you set a goal of writing three pages a day, you'll make your deadline of a first draft in a little over one month. The worst thing you write down on paper (or type on your computer) is always better than the best thing you didn't write down. I'm often amazed at how much better my writing is than I thought it would be, even when I feel that I'm forcing it.

✔ **Get over writer's block.** Writer's block is a familiar condition, but it's really nothing more than procrastination. Don't convince yourself that you have this symptom called writer's block; you'll only make yourself feel intimidated. Instead think of writer's block in your vocabulary as being only a neighborhood of successful writers (and you're one of the writers who lives on that block).

✔ **Always know that writing is rewriting.** Rarely does a person write a letter, story, or screenplay that is ready to be read by all. Knowing that you can rewrite what you wrote is a comfort — even the most brilliant of writers rewrite, often more than beginning writers do! You can, and often will, go back and edit what you've written.

✔ **Just start writing.** Look at it as crossing the bridge. Just cross halfway. Now that you're in the middle, it's the same distance to go back where you started — so why not go the same distance but at least finish crossing the bridge?

Registering your script via the Internet

The main reason for registering your screenplay is to show that you had the idea first — that it is original with you on a certain date. This way, if someone steals your idea or has a similar idea *after* the date that you registered it, you have proof that you had the idea first.

The Writer's Guild of America now has online registration. You can submit your screenplay via an e-mail attachment to the WGA. You pay by credit card and immediately get an online receipt, which you can print to show that your story is registered with the guild. This is the quickest and easiest way to register your script. The cost is $20 for non-WGA members ($10 for members). Go to the WGA Web site at `www.wgaregistry.org` and click Online Registration Service.

If you want to copyright your screenplay through the U.S. Copyright Office (for around $45, but the cost can change, so check on-line), go to `www.copyright.gov`.

You can also do a poor-man's copyright. Seal your script or story idea in a manila envelope, address it to yourself, and take it to the post office to be stamped for registered mail. The U.S. Postal Service is considered a legal entity and can mark your package with its USPS stamp at all the corners and sealed edges. A USPS stamp can be used in a court of law to prove you had the idea first. You don't have to mail it — unless you love getting letters. The post office can hand it right back to you. File it away in a safe place.

Watching words: Closed captions

Want to watch a movie and see the script at the same time? Most TVs nowadays have a closed-caption function that allows you to watch a film or TV show and read along. Closed captioning was established for the hearing impaired, but it's also a great way to study the actual written words while you watch the actors and scenes play out. It lets you compare what you see written on the bottom of the screen — and how delivered dialogue by the actor is written on the page. It makes you realize that everything the actor says is scripted and how the written word is delivered in a natural way following the script verbatim.

Collaborating with writer's software

You can find some great software programs that help you concentrate solely on the creative aspects of your screenplay (leave the formatting for later). Most of the software is very easy to use. Some of these programs offer free trial downloads so you can check them out. Most work for both PCs and Macs. Some of these programs are a little pricey, but the organization you'll gain from the software will save you time and trouble in the long run.

- **Story View** by Write Brothers tracks your story with charts, cards, and color-coding, and literally creates a map of your story that you can stand back and study. Currently Story View only works with PC. The program retails for around $179 , and you can find it at www.storyview.com.

- **Dramatica Pro** by Write Brothers helps you design your story by asking you questions, giving examples, and guiding you through the creative process of writing a screenplay. I like it because it makes you think about your story from every angle, leaving no stone unturned. It's also a lot of fun to use. Dramatica Pro retails for around $135 (Academic version). Go to www.screenplay.com to order.

- **Truby's Blockbuster** software priced at $295 makes for a great writing companion. The program lets you interact with actual examples from many well-known films. It includes Truby's Story Structure Course along with a list of the 22 building blocks of every great story. Add-ons are available that help you write for specific genres such as romance, sci-fi, thriller, action, and so on. Only works on PC, not Mac. Take a look at www.truby.com.

- **Power Structure,** at $179, is a powerful program that encourages you to ask yourself questions and brainstorm ideas to develop a strong structure for your screenplay. Check it out at www.write-brain.com.

> ✔ **Save the Cat** lets you work with index cards and a beat sheet to help structure your screenplay. The program has a *litter box* section for brainstorming and lots of other helpful steps. The software includes tips and a tutorial from screenwriter Blake Snyder www.BlakeSnyder.com for $79.95.

You can also find the preceding software programs and others by visiting The Writer's Store at www.writersstore.com. Many software products have lower-priced Academic versions for students.

Formatting your screenplay

You'll be submitting your screenplay to people who get them every day, so not only does your screenplay idea need to be creative and unique to stand out, but you also need to know the basics of proper screenplay formatting so that when your screenplay comes across the desk of an executive, buyer, or distributor, it looks like the real thing. Take a look at *Screenwriting For Dummies* by Laura Schellhardt (published by Wiley) for the lowdown on formatting as well as writing. Also consider investing in one of the following software programs, which do all the script formatting for you automatically:

> ✔ **Movie Magic Screenwriter** is a formatting program that includes a setting that lets you view your scripts in outline (card) form. I especially like this software because you can export script information, such as location settings, characters, props, and scenes, so that you can begin scheduling your shoot days. I've written most of my scripts using this great software, which costs $249 (under $170 for the Academic version). Free technical support and customer service is great! Check it out at www.screenplay.com.

> ✔ **Final Draft** is similar to Screenwriter. The software includes an "Ask the Expert" by screenwriter and author Syd Field that offers an interactive point-and-click section that helps to answer questions and guide you through the writing process The program retails for $289. ($169 for Academic and Military version). Technical support charges by the minute. Go to www.finaldraft.com.

Regardless of what software you use to write your screenplay (Word, Screenwriter, Final Draft, and so on) always convert it into a PDF file before emailing it to someone. Do *not* send it in the software format that you wrote it in — many recipients may not have the same software you do (and if they do, it's an invitation to edit and manipulate your words) and thus will not be able to open your screenplay file. Of course if you're printing your screenplay out and snail mailing it, or handing it to them in person, you can disregard the PDF warning.

Selling Your Screenplay to a Production Studio, Distributor, or Investor

You can sell your screenplay physically to a studio or distributor, and they will make the picture on their own. Or you can sell a distributor on the idea of your screenplay and story, and the distributor could give you a written commitment to distribute the picture when it's completed. If you get a commitment from a distributor, finding investors willing to take a chance with your film, knowing it already has distribution interest, will be a lot easier.

Selling a production studio or distributor on your idea consists of setting up a meeting to verbally pitch your story. If your idea is well received, the next step is to follow up with either the story in the form of a short one- to two-page synopsis, a *treatment* or *outline* (a detailed synopsis 10 to 20 pages in length), or a copy of an actual screenplay.

Getting your foot (and screenplay) in the door

Some companies receive hundreds of screenplays a month, in addition to one-page summaries from eager screenwriters. The head of the studio or the producer can't possibly read every script that comes in, so the studio hires a script reader to sit all day reading and evaluating screenplays that are submitted to the company. This means you only get one chance at a good first impression. If the reader doesn't like it, your screenplay never goes any farther.

The script reader usually reads your script and then fills out an evaluation page or pages grading your screenplay — similar to what your elementary-school teacher used to do with your assignments. In addition to grading your script, the reader also writes a short synopsis of your story so that the studio executives, producer, or potential buyer can know what your script is about. It's kind of like the *CliffsNotes* of your story. These are some of the things a reader evaluates:

- Is it an interesting story that holds the reader's attention?
- Is it well written?
- Are the characters engaging?
- Does it have commercial potential?
- Is it a "pass" or a "consider for further evaluation"?

If your script does get a thumbs-up from a script reader, you now have to prepare for the rest of the battle. Sharpen your selling skills by warming up for your meeting with an effective pitch that you can deliver in person to close the deal on your great screenplay idea.

Pitching a home run

When you're trying to sell your screenplay to a studio or distributor, you need to throw a powerful *pitch*. A pitch is a verbal sales tool that explains your story and tries to convince the receiver to accept your idea so you can land a distribution deal, a financing commitment from an investor, or a production deal with a studio to produce your film.

Who you make your pitch to is as important as the quality of your pitch. If you pitch to the wrong person, you're wasting your time (and his or hers as well). Many executives in Hollywood are hired just to say "no." You want to give your pitch to someone who can say "yes" or at least to someone who likes your screenplay and has the clout to take it to the person who says "yes." A development executive at a studio or an acquisition person at a production company is usually the person you need to get a meeting with.

The Hollywood Creative Directory puts out several directories, including one of producers and a separate one of distribution companies. The directories also list these companies' past and current projects, so you can decide whether your screenplay is appropriate for them. For more information on the directories, go to Chapter 24 or online at www.hcdonline.com.

Keep the following tips in mind as you prepare and give your pitch:

- ✔ **Identify your film with other successful films.** Hollywood executives need a quick reference point to decide whether your story is something they want to know more about. The quickest way to identify the genre and commercial viability of your screenplay is to cross it with at least two other well-known films.

   Always cross your movie with *successful* films. If your film is the same genre as a film that just bombed at the box office, the executive you're pitching to won't want anything to do with it. My comedy parody *Miss Cast Away & the Island Girls* crosses *Cast Away* with *Miss Congeniality*, along with the crazy humor of *Scary Movie* and *Austin Powers*. Now doesn't that paint a picture with commercial potential?

- ✔ **Keep pitching until you get a home run.** Babe Ruth was known for his homerun record (over 700 throughout his career), but he could have set a record for the most strikeouts, too. You have to keep pitching to get a hit. Selling your screenplay is very similar to baseball. You wind up for the swing, you pitch, and maybe your pitch creates a home run — or at

Pen names

Want to use a different name on your script? Stephen King and many writers have used *pen names* for one reason or another. Maybe you're submitting the same script again with rewrites and you don't want your real name to cross-reference with the new script. Or maybe you have several projects out for consideration and you don't want them to all have your real name on them. Maybe you're not thrilled about the script and don't want to associate with it at all. Here's a suggestion for finding a pen name: Take your middle name, or your best friend's middle name, and then the street you grew up on. For example, my middle name is Michael, and I grew up on Westbrook Drive. So my pen name is Michael Westbrook.

least gets you to first, second, or third base. And then again, maybe you strike out. So you wait for a new game and start all over again. Each time you strike out, go back and work on your pitch so that it's better the next time around.

✔ **Intrigue the listener so that he or she will want to hear more.** A way to do this is to begin your pitch with a question (for example, "What would happen if the sun suddenly burned out?"), and then tell them what happens in your story.

I heard a story once about a frustrated writer who took a famous award-winning film, changed the names, updated the time and locations, and sent it out. It was turned down by every agent and studio in town. *The Wizard of Oz* was turned down by every publisher who didn't have the courage — some had no heart — but L. Frank Baum had the brain to self-publish his stories, which then attracted a publisher to pick up the sequels — and the rest is history. So use a little creativity and keep trying.

Part II

Gearing Up to Make Your Film

The 5th Wave   By Rich Tennant

"Okay, these people are financing a big part of the movie, so during the lovemaking scenes, try not to drop the snow shovels."

In this part . . .

In this part, you discover how to successfully budget and schedule your film and also find secrets for financing your film. This part guides you to the right locations for setting your story and the best cast and crew you can find.

Planning your film with a visual eye before ever stepping on set is important. In this part, I also help you visualize the film through shot-by-shot sketches called *storyboards*.

Chapter 4

Scheduling and Budgeting Your Film

*B*efore you can go out and actually shoot your movie, you have to budget and schedule what you're going to shoot. The schedule helps you figure out what scenes you need to shoot first and the most economical way to get your movie completed. The schedule and budget go hand in hand. Often, you don't have much choice: When you have a set amount to make your movie, you have to make your schedule fit your budget and your budget fit your schedule.

In this chapter, you discover how to accurately budget and schedule your independent film, whether you have no budget, a low budget, or a budget in the millions. You can also find out how to outline your whole shooting schedule on a production board so that you know who's shooting what, where, and when. Finally, I let you in on a few secrets to shooting your film on the cheap.

What comes first — the schedule or the budget?

Which you tackle first — scheduling your film or doing the budget — depends on your situation. It would be nice if you could schedule your film and then see how much money you need, but filmmakers often have only so much money and have to make their films fit the budgets, not their budgets fit their films. It's like trying to pack too many clothes into a small suitcase — you push them in as tight as you can and hope you can still close it. Whatever you can't fit in the case, you have to manage without.

Scheduling your movie lets you know where to direct the money and to which budget categories.

You usually have a set amount of money, and it's the distribution of that amount that is determined by the scheduling — what will be spent where.

By breaking down your script and sorting out cast, crew, props, locations, and shooting days before doing your detailed budget, you leave nothing to chance — this at least lets you know if you have enough money to make your film. You're able to know that what you've scheduled fits within the budget, and so present a more accurate and detailed budget to satisfy your investor, if you're lucky enough to find one.

The Art of Scheduling a Film

Even if you have a definitive budget, you need to break down all the elements of your film to determine how to distribute the money you have. These breakdowns also help you figure out how many days it will take to shoot your film. You have to make your budget fit your schedule, so be prepared to do some juggling. If you're on a tight budget, you won't have the luxury of shooting your film over a period of several months. Your budget may only allow you to schedule a 12-day shoot (every additional day is going to cost you money). Juggling includes consolidating scenes. If you can shoot the scene in the cave in two days instead of three, and the breaking-up scene in the car, instead of in the shopping mall, you'll be able to shorten your schedule, thus saving time and money.

Scheduling a film is like playing with a Rubik's Cube, where you keep turning and adjusting and twisting and tweaking until the elements fall into place. And scheduling your film efficiently is essential to saving time and money. Scheduling your film includes

- *Lining* the script by going through and marking items such as actors, props, wardrobe, and special effects
- Putting those items on individual *breakdown sheets,* each representing one scene from the film
- Transferring the elements on the breakdown sheets to *production board strips*
- Rearranging the order of production strips to find the best shooting schedule

The director and assistant director usually make the schedule together. The process includes figuring out what scenes can be shot together in the same day, scheduling actors to work consecutive days, and deciding how to tighten the schedule so the film can be shot in fewer days. If you don't have an assistant director to help schedule and be on the set to keep things organized, then you have to do the schedule all by yourself.

A calendar is your best friend when scheduling your film. You choose the date to start principal photography and the date the shoot will wrap. By l ooking at a calendar, you see what days the weekends fall on and whether any statutory holidays (like Christmas and Memorial Day) occur that the cast and crew will have off. Calendar programs are also great for reminders and scheduling appointments. Here are two software Web sites to make a date with: www.daychaser.com and www.thecalendarplanner.com. Most computers come with calendar software installed; that might just be all you need.

Lining your script

You break down, or *line,* your script by pulling out elements that affect your budget and schedule. With different-colored highlighters in hand, start combing through your script (or have the assistant director do it, if you have one), highlighting important items with a different color for each category. You end up with a very colorful script after the process is complete. This process is intended to flag the script so accurate breakdowns can be made. The categories to highlight include

- ✔ Actors
- ✔ Extras (background people)
- ✔ Props
- ✔ Wardrobe or special costumes
- ✔ Sets and locations
- ✔ Special effects
- ✔ Vehicles
- ✔ Animals
- ✔ Special equipment
- ✔ Special makeup
- ✔ Optical effects

Breaking into breakdown sheets

After you highlight the various categories of items, transfer the highlighted elements to individual *breakdown sheets* — one for each scene in your film. A breakdown sheet contains separate drawn category boxes to add the elements you've highlighted in the script. You enter each element in the appropriate category box, such as a hammer in the props area, either by hand or by using one of the available software programs (see the section "Scheduling software to make your life easier" later in this chapter).

Number each breakdown sheet so that you can go back and reference it if you need to. Every character in the script is also given a reference number, usually starting with the number 1 for your lead actor. You transfer these numbers to the breakdown sheets and eventually to the individual strips on the production board (more on this in the section "Creating production strips"). Numbering saves space so that you don't have to keep writing the characters' names (plus there wouldn't be enough space on a strip).

A breakdown sheet also has a *header* that includes the following details:

- Scene number
- Script page
- Page count (length of scene divided into eighths — 1½ pages would be 1⅘)
- Location/setting
- Scene description (one sentence)
- Exterior or interior
- Day or night
- Script day (for example, third day in the story when Mary arrives at the plantation)
- Breakdown sheet number

Figure 4-1 shows a sample breakdown sheet from my film *The Dragon's Candle*. Scene 106 has Ghandlin the wizard driving a borrowed police car and zapping traffic out of his way with his magic wand. The breakdown sheet provides separate boxes listing the elements that are needed for this scene.

Scene # 106	THE DRAGON'S CANDLE	Date: 10/5/2002
Script Page: 94	**BREAKDOWN SHEET**	Sheet: 102
Page Count: 2 2/8 pgs.		Int/Ext. EXT
		Day/Night: Day

Scene Description: The Wizard steers the policecar into oncoming traffic   *Page 1*
Setting: Freeway
Location: (Ottawa Queensway)
Sequence: _____ Script Day: 8

Cast Members	**Stunts**	**Vehicles**
1. GHANDLIN 2. RICK	stunt car drivers	Police car
	Props magic wand	**Special Effects** cars zapped out of the way
Extras drivers x 9		
Wardrobe wizards robe	**Makeup**	**Livestock**
Animal Handler	**Music**	**Sound**

Figure 4-1:
A break-
down sheet
created
with Gorilla
production
software.

Courtesy of Gorilla ™ Jungle Software © 2002

Propping up your prop list

Every prop that will appear in your film must be pulled from the script and
added to the props category in your breakdown sheets. A *prop* is defined as
anything your characters interact with, such as guns, cell phones, brooms,
and so on. On a low-budget film, try to borrow your props — especially
if they're contemporary items. For hard-to-find props, you can usually
rent them from a prop house or rental house listed in the Yellow Pages
or the 411 directory in New York (www.ny411.com) and Los Angeles
(www.la411.com). In North Hollywood, California, 20th Century Props
(www.20thcenturyprops.com) has over 100,000 square feet of storage that
houses thousands of props.

Often, props are confused with set dressing, but the difference is that actors don't interact with set dressing. Set dressing includes a picture frame on a mantle or flowers in a vase on a table. The baseball bat in Mel Gibson's film *Signs* would normally have been categorized as set dressing, but because the actors actually interact with the bat (which is displayed on a wall), it is categorized as a prop. You address set dressing in your breakdown sheets only if it's crucial to the story.

Dressing up your wardrobe list

You add certain wardrobe elements to your breakdown sheets, such as costumes, uniforms, or clothes that have to be sewn from scratch. A character's jeans and T-shirt don't need to be entered in the wardrobe box, but a gangster's zoot suit does. Because scenes aren't usually filmed in chronological order, each outfit is given a script day number to ensure that the actor wears the correct wardrobe in each shot. Script days (the timeline of your story) will be part of the breakdown sheets, and if the story takes place over five days, you'll sit down with the wardrobe person and decide what clothing your actors will wear each day if it's not addressed in the script.

Locating locations

You can list your location setting in the heading of each breakdown sheet. Locations dictate a lot regarding scheduling and budget. If you're using software like Entertainment Partners Scheduling, you can cross-reference details about the locations: Are they private or public property? Do you need to secure permits or pay location fees, and how much do they cost? Keep your locations to a minimum; otherwise, you may end up going over budget.

Many states offer incentives to encourage filmmakers to shoot in their cities. See Chapter 6 for more information about location deals.

A "special" on special effects

Scheduling special effects on your breakdown sheets helps you determine what kind of effects you can afford. Keep effects to a minimum if you're working with a lower budget. You may find that designing special effects on a computer fits within your budget better, depending on how elaborate the special effect. If you can get away without special effects and concentrate on a good story, though, I recommend that route. See Chapter 17 for much more on creating special effects for your film.

Creating production strips

After you've copied all the category elements from your screenplay onto your breakdown sheets, you're ready to start transferring these elements to the individual strips that go onto your production board. *Production strips* are about ¼ inch wide and contain the information from your breakdown sheets.

Each strip represents an individual scene and contains all the elements featured in that particular scene, such as location, actors, props, and wardrobe. The header contains the names of your characters in the script with a number assigned to each character. These numbers are added to the strips and line up with the header, so you can see at a glance which scenes each actor appears in.

By having the scenes of your film on individual strips, you can move them around to find the most economical and effective shooting schedule. Films are rarely shot in continuity. Rather, you want to group the same locations together in your shooting schedule so that you don't have to jump back and forth. Shooting the scene at the airport, wrapping up, and then later in the story going back to the airport to shoot more scenes would be silly.

You also want to color-code your strips so that you can step back and see how many interior and exterior scenes you have, making arranging shooting times easier. If the schedule shows you there are more interior scenes, then you know you don't have to worry about weather as much. If the schedule shows you that you have a lot of daytime exterior scenes, then you know you don't have to rent movie lights and a generator — but you do have to be aware of what time the sun sets and when you'll be losing the light. You can choose the color code that works best for you. I usually color-code my strips as follows:

Exterior Day = yellow

Exterior Night = blue

Interior Day = white

Interior Night = green

You schedule as many scenes as you feel you can shoot in one day and group locations, rooms, and so on together. The number of days you shoot has an impact on your budget, so try to fit as much into each shooting day that you feel you can realistically cover without sacrificing the quality of your film. Always allow yourself more time than you think it will take to shoot a scene. If it's a dialogue scene, it may be quicker and easier to shoot than an action scene that needs to be choreographed and covered from several different angles. An experienced assistant director can help you determine if your shooting schedule is realistic or not.

After you've selected the scenes (strips) for each day's shoot, you separate them in your production board with a black strip and then begin the next day's schedule of scenes. You should complete your production board well in advance of shooting (during the preproduction stage) so that everyone on your crew knows ahead of time what is shooting and when.

A production board can be a heavy cardboard or plastic compartment board that allows you to fit your strips into it and see your entire schedule at a glance. You can purchase boards from the Writers Store (www.writersstore.com). They come in 4, 6, and 8 panels and range in price from $65 to $120. If you use a software program like EP Scheduling (www.entertainmentpartners.com) or Gorilla's Scheduling software (www.junglesoftware.com), the board is printed along with your strips onto paper and can be copied and distributed to appropriate crew members.

Stripping down your schedule

Two main factors determine the order in which you shoot your scenes: characters and locations. Start organizing your production strips by grouping the characters that appear in the same scenes together. Then arrange the strips with the same locations as close together as possible.

Actors

Try to schedule your actors so that they work as many consecutive days as possible. Otherwise, you have to drop and then pick up the actors again. In some union agreements, you still have to pay actors who are *on hold* for days they don't work. With non-union agreements, you don't have to worry about this. However, if a union actor is on hold, he or she has to be available at a moment's notice should your schedule change. If you're doing a union production with union actors, special weekly rates will save some money in the budget if you're working an actor more than two or three days at a time.

After you have your production strips in place, you can generate a *day-out-of-days* chart that shows when your actors work during the shooting schedule. You can do this by hand or generate it from the software program you use to produce your production board and strips.

Locations

Grouping the same rooms, buildings, and locations together helps the schedule. Picking up and moving your cast and crew from one location to the next takes time and money. Most films are shot out of continuity for this reason.

Schedule outdoor scenes first. That way, if it rains or the weather isn't appropriate for your shot, you can move indoors and use the time to shoot interior scenes under safe cover. If you start shooting indoors and then go outside, you aren't giving yourself a security blanket for a *cover-set* (backup location). By having a backup interior location when it rains on a day you've scheduled a sunny outdoor scene, you can go into the indoor location without shutting down production, and then go outside again when the weather has cleared up.

Scheduling software to make your life easier

One of the advantages of scheduling your film with a software program as opposed to taping strips of paper onto a piece of poster board is that you can easily group locations and actors and have the software present you with a series of alternative shooting sequences. The other nice thing about scheduling software is that it enables you to generate various lists and customized breakdown sheets. The software automatically transfers the items on your breakdown sheets to your production strips. The following are some great options to consider:

- **Filmmaker Software:** If you go to www.filmmakersoftware.com, you can download, for only $15, Filmmaker Software, which provides every imaginable form and report you'll need to make your film, including breakdown sheets and strip board!

- **Gorilla Production Software:** For $199 student version ($299 standard version), Gorilla (www.junglesoftware.com) includes a scheduling program within its production package software (Gorilla is a full production package that includes budgeting and other reports to assist you in making your film). It's a sophisticated software package that will make the task of scheduling your movie a lot easier!

- **EP Scheduling:** This scheduling software has a form of artificial intelligence. You type in what you want — for the program to group like elements together, giving you all the same sets or actors consecutively in the schedule. The software goes to work sorting and selecting and presents you with a myriad of scheduling options. It lists for $499; you can find it at www.entertainmentpartners.com. Figure 4-2 shows a production board created with EP Scheduling. The Academic version (student) is $195. You can even check out the software by downloading the free demo off their site.

Scheduling software can also be found at specialty stores that cater to filmmakers such as the following:

- **Enterprise Printers:** Enterprise Stationery (www.enterpriseprinters.com) is the leader in entertainment reports, forms, and contracts and has more than 300 production forms, including all the materials you need for breaking down and scheduling your film. You can purchase a four-panel production board for $64.95, a bundle of 50 strips for $5.50, and a header (to list your actors and headings) for $3.50. They also sell the latest budget and scheduling software.

- **The Writers Store:** You can also find a selection of production board and strip products at the Writers Store (www.writersstore.com).

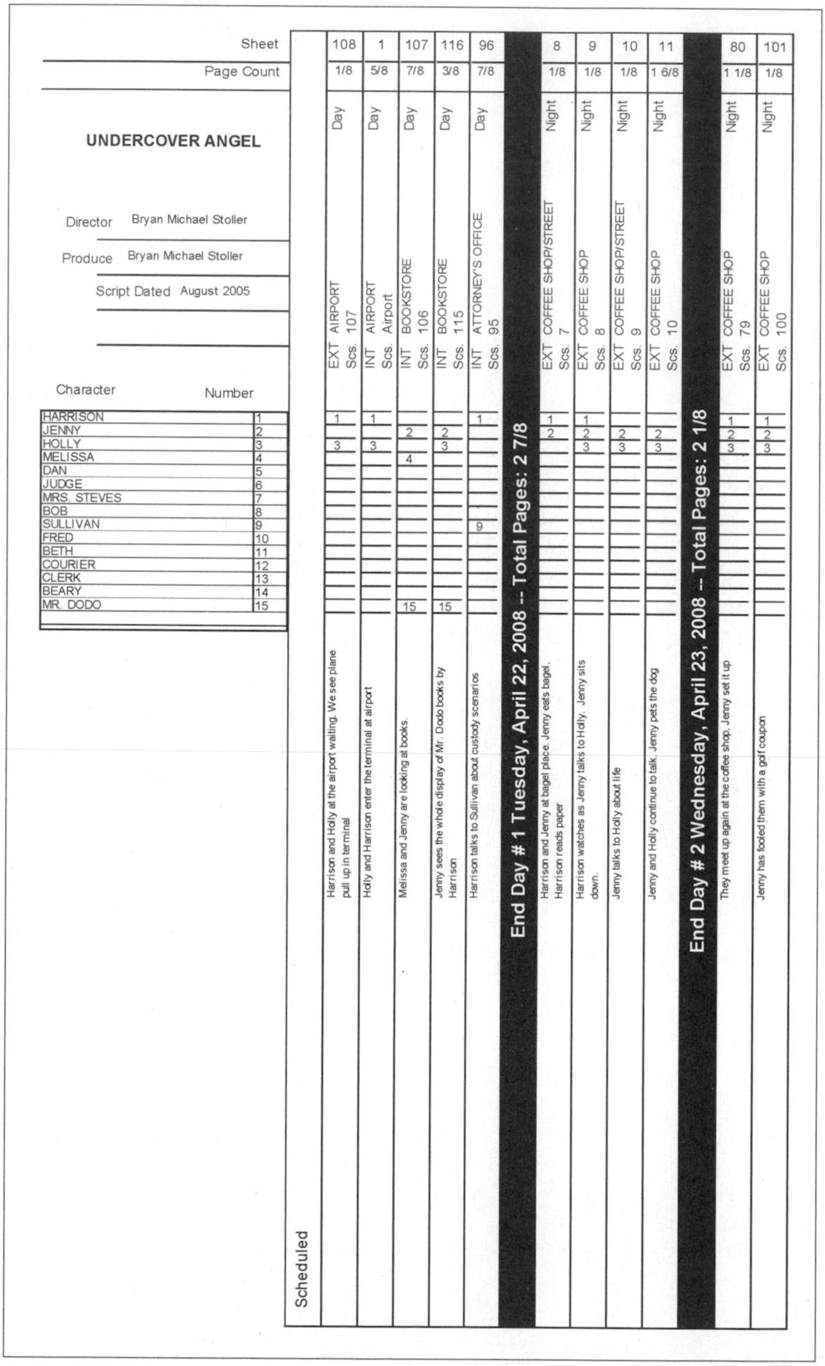

Figure 4-2:
A production board with strips from Entertainment Partners Scheduling Software (with header).

Balancing Your Film Budget

If you're doing a low-budget production, you have a finite amount of money to work with. Therefore, creating a budget and sticking to it is critical; you aren't likely to have a big studio (or a filthy rich uncle) provide you with extra cash if you overspend and come up short. Creating a budget involves allotting the proper amount to each area. Adding at least a 10-percent contingency to your budget to allow for overages is also important; otherwise, you could end up with an unfinished film.

Everything has a price. If you pay full price for everything, your independent budget could end up at $100,000. But if you're a good dealmaker, you may be able to shoot the same film for $50,000. Hollywood spends money and often doesn't have time to work the deals. You, on the other hand, probably have no choice.

If you've already found people to finance your film, they're going to want to see a detailed budget. They'll want to know how you intend to spend their money. So even if the money isn't coming out of your own pocket, you can't escape doing a budget for your film.

Tightrope walking above the line

First, you need to determine what your *above-the-line* numbers are going to be. Above-the-line items include negotiable and influential salaries, such as those paid to the writer, director, producer, and star actors. Your cast is usually found above-the-line because they drive the commercial viability of your film, and their salaries have to be negotiated. If you're doing a studio picture, a star can demand up to $20 million or more these days. On an independent low-budget film, your actors (especially if they're union) are going to up the cost to make your film. The other above-the-line positions like the producer, director, and writer (unless they're all you) are also negotiable, but may be controlled by a union (Director's Guild DGA or Writer's Guild WGA) or agent wanting mucho bucks for his client.

On a non-union film, you can save a lot of money if your cast works for deferred pay, meaning that they don't receive salaries until, and if, the film makes a profit. Getting actors to work deferred is easier than getting crew members to do so, because actors often need the exposure and experience and can add the film to their acting reel and resume.

Starring cameos

If you're creative, you may be able to slip a recognized actor into your film and not have to pay a $20 million salary. If you hire an actor for one day, or even a couple of hours, you can shoot several scenes and insert them throughout the film. I had Dan Aykroyd do the voice of Dexter the computer in my film *The Random Factor.* I spent a little over an hour with him and was able to use about 15 minutes of his voice-over throughout the film. James Earl Jones played a judge in two scenes for my film *Undercover Angel.* I shot with him for a whole day so I only had to pay him a one-day salary. George Carlin performed

a cameo in my American Film Institute student film many years ago. I had the camera set up and ready to go. He came in, did his scene, and we wrapped in less than 45 minutes.

The best way to approach actors is through referrals, or meeting them happenchance in a store or restaurant. (I found Yasmine Bleeth's purse after she left it in a restaurant, and then I asked her to star in my movie *Undercover Angel,* and she did!) You can also write a letter to an actor's agent or manager to see if you can convince him or her to be in your film.

If your cast is union, you can't defer pay (unless it's classified as a short or student film), but you may qualify to do your film under a special agreement with the Screen Actors Guild (SAG) called the SAG Indie Program. This program works with independent filmmakers so that they can afford to use union actors in their films. The agreements that SAG offers to independent filmmakers include

- ✔ **Student Film Agreement:** You don't have to pay the actors to be in your film as long as your film is done under an accredited school and you are a student. The film's budget has to be less than $35,000. The film cannot be sold or distributed (you can use it to showcase your filmmaking skills and help get a paid filmmaking job in the future).

- ✔ **Short Film Agreement:** The budget must be under $50,000 and 35 minutes in length or less. You can defer actors' salaries. If you sell the film, you owe the actors $100 for each day they worked on set. The bonus is that you can use union (SAG) and non-union actors.

- ✔ **Ultra Low Budget:** The total film budget must be under $200,000. You can mix union and non-union actors, and you pay a $100 daily flat rate to your talent. This is the agreement I recommend if your budget is under $200,000 and you're planning on having it distributed.

- ✔ **Modified Low Budget:** The budget must be under $625,000 but may be increased to $937,500 (under special casting considerations). Reduced rates apply for actors, determined by the number of days they work. You must use all union players. Actor's rate is $268 a day.

- ✔ **Low Budget:** The budget for the film must be under $2.5 million. You pay your actors reduced union rates of $504 a day, and you must use all union players.

These agreements pertain to the actors only, not the filmmaker and crew members. For more details on each SAG agreement, go to www.sagindie.org. Always check the SAG Web site because actor's salaries are always changing.

Hanging below the line

Below-the-line items include your more definitive numbers — flat fees and fixed salaries. These usually include your staff and crew, film stock, videotape, memory cards or hard drives, and other categories in which the dollar amounts aren't astronomical and in which you have choices of where to purchase or rent things to fit your budget. On a feature film for which the stars are getting paid millions, the above-the-line numbers can dwarf the below-the-line numbers.

Staffing and crewing

You can find many ways to enlist staff and crew to work on your film. You can pay them something, or you can get them to work for free and defer their pay. The best of both worlds is to pay your crew a little something up front and defer the rest. Getting a staff member or crew person to work deferred is more difficult than getting an actor to work deferred because, unlike the actor, the crew member's work is not as visible on screen. The only advantage for a crew member to work for deferred salary is if he is new to the business and is willing to learn and even apprentice on your film. A crew member may work for less if she is looking to graduate to a higher position and receive a better credit for her resume (for example, moving up from gaffer to cinematographer on the shoot). See Chapter 7 for more about crew members.

You need to negotiate with each crew member and put in writing (a *deal memo*) whether he or she is working by the hour or being paid a flat fee. You can find production forms including crew agreements using Movie Forms Pro (www.movieformspro.com). If you're working with a non-union crew, you have a lot more flexibility in negotiating salaries. Minimum-wage laws will help you set a limited hourly payment (check the minimums in your state) for your crew so they don't feel you're exploiting them. For more information, see www.dol.gov and click on "Wages."

Equipment costs — yes it does!

Equipment costs are also part of the below-the-line expenses. Equipment includes things like sound equipment, cameras, tripod, dolly, and lighting equipment (stands, lights, cables, and so on).

There are lots of camera rental houses that will negotiate with you. Check out rental houses in the Creative Handbook (www.creativehandbook.com). You can make deals on renting or borrowing props, and getting locations to use in your movie through friends and family. (Other categories that you'll find below-the-line are exemplified in Figure 4-3 in the next section, "Budgeting for budget software.")

Actors will work for food

Whether or not your budget allows for your actors to receive salaries, you have to budget to feed them (don't forget to feed your crew too!). Feeding your actors is one of the most important things — don't skimp in this category. People can get very irritable when they haven't eaten properly, and you don't want to fill everyone up on burgers and pizza every day. Budget for not only a great caterer, but for *craft services* (snacks) as well. Being generous when it comes to feeding your actors can make all the difference in the world. Make sure to find out if anyone requires a special diet, such as vegetarian meals or non-dairy. You don't want anyone starving on your shoot.

 If you're doing a low-budget production, look for crew with their own equipment. You may find a cinematographer who has his own camera — especially these days, with 24progressive digital cameras coming down in price. Some cinematographers even own 16mm, 35mm, or digital and HD cameras. Some may have lights and grip equipment, too. Your sound mixer may have her own sound equipment, including a recorder and microphones. (See Chapters 10, 11, and 12 for more on equipment.)

Film stock or digital hard driving

The medium on which you choose to shoot your story affects your budget, whether you shoot super-8, 16mm, 35mm, digital or HD (see Chapter 10). Your *shooting ratio,* or the number of takes in relation to the number of shots you end up using, is also going to determine what you spend on film stock and developing (or digital videotape if shooting video, or hard drive space if shooting in HD) — and ultimately your budget. Do you plan on shooting 1:1 (one take per usable shot) or 3:1 (three takes to get the shot)? Whether this is your first film or last film (just kidding) will determine whether you need to do three takes to get the shot or ten takes to get the shot (even many seasoned directors like to do multiple takes).

To determine the amount of tape film stock or memory cards (that hold your HD digital footage) you need, multiply the number of takes times the total pages of your screenplay (one page averages one minute of screen time). If you plan on 5:1 (five takes to get one shot), multiply 5 times 100 minutes (from a 100-page script) and realize that you need 500 minutes of footage — and then budget accordingly.

Memory cards are used in digital HD cameras instead of video tape. They're like mini hard drives that your camera's high definition footage is recorded and stored on. The content on the memory card can then be transferred to a computer or external hard drive and the card reused. Memory cards come in various sizes starting at 8 gigs.

Topping your budget

The budget *top sheet* is a summary of your budget that lists the main budget categories and the totals of each. You can reference each department by its budget category number assigned on the budget top sheet for a detailed breakdown in the long-form budget. (See Figure 4-3 for a sample budget top sheet created with Easy Budget software, discussed in the following section.) Usually, the top sheet is enough for an investor to see how your film breaks down in terms of cost. Eventually, an investor will want to see the detailed budget and how the categories are broken down.

Each budget item on the top sheet is assigned a category number that helps you reference the details of that category within the long-form detailed budget. It's like a table of contents. For example, Production Staff is category 200-00 and can be found on page 3 of the long-form detailed budget breakdown. On page 3 of the budget detail page, category 200-00 will be broken down listing the individual staff positions and the duration of employment and salary of each. Figure 4-3 also gives you an idea of costs associated with categories like insurance, music score, and so on, on a $214,000 budget.

Budgeting for budget software

Like scheduling software, budgeting software can take a lot of the hard work out of creating a budget for a film. The following are some of the programs available:

- ✔ **Filmmaker Software,** mentioned earlier in this chapter, has a budgeting template included in its production software. A steal at only $15! Go to www.filmmakersoftware.com.

- ✔ **Microsoft Excel** enables you to create your own budget template.

- ✔ **BBP Software** makes a film/TV budgeting template that runs on Microsoft Excel, for the Macintosh and for Windows. It has additional templates for crew and actor contact lists and sells for $99. You can download it from the Web at www.boilerplate.net.

- ✔ **Easy Budget,** which retails for $189.95 at www.easy-budget.com, really is easy to use. Refer to Figure 4-3 to see a budget top sheet created in Easy Budget.

- ✔ **Gorilla** has a budgeting template included in its complete production software package and is available at www.junglesoftware.com for $199 (Student Edition).

- ✔ **EP Budgeting** by Entertainment Partners is the budget software of choice in Hollywood. At $499 , it can be expensive for a low-budget filmmaker, but it's the top of the line if you can afford it. Check it out at www.entertainmentpartners.com. If you're a student (and can prove it) you can get the software for $195 at the Writer's Store (www.writersstore.com).

PRODUCTION BUDGET
Your Movie Title Goes Here

January 1, 2003

ACCOUNT	DESCRIPTION	PAGE	TOTAL
	-Above-the-Line Costs-		
110-00	STORY RIGHTS	1	$5,000.00
120-00	PRODUCER & STAFF	1	$20,000.00
130-00	DIRECTOR	1	$15,000.00
140-00	TALENT	2	$35,000.00
150-00	A-T-L FRINGE BENEFITS	3	$0.00
	Total Above-the-Line Costs:		$75,000.00
	-Production-		
200-00	PRODUCTION STAFF	3	$35,000.00
210-00	EXTRA TALENT	4	$4,000.00
220-00	ART DIRECTION	4	$3,500.00
230-00	SET CONSTRUCTION	5	$3,200.00
240-00	PROPERTY DEPARTMENT	5	$2,300.00
250-00	ANIMALS & ANIMAL HANDLERS	5	$0.00
260-00	STUNTS	6	$0.00
270-00	WARDROBE	6	$2,500.00
280-00	MAKEUP & HAIRDRESSING	6	$1,800.00
290-00	LIGHTING & ELECTRICAL	7	$4,800.00
300-00	GRIP & LABOR	7	$5,500.00
310-00	CAMERA	7	$4,500.00
320-00	PRODUCTION SOUND	8	$3,500.00
330-00	TRANSPORTATION	8	$1,500.00
340-00	LOCATIONS/SET OPERATIONS	8-9	$2,500.00
350-00	FILM & VIDEO PROCESSING	10	$3,500.00
360-00	STUDIO FEES & STAGE RENTAL	10	$0.00
370-00	TESTS & RETAKES	10	$0.00
380-00	SECOND PHOTOGRAPHIC UNIT	10	$1,500.00
	Production Sub Total:		$79,600.00
	-Post Production-		
400-00	EDITORIAL	11	$5,600.00
410-00	MUSIC SCORE	11	$10,000.00
420-00	POST PRODUCTION SOUND	11	$20,000.00
430-00	VISUAL EFFECTS and TITLES	12	$5,000.00
440-00	POST PRODUCTION LAB	12	$0.00
	Post Production Sub Total:		$40,600.00
	-Other Costs-		
500-00	INSURANCE	12	$4,500.00
510-00	B-T-L FRINGE BENEFITS	12	$0.00
520-00	ADVERTISING & PUBLICITY	13	$0.00
530-00	GENERAL OVERHEAD	13	$2,500.00
600-00	CONTINGENCY	13	$12,020.00
700-00	COMPLETION BOND	14	$0.00
	Other Costs Sub Total:		$19,020.00
	Below-The-Line Total:		$139,220.00
	GRAND TOTAL:		$214,220.00

© The Easy Budget Company

Figure 4-3: A sample budget top sheet from Easy Budget software.

The different budgeting software programs are similar, but some are easier to use than others and some have additional applications. Which program you use is usually a matter of personal preference and also depends on how much you want to spend. Entertainment Partners budgeting software has all the categories that you can use or modify. If you use Microsoft Excel, you'll have to design a budgeting template and set up the tables to give you the proper calculations. Some software like BBP Software, mentioned earlier, uses Excel and turns it into a film-budgeting program.

Factoring in a contingency amount

One concern is to make sure you don't go over budget. It happens all the time with studio pictures, but it's not as much a problem for studio pictures as it is for independent films. If a studio picture at $30 million goes over $5 million, the studio usually covers it. If your independent $50,000 movie goes over budget by $10,000, getting that additional funding and completing your movie could become a serious problem. Films often go over budget; rarely do they come in under budget.

Make sure that you allow for a contingency in your budget (usually 5 to 15 percent of the total budget). This will be helpful if and when emergencies come up and things end up costing more than expected, or the schedule changes because of an actor, weather, or some unplanned event. An additional $15,000 contingency on a $150,000 movie could make the difference between having a finished or unfinished movie in the end.

Insurance Is Your Best Policy

An important budget item is insurance for your cast, crew, and equipment. In the long run, insurance *saves* you money, not costs you! It's kind of like wearing your seatbelt: You may not need it, but if you do, you'll be glad that you buckled up for your journey. Better safe than sorry.

Purchasing insurance for a film production is a mix-and-match situation. You need to decide what type of coverage you need and how much of each type of coverage you want. You also need to decide how much of a deductible you're willing to pay (just like with your car or health insurance) if you ever have to activate the policy. You should consider the following types of coverage:

✔ **Cast insurance:** Getting cast insurance usually requires physicals for your actors to make sure that they're starting on your film in a healthy state. If a cast member gets sick (and cannot continue on the film) or dies, cast insurance covers any additional costs that can arise to finish the picture — even if it has to be recast. This coverage can be extremely expensive and should be purchased on an independent film only if a cast member cannot be replaced.

✓ **General liability insurance:** This is required insurance that protects you and your production from claims against you for property damage and claims against you from the public or a third party for injury or accidents incurred on the set.

Make sure that your general liability policy covers any interior locations you shoot at. If you're filming at the art museum and one of your film lights ignites a priceless painting and ends up burning down the museum, you don't want to be stuck without insurance to cover the disaster. No one will let you shoot on their property until you hand them a certificate of insurance, anyway. An average liability policy covers up to $1 million.

✓ **Film and tape coverage:** Though it's still called film and tape coverage, this coverage also now includes all digital, hard drives, and DVD elements used to record your camera footage, as well as processed and captured footage. This covers damage to film or tape and hard drives. A policy can also cover faulty lab work, ruined negatives, bad stock, defective memory cards or hard drives, footage lost during shipping, and so on. Also known as *negative insurance,* it pays for the cost to reshoot footage that was lost or damaged. This is not as crucial for shoots when you're using videotape or hard drives — *if* you make backups of your footage. (If you use video-tape or hard drives, always back up — just in case.)

✓ **Props, wardrobe, and sets coverage:** This covers damage, loss, or theft of important props, wardrobe, and sets. If your film doesn't require expensive props and costumes, you can go without this insurance, or take out a low coverage policy (only insure for the total value of all props, wardrobe, and sets). Don't insure for more than the value — it will cost you more, and it's not necessary (you can only be reimbursed the total value of what you lost, not beyond that).

✓ **Production equipment coverage:** This covers any equipment used on the production. Many rental companies won't rent equipment to you if you don't insure their equipment under a property coverage policy. Most companies request an *insurance certificate,* which is issued from the insurance company showing proof that you have insurance and what your coverage is. On most low-budget productions, a $250,000 minimum coverage should suffice.

✓ **Errors and omissions (E&O) insurance:** Before a distributor or network will show your film, it needs to be protected with errors & omissions insurance, also referred to as E&O insurance. E&O insurance covers lawsuits resulting from copyright infringement and using products or names without permission (usually in bad taste). An E&O policy can run you anywhere between $4,800 and $8,000 depending on the subject material of your film.

You can save a little on your budget by not purchasing E&O insurance until after your film is completed — and let the distributor purchase it (they'll usually deduct the cost from your sales).

✔ **Worker's compensation:** As an employer, you're required to cover your employees under worker's compensation. This protects you and the employees should they have an accident while in your employ. You can buy worker's comp coverage through an insurance agency or payroll company at between 3 to 4 percent of your payroll (the percentage differs in each state). Worker's comp covers people who work as volunteers on your set as well as those who work for pay.

When you take out an insurance policy, you need it only for the dates of your actual production (although for cast and crew insurance, you may want to overlap the weeks or months during pre-production and right through the end of filming your movie). Taking out insurance for a period of a month instead of a year is much more affordable, especially if you're on a tight budget.

When you take out production insurance, you'll have a *deductible* (the amount you have to pay should you have damages and have to activate the policy). Depending on your coverage, a deductible is generally between $2,500 and $5,000. After you pay the deductible, your damages are covered up to the amount of the policy coverage amount. For example, if your camera and tripod fall off a cliff (it happens all the time), the price of the equipment ($30,000) that went over the cliff would be covered, minus the $2,500 deductible. If your cameraman went with the equipment, that's a more serious issue!

Finding an insurance broker

Specific insurance companies specialize in production insurance for your film. (*Note:* Your homeowner's or renter's policy is not appropriate for a film shoot, though it may cover some of your personal items if they're lost, damaged, or stolen while you're on a shoot.)

✔ **Dewitt Stern** offers independent production insurance for around $3,500 to $4,500 depending on the budget and production requirements (www. dewittstern.com).

✔ **ProductionInsurance.com** (a service of Supple-Merrill & Driscoll) is another great place for insurance information: (www.production insurance.com).

✔ **Film Emporium** also provides insurance to independent productions. You can fill out an insurance application form, choose the type of insurance you want, and submit for a quote. Go to the Web site at www. filmemporium.com and click on "Insurance" for more information.

If you find that production insurance is too costly, see if you can go on a *rider*. A rider is what it sounds like: You ride along on someone else's insurance policy. If you're doing the film for a company, chances are you can ride on its insurance policy. Check with the insurance company to make sure that you're covered if you decide to go this route.

Before you go on another company's insurance policy via a rider, make sure that company is legitimately affiliated with you and your production. If you end up having to make an insurance claim, the insurance company will *not* honor the policy if they find out that a company not associated with your production was just letting you use their insurance.

Bond, completion bond

A *completion bond* is an insurance policy that guarantees to the investor or financing source that if your film goes over budget, the completion bond company will finance the difference to complete the picture. The catch is that the completion bond company charges a percentage to do this (usually between 3 and 5 percent of the total budget), whether you need them in the end or not. And if you do go over budget and they have to step in, they can take over the film — and you're history. Usually, films with budgets of less than $1 million are not bonded, so if you're working on a low-budget production, this is not something you need to worry about.

A completion bond company conducts an extensive survey with you and all the production elements. They want to make sure that your budget is realistic. They don't want to have to finance the film — they just want their percentage fee. If you have an underwater fantasy that ends with resurrecting the *Titanic* on a $30,000 budget, they're not going to bond your film.

One of the leading completion bond companies is Film Finances. You can get more information about completion bonds and the services of Film Finances by going to www.ffi.com.

Entitled to a title

Nowadays most distributors require you to provide them with a *title search* and *opinion* on your film's title. The title search shows who else has used the same title, or similar title. This helps a distributor determine whether they want to keep the title, or if it might cause confusion with a similar or identical title. The title *opinion* must be done by an attorney, and it's their legal opinion as to whether they feel there will be any legal concerns using your title (though titles cannot be copyrighted). I've used Suzanne Vaughan for both my title searches and opinions, since she is also an attorney. She can give you a great rate, too, if you contact her at www.clearances.net.

Chapter 5

Financing Your Film

*Y*ou can write a script with virtually no money, but to make a film you need dollars to put it all together. So how do you go about financing your film? Maxing out your credit cards or mortgaging the house is not the smartest or safest way to get the money to make your film. A better idea is to find an investor or investors who are prepared to take the risk of financing a film. Before you even start looking for the film dollars, you need to prepare a professional presentation to show to your potential investors. After you've hooked the money people, you need to offer them a good incentive to believe in you and your project.

In this chapter, I introduce the various ways and places you can find funding for your film. And after you have the funding, I show you how to get started so you can turn the dream of making your film into a reality.

Creating an Enticing Prospectus

Making a film takes money, and that's where the almighty investor comes into the picture. An investor is the person or group that believes in you and your film and has faith in its commercial potential to make money for them. The investor is the one who makes it possible for you to actually produce your film. Without the investor's money, your idea would remain on paper and might never see the light of the projector.

I use the term *investor*, but that doesn't necessarily mean just one investor. Getting people to invest in your film is like selling stock in your film. It's easier to find ten people with $5,000 each than it is to find one with $50,000.

Before you can start looking for investors, you need some ammunition. In order to entice investors, you need to put together a formal written presentation detailing why someone should invest in you and your project. Known as a *prospectus* or *business plan,* this presentation should be informative and entertaining. Putting together a prospectus not only helps get you financing for your film, but it also helps you see your goal more clearly. Keep in mind that, even though the prospectus is a written presentation, you should be prepared to verbally pitch your film idea and its commercial potential to the investor as well.

You can write your own plan from scratch following the advice I give in this section, or you can get software programs with specific templates to help you design an informative plan. For example, you can download PlanMagic at www.planmagic.com for $99.95, or Business Plan Pro at www.business planpro.com for $99.95. If you want a software program specifically geared for a film prospectus only, then Movieplan is a good choice! It's only $39.95, and you can get more details at www.movieplan.net.

The following sections explain what information your package should contain. (***Note:*** Be sure to include a table of contents page directing the investor to the appropriate sections of interest along with page numbers.)

An investor's main focus is to make a good return on his or her investment, while at the same time knowing the associated risk. This is why you should concentrate on presenting to your investor the money-making possibilities should he or she invest in your project. An investor is more concerned with making a profit and looking at your production as an investment; a studio or distributor is looking at the whole picture — a film with a strong story that also has commercial potential.

Synopsis of your film

Most investors are only interested in knowing the gist of your story and the commercial viability of producing it into a film. Your synopsis should include references to the money-making potential of this particular type of story. A page or two is an appropriate length for a synopsis, not much longer than that. At the end of the synopsis, be sure to note that the screenplay is available upon request (be aware that an investor not familiar with screenplay formatting may find the script difficult to read).

Information about you

Your prospectus should include information about your background and achievements. Investors want to know your credits and experience, if any, with regards to filmmaking. If you have made other films before this, list how they faired financially. Also list related skills such as educational background and financial achievements that help support why you're capable of making this film and using the investor's money to finance your production. Be sure to include any documents, such as newspaper articles or copies of award certificates, that support your filmmaking accomplishments and educational degrees.

Info about your cast and crew

If you've already signed on cast and crew, include their resumes. If you don't know for sure who will sign on as members of your cast and crew, list the people you plan to approach. It's only important to list crew like a cinematographer or make-up person who has impressive credits on other successful films that will add to the look of your film.

Also include a *letter of interest* from any actors or name stars who've expressed interest in your project. A letter of interest shows that there is interest from someone who could potentially help the commercial success of your film by appearing in your production. See Chapter 8 for more on letters of interest.

Your budget and profit projections

Investors obviously want to know how much the film will cost to complete. You can include a budget *top sheet,* which is a one-page summary of the entire budget broken into specific categories, or you can provide the full detailed budget with a breakdown of every category. See Chapter 4 for more on budgeting.

Your profit projections estimate how much your film could make in sales, based on other films and studio and/or independent productions similar to your film's budget and genre. You can find this information in the weekly box office reports in *The Hollywood Reporter* or *Daily Variety,* as well as in special marketing issues of these publications.

Investigating Investors

There's an art to finding investors. You need to know who to approach and how much to ask them for, in terms of dollars and cents. You also need to keep their interests in mind when presenting your project. Are they looking to make a lot of money? Or are they satisfied with making a small return on their investment with the association of being involved in the moviemaking business?

Prospecting a Web site

The Internet is a great tool for promoting your film. In the past, filmmakers spent a fortune photocopying their prospectus for their film and then paying for postage or courier charges. Now all you have to do is tell your potential investors to check out your Web site. Investors across the world can check out your project in a matter of seconds, after you tell them about your Web site. (For examples, check out my official Web sites at www.bryanmichaelstoller.com, www.misscastaway.com, and www.lightyearsawaymovie.com). Having a Web site gives you the ability to link to and cross-reference certain information. If you're talking about a particular actor, you can link to the actor's Web site. Or you can create a link to a certain location or piece of equipment that takes the viewer directly to that information.

Locating potential investors: Show me the money!

So who makes a good investor? Anyone! Your parents or relatives, a coworker, an acquaintance you met at a party or seminar, your doctor, lawyer, or dentist, your boyfriend or girlfriend — or their boyfriend or girlfriend, and anyone you do business with, such as the shop owner down the street.

People are always looking for different ways to invest their money. Some play it safe and put it into interest-bearing accounts or long-term CDs. Others like the excitement and risk of playing the stock market, buying property, or the fun of investing in a film. Anyone who has a little (or a lot) of money to invest may be willing to take a chance and back your film; you just have to ask. (I discuss ways to successfully approach potential investors later in this chapter.)

Investors are out there — you just have to find them. And remember, timing is everything. Someone may not be prepared to invest in your film today, but they may be tomorrow. Don't give up — keep asking.

- ✔ **Whether you're at a cocktail party, a screening, or even at the photocopier, let everyone you come into contact with know that you're looking for investors for your film.** You never know who knows whom. Maybe Johnny's dad wants to get involved in financing a small film — you never know until you ask. Word of mouth is the best way to find financing for your film.

- ✔ **Get a mailing list of investors from a mailing list company.** Try Hugo Dunhill Mailing Lists, Inc. (www.hdml.com — look in the index under "Investors"; also try other high-income lists such as "Doctors"). Addresses can be sent to you in the form of mailing labels or email addresses. You pay $75 for every 1,000 names and addresses.

You don't have to find a millionaire to invest in your film. Everyday people are willing to invest some of their savings and/or extra earnings — just look at all those who go to Las Vegas to take a chance on the tables.

Approaching a potential investor

After you know whom to approach for financing, you need to know how to approach them. Meeting an investor is like going out on a first date — you have to impress on the first date, or you don't get a second one. Your first meeting with a potential investor will probably be over the phone. You need to sell him on getting involved with you and your film so that you can move to the next step and have a face-to-face meeting. The potential investor may request a copy of your prospectus or business plan before wanting to meet in person. This is why your presentation package is so important: If it intrigues the investor, you'll get that in-person meeting and have a chance to close the deal.

Keep in mind the following when approaching investors:

- **Be enthusiastic** about your project, but don't be phony.

- **Be honest** and don't guarantee that they'll get rich from investing in your film. If you prove that you can be trusted, they may invest in *you* — and fund your future projects.

Don't ever guarantee investors that they'll recoup their investment and make a profit. Nothing in life is guaranteed, especially getting rich off making a movie. You don't want to mislead them. If you guarantee they'll make money and they don't, they could legally come after you stating you made false promises to them.

- **Be prepared.** Before calling, be ready to answer any questions the investor may ask. This can include what your film's about (be ready to pitch your story), budget amount, shooting schedule, post-production to release schedule, and how long it will take for them to see a return (if any) on their investment. Before your face-to-face meeting, review all the material in your package so that the investor will know that you know what you're talking about.

- **Be respectful.** Assure the investor that you will treat his or her money as if it were your own.

- **Follow up** with a thank-you note to the investor for taking the time to meet with you and for considering your proposal.

You have to look at it as a win-win situation. People get excited about the idea of getting involved in financing a film. It's a lot more exciting (and definitely more glamorous) than buying $5,000 in toilet paper stock. You could be doing the investor a favor. The investor has the potential of making money with your film (also the potential to lose his pants — but you probably don't want to say that). But again, be honest, and let them know investing in a film is a risk — there's no guarantee they'll get their money back or make a profit — but that it's your honest intention to make money for them with your film.

You can also entice your investors by offering to give them an Executive Producer credit in your film's opening credits. If so, be sure to mutually agree in writing the appropriate credit that your investor will receive on the film. You can have as many Executive Producer credits as fits the number of investors.

After you've found investors, a company agreement between you and your investors must be drafted before anyone is going to hand over cash for you to make your film. When the investor agrees to participate in the financing of your film, it's time to move on to forming a company and ironing out the details of putting your project together.

Keeping the Securities and Exchange Commission in mind

To protect investors and investments from misrepresentation or fraud, the Securities and Exchange Commission (SEC) regulates companies or individuals seeking to raise financing. SEC regulations prevent the fund-raising company from misrepresenting the project (and committing other fraudulent acts) so that investors can make informed judgments on whether to invest and how much they want to risk.

As you raise funds for your project, you have to follow SEC rules that ensure potential investors are property informed. These rules deal with things like

✔ How to present your investment opportunity.

✔ How to inform the SEC of your business activities.

✔ How you identify yourself to investors (to make sure that you don't misrepresent your intention and that you conduct all business activities in a legal manner).

If you plan on soliciting money from investors that you do not know personally or if you're soliciting from a number of potential investors (not just one) from a list or through referrals, you need to register with the SEC and follow their rules and regulations. (If the money is from your immediate family, friends, or a limited number of people you know, you don't need to be regulated by the SEC.) The SEC reviews your registration to make sure you're abiding by the rules and regulations of soliciting for funds. You can find all the information you need, along with forms to fill out and register at the Securities and Exchange Commission website (www.sec.gov).

If you should register with the SEC but don't, you could be fined if you don't comply with the rules and regulations of soliciting funds.

Starting a Film Company

When you find an investor who believes in you and your film project, you need to set up a production company through which to run the financing. You often need your investors to help finance the startup of the company as well, so it's best to wait to form the company until you find an investor.

If you don't set up some form of a production company, you're what's called a *sole proprietorship,* and don't have the protection that a production company may provide. Setting up a corporation or limited liability company gives you have a little more protection from lawsuits and other headaches. The company can act as a shield so that, in the event you're sued, only the assets of the company — and not your personal assets — are vulnerable. Each situation is different, so always consult a lawyer about your options and risks.

Being in the right company

You have lots of choices when it comes to the type of company you want to form, each of which has its own advantages and disadvantages:

- General partnership
- Limited partnership
- Corporation
- Limited liability company (LLC)
- Joint venture

As you choose the company that best suits your situation, consider these three main factors:

- ✔ **Liability:** Who will be responsible in case of a lawsuit or bad debts? You and the company partners, or just the company?

- ✔ **Taxes:** What kind of tax structure does the company have? Does the company pay tax or do the taxes flow through to you and your partner's personal taxes?

- ✔ **Ownership:** Who owns the film and any other assets of the company?

Limited partnerships limit the relationship

A *limited partnership* limits one of the partner's liabilities and tax responsibilities (usually the investor in this case). The main or *general partner* is responsible for the company, while the *limited partner* remains silent and lets you do all the work. For example, an investor gives you the money to make your film, but he or she is not involved with the creative decisions or production of the film.

In a limited partnership, only the investor's investment is at risk. Because the investor isn't responsible for any activities that are performed by the limited partnership, he or she isn't liable if there are any lawsuits against the film or the general partner.

Howdy pardner — Striking up a partnership?

A *partnership* is the merging of two or more people with the same goals in business who sign an agreement to achieve those goals together. Also known as a *general partnership,* this agreement gives each partner equal authority and equal liability (as opposed to limited authority in a limited partnership) for the company's activities.

Incorporating the idea of a corporation

A *corporation* is a professional entity that is separate from you as an individual. The corporation reports to the IRS regarding taxes, and it is liable in case of lawsuits, bad debts, and so on. A corporation protects the company owners, the filmmaker (that would be you), and your partners (to an extent) by what's called the *corporate shield.* In the event of a lawsuit, only the corporation assets are liable, not the assets of the individuals who run the company.

The costs of starting a corporation vary, depending on whether you use a corporate attorney or incorporate on your own. It can cost as little as $20 or as much as several hundred dollars, depending on where you incorporate and how. You can incorporate through an online service like www.incorporating.com or www.legalzoom.com that guides you through all the steps of incorporating.

Two good places to incorporate are Nevada and Delaware. Those who form corporations in Nevada, regardless of whether their offices are there or not, do so because the advantages are substantial:

- ✔ There are lower or no tax fees for running the corporation.
- ✔ There are minimal tax obligations (no state taxes).
- ✔ Owners can remain anonymous from the IRS and public records.
- ✔ There is low maintenance in running a Nevada company.
- ✔ Owners don't have to reside in Nevada.

Some people choose to form their corporation in Delaware because, although it has a small fee to incorporate (more than Nevada, but less than any other state) and annual tax obligations, you can incorporate relatively quickly and easily, and company owners remain anonymous. Delaware is also known to have the highest amount of corporations that are *not* physically in the state. All paperwork, which includes setting up the corporation, filing taxes, and accounting, can be done through the mail or online.

Let's see about an LLC: Limited liability company

A *limited liability company* (LLC) combines the best of a corporation and a limited partnership. It protects the filmmaker's assets that are separate from the LLC in case of a liability suit. An LLC is also easier and cheaper to form than a corporation. Usually the owners of the LLC are listed as members without official corporate titles. An LLC is taxed similar to a corporation, or you have the choice of directing profits and expenses through to your personal taxes.

Zooming in on Legalzoom.com

Legalzoom.com was started by a group of lawyers to help make legal advice accessible for everyone using the convenience of the Internet. The site helps you quickly and affordably deal with legal issues, such as starting a business, registering a copyright or trademark and specific contracts — all from the comfort of your home. Legalzoom.com can help you form your production company as an LLC, corporation, partnership, or any of the other business entities mentioned in this chapter. For the appropriate fees, Legalzoom.com will process and file all the appropriate paperwork. It'll even help you file in small claims court if someone owes you money or didn't fulfill a service. The site includes helpful and informative articles and question and answer sections regarding legal issues (www.legalzoom.com).

Joining together: Joint ventures

A *joint venture* usually involves two companies already in business who join together on one production. These companies can be corporations, partnerships, or LLCs. Many studios nowadays are doing joint productions because the cost of a studio film with big-name talent has skyrocketed. A joint venture is similar to the structure of a partnership (it's like a joint partnership).

Other things to do to set up your company

When setting up a company, you need to consider some other items on your to-do list:

- **Opening a checking account (specifically for your production):** If you have a checking account specifically for your production, you can monitor the film's production expenses, and your investors can see a proper accounting of where their dollars were spent.

- **Creating a company name and logo:** A logo gives your production company a professional appearance and credibility, and of course a name identifies it and expresses what kind of company it is.

- **Printing business cards and stationery:** Business cards and stationery add to the professional image of your new production company.

- **Hiring an attorney to look over all agreements:** An attorney can help to protect you from lawsuits and negligence.

Going Escrow

When you've found your financing and set up your production company, as explained in the earlier sections of this chapter, you may want to consider an *escrow account*. An escrow company monitors the bank account that's been set up with the funds for your production. You don't want to be a week into filming and find out your investor hasn't sent the next installment of the budget. Having the money in an escrow account ensures that the money is indeed there and available.

The *escrow holder or agent* follows the specific conditions of a written agreement signed by you and your investors instructing what, where, when, and how the funds will be released. These instructions usually include a payment schedule for disbursement of funds with regards to the production of the film, from preproduction all the way through postproduction. An escrow account is also a security blanket for investors, ensuring them that there will be no suspicious tapping into the bank account.

Fictitiously "doing business as"

If you form a company as a division under someone else's company (or a company you currently own), you may want to use a fictitious business name called a DBA (short for *doing business as*) or sometimes an *AKA* (short for *also known as*). A DBA or AKA is kind of like a pseudonym.

To register a DBA, go to your city's county clerk's office or download the form from the Web site (check your local government Web pages for your county clerk's Web site). A DBA costs between $5 and $187 to register, depending on what state and county you live in, and it expires five years from the date you file it. You can also register and file your DBA using `www.legalzoom.com` (for $99 plus state fees), without leaving your computer. You have to announce the name in a local newspaper to make it official and legal — which costs extra (you run it for four weeks in the new businesses classified section). The clerk's office will give you the information for the newspapers and periodicals that provide this service.

Contracting Your Investor

Drawing up a formal agreement between you and your investors is the final step in securing financing. This agreement is often an adjunct to your business formation agreement (whether it be a corporation, an LLC, or a form of partnership). It spells out exactly the understanding between you and your investors with regards to the financing of your film and the participation (if any) in your company.

Every type of legal agreement has a standard contract. These agreements are called *boilerplate* agreements, meaning all you have to do is fill in the information pertaining to your specific project and budget. You can also add specific items or concerns that you or your investor want to address. You can find boilerplate agreements in Mark Litwak's book, *Contracts for Film and Television* (for more information go to `www.marklitwak.com`). *The Complete Film Production Handbook* also has every conceivable agreement relating to film production including a CD-ROM with printable forms, all for under $40. Movieplan is another software program with investor and company formation agreements (`www.movieplan.net`).

 Even if you do use boilerplate agreements, I recommend that you have them reviewed by an attorney to make sure you've covered yourself. (You also have the choice of using an attorney to prepare your contract from scratch, but this will cost you more than starting with a boilerplate agreement.)

All investor agreements should include the following information:

✔ **Profit:** Usually profits are shared 50/50 between the investors and you and your production company.

- ✔ **Responsibilities:** Spell out the responsibilities of you and your company and the responsibilities of the investor regarding financing.

- ✔ **Recoupment:** This is when and how long it will take before the investors will see their investment back (but never guarantee they will), plus any profits, and how it will be dispersed between you and the investors. Recoupment, if any, can happen soon after the film is completed, or it may take a year or more, depending on the commercial viability of the film and the aggressiveness of your distributor.

- ✔ **Expenses:** Expenses can include your company overhead, distributor's percentage fee, distributor's advertising and marketing costs for your film, travel costs, film market costs, and any other expenses you specify in the agreement pertaining to the production.

- ✔ **Auditing:** Does the investor have the right to audit? If not, who does?

- ✔ **Bonus:** As an incentive to your investor to want to invest in your project, you may want to include a special added bonus on top of the investor's standard recoupment of his investment. A bonus can be in the form of an additional percentage on profits, or a quicker return of his investment before certain expenses are paid, and so on.

Tapping into Alternative Sources

If you aren't having much luck finding private investors, or you need supplemental funding to match funds you've already raised, you do have some additional options.

Pre-selling your film

You may be able to *pre-sell* your film, based on a great script or star talent. You first find a distributor, who then takes your film idea, the script, or the trailer and gets deposits upfront (usually 20 percent of the total selling price) from buyers who like the idea and who will pay the balance (the remaining 80 percent) when the film is delivered to them (see Chapter 19). By having a distributor pre-sell your film, it gives you some money to start your film, and shows that the buyers are seriously interested.

A three-minute trailer (a commercial for your film showing the highlights — see Chapter 19) or a scene from your script, can help pre-sell your film to potential investors or buyers (such as a studio or distributor). A trailer can be shot for little or no money, by getting your actors to work for deferred pay (see Chapter 4) and getting your equipment and locations donated.

Dolly Parton wrote and recorded four holiday songs for one of my films in development. These songs (and her name) were a great promotional tool when putting the production together. Dan Aykroyd provided the voice of Dexter the Computer in my feature film, *The Random Factor,* which gave me a bit of star power to entice a distributor to pick up the film.

Getting a grant

When I was 13 years old, I applied to a government council that financed short films. I was turned down because I was too young. I then applied to a fund that encouraged children to make their own films — they, too, turned me down, telling me I was too old. That was my first and last attempt at trying to get a grant. I don't recommend this route because it involves a lot of time, research, and paperwork — not to mention waiting (as long as two years) to know if you received the grant. But, on the other hand, you may get lucky and find it's just the thing for you.

A grant is easier to obtain if your film is about a cause or supports a charity and if it's a short film or public service announcement (PSA).

Getting a loan

One alternative to private financing is applying for a loan. Your bank may mortgage your home to give you some extra cash, or your credit-card company may increase your credit limit to give you more room for charges on your account.

Although mortgaging your home or upping your credit-card limit will help finance your project, I don't recommend going this route because the risk is too great. Think about it: If you borrow heavily on your credit card, you're going to have some astronomical monthly payments that you'll have to make until you break even on your film, which may never happen. And if you mortgage your home, the worst-case scenario is that you could lose your home — don't do it!

Bartering: Trade you this for that

Bartering is a form of trading. In bartering for a film, a company gives you the use of its product (on loan or to keep, depending on what it is), or an individual lets you use a particular element (like a location or prop) that you want to use in your film in exchange for a credit or placing the company's product on camera. Bartering is one way to bring your budget down, but it's not the way to finance your entire film.

When I was 11 years old, I used to finance my little Super 8 movies by barter-ing. For my film stock, I contacted different camera stores that sold Super 8 film. If they would donate ten rolls of film for me to make my movie, I would list them in the ending film credits. All through my teens, I bartered for on-camera products, including film stock. When I was 17, I made a film called *Superham* and raised some of the financing from a local car dealer. In exchange, the car dealer got a front presentation credit introducing the film. You can try bartering for the following products and services:

- ✔ Clothing
- ✔ Editing equipment and/or an editor
- ✔ Film stock, video tape, hard drives
- ✔ Food and drinks
- ✔ Hotel accommodations
- ✔ Laboratory film developing
- ✔ Locations
- ✔ Products featured in actual scenes
- ✔ Transportation (including cars for the production and airline tickets)

Bartering in the movie business is also known as *product placement*. Product placement is when a company places its product in your film and either lends it to you, gives it to you, or pays you for featuring it in your film (especially if a major star interacts with the product). For example, while shooting my film *Miss Cast Away and the Island Girls,* I approached The Sharper Image about fea-turing a remote control robot in the film. The company was excited about the product exposure and provided two robots to use in the film at no charge.

Product placement in the form of goods and services can save you hundreds, even thousands of dollars depending on what they are and what it would cost you if you had to actually pay for their use. If a food company donates sand-wiches, this could save you hundreds of dollars in feeding your cast and crew.

Some companies, such as Premier Entertainment Services of North Hollywood, California, specialize in placing products in films (check it out at www.pes filmtv.com). If you contact a product-placement company, it will request a copy of your script and comb through it, deciding where it may be able to provide on-camera product for you, based on the client products it represents. There is usually not a charge for this service as the product placement com-pany gets their fee from the companies that provide the products for your film.

Chapter 6

Location, Location, Location

In This Chapter

▶ Finding the perfect locations

▶ Filming at home or out of the country

▶ Creating locations on your computer

▶ Using stock footage

▶ Getting permits and fee waivers

*A*s a filmmaker, you have the power to take your audience on a trip to exotic locales — a remote island, a picturesque small town, or deep into outer space. Therefore, picking the right locations at which to shoot — or creating just the right environments on soundstages or on your computer — is very important to your film's success.

In this chapter, you find out how to discover great locations to use in your film — some of them free of charge. Depending on your budget and the setting of your film, you need to decide whether to shoot on location or on a controlled indoor soundstage, so I give you some advice about making that choice as well. Finally, to make sure that you and your film are protected, I explain the types of insurance and city permits that are usually required when filming on location. Police and firemen may be required, too, and they may show up if you *don't* hire them!

Locating Locations

After you've locked down your script — meaning there are no more changes — comb through it and determine where you want to shoot your scenes. Some software programs, like Movie Magic Screenwriter (www. screenplay.com), actually break down your script for you by pulling out all your scene headings and generating a list of settings from your screenplay. Of course, you can also go through the script yourself and jot down all the locations without having to use a computer. After you have a list of the settings for your film, you can start looking for the actual locations that will fit your story.

You may be able to get a location for free if you can offer something in exchange. If you're filming away from home and you give a hotel a credit or even feature the hotel on camera, you could get free accommodations or at least a discount for your cast and crew to stay there. Lodging can be expensive, and many independent films can't afford to put up cast and crew. So writing in a scene where you actually see the hotel, or adding a big thank you in the end credits, may be worth it.

Taking a picture: Say "cheese" and "thank you"

With the advent of digital still cameras, you can snap some great location pictures to show your cinematographer and other crew members what locations you have to choose from. And you can download the images to a computer and e-mail them in full, crisp color to whomever needs to see them — whether they're across town or across the world! Photos are also helpful in planning your shots after you choose the locations you want to use. With Gorilla software, you can even import your actual location photos right into the project management section; include details on your location as well as driving directions.

I use the Kyocera Finecam M400R, a 4.0-megapixel portable digital camera that takes magazine-quality photos (check out www.kyocera.com) and is small enough to fit in a handbag or jacket pocket. A digital camera like the Kyocera is an invaluable tool for any filmmaker — and not just for location scouting (I talk about other uses for a digital still camera for setting up special-effects shots in Chapter 17 and publicity pictures for your film in Chapter 19).

Sounding Off about Soundstages

Soundstages are a convenient way to shoot interior scenes mainly because you don't have to worry about unplanned sounds interrupting your takes. A soundstage is basically a soundproofed room. All exterior sounds are blocked out of an industrial soundstage after the doors are closed. A soundstage is an acoustic environment that has padded walls that absorb sound to prevent an echo or reverb in your dialogue, as would happen if you filmed in an uncarpeted room. Another advantage of shooting on a soundstage is that you can set up several interior sets for different locations in your script without having to move your whole production team. You can have a courtroom, a cell block, an apartment, a coffee shop, and an interior fast-food restaurant all on the same soundstage.

Finding — or creating — a sound stage

When you see an airport and airplane scene in a film, chances are it was shot on a controlled sound stage. Air Hollywood in Los Angeles (www.airholly wood.com) houses several airplane bodies that have removable walls and seats for convenient filming. Air Hollywood also has a full airport terminal that includes X-ray machines, a magazine store, and a bar. I like shooting at Air Hollywood because I've never experienced a flight delay or had to use the air-sickness bag, and they've never lost my luggage either! And 20th Century Props (www.20thcenturyprops.com) has pre-built sets like a full-scale submarine in its parking lot (I used it in my film *Silly Movie 2*).

To find a sound stage, do a search on the Internet (look for "sound stages"), check your local yellow pages, or order a copy of the *Creative Handbook*, which lists sound stages in Los Angeles (at www.creativehandbook.com; the *Handbook* is free if you meet their criteria).

A sound stage can also be a warehouse, a school gym, or a vacant apartment — any place where you can build sets and hold a decent-size crew. Of course, if the room or building is not soundproofed, you have to deal with outside noises. I once shot an office scene in an IKEA store where mock-up rooms are set up for customers. Many furniture stores use these type of displays, which make perfect sets — if you can get permission from the store and keep the customers quiet (and don't forget to hide the price tags!).

You can make your own soundproofed room, or at least cut down on the reverb, by putting up *foam sheets* on the walls, or on stands (outside of the camera's view) close to where the actors perform their dialogue. These foam sheets absorb reverb and prevent sounds from bouncing back. You can also rent *sound blankets* (the kind used by moving companies). Sound blankets also help to prevent echo and reverb by absorbing sound the way carpeting does. You can hang them outside of the shot or lay them on bare floors (when you're not showing the floor in your shot).

Putting up walls: Using flats

If you're going to shoot on a soundstage or in a warehouse, you have to construct your sets from scratch. You may need to hire carpenters or people with construction knowledge, or you can do the building yourself with the assistance of volunteers. If your budget allows, you could bring in a *production designer* (sort of like an interior designer) and maybe even a person versed in architectural design.

AFCI.org

The Association of Film Commissioners International (AFCI) can help you find answers to important location questions and even put you in contact with worldwide government contacts for on-location shooting. AFCI also puts on location trade shows, where you can meet state and worldwide film commissions all under one roof; check its Web site at www.afci.org for dates and locations. AFCI also publishes the informative *Locations Magazine.* For a subscription, go to the Web site.

Soundstage sets usually involve *flats,* which are separate moveable walls constructed of wooden frames with support stands to keep them upright. When you go to a theater to see a stage play, you often see sets created with flats. Putting together a simple room, such as an apartment, by using flats is fairly easy. Flats can also simulate exterior walls made of brick, logs, concrete, or stucco. Of course, if you have an elaborate set, like the interior of a dry cleaner or an ancient church, using the actual location is easier and cheaper (refer to the earlier section "Locating Locations" for details).

The advantage of filming on a soundstage using a set constructed with flats is that you can remove the fourth wall where the camera is, which allows more room for your crew and equipment to comfortably shoot the film. The problem with flats is that they're big and bulky; you need a truck to transport them and several helpers to carry and set them up.

You can build your own flats or find them at your local theater company. If you're in Los Angeles or New York, try one of the movie studios for renting flats, or you can find scenery houses and set-design companies listed in the Yellow Pages or an entertainment directory like the Los Angeles 411 (www.la411.com), New York 411 (www.newyork411.com), or the *Creative Handbook* (www.creativehandbook.com).

You can make your own flats by building a wood frame out of light plywood. Then you paint or wallpaper it, set it up, and bring in some furniture and set decoration — sort of like home decorating. If you're looking to create an exterior scene, you can attach paneling that resembles brick, log, concrete, or some other surface. You can cut out your own windows and put a scenic background outside the window to simulate an outside setting (or put some branches outside the window to suggest a tree). You can see how to construct sturdy flats in the *Stock Scenery Construction Handbook* by Bill Raoul (Broadway Press, 1990). Figure 6-1 shows a basic example of a flat and how it should be supported.

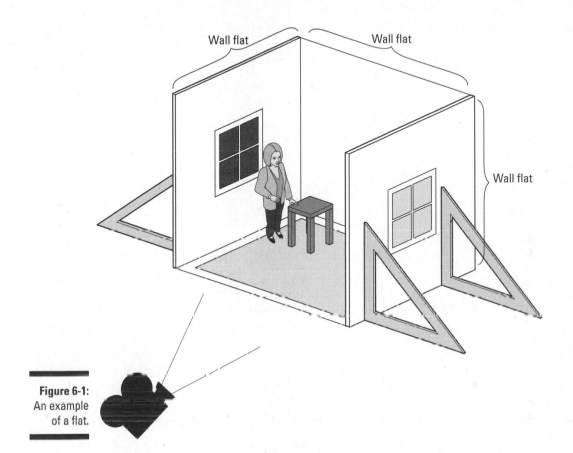

Figure 6-1:
An example
of a flat.

Shooting in the United States or Crossing the Border?

You may not have the luxury of deciding where to shoot your film: Your hometown may be all that you can afford. However, you may face the decision whether to film on locations in the United States or take your production to Canada to take advantage of the exceptional government rebates and funding programs. For information about shooting in Canada, go to these Web sites: www.telefilm.gc.ca, www.cftpa.ca, or www.omdc.on.ca. You may even be able to consider going somewhere else in the world (if the cost of transportation and accommodations is still less than shooting in your hometown). This section examines the pros and cons of both options.

Shooting outdoors

Weather is the number-one concern when shooting outdoors (unless you live in California, where it never rains, at least according to song). Your favorite cable network becomes the Weather Channel. Rain, snow, hail, and wind can ruin any shoot, or at least make it extremely difficult. Hot or cold environments can also affect your camera's performance. Condensation can form on the camera's lens when moving from a cool outside environment to a heated interior. Be prepared to shoot indoors at the last minute (with a backup secured location standing by) if you do get rained out, or be prepared to shoot your scene and have your actors acknowledge the weather in the scene if it is windy or storming.

Researching U.S. government incentives

Shooting outside the United States — often in Canada — has become much more common because of the many government incentives (tax and labor rebates). This phenomenon, known as *runaway production,* has become a concern for cast and crew in the U.S. who lose work to foreign workers. Runaway production is also a government concern, and local agencies are interested in keeping the film industry within the United States by sponsoring incentives to encourage filmmakers to shoot locally.

Making films is good for the economy; businesses, including restaurants, hotels, and parks, benefit from it. To entice filmmakers, many states (including California) offer some of these perks, but check first to make sure:

- ✔ They may not charge location fees for state owned property.
- ✔ They may offer tax rebates to filmmakers who shoot locally. A tax rebate reimburses the sales tax you paid for expenses related to your production.

   Tax incentive programs are always changing, so always check for updates. Usually, you're reimbursed after submitting receipts and proof of sales tax payment.

If you aren't located in a major city that has a film commission set up by the government, you can contact your local city hall to find out if there are any incentives for filming locally (waived permits, tax rebates, and free locations, for example).

Traveling to Canada

Sometimes shooting a film in Canada, as many U.S. studio movies and television shows are doing, has its advantages. They include:

✔ Rebates on federal and provincial sales tax

✔ Lower rental costs on locations

✔ Government rebates on labor (up to 35 percent)

✔ Rebates on labs, Digital Animation and Visual Effects (DAVE tax credit program).

The downfall of shooting in Canada is the added expense of having to fly your cast and crew there (unless you hire them locally) and put everyone up in a hotel. You need to decide whether it's more economical to shoot in Canada or stay at home.

Locating Stock Footage

Want an aerial shot of a city lit up at night? An explosion over the ocean? Chances are you can find the perfect footage already shot and just insert it into your film. That's what *stock footage libraries* are all about. Just like locating a sound effect from a sound effects library or a piece of music from a music library (see Chapter 16 for more on sound and music libraries), you can license existing footage (usually without actors in the shot) to integrate perfectly into your film. A *license* gives you permission to feature particular footage from a film library in your film for a specific fee. Digital Juice has the Videotraxx Film & Video Library (www.digitaljuice.com). I recently used stock footage from Time Image, which has a vast library and some unique location shots I couldn't find anywhere else (www.timeimage.com).

I've used stock footage from the Artbeats Digital Film Library (www.artbeats.com) in many of my projects. They have every piece of footage imaginable, from old black-and-white vintage scenes to astronauts and outer-space footage. You can view its entire digital library online and even purchase and download the footage on your computer. I recommend ordering its free demo CD-ROM or DVD. Most footage is now available in both SD (standard definition) or HD (high definition). Library packages start at around $199. After you license the footage, you have nonexclusive rights to use it in your film.

Stock footage can raise the production value of your film and make it look like a much higher budget film. If you have an aerial opening shot, the audience isn't going to know that you didn't shoot it, or that you paid less than $400 for the footage from a stock footage library.

Some footage from a stock library has been shot on film, and other footage on video (standard or high definition). If you're shooting on film or with a digital 24p camera and you buy footage on video, you can use software like Magic Bullet Frames, available at www.redgiantsoftware.com, to make the video footage look more like it was shot on film. This helps disguise the fact that you have intercut stock footage into your production. (See Chapter 10 for more on choosing a medium in which to shoot your film.)

Stock footage libraries don't just license their footage; they're always looking to buy footage to add to their extensive libraries. Have you shot anything that may work for a stock footage library? You can earn a little money back to cover the expense of shooting the footage and possibly make a little profit, too. My movie *The Random Factor* (with Dan Aykroyd as the voice of "Dexter") required an opening scene with an ambulance racing through the streets. I couldn't find a film library that had all the shots I needed, so I shot the footage myself, used it in my movie, and then ended up licensing it to a stock footage house.

Virtual Locations: Creating New Worlds on a Computer

Need to shoot on another planet? Traveling to the moon isn't economical, and besides, you get motion sickness in outer space. Does the location you need exist only in your mind? Try creating it on your computer.

Bryce, a great software program by Daz 3D (www.daz3d.com), enables you to create realistic-looking scenic backgrounds, from tree-topped mountains and rolling hills to alien outer space terrain complete with hovering planets. Figure 6-2 features a frame from my sci-fi film *Light Years Away* starring Christopher Knight (aka Peter Brady) and Meadow Williams *(Apollo 13)*. You can create your virtual locations in Bryce and then superimpose your actors onto the background using a blue- or green-screen process (see Chapter 17 for more information about blue-screen).

Gee! PS

I have one in my car, and now I can't live without it. It's a GPS (Global Positioning Satellite System) device. They're portable, so you can pack it in your suitcase and pop it in your rental car in another city. The service is free (no monthly satellite fees), unless you want additional services like real-time traffic alert. To use it, you just punch in your final address, and the device calculates your trip. Whether you're trying to find a location in your city or one across the country, the GPS device knows exactly where you are and directs you to your final destination. Most devices have millions of points of interest (POI). You can find local restaurants, hospitals, police stations, gas stations, and more in your immediate vicinity. Many GPS units speak in friendly voices and even recite the street names — and don't worry, they'll never talk to you like a backseat driver.

Figure 6-2:
A virtual alien location created with Daz 3D's Bryce software.

© Astrolite Ent. 2008 Light Years Away — Christopher Knight, Meadow Williams

Securing Your Locations

After you find the ideal locations for your film, you need to have a formal written agreement between you and the property owners granting you permission to film at the location and outlining the specifics (for how long, how much, and any restrictions). You need to be guaranteed the use of the property and make sure that no surprises await you when you show up to start filming. There are services that can assist you in securing locations, either through the city's permit office, a location service, or your local film commission (which you can find by contacting your local city hall office).

Make sure that the person who signs the agreement to let you use the location has the full authority to do so. There should be a clause in the agreement that clarifies the person signing is an authorized signatory, so he's held responsible if it turns out he misled you.

You can have an attorney draft a one-page location contract, or Movie Forms Pro has 110 production forms which include a location agreement (www.movieforms.com). You can also use Enterprise Printers, which has location agreements in addition to more than 400 other entertainment forms, including contracts and releases. For more information, go to www.enterpriseprinters.com.

Acquiring permits

To shoot on most public locations, you need a permit from the city or state (this is separate from the agreement with the location owner), whether you're filming outside or inside. You don't want to be filming with cast and crew and have a police officer show up asking for a permit and you don't have one. If this happens, you could be asked to leave, leaving you and your cast and crew out in the cold. Permits are usually inexpensive, averaging a few hundred dollars; many cities' film commissions encourage filming and waive the permit fee. Check with the city or state permit office to find out if the fee can be waived. If you can't find a permit office, start by calling city hall.

If you're in Los Angeles and have problems finding the permit office, it's because it's listed under Entertainment Industry Development Office. The official Web site is www.eidc.com. For New York City, go to www.nyc.gov and in the City Agencies drop-down list, select "Film/Theatre."

Under no circumstances should you ever sneak onto private property. Trespassing is illegal, and you could be arrested and thrown in jail. Your cinematographer can roll the camera documenting you being hauled off to prison, and you will end up calling your attorney from your "cell" phone.

Ensuring you're insured

What if someone trips and knocks over a light stand, causing the hot light to ignite the drapes and burn down the location? This is when you'll be glad you bought location insurance under general liability coverage. If people know better, they won't let you film on their property until you present them with a *certificate of insurance*. This certificate is issued by an insurance carrier under a general liability policy, proving that the location you're using is covered in case you or your production company cause damage. General liability insurance doesn't really cost you money — it saves you money in the long run. See Chapter 4 for more information about all the insurance you should consider purchasing for your film.

Mapping out your locations

When your locations are set, you need to make sure that your cast and crew can find them. Usually the first or second assistant director supplies location maps to the cast and crew. Photocopy specific pages from the local city guide and also write down the directions. Internet mapping sites such as www.mapquest.com and www.maps.com are also handy — but always double-check Internet directions. If you use www.maps.google.com, you can not only get turn-by-turn directions, you can even click on "Satellite" and see aerial photographs of the location. Click on "Street View" to see an actual street level photo of the address.

Policing your locations

If you need to stop cars or direct traffic around the area you're filming, police may be required. Police are usually required when you're shooting on city or state properties as well (be careful when using the word *shooting* around police officers). Some states offer discounts and rebates on police officers' salaries when filming on government property.

Always have the police direct or stop traffic. You have no authority to do so, and you will either get arrested or some angry commuter will give you a hands-on lesson in road rage. Also, my mom taught me to never play in traffic.

Fire!

If you're dealing with explosions, firearms, or any potential fire hazard, you're required to have a firefighter on the set (and, of course, a pyrotechnician who is skilled with explosives and gunpowder and, if required by law in your area, licensed). Depending on which city you film in, you may get a reimbursement or rebate on the salary you pay to a firefighter.

Shooting Second-Unit Locations

Second-unit photography is footage that isn't filmed at the same time as your principal photography and usually doesn't require your main actors (or allows you to use doubles for a distant shot). Second unit is often filmed after your main shoot, when you've had a chance to make a list of additional shots to weave into your main shots, such as establishing exterior shots of certain locations.

Movie trailers (not the coming-attraction kind)

A movie trailer can be a midsized RV or an oversized Winnebago. A trailer is a luxury not always available to the low-budget filmmaker. On studio pictures, the stars always have their own private trailers with all the comforts of home: a kitchen, a bathroom with shower, and a bed. But even on a low-budget production, trying to get even a small RV to use as a production trailer when you're on location isn't a bad idea. The trailer can be a sheltered place to take meetings, a place for actors to have some private space or even take a nap between takes if they don't have their own trailers. Also, a trailer can be a place of refuge when the weather is bad or a good place to retreat when you need to get your bearings for the next shot.

If your story is supposed to take place in New York, but you live in a small town in the Midwest and you're on a tiny budget, you can't afford to take your whole cast and crew to New York to film, for example. Instead, buy yourself one plane ticket. Pack your digital video camera and shoot some establishing shots that you can cut into your film.

For my film *Miss Cast Away and the Island Girls (*aka *Silly Movie 2),* we shot most of the footage along the beaches of California to save money but went to Hawaii for second-unit footage. We shot actual helicopter footage of the islands (through a helicopter tour guide service) and establishing shots of the ocean waves hitting the tropical shores and cut these into the final film.

Keying in backgrounds

Another inexpensive way to look like you shot your film in another town or abroad, is to *key* them in (the process known as *chroma key*). Shoot your actors against a blue or green fabric background and then superimpose (place) them over any static background footage. You then remove (make transparent) the blue or green behind the actors, allowing your scenic background footage to appear behind them instead. See Chapter 17 for details on using blue or green screen.

Here's a scene from my film *Teddy: First Dog* with my dog Little Bear shot in front of a blue background (using the Reflecmedia kit; www.reflecmedia.com) and then superimposed in front of my second unit footage of the White House. You can also buy footage from a stock footage library and superimpose your actors in front of that footage without having to leave your house.

Courtesy Stellar Entertainment/First Films ©2008

Chapter 7

Crewing Up: Hiring Your Crew

In This Chapter

▶ Finding your crew members

▶ Interviewing potential players

▶ Paying your crew what they're worth

As a filmmaker, you may be the creative driving force and the master of many, or Jack of all trades, but you can't make a film all by yourself. Whether you have a 2-person crew or 30 people assisting you in your vision, you need to find people who are as passionate about your film as you are. In this chapter, I list the positions required on an independent production along with a description of each crew position and what traits, skills, and knowledge are needed. You discover the advantages and disadvantages of hiring an independent contractor versus an employee, along with great tips regarding crew members who may take a pay cut if they get other perks. You can be the producer, director, cinematographer, writer, editor, and even the star of your film — but you can't go it alone: You need a crew to help with lighting, grip equipment, props, wardrobe, sound, and so on.

Something to Crew About

Every film needs a crew, because one person alone just can't do everything. An independent production, especially one that's shooting with a digital video camera (which includes capturing digital footage to memory cards or a hard drive), doesn't require as large a crew as is necessary when you shoot with film. When shooting video, you have sound and picture together and may not need a separate sound mixer. You also don't need a second assistant cameraperson (unless you're shooting HD and you want someone download-ing your digital files) because there are no film reels to load or film reports to send to a lab. Video also requires less lighting than film, which helps cut down on lighting and grip equipment. If you love overworking yourself, you can even operate the camera and sound yourself, as well as position the lights and move the equipment around. Even if you're shooting film, you can still get away with a small crew.

The following sections list the main production team you should try to assemble, whether you're shooting film or video. Having some understanding of what the other people on your crew do — like the cinematographer, the producer, the editor, the dolly grip, and the prop or wardrobe person — can improve your working relationship with them and, in the end, result in a better film.

To decide what role *you* take, think about what you enjoy doing most. If you like putting things together and making them happen, then you'd probably make a great producer. If you like things in a certain way, can envision things as they should be, and love working with people, then your calling may be directing. If you love telling stories and are always jotting down great ideas that come to you, writing screenplays may be for you. Maybe you're a "triple-threat"—someone who writes, produces, and directs.

Producing the producer

A *producer* is responsible for putting the project together and sometimes finding the financing. Without the right producer, the film may never come to fruition. A producer, who is often the filmmaker (the person responsible for the project being produced in the first place), is the first one on the project and the last one to leave. The producer is responsible for hiring the crew and working with the director to hire the actors. The producer helps "produce" all the elements required to put the production together.

Some projects have an *executive producer.* This person earns the title by either handling the business of the production, being the actual financier of the project, or being someone without whom the film would never have come to fruition. In television and studio features, the executive producer is often a representative of the studio or network who carries a lot of authority.

An *associate producer* is usually a glorified title reserved for someone who contributes an important element to the production — such as finding the financing or the name stars. Agents and managers often get an associate producer credit for bringing a star or major element to a project.

The filmmaker's apprentice

An *apprentice* is usually someone new to the world of filmmaking but who wants to be a successful filmmaker one day. He or she is usually willing to work for free in exchange for learning everything possible on the set and being mentored by the director or producer. An apprentice's tasks usually include running errands, making phone calls, and just being by the producer or director's side.

Directing the direction

Everyone wants to direct, don't they? Even my dog has a T-shirt that says, "What I really want to do is direct." A *director* has to be a multitalented multitasker. The director is captain of the ship, the leader of the pack, and is responsible for making all the creative elements come together (see Chapters 13 and 14 for more on what a director does). Many first-time filmmakers can take on the job of directing, and if you do your homework (like reading this book) and are passionate about making your film, you'll find it a rewarding experience. If you'd rather hire someone else to direct, start collecting demo reels — whether they're short films, features, or commercials — from prospective directors.

When searching for a director, ask these questions:

- ✔ **Does he or she tell a story well?** Is the film logical in its sequence of events? Did the director tell an intriguing story?

- ✔ **Are the actors' performances believable?** Do they come across as sincere? Do you care about the characters in the film?

- ✔ **Are camera shots and movement effective?** Does the director use effective angles? Are the shots interesting but not distracting to the story? Does the camera movement enhance the shots?

- ✔ **If the film's a comedy, is it funny?** Does the director have a good sense of comedic timing? Is the comedy funny or too silly?

- ✔ **Is the direction consistent?** Do the shots have a certain style? Do all the elements, shots, dialogue, setting, and so on have consistency, or does the work seem all over the place?

Assistant director

Many people have a misconception of what an assistant director does. He or she does *not* assist in directing the film. An *assistant director* (also known as the A.D.) is more of an assistant *to* the director. The assistant director keeps the set moving and the film on schedule. The assistant director's duties include

- ✔ Breaking down the script with the director (to schedule the shoot days).

- ✔ Relaying the director's technical instructions to the cast and crew.

- ✔ Getting the shots ready by making sure that all production personnel and actors are in place and ready when the director needs them.

- ✔ Working with the extras on a small budget, and relaying instructions for the extras to the second assistant director on a bigger production.

✔ Making up the *call sheets* (lists of which cast members work the next day and any special equipment or elements needed for the shooting). On bigger productions this is usually handed off by the first assistant director to the unit production manager.

✔ Calling the actors who need to work the next day (on larger productions, this task is performed by the unit production manager).

✔ Getting the set settled to start filming (asking if sound and camera are ready and then calling to the mixer to roll sound and the camera operator to roll camera—things that must be done before the director cues the actors or action begins).

The director — never the assistant director — calls "action" and "cut." The assistant director's authority ends when the director calls for *Action!*

Second assistant director

The *second assistant director* (the second A.D.) is an assistant to the assistant director and is also responsible for a fair amount of paperwork — especially if it's a union shoot, because there are strict rules and regulations, and everything has to be documented properly. I liken a second A.D. to an executive assistant — this person does paperwork, works on the computer, and helps to make the boss's job easier.

Some of the second A.D.'s paperwork includes handling call sheets, collecting from the camera department the *camera reports* (shots and footage for the day's shoot), collecting talent releases for background players, and so on. The second assistant checks everyone in at the beginning of each day's shoot, calls the actors for camera when they're needed on the set, and then checks everyone out at the end of the shoot.

My sister Nancy was the second A.D for my film *Undercover Angel,* and her job was crowd control. For the final dramatic scene in the film, Nancy rounded up almost 1,000 extras, which was no small task.

Stepping over the line producer

The *line producer's* job is to work with the budget and line up, and keep tabs on the items in the budget categories that make up your film. The line producer works with the producer in getting good deals on equipment, props, locations, and other elements that make up the budget. On a small production, the line producer can often have the job of producer and even unit production manager. On bigger-budget projects, each is a separate position.

Line producing an independent low-budget film is actually an art form; it requires great skill because you have to work with what you have and can afford. When interviewing potential line producers, find out what budget amounts they've worked with on past productions. Have they worked on budgets similar to yours? If you're shooting a low-budget film, you need to hire someone who's had the experience of line producing an independent film. A line producer who has worked on a multimillion-dollar budget may have difficulty relating to a small budget. Also make sure you get references from a producer or director whom your prospective line producer worked with in the past.

You can find a qualified line-producer (and many other crew and staff positions) by checking out the Los Angeles 411 (www.la411.com) or the New York 411 (www.newyork411.com). These industry directories are some of the finest resources for productions in the film and television industry.

Uniting with a production manager

The *unit production manager,* also known as the UPM, works closely with the line producer and assists in getting good deals on equipment and other elements for the shoot. The UPM also ensures that all equipment is on set, on time. A UPM is kind of a co-line producer (in fact, most low-budget productions have no UPM, only a line producer). A UPM on a low-budget production will often take a lower salary to get a better credit as a line producer.

Supervising the script

Someone with a good eye, a decent memory, a knack for recalling details, and a keen sense of observation is the kind of person you need for *script supervising.* Also known as the *continuity person,* a script supervisor must know the script inside and out to ensure that wardrobe, props, and hair match from shot to shot. Without the script supervisor, cups of coffee may leap into actors' hands, props may simply disappear mid-scene, and chairs may rearrange themselves. Preventing this from happening is the job of the script supervisor. That's why she takes those Polaroid pictures (many now use digital still cameras) to remember what the set was like the last time the camera rolled.

Some of the script supervisor's duties include making sure

- Action matches from shot to shot.
- Screen direction is correct (see Chapter 14), meaning when one actor is supposed to be looking at another actor, they're facing the right direction.
- Wardrobe, props, hair, and make-up match from shot to shot (still photos help match actors' appearance from shot to shot).

- The director has shot enough coverage for each scene (for example, that appropriate close-ups were shot for important emotions, or certain angles were shot to show the full impact of the action).

- Actors say their lines verbatim from the script and are corrected if they change a line or assisted if they forget a line or two (or three).

- Lenses and frame sizes used for each shot are noted so the director will know whether he has shot enough coverage. This is also helpful to the editor when cutting the picture together and knowing what coverage there was for the scene (giving the editor more cutting options).

- The editor receives assistance with scene notes and other details to help edit the picture together in a coherent fashion.

Ask to see a candidate's script-continuity notes to see whether the candidate is organized and his writing legible. Getting referrals and talking to a director who's previously worked with this script supervisor is always a good idea.

Directing photography with a cinematographer

The *director of photography* sees the world through the single eye of the camera and helps you envision your film from script to screen. On low-budget productions, *you* may even be the director of photography. The director of photography is often referred to as the D.P. (or the D.O.P. in Canada) and is also called the *cinematographer.* If you're shooting a low-budget production, your cinematographer will often be the camera operator, as well. Only on bigger-budget productions does the cinematographer have someone else operate the camera.

If you're interviewing potential cinematographers, request a *demo reel* (a DVD that features samples of the cinematographer's work). Usually, a reel will have short samples of the D.P.'s work from different projects, preferably showing a diverse style from film to film. Maybe you can see a sample of a candidate's work on his or her website or on YouTube (www.youtube.com). Every cinematographer has a demo reel — if the one you're talking to doesn't, beware. That's like a screenwriter without a script. Also see whether he or she has references from other filmmakers.

Your cinematographer is one of the most important players on your team. After all, the audience doesn't care how much work went into getting each shot; all they see is the final product. So look for the following attributes when choosing a director of photography:

✔ Does their demo reel reflect a style that you like?

✔ Do they know how to light scenes to convey the appropriate mood — or is their lighting flat?

✔ Are shots framed esthetically, or are they awkward? Is the camera movement subtle or jarring?

✔ Are they pleasant and personable? Will they be easy to work with?

✔ Are they knowledgeable about the technicalities of the camera, and can they work quickly without compromising quality?

✔ Do they have a gaffer and other crew members they like to work with?

✔ Are they willing to work long hours with low pay? Will they work on deferment (meaning some of their salary is deferred)?

✔ Do they own a film, video, or digital HD camera to use on your production?

Nowadays, many cinematographers have their own 35mm, 16mm motion-picture cameras. Some own video cameras, including digital video 24p cinema camcorders and even tapeless HD cameras. You may be able to get both a camera and a cinematographer for the price of one — definitely a plus on a low budget. (For more on motion-picture and digital video cameras, including HD, see Chapter 10.)

First assistant camera

The *first assistant cameraperson,* or first A.C., works alongside the camera operator or director of photography — whoever is operating the camera — and changes camera lenses, inserts camera filters, cleans the shutter gate for dust and particles (if it's a film camera), and adjusts the focus. This position is also referred to as the *focus-puller,* because that's the most important duty of the first A.C.: to make sure everything that's supposed to be in focus is in focus.

An assistant cameraperson on a film camera uses a tape measure and a precision focus knob on the camera to ensure that all images that are supposed to be in focus are. They should be prepared to *rack-focus,* meaning focus from one element in the same shot to another, with precise timing and accuracy. An assistant cameraperson on a video production often takes measurements using the camera's focus through the lens by using a video monitor to see what the camera sees. Many digital camcorders have visual focus numbers in the frame (which are not recorded on tape or file), that the A.C. can dial in after rehearsing a focus point before the camera starts recording.

Second assistant camera

The *second assistant cameraperson,* also known as the second A.C., is required to load and unload the film magazines (if you're shooting film rather than video), being extremely careful not to expose your precious film to the light as he or she unloads your footage and readies it for development at the film lab. If you're recording to memory cards for digital HD, the second A.C. transfers the footage to an external hard drive so you can reuse the cards. The second A.C. is also responsible for slating the clapboard for syncing sound to picture when shooting film (see Chapter 12 for more on syncing sound), and for recording camera reports that detail what shot was recorded on what film roll (or video cassette, if you're shooting video). When shooting film, camera reports are crucial because they accompany the exposed film to the lab and provide instructions if any special developing and/or printing is required.

If you're shooting digital video with a small crew, you usually don't need a second assistant cameraperson (unless it's tapeless and you want someone to transfer the memory cards to a hard drive).

Going with your gaffer

Your *gaffer* works closely with your cinematographer to make sure the mood and lighting of each scene works effectively. Often the gaffer is also an electrician or has experience and knowledge of electricity and voltage. (Ask your cinematographer if he or she has enjoyed working with a certain gaffer in the past. This saves you a lot of time and trouble. You want to have people who are familiar and comfortable working with each other.)

Best boy is your best man

The *best boy* works closely with the gaffer, dealing with electricity and powering the lights. He or she (yes, a best boy can be a woman) also runs the extension cords and checks that everything is plugged in correctly. The gaffer sometimes can recommend a best boy he or she has worked with. If not, ask the cinematographer or another crew person. In the end credits on all my movies, my dog gets a credit as *good boy* next to the best boy's credit.

Electrician is electrifying

An *electrician's* main job is tying your lights directly into the electrical circuit box to avoid a power overload. If you're doing a video shoot in a small location and only using two or three lights, you may be able to plug directly into the wall plugs and not need an electrician to monitor the set. Checking with an electrician first isn't a bad idea, though. You don't want to blow a fuse or, even worse, start a fire. On a smaller shoot, you can hire an electrician from the Yellow Pages and pay him or her for only an hour or two of work at each new location.

Getting a grip

Grips are the film set's manpower: They move equipment and help position lights according to the gaffer and cinematographer's instructions. Having a few grips on hand speeds up your setup and saves time and money. My friend Peter Emslie wanted to work on a project I was developing for Dolly Parton, and he eagerly volunteered to be the dolly grip! A *dolly grip* is in charge of setting up the *dolly* (which is used to move the camera during shots) and the tracks the dolly moves on; he or she skillfully pushes the dolly while filming.

Sounding like your sound mixer

Sound is very important in any film. The *sound mixer* is responsible for recording the actors' dialogue on set and ensuring that it's clear and comprehensible. The sound mixer on a film has a separate sound machine, either a DAT recorder or a Nagra, or will record to a hard drive (see Chapter 12). The sound mixer also has a mixing board that allows him to input several microphones (for several microphone placements within the scene) and mix them into the recorder to get the appropriate balance of all mics. Sound mixers also make sure that the recording is free from interference (background noise that interrupts the dialogue, for example, or hissing or electrical interference on the actual line).

I've worked with sound mixers like Al Samuels, who did the film *Swingers*. Al's production sound was so good that little or no re-dubbing of dialogue was required by the actors in postproduction. I've also worked with sound mixers who recorded unusable sound on set because they didn't know how to mix correctly or how to instruct the *boom* person (see the following section) to position the microphone correctly, resulting in most of the dialogue having to be re-recorded during postproduction (see Chapter 16 sound mixing).

Booming the sound

A *boom person* anticipates the actor's performance on set in order to position the microphone at the right distance and angle to get clear, crisp dialogue while at the same time not letting the mic and boom creep into the shot. The boom held by the boom person is a long pole (sometimes called a *fishpole*) with the microphone positioned on the end. The job requires skill, and without the right operator, the recording will suffer. Because the boom person and the sound mixer must communicate clearly with each other, your sound mixer often recommends or brings his own boom person — someone he has worked with before.

Propping up the prop master

The *prop master* is in charge of any object that an actor interacts with — such as a telephone, a lamp, a gun, or a glass of champagne. On smaller productions, the prop person can also be the *set dresser* (the person responsible for items the actors don't interact with, such as flowers on a shelf, placemats on a table, picture frames on a mantle). The prop master can also double as the *greensman,* in charge of plants, flowers, even trees — anything that requires a hand with a green thumb.

When interviewing people for the position of prop master, you want to know whether the person has access to *prop houses* (like 20th Century Props, www.20thcenturyprops.com) or other places that can provide props for free or at a low rental cost. A prop person also needs to be organized, reliable, and detail oriented. If you're not close to any major production centers, check into local theater groups where you'll likely find a candidate to provide you with props for your film.

Dressing up the wardrobe department

Your *wardrobe person* should have the skill to sew from scratch; on an independent budget you can't always afford to purchase or rent certain wardrobe or costumes. It's also helpful if this person has contacts for inexpensive clothing rentals. The wardrobe person is also in charge of making sure the actors are wearing the appropriate wardrobe in each scene to match continuity. They number the wardrobe or outfits for each scene and keep track of what the actors were wearing in the last scene and whether there are any wardrobe changes for the next scene.

On low-budget productions, the actors usually wear their own clothes, which the wardrobe person has selected by looking through their closets (with their permission, of course). Wardrobe has to be checked out each day and checked in at the end of each day — even something as simple as boots (if the actor takes them home and forgets them the next day, continuity won't match). The wardrobe person keeps clothes hanging on a wheeled rack like the ones you see in a department store. Each piece of wardrobe is tagged and marked for which scenes it is to be worn in. The wardrobe person also makes sure the actor's wardrobe is kept clean (or dirty, depending on what the scene requires).

Making up is hard to do

Make-up is often overlooked on low-budget productions, but it shouldn't be. The wrong make-up or coloring can cause disastrous results on film or video. An experienced make-up artist knows how to work with different skin tones and make them look even under different lighting conditions. Make-up can make circles under the eyes vanish, blotchiness on the skin disappear, blemishes go away, or bruises appear. Never use an inexperienced make-up person. With special effects make-up, your make-up artist can create a deformed character, age an actor, and make creatures come to life with the aid of *prosthetics* (latex appliances attached to the face — see Chapter 17).

Be sure to allow for a make-up kit rental fee in the budget for make-up supplies including sponges, powder, puffs, and tissues.

Gopher this, gopher that

A *gopher,* professionally called a *production assistant* but also known as a *runner,* is usually a student or eager beaver who wants to get on a film set. They go-pher this and go-pher that. The position doesn't require skill as much as it does eagerness to work on a film set. Reliability and hard work are the main prerequisites of a good gopher. The difference between a gopher and an apprentice is that the gopher is hired to work on the set, and often an apprentice is working for free to gain the experience and to learn about the filmmaking process hands-on.

Gophers are easy to find. Post ads at the local colleges and in trade magazines flyers and on Internet film blog and crew sites like www.crewnet.com and www.productionhub.com. Also check out www.studentfilmmakers.com for crew posting under their Classifieds section.

Keeping your composer

The *composer* scores music to accompany the images of your film and to help set a mood. Finding a composer is a lot like finding your cinematographer: As soon as you hear a sample of a composer's sound, you'll know immediately whether you like what you hear. Collect CD samples from composers to hear their work. You can find composers through the various music organizations — BMI, ASCAP, and SOCAN (see Chapter 16). If you go to www.crewnet.com, you can click on "Composers" and find a list of potential people who could score your film.

The composer sets the mood of your film, so liking his or her style and sound is very important. You want to make sure you both have the same vision for the film. After you select someone, sit down and discuss the type of music you hear in your head for certain scenes. I often give my composer a rough tape or CD of songs and movie soundtracks I like, and tell him or her to compose in that style. For my film *Turn of the Blade,* I told my composer, Greg Edmonson, that I liked the sexy sound of the saxophone used in the *Lethal Weapon* soundtrack. This gave him an idea of the style I wanted, and he was able to give me a similar feel for my film.

Never use copyrighted music without permission. If you want to use a commercial song or soundtrack, you need to license it (see Chapter 16). You can be inspired by music that's out there, but don't copy it or even get too close to copying it — you don't want any legal problems.

Editing: Cut that out!

When interviewing a potential *picture editor,* a person who is experienced at cutting film or video images together to form a visual story, ask to see a sample of something he or she has cut together — either a short film or a feature-length film. Ask if any of her clips are on youtube.com to view. Here's a list of things to look for when interviewing a potential picture editor for your film:

- **Technical knowledge of non-linear editing software** (including expertise in all aspects of exporting final footage for distribution). Non-linear is the technique of having your individual shots as separate entities and available to be assembled in any order.

- **A non-linear editing system,** which is usually a desktop or laptop computer with adequate speed and memory.

- **Good pacing (timing)** to their cutting (with no lags or slow spots in the action).

- **Effective use of cutaways** (reaction shots, parallel scenes happening at the same time).

- **Seamless cuts** (no jarring cuts or jump-cuts that look like frames are missing).

- **Tight scenes** (no laborious entering and exiting of actors).

- **Effective transitions** from one scene to another.

And the rest . . .

Depending on the size of your budget, there are other positions that you may need to fill. On a low-budget production, many of the following could be you or someone filling one of the positions mentioned earlier in this chapter:

- **Casting director:** This person breaks down the script and suggests actors suitable for each role. The casting director looks at submitted headshots and resumes and selects actors to come in to audition. Often, in a low-budget production, the filmmaker is also the casting director.

- **Location scout:** The location scout breaks down all the locations in the script and finds the actual locations to shoot the movie. The filmmaker can also be the location scout. I've driven around town many times looking for the perfect place to shoot.

- **Transportation person:** This person is solely dedicated to driving the crew and cast around from hotel to set or parking area to set. If it's a small production, everyone usually drives his or her own car, or sometimes you have another crew member pick you up, and you carpool!

- **Production designer:** A production designer designs the overall look of a film. Although some films (for example, *Batman,* where a whole world had to be created from scratch) depend on a production designer, most small-budget films don't have the luxury of having one.

- **Stunt coordinator:** This person is skilled to either perform stunts himor herself or coordinates with others who are trained stunt people. If your film includes stunts, don't try to save money here. Always hire a professional stunt person who is skilled in even the most basic of stunts. Try to avoid stunts on a low-budget film; they can be expensive and risky *and* raise your insurance package.

- **Postproduction coordinator:** The postproduction coordinator coordinates the completion of the film, schedules when the picture editing and sound elements are to be done, and sets a finishing date for the final production so distribution plans can begin. On a low-budget film, having a dedicated postproduction coordinator is a luxury. Usually, the filmmaker performs these tasks.

- **Still photographer:** You need to think ahead and hire an on-set still photographer to take photos that can be used for publicity and eventually in the artwork on the DVD. Distributors (Chapter 19), request production stills to use in posters and in *one-sheets*, also called *sales-sheets*, which are flyers advertising your film. You also need photos for film festivals and newspaper and magazine articles.

Finding and Interviewing Your Crew

You're ready to make your film and you know the positions you want to fill. Now how are you going to find the people to help you put it all together?

- ✔ **Run an ad requesting that people apply for crewing your film.** You can run an ad in one of the trade publications, like *The Hollywood Reporter, Daily Variety,* or *Backstage West* (if you live in Los Angeles or New York). If you live outside of the Hollywood area, run an ad in your local newspaper or neighborhood flyer. Go on a local TV show or news program and get the word out that you're looking for crew. Post ads at local schools and colleges.

- ✔ **Get ahold of the Los Angeles 411 or New York 411 directory.** In addition to crew listings, these directories list other production resources. Check out www.la411.com or www.newyork411.com. Also try Craig's List (www.craigslist.org): Click on your town or city and then, under the Jobs listing, click the category TV/film/video.

- ✔ **To find crew all over the United States and Canada, go to www.crewnet.com.** You can also try www.media-match.com and www.productionhub.com. You can post a free ad on the sites and request resumes via e-mail or fax.

After you start getting resumes from potential crew members, you're ready for the interview process. You're not just looking for skills, but also for personality and temperament. For the types of questions to ask and skills to verify, see the earlier discussions on the respective positions.

Get references from all potential crew members, even if you don't plan on contacting their references. If they have nothing to hide, they'll gladly volunteer letters of reference or contact names. If they say they have no references, beware!

Let's make contact

A great multifaceted program called Gorilla includes a template for crew (and cast) contact information (plus a complete production-management program for scheduling and budgeting for the independent filmmaker — see Chapter 4). You can also create your own contact list using Excel or any spreadsheet program. A contact list is invaluable, because it contains the names, phone numbers (home, fax and cell), emails, mailing addresses, and other pertinent information of your new family, all in one place. You'll eventually distribute this contact list to your cast and crew so they can communicate with all the departments and actors regarding the production.

Creative Ways to Pay Your Crew

Now that you've found your crew, you have to figure out how to pay them. When you're shooting a low or no-budget film, you don't have a lot of money to throw around, if any. No one is being forced to work on your production, especially if there is low or no pay. But you can save dollars on hiring your crew and still have a win-win situation for both parties.

Paying later: Deferments or points

One of the ways to save money on cast and crew is to set up an arrangement whereby you pay crew members some of their pay later for the work they perform on your film. There are two ways you can do this:

- ✔ **Deferments:** With *deferments,* you *defer some of* the crew members' salaries. Deferments work by paying your crew a small amount up front (if possible) and a larger amount in deferred pay if and when you start seeing a profit from your film's sales. I recommend using deferments especially if you can pay something small up front; that way, you haven't taken advantage of the crew member.

- ✔ **Points:** *Points* are similar to deferments, except that instead of a deferred salary of a specific amount, you reward the crew with one or more points to be paid if and when the film starts to make money. One *point* may be 1 percent of the profits of the film. If the film makes a lot of money, points continue to add up and continue to be paid as long as the film makes money.

Offering points or negotiating deferments are good incentives to offer crew when you don't have enough money to pay them what they're worth up front. Doing so also lets you save money up front, money that you can put up on the screen (into the actual production) and enhance the production values of your film.

I recommend deferments over points, because points obligate you to pay out every time money comes in from the picture, which can be a lot of extra paperwork and expense to keep track of. Deferments, on the other hand, are usually a specific dollar amount; when that amount is reached, your obligation is fulfilled and the crew member doesn't receive any more.

Giving 'em credit

Your potential crew may not be excited about the pay, if there is any, but you may get them excited about working on your film by giving them a credit that they haven't been able to earn yet.

Getting a credit with more prestige on your film can help your crew get better positions on the next film they work. For example, a gaffer who has studied to be a cinematographer may take a cut in pay, or no pay, if he or she gets a chance to be the director of photography on your film (make sure he or she is qualified though). An art director may be excited — and willing to accept less compensation — to get a production designer credit.

Hiring student bodies

Another way to save on your budget is to go to school. Many students still in or fresh out of college would love to work on a production to gain experience and get their first film credit on their resume. Some colleges even let their students earn a school credit if your film meets their educational requirements. If you're making a low- or no-budget film, a student assistant in each department can be an asset to your production.

Paying a kit fee

Another way to save a little bit of money is to split up the salary you pay your crew member by paying him a kit fee. A *kit fee* is like a rental fee for the equipment that the crew member brings to your production. What's great about a kit fee is that it can save crew members on taxes that would otherwise be taken out of their salary, because rental fees don't count as crew labor — and so they may agree to give you a discount on their salary for paying them this way. You can pay kit fees for

- ✔ Your make-up artist's kit with make-up supplies
- ✔ Camera equipment from your cinematographer
- ✔ Lighting equipment from your cinematographer or gaffer
- ✔ Props provided by your prop master
- ✔ Your sound mixer's own equipment

Hiring crew as independent contractors

You can save yourself and crew members a little money and extra paperwork if you're able to hire each crew member as an *independent contractor*. This way you don't have to withhold any taxes on crew members' salaries, and you don't have to pay social security and benefits since they're operating as freelance workers. An *independent contractor* works independently without an employer constantly looking over his or her shoulder. Location scouts, wardrobe designers, freelance writers, and storyboard artists can all easily be independent contractors.

You have to send each independent contractor a 1099 tax form at the end of each year in which they worked for any payment over $600. You can get standard 1099 tax forms at any stationery or office store or from various tax software programs like www.turbotax.com.

When crew have to work specific hours on set, as opposed to working on their own time, you may have to hire them as employees. At that point, you're required to issue W2 forms, which then requires either hiring a payroll company or enlisting a bookkeeper or accountant to do all the payments and tax withholding, including workman's compensation and so on. Check with an accountant who can advise you which crew members can be hired as independent contractors and which ones should be hired as employees.

Union or non-union — that's the question

If you're doing an independent low-budget film, you may not want to deal with the additional expense and paperwork involved with hiring a union crew. Unions are very strict, and if you default on any of their regulations, it could slow down, or shut down, your production. Plus, unions require you to pay minimum salaries, which may not be in your budget.

A lot of independent films can't afford to shoot with union employees and have to pass up experienced union crew, unless that union member wants to work on the production and take a pay cut in doing so. If you do a union production, you have to follow all union rules to a 'T'. And be prepared for penalties, including paying for overtime, and so on. You don't need that headache on an independent production — and most of the time you can't afford it anyway.

Putting a Contract Out on Your Crew

You should always have a signed agreement between you and each crew member. Movie Forms Pro (www.movieforms.com) has crew deal memos.

Whether the crew member is an independent contractor or an employee, a written agreement prevents any misunderstandings and clearly spells out exactly what's expected of the crew member, including the following:

- **Position and title:** Define the title they get in the production credits.
- **Salary:** Specify what they are getting paid (if anything) or getting in deferred pay or points (if any). Note that you may be able to pay non-union independent contractors a flat fee, whereas union employees usually require hourly pay. See the next section for more on union employees.

✔ **Employment status:** Specify whether the crew are working as independent contractors or employees. Make sure everyone fills out a W9 form, with their correct contact info and social security number (download and print out copies of the W9 form at `www.irs.gov/pub/irs-pdf/fw9.pdf`).

✔ **Work hours and work week:** Set out how many hours a day (8 to 12) and how many days a week (5 to 6) are required during production.

Specify *turnaround* time (time off between shoots) in the crew contracts — and make sure it's enough. Turnaround time usually means at least ten hours before the crew member has to return to the set. You need to respect your crew and show you appreciate their dedication to your film, especially if they're working hard for little money.

✔ **Copy of completed project on DVD:** Promise the crew member a copy of the film on DVD when it's completed.

Boilerplates are preexisting contracts that have already been drawn up by an attorney or used for previous productions. All you have to do is fill in the blanks with the crew person's name and other relevant information. My recommendation: Use boilerplates as a guide and then consult an entertainment attorney who can review them and add or subtract where necessary.

One book that I find very informative is *Contracts for the Film & Television Industry* by Mark Litwak (published by Silman-James Press). Mark is a prominent entertainment attorney in Los Angeles who works very closely with independent filmmakers. In addition to his series of legal books, check out his Web site at `www.marklitwak.com`. Mark's industry book contains 40 contracts that are useful for TV and film production, including a 3-page crew deal memo (again, I recommend consulting a lawyer to review any boilerplate contract before using it — doing so protects all parties).

Contracts need to be specifically tailored to your production. If you're in a town that doesn't have an entertainment attorney, you can always find an attorney who is familiar with the film industry via the Internet in Los Angeles, New York, or Toronto. You don't even have to meet face to face. You can send forms and contracts via e-mail and fax machines. I'm in Los Angeles and so is my entertainment attorney — and in a year's time I've only seen him in person twice (and one of those times was when I ran into him at a department store).

Chapter 8

Assembling Your Cast of Characters

The time has come to breathe life into your screenplay's characters and have them jump off the page. In this chapter, you discover how to find the perfect cast for your film and how to talk to agents, managers, and casting directors. You find out what to look for in actors (and their resumes), what to expect when you meet actors, and how to read them for the part. I also give you some important tips to relay to your actors so that you get the best audition from them. You may just discover the next Al Pacino or Meryl Streep. You may also want to pick up a copy of *Breaking Into Acting For Dummies* by Larry Garrison and Wallace Wang (published by Wiley) for more tips on the auditioning and casting process.

Hooking Your Cast and Reeling Them In

Casting is one of the most important decisions you make when putting your film together — it's half the game. So how do you go about finding your cast of characters? There's no shortage of actors (or wannabes), and there's no shortage of places to find them. You can discover your leading lady or leading man on the street, through a mutual friend, at a talent showcase, online, or even at your family reunion (who knew Cousin Benny had that star quality you were looking for all along?). You can also find actors by contacting agents, managers, and casting directors; calling casting services; and scouring actor directories (including those on the internet). The following sections tells you how.

I'm D.B.

A service that everyone in the film industry uses is the IMDb, which stands for *Internet Movie Database* (www.imdb.com and www.imdb pro.com). Every actor who has ever worked is listed on IMDb. Not only can you get actors' complete resumes of films, TV, and stage work, but if you subscribe to *IMDbPro,* you can find out who represents and/or manages them along with contact info. The site also lists production companies, distributors, producers, directors, writers, and films. It's a plethora of information right at one main Internet address. *IMDb* is free, and *IMDbPro* is $12.95 a month, but you can get a free two week trial by signing up.

Calling all agents

Just because an actor has an agent doesn't mean the actor is working a lot. An agent is more of a legal representative for actors — someone to protect the actor from being taken advantage of on the set and to make sure she receives payment for services rendered. An agent usually does all the contractual work with you for the actor he or she represents, whether it's a detailed agreement or a simple one-page *deal memo* (see "Handling Actors' Agreements" later in this chapter).

An agent usually collects the actor's payment and takes a 10 percent agent commission fee before paying the performer. A manager can charge 15 percent or more as a commission fee. This is important for you to know, because sometimes an agent and/or manager asks for the actor's fee, *plus* the agent and manager fees on top.

Most agents won't consider a project for a client until they've received and read the screenplay, along with a written offer. If the agent doesn't like the script (or the offer) or thinks her client isn't appropriate for the project or part, she'll decline.

If the agent *likes* your project, this is a good time to ask who else he or she represents that may be good for your film. For my movie *Undercover Angel,* I asked the agent who represented Yasmine Bleeth (the actress playing the lead in my film) who else he represented that he could recommend to play the male lead opposite her. This is how I ended up casting Dean Winters (of HBO's *OZ, 30 Rock, Law & Order*).

Casting through casting directors

Casting directors are always on the lookout for new talent to feed the myriad productions being produced. In Hollywood, the casting director has a lot of power because if an actor doesn't get past her, he'll never have a chance to meet the filmmakers. A casting director not only filters the piles of pictures and résumés that are submitted but also schedules auditions with the chosen ones. This saves the filmmaker from having to see everyone who walks through the door — even the ones who can't act their way out of a paper bag (which by the way my dog can do very well). A casting director also builds relationships with talented actors whom he's seen perform in the past, and he keeps a roster of these talented individuals should an appropriate part come along for them to try out for.

The casting director is only the guard at the gate — the bouncer outside the club — who the actor needs to get past in order to get to you, the filmmaker. The casting director does *not* make the final casting decision; she only filters the talent or suggests name actors that she can approach for your film. The director or producer makes the final decision on cast.

Placing casting ads

One way to find talent for your film is to place casting ads. A *casting ad* is similar to a job classified ad, but instead of seeking someone for an office position with the proper qualifications, you're seeking an actor with acting experience who qualifies for a very specific acting role. You can place an ad on a job board at a theater company or at local colleges and high schools. Some larger cities even have periodicals devoted to scouting talent. For example, if you're in a major city like Los Angeles, you can place an ad in *Backstage*, a weekly periodical for actors and industry professionals. The magazine is predominately for Los Angeles and New York casting, but anybody can subscribe to it, and you can place a casting ad no matter where you reside. *Backstage* also has an online service where you post your casting ads immediately, making them available to online subscribers (www.backstage.com).

When you post an ad looking for actors for your film, list the following information:

- ✔ Log line of your film (one- or two-line synopsis of the story)
- ✔ Character's name and age range (such as 24 to 29)
- ✔ Character's body type (balding, skinny, chesty — preferably not all three!)
- ✔ Character's idiosyncrasies (knowing that the character has a lisp, a twitch, or a type of attitude is helpful to the actor in the audition)
- ✔ Character role (lead, supporting, or day player)
- ✔ Acting experience (required or not)
- ✔ Whether you're seeking union or non-union actors (many independent low-budget films can't afford to hire union actors and follow union regulations under the restraints of a small production — see Chapter 4)
- ✔ Pay or no pay (important to mention)

Cattle calling

Round 'em up! A *cattle call* is a casting call where anyone can show up and be seen by the producers (like you've seen on *American Idol*). My dog recently went to a cattle call for canines (he has his Dog Actors Guild {DAG} card). You can place a cattle call casting ad in your local newspaper, in an entertainment trade magazine, on the internet, or through a casting service. Depending on the film and the roll being offered, lines can wind around the block. If you're offering generic parts that can be filled by almost anyone, your cattle call could cause a stampede!

✔ Benefits such as a copy of the film and meals on set (important, especially if you offer no or low pay)

✔ Contact information (where actors can send their pictures and resumes)

With the advent of the Internet, picture and résumé submissions can be delivered in seconds instead of hours or days. Nowadays, an attached e-mail photo can be viewed immediately and in high photo quality.

Calling casting services

A casting service is a service that hooks the filmmaker up with the actor — a win-win situation. A filmmaker puts out a call for a particular type of acting role, and a casting service gets that call out to the agents, managers, and actors who could fill that role. Nowadays, many casting services use the Internet, because it's faster than using snail mail or courier services. Many cities have casting services, and the best way to find out is to talk to agents in your area. If any type of casting service is available, agents will be using it.

Accessing actor directories

If you're looking for an apartment, you can browse through a rental directory, complete with photos. If you're looking to buy a new home, you can look through a real-estate guide. Well, actors have their own directory, too. You can flip through pages of a directory that features actors' photos and contact information, all at your fingertips. The Academy of Television Arts and Sciences puts out the *Players Directory,* a series of books categorized by leading, *ingenue* (roles played by young women), and character actors. You can also access it online at www.playersdirectory.com. The books and Internet access cost $75 per set. Most actors in the directory are located in or near the Los Angeles or New York areas (but most are willing to travel for a great role).

Screening an Actor's Information

After you've received an actor's submission, you need to evaluate whether this actor is a potential candidate for one of the roles in your film. Some of the things you'll consider as you review the actor's picture and résumé:

✔ Does the actor look the part?

✔ Does she have the qualifications (acting experience) and/or some professional training?

✔ Does she have any special skills listed that may help add believability to playing that part? (Can she roller-skate? Juggle? Do accents?)

✔ If the actor submitted a demo reel, is his performance believable?

✔ Is the actor union or non-union? If an actor is union, you have to follow union rules and pay the actor appropriately (see Chapter 4). Many low budget films can't afford to hire union actors. Some union actors are willing to work non-union (which the unions don't encourage).

Headshots and résumés

You can tell how serious an actor is by how he submits his picture (called a *headshot*) and résumé. I've received folded photocopies of pictures in letter-size envelopes (saving the sender on postage). If an actor doesn't take him- or herself seriously enough to submit professional materials, you can't take him or her seriously either. The only actors who probably don't need a professional headshot are those auditioning for the role of the headless horseman in *Sleepy Hollow!*

When you receive pictures and résumés from actors, especially if you receive them in the mail, make sure all pertinent information is on the résumé, including a contact number for the agent, manager, or actor. More than once I've received résumé that didn't include the actors' contact information — not even a phone number! Since I couldn't call these actors in for an audition, I had to cast them into a trash can instead.

Also, make sure the pictures and résumés you receive in the mail are stapled together. If not, you may want to staple them yourself (and deduct the staple from their salary if they get the job). That way you don't lose track of what résumé belongs with which picture.

TIP

Breaking into Breakdown Services

If you're in the Los Angeles, New York, Toronto, or Vancouver areas, I suggest contacting Breakdown Services. Breakdown Services lets casting directors, producers, and directors send out a call for a certain type of character(s) needed for a film or TV production. The specified criteria relate to physical description and acting abilities.

You submit a breakdown of your cast to Breakdown Services, which then posts the list on its site, Breakdown Express (www.break downexpress.com). The many agents and

managers who subscribe to the breakdowns can then access it. Breakdown Services also has a service called Actor Access (www. actorsaccess.com), which allows actors to see certain casting notices on the Breakdown Services Breakdown Express Web site.

Placing a breakdown ad is free if your production is union; if your production is non-union, the fee is $100 unless you're paying actors at least $100 a day; then the casting ad is free.

Reading and reviewing résumés

Following are things you should find on an actor's résumé that will help determine whether he or she is qualified for one of the roles in your film:

- **Height, weight, hair and eye color.** Since the photo doesn't say, "actual size," the resume should include height. And because most photos are in black and white, hair and eye color should be included, too.

- **Union affiliations if any.** Don't let non-union status cause you to reject an actor. Just because an actor may not be in a union doesn't mean he isn't a good actor. Every successful actor at one time was not in a union.

- **List of credits.** See what experience the actor has. Just as important as acting experience is the experience of being on a set and knowing the rituals.

- **Commercial credits.** Usually a résumé says, "Commercial credits upon request." You are welcome to request them.

- **Stage work.** Lets you know whether the actor has any live-performance experience (keep in mind that stage acting is quite different from film acting).

- **Training and special skills.** Anything that may enhance the character you're considering the actor for.

- **Contact information (agent, manager, sometimes cell phone, and e-mail address).** Many good actors don't have an agent or manager; you can contact them directly.

Sometimes you find an actor with little experience who ends up being perfect for the part. I never judge an actor by a lack of credits on his or her résumé. Call them in — you can't tell personality from a résumé.

Heading toward headshots

An actor's *headshot* is usually an 8-x-10-inch black-and-white photo with a résumé stapled to the back. Rarely does an actor need a color picture — you expect the actors themselves to be in color. Redheads tend to send color pictures because they feel they are a minority (everyone else is blonde in Hollywood), and their hair color may help them land a part. (*Zed cards* are a series of different shots on one card. Even though they're submitted more for modeling work, I like to see several shots of an actor, if available, just to get a better idea of what he or she looks like.)

I've rarely met an actor who looks exactly like his or her photo. Don't hire an actor based solely on the headshot — always meet him or her in person! I've made this mistake and regretted it.

When you look at an actor's photo, do you see some personality? Is there a gleam in the eye? I've received headshots where the actor looks like he's a frightened deer in a tractor-trailer's headlights, or she's putting on a goofy face that immediately warns me she may be an over-actor.

Taping their act

An actor may submit a *demo reel* with his résumé and headshot. A demo reel is usually a DVD (or a clip available for viewing on YouTube [www.youtube.com] or MySpace [www.myspace.com]) that features a selection of acting scenes, usually between 3 and 5 minutes in length, that the actor appears in.

Spinning an actor's Web site

Not only do the actor's tools include a headshot, résumé, and a demo reel, but many also have either a personal Web page or a Web site. Many actors' Internet sites put up pictures (including headshots) and résumés for filmmakers to reference. One such service is www.hollywoodsuccess.com, which posts actors' pictures and résumés from all over the country.

You'll know an actor is serious and professional about her career if she also has an electronic résumé on a personal Web page with the following:

- Several photos to give you an idea of her look
- An updated list of credits and skills to get an idea of her experience in front of the camera

✔ Her e-mail address, as well as her agent's e-mail address so that you can easily make contact

✔ A streaming demo reel to give you an idea immediately of her on-camera persona (many actors' Web sites now link to YouTube or MySpace, where you can see scenes they've uploaded of their performances)

Auditioning Your Potential Cast

The audition is the first face-to-face meeting between you and the actor. First impressions are always the most important — especially in the casting process. The audition not only gives you a chance to "test" the actor, but it also lets you see if he really does resemble his photo — minus the magic of a professional photographer and airbrush artist — and gives you an idea of whether this person can take direction. Have him read some lines from the script, and then tell him to try it a different way — with an accent or using a different tone or attitude.

Nothing compares to a meeting in person, but if distance is a problem, a webcam meeting is the next best thing! I've even auditioned actors via computer-to-computer webcams using *Skype* and *iChat* (free Internet video-calling services). Auditioning remotely is very similar to conducting an in-person audition, and you can get a good sense of the actor's personality.

Creating a friendly environment

Always conduct auditions in a place of business — never in your home, no matter how small your production. Having people come to your home is a bit suspicious and, besides, it's not professional. Why would you want every Tom, Dick, and Harriet coming to your private residence anyway? You can find an office, conference room, dance studio, or rehearsal hall to rent for a few hours at a reasonable price ($10 to $40 per hour), or borrow an office space through a friend.

If you're personable with the actors, they'll be much more comfortable talking with you and more likely to be themselves. People tend to mirror people — so if you're uptight, they'll be uptight or uncomfortable. Be professional, but be respectful and friendly; not only will the casting process be easier for the actors, but it will also be more effective for you.

Inspecting an actor's etiquette

When you meet an actor for the first time, he or she should make an impression on you. Is this someone you would like to work with? There are several things you should look for in an actor:

✔ **Is he punctual?** Does he show up on time for the audition? If not, this could be an indication that he's not reliable or at least not punctual.

✔ **Does she have personality?** The number-one most important trait of an actor is personality. A strong personality in general helps infuse personality into the character the actor is playing.

✔ **What is he like before the reading and after?** How an actor acts before and after the reading often impresses me more than the reading itself. It gives you a chance to see if that person has a sense of humor, funny quirks, or interesting mannerisms.

✔ **How is she dressed?** An actor should dress appropriately for an audition. She doesn't have to wear a uniform or costume that suits the character, but if she's trying out for a biker chick role, leather pants and a sleeveless shirt is okay. If the role is an attorney, wearing a suit helps the casting director "see" that actor in the role a lot easier.

✔ **Does he conduct himself professionally?** An actor should be polite, cordial, and pleasant at an audition.

Actors who send a thank-you note (or postcard or email with their photo) after you've met always stand out. Less than 10 percent of actors have sent me thank-you notes over the past 20 years, but I've actually singled out actors who do and hired them because their note reminded me of our meeting. It tells me they're thoughtful, probably reliable, and they take their acting career seriously. This is someone I want to have on my set.

Slating on video

You may want to videotape the auditions so that you have a video reference of all the people you audition. When you videotape auditions, always have the actor start by *slating*. *Slating* means that the actor introduces him- or herself on camera and then gives a contact number (cell phone, voice-mail, or agent or manager numbers). Slating saves you the time and trouble of tracking down pictures and résumés.

Avoiding bitter-cold readings

Some directors have actors do a cold reading of *sides* (two or three pages from the script) without any study time on a first audition. This is effective when you want to see how actors work with no preparation. If you want to get a better idea of their performance abilities, then give them at least ten minutes with the material before expecting them to perform it for you.

To help calm the actors' nerves and bring out their personality, talk to them for a few minutes before they read; doing so helps you see whether they're personable and have a quality that the audience will be attracted to. Then have them read to see whether they can inject their personality into their reading. I often tell actors it's okay if they miss or add some words if it keeps them from staring at the script pages. I'm not looking to see how well they can read words; I'm looking for a natural performance that impresses me during the audition phase.

Monologues leave you all by yourself

Actors have been conditioned to bring *monologues* to perform at auditions for the casting director, producer, or director. I'm not a fan of monologues because rarely do you have a film where the actor is talking for three minutes straight with no interaction from other characters. Monologues are more suited in auditioning for stage plays, as they tend to make the actor *project* (reach and speak louder).

When an actor prefers to do a monologue, do what I do: Have the actor pick someone in the room to talk to, and then have that person sit or stand at the distance he would if he were in the actual scene. This helps the actor better target his voice level and emotions. You can also have the other person silently react, so the performing actor has some interaction with a live person. Doing this eliminates another problem: Many actors who perform monologues make the mistake of talking to the casting director or person conducting the auditions (the director or producer) — something akin to looking straight into the camera, which is a no-no! If you're conducting the auditions, you want to observe the performance, not feel like you're part of it.

Making the Cut: Picking Your Cast

Choosing your final cast is not always the easiest job for the filmmaker. The actors you decide on have the responsibility of carrying your film. They are the blood that keeps your film alive.

Calling back

When you like an actor who has come in for an audition, you call her back for a more personal meeting. This is appropriately called a *call back*. The call back gives you and the actor a second chance to become familiar with each other and for you to see whether she's appropriate for the role you're considering her for. During a call back, you usually have more time to sit down and talk to the actor and get a better feel of her personality. You can take time to have her read some pages from the script as well.

Screen testing

A *screen test* is an actual dialogue scene from your film that you have the actor perform so that you can see how he comes across on camera. A screen testing usually occurs only when you're seriously considering a particular actor but aren't sure whether he can effectively play the role. Screen testing also lets you see how comfortable the actor is in front of the camera and how well he takes direction.

Shoot an inexpensive screen test with a video camcorder. The picture quality and lighting aren't important. You are looking only at performance here.

And the winners are . . .

After you've found the actor who's going to breathe life into the character, the first thing you have to do to hire that actor is call the actor's agent (if he is represented by one) and tell her you're interested in casting her client. The agent then contacts the actor and tells him the good news. If an actor doesn't have representation, you can call him directly and personally tell him that you're looking forward to working with him.

Make sure that the actor or the actor's representatives understand all the details of the job. Be up front. If there's low pay or no pay, let them know this right away. (Some agents want their actor clients to get parts and build up a *reel,* various scenes of their work on DVD, and they're glad to negotiate a deal that you can afford.) Let them know that you will give them a DVD copy of their scene, and that you'll feed them on the set.

The next thing you need to do is contract that actor, which means arranging a legal agreement between you or your company and the actor. You can find more information about agreements in the next section.

After you select your actor(s), contact the other actors that you seriously considered before you chose someone else. Actors are sensitive, and knowing that they were seriously being considered lets them know they are worthy. You can even let them know that you will keep them in mind as a backup should your first choice not work out and that you may possibly cast them in future projects. Don't turn down second choices until your first-choice actor has agreed to do the film. You still have to deal with egos, agents, and managers, and your first-choice actor may suddenly not be available.

Agreeing with Actors' Agreements

Once you cast an actor, it's important to get a written agreement between you and the actor, and/or her representative (agent). The agreement protects both the actor and you, the filmmaker. It spells out the terms regarding what's expected of both parties and is signed by you and the actor. The actor plays the assigned role, for a certain period of time, and gets paid (or doesn't). This agreement also contractually obligates the actor to your film; she can't take another project unless you don't fulfill your end of the agreement.

If the actor is a minor (and I don't mean a coal miner), a guardian over the age of 18 must sign on his or her behalf. Otherwise, the contract can't be enforced — it's like not having a contract at all. Without a contract, a minor actor has no obligation to you or the production. He can even not show up on set and demand more money, and you don't have a legal document to enforce.

Contracting union players

If you're hiring union actors with the Screen Actors Guild (SAG), you have to use its contracts, which lay out strict rules and regulations that you have to abide by, including minimum salaries (close to $800 a day) to its union members. There are special SAG agreements for independent productions that may fit into your budget; you can read about these in Chapter 4.

If you're doing a union production using SAG (www.sag.org), the American Federation of Television and Radio Artists (AFTRA, www.aftra.org), or the Alliance of Canadian Cinema, Television & Radio Artists (ACTRA, www.actra.ca), you have contractual union stipulations to abide by. You can get details on the various contract agreements on their Web sites. If you're shooting a very low-budget production, you may want to avoid the paperwork hassles and extra costs of becoming a signatory to one of the unions. The Screen Actors Guild has several special contracts for lower-budget productions (www.sagindie.org) (see Chapter 4); check out its Web site for details.

Contracting non-union players

A non-union actor's agreement can be issued in two phases. The first phase involves a *deal memo*. The second phase involves the formal *long-form agreement*. Both of these are explained in the following sections.

The deal memo

The deal memo is a short, preliminary contract or agreement usually made up of a few sentences stating that you're interested in hiring the actor for your film and that a more formal agreement will be drawn up in the near future. The main purpose of a deal memo is to outline the main points of your deal without having to wait for the attorneys to do their thing. You may be able to find an appropriate agreement from an entertainment book, such as Mark Litwak's *Contracts for the Film & Television Industry* (see his Web site, www.marklitwak.com). Regardless of where you get your contracts, always have an attorney review them before sending them out to be signed.

In addition to a deal memo, you may want to give the actor a monetary retainer to show that you're serious about hiring him. The retainer can be $1, $100, or a $1,000 — depending on how badly you want that particular actor for the part. The retainer legally attaches the actor to your project so you can start planning your shooting schedule or concentrate on casting the other roles. If the actor has name value, having him committed to your film may be of interest to potential distributors and/or investors.

If you're lucky enough to interest a big-name actor in your film, ask her for a *letter of interest,* which is a letter from the talent saying that she is aware of the project and is interested in being a part of your production contingent on salary requirements and schedule. (Usually, you write the letter, and the actor signs it.) Often, the first thing a distributor or studio asks is not "What's the story about?" but "Who's in it?" A letter of interest from a recognized actor could help get you financing and distribution.

The long-form agreement

After contract points are negotiated in detail, a formal agreement, usually called the *long-form agreement,* is drawn up by your attorney. An actor's formal long-form agreement should include the following points:

- ✔ Name of the character role the actor will play
- ✔ The number of shooting days or weeks involved
- ✔ Salary (plus any deferments, and/or points)
- ✔ *Per diem* (pocket money if on location)
- ✔ Perks (such as a trailer, a manicurist, a masseuse, or candy!)
- ✔ Automatic Dialogue Replacement (ADR) availability (for re-recording additional actor's dialogue in postproduction over the picture)
- ✔ How the actor will be billed on the film and poster

In addition, the contract could specify that the actor will receive a DVD copy of the project when it is completed.

Make sure that your agreements let you use the actors' *likeness* in *perpetuity,* which means forever. You don't want to have to track them down ten years later to renew.

Securing releases from extras

In addition to written agreements with your main talent, you also need to have releases signed by *extras* (any other individuals appearing on camera). Yes, *everyone*. Even if people are walking by in the background or sitting at a bar, you need to have them sign a release. A release can be a simple one-paragraph letter giving you permission to use the actor's likeness in your film. (Don't forget: As with lead roles, an extra's release should allow you to use his or her likeness *in perpetuity* so you don't have to track him or her down years later to renew your rights.) A studio or distributor releasing your film will require that you have these releases.

A short release can read as follows:

> For value received, I, [PERSON'S NAME] hereby consent that all photographs and/or images of me and/or voice recordings in whole or in part for [YOU THE FILMMAKER], may be used by [YOU THE FILMMAKER] and/or others with its consent for the purposes of illustration, advertising, broadcast or publication in any manner in perpetuity.

Make sure to include the date and have both parties sign the agreement. Having an attorney review this and any other agreements with regards to your production is always a smart idea.

If you feature people in your film who didn't sign a release, they can legally keep you from showing the footage that they appear in. So don't forget, always get a signed release — even from your mother, if she's in the film!

Union actors working in non-union productions

A union actor may decide to do your film even if it's non-union. *Financial core* was established by the Supreme Court to protect union members from coming under fire from their own union if they take non-union jobs. Financial core encompasses all U.S. unions, not just the ones related to entertainment. Search the Internet for "financial core" to get the latest updates on this controversial topic.

Many times low-budget productions only go union if they have name actors (who can make your film more commercial to distributors). Many actors will work non-union to get a good part (though the unions definitely discourage it). The Screen Actors Guild puts out some low-budget agreements to help independent filmmakers cast union members in low-budget productions and still allows you to use non-union actors in the same film as well (see the guild's Web site, www.sagindie.org). Also see Chapter 4 for more information on low-budget agreements.

Chapter 9

Storyboarding Your Film

In This Chapter

▶ Picturing the importance of storyboarding

▶ Breaking down your film into storyboard panels

▶ Making your own storyboards

▶ Finding a storyboard artist

*I*f a picture is worth a thousand words, then a storyboard literally speaks volumes about your film. What's a storyboard? A visual illustration (hand drawn or created with computer software) of the separate shots that will make up your film. If you've ever read the Sunday comics, you're already familiar with storyboards.

This chapter shows you the advantages of storyboarding and how to break your script down into separate shots that become illustrated panels. You find out about the elements that make up a storyboard panel and the different sizes they come in and why. You see how a professional presentation of your film in the visual form of a storyboard helps you sell your concept to an investor or studio. Don't think you can draw well enough? I provide suggestions for making your own storyboards with the help of some great software products. If you don't want to draw or use software products, I tell you how to find the right artist for your project and what you should expect to pay.

Understanding the Basics and Benefits of Storyboarding

Storyboards, which consist of a series of separate panels or frames, each one representing individual shots in your film, provide an illustrated version of your screenplay — they tell your story with pictures. By storyboarding your film, you, the cast, and the crew can visualize what the film is going to look like before you even start shooting.

Storyboards serve as a visual reference and are helpful in the following situations:

- ✔ Making a presentation to a client, such as an investor or a studio
- ✔ Helping your cast and crew see your vision of the film so that they're on the same page you're on
- ✔ Showing your cameraman (director of photography) exactly what type of framing you want for each shot (more on framing later in this chapter)
- ✔ Scheduling your shots for each day
- ✔ Determining whether you have any unique shots that require action or special effects
- ✔ Budgeting (planning ahead with storyboards saves you time and money)

Having trouble picturing what a storyboard is? Look at the DVD menu section of your favorite film. It probably gives you a choice of chapters and shows you the still frame that begins each scene or chapter. The same idea of frames is used in storyboarding, only the storyboard frame or panel represents the first frame of each individual, continuous shot.

The storyboard's individual shots make up scenes, and scenes make up the whole film. You can have a few dozen storyboards, or 1,200 designed for your film — it all depends on the type of material you're storyboarding. For example, an action picture requires more precise planning; extensively storyboarding these films makes it easier to see and coordinate the shots. It also lets you cover the action from numerous angles and preplan those angles to heighten the excitement. You can also storyboard any stunts, so the crew can see exactly what's going to happen on set. Steven Spielberg storyboarded almost 70 percent of his shots for *Indiana Jones and the Temple of Doom.* (He had help — although Spielberg draws initial concepts for his storyboards, he usually enlists the skills of a seasoned storyboard artist to realize his vision even further. I discuss the benefits of hiring a storyboard artist later in this chapter.)

On the other hand, not every filmmaker relies on storyboards. Sometimes the story doesn't require the details of each shot to be illustrated. A love story, such as the romantic comedy *When Harry Met Sally. . .,* may not demand hundreds of complex storyboards because the shots are not as complex as those in an action or effects picture, although some simple storyboards showing angles and types of shots are always helpful.

Each panel of a storyboard shows you exactly what's needed for that particular shot, eliminating the guesswork for you and your crew. For example, storyboards let you know how big your set needs to be. If you plan to have aliens exit a spaceship, storyboards give you and your crew an idea about whether you need to build the whole ship or just the door area. Another example — does your storyboard show a crowd in the stands watching a football game? From your storyboard panel, you know that you only need a small crowd and not a whole stadium full!

Storyboards are just like comic books

When I was a kid growing up in the '60s, I was an avid reader and collector of comic books. I spent endless hours absorbed in my Spider-Man, Batman, Richie Rich, and Archie comics. Little did I know that years later I would work with comic panels, or storyboards, to map out my shots for a film. Reading comic books at a young age taught me how to break a story into shots and angles — and I was learning about movement within a single shot or panel that I would one day apply to my filmmaking ventures. Once you start storyboarding, you'll never look at the Sunday comics the same way again!

You don't need to have storyboards rendered in full color unless you use them to impress a client or investor when selling your idea. Often, completed panels are acceptable in pencil, ink, or even charcoal — as long as they depict your vision as the director accurately.

Setting Up to Storyboard

Before you create your storyboards, you have to perform certain tasks and make certain decisions. First, begin by evaluating your screenplay and picturing it in terms of separate shots that can be visually translated into individual storyboard panels. Then you determine what makes up each shot and also which images need to be storyboarded and which ones don't. After you start storyboarding, you'll need to determine whether you're shooting for a TV movie or a theatrical release, which may affect the frame dimensions of your panels. Read on for the details!

Breaking down your script

The task of turning your screenplay into a movie can be very overwhelming. But remember, a long journey begins with a single step, so begin by breaking the screenplay down into small steps, or shots. A *shot* is defined from the time the camera turns on to cover the action to the time it's turned off — in other words, continuous footage with no cuts. Figure out what you want these shots to entail and then transform those ideas into a series of storyboard panels. Stepping back and seeing your film in individual panels makes the project much less overwhelming.

Evaluating each shot

You have several elements to consider when preparing your storyboards. You first need to evaluate your script and break it down into shots. Then, as you plan each shot panel, ask yourself the following questions:

- ✔ What is the location setting?

- ✔ How many actors are needed in the shot?

- ✔ Do you need any important props or vehicles in the shot?

- ✔ What type of shot (close-up, wide-shot, establishing shot, and so on) do you need? (See Chapter 14 for specific information about shots.)

- ✔ What is the shot's *angle* (where the camera is shooting from)? Is it a high angle? A low angle? (Chapter 14 has more on angles.)

- ✔ Do any actors or vehicles need to move within a frame, and what is the direction of that action?

- ✔ Do you need any camera movement to add motion to this shot? Does the camera follow the actor or vehicles in the shot, and in what direction?

- ✔ Do you need any special lighting? The lighting depends on what type of mood you're trying to convey (for example, you may need candlelight, moonlight, a dark alley, or a bright sunny day).

- ✔ Do you need any special effects? Illustrating special effects is important to deciding whether you have to hire a special-effects person. Special effects can include gunfire, explosions, and computer-generated effects.

Organizing a shot list

After you determine what makes up each shot, decide whether you want to storyboard every shot or just the ones that require special planning, like action or special effects. If you want to keep a certain style throughout the film — like low angles, special lenses, or a certain lighting style (for example, shadows) — then you may want to storyboard every shot. If you only want to storyboard certain scenes that may require special planning, keep a *shot list* of all the events or scenes that jump out at you so that you can translate them into separate storyboard panels.

Even if you've already created your shot list, you aren't locked into it. Inspiration for a new shot often hits while you're on set and your creative juices are flowing. If you have time and money, and the schedule and budget allow, try out that inspiration!

Framing storyboard panels

Before you actually draw your storyboards, you need to create a space for them to call home. The shape and dimensions of your storyboard panels will be determined by whether your movie is going to the standard TV screen, high definition TV screen, or theatrical screen. These different dimensions affect how much information is drawn into your storyboards and what will ultimately be seen on the appropriate screen.

A storyboard panel is basically just a box containing the illustration of each individual shot (one of many that you envision for your film). Here are some quick steps to design your own storyboard panels:

1. **Decide which shape and size of panel to use.**

   A television storyboard panel, like the screen on a standard television set, resembles a square, only slightly wider (4:3 dimensions). Theatrical feature-film storyboards are rectangular in shape and almost twice as wide as a standard television screen (see Figure 9-1). Many filmmakers now shoot for the wider framing which works well for theatrical films and high definition TV's and can be reduced or cropped to fit standard sets.

   You can purchase pads of storyboard panels in different format sizes at many art and business stores. If you don't want to spend extra dollars on a pad of professional storyboard paper, you can draw your own panels — four to six on a regular 8½-x-11-inch piece of paper (keeping them at a legible size), or you can even print blank storyboard panels using your desktop computer.

2. **Draw the shape of the panel and add a thick black or grey border (approximately ¹/₂ inch in width) around the square or rectangle.**

   Placing a border around each panel helps you to see each panel as a definitive separate shot and subliminally creates the illusion of a TV or darkened theater around your shot, giving you an idea of what that individual image will look like. With theatrical panels you may want to avoid the thick border to save on page space (and ink!).

3. **Create a *description panel* by drawing an empty box just below the bottom of the frame panel.**

   Use the *description box* to write down important information that describes in detail what the illustration doesn't show or enhances what is drawn in the frame (see Figure 9-1). For example, include any important dialogue, camera directions, scene numbers, or special-effects instructions.

Figure 9-1:
A story-
board
standard
TV panel
from *The
Frog Prince,*
and a wide
screen
panel from
*Miss Cast
Away and
the Island
Girls.*

The Frog Prince -- TV panel

SUDDENLY A FLY BUZZES AROUND THEIR HEADS. PRINCE ZAPS THE FLY WITH HIS TONGUE.

Shot #   Miss Cast Away -- theatrical panel

The girls are positioning some chopped trees into place........

© Stellar Entertainment (Artist: Tom Decker)
© Stellar Entertainment (Artist: Cuong Huynh)

Deciding What to Include in Each Panel: Putting Pencil to Paper

After you create your storyboard panels, you need to decide exactly what you want your shots to look like. First, determine what the best angle is to capture the drama in a particular shot and whether you're going to move the camera. Also, think about lighting effects (shadows, special lighting, and so on) and other special effects that can be clearly exemplified in your boards. You should also draw any physical elements that will be inside the frame, including special props and, of course, your actors.

Choosing the right angles

You need to decide where you want to position the camera for the best *coverage* (the best angle to see the action). Angles have a subliminal effect on your audience (see Chapter 14 for examples of what the various camera angles look like in the frame and what effects they have):

✔ **A low angle,** in which the camera is positioned on the floor looking up at the actor, can make an actor appear bigger and more menacing. So in your storyboard panel, you draw the low angle looking up at the actor with the ceiling behind him.

TECHNICAL STUFF

Widening the screen to be seen

Standard TVs have an aspect ratio of 4:3. The picture is slightly wider than it is high. This is the aspect ratio that has been designated to conventional television since the advent of the medium. The dimensions for high definition is 16:9, where the width is almost twice the height of the TV screen. Motion pictures are projected in theatres in a 1:85 ratio which is approximately two and half times the width by height (often referred to as *letter box* or *wide screen*). Motion pictures conform well on HD 16:9 televisions. Some foreign countries use different aspect ratios such as 1:66 and 1:78 which are variables on the letterbox format and can be reduced (or cropped) to fit on virtually any television set.

> ✔ **A high angle** that looks down on an actor can make the character appear innocent, small, or weak. The storyboard sketch must make it clear that you need to have the camera up high.

Make a note if you will require special equipment, such as a high tripod or a crane to get your high-angle shot (check out Chapter 14 for more information about types of dollies and cranes).

Imagining camera and actor movement

Camera movement emphasizes a feeling or mood in a scene, and your storyboard panels need to depict any such movement in each shot. (Check out Chapter 13 for additional tips on camera movement.) This is also a good time to decide if your actors are going to move within the frame as well. You can plan basic actor movement in the storyboards and save detailed movement of your actors, called *blocking* (see Chapter 13), for when you're actually on the set.

Three-dimensional arrows usually show movement within a panel. The arrows point in the direction of your camera movement, whether it pans up, down, left, or right. They also convey the camera moving in or out of the shot or leading or following an actor or vehicle. They can even show the camera in a spin when you want to create a dizzying effect. Figure 9-2 illustrates the use of arrows in a storyboard panel from my sci-fi fantasy *Light Years Away*. Notice that the larger arrow shows the direction the character is moving within the shot, and the smaller arrow shows the movement of the camera following the action.

Figure 9-2:
The use of
arrows for
movement.

David sees Misty in the beam of light from the heavens.

(as David approaches, Camera moves around Misty in the light)

Boarding your special effects

Special effects can be costly if they aren't planned properly. By storyboarding your special effects, you see exactly what they entail. For example, if a giant dinosaur looms up into the frame, you know the shot requires at least the head of the creature and some blue sky behind it. You and your special-effects team know exactly the elements you need for the shot (and the creature knows he doesn't have to worry about what shoes to wear that day). Now, if in the next frame, you have the monster from head to toe, chasing the villagers, your special-effects team has a lot more work to do.

Storyboarding is also important to see how the camera needs to move during the effect, which can be tricky when the frame has computer-generated images. If the shot consists of an explosion with an actor in the same shot, then you can see by this panel that either you have to have the actor as far away from the explosion as possible (unless you don't plan on using the actor in any more shots — just kidding!) or you need to add the actor to the shot during postproduction. By illustrating these effects or stunts in a storyboard panel, you have a better opportunity to actually see what elements are in the shot and what safety precautions may be required.

Animating animatics

Animatics is a form of storyboarding that incorporates your individual panels and turns them into a moving picture show. Animatics can be as simple as a video presentation with zooms and pans of the storyboard frames. On a more sophisticated level, you can animate your storyboard panels, with your characters and vehicles moving within the panels, and add in narration or dialogue.

The DVD of Pixar's *Monster's, Inc.* shows the actual animatics for the film. Many animated films use animatics because the character styles already exist (although cruder and simpler drawings are used to illustrate the characters' movements within the shots). TV

commercials also rely heavily on animatics because a client is more easily convinced if he can see a moving visual presentation that resembles the final product. Of course, it's also easier to do an animatic for a 30-second commercial than a 2-hour film.

StageTools makes two popular software programs that can help you design animatics for your film. Check out www.stagetools. com for MovingPicture, MovingPicture Producer, and MovingParts for free software demo downloads. You can also check out Storyboard Artist for interactive storyboards from www.powerproduction.com.

Use the description panel (explained in the earlier section "Framing storyboard panels") to detail exactly what is required for a shot. In the previous example, the description panel would note that explosives are set in the alley behind the dumpster and that you will superimpose the actor into the shot during postproduction. Additional information may mention that the dumpster lid is made of light plastic, and it isn't hinged to the bin, so it can fly into the air on detonation (that reminds me, I forgot to take out the garbage).

Sketching out the actors, props, and vehicles

As you inspect each shot, you see what actors, props, and vehicles are required. If you decide that one storyboard panel is a close-up of an actor, you sketch that one actor, and only that actor, in the panel. You may decide that you want a two-shot (see Chapter 14 for more information on different types of shots), so you need to frame two actors in this panel.

Looking at lighting and location

Lighting can emphasize a certain mood or tone in a shot. So when drawing your panels, point out any special lighting techniques. If it's a dark chase through an alley, cryptic shadows and darkness add to the suspense and need to be illustrated in your storyboards. You can give more detail in the description box below each storyboard panel about what you're trying to show in the illustration.

You don't need to draw actual locations in detail unless something in the setting is crucial to the shot, or a character interacts with it somehow. If a car is driving down the road, you only need to draw the road and not the surrounding trees and buildings. If an actor enters a room, you only need to draw the door from which the actor enters. Some scribbles or lines on the walls can show that the scene is taking place inside. If you're using a software program to design your storyboards, the program can repeat a background location so that you don't have to draw it by hand every time (see "Designing with storyboard software" later in this chapter for more information).

I Can't Draw, Even If My Life Depended on It

Many people are not trained artists, and some of us can only draw stick people (who look like skinny actors who don't eat — I know a few of those). But never fear, in the following sections, I outline a few solutions — like using storyboard software or hiring an artist — for the artistically challenged.

Designing with storyboard software

If you're not satisfied with drawing happy faces on stick people, but you still want to create the storyboards yourself, try using storyboard software. Storyboard programs give you a library of pre-drawn generic characters (male, female, children, animals) that you can choose, click on, and drop right into your storyboard frames. You can manipulate the size and shape of each character and even rotate each character's position. Along with a cast of characters, these programs also usually provide a library of common props and generic locations to place in your frames as well. A few different software programs are available to help you out:

✔ **Atomic Storyboard** is a free software program that you can download at www.atomiclearning.com/k12/storyboardpro. The price is right!

✔ **Storyboard Quick** from PowerProduction (www.storyboardquick.com) costs $299.99. This easy-to-use program makes for quick storyboarding.

Storyboarding with Storyboard Quick

One of my favorite storyboard software programs is Storyboard Quick by PowerProduction Software. A great feature of Storyboard Quick is that you can input your entire screenplay so that every piece of dialogue has its own storyboard panel. It's a great way to break down your script. Storyboard Quick works for both PCs and Macs.

After storyboarding every shot, Storyboard Quick then lets you choose what elements you want in your separate panels. You can drag and drop illustrations of different characters and put them anywhere within the frame. You can resize your characters to any size and turn and flip them in any direction. Storyboard Quick comes with libraries of images that include characters, props, and locations (such as various rooms, beaches, mountains, deserts, and even interiors of vehicles). You can also buy add-on libraries for additional prop, character, and location images. You can get more information on Storyboard Quick and buy a copy at `www.storyboardquick.com`.

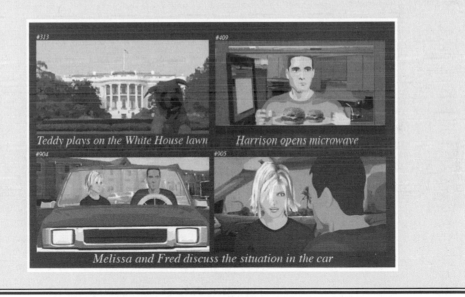

Teddy plays on the White House lawn

Harrison opens microwave

Melissa and Fred discuss the situation in the car

✔ **Storyboard Lite** is a cool software program (costing $250) that allows you to create realistic three-dimensional characters and objects within your storyboards. It's available at `www.zebradevelopment.com`.

✔ **FrameForge 3D** is the Ferrari of storyboard software (`www.frameforge3d.com`). The program turns your storyboard elements into a virtual world, allowing you to manipulate your actors, angles, and even lenses without having to redraw them every time.

Another way to create storyboards if you're not an artist is to take photographs! Get several of your friends together and have them act out your screenplay in pictures. The most economical way to do this is to get your hands on a digital still camera (I use the Kyocera Finecam SL400, www.kyocera.com). Have no friends? Use dolls, toy soldiers, or puppets — whoever your real friends are. George Lucas shoots amusing low-budget video storyboards with dolls of his Star Wars characters for his sci-fi *Star Wars* epics.

Drawing the help of a professional artist

You've been reading this chapter and thinking to yourself, "I can't draw well enough to put my shots into storyboards" or, "I'm not computer literate; I won't be able to run the storyboard software programs." Don't panic! If you aren't happy with your stick characters in your frames, and you can afford it, you can always hire a professional storyboard artist.

A storyboard artist is very much like a crime sketch artist. You describe in detail what your shot looks like, and the artist does his best to put your vision on the page. The artist starts by sketching very rough pencil drawings and making any special notes during your meeting — with you looking over his shoulder to see that he's on the right track. He then goes home (or wherever he feels most comfortable drawing) and returns later with the completed panels. A storyboard artist can ink in the pencil drawings or leave them a little rough, depending on your taste.

If you ask a storyboard artist to *conceptualize* (meaning to design the look of a piece of equipment, a wardrobe, or a vehicle, like a spaceship), you want him to render it in full detail and color for optimum presentation.

Discovering an artist

Lots of talented artists are out there who would be glad to storyboard your film. Even an artist who has never done storyboards can still sketch some great panels after getting a basic understanding of camera shots and lenses. If you decide to hire a professional artist, there are several ways to find one:

- ✔ Art schools are a good place to find budding talent.
- ✔ Cartoonists who work for a local newspaper may enjoy a change of pace.
- ✔ *Picture Book* is an annual reference guide (specializing in children's illustrations) packed with hundreds of artists' samples and contact information. You can check it out at www.picture-book.com or call 888-490-0100.

- *RSVP: The Directory of Illustration and Design* is similar to *Picture Book* and also features hundreds of artists' sample work. You can find out more information at the Web site at www.rsvpdirectory.com or send an e-mail to info@rsvpdirectory.com.

- Famous Frames, Inc. is a company that specializes in providing storyboard artists for independent and studio feature films. Find the company at www.famousframes.com.

- *Animation Magazine* features interviews and articles on cartoonists and also has helpful ads and classified sections that list artists available for freelance work. For subscription information, call 818-991-2884 or go to www.animationmagazine.net.

- An Internet search for "Artists" and "Cartoonists" can also turn up some valuable contacts.

Assessing the artist's qualifications

You need to keep in mind several things when interviewing professional artists to storyboard your film:

- **Be sure to ask whether he or she has ever drawn storyboards before.** Working with a storyboard artist who is versed in camera angles and lenses and has a basic knowledge of cinematic language is best.

- **Make sure the artist draws in a style that works aesthetically for the style of your film.** If the film is a comedy, the style should be light and even have a slight cartoonish feel to it. If it's a serious drama, the illustrations should depict a more formal style with shadows and more serious undertones.

    Request samples from other films the artist has storyboarded to see not only whether you like her style but also whether she has an understanding of the process. Her current work should speak for itself.

- **Assess your compatibility.** It's very important that you get along as a team so that the artist can translate your shots more accurately and effectively into the storyboard panels. Keep in mind that even though you call the shots, you may get some great ideas from the artist.

- **Negotiate a fair price.** You want an artist who will work at a reasonable rate that fits within your budget. Often on independent films, storyboards are a luxury, so you want to make sure you have enough money to pay for a storyboard artist. Sketches per panel can range from $3 for a rough thumbnail pencil sketch to $50 for a detailed black-and-white ink rendering. Remember, though, the price is completely negotiable between you and the artist.

Frame Forging in 3D

FrameForge 3D Studio 2 is a phenomenal 3D storyboarding program that creates a virtual world of your movie. You build your sets, create your characters, and add props and vehicles, all in a 3D virtual world. Once you build each set/location and cast your storyboards, all you have to do is move the virtual camera, and the program creates your angles and camera shots for you. Input your lenses and shot sizes, and the images in your storyboard panels will show the correct dimensions, emulating what they would look like with those actual lenses and shot sizes (lens and angle perception). With a simple click of your mouse, you can even change the three-dimensional panels to look more like two-dimensional artist sketches.

The program is $399 ($179 for the Academic version). You can order expansion packs (at additional cost) that include Crime & Justice (police and swat teams), Military Pack (soldiers, terrorists, battlefield armaments, and military vehicles), and Stock Set (furniture, landscaping elements, and structural elements). You can also order the Directors Pad — a dedicated handheld controller with buttons and a joystick that lets you control and experiment with all your camera angles and object functions (www. frameforge3d.com).

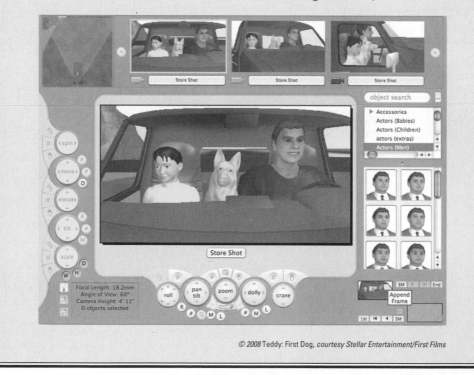

© 2008 Teddy: First Dog, courtesy Stellar Entertainment/First Films

✔ **Make sure that the artist's turnaround time works for your schedule.** *Turnaround* means the time it takes from working on the rough sketches with the artist until the artist comes back to you with the final rendered storyboard panels.

Don't limit yourself to only local artists. You can work with an artist via e-mail and have the storyboards scanned and sent to you as an attachment. If you go this route, discuss the shots and style in detail with the artist first and make sure his rough sketches match your expectations — he can then e-mail you what he's working on so that you can verify he's on the right track. You can even pay your artist using PayPal (an internet service that lets you send or receive payments anywhere in the world). All you need is his e-mail address. Check out PayPal (`www.paypal.com`) for more information on this payment option.

Part III

Ready to Roll: Starting Production on Your Film

In this part . . .

Hold onto your director's cap because you're going to discover some pretty amazing stuff in this part. What was once unattainable to the independent low-budget or no-budget filmmaker is now attainable. Welcome to the future!

In this part, you see that the creative elements to making a movie are the same whether you shoot with a traditional film camera, a basic camcorder, or a high definition digital 24-frame camcorder that emulates the look of film.

This part takes you behind the scenes and shows you the meaning of "Lights, camera, action!" You're sure to find the chapter on lighting illuminating, and I'll have you tuned in on the sound production chapter. I give you the right directions in Chapter 13 on directing your actors and then direct you onto your film set in Chapter 14.

Chapter 10

Shooting through the Looking Glass

*W*ith the magical box called the movie camera, you can capture your story, turn it into pictures, and show it to audiences all over the world. In this chapter, you see the difference between motion-picture film cameras and video camcorders, including advanced digital cinema camcorders (standard and high definition). This chapter also explains how the single eye of the camera sees and how you can harness that distinctive eye to get the best picture possible. I help you choose the correct lenses to capture your shots and use them to their full benefit. Finally, you find out how to add filters and other accessories to your filmmaking toolbox.

The 21st century has brought some amazing technological advances to mankind, including digital filmmaking. All the filmmaking techniques and creative skills described throughout this book can be applied to digital filmmaking. The only difference is in the type of equipment and the technical means of getting a finished product.

Choosing the Right Camera

Before shooting your film, you need to decide whether you want to use a traditional film camera (that uses film *celluloid*), an analog consumer video camcorder (the type you use to record family events), or the advanced technology of digital camcorders (including digital 24p cinema camcorders that closely emulate the look of shooting with a film camera).

Rolling with film cameras

The *film camera* (also referred to as the *motion-picture film camera*) has been around since the late 1800s. Because the film camera runs film stock through its housing, it's a much bigger and heavier piece of equipment than a video camcorder. Film cameras generally rely on manual focus, exposure, and settings.

Film has a nostalgic feel to it, creating the illusion of something that's happened in the past — the feeling of reflecting on a cherished memory. Film photographs a softer, more surreal image than the sharp, sometimes harsh and unflattering picture that video camcorders present.

Film cameras come in various formats that use different film stock sizes, depending on which camera you choose to shoot with:

- ✔ **Super 8:** Film stock that's 8mm in width. This small format is usually used for home movies and documentaries, and it has a flatter image than other film types. It's the least expensive route when shooting with film and costs approximately $10 per minute of film, including developing. Check out Pro8mm (www.pro8mm.com), the leader in professional Super 8 services.

- ✔ **16mm:** Film stock that's 16mm in width. This film allows for more depth in picture quality than does Super 8. It's often used for TV, low-budget features, student films, and documentaries. The cost is approximately $15 per minute of film, including developing.

  My friend Anthony Santa Croce produces the television series *Monk* starring Tony Shalhoub, and they shoot their episodes on Super 16mm. Shooting Super 16mm is an ideal format if the final product is going to television broadcast and DVD rather than to the large theatrical screen. It's also more affordable for productions on limited budgets. Anthony also produced *Tales from the Darkside.* When I directed an episode back in the late '80s, we shot on 16mm on extremely tight budgets.

- ✔ **35mm:** Film stock that's 35mm in width. It's used for TV and feature films. Considered a professional format, 35mm film is the most commonly used film stock by motion-picture studios. The cost is approximately $65 per minute of film, including developing.

You can cut your film costs by buying 16mm or 35mm *recans,* rolls of film that have been put back in the film can by a production company that ended up not using all the film stock it purchased. You can buy recans or film ends (under 400-foot reels) at prices much cheaper than the cost of new film stock. Film Emporium (www.filmemporium.com) is a reliable company that guarantees its short ends and recans. You can get brand new film stock up to 30 percent off retail prices if you're a student with I.D. — through special student programs offered by both Kodak and Fuji Film. Check out their respective Web sites at www.motion.kodak.com and www.fujifilmusa.com.

Staying up to standards with ASA and ISO

You can buy film for your camera in a variety of speeds. *Film speed,* in relation to American Standards Association (ASA) and International Standards Organization (ISO), refers to how quickly the film responds to light. The higher the ASA or ISO rating, the more sensitive the film stock is to light. Some films can actually "see in the dark." An ASA of 800 is more light sensitive and can expose darker images than, say, a film speed of 200 ASA. (When you buy film for your 35mm still camera, you have the same choices of ASAs as well.)

In the past, higher ASA films that worked well in shooting low-light situations often had a grainy picture quality. Kodak has made some amazing developments over the years, producing high-speed films such as Vision3 500T color negative in 16mm and 35mm formats with much less grain and very sharp, crisp picture quality.

In terms of digital camcorders, light sensitivity is determined by the camera's CCD and Lux capability and not by the videotape stock (see Chapter 11 for more information on Lux).

Reading the camera magazine

You can't read a camera magazine because it's not the type of magazine you may be thinking of. Instead, a *camera magazine* is a housing that looks like Mickey Mouse ears on the top of the motion-picture film camera; it holds the raw (undeveloped) film that winds off the reels into the camera and past the exposure gate. The magazine is sealed tight and perfectly light-proof (so the film isn't accidentally exposed and ruined by the light). After the film winds up on the back magazine during shooting, it can be detached easily from the camera and downloaded by the assistant cameraperson (see Chapter 7 for details on crew responsibilities). The exposed film is then sealed in a film can and sent to the lab for developing.

Video tapping

With a film camera, you can record the image on film and onto videotape at the same time, if you have a *video tap,* also known as *video assist.* Nowadays, most film cameras come with a video tap, which enables a video signal to record exactly what the film camera is seeing through the lens. Video assist can save time and money on the set, by letting the director see on a TV monitor the actual camera movement and framing by the cinematographer. If it was recorded to a tape deck or hard drive, you can also play back a shot on the monitor so that you can decide whether it needs be reshot.

One of the advantages of shooting your movie with a camcorder is you automatically have your video assist!

Video assisting Jerry Lewis

Jerry Lewis directed and starred in many of his films, but he had difficulty gauging his performance while doing double-duty as director. He needed to find a way to see what he shot while he was filming it and not be surprised a day later when the footage came back after being developed at the lab.

In 1956, Jerry attached a video camera to the film camera so that he could capture his scenes on video at the same time the film camera was rolling. This is how *video assist* was born. Jerry Lewis created a new technique that virtually every filmmaker shooting with a film camera uses to this day.

Recording with digital camcorders

Video images are captured by a video camera that's connected to a recording deck or by a camcorder that houses both the camera and recorder (hence the name *camcorder*) in one unit and records images in an electronic environment. When using a digital camera, you also have several types of digital formats, which can determine how the final image looks:

- **Digital camcorders:** These cameras are better than analog video camcorders because the digital technology records a sharper picture image that doesn't degrade during copying to other digital tapes. Digital camcorders have exceptional image quality (especially if they record in high definition) and can be used in most professional applications that are appropriate for video recording, such as news footage, documentaries, and entertainment programming. Digital camcorders can record to different types of tape formats including mini-DV, digital betacam, and DVCAM. Certain digital camcorders record in high definition directly to memory cards or an external hard drive. There are a few consumer camcorders that record directly to DVD discs.

- **Digital 24p cinema camcorder:** This is also a digital camcorder, but it can closely emulate the look of a film camera without the expense of film stock, lab and printing costs, or *telecine* (transferring-to-video) costs. By recording the equivalent of 24 frames per second, this type of camera gives the video image more of the soft and pleasing look associated with film. Digital 24p camcorders share many of the same tape and digital formats as non-24-frame digital camcorders, and many can also record in high definition for exceptional image quality.

The "p" in 24p, stands for *progressive*. What it means is that each frame is scanned in a progressive continuous manner, resulting in a better quality image (higher resolution), as opposed to *interlace,* which scans and processes every other frame and then interlaces the missing frames to fill in the gaps. Progressive requires more processing, which in turn requires more memory and demands more storage. The advantage of interlace is less processing and memory, but it compromises picture quality, with the possibility of artifacts, flickering, or strobing.

Digital consumer camcorders start as low as $600 (including high definition models) and average around $3,000 and up for prosumer or professional camcorders. Prices are definitely becoming affordable for the independent filmmaker. (*Prosumer* is a term coined by certain manufacturers to mean a cross between a professional and consumer level product. A prosumer camcorder can be used in a professional capacity — exceeding home-movie standards in terms of picture quality and end use — but is also more affordable, falling within the consumer price range.)

Going over the advantages of video camcorders

Shooting your film with a camcorder has many advantages:

- ✔ **A camcorder is lighter and smaller (and more portable) than a film camera.** A camcorder can be between 1–8 pounds. A film camera (with film magazine & lenses) can weigh 15–40 pounds.

- ✔ **You don't have to reload every ten minutes as you have to with film magazines.** For digital camcorders, each mini-DV tape is one hour, and it's easy to pop in and out, just like with a VCR.

- ✔ **Tape is cheaper than film.** Mini-DV tapes sell for around $3 each.

- ✔ **You can save tape or memory cards and reuse them.** If you don't like the take, record over it, or you can reuse older tapes that you're finished with and want to erase. Memory cards (containing your footage) are usually transferred to a hard drive so the memory card can be used again with the camcorder.

Analog video camcorders use either VHS or Beta tapes, formats that are slowly fading away. Camcorders that record digital files use interchangeable memory cards, and/or can record to external hard drives that connect to the camcorder.

- ✔ **You see the image instantly on the camcorder's LCD built-in screen.** With this capability, you don't need a video assist tap (see the earlier section "Video tapping" for details). You can also plug in an external monitor to your camcorder to view a larger image.

Century Optics makes an LCD Magnifier that works on specific camcorders, enlarging the image and shading it from the sun so you can see the image and be able to better determine if your exposure and focus are correct. Check it out at www.centuryoptics.com. You may want to connect a small television monitor to your camera to get a better idea of what your final picture will look like. Make sure your TV monitor has been set correctly for proper skin tones and other coloration. If you're recording in high definition and want to view your footage on a separate monitor in full high def, you need to connect to an HD monitor. Many HD camcorders include a down converter for viewing your footage on a standard TV monitor (but you won't see the details of the HD quality).

✔ **You can plug in a microphone and use the digital sound from the camera.** If using a digital camcorder, your sound will be professional digital quality!

Make sure the camera has an input for a separate microphone (most do). You rarely want to use the microphone that comes attached to the camera because you'll hear everything in front of and behind the camera (this is called an *omni-directional microphone*). See Chapter 12 for more on microphones.

✔ **You don't have to take the footage into a lab and have it developed.** This saves time, money. and hassle.

✔ **You can import the footage directly into your editing system.** You don't have to transfer it to tape from film — it's already on tape, or in a digital format, and you can start editing!

✔ **You can manipulate it to more closely resemble film shots.** Software programs like Magic Bullet Frames from Red Giant Software (www.redgiantsoftware.com) can make your analog or digital video footage look more like you shot it on film if you aren't using a digital 24p camcorder or if you want to experiment with the color, texture, and mood of your images. There's also a company called Filmlook (www.filmlook.com) that can run your movie through its patented digital process (and also color-correct) to make it look more like it was shot on film. There are digital camcorders that simulate film and 24-frame motion (see the following section). Red Giant Software also makes a product called Instant HD that can emulate the look of high definition from footage you originally shot in standard definition.

Taking a close-up look at digital cinema camcorders (24p)

Panasonic has a 24p (24-frame progressive) camera called the AG-HVX200 (see Figure 10-1). Priced around $4,000, this camcorder can give you a traditional video look equivalent to 30 frames a second or, at the switch of a button, it can emulate 24 frames per second to resemble the texture and look associated with a celluloid film image. The AG-HVX200A, part of Panasonic's P2 series, can use either mini-DV tapes for standard recording or P2 memory cards to record in high definition. Sony, Canon, and JVC also make affordable 24p digital camcorders that are worth investigating.

The Panasonic AG-HVX200A camera uses technology similar to the digital cameras George Lucas used in his *Star Wars* films *The Phantom Menace* and *Attack of the Clones,* in which Lucas proved that the picture quality of digital cinema camcorders can emulate closely the look of film. Robert Rodriguez shot *Spy Kids 2* entirely with digital camcorders and has said that he'll never use film again.

Seeing red with the Red Cam

Hollywood is all abuzz with the advent of the Red Cam. It's not an analog camera, and it's not a high definition camera. It's a 4K (four thousand pixels) camera that's four times sharper in image than HD (the more pixels, the higher the resolution). It was developed to aggressively compete with motion picture film cameras, without having to use film stock. The movie *Jumper* starring Samuel L. Jackson was shot with the Red Cam. The camera starts at $18,000 and will put you back another few thousand on accessories and lenses.

Director Peter Jackson (*King Kong, Lord of the Rings*) shot footage for *Crossing the Line* using the Red Cam. At NAB (National Association of Broadcasters) in Las Vegas 2008, Red Digital Cinema introduced the *Scarlet* camcorder. For under $3,000, it's an affordable professional 3K (three thousand pixels) camera for the independent filmmaker! Check out the Red Cam, the Scarlet, and other new stuff coming from Red Digital Cinema at www.red.com.

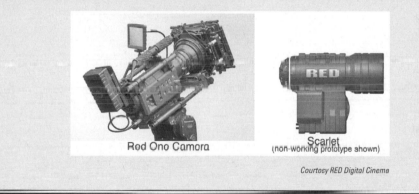

Red One Camera

Scarlet
(non-working prototype shown)

Courtesy RED Digital Cinema

Shooting on video or on digital files with a digital cinema camcorder saves you a lot of money over shooting on film. If you can't afford to buy a digital cinema camera like the AG-DVX100B (standard definition only) for around $2,500 or the AG-HVX200A (standard and high def) for around $4,000, you may want to rent one from a camera rental house or your local TV station. Or better yet, find a cinematographer who owns one of these camcorders.

With the advent of digital technology using 24p to emulate a film-look (without having to use film), more and more productions are being produced on video or digital files. However, all these productions have to be transferred to film for theatrical release, unless they're projected by video projectors, which only a minority of theaters and auditoriums can do (but this is quickly changing). Many productions will never make it to a movie screen, however, and if shot with a camcorder (video or digital files) with the 24p cinema look, they'll be fine for a television screen.

Figure 10-1:
The
Panasonic
AG-HVX200
camcorder.

Courtesy of Panasonic Broadcast

Most standard digital camcorders (including the 24p cinema versions) allow you to emulate a wide-screen image similar to the shape of the widescreen in a movie theater (this is also helpful if you're planning on blowing up your 24p digital video to 35mm film to show in movie theaters). The camcorder puts a black border at the top and bottom of the screen and creates a rectangular shaped frame, rather than the squarish dimensions of a standard TV set (see Figure 10-2). Many films on DVD give you the option to view the film in the widescreen format, also referred to as *letterbox*. Chapter 9 shows you the various screen shapes. If you shoot with a high definition camcorder, the frame dimensions will automatically be in the widescreen format of 16x9.

Figure 10-2:
A standard
camcorder
image with
the wide-
screen
(letterbox)
frame
turned on.

Do You Need Glasses? Types of Lenses and What They Do

Camera lenses are sized in millimeters, which represent the circumference of the lens or the ring size that attaches to the camera housing, in order to control the size of your shots. (Note that camera formats are also referred to in millimeters, as in 35mm, 16mm, and Super 8mm; here, millimeters refer to the width of the film stock the camera uses — are you confused yet?) The assortment of lens sizes needed depends on the camera format being used. For 35mm film cameras, a set of standard lenses for picture area consists of the following: 18mm, 25mm, 35mm, 40mm, 50mm, 75mm, and 100mm (see Figure 10-3 for examples).

Figure 10-3:
A wide, medium, and telephoto lens for an older model 35mm Arri camera.

100mm lens
50mm lens
25mm lens

Each lens serves a purpose and gives a different image size when attached to the camera. A lens can also change the characteristics of the image. For example, a wide lens like the 18mm makes things appear more spacious by slightly bending the image (squeezing more information into the shot). A wide lens is effective for shooting establishing shots to make rooms and areas look roomier than they really are. A telephoto lens tends to flatten and compress images and make things appear closer together. Telephoto lenses are good for bringing distant objects closer to the camera (using magnification).

Lower-priced camcorders come with a fixed lens that is a permanent part of the camera and can't be detached (unless you take a hacksaw and cut it off — but you don't want to do that now, do you?). Professional-model and higher-priced camcorders, like the Canon XL- 2, use *interchangeable lenses,* which allow you to detach the existing lens and screw on different-sized lenses (telephoto, wide-angle, zoom, and so on). In most digital camcorders, the lens functions are similar to a film camera's lenses (if the camera accepts interchangeable lenses), but they are measured differently. The measurement used to determine a consumer digital video camera lens for image size can be eight times less than a film camera lens measurement (depending on the make and model of the camcorder). Therefore, a 4.5mm wide-angle lens on a digital camcorder is equivalent to a 32.5mm lens on a 35mm film camera.

A revolutionary adapter called the Letus35 allows you to add a variety of individual lenses to most consumer camcorders that have a fixed lens. This allows the filmmaker to have more control over depth of field (sharp focus on certain subjects, and blur out backgrounds for example — which is normally limited on a consumer camcorder with a fixed lens). The adapter attaches to the camera's permanent lens, and with this technology the camera's optics work in conjunction with the Letus35 adapter as if it were a professional line camcorder with add-on lens capability. Not only can you then attach additional lenses to your lower-priced consumer camera, but the image will also be softened to have more of the look and feel of film — rather than a harsh video image. Check out the Letus35 at www.Letus35.com. The adapters start at $1,100.

The normal lens

A 50mm lens on a 35mm film camera or 35mm still camera is known as the *normal lens.* It's equivalent to what your eye sees (look through the lens and open your other eye, and you will be seeing about the same size image). This normal lens does not create any distortion and presents an image that most closely resembles what you see without the camera. Many filmmakers prefer this lens when shooting actors. Depending on your subject, a normal 50mm lens can be more complimentary to your actor's features (a wide lens may make your actor look heavier or distorted, a telephoto lens may flatten your actor's features).

For cameras other than 35mm film cameras, the size of the normal (50mm) lens is smaller. Table 10-1 shows the measurement of normal, wide-angle, and telephoto lenses for various types of cameras.

Table 10-1	Normal Lens (50mm) Measurements for Various Camera Formats	
Camera	*Type of Lens*	*Measurement*
35mm	Normal lens	50mm
	Wide-angle lens	18mm
	Telephoto lens	100mm
16mm	Normal lens	25mm
	Wide-angle lens	9mm

Camera	Type of Lens	Measurement
	Telephoto lens	50mm
Super 8mm	Normal lens	15mm
	Wide-angle lens	7.5mm
	Telephoto lens	30mm
Digital consumer video	Normal lens	5.5mm
	Wide-angle lens	3.4mm
	Telephoto lens	20mm

Digital video lenses on consumer camcorders vary in sizes depending on the particular make and type of camcorder, so check the manual that comes with the camera. Most professional digital camcorders, including standard and high definition, use PL (positive lock) mounts and can therefore use a variety of 16mm or 35mm motion picture lenses.

Short or wide-angle lens

A *wide-angle lens,* also called a *short lens,* consists of a curved glass that bends the light coming into the camera and pushes the picture back to create a wider frame than what you see with the naked eye.

When using a 35mm camera, a wide-angle lens is lower in number than the 50mm normal lens. (For other type of cameras, the numbers for a wide-angle lens are much lower — refer to Table 10-1.) Therefore, a 40mm or 25mm lens (on a 35mm film camera) pushes the image farther back to appear as if you're farther away than you really are. The image is reduced so that more of your subject or scenery can fit into the frame. Wide-angle lenses make locations and sets appear more expansive (more picture information is squeezed into the frame). However, wide-angle lenses can create some distortion, so the closer you are to the subject, the more noticeable the distortion is.

A *super wide-angle lens* is sometimes referred to as a *fisheye* lens because it resembles a bulbous fish eye. Often these lenses are 18mm or lower for a 35mm camera. This type of lens (see Figure 10-4) distorts the picture and makes everything look rounder. Usually you only want to use a really wide lens when you want to create an effect like someone looking through a peephole in a door, or for comic effect when you want a character's nose to be bigger and his or her face distorted.

You can add a wide-angle lens to your consumer camcorder by screwing a *converter lens* (with threads) onto your existing camera lens so that you can go even wider than the permanent lens on your camera allows.

Super wide-angle lens

Super wide-angle lens in action

Figure 10-4: A super wide-angle lens (left), and a super wide-angle lens in action (right).

Going long with telephoto

A *telephoto lens* (also called a *long lens*) is higher in number than 50mm for 35mm film cameras. Therefore, a 75mm lens gives you an image that appears to be closer than the normal lens (50mm) does. If you look through the camera with a 75mm lens and open your other eye, you'll see the image closer in the viewfinder than it really is in person.

A telephoto lens is often used for close-up shots, throwing the background out of focus. An out-of-focus background lets the audience concentrate on an actor or object in the frame without being distracted by the surroundings. A telephoto lens is also used to capture close-ups of buildings or objects that are at a fair distance from the camera. A pair of binoculars works similar to a telephoto lens by bringing the subject closer. Explosions, car stunts, and other dangerous situations can be safely captured on film from a distance using a long lens.

Zooming in on zoom lenses

A *zoom lens* does the work of several lenses in one. You can frame a wide-shot, a medium shot (usually framing your subject just above the waist to slightly above his or her head), and also a telephoto close-up shot by using a single zoom lens. Most consumer camcorders come with a zoom lens that's permanently attached to the camera. A zoom lens saves the time of removing and attaching different lenses and of having to make sure no dust gets in the camera while changing lenses.

Clearing the Air about Filters

You've heard the term, "seeing life through rose-colored glasses." Well, in a nutshell, that's what *lens filters* are all about. They're like sunglasses for your camera. But each lens serves a different purpose: You can change colors, set moods, and correct the picture. By placing a filter in front of your camera lens, you can magically change or enhance an image by

- ✔ Removing annoying glare
- ✔ Changing the color of the sky
- ✔ Softening the subject through the lens
- ✔ Adjusting the exposure (darker)
- ✔ Correcting the image color
- ✔ Making colors pop (stand out)

The Tiffen Company (www.tiffen.com), one of the largest and most recognized filter companies, puts out a line of quality filters. Table 10-2 gives you some examples of what Tiffen filters can do. Tiffen also puts out a software program called Dfx that allows you to create virtual filter effects in the post-production phase right in your computer.

Table 10-2	Tiffen Company Filters
Filter	*Effect*
Pro-mist	Softens the image
Polarizer	Reduces or eliminates glare
Star	Causes light sources to sparkle
Neutral Density (ND)	Lowers the exposure, making the picture darker
85 and 80	Color-corrects the image
Sunrise (half)	Adds warm sunrise degradation to the sky (the bottom part of the filter is clear, and a warm color — orange or yellow — gradually gets deeper toward the top of the filter)
Blue Sky (half)	Adds richer blue to the sky (the bottom half of the filter is clear, and the upper half gradually becomes a deep sky blue)
Full Orange	Warms the entire image
Full Blue	Cools the entire image (also emulates nighttime)

Lee Filters (www.leefilters.com) is a company that offers similar filters, as does Schneider Optics (www.schneideroptics.com). Samy's Camera (www.samys.com) also carries a wide variety of filters and camera accessories.

Sliding-in or screwing-on: Types of filters

Filters come in two format types and can be used on both film cameras and video camcorders: Slide-in and screw-on. Each has it advantages, as explained in the following sections.

Whenever you put a filter or additional lens over your camera lens, you need to adjust the exposure because the camera is now working through more levels of lenses to give you a good picture (see the "Exposing Yourself to Exposures" section later in this chapter).

Screw-on filters

You screw a screw-on filter directly onto the camera lens (you need to match the lens circumference millimeter size to fit your specific camera). Screw-on lenses don't require a bulky matte box, as do slide-in filters, which keeps the camera portable and lightweight.

Slide-in filters

Slide-in filters require a *matte box,* a device that you mount in front of your camera lens. The filters, which are approximately ¹/₄-inch thick and 4x4 inches in size, conveniently slide in and out of the matte box. A matte box can also be used for inserting effects masks, which suggest looking through keyholes, binoculars, or a telescope view. The Tiffen Company, in addition to making screw-on filters, also makes slide-in filters, which can be used with its FilterFlex matte box (see Figure 10-5).

The advantage of a slide-in filter is that it works with any camera (and lens), because it doesn't depend on having to screw a fitted sized lens directly onto the camera. Instead a standard 4x4-inch filter slides into the matte box. Also, using multiple filters in a matte box is easier.

Slide-in filters for the matte box are quicker and more convenient than screw-on filters — you just drop the filter in the slot. Slide-in filters can also be turned sideways, something you can't do with screw-on filters. Both types, however, allow you to use multiple filters at the same time if you want to use a combination of filter effects like a warm color filter, plus a filter that softens the picture image.

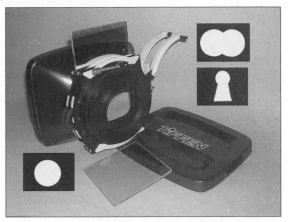

Figure 10-5:
A matte box with slide-in filters, and an example of visual effects masks to suggest looking through binoculars, a keyhole, or a telescope.

Courtesy of Tiffen

Coloring with filters

The main purpose of color filters is to correct the film or video image so that the colors resemble what the human eye sees, whether you're shooting indoors or outdoors. Without proper color balance, your picture will have a slight off-colored tint to it.

On a film camera, the color filters you use depend on the film stock you're using and the color temperature of your lighting source (see Chapter 11 for details on color temperature). For example, a number *85 filter* color balances *tungsten* (film stock designed to be used indoors) for outdoor filming so that your scenes don't have a blue hue to them. A number *80 filter* color-corrects daylight film being used indoors so you don't have a yellow, red, or orange tint to your picture. Chapter 11 also discusses color corrections and effects using *gels,* which you can place in front of your film lights. In addition, your film footage is color-corrected or adjusted by the timer in the lab or while transferring your film footage to video via telecine (see Chapter 15).

If you're using a digital camcorder, you can manually set the color balance by pointing the camera at a white card or object to establish a point of reference for your camera. Or you can use the automatic white balance that sets the correct color balance for you (but the exposure can fluctuate if you move the camera within different lighting conditions). After establishing what the color "white" should look like, your camcorder then recognizes the correct colors of other objects.

One of the advantages that digital has over film is that you immediately see on your LCD or TV monitor the results of the color correction. You don't have to wait for the film to come back from the lab to see whether you got it right. In the post production stage, you can do additional color-correction tweaking right on your computer. Most editing software like Final Cut comes with color-correcting software.

Get a color chart from Kodak (it resembles a colored checkerboard) or the *Macbeth* color chart (you can purchase this chart at Samy's Camera, www.samys.com, for under $60). You can photograph the chart at the beginning of each film roll or digital recording to use as a color reference when color-correcting in postproduction.

Day for night and night for day

Sometimes you can't conveniently shoot a night scene at night or a day scene during the day. By putting on a blue filter during an overcast day (and avoiding showing the sky in the scene), you can fool your audience into believing that the blue cast is night.

To create the look of daytime after the sun has gone down, you use large lights called *HMIs,* which simulate sunlight and also use a warm-colored filter to enhance the effect. By keeping your shots fairly close on your subjects and avoiding the horizon in the frame (such as keeping the actor against a building), your audience will think the scenes were shot during daylight hours.

Neutral about Neutral density filters

A *neutral density filter,* also known as an ND filter, is used to reduce the amount of light coming into the camera lens — much like a pair of sunglasses cuts down on the amount of light hitting your eyes. In bright-light situations, an ND filter helps to avoid an overexposed picture. These filters come in various gradations, each one darker than the next. You screw on, or slide in (if using a matte box), a neutral density filter in front of the film camera lens. If you're shooting with a digital camcorder, you can turn on the neutral density filter electronically by flipping a switch.

Polarizers

Certain surfaces, like a metallic robot, a shiny car, or sparkling windows, can cause distracting reflections. *Polarizers* usually take care of this problem. If you're filming someone through a car windshield, for example, you often get a glare, making the driver difficult to see in the car (see Figure 10-6). A polarizing filter can be adjusted until the glare is minimal or completely eliminated.

Figure 10-6: Without polarizer (left) and with polarizer (right).

Exposing Yourself to Exposures

Exposures control the amount of light entering the *iris* (also called the *aperture*) of the camera lens, which reacts to the light and opens and closes to allow more or less light into the camera. The human eye iris works similarly, but the response is automatic. The film camera's eye needs human assistance to adjust the settings for focus, exposures, and so on. Most digital camcorders have advanced circuitry and do a lot of this for you (when set on automatic).

When you look outside on a bright day, the iris of your eye shrinks to a smaller circle because the eye has plenty of light to see. The iris of the camera works the same way; concentrated light is directed through the tiny aperture of the camera causing objects to appear in sharp focus (this is also why people who don't have 20/20 vision see better during daylight hours than at night). Have you ever noticed that when you turn off the lights in a room, your eyes take a moment to adjust? That's because your brain is telling your iris that it needs to open wider to compensate for the lack of light. The iris of the camera works the same way and has to be opened up wider to allow for more light to enter the lens to be able to expose an image with enough light.

F-stopping to a "t"

The various sizes of the iris as it opens and closes to light are measured in f-stops. You can manually set these settings to get a proper exposure (allowing enough light to enter the lens to record a proper image — not too dark, not too light). Or you can use the automatic setting on your camera. The disadvantage to using the automatic setting is that the lighting will fluctuate as you move the camera within different lighting conditions. (If you take a film lens and adjust the f-stops while looking into the lens, you can actually see the iris adjusting in size, similar to the iris of your eye as it adjusts to light.)

Figure 10-7 illustrates the *aperture* opening of different exposures. The higher the number, the smaller the opening of the iris. F-stops are also measured in t-stops, which are more accurate. Most film cameras are marked with both f- and t-stops on the side of the lens.

Figure 10-7:
A series of
aperture
settings at
different
exposures.

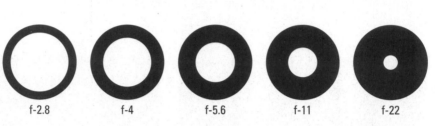

f-2.8   f-4   f-5.6   f-11   f-22

Shuttering to think

Shutter speed affects how the motion of an image is captured on film celluloid or recorded on videotape or digital files. High shutter speeds are appropriate for shooting fast-moving subjects, such as a car chase or a competitive sporting event. By setting your camera for a higher shutter speed, you avoid having your subject blur or smear in the frame. For example, if you pause the footage on your DVD player, the subject looks like a clear still photograph, rather than a blurred image moving across the frame. Slower shutter speeds are best for low-light situations where the image needs adequate light to get a properly exposed picture.

On a film camera, the standard shutter speed at 24 frames per second is $^1/_{50}$ of a second. You can adjust the film camera shutter up to $^1/_{1,700}$ of a second. On a camcorder, the standard shutter is $^1/_{60}$ of a second (equivalent to a video camera shooting 30 frames per second), and on some cameras, like the Canon GL-2, the shutter speed can be adjusted as fast as $^1/_{15,000}$ of a second.

Focusing a Sharper Image: Depth of Field

Depth of field deals with the depth of focus in your shot. In other words, what distance in front of and behind your subject are in acceptable focus? Knowing how depth of field works helps you to compose more interesting shots. The left shot in Figure 10-8 was taken with a 50mm lens set at 8 feet (with a small aperture setting of f-16) resulting in the actress and background both being in focus. The right shot was taken with a 100mm lens (with an f-stop of f-4) with the actor 25 feet from the camera. Notice that the actor is in focus, but the background is out of focus.

Figure 10-8:
With a medium (50mm) lens, everything is in focus (left). With a telephoto (100mm long lens), the background is out of focus (right).

©2000 Astrolite Ent./Stellar Ent. Meadow Williams & Christopher Knight in Light Years Away

Make sure the eyepiece on your camera is focused to your eye. Otherwise, you can't tell if your subject is in proper focus.

The type of lens, shutter speed, and f-stop all affect the area in the frame that will be in focus. Table 10-3 shows the range of focus (what will be in focus at different exposure f-stop settings) within the frame, using a 50mm lens (normal lens) on a 35mm film.

Table 10-3	The Distance Range in Focus at Different F-Stops			
Lens Setting	*f-4*	*f-5.6*	*f-11*	*f-22*
15 ft.	11 ft. to 23 ft. 8 in.	9 ft. 11 in. to 30 ft. 9 in.	7 ft. 6 in. to 20 ft. 8 in.	5 ft. to infinity
8 ft.	6 ft. 8in. to 9 ft. 11 in.	6 ft. 4 in. to 11 ft.	5 ft. 3 in. to 16 ft. 11in.	3 ft. 11in. to infinity
5 ft.	4 ft. 6 in. to 5 ft. 8 in.	4 ft. 3 in. to 6 ft.	3 ft. 9 in. to 7 ft. 5 in.	3 ft. to 14 ft. 1 in.
2 ft.	1 ft. 11 in. to 2 ft. 1 in.	1 ft. 11 in. to 2 ft. 2 in.	1 ft. 9 in. to 2 ft. 3 in.	1 ft. 7 in. to 2 ft. 8 in.

The higher the f-stop, the larger the area that the camera sees in sharp focus. You can find cinematography books at your library or local bookstore that contain every conceivable depth-of-field chart for film and video cameras and the various lens and exposure settings. *The American Cinematographer Manual,* edited by Stephen H. Burum (published by A.S.C. Holding Corporation), makes a great reference book as well.

Most camcorders give you the option to focus manually, and this is your best bet. Zoom in as close as you can to the object you want to concentrate on, focus as clearly and precisely as you can, then zoom out and frame your image. Now you know your subject is in focus, regardless of objects or things moving behind or in front.

You have to be careful if you use the automatic focus because certain situations can fool it:

- **Shooting through a cage or a fence:** The camera doesn't know whether to focus on the bars or the object behind it.

- **Images that aren't centered in the frame:** The camera may try to focus on an image that's in the foreground or background but not the main subject.

- **Fast-moving objects:** These can trick your auto focus into trying to follow-focus the image.

Chapter 11

Let There Be Lighting!

*L*ittle did Thomas Edison know that the simple light bulb he invented in 1879 would take on so many shapes and color temperatures and be instrumental in controlling the look of every image captured on film or video. Without the proper lighting and exposure, your actors will be sitting (or standing) in the dark.

Lighting, the focus of this chapter, is the technique of creating a mood. Here, you develop a feel for composition, color temperatures, and the distribution of light and dark. You also get a short primer on lighting safety.

Lighting Up Your Life

Lighting brings life to your shots. Light lets your audience "see" where your actors are and where they're going. Instead of just flipping on a light switch in a room with one overhead light, you have the power to control the lighting in your shots by positioning a myriad of lights (on stands) virtually anywhere to illuminate your scene. Lighting can bring aesthetic beauty to your shots, or true ugliness, depending on the final results you're looking to achieve. When lit correctly, your lighting will pull your actors away from the walls and furniture. Creative lighting can reach behind your actors and separate them from the background. You can create depth and perspective with proper lighting and control the mood of the scene by coloring your lights.

Don't be afraid to experiment with light. Pick up your lights on their stands and move them around your subjects. Watch what light does to your actors as you lower, raise, and tilt your movie lights at different angles toward your subjects. See how you can create a mood with shadows and make your actors look more pleasing by bouncing light off the ceiling or using other lighting tricks and tools, like scrims and glass diffusion, discussed later in this chapter.

Shedding Some Light on Lighting Jargon

Before delving deeply into this chapter, take a minute to review two important lighting terms.

Big Foot-candles: Lighting for film cameras

Motion-picture film cameras measure the illumination of light falling on a subject in *foot-candles.* One foot-candle is the amount of illumination produced by a single candle at a distance of 1 foot away from the subject. For example, if your light meter (see the "Measuring with light meters" section later in this chapter) reads 200 foot-candles, that means that your light source is equivalent to the illumination of 200 candles falling on your subject from 1 foot away. The exposure is also determined by the speed of the film, which in turn controls your exposure (see Chapter 10 for information on stops and exposures).

Lux (and cream cheese): Lighting for digital (SD and HD)

A *lux* is the European equivalent of a foot-candle, but instead of being the equivalent of a single candle at a distance of 1 foot, one lux is the illumination of 1 square meter (European measurement) per single candle. Digital (standard definition and high definition) cameras measure light in lux.

Standard digital camcorders are much more sensitive to light than motion-picture film cameras are, so you can more easily shoot in low-light situations (though high def cameras require more light than standard def). Lux allows the camera to dig into the darkness and gives you an acceptable image that's not grainy or muddy in appearance. This is similar to the newer fast-speed films, with less grain, which have been developed for motion-picture cameras (see Chapter 10). *Fast-speed film* refers to the film stock's ability to respond to light, not to how fast the film moves in the camera.

Digital cameras contain chips — not potato chips, but digital chips — known as *CCDs.* CCD stands for *charge-coupled device* and is a circuit that stores data and converts what the camera records into an electrical image. CCDs are also light sensitive, allowing the camera to "see" into dimmer environments and produce acceptable images. A one-chip camera lends itself to home movies and non-broadcast projects, while a three-chip camera is suitable for professional broadcast with colors and a digital image that is cleaner and sharper than one-chip cameras. Three-chip cameras are more expensive, so if you decide you want one, you have to dip deeper into your wallet (chip and dip).

A standard lux rating averages around three lux and is affected by the CCD and the lens speed. CCDs are light sensitive and determine the lux in a digital camera. A 60-watt light bulb is equivalent to 10 lux, so a 3-lux camera is extremely sensitive to light when recording.

Taking your color temperature

Different types of light radiate different color intensities, called *color temperatures,* which affect how the camera records the light. The color temperature of the lighting affects the final colors in your film. Color temperature is determined by the intensity of light that radiates from your movie lights; don't confuse it with thermal temperature that measures hot and cold.

When you're imagining how color temperature works, think of a blacksmith heating up and shaping a horseshoe in a forge. As the black mass heats up, it turns different colors. This is how color temperature works.

Our eyes adjust to the colors of light, something the camera can't do without some assistance. That's why gels, white balance, and filters (see Chapter 10) are used to get the film or video camera to see what the human eye sees. The camera has a mechanical eye (with film cameras) or an electronic eye (with digital cameras) that has to be programmed so that lighting will look natural to what the human eye sees. Many camcorders do emulate the human eye when you set them on automatic.

Every color has a temperature that's measured in *Kelvins* (named after Lord Kelvin, who discovered the system). Kelvin is a rate of measurement in degrees, similar to Fahrenheit and Celsius, and it's usually shortened to °K. Warmer colors like red and amber have lower Kelvin ratings. For example, sunlight is yellow, orange, and red — a lower Kelvin rating than the blue Kelvin rating of the moonlight. Film is a sensitive material that lets light burn its color into it. The higher the temperature in °K, the cooler the color. In other words, the hotter the temperature, the bluer the hue; the lower the temperature, the warmer the hue (reds, oranges, yellows). Table 11-1 shows standard Kelvin ratings.

Table 11-1	Kelvin Ratings of Light
Light Source	*Average Color Temperature (in °K)*
Candle	1,600
Sunrise/sunset	2,000
3,200 Tungsten (incandescent) lights	3,200
Early-morning/late-afternoon sunlight	4,200
Midday sunlight (hottest)	6,000
Light shade/overcast	7,200
Full shade/hazy day	8,000
Dusk	9,500
Early evening	13,000

The average indoor color temperature of your lights is 3,200°K, and the average lighting provided by the sun during daylight hours is about 6,000°K.

Illuminating with soft light versus hard light

Soft light is any light source bounced off a reflective surface and then onto your actors, thus creating a softer effect. You can create soft light in a number of ways:

- By simply bouncing light off a ceiling or a white card or by using a portable lighting device that has the bulb facing into a reflective housing that bounces the light back out.

- By placing a translucent cloth-like material in front of the bulb to filter any hard direct light from falling on your subject — this is called *diffusion*. A lampshade is a perfect example of this type of soft light; rarely does a room have exposed light bulbs (naked bulbs should not be seen in public!). The company Rosco, www.rosco.com, makes a line of light control filters called Cinegels, which includes cloth diffusers. Photoflex (www.photoflex.com) makes a soft-light fixture (called a soft box) that houses a 1,000-watt bulb in a soft covering to diffuse and soften the illumination of the subject (see Figure 11-1).

Figure 11-1:
WhiteDome
light by
Photoflex.

Hard light creates a harsh, bright look on your subject and should be avoided — it's not flattering to most subjects. An example of hard light is the intense rays of the sun. Most professional cinematographers prefer filming outside on cloudy days (rather than sunny days), because the clouds diffuse the sunlight and add softness to everything. On larger productions, the lighting crew actually stretches a large white translucent tarp on a metal frame over the scene to diffuse the harsh rays of the sun falling on the actors. On close-up shots, you can easily hold a translucent cloth in the path of the sun above the actor to diffuse the harsh sunlight and create a soft light on your actor's face.

Seeing your iLite

The sparkle in an actor's eye can make or break a close-up. A small light, called an *eye light*, often attached to the camera can help bring life to an actor's eyes by brightening them up and adding a little glint. Litepanels makes a mini-light called the Litepanels Micro (see Figure 11-2). It's a small, extremely lightweight light about the size of a deck of cards. It fits on most camcorders and helps naturally brighten any subject in a close-up and helps to fill in shadows on the face. The heat-free litepanels Micro uses LED bulbs and runs on regular AA batteries (that last up to eight hours). It retails for under $350, and you can get it at www.litepanels.com.

A little trick that I've discovered is using my iPhone to reflect an eye light or fill light onto my close-up subject. It's pocket portable, doesn't need to be plugged in, and if I open a blank screen and turn the brightness up, it's surprising how much illumination it throws on my subject!

Figure 11-2:
Litepanels
Micro.

Painting with Light

Lighting your film is similar to painting a picture with brush strokes onto a blank canvas. An artist brushes on light to create a mood and cast light on the subject or objects in the painting in much the same way you set up and position your movie lights. You throw light onto your set and subjects. In order to create a three-dimensional look to your shots, you need to understand the basic lighting setup, shown in Figure 11-3, that helps separate your subjects from the background that could otherwise cause a flat-looking image:

- **Key light:** The main light (and often the brighter source than your other lights) that you set up first and then supplement with two or more other types of lights.

- **Back light:** Also used as a *hairlight,* the back light is directed at the back of your actors to pull them out of the background. It can also create a soft halo around your subjects.

- **Fill light:** You use the fill light to fill in or supplement the other lights for a more natural look. This light also helps soften shadows.

- **Background light:** As its name implies, the background light lights your background to separate it from your actors and to create more depth in the shot.

Figure 11-3:
A basic
lighting
setup using
a key light,
a fill light, a
backlight,
and a back-
ground light.

Spotlight on Lighting Equipment

You can light a scene in many ways. Turn on a corner lamp. See the light find your subject. Now turn on an overhead light. Each lighting source enhances and sets a mood for your shot. A candlelit dinner wouldn't be half as romantic if the room were bathed in bright light. A haunted house wouldn't be nearly as scary if it were as bright as day inside.

Lowel, a popular lighting company, makes some great portable kits like the DV Creator 55 kit that includes accessories like reflectors, gels, and barn doors with its lights (all of these are discussed in this section). You can view the company's catalog at www.lowel.com. Samy's Cameras (www.samys.com) also carries a wide variety of lighting equipment.

Shining light on halogens, incandescents, fluorescents, and HMIs

Most movie lights use *halogen* bulbs (also called *halogen quartz*), which are usually at a color balance of 3,200°K (see the section "Taking your color temperature" earlier in this chapter). Inside each bulb is a *tungsten coil* that heats up the halogen gas in the bulb to create a steady, consistent light, giving an even color temperature — thus, ensuring a consistent color balance for the scene.

An *incandescent (tungsten)* light is a light source that you probably use every day in the form of your household light bulb. An incandescent also contains a tungsten wire filament that heats up, but unlike the halogen lamp, the bulb doesn't contain halogen gas and so isn't as energy-efficient as halogen bulbs. Household incandescent lamps have color temperatures of around 3,000°K, depending on the wattage. Halogen bulbs last two to three times longer than a regular incandescent light bulb and burn at higher temperatures.

Don't ever touch a halogen bulb with your bare hands — even if the bulb is cool. The oil on your fingers creates a spot on the surface of the bulb that eventually weakens the glass and causes the light to explode. Also, halogen bulbs can be extremely hot and can burn you!

Fluorescent lights, often called CFL (Compact Fluorescent Light), are energy-efficient bulbs that last up to ten times longer than incandescent bulbs and give out less heat. The color temperature of fluorescent bulbs are close to incandescent/tungsten Kelvin ratings.

An *HMI* (short for *halogen metal iodide*) is a powerful, expensive, bulky light used to emulate sunlight (it has the same color temperature as sunlight). Use it to supplement real sunlight when the sun is setting or on overcast days. You can also shine an HMI through the windows on your indoor set to create the appearance of bright sunshine beaming in, or you can place it outside a window at night to simulate daylight outside. You can also use an HMI to fill in shadows on an actor's face caused by the sun.

When you're working on smaller interior sets, like an office or bedroom, a portable lighting kit usually suffices. A *lighting kit* typically consists of three to four small halogen lights with collapsible stands that you can adjust to whatever height you need. I have several great lighting kits that I ordered off the Internet from Lowel Lighting (www.lowel.com) and PhotoFlex (www.photoflex.com). Lighting kits, like the one shown in Figure 11-4, usually come neatly encased in a sturdy case or canvas bag that you can carry conveniently.

Pick up a couple of halogen lamps for under $40 from your local hardware store; they're cheaper than renting professional studio lights or a complete lighting kit. Often called *work-lamps*, they come with sturdy stands, and the lights are bright enough to light a small outdoor parking lot.

Figure 11-4:
A Lowel DV Creator 55 portable lighting kit that includes a reflective umbrella and a convenient tough carrying case.

Image courtesy of Lowel-Light Mfg, Inc.

Filming the light of day

If you're shooting with a motion-picture film camera, you need to make sure the color temperature of the film stock matches the color temperature of the light you're filming under. *Daylight* film is color balanced for the Kelvin temperatures radiated by the sun.

Indoor film is balanced for tungsten lights. Tungsten halogen lights are usually rated at 3,200°Kelvin and are consistent in the color temperature they radiate. Household incandescent lamps have a color temperature of around 3,000°K, depending on the wattage.

If you're using indoor film and you have sunlight coming through the windows, you need to use an 85 (amber-colored) filter (see Chapter 10) to color-correct the daylight. If you're using outdoor film indoors, you use an 80 (blue-colored) filter to color-correct your halogen indoor lights for the outdoor (daylight) film stock.

You're on a roll with gels

Instead of, or in addition to, using filters over the camera lens (see Chapter 10), you can change the color on the set by placing rolls of colored *gels* over the lights (or in the case of sunlight, over windows). You can mix and match different colored gels with different lights and pinpoint certain colors on certain objects or people in the scene. For example:

- A blue gel on a light creates a blue hue to simulate a moonlit night.
- A warm yellow/orange gel can add to the warmth of a romantic scene in front of the fireplace.

Gels are often used to color-correct light sources in order to balance the film stock. An 85 amber gel converts incoming sunlight to indoor color balance to give you correct coloring with your tungsten lamps for your indoor scene.

Gels create artistic hues on set, diffusing and controlling the lighting environment designed by the cinematographer and the gaffer. The company Rosco puts out a free color-swatch booklet that has close to 300 gels, called Cinegels, with diffusion samples in a little flip book — visit Rosco's Web site at www.rosco.com to request the free swatch book.

Gels come in rolls for a reason: You may need to use a lot of them. For example, if you're filming indoors and have a big, bright window in the shot, you're going to get a blast of overexposed light if you don't do something. You can put a gel over the window to color correct and also cut down the light.

Reflecting on reflector boards

You can't control the sun when you're filming outside, other than knowing what position it will be at any given time of day. But you can control the direction of the sun with a little portable shiny device called a *reflector*. If your subject can't face the sun, you use a reflector board to catch the sun's rays and bounce the light back onto your subject (see Figure 11-5).

Photoflex makes a portable pop-open reflector disc called the MultiDisc that collapses to the size of a steering wheel and comes in three sizes: 22-inch, 32-inch, and 42-inch. It also includes additional white, soft gold, silver, and translucent reflective surfaces. You can also diffuse the sun's harshness by placing the translucent MultiDisc between the sun's rays and your subject. Check out the MultiDisc at www.photoflex.com (click on "Products" and then "Reflectors").

Figure 11-5: An otherwise dark subject receives a boost of reflected illumination from the sun with the help of a reflector.

You don't need to run out and buy a professional reflector board if it's not in your budget. Instead, you can use a white foam card or flexible piece of shiny aluminum. Mother Nature herself makes a great reflector in the wintertime — it's called snow. (Even Mother Nature is into snowbusiness.) The white snow helps to reflect sunlight off the ground and upward to get rid of shadows under an actor's eyes, nose, and chin.

If the sun is behind your actor and you don't use a reflector board, you'll most often end up with a silhouette of your actor (referred to as *backlit*) because the light of the sun behind the actor is brighter than the light in front of your actor. The camera exposes for the brighter image and leaves your subject in the dark. Silhouette shots can be effective for scenes such as an actor on a camel crossing the hilltops against the sun.

Do you have a decent broad?

A *broad* is a light that has an open-faced reflector housing and can illuminate a wide area. The light from a broad has little control, unless you use barn doors, or flags, to help direct the light, because the lamp doesn't have an adjustment to focus the intensity of its beam.

Opening barn doors: No cows or chickens here

You may need to control the spread of light falling on your subject from a lamp with *barn doors*. Barn doors resemble miniature black flags and shade the light as it beams out of its housing. A typical barn door has between two and four metal, hinged doors that open up like — you guessed it! — barn doors.

Cooking with cookies, scrims, and diffused glass

When using movie lights, sometimes the light is too bright and you want to control the intensity. There are many ways to do that: using cookies, scrims, and diffused glass placed over the lights to soften or create a lighting effect:

- **Cookies:** These *cookies* aren't edible, but they are kind of like a cookie cutter. Cookies break up light or simulate the shadow of tree branches, window blinds, and so on. They come in a variety of shapes, and you can easily make your own.

  For an inexpensive cookie, take a small branch off a tree (the one the gardener was going to trim anyway) and clamp it to a stand, putting it in the path of your light. The branch casts an abstract shadow, simulating a tree outside a window.

- **Scrims:** *Scrims* resemble the screen in a screen door or window. They cut down on the intensity from hot set lights and are placed in a holder or on a stand in front of the lamp.

  For an inexpensive scrim, go to your local hardware store and buy some black mesh used for patio screen doors or windows. Cut it to fit in front of your lights, and clamp it in place with a black binding clamp from an office-supply store.

✔ **Diffused glass:** *Diffused glass* diffuses the light source when you place it in front of your light. Diffused glass may be frosted, bubbled, or textured like a glass shower door. This texturing creates a softer light on your subjects that makes them look better than under a harsh light with no diffusion.

Waving flags and snoots

If the first thing you think of when you hear the word *snoot* is an elephant or an anteater, you're not far off. A *snoot* directs light through its trunk-shaped funnel and produces a concentrated beam of light similar to a spotlight. It is used a lot in shooting miniatures, because the light can be pinpointed on small areas.

A *flag*, on the other hand, probably makes you think of the country's flag flapping in the wind with the sun shining brightly behind it. In filmmaking, however, the sun can be flagged by a flag. A flag is a (usually) black, opaque piece of material that you stretch over a wire frame to block light from a movie light or the sun that's glaring into the camera lens. A flag works just like your hand does when you use it to keep the sun's glare out of your eyes or like your car visor does when you flip it down while you're driving.

Measuring with light meters

To accurately record an image on film, you need to use a light meter. A *light meter* resembles a battery tester, only you dial the film stock you're using into the meter and then take a light-meter reading of the lighting on your set. The meter tells you the correct exposure to set your camera at.

Light meters read the intensity of the light on the subject in foot-candles, letting the cinematographer know what his *f-stop* or *t-stop* setting should be (more on *f-* and *t-stops* in Chapter 10).

Some light meters give you both *reflective* and *incidental* readings (see Figure 11-6):

✔ **Incidental light meter:** An *incidental light meter* reads direct light shining into the meter from the actual light source. These meters are quite accurate and aren't fooled by large areas of light and dark in the same shot.

✔ **Reflective light meter:** A *reflective light meter* measures the reflected light off the subject and back into the meter. A *spot meter* is a reflective meter that reads the light in a particular spot so that you know how light falls in different places over your subject and can choose an average reading — even if you have large light and dark areas that normally confuse a meter. A digital camera works similarly to a spot meter. It allows you to zoom in on a particular spot and get an accurate reading without having to use a separate light meter.

When you're using a digital camera, take a light reading and then set your exposure manually. This way, if the camera follows a subject or a brighter or darker object enters the frame, the camera doesn't try to automatically adjust the exposure and cause the picture to flutter between light and dark.

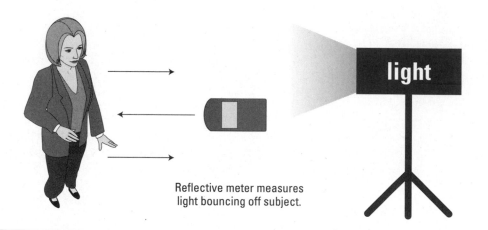

Reflective meter measures
light bouncing off subject.

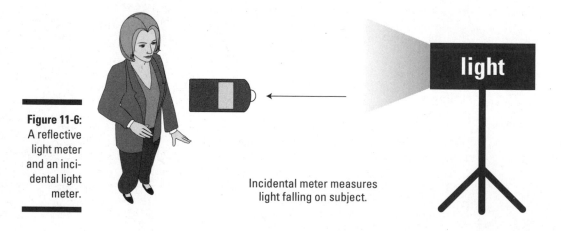

Figure 11-6:
A reflective
light meter
and an inci-
dental light
meter.

Incidental meter measures
light falling on subject.

Gathering light on accessories

In addition to all the complex, technical lighting tools detailed in the preceding sections, you also need to think about a few low-cost, simple accessories that are a necessity on the set.

An *expendable* refers to an element that can be used up and replaced. Light bulbs (halogen, fluorescent, incandescent) eventually burn out, break, or just plain don't work. They are expendable and have to be replaced. Tape, glue, batteries, and even gels (which eventually fade, melt, or wear out) fall into the expendable category, as well.

- ✔ **Clamps and clothespins:** You use clamps and clothespins to hold diffusion cloths or scrims over your lights, as well as to clamp things to your C-stands. Clothespins can be helpful to clip light things together, attach or hang props, and so on. Your local hardware store has a variety of grips and clamps in all shapes and sizes.

- ✔ **C-stands and lighting stands:** *C-stands* can be lifesavers. You can adjust these stands to varying heights, as well as adjust the extended folding arm post into many positions for holding flags, cookies, *scenic backdrops* (see Chapter 17), or props. *Light stands* are adjustable in height and usually have three extended legs that spread out to help balance the weight of the light securely so it doesn't topple over.

- ✔ **Sandbags:** *Sandbags* may not seem important — after all, they just lie there like a lump and don't look very impressive. But when you have unbalanced light stands and other pieces of equipment tipping over, you may wonder how you ever survived without them. A sandbag is simply a filmmaker's paperweight. A standard sandbag weighs about 15 pounds and resembles a saddlebag.

  You can rent sandbags, buy them for about a dollar a pound, or make your own. To make your own, fill empty plastic sandbags (you can find these at most hardware stores for under $1 each) with play sand (you can buy 50 pounds for around $4).

- ✔ **Gaffer's tapes:** Your *gaffer* works closely with you or your cinematographer to perfect the lighting of your scenes (see Chapter 7 for details on the gaffer's job). Included in the gaffer's arsenal of tapes are masking tape, Scotch tape, double-sided tape, and spray-on glue.

Blowing a Fuse: Taking Safety Precautions

Gaffers and electricians (see Chapter 7) are trained to not overload the electrical circuits. Lights use a lot of voltage and need to be distributed properly. You don't want the fire department showing up after you've blown the fuse for your entire neighborhood.

Plug in your lights using several different circuits. Don't plug them in using the wall plugs in the same room. Be creative in your distribution. Get a lot of extension cords and plug into different rooms, so you don't overload one individual circuit. You may have to have your electrician do a *tie-in*. This means that he plugs the lights directly into the fuse box and surpasses the electrical outlets at your location.

You're not always going to be near an electrical outlet, and if you're shooting outdoors as night is falling, you may need to supplement your lighting. Even if you're shooting a night scene, you still need lights to get a properly exposed image. Some indoor locations may not let you use the electricity, or you may be filming in an older house or building that can't take the voltage required by your lights. These are times when you need a portable generator. Generators run on gasoline. Don't forget to have a can of gas ready to refill the generator. You don't want to use the old excuse, "We ran out of gas."

Chapter 12

Sound Advice: Production Sound

You've heard the expression "A picture is worth a thousand words." But with the right sound accompanying the picture, it can be worth 10,000 words! The right music or soundtrack can enhance even the dullest images. Sound and picture should complement each other. It's kind of like a relationship: You may be all right on your own, but together you're a dynamite team. Radio dramas were exciting to listen to, and silent pictures entertained audiences, but it wasn't until radio and silent pictures were married that things really started to sizzle. And the honeymoon is still going strong.

Getting a clear professional dialogue track on your film requires the expertise of someone skilled in the art of sound recording. A *production sound mixer* will have the knowledge of what microphones to use and how to control the audio levels to give you the cleanest audio tracks. If you don't have the budget to hire a professional sound mixer, you can train yourself, or hire someone interested in taking on the task of recording your audio — but you have to read this chapter first!

Testing, Testing, 1, 2, 3

Without sound you're just shooting a silent movie, and silent movies are a thing of the past. The sound elements for your film are made up of a series of sounds:

✔ Actors' dialogue

✔ Environmental atmosphere (ambience)

✔ On-camera sound effects

These elements have to be recorded properly to create a pristine soundtrack for your film. If you're making your film with a camcorder, then you can record the sound onto the same tape or digital file that records your images, keeping picture and sound as one. If you're shooting with a motion picture film camera, then you'll have a separate sound system recording your audio, which will be married to your film in the postproduction phase.

Assembling a Sound Team

Just as it's important to have someone who knows how to operate the camera and give you great-looking images (see Chapter 7), it's also important to have someone skilled at recording production sound so that the audience "hears" your film. You can record the sound yourself or hire someone eager to do sound for you, but if you can hire someone experienced in this field you'll have fewer headaches in the end (getting clear crisp sound for the final product). The other advantage to hiring a skilled sound mixer is that he or she may own a recorder and microphones, saving you the time and trouble of renting or buying them elsewhere.

Mixing it up with your mixer

No, a mixer is not your personal bartender on the set. A mixer mixes the sound elements on set, which consist of dialogue between actors and accompanying production sounds, like footsteps or doors closing, that help guide the addition of enhanced sound effects in postproduction.

A *sound mixer* uses a mixing board to control and adjust volume levels and the quality of the sound — not too low, not too high, no interference, and so on. When shooting on film, the mixing board is connected to the sound recorder; when shooting digital (standard or high definition), it's connected to your camcorder. Sound mixers train their ears to pick up any distracting noise, such as background noise or hissing, that can ruin the recording of sound during a shot, and then they adjust it out of the sound mix.

The sound mixer's duties also include

- Recording usable actor dialogue and room tone (known as *ambience*)

- Announcing each take (called *slating* the take) and keeping a written log for the picture editor to follow in postproduction (see Chapter 15)

- Recording any necessary voice-over (off-camera narration heard over a scene) or *wild lines,* lines repeated for clarity after the scene has been shot

- Recording special sound effects on set that can be used in the final film or replaced and/or enhanced with an effect from a sound-effects library
- Playing back music and lyrics for lip-syncing (on music videos)

Making room for the boom operator

The job of a *boom operator* is to hold the microphone attached to the tip of a pole called the *boom* (often referred to as a *fishpole,* because it resembles one) out over the actors (or just out of camera frame so it's not in the shot) and to find the best direction from which to capture the actors' dialogue. The boom operator works closely with the sound mixer and is usually guided by the mixer (through headphones) as to where to point the microphone for optimum dialogue recording.

The duties of the boom person include

- Directing the boom and mic in the most favorable position to pick up the best dialogue recording
- Being familiar with the scenes, knowing which actor speaks next, and pointing the microphone directly at that actor from above or below the camera frame
- Placing hidden mics or lapel mics on the actors when it's difficult to pick up good sound with the mic outside of the shot (especially in wide shots)
- Setting up and testing the wireless mics used in wide shots

---

Wild and crazy lines

Dialogue has to be clear. If the audience can't hear an actor's dialogue, they'll lean over to the person next to them and say, "What'd he say?" and miss the next bit of dialogue. You don't want that to happen. If the sound mixer thinks that a line has been stepped on by another actor or that some background noise interfered, he or she has the actor repeat the lines, now called *wild lines,* after the director has yelled "Cut!" and the camera has stopped rolling. Replacing those lines in postproduction is easier than reshooting the whole take if it's otherwise usable except for that line or two. Recording the actor's line on set ensures that the sound can be easily matched into the existing take.

Don't underestimate the skill of the boom operator. On my film *Turn of the Blade,* we had someone fill in for my boom man one day. This guy was so bad, he kept creeping into every shot — he almost became part of the cast. Often, your mixer can recommend someone he or she has worked with before who doesn't need to be fitted by your wardrobe person.

Choosing Analog or Digital Sound

Just as you have a choice of film, video, or digital formats (see Chapter 10), you have a choice of audio-recording formats: analog or digital. As you've probably discovered, your music CDs sound better than your cassette tapes. CDs are in the digital domain, and you don't lose any generation in quality when making copies as you do when dubbing analog cassette tapes.

With digital technology rapidly advancing, it's much easier to record your audio using digital equipment and spare the trouble of using older analog technology and lower audio quality. Digital machines are more compact, they use fewer batteries than some of the older bulkier analog recorders, and most now record to hard drives. Finding a digital recorder in a small town is also easier than finding an analog recorder for film use. If you're shooting with a digital camcorder, your camcorder acts as a camera and a recorder all in one unit, and your sound will automatically be in the digital realm.

Analog: The sound of Nagra Falls

The Polish word *Nagra* means "to record." A Nagra, from the company of the same name, is an analog recorder that uses ¼-inch magnetic tape on reel to reel (Nagra makes digital recorders as well). Analog Nagras were once the choice of recording mixers on almost every film ever made in Hollywood, but now with the advent of digital technology, filmmakers have more choices (and less-expensive alternatives) when choosing a recording machine for their productions. An analog Nagra keeps in perfect sync with the film camera because it has a crystal-sync device within its housing. *Crystal sync* is an electronic device that is found in both the motion-picture film camera and the separate sound recorder and provides for precise speed control.

A Nagra requires up to 12 batteries at a time, and those 12 batteries may have to be replaced every day. My advice is to move up to the new technology of digital audio recording and leave analog behind.

DAT recorders and dat's not all

DAT stands for *digital audio tape*. A DAT is similar in size to a mini-digital videotape that you'd use in a digital camcorder. DAT recorders are compact and portable and work with batteries or an AC adapter. If you use the right microphone (see the later section, "Recording with Microphones"), you get audio that's as pristine and professional as the audio in any studio feature film.

DAT recorders are harder to find now, and most filmmakers now use digital field recorders that record to sound files on memory cards or a hard drive. This also saves you the step of having to transfer DAT tapes onto a hard drive into digital audio files. If you want to record on DAT, you can find used recorders on www.ebay.com at affordable prices.

In the field with digital recorders

Digital field recorders look like a portable tape recorder but have no moving parts. Audio is recorded onto a memory card or internal hard drive. The audio files can then be transferred to an external hard drive or to a DVD data disc (you get about 85 minutes of sound recording on a DVD). Fostex (www.fostexusa.com) and Edirol (www.edirol.com) are two popular recorder brands used in the field. The audio recorders can be expensive, anywhere from several hundred dollars to a few thousand dollars to buy. Roland (www.rolandus.com) makes the CD-2c Recorder for $699. It records to CD discs or memory cards.

If you're in Los Angeles, you can find sound houses that rent digital field recorders. If you're in a smaller town, you may find a local music equipment store that can rent you a digital recorder. If you hire a professional sound mixer, chances are he'll have all his own equipment, including a sound recorder and a set of appropriate microphones.

You don't have to worry about buying or renting a digital field recorder if you're shooting with a digital camera. You can plug your sound directly into your camcorder (standard or high definition) and you'll get pristine high quality sound married to your visual footage. Having a separate sound recorder is more of a security backup should something happen to the audio recording that's going into the camera.

If you want to record separate digital audio but can't afford to buy an expensive system or rent one, you can purchase a digital voice recorder at your local electronics store. These devices record to built-in hard drives and hold up to 130 hours recording time (in LP mode). Just make sure the mini-recorder has an input jack for a microphone. Olympus (www.olympusamerica.com) makes the WS-210M Digital Voice Recorder for $99. It has a USB input which plugs directly into your computer to transfer the recorded audio files to your hard drive.

BWF stands for *Broadcast Wave File.* This is the type of file format that sound is recorded to for television or motion picture productions. The BWF files contain the digital sound recordings along with accurate timecode numbers. Similar to WAV (short for Waveform) audio format for PCs, BWF audio files can be recorded to a hard drive, memory card, or CD/DVD data discs.

Recording with Microphones

Recording crisp, clear dialogue is an art because sound is a very sensitive element, moving in waves similar to the circular ripples that spread out when you drop a rock in water. Recording these sound waves — as dialogue or other audio elements — so that they can be heard with optimum quality requires the proper microphone. If you're shooting on digital, you can plug the appropriate external microphone directly into the camcorder for better audio-recording results and override the camcorder microphone.

Dialogue, background sounds, crowd noise, or a live musical performance all require a different type of microphone. And a sound mixer is trained to know which type of microphone is appropriate for each situation. The sound mixer's arsenal of microphones includes

- Shotgun microphone (a directional microphone)
- Omni-directional microphone
- Lapel (lavaliere) microphone

The following sections describe how these microphones work.

Every type of microphone has a *listening pattern* that determines from which direction the microphone hears sound. For example, if you have a shotgun or directional microphone, its listening pattern is that of a narrow tube; it hears only what's directly in front of it. Anything outside this directional pattern can't be heard clearly by this type of microphone. Figure 12-1 shows what the listening patterns look like for omni-directional and directional microphones. You can often find an illustrated pattern of your microphone's listening pattern in the manual that comes with it.

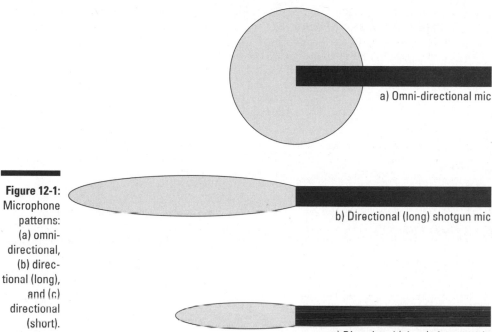

a) Omni-directional mic

b) Directional (long) shotgun mic

c) Directional (short) shotgun mic

Figure 12-1:
Microphone
patterns:
(a) omni-
directional,
(b) direc-
tional (long),
and (c)
directional
(short).

All types of microphones can usually be rented from your local instrument music store or a sound rental house, if you have one in your area.

The microphone that comes attached to your camcorder is not very good for professional sound recording. The main reason is that many camcorders have an omni-directional mic that picks up sound not just in front of the camera but from the sides and behind. That means the mic will pick up everything — from you behind the camera whispering to yourself, to Joe flushing the toilet in the next room. That's why most camcorders have an input to plug in an external microphone. The microphone that comes attached to your camcorder is usually appropriate only for recording events such as parades, birthday parties, vacations, and family get-togethers.

Shooting with shotgun microphones

A *shotgun microphone* resembles Han Solo's light saber, only it doesn't light up — and it doesn't make a very good weapon. This type of microphone has a shock mount holder (suspended by rubber bands for shock absorption). It may also have a shoe for mounting the microphone on a boom, camera, or tripod.

A shotgun is a *directional* microphone, meaning that it only picks up sounds directly in front of it, and it filters out sounds to the sides and back. It's like a bullet being shot from a gun — the line the bullet travels is the direction from which the microphone picks up sound. You use directional microphones to record actors' dialogue.

Shotgun mics come in two types:

- ✔ **Long shotgun** has a long, narrow directional pattern that picks up sounds at a distance directly in front of the microphone, which is effective when actors are in a wide shot and the microphone can't get too close without ending up in the shot.

- ✔ **Short shotgun** has a narrow directional pattern with a shorter reach for sounds closer to the microphone. This mic works well for medium and close-up shots when the microphone can be closer to the actors and still be out of the shot. This is the most common type of microphone used for recording actors' dialogue on set. If you can only afford to buy or rent one, this is it!

A shotgun microphone (see Figure 12-2) is usually covered by a *windscreen* (a tube-shaped piece of foam that slides over the length of the microphone). If you don't protect your microphone with a windscreen, you'll hear a shallow, soft banging from the air movement. A windscreen helps to absorb or filter out wind, as well as an actor breathing too closely to the mic. On windy, outdoor shoots, you use a windscreen resembling a furry ferret that absorbs wind before it hits the mic's sensitive diaphragm.

Figure 12-2:
A shotgun (directional) microphone from Azden.

Omni-directional mics

Omni means "all," and that's exactly what an *omni-directional* mic hears. Like the human ear, this mic is unable to decide which sounds to listen to and hears everything at once — and at the same volume level. Use omni-directional mics for events, crowds, plays, and environmental background recordings (see the sections "Recording with Microphones" earlier in this chapter and "Capturing On-Set Ambience" later in this chapter). Most built-in microphones on camcorders are omni-directional.

Lapel microphones

A lapel microphone (also known as a *lavaliere,* or *lav* on set) can be worn on a lapel or cleverly hidden in a person's clothing, such as on a tie or in a pocket, and is small enough to not be intrusive. Wireless lapel mics are often used on actors for distant shots requiring dialogue. Most sit-down interviews on television and documentaries use lapel mics.

The Azden Corporation (www.azdencorp.com) makes a high-quality broad cast standard WLX-Pro VHF wireless system. It comes with the lapel microphone and receiver and has a range up to 250 feet.

Wireless microphones

Shotgun and other microphone types (including lapel mics) can be wireless and work on radio frequencies. Wireless mics are usually used only to pick up the actors' dialogue for distant shots, when a boom or mic cables would otherwise end up in the shot.

Carting all that sound around

With sound recording, there's a lot of equipment to carry around. That's why professional sound mixers use a *sound cart,* which is a portable table on wheels that holds all the equipment, including cables, boom pole, adapters, mixer, and coffee and donuts, too. The sound cart serves as the mixer's moveable desk, with everything at his disposal. It also enables him to quickly wheel his equipment out of the way of the camera, should the director want to shoot in his direction!

Using Your Headphones

You and your boom operator should always use professional cushioned *headphones,* which cup the ear and block outside noise to make sure that your sound is coming through clearly and that there's no interference or buzzing on the line. You can use *earbuds* (which fit in the ear), but you get a less accurate indication of the sound recording because some background noise still makes its way in.

Always verify your sound recording through headphones. At the start of each day's shoot, record some test audio and play it back in the headphones to make sure your microphone and recorder are working properly (this includes your camcorder's audio if you're shooting on video or digital). I've had too many shoots where I forgot to bring headphones or earphones, and just assumed that the camera was recording sound. One time, the microphone didn't have a battery and didn't record any audio. Another time, the external microphone wasn't plugged in properly to my camcorder; instead the camera was picking up sound with the built-in camcorder mic, and you could hear everything in front of and behind the camera (all of it louder than the talent on camera).

Walking and Talking: Walkie-Talkies on Set

Even though walkie-talkies aren't used to record dialogue or sounds for a film, it would be difficult to run your set without them, so I mention them here. You would probably lose your voice after yelling back and forth on the set without them. Walkie-talkies or two-way radios are helpful for

✔ Communicating at a distance with crew who can be scattered about

✔ Driving scenes (when the camera and the actors are in separate vehicles)

✔ Helicopter shots (for communicating with the ground crew)

✔ Signaling the police (or an assistant) to hold traffic or pedestrians during a shot

Instead of renting walkie-talkies for your shoot, go to your local electronics or department store and pick up some consumer walkie-talkies. They'll cost you less than a day's rental from a sound rental house — and you get to keep them! I've used two-way compact radios from Midland Radio (www.midland radio.com) that have up to a 16 mile range and are priced at $29.99. An optional earbud and a lapel microphone allow for hands-free, voice-activated operation. Cell phones are another alternative (though you can only talk to one person at a time), but don't forget to turn them off during a sound take!

Listening for Quiet

In addition to the windscreens used with shotgun microphones to keep the wind from becoming part of a film's soundtrack (refer to the earlier section "Shooting with shotgun microphones"), sound teams use additional equipment to ensure that the actors' dialogue comes through loud and clear.

Shushing the camera: Barney hears you

A *blimp* or *barney* is a casing that fits snuggly over the film camera magazine reels to muffle the sound of the camera — kind of like a silencer for the camera. If you use a digital camcorder, you don't have to use a barney because camcorders are usually silent.

Silencing footsteps with sound blankets and foot foam

If you have actors walking on hardwood floors or concrete, especially women in high heels, you need to put *sound blankets* on the floor. Sound blankets are like the heavy padded sheets used in moving vans for covering furniture. Sound blankets absorb the sound of the actors' footsteps on a bare floor, preventing the actors from stepping on their lines — literally. These blankets absorb errant sound waves and prevent your dialogue from sounding tinny or picking up too much reverberation. Of course, you only put sound blankets on the floor when the actors' feet are not in the shot. You can also drape sound blankets over vertical stands or hang from the walls to help absorb reverb off bare walls.

You can also purchase *foot foam* from any sound rental company. This product is a foam rubber of varying thickness that can be cut and adhered to the bottom of your actors' shoes, enabling them to walk on hard surfaces without making excessive noise and allowing the camera to show their feet as well.

If you're on a limited budget, you can silence your actors' shoes by using double-sided tape or glue to attach thin pieces of carpet padding to the bottoms of their shoes. Applying the soft fuzzy side of velcro to the bottom of footwear is another good trick.

Acoustics and carpeting

Recording sound in a gymnasium or a house with hardwood floors makes it difficult to record proper sound without getting a tinny sound or reverb. The sound bounces off the reflective surfaces like radar. If you have a choice, film your scenes in carpeted rooms or be prepared to put down sound blankets. Also, hang some blankets or foam sheets over stands to absorb some of the sound that bounces off the walls and floor.

Getting Up to Speed Safe and Sound

Tape takes time to get up to speed (whether it's analog or digital), just like it takes your car time to get up to 60 miles an hour. That's why the sound mixer has to yell out the word "speed" so you know that the audio will be usable. This is required when shooting motion picture film and using a separate sound recorder, but you should also give a few seconds to get up to speed when shooting with a video camcorder, or digitally recording to a hard drive, even though the sound and picture are one.

Slating with the clapper board

Slating is a familiar sight to most people, although many probably don't know what it's for. A person with a black-and-white board, called a *clapper board,* stands in front of the camera and says something like, "Scene 1, Take 3," claps the board down creating a loud "clap," and then ducks out of the way. Slating not only visually identifies the scene number, shot number, and production information, but it also is used to sync up picture to sound when using a film camera or separate audio with a digital camera (as explained in the following section).

When shooting motion picture film and separate sound (or digital and a separate audio recorder), you match up picture to sound by matching the sound of the clapper clapping down with the image of the clapper board completely closed in the first frame. Syncing the clap with the picture in this one frame marries the sound and picture and puts it perfectly in sync.

If you've misplaced your clapper board or can't afford one, you can clap your hands together (just once — don't applaud!) to give a sync mark to match the sound to the picture. You won't be able to identify the scene number and shot number, though, unless you announce it or write it on your hand each time.

Sounds like MOS

The abbreviation *MOS* comes from a German director (with contradicting opinions as to whom that German director was) who said, "Mit out sound," when a take was to be filmed without recording sound. If a scene contains no dialogue, you can often film MOS and not have to worry about disruptive sounds like planes flying overhead, dogs barking down the street, or the sound of the noisy generator running the lights. You may even be able to let your sound mixer and boom operator go home early!

Syncing picture and sound with timecode

Timecode is a series of electronic-generated numbers — hours, minutes, seconds, and frames (for example, 10:28:22:06) — each representing a specific frame of your movie when recorded into digital files or when transferred onto videotape. Even if you have thousands of frames in your film, after it's transferred to tape or recorded onto digital media (smart cards or hard drive), each frame has its own personal identification number that can be punched into a computer to pinpoint that specific frame. These timecode numbers are generated on BWF audio files (explained in the earlier section "In the field with digital recorders").

Timecode numbers can be used to sync shots (which is quicker than eyeballing the clapper board and matching it with the sound of the clap) if you're using a *timecode slate* (a clapper board that displays the timecode numbers read from a timecode audio recorder). You simply punch in the timecode numbers displayed on the special timecode slate, and the picture and sound automatically sync up.

Capturing On-Set Ambience

Ambience is the background sound of a particular environment. These distinctive, individual sounds accentuate a scene and help dialogue and sound effects blend together, while smoothing out the soundtrack to sound rich and full. You need to record ambient sounds just as you do dialogue.

While shooting on location, the sound mixer usually has the cast and crew be quiet for a moment or so and records *room tone* (recording outside ambience is called a *presence track*). Room tone can include the low hum of an air-conditioner, the almost inaudible sound of a refrigerator, or ocean waves. The ambient sound can then be *looped* (repeated over and over in post-production) and layered under the dialogue, which is recorded separately, to create a realistic-sounding scene. Ambient sounds include

- **Factory:** Sound of machines whirring and air conditioning buzzing
- **Carnival:** People laughing and tinny carnival music playing
- **Library:** People whispering, pages turning, clock ticking (yes, even a quiet library has ambient sounds)
- **Freeway:** Sound of bustling traffic and horns honking
- **Meandering stream:** Sound of water babbling and birds chirping
- **Restaurant:** People talking and utensils clattering

If you can't afford to shoot in an actual restaurant, you can fake it right in your own house or apartment. Set up a corner with a table and chairs and add ambient sounds that you've recorded at a busy restaurant. When you add the ambient sound in postproduction, it will seem like your actors are in a corner of a busy restaurant. Just don't pull back with the camera and reveal your dog sitting on the stairway waiting for table scraps.

Reporting Your Sound

Sound reports are production forms that the sound mixer fills out. They provide information about the audio recorded on set, including which tapes, digital files, or reels contain which sound takes. Making sure that sound reports are filled out properly is critical for providing precise notes to the editor when matching up the sound to the picture. You can get sound report forms where you rent your sound equipment, but your sound mixer will probably have them, too.

I recommend you always back up your sound files, whether you're recording to digital audio tape (DAT) or to digital files on a hard drive or memory cards. It's inexpensive to clone your hard drive files to another backup drive or transfer your sound files to CD or DVD discs. Just as you should backup your computer files for security, you should back up your sound files without exception. Better safe and sound than sorry.

Chapter 13

Directing Your Actors: . . . And Action!

In This Chapter

▶ Reading through the script with your actors

▶ Establishing authority and gaining the actors' respect

▶ Rehearsing your film's scenes

▶ Directing your actors on set

When I was 8 years old, I was fascinated with magic and puppets. Then I picked up my dad's Super 8 movie camera and learned to manipulate my puppets on camera. The magic of filmmaking! Actors are kind of like puppets, and the director is the puppeteer pulling the strings through the magic of the movie camera.

The filmmaker in the world of low-budget filmmaking is often known as a triple-threat — producer, director, and writer. So when I talk about the "director," I'm referring to the filmmaker as well. Chances are you're at least one of these — or possibly all three.

This chapter uncovers the secrets of working with actors after you've cast them in your film. Your actors will look to you, the director, for advice and guidance. Discover how to create a comfortable environment in which the actors' trust you. Find out how to speak the actors' language, explore the story's subtext, and define each character's backstory with your cast. See how *blocking* (where your actors move on set) can enhance a scene, and discover how to pull the best performances from your actors.

Getting Your Actors Familiar with the Material — and Each Other

The director's job is to understand the script and to make sure that the actors comprehend the overall story and how the characters they're playing fit into it. You as director need to discuss certain things with each actor to make the character clearer in the actor's mind:

- **The character's goals:** What drives or motivates the character and makes him or her tick?

- **The *subtext* (what the character isn't saying):** What is the character saying indirectly (not through right-on-the-nose dialogue)?

- **The *backstory* or *ghost* (the character's past):** How is the character affected by his or her upbringing?

- **Idiosyncrasies of the character:** Does the character have any unique quirks — special personality traits that stand out and make him or her different?

- **The introversion or extroversion of the character:** How would the character behave in a situation? (Would the character step back or step forward?)

- **The character's dress and grooming style:** Is the character neat or a slob? Does he or she care?

- **The character's views on life:** Does the character have strong opinions? Is the character a leader or a follower?

- **The theme of the story as it relates to the character:** Is accomplishing the goal necessary to the character's survival?

I talk more about helping actors prepare for their characters in the section "Preparing Your Actors before the Shoot" later in this chapter.

Remembering that familiarity breeds content

The director's first job is to make the actors feel comfortable because the actor/director relationship determines whether the performances and relationships on screen are believable.

An ensemble show like *Friends* had a successful cast that worked perfectly together — they really were friends, even after working together for so many seasons. But when making a film, you don't have the luxury of the cast getting to spend a lot of time together, so arranging a few informal gatherings for your film cast is a good idea. A launch party for the film is always a good idea because it gives everyone a chance to meet and greet before starting work on the film. Dinner with the main cast, coffee, or even a walk around the block helps break the ice and can make a big difference when the actors do scenes together.

Reading through the script: The table read

The *table read* is an informal get-together for the cast and director (and other prime production people) in which they sit down and read the script from beginning to end. This is the first time you'll hear the script come to life — kind of like a radio drama without the sound effects and music — and it's an important stage during which the actors are heard together in one sitting. Have the actors read through the script several times and study their characters before coming to the table read.

The whole cast should be at the table read. This is the one rare occasion when the entire cast and the director are in the same room together. Because most films are shot out of context, it also may be the only time the actors hear the story from beginning to end, giving them, and you, a sense of the story's continuity. This helps the actors make choices and understand the story better when on the set and shooting a scene out of context. The actors can refer to the table read and know what came before and what follows after.

During the table read, you hear what works and what doesn't. If it's a comedy, does everyone find it funny? This is also the opportune time to answer questions from the cast as they read through the script together.

Adjusting dialogue to make it read naturally

Often, a screenplay contains dialogue that doesn't quite sound natural because the writer couldn't try it out with real actors. If an actor is uncomfortable saying a line, you should probably change it — you don't want an awkward performance that doesn't come across as believable. Use the table read, discussed in the preceding section, to discover and correct these types of problems instead of waiting until you're on the set. The table-read may also spark some additional ideas, in addition to dialogue adjustments, that you may want to make a note of.

Being a Parent and Mentor to Your Actors — with No Allowance

Actors work from inside their character and can't see how their performance is being perceived. Even the most successful actors need guidance from their director. Many actors admit that they're like lost children: They are vulnerable, sensitive, and open to guidance — all assets of a great actor.

Above all else, to get the proper performance, trust must exist between you and the actors. The more the actors trust you, the more they will allow you to dig in deep and pull great performances out of them. The actors also need to respect you as they would a parent and a mentor. Without the actors' respect, gaining their trust and getting great performances from them is very difficult.

A director needs to understand actors. Read about acting. Observe acting classes and study actors in films and on TV. Doing so conditions you to appreciate where an actor is coming from. Empathizing with your actors more helps you make better choices when directing your actors. Also, check out the book *Breaking into Acting For Dummies* by Larry Garrison and Wallace Wang (published by Wiley) to get a better handle on the actor's side of things.

I adopted a puppy (during the course of writing this book, he's eaten five pairs of shoes). Without meaning to be condescending, I've found that raising a puppy is similar to working with an actor:

- ✔ The director has to be patient.
- ✔ The actors need discipline.
- ✔ The director must employ repetition to help the actors learn.
- ✔ The actors need to be rewarded (praised).
- ✔ The actors need to feel appreciated and loved.
- ✔ The actors need guidance.
- ✔ The director needs to be able to teach the actors new tricks.
- ✔ The director needs to show the actors the right way to do things.
- ✔ The director sometimes needs to reprimand the actors (civilly).
- ✔ The director sometimes needs to send the actors to their trailer (cage) when they misbehave.

The actor should be treated with respect. A director gives guidance and support. The director is *not* a dictator!

Preparing Your Actors before the Shoot

You've done the table read and, if you're lucky, you have a little time to work with the actors one-on-one before everyone sets foot on the set. Preparing your actors includes rehearsing, but rehearsing is only a small part of the preparation. You need to share tips and tricks with the actors so that they give the best and most believable performances in your film.

Life's a stage

We've all been actors at least once in our lifetime. At the age of 5, you probably put on your best performance for that trip to the ice-cream shop or feigned a temperature to get out of going to school. Remember that dramatic temper tantrum at 6, when you had to go to the dentist or get your hair cut? When you were young, you had no inhibitions and you weren't self-conscious — that's why children often make great actors.

Actors are really just hypnotizing themselves into believing that they are the character in the screenplay. (In high school, I tried hypnotizing all the girls in my history class, but it didn't work.)

What about in the courtroom? The lawyers who present their cases, and their clients — guilty or not guilty — often pour out believable performances to influence the judge and jury. Many people who are psychosomatic actually get sick because they've convinced themselves that they're sick. The mind is a powerful thing. William Shakespeare said, "Nothing is good or bad, but thinking makes it so." If you believe it, it must be true. An actor can use this power of the mind when adapting a character.

As explained earlier in this chapter, the director makes sure that the actors understand the characters' goals, desires, and purposes in each scene. The actors and director need to be on the same page and agree on the meaning of each scene.

Casting is half the game. A director shouldn't have to teach actors to act. A director should guide and give direction only. It's up to the actors to come to the set as professionals and know how to utilize an actor's tools. See Chapter 8 for details about casting the right actors in your film.

Rehearsals, yea or nay?

Preparing your actors for the shoot involves some form of rehearsal. You can repeat each scene until it feels right. Or you can do exercises and give tips to loosen up the actors. Rehearsing can mean having the actors — especially those who have a friendship or association on screen — spend time with each other in order to become more comfortable around one other. It can be *blocking* the actors' movements for the camera (see the section "Blocking, walking, and talking" later in this chapter) and coming up with the right *business* for each actor in each scene (see the section "Taking care of business" later in this chapter). If you do rehearse with your actors, remember that the purpose of rehearsing is to make the planned look unplanned.

Too much rehearsing can take away a scene's freshness and spontaneity. Steven Spielberg, like many other directors, is not a big fan of rehearsing too much. The other problem with over-rehearsing is that if you see a better choice for blocking, dialogue, and so on during filming, it may be hard for the actors to change what they've conditioned themselves to do during rehearsals.

Sometimes you can use *not* rehearsing to your benefit. One of my films featured a musical number spoofing *The Pirates of Penzance,* and I wanted it to be an uncoordinated dance number. My sister Marlene asked when we were rehearsing, and I told her we weren't!

Not every scene needs a rehearsal, just like not every scene needs to be storyboarded (see Chapter 9 for more on storyboarding). Don't beat a scene to death. I like to let the actors give their rendition of the performance — that gives me something to mold and shape from a director's point of view.

Some actors require a lot of rehearsal, and others prefer very little. An actor may need rehearsals even if the director doesn't like to rehearse. Some actors' performances get better the more they rehearse, and some get worse (they become less believable, and their performance becomes flat). An actor's training and experience can determine how much rehearsal time, if any, he or she requires. By being observant, you can see whether the actor needs time to warm up or if she's up to speed on the first take.

When you rehearse with your actors, let them hold something back from their performance. Have them save a freshness for the camera.

Rehearsing the characters, not just the lines

The actors should think about the characters they're playing, not just the words they say. An actor needs to imagine himself or herself as the character and figure out what the character wears, what the character's opinions are, and how the character reacts in certain situations. An actor can rehearse a character while driving, having lunch, and so on without having to study the script or the character's dialogue.

As the director, you can direct the actors to inject their personality into the characters — to imagine their blood pumping in the characters' veins. Encourage them to become their characters, to pull their characters off the page and bring them to life!

Actors should study people's quirks and idiosyncrasies and find little unique traits to add humanity and dimension to the characters they play. Frank

Abagnale, Leonardo DiCaprio's character in *Catch Me If You Can,* always peels the labels off bottles, telegraphing his nervousness and youthful energy. It also shows Tom Hanks's FBI agent, Hanratty (who knows of Abagnale's label-peeling habit), that Frank is nearby. My friend Donald Petrie, who directed *Miss Congeniality,* was with Sandra Bullock at dinner one night when she laughed and let out a loud snort. Don told her that would be great for her character — and it ended up in the film.

Discovering the characters' backstories

Backstory is the history of a character. It's also referred to as the *ghost.* What haunts the character from childhood? What kind of family did he have? What type of upbringing?

The director should encourage each actor to imagine and develop the ghost of his or her character, but the actor doesn't need to share it with the director as long as the history works for the actor and helps bring dimension to his or her performance. The backstory can become the actor's personal secret, making the fictional character more real to the actor.

Knowing the backstory or ghost helps an actor make dramatic choices for the character during each scene when decisions need to be made. For example, if Jonathan was abused as a child, now as an adult he may flinch every time someone makes a sudden move around him.

Prompting dialogue

Sometimes an actor needs help delivering a speech during a scene, reciting a lot of words and facts that are difficult to memorize, or, if you're shooting a documentary or infommerical, talking into the camera. The solution? A teleprompter.

You see actors reading off teleprompters all the time on TV. All the awards shows prompt the actors with their intros and presentations, and most times when you see a political candidate or a host talking into the camera, chances are, they've never memorized a word they're saying — they're reading it word for word off a teleprompter screen.

DV Prompt developed teleprompter software that lets you feed a script into your desktop computer or portable laptop. The software displays the words of your script in virtually any size font, lets you control the speed of the scroll, change the colors, and so on. You can get DV Prompt software for only $60 at www.dv creators.net/dvcprompt or try out the free download trial first — and be prompt!

Reading between the lines: Subtext

Subtext is what's being said between the lines. Rarely does a multidimensional character say things right on the nose (although they do it all the time in bad scripts). Subtext is an element that an actor's character will probably deliver through many passages of dialogue. It's important for the director to make sure that every actor understands the subtext of the scene.

Subtext is relayed onscreen through the actors' body language and the dialogue metaphors that their characters choose during the scene. When a character says that she doesn't mind, does she? When Sally says she's really happy that Noah's getting married, is she *really* happy for him? What does her body language tell us as we see her twisting a paperclip into a pretzel as she says, "Everything's fine"?

In *The Big Picture,* Kevin Bacon's character, Nick, is making lunch for his girlfriend, Susan (Emily Longstreth), whom he broke up with earlier in the film. The two are talking about their grilled-cheese sandwiches, but the dialogue and action in the scene are actually revealing the subtext of them starting up their relationship again.

Exercising and warming up your actors

Much like going to the gym, an actor needs to warm up both physically and mentally before getting into the real workout of filming. Stretching limbers up the body, and doing breathing exercises opens up the mind. Many actors forget to breathe properly before starting their scenes. It's amazing what a few deep breaths can do to calm an actor before performing a scene or getting into character.

Keeping it natural, naturally

A great exercise is to have your actors whisper their lines in rehearsal and then perform the scene again using normal volume. Overacting is much harder when you whisper, and it's always easier to bring up a performance than to bring it down. Bruce Willis was very believable in *The Sixth Sense,* and he virtually whispered his whole performance.

Another thing to note is the distance between your actors. If they're in close proximity to each other, they don't need to raise their voices for everyone in the room to hear. I was working with two actors who were speaking too loudly across a table, which made the performance unnatural. So I told them to pretend they were in a busy restaurant and didn't want anyone eavesdropping on their conversation. It worked like a charm. Lowering their voices toned down their overacting.

Being objective about subjective acting

Objective acting is when an actor is aware of his or her performance. The actor is conscious of the audience or camera and aware that he or she is being observed. The actor is not affected by the emotions of the character because he or she is being objective and can feel only sympathy, not empathy, toward the character. This is not the right way to carry a performance.

Subjective acting is when an actor is totally immersed in the feelings and emotions of the character in the scene, and the audience feels like voyeurs into the private life of the character being portrayed. The actor is acting internally, as if the audience and the camera don't exist. When the actor becomes the character and believes his own performance, so does the audience!

I discovered an exercise that helps actors play more naturally. If you're not getting a realistic performance from your actors, give each one a yo-yo. Have them recite their lines while trying to do tricks with the yo-yo. It's some kind of left brain, right brain (no brain) exercise that I've found takes the actors' minds off trying too hard.

Improving through improvisation: "I made that up"

An excellent exercise to get actors to think beyond what's written in the script and delve into what a scene is really about is to have them ad-lib or improvise the scene. Doing the scene without the script — just making up what the scene is about — helps the actors feel the emotion and sense of the scene. When you feel that the actors have gained some insight by improvising, have them follow the script again.

Acting is reacting

Many actors are too focused on anticipating their lines and don't listen to the other actors. But acting is like Ping-Pong or tennis: You have to react to the ball coming at you or you miss it every time. Speechless characters can be just as intriguing in films as those who speak. Without dialogue, a character is a sounding board for another character, and someone who communicates through her physical expression, which can be as powerful as her verbal expressions. Good actors emote without saying a word.

As a director, become more aware about how you act and react to things every waking hour. Acknowledge how everyday things affect your emotions. This sensitizes you to how an actor works. Which emotions are verbalized and which ones are shown through expression? Which ones are subtle and which ones are over the top? Use these feelings to help get your thoughts across to your actors when directing them.

Speaking with body language

Have your actors study body language. An actor not only speaks with words but with his or her body. Body language can be very powerful. People cross their arms when they're shy or being defensive. They slump when they're feeling down or have no energy. People move differently when they flirt. Turn the TV's sound off and watch for body language. It's a universal language without words. Notice how you can even tell how a dog is feeling by its body language.

Remind your actors that true character is revealed more by what a character's actions are when he or she is alone than when around others. The tough biker enters his apartment, sits down next to his cat on the couch, and pets the animal in a very caring manner — showing a sensitive side that no one sees when he's in public.

Directing Actors during the Shoot

Directing actors on set involves more than just helping them perform in character. It includes telling them where to move within the frame, giving them proper direction and motivation for the scene, and answering any questions that help the actor better his or her performance. The actor should trust you and look to you for guidance.

Never yell at your actors. If an actor is doing a scene incorrectly or not to your satisfaction, take him or her aside quietly and discuss the situation in private. Do not correct or critique an actor's performance in front of the rest of the cast and crew. The actor will appreciate the fact that you discuss direction in private. Actors especially are self-conscious. You don't want to embarrass them in front of the rest of the cast and crew or upset them and have to deal with a moody actor who won't come out of his trailer.

Encouraging your actors to ask questions — but not too many

You want your actors to feel that they can ask questions because you don't want them second-guessing things on the set. But if an actor gets too dependent on the director and asks questions before every take, encourage the actor to start trusting his or her performance and answer some of those questions on his own. To keep the need for questions to a minimum, be specific in your directions. Ambiguous directions can cost extra takes when an actor misunderstands you.

Remind the actors before shooting a scene where the scene is in the story and what came before it, especially if you're shooting out of order. Doing so helps the actor recall how she felt in the scene before this one and match her emotions to reflect the former scene. If Mary was sullen in the last scene because Gary had to fly out of town, then Mary would still be holding her feelings in the next scene.

Reminding your actors that less is more — more or less

Sometimes it's better for actors to do less in terms of expression and emphasis in their dialogue. They should feel the emotion and let their body language and tone set the mood (but without exaggerating their body movements either — like waving their arms around or using their hands too much when talking).

Stage actors have to *project* their performance to a live audience, which involves emphasizing dialogue and increasing volume because the audience is at a distance. Yet when an actor projects in front of a camera, the performance can come across as stagy or not believable. A camera can pick up subtle emotional clues: a blink, a tear in the eye, or a simple twitch. So giving less is more in film. Let the projector project, and not the actor.

I once read a newspaper review of a film that said, "Great acting!" To me, that's a contradiction. Great acting should be invisible. Last time I was in an office store, I complained to the store clerk that I couldn't find the invisible tape. Get the idea? If it's invisible, you shouldn't see it.

When it comes time for an actor to let loose for a big scene, make sure that you keep that actor fresh until the big moment. Save an actor's emotional performance for the close-up. If you know that you're going to go into a close-up when the actor wells up with tears, you don't want the actor to give her best performance in the wide shot. You still want to shoot the wide shot, so your editor can cut into the close-up on movement.

Also make sure that your actors flow each mood into the next. They'll need your guidance on this. When happiness turns to anger, the audience needs to see it building up — it can't just come out of nowhere. It's like a teapot coming to the point of boiling: It happens gradually until finally the steam shoots out under the pressure. When a singer carries a note higher and higher, it's a gradual ascension. A character would only "snap" from one mood to another if he were crazy or unstable.

Feeling the words, not just memorizing

What did you have for lunch three days ago? I can guarantee that you had to think about that. It took some *pre-thought*. Did you look down or away to catch your thoughts? As a director, remind your actors to use pre-thought when recalling things. Too many actors seem to roll off numbers and recall incidents without any pre-thought because they've memorized the script so well. They don't show that they're thinking — only acting.

Along those same lines, many actors enter a scene and put too much into a simple "hello." Direct your actors to have a more matter-of-fact delivery. Don't enter the scene saying "hello" like you've rehearsed it 100 times, and it's the most important thing in the world.

Also make your actors aware if they're enunciating each word too perfectly. Precise enunciation is reserved for narration, professional speeches, and presentations. Let the actors run their words together. Many actors tend to put too much space between words to make sure that they're being clear, but it doesn't sound natural or believable in films.

Blocking, walking, and talking

Blocking is how the actors move on set and how the camera covers that movement. The blocking for a scene is sometimes done in rehearsal, but often it's done on the set just before filming (see Chapter 14).

Establishing blocking is like breaking down a scene into separate blocks. An actor moves first from the window to the table, then from the table to a chair, and then from the chair to the door. Movement keeps a scene from becoming too static and makes the actors' performances seem more real. In real life, people rarely stand or sit in one place too long.

Robotic performance

Without an on-screen personality, an actor comes across as a robot, programmed to recite words without feeling or expression. Encourage your actors to bring their uniqueness to the role, to plug their own DNA into the character they're playing. Think of an actor as an empty computer with unlimited software choices.

Look at successful and unique actors like Arnold Schwarzenegger, Steve Martin, Sandra Bullock, and Clint Eastwood. All could have followed earlier advice to get rid of the accent, the white hair, the attitude, acting style and so on, but they retained their own looks and personalities with great success.

The best time to decide on blocking is when you have the actors together for rehearsal, or on the set as the camera and lights are being set. Have the actors do their lines and see what motivates their movement. Often blocking comes automatically. It feels right for the actor to stand up at this point, or sit down, or move toward the window during a specific piece of dialogue.

Cheating is a technical term for framing things better for the camera, or for making the shot look more aesthetically pleasing — when an actor needs to turn slightly to one side for a better shot, for example, or when two actors need to move closer together to make a shot work. You cheat the lamp into the shot behind the actor's close-up so that it frames better in the picture, for example.

Taking care of business

An actor's performance is made more real when he or she is preoccupied with moving and doing *business*. Business is what actors do with their hands, or the action that occupies them while they're performing a scene, such as drinking, fiddling with keys, doing the dishes, or tidying up. A director usually gives each actor an idea for his or her business, but sometimes the actor has a good suggestion as well.

Business takes away from an actor's self-consciousness. It gives the actor something to do with his or her hands. Some actors use their hands too much, waving them all over the place. By holding a book, a pen, or a drink, the actor doesn't have to worry about what to do with her hands. It's a diversion, like the yo-yo exercise mentioned earlier in this chapter.

Matching actors' actions

Make sure that your actors repeat the same blocking and business when filming from different angles. In postproduction, the editor needs to cut the two angles together, and as long as the actor does the same thing in both shots, the editor can have a choice of where to cut. If an actor is talking and raises a coffee cup to his lips, it has to match other camera shots taken from another angle. The actor has to raise the cup at the exact same line of dialogue, or the two shots won't cut together properly (and this will really frustrate the editor, who may not be able to cut the two shots together smoothly). The script supervisor helps the actors remember what their actions were in each shot so they match when the scene is shot from a different angle. (You can find more on the script supervisor's assistance to the actors and director in Chapter 14.)

Gorilla training

Sometimes an actor has to wear heavy prosthetic makeup (like a mask) or a complete body costume, like a monster or gorilla suit. Body language can have a big impact on a performance, especially when make up limits facial expressions.

I did a cameo in the film *Naked Gun 2½,* playing a gorilla when Leslie Nielsen comes crashing out of the zoo entrance in a tank followed by runaway elephants, giraffes, and two gorillas. (The gorillas had to be actors in suits because using the real animals wasn't safe.) For a week, I studied the mannerisms and body language of a gorilla — I was in "gorilla" training!

In a full body suit, an actor has to project his emotions to reflect how the character is feeling. Robin Williams had to perform as a robot in *Bicentennial Man,* and Jim Carrey gave an animated performance under the furry makeup of *The Grinch.* Sometimes an actor's mannerisms and body language are transferred to a computer-generated character, as was done with Gollum in *Lord of the Rings: The Two Towers.* Andy Serkis, acting as Gollum via computer motion-capture, received a lot of praise for his performance and garnered a lot of awards.

Continuity mistakes can make a film look really unprofessional — even though the pros make them all the time. Continuity means that things need to remain consistent from one angle to another, or the audience will get confused. A sandwich has to have the same bites taken out of it when covered from a different angle. An unwrapped present shouldn't still be wrapped in a different angle. If an actor exits one room wearing a blue shirt, he should enter the next room wearing the same blue shirt.

Commending the actors

Giving your actors feedback after you shoot each scene is very important. An actor is always looking for a response — attention is one of the reasons people become actors. Actors often feel isolated and hurt if they don't receive acknowledgment.

If an actor doesn't receive any feedback from you, even a simple, "That was great," she'll feel that her performance didn't live up to your expectations. If you believe that your actors can do a better take, tell them, "That was good, but I know you can do better." Treat the actors delicately, and you'll get great performances from them.

A professional and thoughtful director compliments the actors' work and encourages them to give the best performances possible, but rarely will an actor return the compliment. The filmmaker usually gets his praise at the film's premiere.

Chapter 14

A Sense of Direction: Directing Your Film

In This Chapter

▶ Understanding what a director is and does

▶ Translating script to screen

▶ Choosing your shots

▶ Moving the camera

A director is an *auteur* — the true author of a film. He or she is not unlike a god, a creator, a leader who takes all the credit — or all the blame! If you as a filmmaker take on the task of the director, shaping and molding all the elements into a movie, your passion for the story should be undeniable; you'll be involved with it for quite some time. A director lives film in the daytime and dreams film in the nighttime.

This chapter breaks down the mystery behind what a director does to produce a film. You see what makes a great director and how to translate a script to the screen. You discover the cinematic language of directors, from making decisions on the set to subtext, symbolism, and pacing.

You also find out when to move the camera (after all, it's a *motion* picture) and why, as well as what special equipment, including tripods, dollies, and cranes, helps you get the desired shot. Directing a film is a laborious task, so be prepared to run an exhausting, but exciting, marathon.

Focusing on Directing

The director of a film must work closely with the actors in a creative capacity, pulling the best performances from them (see Chapter 13, which talks about directing actors). The director also needs to have some knowledge of the camera and lenses, and how to use them to set a mood in a scene. Having the final say on the locations, casting, script, and often editing of the final picture makes the director the keeper of the film and stamps it with his or her personal signature.

Directing traits

A director is a father, mother, psychologist, mentor, and ship's captain. To succeed in this role, you must be good at giving directions in an authoritative manner — without being a dictator. Certain traits make for a successful director. Some people are born with these traits; others acquire them through observing and studying and learning to be more aware of everything around them. The following list of traits will help you be a better director:

- ✔ **Being mentally strong:** The director needs to be emotionally and mentally strong in the sense that he can control his emotions. By keeping calm, the actors remain calm. If the director is uneasy, the actors pick up on this. It's very similar to a dog watching his master and sensing that something is wrong. It's important to be sensitive to the actors' needs. A director should also never lose his sense of humor (hopefully he has one in the first place!).

- ✔ **Being a problem-solver:** A big part of a director's job is problem-solving — and doing it on the spot. You need to make decisions quickly and wisely, because not making a decision is a decision. Take a deep breath, make a decision, and move on.

- ✔ **Setting the tone:** The director sets the tone on set with the cast and crew. A friendly family atmosphere creates camaraderie among the cast and crew that is reflected in the final production. Actors often subliminally mirror their director. If the director is frantic, uptight, and nervous, the actors' performances are affected. If the director is confident, organized, and decisive, the actors feel a sense of security. And if the director earns an actor's trust, the actor is more willing to try different things.

  As your film's director, you need to show confidence. You are the leader, and the cast (and crew) will look up to you.

- ✔ **Having an eye for detail:** A good director has an eye for detail and can visualize the screenplay as a moving picture even before setting foot on the set. The director can help the actor find little nuances, subtle expressions to make his or her performance unique. When deciding on props and set design, the director looks for details that add character and dimension to be used in the scenes.

- ✔ **Timing and pacing things right:** With the help of the script supervisor (see Chapter 7), the director makes sure that the shots and scenes are filmed at a proper pace. The script supervisor carries a stopwatch and accurately times each shot to get a better sense of how long the scene will run on screen.

The world tends to slow down on screen — probably because the audience's attention is concentrated solely on the screen and the camera doesn't blink. The director's job is to pace the film by controlling the pacing of the actors' performances and the number of shots in each scene. The more shots in a scene, the faster the pace feels and the less it seems to lag.

Training yourself as a director

A director, no matter how experienced or successful, is a student of film. You are continuously learning and studying — experiencing life and bringing those experiences to your work. One of the most important things you can do to become a better director is to study films and cinematography to see how others tell their stories cinematically and figure out at least the basics of lenses and shot composition.

Seeing what other directors do can trigger new and original ideas, especially if you study films in your genre (see Chapter 2 on film genres). That's why you should watch films — not to copy, but to be inspired. Here are a couple of tips to use when watching films and TV shows:

- **Read the script in closed caption.** One of my favorite things to do when I have time to watch TV or rent a movie is to view the closed-captioning. Doing so enables me to read the script on the bottom of the screen as the story unfolds. You can study performances (as well as camera moves) and see how the script is structured — literally.

- **Watch a silent film.** I like to turn the sound off once in a while when watching films (no one wants to watch films with me for some reason). Films are all about motion. If a film is done right, you can tell what the story is about by the visuals. If you watch *The Green Mile, E.T.,* or *The Sixth Sense* with the sound off, for example, you get a sense of what the characters are going through, the emotions, and so on. If you watch a soap opera on TV and turn the sound off, though, all you get are talking heads — and no idea what's going on.

Here are some other things you can do that can translate into making you a more effective director:

- **Read books.** Read voraciously and on every topic; you never know what may come in handy.

- **Watch people.** See how their moods affect their body language and how they react to strangers and to friends.

- **Experience life.** Take in the world around you. The more experiences you have, the more original ideas you can bring to your films.

- ✔ **Ask questions.** It's the only way to get the answers.

- ✔ **Observe acting classes.** See how acting coaches teach.

- ✔ **Take classes.** Force yourself to study subjects you normally would have no interest in. When you take active interest in a topic, you'll be surprised at the curiosity it generates in you.

- ✔ **Travel.** See the world and the lifestyles of other countries.

- ✔ **Study paintings.** Look for inspiration in terms of composition and lighting.

Translating Script to Screen

A screenplay is the blueprint of what ultimately becomes a motion picture. The director's task is to translate this blueprint to the screen — to "build" the film. Each scene can be interpreted in many different ways, and if the director is not the screenwriter, he or she must understand what the writer is trying to say. The director also needs to fix any holes in the story, know how to translate words into visuals, and add or delete scenes to make the story stronger.

As a director, you have to be passionate about the material — dissect it, understand it completely.

Directing your sleep, exercise, and eating

Directing a film is like going into battle (with a small army). You've got to be well prepared. Exercising, eating right, and getting plenty of sleep is crucial to being a strong director and leader on your film. You're training for a marathon and you need to get in shape and be alert with all your senses if you want to survive your shoot and make a great film.

When I start preproduction on my films, I use a company called Chef's Diet (www.chefs diet.com). They prepare three healthy meals a day (starting at $20.95 a day) including two great snacks (or two meals starting at $14.95 a day) and have it delivered to my door every morning in a cooler. I can't use the excuse I've forgotten to eat or didn't have time. Check out Chef's Diet; you'll see many celebrities and industry people on their endorsement page who've had the same idea to eat right during their movie-making adventures.

Understanding the screenplay

As a director, you need to understand exactly what the story is about and what the motivation and goals of each character are. A director looks at each scene and asks, "What's the purpose of this scene? What's the underlining reason — to impress the girl, to prepare for the big race?" Just as the actor asks the question, "How does this scene relate to my character?" the director asks a broader question, "How does this scene relate to the story as a whole?" Sometimes the director finds that the scene doesn't add anything to the story and ends up cutting it. Other times, the scene may need to be enhanced or another scene or two may need to be added before or after this particular scene to strengthen it and the story.

By asking questions, you're forced to seek the answers. This adds more dimension to the story and characters. It helps you make choices in your direction and step back to see the whole picture.

A scene's underlying purpose is often revealed by subtext. *Subtext* is the meaning behind the words — it's reading between the lines. You need to understand not only what the characters are saying, but also what the subtext reveals. What does the scene really mean? How do the characters really feel? Subtext can mean the opposite of what a character says verbally. A character may say, "I hate you!" when his actions reveal the opposite emotion. Meaning conveyed through subtext can also be more powerful than meaning conveyed through dialogue. Instead of Karen saying she misses her daughter, it's much more effective to use a visual of her picking up her child's favorite doll and looking at it sadly.

Symbolism is a type of metaphor in which one thing is used to represent something else, such as an idea or an emotional state, or to convey a deeper truth. In cinema, visuals are often used symbolically and can be very powerful. In the screenplay I adapted for *They Cage the Animals at Night* from the novel by Jennings Michael Burch, I incorporated symbolism in these ways:

✔ Little Jennings is locked in his room with the same key that was used to lock the stuffed animals in the cabinet at night. In this instance, the use of the key symbolizes that Jennings is just like a caged animal.

✔ The setting of the orphanage resembles a prison with barbed wire around it. Without ever stating the fact in words, the orphanage's setting symbolizes the imprisonment of the orphans.

Rewriting or adjusting the script

If the director isn't the screenwriter, he or she often embellishes the story and adds his or her own creative vision and style to the script. Enhancements to the script include adding or deleting scenes to support other scenes in the story, along with filling any holes in the story. In addition to strengthening the script in terms of better character development (Jimmy finally realizes he can do it on his own at the end) or story repairs (Sarah shouldn't run into Mark at the train station because it's too contrived to the story), you may also need to do some adjusting because of budget limitations.

As you're prepping the film, you may find that consolidating several locations into one makes the production more economical. You also may find that you eliminate some of the secondary characters that aren't crucial to the story and save having to pay additional actors.

Visualizing your screenplay

After you've done your directorial homework of understanding the emotional and psychological aspects of the screenplay, you now must turn the words on paper into visual shots. As you read your screenplay with your visual mind open, certain portions will jump out at you, calling for a specific shot or a certain angle to express what's going on in that particular scene. Sometimes it's a simple *close-up* or *two shot* (see later in this chapter) or it's a dramatic image that calls out, like the powerful end shot in the original *Planet of the Apes* (1968) when the camera pulls back to reveal the Statue of Liberty half-submerged in the sand by the ocean's shore.

Translating the script into visuals is something that the director does alone, unlike the table read, which involves the entire cast (see Chapter 13 on actors). To get the creative juices flowing and to better understand the characters and story, isolate yourself from civilization and escape into the world of the screenplay.

Take a pencil and a ruler and partition the individual scenes in the script. Draw a solid line across the page at the beginning of each scene. Separating your film into separate blocks makes tackling the scenes one at a time easier.

Mapping Out Your Plans for the Camera

Part of a director's homework includes making notes, sketches, or diagrams of how he or she envisions the shots in each scene. You can use various techniques to plan shots, including storyboards, written shot lists, schematics, notations on the script, and models.

Designing storyboards

Some directors start directing even before stepping onto the set by creating a comic-book version of the film utilizing *storyboards*. Storyboards are visual frames that outline the composition of each shot. Some directors prefer to design shots with storyboards, but they require a lot of time and an artist's hand (although you can draw stick figures or use storyboard software). Other directors prefer to save storyboarding for special-effect shots and action scenes only (see Chapter 9 for more on storyboarding).

Creating a shot list

A shot list, sometimes referred to as a *dance card,* consists of written directions that describe the details of each shot. Usually, it is scribbled on index cards for convenience. Sometimes the director prepares the shot list well in advance, and sometimes it's done right before the next day's shoot. A shot list contains the scene and shot number, which the director checks off as shots are completed. Here's an example of a shot list for Scene 45 from my film *Undercover Angel* (more on types of shots in the section "Taking Your Best Shot" later in this chapter):

> *Harrison* looks up from typewriter — **camera dollies** in for a **close-up**.
>
> *Jenny* gets up and goes to the door — **camera follows** her and stops.
>
> *Harrison* gets up — **camera leads** him to *Jenny* at the door.
>
> Two shot — **over the shoulder** of *Harrison* talking to *Jenny*

As the director, you may want to do both a shot list and storyboard your scenes to illustrate the actual framing and position of the action.

Sketching schematics

Schematics show a basic floor plan with an overhead view of where the camera and actors will be placed for each shot within a scene. I use dotted lines with directional arrows showing actors' movement. If you have several camera angles, number each camera shot in the schematics to show exactly where the camera will be placed.

You can draw schematics on separate pieces of paper and numbered to each shot and scene or you can sketch them on the page opposite the scene in the screenplay. In Figure 14-1, the director's schematic shows the actor's position and direction of movement with the camera placement and movement as well. If you prefer to use a software program, Smartdraw ($197) provides various floor-plan layouts and hundreds of images, including a camera icon that you can use to design your shots from an aerial point of view. For a free trial download, go to `www.smartdraw.com`. FrameForge 3D (which I talk about in Chapter 9) not only creates virtual three-dimensional storyboards, but it also creates accurate overhead schematics of all your camera setups (`www.frameforge3d.com`).

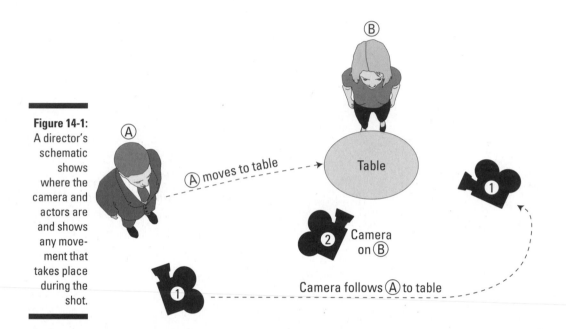

Figure 14-1: A director's schematic shows where the camera and actors are and shows any movement that takes place during the shot.

When planning your schematics, you can use different-sized coins (pennies, dimes, and nickels) to represent different actors and move them around on your floor plan. After you decide on the actors' movement within the scene, circle the coins in place and then choose the best camera placement to cover the action (but then put those coins into your budget — you're going to need every penny!).

Making notes on the script

You can circle, box, underline, and highlight certain words in the script to show different instructions, such as when to use a close-up, dolly-in, or tracking shot. (See "Taking Your Best Shot," later in this chapter, for information about the different types of shots directors use.)

Planning with models (not the high-fashion kind)

To get a three-dimensional idea for your shots, you can place dolls or miniature plastic soldiers on a tabletop to find the best camera angles. Doing so helps you visualize where to position the actors to get the best coverage. Just be prepared to explain why you're playing with dolls when someone walks into the room unexpectedly.

Continuing Continuity with Your Script Supervisor

Directing a film is like piecing a jigsaw puzzle together. It's up to the director and the script supervisor to make sense of it all (see Chapter 7 for information about hiring your crew). The *script supervisor* works alongside the director, keeping track of *continuity* (the logical order of things, actions, wardrobe, and characters that need to be consistent from shot to shot or scene to scene) and following the script to make sure that the director doesn't miss a scene or a planned shot.

Forgetting a scene is very easy because a script is usually shot out of sequence. Without a script supervisor to mark the script and follow what has been shot, it's not uncommon for a scene or two to be forgotten. Even the lowest budgeted film should have a script supervisor. The director has enough things to worry about, and forgetting whether the actor exited right or left in the last shot is very easy to do — but it's the script supervisor's job to remember those types of details and more. The script supervisor can be the director's best friend (next to his dog).

Got a match?

The director sometimes has an actor repeat his actions so they match when the same action is filmed from a different camera angle or with a different shot size. This is called *matching*. It's important for the actor to match his actions exactly so that the two shots can be cut together seamlessly, ensuring continuity. An effective way to cut shots together is during movement on camera; if an actor lifts a coffee cup to his lips in a wide shot, the filmmaker (or your editor) may choose to cut to a close-up of the cup coming up to the actor's lips. But the action must be repeated exactly in the wide shot and again in the close-up for it to match in the editing room. The script supervisor takes note of the actor's *business* (see Chapter 13) and reminds the actor to repeat the same action at the new angle.

Inserting coverage and cutaways

As the director, you should be versed in the power of coverage, cutaways, and inserts — and know the difference between them.

Coverage

Coverage is catching the same action from different angles so that the continuity of the shots is logical. It can be done with several cameras or, as is often done on low-budget productions, by placing the camera in different positions and repeating the action.

TIP

When covering the action, the director needs to set a shooting ratio (how much film or video to usable footage). An average shooting ratio on a low-budget film is 3:1 — three takes to get one good one. Setting a shooting ratio is important, because this lets you pace how much raw film or tape you need to purchase (and what to budget for). If shooting to digital files, then you only need to be concerned about having the appropriate size hard drives, and how many. A production that is budgeted for 3 takes per shot needs to have approximately 270 minutes of film or video stock to end up with roughly a 90-minute finished film (3 takes × 90 minutes = 270 minutes of stock needed).

If you're shooting on video, you have more leeway because tape is cheaper than film stock — and you can even play back the shot right away to see whether it worked to your satisfaction and then decide if you want to try another take. If you're shooting on digital (standard or high def), you need to budget for memory cards and external hard drives.

Cutaway

A *cutaway* is a shot of something the actor looks at or something that is not part of the main shot — such as a clock on the wall or another actor reacting to what's going on in the scene. You can use a cutaway to save a shot that doesn't work in one take and to hide what would otherwise end up being a *jump-cut* (the action appears to be missing frames and jumps). You can use part of Take 1 before the cutaway and the end of Take 2 after the cutaway, for example. Cutaways are often used in interview situations: the guest speaks and then there's a cutaway to the interviewer nodding (this allows tighter editing of the guest's answers).

Use a cutaway after a gag to show a reaction. It helps to emphasize a funny moment for the audience, allowing them to share their reaction with an on-screen character. Showing a reaction also lets the audience know how to react to something if it can be interpreted in several ways. An effective use of a cutaway is the Wicked Witch in the *Wizard of Oz* watching Dorothy and her friends through a crystal ball. You can also use a cutaway to condense time — he walks toward the exit, cut to a cutaway of him being watched by the cat from the stairs, and then cut back to the actor now on the street and getting into his car.

Insert

An *insert* is similar to a cutaway, except that it's usually part of the same location where the dialogue or action is taking place, but often shot separately from the main shoot or after the actors have left the set. An insert is usually a close-up of a watch, a letter (like the one Harry Potter received notifying him he was accepted at the Hogwarts School of Witchcraft and Wizardry), or someone holding an object, like the remote control for the time-machine Dolorean that Doc operated in *Back to the Future.* When you do an insert of someone turning pages in a book, for example, or a close-up of a watch on a wrist, you can use a someone other than your main actor. Just remember to make sure the hands are alike: same gender, similar appearance, and wearing identical rings or jewelry.

Screen direction: Your other left

Screen direction is an important element to be aware of. If a car is driving right to left in one shot, the car should continue to travel in the same direction to its destination. If the camera crosses the *line of action* to the opposite side of the car and shoots it going left to right, the car will appear to be going in the opposite direction, as if it were heading back to where it started from. Paying attention to the line of action, also known as the *action axis* or *180-degree rule,* helps keep the direction of your actors and movement consistent so the audience doesn't get confused.

When one actor speaks to her left, you expect the actor to whom she's speaking to look to his right. You create an imaginary line and keep all your elements on one side of the line or the other — but you have to remain consistent, otherwise you'll be *crossing the line* and the on-screen direction will be flipped. If you film both actors as though they're looking to their left, it will appear as though they're looking at something to their left, and not at each other. The camera should not cross the line of action. Many amateur filmmakers often make the mistake of *crossing the line.* See Figure 14-2 for an example.

You can cross the line of action while the camera is in motion (where the change of direction is seen on-screen) because then the audience sees that the camera has stepped over the line, and you don't have an abrupt cut that can be disorienting.

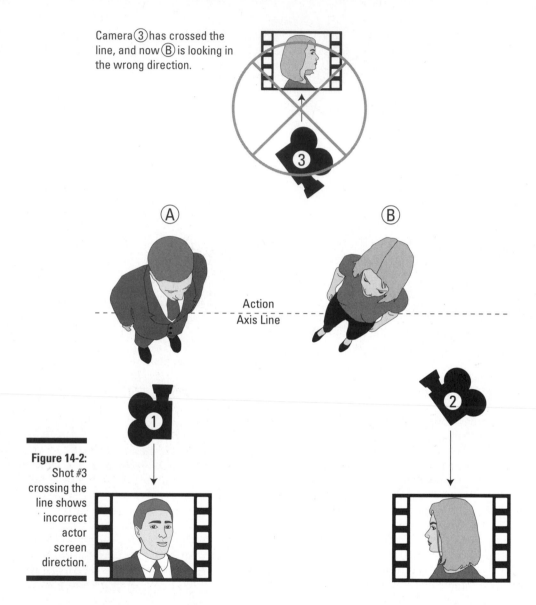

Camera ③ has crossed the line, and now Ⓑ is looking in the wrong direction.

Action
Axis Line

Figure 14-2:
Shot #3 crossing the line shows incorrect actor screen direction.

Taking Your Best Shot

The camera never blinks. That's what cuts (changing from one shot to another shot) are for. But to cut from one shot to another, you have to vary your shots by size and angle so that you don't end up with a *jump-cut,* which would appear as if the shot were missing some frames (see Chapter 15 for more on film editing). Shot compositions, sizes, and angles enhance how you tell your story. You may want a close-up when two actors are talking if the conversation is an intimate one. A wide establishing shot may be appropriate if you want to show that the actors are surrounded by a barren wasteland. A great book to study composition of shots is *The Five C's of Cinematography,* by Joseph V. Mascelli (published by Siles Press).

As a director, knowing at least the basics of the camera and lenses is advantageous. You should hire someone who is skilled in shooting video and/or film if you want your production to look professional. The cinematographer's job is to be educated about lenses, exposures, and how the camera functions (see Chapter 10), but you'll be better able to convey your story visually if you have a sense of what the camera can do.

Each cinematographer and director has a slightly different definition of framing and shot sizes, but the definitions are similar enough to warrant the following list of traditional shots, explained in the following sections:

- ✔ Wide shot (which can also work as an establishing shot)
- ✔ Medium shot
- ✔ Two shot
- ✔ Close-up

Where the heck are we? Establishing a wide shot

A *wide shot* (WS) reveals where the scene is taking place. Also referred to as a *long shot* or *master shot,* a wide shot helps orient the audience. A wide shot also gives the actors room to move within a shot, without the camera having to follow them. Medium shots and close-ups (explained later in this chapter) are often cut into a wide shot for variation.

An *establishing shot* is a type of wide shot that can establish a building before the camera cuts to an interior office. Figure 14-3 shows a wide shot from my film *Undercover Angel* in TV format (close to the dimensions of a square) and a wide shot from my film *The Random Factor* in the wider theatrical format that is an oblong rectangular frame size.

Figure 14-3:
A wide shot in TV standard format size (left) and an establishing shot in theatrical format frame size (right).

Photo of Dean Winters and Emily Mae Young in Undercover Angel, *courtesy of Sunland Studios/Stellar Entertainment*
Photo of Andrew Divoff and William Richert in The Random Factor, *courtesy of Showbuzz and Gloria Everett*

You don't have to be a psychic to get a medium shot

A *medium shot* (MS) is a standard shot that usually shows a character from belly button to slightly above the actor's head. A medium shot is more intimate than a wide shot, but provides more breathing space for the actor than a close-up. It's also used when you have an actor holding something in the frame or elaborating with his hands. Figure 14-4 shows a medium shot from my film *Undercover Angel*.

Two shot: Three's a crowd

A *two shot* can either be a form of a medium shot that has two actors standing or sitting next to each other or an over-the-shoulder shot where one actor's back or profile is closer to the camera than the other actor facing the camera. A two shot can save time and money when you have a dialogue scene between two actors by having them both in the frame as they carry on their conversation. The audience diverts their attention to each actor as he or she speaks, instead of having the camera cut to individual shots of each actor speaking. A two-shot is also effective when two characters are walking and talking side by side. Figure 14-5 shows a two shot from *Undercover Angel*.

Figure 14-4:
A medium
shot.

Photo of Dean Winters in Undercover Angel, *courtesy of Sunland Studios/Stellar Entertainment (UA photos by Bill Grimshaw)*

Figure 14-5:
A two shot.

Photo of Dean Winters and Yasmine Bleeth in Undercover Angel, *courtesy of Sunland Studios/Stellar Entertainment*

I'm ready for my close-up

A *close-up shot* (CU), or *single,* is usually from above a person's chest or the nape of her neck to just slightly above the top of her head. If you get in closer, so that the actor's head fills most of the frame, you have a *tight close-up.* Going in even tighter, to a person's eyes or mouth, gives you an *extreme close-up.* Close-ups create a sense of intimacy and the feeling that you're involved in the scene. They also reveal emotion in the eyes or the hint of a smile. Figure 14-6 shows both a close-up and a tight close-up.

The director often chooses a close-up to emphasize the intensity of a scene. Emotional or sensitive dialogue is often shot in a tight close-up to emphasize the importance of what's being said.

Figure 14-6:
A loose
close-up
(left) and
a tighter
close-up
(right).
Notice the
breathing
room to the
left of the
actors.

James Earl Jones in Undercover Angel, *courtesy of Sunland Studios/Stellar Entertainment (photo by Bill Grimshaw)*
Crystal Owens in Turn of the Blade, *courtesy of Northstar Entertainment*

When framing an actor in a close-up, give him some *breathing room.* Breathing room puts more space in front of the actor's face in the direction he's looking or talking than behind him. If you don't allow this space, the shot will have a claustrophobic feel to it. Also, never center a head in the middle of the frame unless it's a news reporter talking into the camera. Centering someone in the middle of the frame creates an awkward composition and creates an off-balance feeling to the shot.

Teeter-tottering angles: Are you high or low?

A *high angle* is usually shot using a crane, standing on a hill, or looking out a window of a high-rise to get an angle looking down. When you shoot from a high angle, your subjects look smaller and therefore insignificant.

In contrast, you shoot a *low angle* from below your subject's height — as low as the ground (or lower if you dig yourself a hole). Low angles tend to make subjects look bigger and more powerful. A character appears intimidating if you use a low-angle shot. Figure 14-7 shows an example of each type.

Here's an inexpensive way to get a low-angle shot from the ground: Get one of those beanbag pillows and lay your camera on it. Shape the pillow to cradle your camera safely and align it so that the shot isn't crooked (unless you want it to be).

Figure 14-7:
High-angle shots make subjects look smaller and less significant (left). Low-angle shots make subjects look more imposing (right).

I'm high on you: The God shot

In a *God shot,* the camera looks straight down on a scene, symbolizing God's point of view looking down on his creation — also showing the audience the big picture. This can be an interior shot or a very effective exterior shot from the sky. It is often used in films to remind us that a central character is human and sometimes insignificant. The God shot was used effectively in *The Truman Show* to symbolize the God complex of Christof who created and directed the ultimate reality show documenting the real life of Burbank Truman and televising his personal life unfolding in front of the entire world.

To accomplish a God shot, you need a camera crane. A cheaper way to go is to shoot looking down from a tall structure.

Finding the director's viewfinder

Kish Optics makes the Personal Director's Finder, a precision viewfinder that enables you to see the world through the eyes of a lens. The Director's Finder has built-in interchangeable aspect ratios that you can resize with a simple twist (for framing standard TV or HDTV and theatrical-screen shots). The finder allows you to "see" through different size lenses that a film or video camera uses without having to carry a camera around with you. These finders are light enough to hang around your neck or keep in a handbag. Check out www.kishoptics.com for other types of finders, including the Ultimate, the Ultimate16, and the MiniFinder.

Picture This: Deciding When to Move the Camera and Why

Fred Astaire said that if he didn't dance in a scene, the camera should. Keeping motion in a shot is like choreography for the camera. If you stand still too long and your camera remains static, your audience gets restless. It's as if you're having a stare-down with the image because the camera never blinks. A moving camera, however, brings energy to the scene. So, when you have a good reason to move the camera, let it dance! It's appropriate to move the camera when

- ✔ Following a character
- ✔ Revealing something
- ✔ Emphasizing a character's reaction
- ✔ Underlining a dramatic effect
- ✔ Creating a sense of chaos or excitement

An actor's actions should motivate the camera. Start to move the camera at the same time the actor moves to create seamless camera motion.

Playing with dollies

A camera that needs to be moved is placed on a *dolly* so that the motion is fluid and doesn't bump around. You can rent a professional dolly with a hydraulic stand that acts as a motion tripod, or you can make your own by fitting a flat board with rugged wheels. Put a tripod on the board, and you have yourself a dolly. I use a Bogen Manfrotto tripod (www.bogenphoto.com), which I secure to the dolly. It's a lightweight but sturdy tripod that has a great fluid head for effortless panning and tilting of the camera.

If you're working on an uneven surface, you need to lay down *dolly tracks*. You can rent them with the dolly, or you can put down boards or mats on the ground to create a smooth surface for the dolly wheels to roll over. ProMax Systems (www.promax.com) makes a lightweight tracking dolly with super-smooth dolling motion. The package comes with 15 feet of track that breaks down into 5-foot sections for travel or storage. It's priced at $399.

If you can't afford a dolly, borrow a wheelchair. Sit in the wheelchair with the camera (get one of those beanbag pillows to rest the camera on to absorb the shock) and have someone push you for a smooth dolly shot.

I once needed a shot that moved in over a conference table during a scene of the boss talking to his board members. I wanted the camera to move toward the boss at the head of the table. We put the camera on an inexpensive skateboard and slowly moved it over the surface of the table toward the actor. It was one of the smoothest shots in the film!

Craning to get a high shot

A camera *crane* allows you to raise or lower ("boom") the camera while filming to get a more dramatic shot. ProMax Systems makes a series of cranes that includes the *CobraCrane*, a 5-foot crane (it can reach up to 9 feet in the air, depending on the height of your tripod). The CobraCrane uses a cable-and-pulley system with roller bearings, allowing you to tilt the camera for extremely smooth angles in all directions. Check out the CobraCrane, which starts at $399, at www.promax.com.

When shooting from a crane, you need to be able to view the shot so that you can manipulate it properly. Otherwise, you could end up with something that's unusable (at worst) or not quite what you wanted (at best). When shooting video or to digital files using a crane, you need to run a video cable from the camera to a TV monitor. If you're using a film camera, then you need to have a *video assist* unit (see Chapter 10 for more information on video assist). I use a portable LCD mini flat screen to watch and play back the crane footage. You also need a set of free weights (from a sporting goods store) to counterbalance the crane to keep your camera in the air, kind of like a teeter-totter.

Steadying the camera

A camera steadying device attaches to your body (or the cinematographer's) with a harness and turns the camera into a fluid floating machine. Think of it as a shock absorber for the camera. The brand commonly used in Hollywood is called a *Steadicam,* made by the Tiffen Company (www.tiffen.com). Instead of laying down dolly tracks, the camera operator just walks with the camera "floating" in the Steadicam harness. A Steadicam is great for walking and talking shots with your actors. Tiffen also makes the Steadicam Merlin (at $849) for camcorders weighing up to five pounds.

ProMax puts out the impressive Steadytracker that works for video camcorders. It balances the camera, giving it weightlessness and the appearance that it's effortlessly gliding through your shots. You can purchase a Steadytracker starting at $199 at www.promax.com.

I discovered an interesting new device called the DvRigPro. It's an advanced shock absorbing shoulder mount for the camera. It works very similar to the Steadicam but is less bulky, simpler in design, and less expensive. It costs around $485. You can get more info at www.dvtec.tv.

Bogen puts out the Fig Rig, which resembles a steering wheel (at $317); see Figure 14-8. You can attach small lights, microphone, and even a camera remote conveniently on the handle for turning the camera on and off and controlling the zoom. Steer yourself to Bogen's website at www.bogen imaging.com.

Figure 14-8:
The author using the Fig Rig on set.

Part IV
Finishing Your Film in Post

In this part . . .

Welcome to the world of postproduction. Editing a film has become easier and less expensive over the last few years as filmmaking has entered the digital computer age — this is a marriage that will last forever. You discover in this part that you can edit your film like the big studios do, right on your desktop computer.

Postproduction audio, such as sound effects and musical compositions, is an important element for making your film sizzle with great sound. Special visual effects have been greatly influenced by the computer age, but with some ingenuity, you can still create some incredible effects with the camera without exploding your budget. In this part, I also discuss the title of your film and the proper credit recognition for all the cast, crew, and contacts who help bring your film to fruition.

Chapter 15

Cut to: Editing Your Film Frame by Frame

. . . .

In This Chapter

▶ Working in a linear or non-linear environment

▶ Editing your film on a computer

▶ Cutting creatively

▶ Burning your finished film into the digital domain

. . . .

After you've shot your film, you're ready to *cut* (edit) it together. You can edit your film on your computer and do it affordably. In this chapter, I introduce you to the various software programs that enable you to cut your film without leaving your desk.

In this chapter, you also see how the worlds of linear and non-linear editing work and discover the secrets to cutting your picture for the optimum effect — by controlling the story, changing the sequence of events, and playing with time. Sound editing is also important when cutting together dialogue, sound effects, and music; so you see (and hear) all about that, too. I also introduce you to the duties of your film laboratory and show you how to *develop* a great relationship.

Editing Your Film: Putting One Frame in Front of the Other

Editing is more than just piecing together shots into scenes. Understanding the story and the best way to tell it is an art. Editing controls the feel of your film and can make or break the illusion. To edit well, you need to know on what frame to start your scene and on what frame to end it, when to cut to the *reaction shot* (a visual response from another actor in the scene), and when to stay on the main character.

Some of the elements you need to consider when editing are

- ✔ **Pacing:** The length of shots and scenes gives the entire film a pace — a feeling of moving fast or slow. You don't want the film to lag.

- ✔ **Scene length:** Keep scenes under three minutes, if possible, so that they don't drag on and seem monotonous.

- ✔ **Order of shots and scenes:** By arranging your shots in a particular sequence, you can dramatically affect a scene's meaning. See the later section "Linear versus Non-Linear Editing" for details.

- ✔ **Cutting on action:** Most shots cut (or edit) better on action. If your actor is picking up a coffee cup, have him or her repeat the action while you film it from different angles or shot sizes (such as a close-up or a wide shot). You then can overlap the shots as you cut on the motion. This is also called _matching,_ and it helps hide the cut, making the transition appear seamless.

- ✔ **Matching shots:** You want to join static shots with static shots, and moving shots next to other moving shots. If you have a fast-paced car-chase scene and the camera is moving wildly to follow the action, a sudden static shot of a car sitting quietly at a stop light will be jarring. (Of course, that may be the effect you want.)

- ✔ **Varying the angle and size of shots:** A _jump-cut_ happens when shots that are too similar in appearance are cut together, making the picture look as if it has jumped, or that the actor has popped from one spot to another. In order to avoid a jump-cut, you need to vary the angle and size of the next shot. One way to avoid a jump-cut is to shoot a cutaway of an actor's reaction or of a significant object on set that you can use to tie two different shots together. An appropriate cutaway can often save the day.

- ✔ **Showing simultaneous action:** You can cut back and forth between scenes happening at the same time. This is called _cross-cutting._ Or you can make a _parallel cut,_ which is showing the simultaneous action with a split screen. This is often done on the TV show _24._

- ✔ **Choosing the best take (or combining the best of several takes):** You shoot several takes of a particular scene so that you have a choice in the editing room. Obviously, the more takes you have, the more choices. You can also combine parts of various takes — the beginning of one take, and the end of another, for example, if you have a cutaway to insert between them — to create the effect you want.

Choosing an editor: Who cut this?

You need to decide whether you're going to edit the film yourself or get a fresh pair of eyes to do it for you. Many directors avoid editing their films because they're too close to the material and want to bring another perspective to the story. That's why, on a big studio film, a picture editor starts assembling your shots and scenes together as you're shooting, and a sound editor edits the dialogue and other sound elements.

You can place an ad seeking an editor in the classified section of many film and trade magazines like *Backstage* (www.backstage.com) or search online at www.crewnet.com for an editor near you. Look for someone who has at least a few films under his belt and ask to see a sample of his work — does he cut scenes tight so they don't lag? But if you're on a small production, you're probably your own editor. You're in good company, though. Robert Rodriguez *(El Mariachi* and *Spy Kids)* prefers to cut his own films. For more on hiring an editor for your team, check out Chapter 7.

One of the advantages of hiring an editor is that he or she can start assembling what you've shot immediately after the first day on the set. This means that your editor can tell you while you're filming whether you need extra footage: a *cutaway* (a reaction shot or something that helps piece two other shots together seamlessly) to make a scene work better, a close-up of some person or object, or an *establishing shot* (a wide shot of the location that orientates the audience to where the scene is taking place).

Shooting enough coverage

You need to shoot enough *coverage* so that you have plenty of different takes and interesting angles to choose from. Every time you add another angle to a scene, you make it more interesting and less monotonous. Using just one shot in a two-minute scene is like having a stare-down — and that's just dull and annoying (unless it's a bet to see who wins). The camera never blinks — that's what cutting is for. Cutting is like blinking from one shot to the next. When you watch a play, you don't stare at the stage as a whole the entire time; you concentrate on the individual actors as they speak, or on a prop or action sequence that catches your attention.

If you don't have time to shoot several angles, then create movement in the shot, such as having the camera follow or lead your actors as they're walking and talking.

Some directors shoot a ratio of three takes to get one shot (3:1), and some shoot ten or more. The editor's job is to find the best take or to combine the best of two takes with a cutaway. As you start to piece the film together, it magically begins to take on a shape of its own, and the story starts to make sense.

Assembling a first cut

The first step is piecing together what is called an *assembly cut, rough cut,* or *first cut.* This is the most basic cut possible, showing the story in continuity (because often the scenes are shot out of order, out of continuity).

Editing the picture of your film is very similar to writing a screenplay. The first assembly of footage is like the first rough draft, putting things into perspective and giving you a feel for your film. After you have your basic cut, you start shaping, trimming, and cutting until your piece feels complete. Like dancing, there's a rhythm to cutting — it flows, and everything feels like it's falling into place.

Don't be discouraged if the first cut doesn't excite you. The pacing may seem too slow, the performances may appear dull. I've often been disappointed with a first cut. After your first cut, you start to get a sense of how to tighten up the picture. You start to cut out long boring exits to the door, pauses that are too long between lines, or a scene that isn't working and that won't be missed if you cut it out entirely. You need to do a lot of shaping and adjusting before your masterpiece shines through. It's like molding something out of clay — you have to keep chipping away until you like what you see.

Building a director's cut

The director's contract usually stipulates whether he gets to make sure his vision is followed in the editing room by approving the final cut of the film. This final, director-approved cut is called a *director's cut.* The director usually views an assembly, or first, cut (scenes assembled loosely in continuity according to the screenplay; see the preceding section) by the picture editor. The director then gives the editor suggestions on where to place specific shots, close-ups, and establishing shots; how to change the order of things; how to tighten a scene; and so on.

Usually, a director gets a director's cut based on his clout in the industry. Ultimately, the studio has the final say in the cutting of a picture if the director doesn't contractually have final cut. Steven Spielberg always gets final say because he's earned that honor and proven himself to know what works and what doesn't. George Lucas always has the final cut because he doesn't report to anyone but himself! With the release of most films on DVD now, many directors who didn't have the clout to get a director's cut theatrically in their studio contract, now have the opportunity to get a director's cut featured as one of the bonuses on the DVD.

The cutting-room floor

Many actors in Hollywood have unfortunately only made the *cutting-room floor*. This expression started in the days when editors physically cut film and literally threw the discarded scenes on the editing-room floor. Today, very few film scenes are discarded entirely. Instead, these unused scenes are saved on a computer hard drive and often incorporated into the bonus section of the film's DVD release (including outtake flubs by the actors).

Photo finish: Finalizing a final cut

Many times a studio screens a version of the film to a *test audience* (a group of people paid to watch and rate the film). The audience members take notes, and the studio (or the director, if she has final cut) evaluates all the comments on the picture and may re-edit accordingly.

After all the editing is finished and approved, you create the final, *locked* picture approved by the studio — or by the director if he has the authority to make the final cut (which you probably do have if you're an independent director). Now the postproduction work on sound begins, and the composer can start timing the scenes that will be *scored* (set to music).

Listening to the sound editor

In addition to editing the picture on your film, you have to assemble and edit the sound elements. These elements are prepared by the sound editor, who is most often the picture editor and even the final postproduction sound mixer on an independent film. The sound elements are put onto separate audio channels (called *tracks*) and then mixed down into a final soundtrack that combines all channels mixed together. Some of those edited sound elements include

- Dialogue (may have separate dialogue tracks for each actor)
- Sound effects (can have unlimited sound-effects tracks)
- Music (usually one or two tracks for music)
- Ambience (background sounds like birds chirping, an air-conditioner humming, ocean waves crashing, and so on)

Flatlining the flatbed and moviola

Not too long ago, editors would cut their films by actually handling the film itself and physically cutting it, where necessary. They would trim the celluloid and glue or tape the scenes together on a moviola or flatbed, which would run the film at the proper speed to see what the final results looked like, and how the picture timed out.

A *moviola* is an upright editing system that resembles a projector. The actual film is projected into a viewer as it spools onto a top reel. The picture editor physically cuts the film into individual shots and hangs the film strips in a

bin for reassembling. A *flatbed* editing system works similar to the moviola, but instead of being vertical, it's a horizontal table with the film reels lying on the surface.

Although physically cutting the film is considered non-linear editing because the individual shots and scenes are rearranged like individual blocks, the process isn't nearly as quick and effective as rearranging the clips digitally on a non-linear editing system. Editing on a moviola or a flatbed has pretty much been replaced by digital non-linear editing on a computer.

Dialogue editing is as important as your picture edit. The sound editor has a variety of elements to consider, such as overlapping conversations or starting a character's dialogue over the end of another character's shot. Check out Chapter 16 for more on dialogue and sound editing.

Linear versus Non-Linear Editing

Imagine that you've sorted through a set of your recent vacation photos and slipped them into a photo album, one picture per page. You just created a sequential order to your sightseeing photos. But say your mood changes or you decide that the picture of the huge fish you caught looks much better facing the photo of Uncle Bob's minnow, even though he caught it several days before your catch and before the trip to Disney World. No problem. You can just slide the photos out of their pockets and rearrange them. This is non-linear organization. Of course, if the photos are glued into the pockets, you can't rearrange them. They're now treated together as a whole, and not as individual shots — they're stuck in a linear world and can't be rearranged.

Editing in linear

Linear editing means that you assemble your shots one after another in consecutive order. Linear editing takes longer than the alternative (non-linear editing, explained in the next section).

The only time you *have* to edit linearly is if you edit directly onto videotape. A video deck, used as a *player,* allows you to transfer footage to a video *recorder* deck that puts one shot at the end of another shot. Videotape can't be cut physically, so if you want to remove or add just one shot somewhere in the middle of your edits, you have to start over again.

Editing in non-linear

Digital non-linear editing, first pioneered by George Lucas's Editroid system, has opened a new world for the editor. A single editor can now quickly experiment with different variations of a picture that would otherwise have taken a dozen editors many hours, or days, to perform.

In *non-linear editing,* each shot, and each scene, is its own separate compartment and can be moved around in any order within your film. Even the opening scene can easily be moved to the end in the editing room. Non-linear editing is easier and quicker; it also allows you to be more creative than linear editing does.

Sometimes the order of your shots is dictated by the obvious — like the order of events when getting dressed: You put on your underwear first and your pants second — at least I hope you do. But if you rearrange the order of shots or events, you can change the psychology of your scene. For example, here are three shots in a particular order in your film:

1. A baby crying

2. The family cat hanging from the ceiling fan

3. A baby laughing

If you start with the baby crying, then in this order, the effect is the cat has stopped the baby from crying, and the child is now amused. Now see what happens when you change the order:

1. A baby laughing

2. The family cat hanging from the ceiling fan

3. A baby crying

Having the baby laughing at the beginning and crying at the end creates the effect that the child is now frightened for (or of) the animal. Quentin Tarantino put the ending of his film, *Pulp Fiction,* at the beginning of the film, and let the story progress until it picked up the beginning at the ending.

When you shoot footage with your camera, you're shooting in a linear fashion. For example, if you're filming the birth of a baby, everything you film shows the birthing process in order. But if you go into the editing room and decide to edit in non-linear, you can change the order of real time and have the baby go back to the mother's womb (go to your womb!). With digital technology, you can shoot in linear fashion and cut in non-linear style.

Editing on Your Computer

The same computer on which you write letters, organize your bank account, surf the Internet, and maybe even write your script can now easily be turned into a powerful editing machine. Most computers, both PC and Apple computers, are able to edit a film in a non-linear environment and are limited only by the size of their hard drives (but unlimited when using external hard drives).

In non-linear editing, you take all your separate shots, arrange them in any order, and then play them consecutively to form a scene. Every frame has its own individual set of *time-code numbers* (numbers generated electronically on the video image or in a computer) or *edge-code numbers* (numbers printed on the actual film stock) that pinpoint its exact starting and ending frames. Computer software can then generate an *edit list* that accurately contains the hour, minutes, seconds, and frames of your shots and identifies each cut made by the editor. With the right editing software, you have the capability to edit your film without leaving your computer. (For technical tips on setting up your own editing studio, check out *Digital Video For Dummies* by Keith Underdahl, published by Wiley.)

You can also purchase third-party software programs to perform additional functions like special effects, mattes, and process video or digital footage to look more like motion picture film. (See "Simulating cinema with software" later in this chapter. Also see Chapter 17 for more on software used for special effects in the postproduction phase.)

Hard driving

Your computer hard drive stores all your picture information. Because you'll probably need more hard drive space than the amount that's in your internal hard drive, you may want to purchase an external hard drive. An external hard drive is often compact — about the size of a paperback novel or hardcover book (or larger depending on the storage size of the drive). Iomega (www.iomega.com), which makes the popular Zip drives and discs, also makes slick-looking, dependable external hard drives that plug into your computer. Seagate makes a line of hard drives called Maxtor (www.maxtor.com), which are extremely reliable and easy to set up. The Maxtor OneTouch Mini with 250 gigabytes is about the size of a deck of cards! External hard drives connect to your computer via USB cables, or *firewire* for speedy data transfer.

Most external hard drives come with setup software and usually work for both PC and Mac platforms. When set on *standard broadcast-quality* in your computer (the highest quality picture for television broadcast), you can capture anywhere from five to ten minutes of standard digital footage per gigabyte of hard drive space. Therefore, an 80GB drive lets you hold up to 13 hours of footage. If you're capturing high definition (depending on the compression), it can equate to around one gig per minute (or less) — so an 80GB drive in high def can give you up 80 minutes. (I have a one terabyte also known as 1TB — 1,000 gigabytes — drive from Maxtor.)

Cutting it with editing software

Without software, a computer has no personality. Add film-editing software, and it becomes a complete postproduction editing suite within the confines of your desk space. You can choose from a myriad of editing software that allow you to affordably edit your film or video footage in a non-linear environment. Many computers even come with free editing software.

Most software-editing programs use these basic components of non-linear editing:

- A bin to hold your individual shots
- A timeline that allows you to assemble your shots in any order (It resembles storyboard panels — see Chapter 9)
- A main window that plays back your edited footage
- Titling and transition options

Wired for firewire

Firewire is a digital connection (a special cable) that transfers the information from your digital camcorder to your computer, to an external hard drive, or to other equipment with no degradation in picture quality. Most computers now have firewire inputs so that you can plug your camcorder directly into them and transfer your footage. The data speed transfer of firewire comes in two speeds: 400 MBPS (megabytes per second) and 800 MBPS (which is twice as fast). The higher the MBPS, the faster the data transfer — which is a good thing if you get impatient easily.

Firewire external hard drives are able to move information faster than USB drives (which transfer data at least 30 times slower than firewire) and are almost a necessity when editing large project files.

Most editing software now accepts not only standard quality footage, but high definition footage as well.

iMovie

Many Apple computers come with iMovie, a simple-to-use, non-linear editing software that allows you to cut your movie on your computer (see Figure 15-1). Check out *Digital Video For Dummies* by Keith Underdahl (published by Wiley), which guides you through the steps of using this effective and easy-to-use software to edit your projects.

Figure 15-1: The iMovie 8 editing software program and its functions.

iMovie screenshot reprinted by permission of Apple Computer, Inc.

An Avid Fan

Avid, a name synonymous with non-linear editing, makes Avid Media Composer software, which works with Mac or PC platforms and accommodates SD and HD formats. Many studio feature films have been edited using Avid software to cut picture and sound. Media Composer is more sophisticated than other lower-priced editing software, and with a price under $2,300, you can't beat the professional editing it lets you perform. The software includes audio tools for post sound. It also includes titling and graphics, along with a variety of real-time effects. You can get more details on Media Composer at www.avid.com.

Becoming a Pro with Final Cut

Final Cut Studio 2, available for Apple computers for under $1,300, is a professional and powerful non-linear software program for cutting picture and audio. It's much more sophisticated than iMovie or some of the other non-linear software, and it can produce some amazing results, including titles, effects, and transitions. The Studio 2 package consists of Final Cut Pro (editing program); Color (color correction); Motion (3D graphics and animation); Soundtrack Pro (post soundtrack mixing for finalizing audio), which includes an extensive sound effects and music library; Compressor, which lets you format your final product for delivery in broadcast standard or high definition; and DVD Studio Pro, which allows you to author and burn DVDs of your final product with sophisticated DVD menus (check it out at www.apple.com/finalcutstudio).

Apple has also come out with Final Cut Express, a less expensive, simpler and easier-to-use version of Final Cut Pro, for $199. This is a perfect non-linear editing software for the novice independent filmmaker. The software also works with standard and high definition footage and includes enhanced audio controls. Also check out *Final Cut Pro HD For Dummies* (Wiley) for helpful tips on using this phenomenal software.

Premiering Adobe

Adobe makes popular software programs for the editing world: Adobe Premiere Pro for picture and sound editing (priced at $799), which includes an audio mixer for professional soundtrack results, and After Effects (at $999), which is kind of like Photoshop, but with motion. Check out Adobe's products at www.adobe.com. The software is standard and high definition ready.

Jumping back with the Editor's Tool Kit

Digital Juice puts out The Editor's Tool Kit Pro (starting at $249 for each volume), an invaluable tool for creating titles and credits. Each of the five sets provide seamless animated backgrounds and lower thirds on DVD-ROM discs (where you key in titles and credits), along with royalty-free graphics and animations in standard and high definition. You also get a myriad of fonts to choose from for your credits and titling needs. This is a great tool for any editor!

Digital Juice also puts out Jump Backs (starting at $69 per volume), which provides lively animated motion backgrounds that can be looped seamlessly (repeated without a definitive end to the footage) to enhance any video or film project in the editing room (see Chapter 18). Jump Backs comes on DVD ROM with Juicer software, which lets you process the animations on any computer. Jump Backs is available in standard and high definition formats. Digital Juice also puts out Swipes and Particle Illusion, which can add some cool magic to your productions. To discover more about all these great Digital Juice products, go to www.digitaljuice.com.

Simulating cinema with software

Many independent filmmakers desperately want to make a movie that looks like it was shot on 35mm film — but they can't afford the expense that comes with shooting on motion picture film stock. There are now software programs that will process your video or digital footage in the postproduction phase and create the illusion that you shot on 35mm film. These programs emulate the characteristics associated with the look of film stock, such as grain, softness, subtle flutter, and saturated colors. The software also pulls down the equivalent 30-frame video footage to emulate the 24 standard frames used with motion picture film cameras.

Magic Bullet Frames and Magic Bullet Looks by Red Giant Software (www. redgiantsoftware.com) gives your harsh-looking video or digitally captured footage the soft romantic look of 35mm film. This third-party film-simulation software works with most editing programs, such as Final Cut Pro, Adobe Premiere, and Media Composer.

Red Giant Software also makes a product called Instant HD. It takes your standard quality footage, up-rezzes it, and converts it to look like you shot in sharp high definition. The software is only $99. For more info, go to www. redgiantsoftware.com.

Posting your production in your computer

After you finish editing all the dialogue and picture elements for your movie in your computer, you're ready to marry your picture and sound together. If the final production is going to television and DVD distribution (and not a theatrical release), then you can continue to do most of your final preparations in the computer (color correcting, titles, and so on). If you plan on getting a theatrical release for your picture, then you'll be working further with your film laboratory to prepare the appropriate film elements for a theatrical release (see the section "Developing a Relationship with Your Film Lab" for details.).

Outputting formats

Once you've completed your final cut, you then have to figure out how you're going to get your movie out of your computer. There's a variety of ways to output your film. One way is to make a QuickTime file. This file can be exported to an external hard drive or onto a standard DVD or Blu-ray disc (depending on the size of the file). A small QuickTime file can even be uploaded and showcased on YouTube (www.youtube.com) or MySpace (www.myspace.com).

If you want to export your edited movie from your computer directly to analog or digital tape, including digibeta, then you have several options. AJA makes a line of Kona video cards (containing circuit boards) that you have to physically install into your computer. On one end of the card is a variety of different patch cords, giving you many choices to transfer your edited project out to different tape formats. Another option is the Io HD from AJA. The Io HD is a separate device that simply plugs into your computer's firewire port, saving you the time and hassle of having to install a video card, and it's the easiest way for outputting your edited projects. The great thing is the Io HD works with portable laptops as well. Check out the AJA products at www.aja.com. If you don't have an AJA card or other device to export your QuickTime file out of your computer, you can take that QuickTime file to a professional post-production facility and have the people there transfer the QuickTime file to digital videotape for you.

If you've ever had the challenge of trying to send a digital file to someone via email but the file was too big, here's a little secret: Check out www.you sendit.com. This site allows you to upload and download files. The cost? Files up to two gigabytes are $9.99 a month; files up to 100mb are free!

Developing a Relationship with Your Film Lab

If you're working with actual film celluloid, you need a film laboratory. You can find a film laboratory in the Yellow Pages or by surfing the Internet under "Film Laboratories" or "Motion Picture Film Services." If your town doesn't have a film lab, you may want to call a laboratory in Los Angeles or New York. In L.A., try Deluxe Labs (www.bydeluxe.com) or Technicolor (www.technicolor.com). In New York, try Colorlab (www.colorlab.com) or DuArt Film and Video (www.duart.com) and arrange to have your film shipped for developing. When I shot my film *Undercover Angel* in Ottawa, Ontario, I shipped my film by bus to Deluxe Laboratories in Toronto. The lab developed my film stock and shipped back the *dailies* (see the next section "Developing negatives, producing prints, and more") by overnight express.

A good relationship with your lab ensures that the services it performs — including developing your film negative; transferring your film to videotape, DVDs, or hard drives (for dailies as well as the final product for TV and DVD release); transferring your movie shot on videotape or digital files to film stock (for a theatrical release); and printing your film — are performed properly and on a timely basis. Also, don't be afraid to negotiate for the best price you can. Laboratories often give discounts to first-time or independent filmmakers. All you have to do is ask!

Film labs offer the services and equipment outlined in the following sections.

If you're working solely with digital and/or videotape, you don't need the services of a film lab. At some point, you may need a master digital video tape and/or DVD or video dubs of your final movie; if you don't do this yourself, you can have it done at a duplicating or postproduction transfer house, as explained in the later sections "Cloning, Not Copying; Cloning, Not Copying."

Developing negatives, producing prints, and more

If you shoot on film and then edit in your computer, you need the services of a film lab to develop your film negative and then transfer that footage to digital media (DVDs or hard drive) so you can then input that footage into your computer that contains your editing software.

If you shoot your movie on film or on digital with plans for a possible 35mm theatrical release, the film lab will develop your film negative and make a separate film print — good if you're cutting the actual film or going for a theatrical release. The process is similar to the developing process of still photos in which the negatives are developed to make photo prints.

If you're going directly to TV or DVD distribution, you can skip the process of printing your film stock and actually turn your developed negative into a positive image in the telecine stage. *Telecine* is the procedure of transferring your 16mm or 35mm film stock footage directly onto videotape or digital files. Nowadays most film labs have telecine bays (or work closely with companies that do) where you can transfer your developed film footage to videotape or digital files. In telecine, you can play with the colors, correct the exposure, and do lots of other picture enhancements, as well.

Dailies consist of the footage that you shot the day before, which has already been developed by the lab. If you're shooting with a camcorder, your results are immediate, and you have no dailies to speak of — you just rewind the tape or click on the appropriate digital file and watch what you've shot.

Being positive about a negative cutter

If you originally shot on motion picture film, cutting the film negative is one of the last steps before you're ready to make prints of your film for theatrical distribution. The negative cutter follows your *edit decision list* (EDL), which is an electronic printout of numbers that relate to each edit if your movie was cut on a non-linear system, or the actual edge-code numbers printed on your *film work-print* (a print of your film that can be handled) if you're physically cutting the actual celluloid film.

The EDL on computer disc can also instruct a computer in a professional postproduction editing bay to assemble your project into a final edited production onto videotape or a digital file. It finds the shots that are to be edited together and matches up the correct numbers at the end of one cut and the numbers assigned to the new cut. (This is usually done in a professional editing bay if you off-lined your movie on your computer in a lower picture resolution — possibly because you didn't have the hard drive space to do higher picture resolution — especially if you shot it in HD.)

The best place to find a negative cutter is through your film laboratory's recommendation. You want a good negative cutter who will delicately cut your film negative, keeping it safe from dust and scratches.

Color-correcting your film: As plain as black and white

Before you make your final film print, your film footage has to be color-corrected scene by scene so that the shots match perfectly. For example, when you're shooting outside, the sun is constantly moving and changing the color temperature of your footage (see Chapter 11 for color temperature info). One shot may not match a previous shot because the tint is slightly different.

You may want to enhance the color of your scenes, such as make your skies bluer or add more saturation of colors to your footage that requires shot-by-shot adjustment. If you're making a Western or period piece, you may want to pull out some of the color or infuse a sepia tone into the entire production.

When color-correcting the actual film negative, a machine called a *hazeltine* or *color analyzer* calibrates the settings of color correction and exposures, which the printing department follows. Your negative footage appears on a monitor showing how the positive picture and color will look when projected on the screen. The person working for the lab who corrects the color is called the *timer.* If you color-correct your film for video or TV release, the color corrector is called a *telecine operator* or *colorist.*

If you're editing your film or video on a non-linear system in your computer, you can also control and correct the image color with the editing software or with a third-party software. Video doesn't require as extensive color-correcting as film stock because you can do the adjustments in the camera and see the results immediately. The correction that you make in the postproduction stage is usually to enhance the image colors or to change them completely for effect.

Answering your first film print

After your negative cutter puts together your final negative cut (if you're planning a theatrical release) and your color corrections have been made, the film lab develops the first positive print of your film which is called an *answer print.* You usually get to screen the film in one of the lab's screening rooms to check the picture for proper exposure and color correction. You make a note of any adjustments and send the notes to the lab to correct.

After you accept the adjustments to the answer print, you then make your final *composite,* which contains the picture and sound together. You're now ready to make theatrical prints for your distributor or to send to the theaters, depending on your distribution plan (see Chapter 19). This process is used only if your film is going to be screened in movie theaters.

Cloning, Not Copying;
Cloning, Not Copying

In the past, making a *dub* (copy) of your VHS tape (now an archaic format) was as simple as taping from one machine to another or taking the tape to a video-dubbing company (which makes dubs in quantity at one time). But the dub never looked as good as the original. It was always grainy and softer in focus — kind of like a photocopy of a photocopy that gets more and more fuzzy. But now, when you make a copy from a digital tape to another digital tape or to a DVD, you're making an exact duplicate of the original material. You're actually making a *clone* — a copy of the original with no degradation in picture quality. So the clone you send to people looks as good as the original footage.

Most film laboratories offer this service either in-house or through an affiliated company, but you can also do it on your own. Most PC and Mac computers make it easy for you to burn your own DVDs right on your computer. Apple software puts out iDVD and DVD Studio Pro, which let you create menus and chapters and put an entire film or project, up to two hours in length (longer if highly compressed or on a Blu-ray disc), on a DVD-R. MyDVD for the PC by Roxio retails for $49.99 and does all the DVD authoring you need (www.roxio.com).

DVD blank media discs have come down drastically in price over the years. You can get them as low as .20 cents each. Usually you buy them in bulk on spools of 50 or 100. If you have a DVD printing and duplicating machine, like the Primera Disc Publisher SE (www.Primera.com), shown in Figure 15-2, you can use printable DVD blank discs to print your own artwork directly on the disc after it burns your footage onto the DVD. I get my blank DVD discs from www.americal.com at a great price — and they can ship to you too.

Figure 15-2:
The Primera
Disc
Publisher
SE (prints
and burns
DVDs).

Courtesy Primera Technology, Inc.

You can make your own DVD labels with CD label kits and personalize your DVDs with a selected still photo printed on the CD label from your film.

If you don't have a DVD burner in your computer or you're still afraid of the technology of DVD burning, don't worry, DVD player/recorders have popped up on the market. Making DVD copies of your film is as easy as pushing the record button! These DVD player/recorders look like regular DVD players, but they can burn DVDs as easy as making a VHS dub. They have analog and firewire inputs (for true digital transferring with no picture loss). Some DVD recorders also have a VHS player in them that allows you to dub your old VHS tapes to DVD discs.

With the high definition wars behind us, Blu-ray has come out the victor (beating out the format called DVD HD). *Blu-ray* is a high definition DVD optical disc format that was developed to not only hold more digital information (more than 10 times that of regular DVD discs), but to also hold programs and movies at the highest HD quality available (more on this in Chapter 19 on distribution). The name Blu-ray derives from the blue laser light used to read this type of disc. All studio releases will be available on Blu-ray format now (in addition to regular DVD).

Interview with a studio head

I sat with Alan Horn, President & Chief Operating Officer, Warner Bros. Entertainment, one day for an interview. As president and COO, Horn is responsible for a variety of Warner Bros. business divisions, including its motion picture division, and has final green-light authority over all Warner Bros. movies that get made. "This process gives us consistent oversight of our films," he says. His successes include many box office and critically acclaimed hits such as the *Harry Potter* and *Batman* franchises, as well as Academy Award-winning films such as *Million Dollar Baby*, *Happy Feet*, and *The Departed*. A chess enthusiast, Horn makes use of these same skills — savvy calculation and strategic planning — in running the studio and releasing theatrical feature films successfully.

Horn has been in the industry for many years, having co-founded with his friend, director Rob Reiner, Castle Rock Entertainment in 1987 (which produced many successful films like *When Harry Met Sally. . . , City Slickers*, and *A Few Good Men*, as well as the hit TV series *Seinfeld*). I asked him how the industry has changed over the years.

Without hesitation, Horn said, "Technology — the technology that manifests itself in the production process — in the making of the movies and in the completion of the movies. The special effects technology now is stunningly good and it's seamless; the audience has come to expect first class technology. They expect to see a tiger and not be able to tell if the tiger's real or not." To make his point, he told me about a "little movie" the studio just did: *The Bucket List*, starring Jack Nicholson and Morgan Freeman and directed by Rob Reiner. "In the movie, these two characters travel all over the world, but the actors actually never went anywhere. So when we tell people, no, they didn't go to the Pyramids — it's such a shock. It's all green screen. It really is amazing what they can do nowadays." Horn laughingly recalled being

on the set of *300* and seeing "twenty buffed-out guys charging each other in an empty warehouse with a bunch of fake rocks!"

I asked Horn what he looked for in a screenplay. "The most important thing is a good story," Horn said. "I'd like to see a screenplay that is about something. It doesn't have to have a message in it, but it needs to have a good story. It's easy to get sidetracked by the spectacularity that exists in special effects and technology and lose the story to that." Horn continued, "It's always about the story. If it's supposed to be a comedy, then it ought to be funny; if it's a horror movie, it ought to be scary; if it's a dramatic movie, it ought to be dramatically compelling. If it isn't, you wind up with what I call a 'feathered fish,' which is just a little bit funny and a little bit dramatic and a little bit this and a little bit that — and I think you have a problem."

When asked about advice he'd give for filmmakers just starting out, Horn said, "Filmmakers need to understand and have a comfort with technology, but it's always back to basics. A filmmaker should find something about which he or she is passionate. Everything flows from passion. Mr. Shakespeare said many years ago, 'The play's the thing.' Filmmakers have to find something that interests them, and they should build on their strengths." He went on to say that the filmmaker should strengthen his or her weaknesses and make his or her strengths "super strengths."

I agreed with Horn, especially that it takes passion to be successful, and I could have asked him many more questions. And though Horn seemed in no hurry to end the interview, I didn't want to overstay my welcome. Because in addition to being the President, COO, adroit chess player, and gracious interview subject, Horn also holds a third-degree Black Belt in Taekwondo (although that was back in the day)!

Chapter 16

Posting Your Film's Soundtrack: Adding Music & Effects to the Mix

· ·

In This Chapter

▶ Mixing dialogue, sound effects, and music together

▶ Sounding off on sound effects

▶ Adding music that's music to your audience's ears

▶ Marrying picture to sound

· ·

More than 80 percent of the sound in a film is added *after* shooting, during postproduction. All the different types of sound — dialogue, sound effects, music, and so on — are recorded separately and then mixed together to create one soundtrack. If you really want to take notice of sound that's been added, watch an animated film like *Shrek, The Simpson Movie, WALL-E,* or *Horton Hears a Who!,* for which 100 percent of the sound was created (an animated picture requires all sounds to be created from scratch to match the images).

Even if your film features live actors, you need to add sound effects, music, and other sound elements in order to strengthen the production value of your film. Sound effects enhance visual elements, putting some real *punch* into a punch, for example. Music, whether it's licensed songs or composed specifically for the picture, enhances the mood of a film. This chapter explains what these other sound elements are, how to record or acquire them, and how to mix it all together yourself or find a professional sound mixer to make your film's soundtrack sound great.

Finishing Sound in Postproduction

After your film's picture is *locked* (picture editing and timing of the film will not change, and dialogue is synced up with the picture; see Chapter 15 for details), you're ready to start adding another dimension to your baby: sound design.

The *re-recording mixer,* also known as the *postproduction sound mixer,* takes all the sound elements of your production and mixes them down into one master soundtrack that complements the picture. On a tiny budget, you may be the sound mixer, but the job requires some technical know-how and artistic skills and may be too ambitious an undertaking. Finding someone with experience, if you can, is the best route to go. On bigger budget productions, you may have a team that includes three mixers working together. One controls the music, one mixes sound effects, and another handles the dialogue.

The key to mixing the final elements is knowing how and when to feature different sounds and controlling the volume of each element. When dialogue comes in while music is playing, the mixer needs to find an appropriate volume level so that the music doesn't drown out the dialogue or disappear behind the scene. A sound that is too loud or too soft can distract from the action. Sound-mixing a film is similar to sound-mixing a song in which lyrics and instrumentation are combined and balanced so all the elements are heard clearly.

The more layering of sound you have, the more professional your soundtrack will seem. The effect is subliminal. A good sound mix is invisible to your audience — but they're sure to notice a bad mix.

Stirring up the mixer's toolbox

The mixer brings artistic and technical skills to the mix, but the following tools make the job easier:

- Mixing board (if not part of your sound software)
- Computer (most home computers can accommodate sound software)
- Sound mixing software
- Digital audio tape (DAT) recorder, or hard drive for output to your final film or video project

If using a computer, you input the separate audio tracks — containing dialogue, sound effects, songs, and musical score — into the computer and mix them by using special sound-mixing software (again it's recommended you hire a professional mixer if you're not versed on the technical aspects of sound mixing). The tracks are then balanced and output to a final recording device. From there, the sound can be transferred to a finished video master or to the optical track of your film print. (See the section "Outputting Your Final Mix," later in this chapter for more information.)

Pro Tools has been the sound-mixing software of choice for professional sound designers. It's the sound equivalent of a picture-editing system like Avid or Final Cut Pro (see Chapter 15). You can order Pro Tools for $199 from www.digidesign.com. Final Cut Studio comes with Soundtrack Pro, which features powerful audio editing and software tools to mix a final professional soundtrack to your movie. It also includes a royalty-free library of over 5,000 sound effects.

If you want (or need) to hire a seasoned postproduction sound mixer, call local sound studios and ask for contact numbers. You can also look for a sound mixer at www.crewnet.com and www.media-match.com, which lets you search for any crew position by city or state.

Mixing the right balance

The sound mixer plays each scene of your film repeatedly as he or she mixes and syncs the sound elements. These elements consist of

- Dialogue
- Sound effects
- Foley (footsteps, falls, fight sounds, hand props, and so on that are matched perfectly to the actor's on-screen actions by Foley artists — see "Getting to know Jack Foley" later in this chapter)
- Musical score (including songs)
- Voice-over narration
- Ambience (background environmental sounds)
- Source music or songs within the scene (on radio, TV, or a performing band), which has to be recorded specifically for the film or with permission to use the source from the originator or owner of the source music

The sound mixer must make sure the dialogue, music, and effects aren't competing with each other, controlling the audio levels so that the sounds balance one another. On a small production, the sound mixer is usually in charge of mixing all the elements, which include dialogue, music and songs, sound effects, Foley, and ambience. The key to a good sound mix is staying focused on the picture so that the audience can stay focused on your story.

The mixer controls a separate track for each individual element, including several tracks of dialogue. The dialogue editor prepares a separate audio track for each actor's dialogue so that the sound mixer can control each actor's dialogue in terms of audio level and equalization individually to get clear-sounding dialogue. On a small production, your dialogue editor is often the same person who edits your picture. Each sound category is marked on the mixing board so that the mixer knows which volume slider controls which track. A film soundtrack can have unlimited individual audio tracks on top of each other containing different sound elements, as the mixer can keep layering and mixing (adjusting appropriate audio levels), on as many different tracks until you've got one complete master soundtrack.

The sound mixer can emulate certain effects through the mixing board or a software program; for example, a *telephone filter* can make a voice sound as though it's coming through a telephone. *Reverb* can add an echo to a voice to make it sound like the actor is speaking in an auditorium, and even make voices sound like they're a fair distance away. In addition to these specialty effects, audio filtering can be adjusted to minimize any *noise,* or hissing, that may be on the recorded audio track.

The mixer also prepares *music and effects* (M&E) *tracks* without the actors' dialogue so that, if the film is purchased for distribution in a non-English-speaking country, it can be dubbed in the language of choice and still retain the music and sound effects. You can find further details on M&E in the section "Separating music and effects tracks for foreign release," later in this chapter.

A qualified sound mixer has an "ear" for mixing the right volume levels and finding a happy medium between the dialogue, music, and sound effects so they aren't competing with each other. To help ride the proper audio levels of each sound element, the sound mixer refers to a cue sheet prepared by the sound editor that indicates when each effect will be coming up (so the mixer can anticipate lowering or raising the volume of the upcoming sound element).

Looping the loop

Looping, also called *ADR* (automatic dialogue replacement), is the art of replacing dialogue that wasn't recorded clearly on the set or couldn't be recorded properly because the location was too noisy to get good audio. The actor watches on a monitor or movie screen the shot or scene for which dialogue needs to be replaced. Through a set of headphones, the actor listens to the unusable audio replayed over and over again (looped) and then repeats the lines for re-recording, trying to match what's on the screen. The best audio take is kept and edited to match the picture as closely as possible. The mixer works magic with equalization and reverb to make it sound as close to the previously recorded on-set dialogue as possible.

If an actor steps on a line, stutters, or screws up a word during actual filming, it can be re-recorded in an ADR session and mixed back into the dialogue tracks. Often times, it's not the actor's fault; instead a plane flies overhead, a garbage truck reveals it's grinding presence outside, or some crew member talks over a take with "When's lunch?"

Creating Sound Effects with a Bang

Try turning the TV sound off, and you realize how much less dramatic the action seems without sound effects (or music or dialogue). Sound effects can be very subtle, like a key jiggling in a lock, or very dramatic, like a thunderous explosion of a missile strike. Almost all the sound effects that accompany a film are added or re-created in postproduction. Dialogue is the only sound from the actual filming that's retained all the way to the final picture — but not without enhancement.

Using a sound effect to suggest an action or event that you can't afford to shoot is often just as effective as showing the whole event. For example, say you want to include a car crash in your film. A car drives out of the frame, and a few seconds later you hear a terrible crash (another sound effect) — and then a lone tire rolls into the frame. You've created a believable effect — without totaling the car! You can create your own sound effects or license them from a sound-effects library.

Listening to sound-effects libraries

You can find almost every sound effect imaginable in sound-effects libraries. Sound Ideas is one of the world's largest publishers of sound-effects libraries. I'm currently using one of its sound packages called the General 6000 Series. This series contains every imaginable sound effect; you have 40 CDs' worth of sounds to choose from. Check out the Web site at www.sound-ideas.com to see the different sound-effects libraries offered. The sound effects are all digitally mastered and include these categories:

- **Animals:** Dogs, cats, birds, exotic animals
- **Devices:** Telephones, cell phones, fax machines, coffee makers
- **Fights:** Punches, jumps, falls
- **Locations:** Airports, restaurants, schools, playgrounds
- **Office environments:** Office machines, printers, elevators
- **People:** Crowds, applause, footsteps, laughing, crying
- **Toys:** Wind-up toys, race cars, spring-action toys
- **Vehicles:** Planes, trains, automobiles, boats

Some sound-effects libraries let you download individual sound effects for as little as $5 an effect. You can also buy individual sound effect CDs at most music stores for under $20. (I like to have the actual CDs and use the category listings and track numbers, but you can also download sound effects at www.sounddogs.com.)

A professional sound-effects library on CD can cost anywhere from $200 and up, depending on how extensive it is. I use the Digital Juice sound-effects libraries. When you run them through the "Juicer" (software engine), you can browse, search, and preview up to 35,000 sound effects right on your desktop!

Another sound-effects company, Hollywood Edge, carries some great sound-effects libraries online at www.hollywoodedge.com. Sonomic (www.sonomic.com) lets you search for the exact sound effect you're looking for, listen to it, and download it to your hard drive immediately (after using your credit card and paying for individual sound effects or entire CDs, of course). You can then output it to a digital editing program, tape source, or onto a recordable CD.

If you're mixing your film at a professional mixing studio, most times you can use its sound-effects library for a minimal charge — usually by the individual sound effects or a negotiated flat fee.

Creating and recording your own sound effects

If you want to save money and have some fun, you can record your own sound effects. I did that for my independent film *Turn of the Blade*. I went to the airport and recorded sounds of planes and helicopters taking off and landing, along with other airport sounds, on a portable DAT (digital audio tape) recorder. These tapes are similar in size to mini-digital video (DV) tapes. Because DAT is in the digital domain, you get pristine, high-quality audio when recording and don't lose any quality when making dubs of your sound mix (in the digital world, *dubs* are clones; you get an exact duplicate of the master).

Can't afford a DAT recorder but own a digital video camera? Record your sound effects onto the audio portion of your mini-DV tape. Just make sure that you use a good external microphone appropriate for recording the particular sound effect you want. (Use a directional microphone for concentrated sounds like keys dropping on the ground and omni-directional for recording ambient sounds like the ocean. See Chapter 12 for more on microphones.) You may want to keep the cap on the camera so you know that you were recording for audio purposes only (but remember to take the cap off while shooting your actual film!).

You can also record on a portable mini-recorder that has a built-in hard drive for professional digital quality sound. Olympus makes a palm-sized digital voice recorder for around $100 that can be plugged directly into your computer's USB port to download your audio files. With a decent microphone you can even use your iPod to record in certain situations!

Don't be afraid to experiment when creating sound effects. Emulate skaters on an ice rink by scraping knives together and punches by slamming dough on a counter. Make alien sound effects by slowing down, speeding up, or mixing several sounds together. Need the sound of a roaring fire but the real thing doesn't roar? Try crumpling paper into a ball close to a microphone. Waiting for the thunder in a rainstorm? Wait no longer; get a piece of tin or even a cookie sheet and flap it around. Voilà — thunder inside your house!

Getting to know Jack Foley

Named after its innovator, Jack Foley, *Foley walking* is a precise sound-effects technique where an artist (also called a Foley artist) watches the screen and reenacts the actors' interaction with items to re-create the sound effects that accompany the images on the screen. Foley effects include footsteps, clothes rustling, objects being handled, and body impacts.

Foley walkers often use a Foley pit (sophisticated audio postproduction facilities usually have such a pit available). A Foley pit consists of separate floor panels with different surfaces such as hardwood flooring, carpeting, concrete, and even water. The Foley walker has different surfaces at his or her disposal and walks "in place" on these surfaces while watching the actors on screen. A skilled Foley artist usually watches the scene a few times before acting out the action and then creates the Foley sounds at the same time as the action is playing out on the screen while it's being recorded to audio tape or digital files.

A Foley artist often brings a large suitcase containing items to assist him or her in re-creating sound effects to match the picture, such as various shoes, an assortment of hand props (paper, cutlery, stapler, and so on). Letting the Foley artist know what special elements may be helpful to bring when adding Foley to your picture (for example, coconut shells cut in half can emulate horses hoofs trotting across the pavement) is also helpful. I've seen a few burly Foley walkers put on women's shoes to emulate a woman on screen trekking down the street in high heels. (I can imagine a Foley walker's business card with the slogan, "I'm not a cross-dresser, but I may need to put on high heels.")

Foley is different from using a sound-effects library because it's easier to emulate someone walking up a flight of metal stairs and matching it in one take with a Foley walker. With a sound-effects library, you would have to find individual footsteps and match each one every time the actor moved up one step. This would take more time and more work to sync up.

The best way to locate a Foley artist is by contacting a local sound studio or TV station and asking if it has a list of professional Foley artists. You can also log on to www.crewnet.com and see if a Foley artist is in your neighborhood.

If you can't afford a professional Foley artist (which could cost upwards of $25 an hour), you can have fun doing your own Foley. You'll just have to do a lot of practicing. You can put together your own Foley pit by using a square foot or two of different surfaces like tile, wood, concrete, and carpet, plus a bucket with water (for splashing sounds). Create your own fight sounds by punching into a bag of flour or sand. You can use household items to enhance sounds made by your actors interacting with items on screen, like keys jingling, pens clicking, and cutlery clinking.

Adding room tone: Ambience or background sounds

Ambience is the background sound that gives your soundtrack fullness and enhances the location environment. Ambient sounds can be the buzzing of an air-conditioner working overtime, dogs barking in a neighborhood, or water dripping in the kitchen sink. Often, the production sound mixer records a loopable ambient track at the shoot (see Chapter 12). The postproduction sound mixer can also enhance a scene by adding ambience from a sound-effects library that may have a fuller sound than the original location — like sounds of birds chirping in a park, or a nearby cascading waterfall.

Scoring Big with Music

Turn on a classical radio station and close your eyes while the orchestral pieces play — you can't help but imagine visual images created by the music. Instrumental music can help evoke a mood in each scene of the film and create an underlying emotion that the audience can feel. Add some songs with lyrics, and you've got a film soundtrack.

Conducting a composer to set the mood

A *composer* can write an original music score to fit your film perfectly. He or she composes a theme that identifies your film and enhances the emotion and subtext of your story. The composer should write music appropriate to each scene. You don't want pounding rap music during a romantic interaction of two people having a candlelit dinner. Some musical scores, such as the scores from *Jaws, E.T.*, and the emotional orchestral score of *Schindler's List,* have become easily identifiable because they capture the style and theme of each film so well.

Nowadays, composers can record an entire film soundtrack without leaving their garage or studio — and without hiring a single live musician. But while synthesizers and samplers have gotten better, they still can't replace the sensation of human breath filling an acoustical instrument. Hiring musicians can be expensive, however; so a synthesized orchestra is often a cheaper way to go. Or you can combine synthesized music with real musicians. That's what composer Greg Edmonson did on my film *Turn of the Blade* to create a score that sounded more like a real orchestra.

With the sophistication of today's computers and digital technology, almost every film's music design is done digitally (on a computer) by using a software program like Pro Tools. Sound can be processed, manipulated, and adjusted quickly, so the composer can hear the results immediately and continue to make adjustments if necessary.

The best way to look for a composer is by calling the local sound-recording facilities in your area. Your local TV station may recommend a composer who works in your town. *The Hollywood Reporter* (www.hollywood reporter.com) has special film and TV music issues that come out several times a year. The issues list composers alphabetically along with their credits. You can also contact the various music organizations (BMI, ASCAP, and SOCAN) and get a free list of their members — composers, musicians, and songwriters. Crew Net (www.crewnet.com) is a free service that lets you search for a composer (and other crew positions) by city or state. Media-Match (www.media-match.com) also provides a similar service via the Internet. I've discovered some great musical talent (composers and song artists) at VersusMedia (www.versusmedia.com).

If you plan on using any music you didn't commission and pay for, be sure it's in the public domain (see "Singing songs in the public domain" and "Orchestrating the rights to popular music" later in this chapter). If you're not sure of the rights or you didn't pay to use someone else's music, you're making yourself liable for a lawsuit — don't take a chance!

Composing your own music

You can use music software programs that put you at the keyboard — and you don't even have to read music or have ever played a note in your life. SmartSound makes Sonicfire Pro, which enables you to become your own composer, using your own computer (see Figure 16-1). The program gives you custom control over genre, style, and duration. You don't have to be a musician or know how to read music to get professional results. It's easy to use and starts at $99.95 (depending on how many library music discs you buy with the software). You just input your picture footage into Sonicfire Pro, choose from the music library selections that you own for the style of music (scary, happy, energetic, romantic, thriller), then point and click to cut, rearrange, and control the music to match your picture perfectly! Check out Sonicfire Pro at `www.smartsound.com`.

Figure 16-1: Sonicfire Pro makes importing your movie and then customizing your own music easy. Here I am at a *For Dummies* book signing with a friend.

The sound of music libraries

If you're on a limited budget, you may not be able to afford a composer to write and score original music for your film or video project, and you may not have the patience to use a music program like Sonicfire Pro. That's where music libraries come to the rescue. Just as you can get sound effects from a CD library, you can get music of every conceivable type, which you pay a fee to use in your film. Your project will sound very professional if you use music from a music library.

Some music libraries charge a *needle-drop fee,* which is a fee charged literally every time a music cue starts and stops in your film. But most provide *royalty-free* music, meaning that after you buy the CD, you get a lifetime of unlimited use of the music on that CD — so get out your library card! Digital Juice has a series of music libraries called BackTraxx. You can also get Cinematic

Stacks that you can layer into the BackTraxx selections and customize your own unique versions and specific lengths of musical cuts to fit your footage.

Companies such as Music Bakery (www.musicbakery.com) provide CDs with a wide variety of music cues to choose from for your film project. CDs start at $147. I've been using Music Bakery's CDs for years, and I've always been impressed with the selection. Some of the categories that music libraries offer include a variety of musical styles and genres: jazz and blues, orchestral, rock and urban, corporate image music (short music intros appropriate for logos), drama and suspense, and more.

Some music libraries allow you to sample their music via the Internet so that you can select tracks for your project without having to buy the CD before you hear it. For example, Creative Support Services (CSS) is another music library that provides a broad range of music for film and video projects. At the Web site (www.cssmusic.com), you can listen to up to 10,000 tracks — if you have the time.

Playing with original songs

You can enhance your film and add some energy to certain scenes by slipping in some songs. Finding new talent in clubs and showcases (maybe you'll find the next Beatles) can be a lot of fun — not to mention cheaper than having to license a well-known song from a major recording label. You're sure to find bands that will be excited to have one of their songs in your film. If you offer to let them keep the rights to the song, they may let you use it for free.

Versus Media (www.VersusMedia.com) is a one-stop website to find song artists looking to provide existing or original songs for film productions. Zero Fee Music (www.ZeroFeeMusic.com) provides free songs (to eligible film-makers) from their song catalog. You only have to list their songs on your music cue sheets (see "Cueing up cue sheets" later in this chapter), and when you sell your movie to television, the TV station pays the royalties to the artist's music organization.

Always have some written agreement between yourself and the band. It's best to have an attorney versed in entertainment or music contracts write it up for you. You can find music and song agreements in *Contracts for the Film & Television Industry* by Mark Litwak, along with other staff and crew contract information. Your agreement should clearly state that the band is providing you the original lyrics and music in a recording that you can use in your film (for no charge, or a nominal fee), and the band owns the song that can be used in the context of your film. Any royalties paid by the band's music association (BMI, ASCAP, or SOCAN) is paid from the TV network that licenses the film and follows the music cue sheets to see who gets paid for the music.

BMI, ASCAP, and SOCAN

BMI, ASCAP, and SOCAN (a Canadian association) are music performance rights organizations that collect royalties for songs, soundtracks, and any other music sources created by their members (composers, songwriters, and musicians) that appear in any published work. They monitor the information through the cue sheets (see "Cueing up cue sheets" in this chapter) that the film's composer or production company provides to each buyer or distributor. These performance rights organizations send their members quarterly statements listing the distribution of the projects in which the members' music has been heard. The composer or songwriter receives a royalty (a fee paid each time, by the TV station, when his or her work is heard) in a particular production.

Orchestrating the rights to popular music

Music companies have dedicated licensing departments for the very purpose of licensing songs for use in films, TV, and commercials. A well-placed song can be as lucrative for a band and its recording company in a soundtrack that sells at a music store as it is having the song in the finished film. But recording companies don't just let you use their music for free; you have to pay a licensing fee. Every music label has a licensing department that deals specifically with licensing their songs to film, TV, and commercial properties.

Using a recognizable song in your film can cost upwards of $20,000 for the *synchronization rights* (connecting musical recordings up with film or TV works). You can save some money if you use the lyrics from the song but have your newly discovered band do its own rendition (you still need to license permission to use the lyrics). Many bands have their own garage sound studio where they can record a song or two for relatively little money, or they have contacts with professional sound studios that may give them a discount.

Even the song "Happy Birthday" is protected by copyright. You would need permission to use the lyrics or music in your film even if one of your actors sings it or any part of the song. It's easier to write your own birthday song — and then copyright it so that no one else can use it without paying you!

Cueing up cue sheets

When you sell your film to a distributor, you need to provide a *cue sheet*. This sheet, usually prepared by the composer, is simply a listing of all the music cues in your film. A cue sheet lists the cue number, the time length of the cue, and a brief title or description of what the music piece relates to in the film (for example, David meets Misty). Cue sheets help the music organizations like BMI, ASCAP, and SOCAN monitor their members' contributions to various projects and receive proper royalties for the use of their music.

Singing songs in the public domain

Seventy-five years after a song is written, its copyright expires, and the song enters the *public domain.* Anyone can use material in the public domain without having to license it from the owner or get permission to use it for professional (and profitable) purposes. Most of Gilbert and Sullivan's famous songs, such as "The Modern Major General," are in the public domain. Titles such as "Pop Goes the Weasel" and "Row, Row, Row Your Boat" are other well-known ditties in the public domain. For various titles that are currently in the public domain, check out www.pdinfo.com.

A song or musical composition may be in the public domain, but the actual recording may be copyrighted, so make sure to do your research. The best thing to do is to have a composer rescore it and hire original singers and musicians to perform it.

Outputting Your Final Mix

Your sound mixer prepares separate tracks known as *stems* for your film. Each set of stems consists of different mixed elements that make up your final mix. One set of stems contains the dialogue, one set is dedicated to music, and another set is for sound effects and Foley. When played together, these stems represent your final mix and are used in the making of your final release.

After you have your dialogue, sound effects, ambience, Foley, and music pulled together into your final mix, or *printmaster,* you're ready to sync sound to picture by transferring the sound to your film negative at the lab. If your sound has been mixed for a digital or video production, the final soundtrack can be transferred directly into a digital-editing system via a hard drive, from storage discs (DVD or CD), or onto a DAT audiotape.

The final output is usually done by someone at the film lab when transferring to film. If you're going to video or into a non-linear digital editing system, you can input it yourself, or if you're using an editor, she can input it and sync it up to the final picture.

When finishing on film, the final sound mix is printed to the *optical track* of your film print. The sound and the film are then married to become one — for better or worse! However, if you want to use a popular sound format that makes your soundtrack really come to life, you need to take your printmaster through a format-specific encoding process. Dolby Labs licenses its popular Dolby Digital 5.1 surround encoding technology, giving a unique dimensional sound quality to your soundtrack.

Surrounding sound

Sound can be exciting to the ears, especially with the advancement of surround sound formats, which include Dolby Digital 5.1 and Sony SDDS 7.1, a three-dimensional sound experience. With three front speakers (left, center, and right), two surround channels (left surround, right surround, and a separate feed for a subwoofer for low-frequency material), you can make your audience feel like they're part of the action. After you've mixed your multichannel surround, you usually also create separate printmasters for four-channel surround (Dolby SR) and stereo masters as well. This is another option if you want to spend the extra dollars and feel that your soundtrack will benefit from using the surround sound technology.

Separating music and effects tracks for foreign release

If you know that you're going to have a distributor sell your film in the foreign markets (overseas), you also need to make two separate printmasters: one that contains only the music and sound effects (M&E tracks) and another with just the English dialogue. Having this version of the printmaster enables a foreign distributor to dub the language of its country into the picture and still have the original music and sound effects tracks behind the dubbed voices. The English dialogue track is used only as a guide.

Next time you're on an airplane that flies to a foreign country, check the audio channels on the in-flight film. You can often switch back and forth between languages, but you'll notice that the music and sound effects are the same on both channels.

Chapter 17

Conjuring Up Special Effects

. . . .

In This Chapter

▶ Creating computer effects for your film

▶ Painting special effects into your shots

▶ Lensing special effects through the camera

▶ Making make-up effects

. . . .

A special effect is something out of the ordinary that entertains, amazes, and adds wonder to the story. Special effects — whether dinosaurs in your kitchen or cars blowing up downtown—don't just happen in front of the camera. They take preparation and skill. Like a magician creating illusions on-stage, you can create illusions for your film. With special effects on set through the camera or in postproduction, you can fool your audience by making some-thing look like it really happened! This chapter tells you what you need to know.

Creating Effects: In or Out of Camera?

You can create special effects in several ways:

✔ **In the camera:** To create effects in the camera, you use lenses and filters or you control exposure (see Chapter 10). You can do double exposures in the camera to create ghost effects, for example, and use forced per-spective to make things appear bigger or smaller than they really are and change their perspective. You can add a photo or miniature close to the lens to appear life-size and real. Playing with speed and motion of the camera is another in-camera trick.

✔ **On the set:** Effects created on the set include things like explosions, fire, and gunshots. Levitation and superhuman leaps can also be created on-set with wires attached to your actors (like Spider-Man leaping from building to building); the wires are removed (erased) in postproduction. You can also use *matte paintings* (elements painted on glass in front of the camera) or front and back projection of locations onto a large reflective screen behind your actors. Weather, such as rain, snow, fog, wind, and lightning are often on-set effects, as well.

- **With make-up:** These types of special effects include horror make-up, latex appliances to the face, and special teeth and contact lenses. Full-body costumes, such as a gorilla suit or the creature costume in *Alien,* also fall under this category.

- **In postproduction:** Using *opticals* (adding images together in the film lab) or compositing images together using blue or green screen. Also CGI (computer-generated images) are very popular (and much more affordable nowadays) for generating special effects and creating images during the postproduction phase. Matte paintings are often composited to the final film image in post-production.

The following sections of this chapter explain these different effect options in detail.

Dropping in Backgrounds

Often on an independent budget you can't afford to travel to a distant location to be used as a backdrop for your film, or the location only exists in your mind (like a desert planet with three moons and a pink horizon). Fortunately, with a little know-how, you can place your actors into backgrounds that have either been filmed separately (without any actors in the shot) or created completely in your computer. This is known as *compositing,* where several elements shot at separate times are combined to look like they were shot together as part of the same shot.

You can combine several different special effects, such as matte painting, blue screen, and background plates, by *layering* them upon each other. It's like laying clear plastic sheets on top of each other, but each one has a different element that complements the previous plastic sheet and its element. After all the elements are blended together, you have a *composite.* dvMatte is an amazing software program that lets you make seamless composites (check out www.dvgarage.com for more information).

Turning blue and green

In the blue-screen process, the actor does the scene in front of a blue (or green) background, which is later replaced with a picture, painting, or computer-generated background (also known as a *background* plate — see the following section on plates). Imagine taking a pair of magic scissors and cutting away everything that's blue or green. You end up with what looks like a cardboard cutout of your actor that is then placed in front of any background. Your actor looks like she's really there and not in front of a screen at all. Green is used a lot now for the screen color, because that particular hue is not a common color that your actors would be wearing.

John Fulton was one of the first effects creators to use what is known as the *traveling matte* using blue screen (green screen is popular now, too). Fulton designed the effects for *The Invisible Man* in 1933 (an updated version, *Memoirs of an Invisible Man,* in 1992, starring Chevy Chase, used the same blue-screen techniques over have a half-century later). George Lucas uses blue screen in his *Star Wars* epics to blend his live-action actors into wondrous sci-fi fantasy locales from his imagination.

Generating computer effects

Almost every film you see nowadays has at least some computer-generated effects — even if you don't notice them. *A Beautiful Mind* has seamless digital effects, such as the seasons that magically change right before the audience's eyes while John Nash (Russell Crowe) sits by his window working on his thesis. Then you have films like *Men in Black* and *The Chronicles of Narnia* that have hundreds of computer-generated effects created in postproduction, after the main photography of the film has been shot. These amazing illusions, like the ones shown here from my film *Silly Movie 2,* can be created entirely on a desktop computer.

I found a fun and amazing software animation program called PQ Talking Photo. You can take virtually any still photograph of a person or animal and make it talk or sing! I was able to make my dog sing a song with just a few clicks (and now he's got a record deal!). You can get a free download of the software at www.pqdvd.com/talking-photo.html

Adobe makes a software program called After Effects that can be used with non-linear editing systems (see more on non-linear editing in Chapter 16) to create many amazing effects. If you're familiar with Adobe's Photoshop CS3, which lets you manipulate photos and images, then imagine After Effects as Photoshop in motion. You can take a still image of a truck, animate the wheels, add suspension in the cab, and create a moving image. For more information, go to www.adobe.com. Studio Artist from Synthetik lets you *morph* (transform one image into another, like the antagonist in *Terminator II* or Dr. Banner in *The Incredible Hulk*). To get more information on Studio Artist, go to www.synthetik.com. Particle Illusion at www.digitaljuice.com is another magical software product you should check out.

© 2008 Bryan Michael Stoller/Island Productions, Silly Movie 2

Pirates of the Caribbean used a screen process called Reflecmedia. You can get an affordable Reflectmedia kit that comes with a special light ring for your camera lens and a highly reflective backdrop material that virtually disappears on camera, creating a flawless composite. The reflective material was also used for Harry Potter's invisible coat. Go to www.reflecmedia.com.

Figure 17-1 shows the prehistoric pig, *Jurassic Pork*, generated on the computer. The second image is me in *Miss Cast Away & the Island Girls (*also known as *Silly Movie 2)* against a blue screen (even though it's a black-and-white photo, I swear it was blue). When the two images are merged together in post-production, you have what is called a *composite* with the action hero and the prehistoric pig appearing as if they are in the same shot together.

You don't have to use a professional blue or green screen — you can just use a plain-colored bed sheet, as long as you don't have that same color in your subject's clothing or hair coloring. Then in postproduction, you remove the screen or sheet color and bring in your background plate to merge the elements together. If you want to purchase an effective and inexpensive blue or green screen (like the one I used in the composite shot in Figure 17-1), Photoflex makes one called Flexdrop2 that pops open to a 5×7-foot screen (it's double-sided with blue on one side, green on the other) and is light and portable so you can take it to the set or stage. Check out the Photoflex Web site at www.photoflex.com.

Figure 17-1:
The author (on right, not left) in a composite shot created from two images.

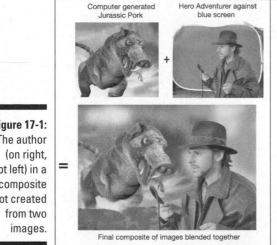

Computer generated Jurassic Pork

Hero Adventurer against blue screen

Final composite of images blended together

© Zandoria Studios/William Sutton
© Concept by Bryan Michael Stoller 2003

Dishing out special-effects plates

Special-effects plates are actually background *plates* — still photos or motion picture shots of a particular location. The still photos or moving footage is then inserted in postproduction behind an actor or characters who performed the scene in front of a blue or green screen. Background plates are usually shot before the main photography of your film so that you know how to line up your actors so that, when they stand in front of the background footage, the scene looks believable. I've used stock footage of distant or difficult locations from Time Image as background plates behind my actors (www.timeimage.com).

Digital cameras are great for taking high-quality pristine photos of locations for background plates. I use the Kyocera Finecam S4 digital still camera (www.kyocera.com). It's a 4-pixel camera, meaning that you can enlarge the photos without losing detail. Most digital still cameras range from 2 pixels to 10 pixels.

Painting scenery into your shots: Matte paintings

Instead of constructing or destroying real cities, buildings, and other backgrounds, you can paint them! In the *Wizard of Oz,* the famous Emerald City is actually a *matte painting.* The grass and field of flowers in the foreground are part of a real set, but the background with the Emerald Castle and sky is painted on glass. A matte painting can actually be in front of the camera, the painted image can be positioned so that the glass is not seen on camera, and the painting on glass looks to be part of the actual shot. A matte painting can also be photographed in postproduction and merged with scenes already shot.

The Gotham City skyline featured in *Batman* used matte paintings. And the film *Earthquake* used matte paintings to simulate earthquake damage to the high-rise buildings by placing paintings over the existing exteriors to simulate gaps, caved-in walls, broken windows, and partially collapsed buildings. Nowadays matte paintings are often painted digitally in the computer and married to the live-action footage in postproduction.

Have you seen scenic backdrops?

Almost every television show or film uses billboard-sized scenic backdrops that either are blown up from an actual location photograph or are painted onto a light-durable material like vinyl and positioned behind the actors on the set. Scenic backdrops are often seen through the windows on stage sets. Or the high-rise building with the huge picture windows and the beautiful city skyline could be a scenic backdrop. An example of a city backdrop at night is the one seen every weeknight behind David Letterman's desk on *The Late Show*. Scenic backdrops are sometimes translucent so they can be backlit to give the image vibrancy. Backdrops save time and money in the long run because they're cheaper. Rather than go to Paris, for example, you can use a scenic backdrop (in a warehouse in your hometown) of the Eiffel Tower outside the restaurant set window.

Scenic backdrops can also be projected from behind or from the front onto a reflected screen behind the actor that accepts a deep sharp image from the projector. Projecting images can be cheaper because you don't have to find a life-size backdrop. The projected image can be from a 1-inch slide or transparency. With the advancements in computer effects, however, most productions (that have the budget and computer equipment and software) prefer to create the backdrop in the computer instead of using front or back projection.

Clipping your magazines

You don't have to be an artist to insert amazing elements into ordinary shots. Go through your magazines and cut out images that would work in your shots. If you have an actor venturing across the world who comes upon a beautiful castle, for example, find a photograph of a castle in a magazine and cut it out (don't venture across the world, unless you really want to for this shot). If you need to enlarge it, go to the color-copy place or scan it into your computer. Then stick the image on a piece of clear glass or mount it on cardboard, stand it up between the camera and your actor, and frame it appropriately in the shot.

Presenting a touch of glass

You can position a painting, miniature, or photograph on a piece of glass in front of the camera to create the appearance of that element being an actual part of the shot. Glass, if lighted properly, is invisible to the camera, so the audience won't see the glass. Remember that you see in three-dimensions, but the camera has only one eye and sees in two dimensions (a flat surface) only. A photograph or painting has the illusion of looking three-dimensional through the camera's single lens, therefore it appears to be part of the actual shot.

In Figure 17-2, you see a magazine picture placed on glass and incorporated into an actual location with the actor. The princess is standing 20 feet *from* the camera and slightly to the left of the castle cutout. The cutout is only 4 feet from the camera and 3 feet high. If the princess were to move to her right, closer to the castle, she would end up behind the cutout.

Figure 17-2:
Magazine picture on glass.

Weathering the storm

Weather is considered a special effect in film because you have to imitate Mother Nature (she doesn't storm on command). Many screenwriters don't think twice about starting a scene with, "It was a dark and stormy night." But unless you want to sit and wait for it to really rain, you have to create the storm yourself, and it's not cheap. Same with wind and snow. So unless it's crucial to the scene, leave it out.

Creating snow or rain outside a window for an indoor scene is a much easier effect to accomplish. Rain is as simple as having someone outside spraying a regular garden hose above the window — the water will fall and look like raindrops against the pane (just don't forget to close the window!). Rain is also easier to see if it's backlit. For snow, you can find various substances like laundry detergent and have someone above the window (on a stepladder) sprinkling the dry soap flakes evenly from above. From inside, it looks like snowflakes are falling. Just make sure you don't mix your soap snowflakes with your garden hose rain — you'll have an outdoor bubble bath flooding the neighborhood!

Downsizing Miniatures

Many amazing effects have been achieved in the movies using *miniatures* (which are relatively small and usually built to scale). The film *Earthquake* had miniature towns, cities, and landscapes built so they could be destroyed easily on film. Steven Spielberg used several miniature sets in his film *1941*. (The scene of the Ferris wheel breaking off its axis and rolling down the Santa Monica Pier into the ocean was a miniature built to scale. It would have been too expensive, too dangerous, and nearly impossible to do that with the real thing — plus, I think I was on that ride a few years ago.) In *E.T. The Extraterrestrial*, Spielberg used miniatures combined with actor close-ups when Elliot and his friends steered their flying bicycles across the sky above their neighborhood. He also used stop-motion animated models (see Chapter 2) in *Indiana Jones and the Temple of Doom* during the high speed coal-mining cart chase.

Looking down on miniatures

You need to keep several things in mind when shooting models and miniatures:

- ✔ **Use pinpoint lighting (because you're lighting small objects) when filming indoor miniatures.** For exterior miniatures, such as towns, landscapes, and roads, build the miniature set outside and take advantage of the real sunlight, as well as the real sky and clouds.

- ✔ **Keep the camera on level with the miniatures, as if you and your camera are to scale with your miniature.** Only shoot higher if you're simulating a shot from a helicopter or tall building.

- ✔ **If you're using miniature vehicles, water, or anything with movement, slow down the action so that the miniature doesn't move unrealistically.** If the miniature is half the size of the real object, you slow the film or digital footage down by half. That is, you shoot at 48 frames per second — twice the speed of the normal 24 frames per second (thus, compacting double the frames in the same amount of time, which creates the illusion of slow motion). If your miniature is one-quarter the size of the real thing, slow it down by four times the actual speed — get the idea? By speeding up the frame rate, you slow down the real-time action when it's played back at the regular 24 frames per second. If you're shooting tape or digital files, you usually control the speed in the postproduction phase. Go the section "Speeding slowly" for more on how to manipulate camera speed.

Speeding up the camera to get slow-motion sounds like a contradiction, but don't be confused. If a film camera is sped up and shoots 120 pictures (frames) a second, the action plays back as slow motion because the projector plays back at a constant speed of 24 frames per second. In other words, it takes the projector about six seconds to show the action that took place in one second.

Keep in mind that the larger in scale your miniature is, the more realistic it will look, and the less chance your audience will think it's a miniature.

Forcing the perspective, forcefully

If you stand at the end of a long road and look off into the distance (which I don't recommend, especially if it's a busy highway), the road appears to narrow as it reaches the horizon. With miniatures, you want to create this effect *without* the distance. This concept is called *forced perspective*. If you want to build a miniature road, for example, you cut out a long triangle instead of a long even strip of road. Position the triangle on the ground and put the camera at the widest end of the triangle. The point of the triangle will look like the road is going off into the distance (see Figure 17-3).

Figure 17-3: A miniature road designed for forced perspective.

Stretched triangle road for forced perspective

Climbing the walls

In my teenage days, I made a short film called *Superham*. In it I had a scene of a Spider-Man-type character climbing what appeared to be the side of a brick building. The effect cost me all of $3. I bought a plastic sheet pressed with miniature bricks at the local hobby store. To defy the laws of gravity, I turned the miniature brick wall sideways, lining the edge up with the top of a short concrete wall 20 feet behind the miniature wall and had my actor crawl across the top of the short wall in the background. I turned the camera sideways, so it looked like my actor was crawling up the brick wall — and of course the miniature bricks turned sideways closer to the camera helped to complete the illusion (see Figure 17-4). The original *Batman* TV series used this simple technique in every episode in which the caped crusader used his bat rope to climb to the top of a building (his cape was held up by a wire).

Storyboard your special effects so that the entire production team can see exactly what the effect is. See more on storyboarding in Chapter 9.

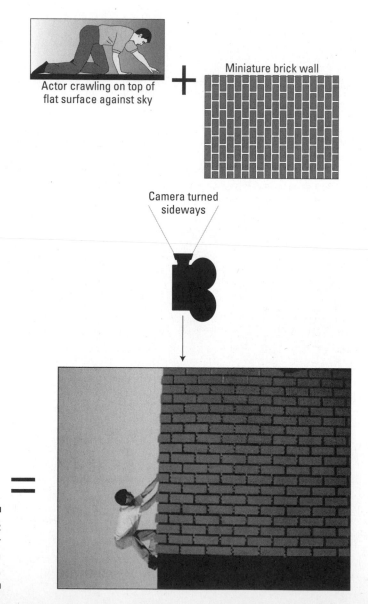

Actor crawling on top of flat surface against sky

Miniature brick wall

Camera turned sideways

Figure 17-4: An actor "climbing" a wall.

Wired for special effects

Wires are a great way to have your actors achieve superhuman feats. Wires were used in *Iron Man* to make it look like Robert Downey Jr. was actually flying in his iron suit. Harry Potter flew successfully on his Nimbus 2000 with the help of wires. *Crouching Tiger, Hidden Dragon* assisted its actors in leaping higher, running along rooftops, and shooting through the trees with the help of wires that were erased during postproduction. Keanu Reeves in *The Matrix* performed some anti-gravity acrobats with the skilled work of wires. Tobey Maguire would have been grounded if it weren't for the application of wirework in his film *Spider-Man.* You can erase the wires from the footage either by having a computer artist simply erase them or by using blue or green wires that can be removed when the image of the actor and the background plate are composited together (like the blue-screen process).

Creating Effects Right in the Camera

Many of today's digital cameras have built-in effects such as fade-in and fade-out, *wipes* (which "wipe" the image to black with a sliding black shape), mosaics, and negative black-and-white images. Many of these effects, such as the wipe (which you can also create by sliding a piece of cardboard across the lens), work great as transitions (smoother cuts) between scenes. When shooting with film, the film lab often creates these effects for you, which are referred to as *optical effects.* Another simple transition is having an actor walk toward the lens until he covers it completely. I once did a film where I had the actor throw his laundry over the lens, causing the scene to go black.

Another effect you can do with the camera is to use a *beam splitter,* which is a half-mirrored piece of glass between the camera and your subject. The glass is positioned at a 45-degree angle to reflect an image that's off-camera into the glass that the camera is shooting through. The half-mirror is invisible to the camera except for the image it's reflecting into the glass. This makes your actor appear in the original shot as a transparent ghost.

Backward about reverse photography

Reverse photography can be as obvious as somebody having a meal backward (you film him or her normally and then just reverse the footage) — it can get a hilarious (or gross) response from your audience. Or you can be more subtle and create an effect that doesn't immediately appear as if the footage were reversed.

I was shooting a commercial in which a superhero emerged from a phone booth and, like Superman, leaped up into the sky. It was a simple effect. My actor stood on top of the phone booth (remember phone booths?), and the camera only framed to just below the top of the booth. The actor then jumped off the top, entering frame, and then straightened up and walked backward into the phone booth. I simply reversed the footage and it appeared as if he walked out of the phone booth and leapt straight up into the air.

In the opening credits of *Austin Powers: The Spy Who Shagged Me,* Austin Powers emerges from an outdoor swimming pool after a synchronized Busby Berkeley-type water folly and rises up into the air — with his hair and clothes completely dry. This was achieved by lowering him into the water, and then simply reversing the footage.

Double exposure, double exposure

A *double exposure* puts two different pictures or scenes together at the same time and runs them parallel to each other. You create a double exposure on film during postproduction in the film lab, or with software on a non-linear editing system. The difference between a double exposure and a true blue- or green-screen composite (see the "Turning blue and green" section earlier in this chapter) is that the double exposure causes the person to look transparent and not a solid part of the scene that it is double-exposed against.

Speeding slowly

Undercranking and *overcranking* refer to manipulating the speed of a camera. You can often change speed on a motion-picture film camera by adjusting the camera itself. To change the speed of a digital camcorder, you usually have to change the speed during the editing postproduction phase. With these methods you can create interesting effects:

- ✔ *Overcranking*, **or speeding up film, creates the illusion of slow motion.** The faster the film runs through the camera, the slower the motion will be. Running the film through the camera quickly gives you more individual frames to play back at regular speed — creating the illusion of slow motion. Overcranking the camera is also a necessity when you're filming miniatures (see the earlier section "Downsizing Miniatures").

- ✔ *Undercranking*, **or slowing down film, speeds up the action in your scene.** Car chases are often undercranked slightly to make cars appear as if they are traveling dangerously fast. *Undercranking* also refers to clicking frame by frame, similar to stop-motion animation (see Chapter 2).

Because the frames end up missing some of the actual action, the actor or vehicle on camera appears animated or sped up.

✔ **Using time-lapse photography captures motion often imperceptible at real-time speeds.** An *intervalometer* is a timer (either attached to or a part of the camera) that can be set to click a frame at specific intervals, such as every second or every 24 hours. You've seen this effect with flowers blooming, clouds twirling through the sky, and buildings being constructed in a matter of seconds.

Creating effects with lenses and filters

Special lenses and filters that you screw onto your camera or use in a matte box (see Chapter 10) can alter or create a special element that you couldn't achieve using a normal lens. The difference between a lens and a filter is that a lens changes the shape of the picture in some way (such as distortion with a super-wide-angle lens — see Chapter 10). A filter usually plays with the color, exposure, or glare coming into the camera.

Special-effect filters change colors in unique ways (these are different from the color-correcting filters that I talk about in Chapter 10). For example, if the bottom part of the lens or filter is blue and the top part is yellow, the ground will appear blue and the sky yellow. Tiffen, one of the top developers and manufacturers of lenses and filters, makes a variety of these effects. Check out www.tiffen.com. Here's a list of common special-effect filters and lenses and what they do:

✔ **Star:** Makes reflective objects in the picture twinkle

✔ **Fog:** Creates a soft fog effect in the scene

✔ **Prism:** Creates multiple images of objects or actors in the frame

✔ **Gradual:** Changes the color of the sky or the upper part of the frame

Tiffen now makes special software called *Dfx Digital Filter Suite* that emulates a variety of Tiffen's camera filters in the digital world that you can experiment with in postproduction. GenArts makes a popular effects and filter simulating software called Sapphire Plug-ins. Check out www.genarts.com. Final-Cut Pro and other editing software often come with their own special effect and filter choices. Most of the software programs mentioned work as plug-ins with the popular editing systems.

Splitting the diopter lens

One of my favorite special-effect lenses is the *split diopter lens*, which Orson Welles used for many of his scenes in *Citizen Kane* to keep both the foreground and background images in perfect focus. When filming at night or indoors, keeping everything in focus is hard. It's like being nearsighted and not seeing things at a distance — or being farsighted and not seeing things close up. A split diopter lens splits up the picture so that a distant object on one side of the frame and a close-up object on the other side can both be in focus in the same shot. It's kind of like a bifocal lens turned sideways for the camera.

I used a split diopter on a comedy short I did called *Monkey USA* where I spoofed *King Kong*. I had an actor sitting in a giant King Kong hand (rented from a studio), which was 30 feet away from the camera on one side of the frame. On the other side of the frame, I had an actor in an ape suit stand about 2 feet away from the camera. Both sides of the frame remained in focus and created the illusion that the giant King Kong hand wrapped around the actor was connected to the gorilla to the right of the frame (see the following figure).

Exploding Effects on Fire

A lot of special effects that look dangerous on film are harmless effects created in the mind of the filmmaker. Explosions, fire, and guns, on the other hand, can be very dangerous. A *pyrotechnician* is trained to work with elements that could be extremely dangerous on your set. Creating explosions and fires and using ammunition are some of the skills a pyrotechnician has been trained for.

Never attempt any fire effects or explosions on your own. Always enlist the skills of a qualified pyrotechnician. You're also required to have a firefighter on set to make sure that everyone remains safe.

You can add fire later with a computer or superimposed by overlapping several images. Or you can actually set a fire in a controlled environment. *Backdraft,* Ron Howard's firefighting film, used many controlled situations to simulate the danger of fire. These scenes were supervised by a firefighter on set along with a skilled pyrotechnician.

At Halloween time, you see fog machines in almost every novelty store. They're small vaporizer-type devices that heat up and expel a harmless smoke-like steam into the air — similar to dry ice but much simpler and safer to use. They cost between $35 and $100, depending on the size of the machine. You can buy fog juice that heats up in the device and turns into fog that can be controlled to shoot out a nozzle in small or large bursts. Great for shooting a foggy night scene or smoking up a bar. Do you remember the flashlight beams cutting through the misty forest in *E.T.?* Fog machines were used to catch the rays of light and enhance the mood of the scene.

Making Up Your Mind about Make-Up Effects

Special effects aren't just limited to illusions that look real only through the camera lens or after the postproduction stage. Make-up is make-believe that can walk and talk without the magic of the camera but through the magic of talented make-up artists. Many people think of beauty makeovers when they think of make-up artists. You don't normally think of monsters, alien creatures, and flesh — but the world of the make-up artist is a broad one.

Applying prosthetics

Prosthetics is a term associated with artificial limbs. In the world of special effects make-up, however, *prostheses* are used to create additional limbs, burn victims, and monster effects (all the sick, gross stuff). Prosthetic pieces, also called *appliances,* are usually made of foam latex, which can move much like human skin and muscles. Make-up effects artist David Miller designed the conehead makeup for Dan Aykroyd and the entire Conehead population in the film *Coneheads.* He also designed Freddy Krueger's make-up for the *Nightmare on Elm Street* films. (Miller was working late one night trying to decide on the look of Freddy Krueger and glanced down at his melted cheese pizza — inspiration hit!)

You can also do mechanical make-up effects, like a head-cast made from an actor with features added to a fake head. I made a cameo appearance as a werewolf in one of my short films several years ago. My sister Marlene, a professional make-up artist, and make-up artist Jack Bricker took a cast of my head by pouring plaster over my face, leaving straws in my nostrils so I could breath (that was the only time in my life that I've ever been plastered). When the plaster dried, they used the mold to design the werewolf head in latex and added hair and an extended muzzle to the *dummy head.* To save time and money, they only made a half-head because the final shot was a profile, and the camera would never see the other side (see Figure 17-5).

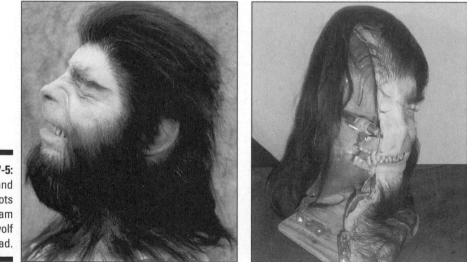

Figure 17-5:
Front and
profile shots
of a foam
werewolf
head.

Capturing motion with motion capture

Motion capture is a technique that captures a live actor's movements into a computer. The realistic movements can then be transferred to a 3-D computer-generated character of virtually any size and proportion, like the CGI dodo shown here. Small tracking sensors are attached to the actor — like connecting the dots on a stick figure. When the actor moves, the computer tracks movements —an elbow bending, a finger pointing, legs running, or arms punching — in real time. Many studio animated CGI (computer generated image) movies use motion capture (*Polar Express, Monster House,* and *Beowulf* to name a few). A company called Naturalpoint makes a motion capture

system called OptiTrack for only $5000 (www. naturalpoint.com/optitrack).

An older technique that's been around since the invention of film is *rotoscoping*. In the old days, animators would trace an actor's actions off a film performance and turn the actual performance into a series of separate drawings. These drawings would then be photographed frame by frame and the end result would be an animated character with very real human motion. Motion capture using a computer and tracking sensors is the 21st century version of rotoscoping — and it's in real time!

© 1998/2008 Mr. Dodo created by Bryan Michael Stoller / CGI by William Sutton/Zandoria Studios

Here's looking at scleral lenses

Remember Michael Jackson in *Thriller?* Jim Carrey in *The Mask* or *The Grinch?* Edward Norton in *The Incredible Hulk?* The apes in *Planet of the Apes?* They all had weird eyes. These eyes are achieved by special contact lenses, called *scleral lenses,* which have funky pupil designs and are fitted to cover the actor's eyes like conventional contact lenses.

Linda Blair wore scleral contact lenses for *The Exorcist* and then again when I revisited her possessed state in my comedy spoof *The Linda Blair Witch Project* (see Figure 17-6), where she finds out she's possessed by famous comedians (did you know that possession is nine-tenths of the law?). You can stream my short on YouTube at www.youtube.com/watch?v=ftqEhTpZtQs.

Be sure to purchase scleral lenses from an optometrist or from eyewear specialists like Dr. Morton Greenspoon and Dr. Richard Silver (www.provision care.com), who have designed and provided special scleral lenses for many Hollywood blockbusters (including *The Grinch* and *Men in Black*). Although specialty stores, especially during Halloween, carry designer effects lenses, you don't know if they're made by a reputable company, and the lenses aren't fitted to your particular eye shape. Not only could they cause discomfort or infection, but worse, damage to your cornea. Always consult an ophthalmologist before putting anything in your eyes!

Figure 17-6: An example of scleral lenses and vampire teeth.

Linda Blair (left), Make-up artist, Marlene Stoller (right)

Take a bite out of this

Another skill of the special-effect make-up artist is designing and creating teeth that fit over the actor's own bite. A mold is taken of the actor's real teeth — very similar to how a dentist takes a mold to fit you for a crown. The artist then sculpts a new set of molars — from ghoulish monster or vampire teeth to rotten buck teeth like Austin Powers. Refer Figure 17-6 for an example of vampire teeth that fit over the actor's own incisors.

Chapter 18

Giving Credit and Titles

In This Chapter

▶ Giving credit where credit is due

▶ Designing titles and credits to fit your film

▶ Creating inexpensive, effective titles

▶ Preparing your film for foreign release

*C*redits (a person's name with his or her position) are important to your cast and crew because everyone likes to be recognized for their hard work, and people who work on films are no exception. Receiving credit on a film gives your cast and crew members credibility and can help get them their next job working on another film after yours. In this chapter, you discover impressive ways to give credit to everyone who worked on your film.

Choosing a main title for your film is important, too, just as important as deciding what to name a baby — after all, your film *is* your baby. In this chapter, you see how to create inexpensive titles that can be shot right in the camera or hire a title house to design your titles. You also find out how to prepare a textless version of your film before it's sent to foreign distributors.

Titling Your Film

Coming up with a good title for your film is more than just picking a catchy name. The right title can help market your film to the right audience. For the re-release of my film, *Miss Castaway*, I changed the title to *Silly Movie 2* because the movie was really silly and the title helped attract the appropriate audience — one that appreciates that type of humor. A film's name also influences what people perceive it to be about. It can be an intriguing title like *Fatal Attraction* or an identifiable title to let the audience know exactly who the film is about, like *King Kong, 101 Dalmatians,* or *The Blues Brothers.*

As you think about the title of your film, keep these things in mind:

- ✔ **Choose something that sounds intriguing:** *The Happening, Meet Dave, 2001: A Space Odyssey,* and *Back to the Future* are examples of intriguing titles.

- ✔ **Keep it short and easy to pronounce:** *Wanted, Die Hard,* and *Get Smart,* for example.

- ✔ **Don't reveal too much about the film through its title (except in rare instances where doing so can be intriguing or fun for the audience):** *Journey to the Center of the Earth* or *Snakes on a Plane,* which tells you exactly what to expect!

- ✔ **Set the tone or genre of the movie:** *You Don't Mess with the Zohan, Kung Fu Panda,* and *Grumpy Old Men* (all comedies); *Schindler's List, The Godfather,* and *All the President's Men* (all dramas, although *All the President's Men* could also be a comedy, I guess!)

A title can't be copywritten, but it's always a good idea to research your title to ensure that it's not the same or similar to another well known movie title. When your film is finished, a distributor will request a *title search* be done to make sure there's no other commercial title in release that could be confused with your title. If a title is identical, a major studio could sic their lawyers on you and pressure you to change the title. That happened with one of my titles, which I ended up changing to avoid being threatened by the studio. (Go to Chapter 19 to find out more about distributing your film.)

Writing a Running List of Names and Positions

From the minute you start thinking of making a film, start jotting down the name of every person and company involved in your production. Remembering to place a name in a credit roll in the first place is always much easier (and cheaper) than finding out later that you forgot someone and having to deal with the consequences.

Spelling it write

Make sure every name in your opening credits and ending credits is spelled correctly. Years ago I made a short film spoofing *Friday the 13th* where Jason joins a hockey team. My composer Alan Fleishman wrote a fantastic orchestral score, and I was really proud of how the music came out. Alan is also a very good friend, and when the film premiered to a large audience, Alan pointed out to me that his name was spelled wrong. I felt terrible. Well, now I have a chance to make it up to him. Here's the correct spelling: Alan Fleishman. (I'm proofreading this chapter before it goes to press, just in case.)

Entitled to a credit

For every favor, product deal, or donation you get, you need to thank people and companies responsible in your film's ending credits. It's cheap to use up a line — it could cost you relationships and friendships if you forget. People and companies like to see their names up on the big screen, and recognizing them in this way shows your appreciation of their contribution to your film (they may contribute to your next one, too!). So credit — don't forget it!

Designing Your Titles and Credits

When you decorate your house or apartment, you pick a style. You should do the same when you design your opening title and credits. Main titles and credits can be presented in many creative styles, limited only by your imagination. Start thinking about a unique style that fits your film.

An appropriately designed main title and credits can convey the feeling of fun with a free-style font, seriousness with a plain unencumbered font, or wild and crazy with letters that look like they want to break free. So make sure the style you choose matches the feel of your movie. If you're filming a murder mystery, for example, you wouldn't want to use cartoon lettering in your opening credits.

Often, an audience doesn't pay too much attention to the fonts of your title and credits, but they have a subliminal effect on the viewer nonetheless. In Michael Jackson's *Thriller,* the title looked like it was scratched in blood — definitely creating a mood. In my film, *Light Years Away,* the main title formed out of stars in the deep void of space. The opening credits to *Spider-Man* were caught in an animated web. Next time you go to the movies or watch a video, notice the stylish fonts used in the title and opening credits; you'll be surprised how different and creative they are.

Digital Juice makes a line of colorful and effective animated backgrounds called Jump Backs (in SD & HD), which add a professional flair to your title and credits. You've probably seen these backgrounds on many TV shows with credits and titles superimposed over them. Instead of setting your title and credits on plain black, you can have them pop and breathe with life, accentuated with lively Jump Backs as your background. Over ninety volumes are available, which add up to more than 2,400 backgrounds. Each animated background is 15 to 30 seconds in length and can be seamlessly looped to go on forever. Digital Juice also makes a series of six volumes called the Editor's Tool Kit Pro, which includes animated backgrounds, *lower thirds* (for adding names and titles anywhere on the screen), and a vast array of font types to superimpose over your images. Checkout www.digitaljuice.com for more details.

I've used a company called VT2 Media Design and Communications (www.vt2.com) of Texas, which designed and created opening titles and credits for some of my films, including the animated logo for one of my projects with Michael Jackson. If a company designs your titles, they usually create storyboard panels illustrating how the titles and credits will look in the final frames of the finished film.

Designing the style with fonts

You can choose from thousands of different font styles to make up your title and credits. You've probably got a few hundred on your computer right now. Each font has a feeling and sets a mood. One may be perfect for your film. For example, in my film *Undercover Angel,* my lead character, Harrison, is a struggling book writer. I chose the Courier font, which looks like it came from a typewriter, for the opening credits of the film. It worked especially well because the film starts off with Harrison at his typewriter shortly after the opening credits end.

You can find some great font software at Web sites like www.fonts.com and www.1001freefonts.com or doing a search on the Internet for "fonts."

Animating your main title and credits

Animation adds life and character to your opening and ending title and credits. *The Pink Panther* films were popular for their amusing animation credits and helped spawn the *Pink Panther* animated cartoon series. Steven Spielberg used a stylized cartoon opening for his film *Catch Me If You Can.* Although a full-length animated film is expensive to produce, a few minutes of animation for opening title and credits is usually affordable enough (especially if you use stop-motion or cut-out animation — see Chapter 2). Spending your money on animation at the beginning of your film rather than the ending is better because most people leave as the end credits begin to roll anyway.

The Animation Factory provides a fun angle on presenting your titles and credits. On its Web site www.animationfactory.com, you have a choice of over 500,000 cycled animations, including high-definition clips that can be incorporated into a Web site announcing your production or used in the opening or ending credits of your film. The Animation Factory has every themed animated image imaginable. For a small annual fee starting at $59.95, you can access the entire library of animations. It's a really fun site — check it out.

Digital or optical credits

You can design your credits right on your computer and transfer them to your digital footage. These are called *digital* or *electronic credits.* Most new computers today have a video card or can have one installed that allows you to input and output digital video.

Optical credits are done at a title company or film lab that specializes in designing and photographing titles and credits. They are then printed on film stock and *superimposed optically* (placed over the appropriate scenes by the film lab) over the opening or ending footage of your movie. They can also be printed as white letters on a black background, which is often the way ending roll credits are presented.

Hollywood has many title houses that can create your opening titles and ending credits. You don't have to live in Los Angeles to hire a title company. You can e-mail and fax all the information, and a title company can shoot your titles and ship them directly to you. Many title companies are eager to help independent filmmakers. Most title companies can convert Microsoft Word or text files containing your titles and credits and selected font styles, and print them to film stock or *telecine* them (electronically place them into your film using a video editing bay) into your finished film or digital production.

When working with a professional title house, you'll always be sent a sample of the copy to proofread. Be sure to read closely — overlooking the obvious (misspellings and typos) is all too easy.

Crediting without a computer

If you don't have a computer to create your own title and credits and you can't afford to hire a title company, you still have hope. Let these ideas spur your own creativity:

- ✔ Go to your stationery or art-supply store and pick up some lettering stencils or vinyl stick-on letters by Letraset. You can even get three-dimensional letters from an art-supply or toy store.

- ✔ If your film is a beach film, write your title and opening credits in the sand and let the tide come in and wash them away.

- ✔ If it's a college or high school film, write your title and credits on a blackboard with chalk.

I did a stop-motion animated film many years ago that retold the story of the Frog Prince. My ending credits looked like they were at the bottom of a pond that rippled between credits. Here's what I did: I placed my credits on a card and took a clear dish and filled it with water. I shot through the water in the dish with my camera and jiggled the water in between credits. The credits looked like they were under water! You've also probably seen many films use the turning pages of a book for the opening credits — it's easy to do, and it never gets old.

Rolling Your Title and Credits

After your film is completed and you've assembled all the elements for your main title and credits, you need to concentrate on the timing, order, and legibility of those credits.

If you make your ending credits interesting, you may be able to keep the audience in their seats. Most people get up and leave the theater (or head to the kitchen or bathroom if they're watching on TV), but you can do some of the following to keep them glued to their seats:

- ✔ Have some type of animation or movement to the ending credits.

- ✔ Intercut scenes from the film in between the end credits or include an *epilogue* (closure for some of the characters) to your movie which fades in during your end credits, then fades out to let your credits continue.

- ✔ Stop the credits to feature funny *bloopers* (flubs or mistakes) from the film (like *Monsters, Inc.*, *Toy Story,* and *Rush Hour* have done). *Evan Almighty* had the cast and crew all doing Steve Carell's dance during the ending credit roll (*Ark Building for Dummies* was featured in the movie!)

Timing the opening and ending credits

The best way to organize and time your title and credits is to storyboard the opening of your film (see Chapter 9 for more on storyboarding). This allows you to pace your opening credits to the visuals of your film's opening scenes. If you have your title and credits over black (that is, without scenes from the film running in the background), you don't have to worry about storyboarding them.

Titles and credits bookend a film, clearly identifying the beginning and "The End" of a film. The opening title and credits begin before the film gets into the meat of the story. The ending credits roll when the film has come to a satisfactory conclusion (at least that's what you hope for!).

Sometimes a film's opening credits don't start until after a prelude scene that grabs the audience from the first frame of the picture. Some movies don't even have credits until the end of the movie — but this is rare with big studio productions because of filmmaking egos who want you to know who made the movie and their titles right from the beginning.

Keep in mind, when timing your ending credits, that you don't want them to roll by too fast or too slow. They should be slow enough to read, but not so slow that you put your audience to sleep.

Ordering your title and credits

Just as you have to think about how your title and credits look and when they appear, you also have to think about the order of the credits themselves. Who (or what) appears first, second, and so on? Read on to find out.

Opening credits

The order of opening credits has no real norm, except that usually a big-name star's credit is one of the first to appear (after the distributor logo). The last credit to appear is usually the director's credit. But in between, a myriad of variations exists. Here's one example of a typical opening-credit order:

- Distributor logo
- Production company presents
- The director or production company's possessory credit ("A film by…")
- Title of the film
- Starring cast
- Casting by
- Executive producer
- Producer
- Co-producer(s)
- Music by, or Original Score by
- Costumes designed by (usually reserved for period pieces or wardrobe-heavy films)
- Visual effects designed by (if a heavy visual effects film)
- Production designer
- Edited by
- Director of Photography
- Screenplay by
- Directed by

If you're making an independent film, chances are you may be a triple-threat, meaning your credit will read, "Written, Produced, and Directed by. . . ."

If you are a triple threat, you may be possessed by the *possessory credit,* which strangely enough has nothing to do with being possessed. (Although I did once direct Linda Blair in a spoof I wrote called *The Linda Blair Witch Project,* which parodied *The Exorcist* and *The Blair Witch Project* and in which Linda Blair was not only possessed but also found out it was hereditary.) A possessory credit is a possessive ownership (auteur) credit that usually belongs to the director of the film, such as "A Steven Spielberg Film." Sometimes it's not a director or individual, but a production company, for example, "A Northstar Production."

Closing credits: The End

The closing credits in a film usually begin with the cast in order of appearance, then a repeat of the opening names and titles, followed by staff and crew names. Next, special effects credits, music and song cues used in the film, and then special thanks. By the end of the credit roll, there is often a disclaimer about any similarities to names or characters being purely coincidental. And then the end credits usually finish up with ownership of the motion picture and copyright date.

Ensuring the safety of your credits

One very common mistake that even the studios make from time to time is forgetting to check for *title safety.* Standard TV sets can vary image size in terms of the edges of a picture. Most of the time you never know that the edges of the picture are cut off, except when there are titles or credits. A universal safety zone for standard televisions was established to protect titles and credits from being cut off within the frame. Figure 18-1 illustrates the space you need to place around your credits so that they remain intact on a standard television screen. These safety lines are usually visible through the eyepiece in motion-picture film cameras. High definition television sets have a 16×9 viewing area and generally do not have a cut off area. Just to be safe though, always allow an invisible border around your titles and credits to ensure they're safe.

Make sure your credits are big enough to read if your movie is broadcast on TV. This was a problem of many of the films I made as a kid. My mom always reminded me to make the lettering legible. To this day I stop to remember her advice — so now my credits are legible on any size screen.

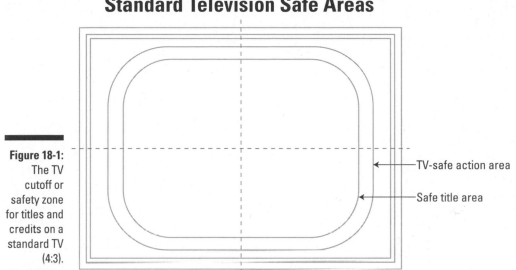

Standard Television Safe Areas

Figure 18-1:
The TV
cutoff or
safety zone
for titles and
credits on a
standard TV
(4:3).

TV-safe action area

Safe title area

Covering Your Eyes: Stripping Titles for Foreign Textless

Textless opening and ending footage is simply the footage from your film before you add the title and credits over the picture. When your film goes to the foreign markets, your cast and crew names remain the same, but the names of each position and your main title are translated into another language.

Non-contractual credits

If you make up an advertising poster for your movie before the film has been shot and before the actor contracts are signed, you want to be aware of the disclaimer *non-contractual credits.* You can put actors' names on the posters (a good idea if some recognizable names are considering roles), but the words, "credits are non-contractual" must be on the poster. This means that you have not contracted the actors to be in your film (but they have given you verbal

or written permission to put their names on the poster), and their names are only appearing on your poster in good faith. This protects you if a distributor demands that you use the actors listed on your poster, or if you have to replace an actor featured on the poster. Put the words "credits are non-contractual" at the bottom-right corner of your poster in very small lettering — just like the fine print the attorney doesn't want you to notice in a contract.

Subject to subtitles

Subtitles are usually reserved for foreign films coming into the English-language market. The English translation appears in the lower part of the screen (in title safe on a standard TV) as the actors speak in their native tongue. This is similar to turning on the closed-caption feature on your TV, which amounts to English subtitles in English-speaking films so that the hearing impaired can follow the dialogue.

Chances are you're not going to use subtitles in your film, unless you're doing it for comedy purposes (as in *Austin Powers in Goldmember*), or when your film includes an alien or a person speaking a foreign language among English-speaking characters (like the natives in *Raiders of the Lost Ark*). Most American films are not subtitled overseas; instead the voices are usually replaced by voiceover actors speaking in their own language (see Chapter 19).

After your film is completed, the film lab makes a *textless* copy of your opening and ending credits footage (if you shot on film). If you edited your film on your computer, you create a *textless* copy of your movie by removing the layer that holds your opening and ending credits. When the foreign distributor receives your film, it places the translated title and credits over the picture. Voilà!

Part V
Finding a Distributor for Your Film

The 5th Wave   By Rich Tennant

"You know that 'buzz' I said our film created here at the festival? Short in the theatre's sound system."

In this part . . .

This is one of the most important parts of this book because, without distribution, the world will never see the masterpiece you worked so hard on. Distribution is getting your film into theatres and into stores on DVD, as well as airing on TV screens all across the globe. With the right distributor, this is all possible.

Film festivals are another avenue for getting your film out in the public eye. You can gain some great recognition as a filmmaker and maybe even win some well-deserved accolades for your creative cinematic endeavors. Film festivals are also a great way for distributors and potential buyers to discover you and your film, and this part gives you the lowdown.

Chapter 19

Distributing Your Film

Distribution is the final stage of the filmmaking process, and it's definitely the most important one. If it isn't distributed, your film will sit on a shelf, and no one will ever see it. In this chapter, I explain the secrets of film distribution. You find out how media rights for theater, television, and video, as well as ancillary rights for merchandising products inspired by your film, are broken down. You see how a distributor markets a film and what you can do to help. I also offer invaluable advice on what to look for in a distribution contract and help you discover the secrets of negotiating the best distribution deal for your film. You also see the advantages of hiring an attorney who's well versed in distribution agreements.

This chapter also provides information about finding a foreign distributor or sales agents who have relationships with worldwide buyers. I tell you about all the possible markets for your film, what each territory pays, and what to expect for your film. I provide firsthand information about the film markets that can introduce your film to foreign buyers, including Cannes and MIPCOM in France, and the American Film Market in Santa Monica, California. And make sure you check out the lists of the top domestic and foreign distributors.

Understanding How Distribution Works

Distributing a film is similar to selling a product. The product needs to get to the customer, and a distributor puts the two together. The world is your potential customer, with global distribution separated into two divisions: domestic and foreign. Including the United States and Canada, more than 65 countries could buy your film. Each country, or *territory,* is a potential paying customer. When a territory purchases your film, it sells it to the various TV, video, and theatrical markets within its country — and it has to negotiate a price with your foreign distributor or sales agent to do so.

To find a distributor, when you have a finished film, you send potential distributors a DVD screener (covered later in this chapter) for distribution consideration. (Many times securing a distributor before the distributor can see a finished product is difficult.) Because there is more demand for product worldwide, you may find it easier to find a foreign distributor first and then find a domestic distributor to cover the United States and Canada (see "Finding a Reliable Distributor or Sales Agent," later in this chapter for details.) You can also enter your film in the various film festivals (see Chapter 20), and let the distributors track *you* down. Or you can hold your own screening and premiere your film to invited distributors.

A film that is distributed overseas usually has to be converted to a system that accommodates the frame rate and scan lines that are compatible with the local broadcasting standards of the specific territory, standards that may be different from those in the United States. A new digital system (introduced in February 2009) replaces the old broadcast system used in North America. The two main worldwide formats are ATSC (replacing NTSC) and PAL:

- **NTSC** (National Television Standards Committee) has been the standard analog broadcasting format since 1940 in North America, most of South America, and Japan. It is based on 525 lines of resolution and is equivalent to 30 frames of video per second. This system is scheduled to be replaced by ATSC, explained shortly.

- **PAL (**Phase Alternation Line) is the analog television display standard that is the predominant video system used in Europe, Asia, and other parts of the world. PAL transmits 25 frames each second and uses 625 individual scan lines of resolution.

- **ATSC** (Advanced Television Systems Committee) will replace the NTSC analog system for digital television, effective February 17, 2009. This broadcast system accommodates standard and high definition wide-screen images of 16:9 images and up to 1920×1080 pixels.

For an NTSC or ATSC video to be viewable overseas, it has to be transferred to PAL format. Your foreign distributor or sales agent usually arranges for the conversion of your film for sale in the overseas territory.

A third option, *streaming* via the Internet, is a universal format that can play footage on virtually any Internet-equipped computer. Streaming is more appropriate for showcasing short films on specialized sites. Check out my parody short *The Linda Blair Witch Project* at www.youtube.com/watch?v=ftqEhTpZtQs.

Presenting Your Film to Distributors

Studio distributors are always on the lookout for little gems to distribute, so creating awareness for your film before and after you shoot it is essential. A film trailer is a great tool to get buyers excited about your film, and designing a poster for your film is the first thing you should think about — even before you start shooting your film.

When searching for a distributor you will hear the term *sales agent* and/or *distributor*. A *sales agent* represents your film like a real estate broker (reel- estate broker) trying to find a domestic or foreign distributor to buy your movie and distribute it. A *distributor* actually distributes your film directly to the consumer. Oftentimes, foreign distributors also call themselves *foreign sales agent* because they're repping your film to individual countries who will buy your film and distribute it within their territory.

Posting a poster of your film

An intriguing poster can excite buyers and raise interest in your film. You may be thinking, "Why make a poster? I haven't even made my film yet." But many films are pre-sold by posters that exist way before the film is ever shot. A poster can give your investors (see Chapter 5) or a potential distributor a taste of what's to come.

Adobe PhotoShop CS3 and Illustrator, part of the Adobe Create Suite (www.adobe.com), are great software programs that you can use to design a poster. Synthetik (www.synthetik.com) makes another great program called Studio Artist that gives you painting and drawing power.

When you make a poster before the film, the credits on the poster are considered *non-contractual*. This means that the people whose names appear in the starring roles and production credits are not officially signed to do the film (but have given you permission to use their names) and could change by the time the film is made. Stating this on the poster protects you and the people whose names appear on the poster from any legal disputes between each other, especially the distributor and/or the buyers.

After you find a distributor, the company may want to design its own poster (even if it was attracted to your film because of *your* poster). Your distributor knows what kind of graphics, colors, and images appeal to global buyers. Figure 19-1 shows two posters, one for my film *Undercover Angel,* designed by the distributor, and one for *Silly Movie 2* designed by my sister Marlene who runs her company MarGraphiX.

Figure 19-1:
The *Undercover Angel* distributor's poster and the poster for *Silly Movie 2.*

Picturing the set photographer

Having someone take professional photos on your set while you're shooting your film is important. These photos will be invaluable when it comes to marketing your film; they're also a mandatory requirement of any distributor. The distributor needs photos showing stills from your film for the promotional flyers. It also uses photos to design your main poster. Don't rely on taking stills off the original footage — the quality isn't very good, and your poster will look cheap and unprofessional.

If you can't afford a professional photographer, get a digital still camera and have someone on your crew with a good eye snap some photos. (Your cinematographer could do this before and after shots.)

Pulling your audience in with a trailer

After you find a distributor and have completed your film, the distributor will want to create a professional film *trailer,* which packs the exciting moments from your film into a commercial. Sometimes a filmmaker will shoot a trailer to try to interest an investor in putting up money to make the actual film. A trailer usually runs one to three minutes in length and features highlights from the film that will spark the interest of buyers. It's also a great idea to post your trailer on www.youtube.com and start a worldwide buzz for your film!

Premiering your film

Showing your film on the big screen in front of a captive audience is a good way to influence potential distributors (as long as the audience's reaction is positive!). If you live in or near Los Angeles or New York, set up a premiere for domestic and foreign distributors, theatrical distributors, TV stations, and DVD home entertainment distributors. If you live outside L.A. or New York, you may want to venture there for the big premiere. The main costs associated with setting up a premiere include rental for a theater and printing and mailing invitations. For a great deal on printed invitations, contact PIP Printing in Burbank at www.pip.com/burbank — tell them I sent you!

If you can't bring buyers to your film, you have to take your film to the buyers. You can get professional-quality dubs of a feature-length film on DVD for less than .40 cents a disc, plus the DVD box and artwork. Now that DVD copies have come down in price, you can send a DVD that has better picture resolution and CD-quality sound (and that requires less postage than an archaic VHS tape). Primera makes a desktop DVD duplicator, the Disc Publisher SE. It burns copies of your movie onto printable DVDs and automatically prints your artwork onto the discs as well. Check out www.Primera.com

Compelling artwork on your DVD cover can go a long way toward catching the eye of potential distributors. You can design your own movie artwork on your computer or scan a color photo from your film. Buy the plastic DVD boxes that have a clear plastic sleeve (like school binders) and slip your artwork into the sleeve. Ten or 20 dubs of your film should be enough to send to distributors. For lists of distributors, turn to "The best domestic distributors" and "The best foreign distributors," later in this chapter.

Before you send screening copies of your film, have the dubbing place superimpose a visual disclaimer across the bottom of the picture that says something like "Screening Copy Only" (if you're using editing software, you can do it yourself). This disclaimer, similar to a watermark on a confidential paper document, prevents thieves from stealing your film and selling it to television or home video — there's no way to get rid of the visual warning unless you cut off the part of the picture that has the disclaimer.

Seeing stars

If you can get a name actor in your film, even in a small part, your film will get more attention and help you get financing or a distributor (depending on the actor you get). Casting directors can usually use their relationships with agents, managers, and talent to help you land some stars. Casting Yasmine Bleeth and James Earl Jones helped get my film *Undercover Angel* off the ground. Having Academy Award-nominee Eric Roberts and Christopher Knight (Peter Brady) in my film *Light Years Away* added credibility to the project. And having Dan Aykroyd as the voice of Dexter the computer in my film *The Random Factor* helped the film find distribution.

Distributing Your Film Domestically

Domestic distribution is the licensing of your film to media outlets in the United States and Canada. Domestic usually encompasses Canada as well as the United States because television broadcasts spill over the border, and satellite can be picked up in both the United States and Canada. TV and satellite are part of the media rights for which a distributor negotiates.

Domestic distribution can account for 50 percent of your film's profits, the other 50 percent being from foreign profits. If your film is picked up by a major motion-picture distributor in the United States for theatrical release, you could receive an advance of $500,000 or more, plus a share of the profits (which is negotiable and varies depending on the distributor, anywhere from 20 to 50 percent). The distributor usually deducts what it paid in an advance from any profits owed to you. Miramax paid $5 million for the independent film *Swingers,* produced on a budget of only $250,000.

DVD home entertainment rights with a major studio distributor can pay an advance of around $300,000, depending on the material and whether any recognizable names appear in the film. In addition to an advance, you could also see profit participation as well. You can get anywhere from $10,000 to $500,000 for a one-time television licensing fee.

Domestic studio distributors may give you a *negative pickup agreement* for your film. A negative pickup guarantees that the distributor will buy your film when you deliver the final product. Raising the money is easier when a studio distributor gives you a negative pickup offer in writing. You can then approach investors and show them the negative pickup agreement from the studio insuring that the film will have distribution when you deliver it.

I did self-distribution my way

When I made my first feature film, I was frustrated because I couldn't find a distributor to pick it up. One day I went into my local video store and, for fun, put a copy of my film (in a video box with artwork) on the shelf so I could tell people that my film was in the video store. A week later, I went into the video store, and my video was gone! I asked the clerk, who looked on the computer and told me that it had been rented! It was an exciting feeling to know that someone actually rented my film. About a year later I finally found a distributor, and the company put my film in major video stores, including Wal-Mart — saving me the trouble!

Minding media rights

When you sign with a distributor, the distributor negotiates *media rights* for your film in each country (also referred to as a *territory*). These rights determine in which of the following outlets your film can be seen in the specific territory and how much is paid for the licensing rights to each medium:

- **Theatrical:** For theatrical screenings to audiences.

- **Home entertainment:** On DVDs, including Blu-ray discs in video stores.

- **Pay-per-view:** For broadcast viewing on a pay-per-view basis. Includes Video on Demand (VOD), which lets you watch it exactly when you want to watch it.

- **Pay television:** For broadcast on pay television that has paid subscribers (such as HBO or Showtime) and usually has no commercials.

- **Satellite:** For TV satellite markets within a territory (broadcast at the same time that pay TV starts).

- **Cable television:** For broadcast to basic cable television subscribers.

- **Free television:** For broadcast on television networks like NBC, ABC, CBS, and FOX.

- **Closed circuit:** For limited exposure in hotels, airplanes, and cruise ships.

- **Internet:** For viewing or downloading off the Internet.

A *window* is the period of time during which a film is available for each media right. For example, a theatrical release usually goes to DVD after a window of six months; DVD usually has a window of 30 days before pay TV can broadcast it. Some TV broadcasters negotiate for an extended window of up to a year or two, depending on what they pay for the licensing of the picture. Each buyer needs to abide by the window so as to not infringe on another buyer's window in a different medium.

IMAX-IMUM

The world's largest film format originating from Ontario, Canada, called IMAX, is a projection system that distributes movies that have been transferred to 70mm, 15 frame perforated stock for large image projection. The projected image is eight stories high by 120 feet wide — obviously requiring a special theatre to accommodate the format (there's close to 300 IMAX theatres worldwide). The film moves horizontally, similar to a train meandering over train tracks. IMAX is best known for its documentaries and travelogue large format movies but also projects studio features digitally remastered onto 70mm film stock for the IMAX experience, including such blockbusters as *Apollo 13, Harry Potter and the Order of the Phoenix, Night at the Museum, Superman Returns, Spider-Man,* and *Batman: The Dark Knight.* IMAX has introduced several digital projection systems and will eventually switch from 70mm film projection systems to all digital projection.

When a film is licensed for a particular medium and has a defined window, the distributor may request a *holdback,* meaning that your film cannot be shown on any other media until a negotiable period of time has lapsed.

Netflix (www.netflix.com) and Blockbuster (www.blockbusteronline.com) both offer a service to rent DVDs by mail. You make your selection on their Web sites after browsing through movie titles — and in a day or so your selection will arrive in the mail. After you watch the DVD, you just return it via the mail. You can even rent my movies, *Undercover Angel* and *Miss Castaway & the Island Girls* at Netflix and Blockbuster online!

Anticipating ancillary rights

Ancillary rights bring in additional income derived from other sources, such as a soundtrack, novelization, comic books, toys, or any type of merchandise inspired by your film. *Star Wars* figurines, *Harry Potter* books and games, and *Transformer* toys and action figures are all part of this merchandising bonanza. You can find *premiums* (inexpensive toys and gadgets) in cereal boxes and kids' meals at fast-food restaurants as cross-promotion for films. Additional ancillary rights can include a sequel to your film, a spin-off television series, or even a stage play (like Disney's stage adaptation of *The Lion King*).

Successful ancillary merchandising on an independent film is much more difficult without the backing of a major studio. However, my independent film, *Undercover Angel* had a character named Mr. Dodo in the film, which created a following and led to the marketing of Dodo dolls and books. You can see Mr. Dodo at www.mrdodo.com.

Laser Light Blue

Blu-ray, the newest DVD high definition format, won the format wars and beat out the competing medium called DVD HD. The Blu-ray name is derived from the laser blue light that reads and can write onto the disc. A Blu-ray disc (the same dimensions as a standard DVD) can hold up to 50 megabytes of high definition footage, as opposed to the limited 4.7 megs on a traditional DVD disc. The good news for all your standard non-high def DVDs — they play just fine (and look even better) in a Blu-ray HD player!

Meeting domestic buyers at the Home Media Expo

The Entertainment Merchant's Association (EMA) holds the Home Media Expo every July in Las Vegas (but may relocate). This expo brings domestic buyers and sellers of films and programming for home-entertainment on DVD to resellers. Attending the Expo are the owners of both the big video chains and ma-and-pa retail stores. Having your film featured at the Home Media Expo usually comes after a domestic distributor has signed a distribution deal with you to represent your film to all the home entertainment retailers. If you haven't found a distributor for your film, the Expo is a good place to network and meet potential distributors to distribute your film on DVD.

Distributing Your Film around the World

Foreign distribution is the licensing of your film to theatrical, TV, and home-entertainment (DVD) buyers overseas in the global market. Your foreign distributor (or sales agent) represents your film to more than 65 countries (also known as *territories*). Each country has individual buyers who purchase film rights for their territories. (**Note:** Some territories group together multiple countries. Check with your foreign distributor for details.)

Foreign sales can account for 50 percent of all worldwide sales (with domestic representing the other 50 percent). Europe accounts for up to 70 percent of all foreign sales. Finding a foreign distributor or sales agent is much the same as finding a domestic distributor — you send a DVD screener of your film to the various foreign distributors (see "The top foreign distributors" later in this chapter) or browse through The Hollywood Creative Directory's distributor guide (www.hcdonline.com) for a listing of every foreign distributor (and domestic ones as well).

Selling your film at the super markets

When you secure a foreign distributor, that distributor is likely to take your film to a market to connect with potential licensors. Three international film markets allow foreign distributors to showcase their library of films for licensing to the global market. These markets are a necessity for foreign distributors to attend, although films are sold between markets as well:

- **The American Film Market (AFM)** takes place in October/November in Santa Monica. Producers, distributors, buyers, sellers, actors, and filmmakers flock to a beachfront hotel for eight days of dealing and networking. More than 300 exhibitors set up offices in suites at the hotel. Local theaters screen films so that buyers can view the distributors' products.

- **The Cannes Film Market** takes place in mid-May for approximately 12 days on the French Riviera, running simultaneously with the Cannes Film Festival (see Chapter 20). The festival is a competition of films, and the market is a film-selling convention. Buyers, distributors, and filmmakers enjoy the festive European culture along with distributor parties on rooftops and luxury cruise boats.

- **MIPCOM,** another popular overseas market, is held in mid-October for five days in Cannes and concentrates on TV series and movies for international television markets. Your foreign distributor can get additional TV sales for your film by taking it to this market. MIP-TV is put on by the same organization and takes place in April.

Your foreign distributor or sales agent may agree to pay your way to one or more of the markets in exchange for distributing your film, or it may deduct your traveling expenses from your film's profits. But hey, wouldn't it be fun to go to France with your film?

If you've made a 35mm print of your film, your distributor will set up screening times for buyers to see your film in a nearby theater. If you don't have a 35mm print, your distributor may pay to have a print made.

If you shot and cut your project on video or digital files, you may need to blow it up to 16mm or 35mm if your film is getting a theatrical release or your foreign distributor wants to screen it for buyers at the various film markets. The delicate and expensive process called *film scanning* can cost from $30,000 to $60,000 for a theatrical-length piece to be blown up to 35mm. To save on this cost, see if your foreign distributor can project your film from a video projector instead, unless the distributor is willing to incur the cost to blow it up.

Projecting your image

Because more and more productions are being shot on video and digital files, many theaters are now equipped to project video. This is a plus when a distributor wants to project your film to potential buyers and you don't have a theatrical print but only a finished copy of your film on video or a hard drive. Your production can be transferred to DVD or digital tape and projected in a theater without the expense of blowing it up to 35mm film stock. Most people won't know the difference, especially if you make your footage look like film, either with software that emulates film, like Magic Bullet Frames (www.redgiantsoftware.com), or with one of the 24progressive digital cinema camcorders, like Panasonic's AG-HVX200. The studios are working on ways to beam film to theaters electronically and do away with the heavy film reels and cans that are currently shipped. It would be similar to how you receive cable television channels or satellite TV.

Negotiating: How much for your film?

Your foreign distributor (or sales agent) makes separate and exclusive deals with each country for all media rights or combinations thereof to your film. As with domestic media rights, each media right is for a certain window of time so as not to infringe on another market's window. Buyers pay a heftier price if your film has a theatrical release before DVD and television.

Usually, filmmakers give foreign distributors (or sales agents) all foreign rights, including all ancillary markets, so the distributor can enter into agreements for TV, theatrical, and DVD rights overseas. Domestic works differently because the filmmaker has more control in distribution at home and can do individual deals for TV, theatrical, and DVD, which would be difficult to track on foreign sales.

Each country pays a different licensing fee for your film, negotiated by your foreign distributor or sales agent. The fee depends on the size of the country and other factors, such as these:

- ✔ **The state of the global economy.** Is the world in good economic state, or dealing with difficult financial times?

- ✔ **The genre of your film.** Action and horror, which translate well visually overseas, tend to bring in higher prices than comedies and family fare.

- ✔ **Whether any name stars or recognizable talent appear in your film.** Name stars add credibility to your film, which can make the difference in getting a sale and also fetching higher licensing fees.

✔ **The production values of your film.** Does it look like it was made on a higher budget?

✔ **What's popular at the time at the world box office.** Is science-fiction popular because a major sci-fi film is doing well at the box-office? Next week it could be fantasy or crime, depending on the success of major studio releases (everyone likes to follow in the trail of a successful genre).

Table 19-1 shows the low and high rates paid by a selection of foreign territories for television and DVD rights. It gives examples of prices that have been paid for independent films with the production values that look like a $1 to $2 million film. As you can see, the numbers really add up. Theatrical rights could pay significantly higher numbers. Note that foreign distribution companies usually deal in U.S. dollars when selling overseas.

Table 19-1	Prices Paid by Foreign Buyers for a Low-Budget Film for TV and DVD Rights
Territory	*For a Film That Looks Like a $1 to 2 Million Budget*
France	$25,000 to $100,000
Germany	$25,000 to $ 150,000
Italy	$25,000 to $100,000
U.K.	$30,000 to $100,000
Japan	$40,000 to $100,000
Mexico	$15,000 to $60,000
Poland	$5,000 to $30,000
Turkey	$15,000 to $40,000

Speaking their language

After your film is sold to a foreign territory, it's dubbed in the language of the country that purchased it. The filmmaker has prepared a music-and-effects (M&E) track (see Chapter 16) that allows the language of the foreign country to be dubbed while retaining the original music and sound-effects tracks. The foreign buyer or territory that licenses your film incurs the cost of translation and dubbing and performs the work in its country.

A separate language dub may not have to be done in each and every country. If your film is sold to France and dubbed in French, your distributor can use that same French version to sell to French-speaking portions of Canada. If you sell to Spain, your distributor will inform the buyers for Mexico that a Spanish version is available for licensing.

Pre-selling a film

Pre-selling is when a distributor sells rights to your film to foreign buyers even before the film is made (see Chapter 5). The distributor takes *advances* (down payments of at least 20 percent), which are presented to the bank or to investors to confirm that your film has buyers waiting to license it after it's completed. Doing pre-sales is much more difficult than it used to be, unless the film has some major stars attached to it.

The English-language dialogue isn't the only thing that has to go when dubbing a film; the English words that visually appear in the film have to be removed as well. When your film goes to another country, you must provide the distributor with a *textless* version with the title and all credits missing. The receiving country translates your film's title, as well as all production credits (of course, the crew and actors' names remain unchanged), into its language. See Chapter 18 for information about credits and titles.

Finding a Reliable Distributor or Sales Agent

Finding a distributor or sales agent can be easy if you've made a very commercial film or difficult if your film can't seem to find an audience. The first thing to do is get a list of distributors (see the Hollywood Creative Directory in the following list) and make an introductory call to see if any may be interested in screening your film. If there is some initial interest, send a DVD screener of your film with a letter stating that you spoke with the distributor on the phone and thanking the distributor for the consideration.

Another way to get a distributor or sales agent interested in your film is to submit to film festivals. If your film is accepted to screen at a major film festival, like the Sundance Film Festival or Toronto Film Fest, then you have a very good chance of having a distributor discover your film. If your film doesn't get accepted or discovered at a film festival, there are other ways to find a distributor:

- ✔ **Film Finders:** This service tracks film rights and availability throughout the world at no charge to you. List with this service, and distributors may be calling you to inquire about your film! Go to www.film finders.com to list your film.

- ✔ **Producer's representative:** A *producer's rep,* also called a *sales rep* or *sales agent,* is an individual or a company, similar to a manager or agent, that helps you find a distributor (though many distributors also call themselves sales agents when repping your film to other territories — the term is often interchangeable). Producer's reps have relationships with various distributors and attend all the major film markets. They can also advise you on distribution contracts and help negotiate the best deal. Bruder Releasing (www.4bri.net) is a producer's rep and a distributor who has represented some of my films for domestic television.

- ✔ **Other filmmakers:** Other filmmakers who have films in distribution may be able to provide you with an introduction to their distributors.

- ✔ **Trade papers:** *The Hollywood Reporter* and *Variety* put out annual foreign-film market issues and domestic distributor listings.

- ✔ **Distribution directories:** The Hollywood Creative Directory (www.hcdonline.com or 800-815-0503) puts out reference directories, including one on distributors. It lists the contact information for more than 800 companies, including film and TV distributors, foreign film buyers, networks, financing companies, and sales agents. The directory is updated several times a year.

See also the lists of the top ten domestic and foreign distributors later in this section.

If a distributor or sales agent is interested in your film, always ask for referrals. Talk to other filmmakers whose films the distributor represents. This lets you know if the distributor is reliable and honest.

The best domestic distributors

The following are the top ten domestic studios that distribute films for theatrical, television, and DVD release in the United States and Canada:

- ✔ **Dreamworks:** 100 Universal City Plaza, Universal City, CA 91608; phone: 818-733-7000; www.dreamworks.com

- ✔ **MGM (Metro Goldwyn Mayer):** 10250 Constellation Blvd., Los Angeles, CA 90067; phone: 310-449-3000; www.mgm.com

- ✔ **Columbia Pictures: 10202 W. Washington Blvd., Culver City, CA 90232**; phone: 310-244-4000; www.sonypictures.com

- ✔ **Lionsgate Films:** 2700 Colorado Ave., Santa Monica, CA 90401; phone: 310-449-9200; www.lionsgate.com

- ✔ **Paramount Pictures:** 5555 Melrose Ave., Los Angeles, CA 90038; phone: 323-956-5000;www.paramount.com

✔ **Sony Pictures Entertainment:** 10202 W. Washington Blvd., Culver City, CA 90232; phone: 310-244-4000; www.sonypictures.com

✔ **Twentieth Century Fox:** 10201 W. Pico Blvd., Los Angeles, CA 90035; phone: 310-369-1000; www.fox.com

✔ **Universal Studios:** 100 Universal City Plaza, Universal City, CA 91608; phone: 818-777-1000; www.universalstudios.com

✔ **Warner Bros.:** 4000 Warner Blvd., Burbank, CA 91522; phone: 818-954-6000; www.warnerbros.com

✔ **The Walt Disney Company:** 55 S. Buena Vista St., Burbank, CA 91521; phone: 818-560-1000; www.disney.com

The best foreign distributors

The following are the top ten companies that distribute films to overseas foreign markets. Foreign territories usually license DVD, television, and theatrical rights:

✔ **Alliance Film:** 121 Bloor St. East, Ste. 1500, Toronto, Ontario Canada, M4W 3M5; phone: 416-967-1174; www.alliancefilms.com

✔ **Crystal Sky Worldwide Sales:** 10203 Santa Monica Blvd., Los Angeles, CA 90067; phone: 310-843-0223; www.crystalsky.com

✔ **Curb Entertainment:** 3907 W. Alameda Ave., Burbank, CA 91505; phone: 818-843-8580; www.curbentertainment.com

✔ **Film Artists Network:** P.O. Box 93032, Hollywood, CA 90093, phone: 818-344-0569; www.filmartistsnetwork.com

✔ **Motion Picture Corporation of America:** 10635 Santa Monica Blvd., Los Angeles, CA 90025,; phone: 310-319-9500; www.mpcafilm.com

✔ **Peace Arch:** 4640 Admiralty Way, Marina del Rey, CA 90292; phone: 310-776-7200; www.peacearch.com

✔ **Morgan Creek International:** 10351 Santa Monica Blvd., Los Angeles, CA 90025; phone: 310-432-4848; www.morgancreek.com

✔ **The Weinstein Co.:**375 Greenwich St., New York, NY 10013; phone 212-941-3800; www.weinsteinco.com

✔ **Nu Image — Millennium Films:** 6423 Wilshire Blvd., Los Angeles, CA 90048; phone: 310-388-6900; www.nuimage.net

✔ **Showcase Entertainment:** Warner Center, 21800 Oxnard St., Ste. 150, Woodland Hills, CA 91367; phone: 818-715-7005; www.showcase entertainment.com

Four-walling has a ceiling

Four-walling refers to distributing your film yourself without the aid of a professional distributor. I don't recommend this route because it's time-consuming and expensive. You have to pay for your own 35mm film prints, place ads in newspapers and magazines (which is not cheap), and make your own posters. You also have to contact the individual theater owners who rent out their facilities to independent films.

Usually, only art houses and small theater chains will consider a film that's not represented by a major distributor. In this case, the filmmaker pays the theater a rental fee. In return, the filmmaker gets the total admission fee paid by the theater patrons but the theatre owner gets to keep the popcorn and soda receipts!

Although setting up your own domestic distribution by dealing with individual TV networks, home entertainment (DVD), and theatrical studios is possible, I don't recommend this approach for foreign distribution. To get your film distributed successfully overseas, you need a qualified and competent foreign distributor or sales agent who can track your film's sales, speak the languages, and benefit from the relationships with the foreign buyers that they deal with on a regular basis. There are also complicated tax and delivery requirements that are a major headache for an independent filmmaker and should be left up to the expertise of a foreign representative.

Demystifying Distribution Contracts

After you settle on a distributor, you must sign a contract. Distribution contracts can be long, detailed, and confusing. When you get to this stage, I suggest that you contact an entertainment attorney or someone versed in distribution contracts. You don't want to lose your film and profits to a distributor because you didn't understand the distribution contract. The following are some of the things a distribution agreement addresses:

✔ **Grant of rights:** What media rights is the domestic distributor taking — TV, theatrical, home entertainment (DVD)? A foreign distributor representing your film overseas usually takes all rights.

✔ **Term:** For how long does the distributor have the right to distribute your film? It can be up to 25 years. If it doesn't fulfill a certain amount of net sales, you, the filmmaker, should have the option to cancel the agreement (in writing, of course).

Whatever deal you strike with a distributor, decide on a minimum dollar amount that it has to reach in net sales (meaning the dollars that you pocket). If the distributor doesn't reach that number in two years from the date of signing, then all distribution rights revert back to you, and you can find another distributor. I usually use a number like $200,000 to $500,000. If you don't reach that, it's time to move on.

✔ **Territory:** Is it for the whole world or just certain territories? Usually with a foreign distributor it's all territories except the United States and Canada, which is usually taken by a domestic distributor.

✔ **Delivery requirements:** What picture elements do you need to provide? A 35mm print? A video copy in high definition? A hard drive containing all your files? Do you have publicity photos, artwork, actor and crew agreements, and an accurate credit list ready to hand over to your new distributor?

✔ **Accounting terms:** You need to have access to the distributor's books regarding the collection of sales on your film. How often do you have access to those books?

✔ **Gross and net dollars:** Look for the definition of *gross receipts* and *net receipts* (after agreed-upon expenses are paid) that will be split between the distributor and you, the filmmaker. You can find further definitions of *gross* and *net* later in this chapter.

✔ **Statement terms:** Does the distributor have an obligation to provide you with producer's statements of any and all sales on your picture? Usually, the distributor provides monthly statements the first year, quarterly the following year, and annually thereafter, but this is negotiable.

✔ **Payment terms:** When is the distributor obligated to pay you your share of the profits from your picture? It's usually after defined expenses (marketing and distributor's fees). Determine the allocation of gross receipts — what's paid out and when. Also determine if an *advance* is paid (upfront money to acquire the rights to distribute your film).

✔ **Marketing expenses:** This category includes prints and advertising costs, film-market expenses, the costs of making the film trailer, and so on. Put a cap on marketing expenses so that your distributor can't spend beyond that point. Prints and advertising usually cost between $50,000 and $100,000 on an independent film.

✔ **Proof of copyright:** The distributor wants to ensure that you are the original owner of the property (the script and completed film should each have their own separate copyright registration).

In perpetuity is a term that's used in distribution contracts. It means "forever," ensuring that the distributor has the rights to your film forever — unless you put a term on it. Agreeing to a limited term, such as ten years with a renewal clause, is to your advantage.

Insuring for errors and omissions

A distributor can purchase *errors and omissions insurance* (E&O) after it decides to distribute your film. E&O protects you and the distributor from being sued by any third party, if someone says that you stole his idea, slandered him in the film, or used something of his in your film without permission. A distributor usually also requests a *title search* done by an attorney before purchasing E&O insurance. Even though you can't copyright a title, the distributor wants to know if other films are out there with similar or competing titles that could cause confusion or concern.

Usually, a distributor makes sure that no such liabilities exist in your film before it takes it on. If it has concerns, it'll ask you to cut out the offending or questionable material. A distributor usually pays the cost of E&O (see Chapter 4), which can run around $8,000 and up, and then deducts it from your profits.

Accounting for creative bookkeeping

Bookkeeping is another reason why you need to have an attorney review your distribution agreement for your film. Distributors can be very creative in their bookkeeping, and your film could end up never seeing a profit in your pocket — no matter how many sales your distributor makes. Expenses have to be clearly defined in your distribution contract. A distributor can charge excess overhead costs and other hidden charges if you aren't careful.

When you receive a contract from a potential distributor or sales agent, it will contain definitions of *gross* and *net.* Your attorney must look over these definitions carefully. *Gross* is all the monies that come in on your film; *net* is what's left after your distributor takes its expenses. Make sure that those expenses are clearly defined. A distributor's expenses consist of

- **Distribution fee:** For a foreign distributor, 20 percent to 30 percent is standard off the top of all gross sales. With a domestic distributor, the fee could be an advance, such as $500,000 paid up front to you to acquire distribution rights to your film, with royalties paid on a percentage of the sales (this is negotiable). Or the distributor may want a *complete buyout* (a flat fee paid with no royalties and the distributor ends up owning your film).

- **Market expenses:** For foreign distributors, these expenses include overseas film-market costs; for domestic distributors, they include conventions or film markets.

✔ **Promotional flyers (also called *one-sheets* or *sell-sheets*):** For handing out to buyers (design and printing costs).

✔ **Posters:** To hang up at the film markets (design and printing costs).

✔ **Trade ads:** To create buyer awareness of your film (design and advertising costs).

✔ **Movie trailer:** To help sell your film to buyers (creative and editing costs).

✔ **Screeners:** DVD screeners of your film provided to potential buyers upon request.

✔ **Travel:** For you to attend an overseas market with your foreign distributor. This can include costs for film market badges as well.

Always put a cap on expenses. Clearly define the amount of expenses the distributor can deduct against the sales on your film. After the defined expenses are recouped (including the distribution fee), you'll begin to share in the profits.

Chapter 20

Exploring and Entering
Film Festivals

In This Chapter
▶ Understanding the benefits of entering and attending film festivals
▶ Finding film festivals that suit your film
▶ Submitting the right materials

*Y*ou've finally completed your film, and you can't wait to win some awards for all your hard work. Film festivals are the perfect place to get your film noticed and perhaps gain some recognition for it. This chapter provides firsthand information about entering and (hopefully) winning film festivals, along with how to choose the best festival and the right category for your film. I also give you some hints about getting a discount on the festival entry fee or even getting the fee waived.

Being accepted at a festival such as the Sundance Film Festival is as important as winning. (It *is* a nomination.) An award or acceptance at a prestigious festival can give you and your film credibility. In this chapter, you find a list of the top ten festivals where you can enter your film and compete for award recognition.

Film festivals are also a great place to network and even commiserate with fellow filmmakers on the trials and tribulations of getting your film completed. If you attend the festival in person, you have a chance to talk with agents, distributors, and other people you wouldn't normally have a chance to hang out with informally in Hollywood or elsewhere.

Demystifying Film Festivals

A film festival is a festival to send your film for possible acceptance with other films. It's a place to compete, be judged, and either place, win, or lose. A film festival is also a spot to meet new friends, watch films that may never make the mainstream market, and make some business contacts that could help further your career.

Film festivals are springing up like weeds all over the world. With so many out there, you're bound to find at least one that will screen your film, regardless of how good or bad it is. Any recognition from a film festival is better than no recognition at all.

Most film festivals are run by committees consisting of the festival director and the organizers, volunteers, and judges. Often, festivals hire judges who are skilled industry craftspeople and can recognize the talents of their peers. Some of the higher-profile festivals involve well-known actors, producers, and directors as judges. These judges are familiar with the process of filmmaking and look for expertise in story structure, direction, acting, editing, and the picture as a whole as well.

Along with the excitement of watching your film with an audience and gauging the reaction, networking is a very important part of attending a film festival. You never know what new friends or business contacts you're going to meet. After all, you'll be around your peers — people who love film as much as you do.

Because many filmmakers are now making their films with digital camcorders (including high definition), most film festivals accept finished product on videotape or DVD — which is screened using video projectors — as opposed to film projection.

Film festivals are often endorsed by the state or city in which they're held, such as the Palm Springs Film Festival and the Santa Barbara Film Festival. The festival promotes tourism and revenues for the city. Some festivals are run by nonprofit organizations.

Film festival recognition adds to your credibility as a filmmaker. If you win just one film festival, you're officially known as "an award-winning filmmaker."

Judging the difference between a film festival and a film market

Many up-and-coming filmmakers get confused by the difference between a film festival and a film market. A *film festival* is a competition of films vying for recognition in the form of awards and acknowledgment. The visibility that filmmakers get and the networking they can do open up the possibilities for finding a distributor, if they don't already have one.

A *film market* is a business convention that showcases films for sale to buyers looking for film product all over the world. At a film market, the films already have representation with distributors or sales reps who are soliciting the films to domestic and international buyers for the TV, DVD, and theatrical outlets. The Cannes Film Festival has a film market that parallels the festival but is a separate entity.

The American Film Market in Santa Monica, California, the Cannes Film Market in France, and MIPCOM (also in France) are the three main worldwide film *markets*. See Chapter 19 for more information about film markets.

Screening the benefits of entering film festivals

Besides being a great place to check out what other independent filmmakers are doing, a film festival serves two main purposes: showcasing films and helping filmmakers find potential distributors for their films. Also keep in mind these other benefits to entering and attending film festivals as you wonder whether your film is good enough to enter:

- **They give you the opportunity to network with other filmmakers.** You can meet your peers and share stories and misadventures.

- **They provide a forum in which you can meet business contacts.** Agents, attorneys, distributors, and studio executives are much more approachable in a festival environment.

- **They give out cash and prizes.** I don't know anyone who's ever complained about winning cash or prizes. Prizes from festivals are often film related, such as free laboratory services, camera and editing equipment, and film books and magazines.

- **They give out statuettes and certificate awards.** Being able to display an award or any type of accolade for your hard work is always nice. An award also gives you and your film credibility.

- **They offer panels and seminars that you can learn from.** Many festivals have credible filmmakers and entertainment-industry guests who offer invaluable insights and answer questions.

- **They can help generate publicity for your film.** Your film could get written up in the local paper of the festival or even get a review (hopefully a good one) from one of the major trade papers like *The Hollywood Reporter* or *Variety*. Local news and entertainment shows may interview you on camera and ask you about your film.

- **Festival parties are fun.** People (especially agents and distributors) are often more relaxed and approachable after a few drinks and some good music. Just don't drink too much and make a fool of yourself by dancing on the tables. You want your *film* to be judged — not *you!*

Don't be intimidated by film festivals. Your film may be the little gem a particular festival is looking for. Anyone can enter a film festival as long as he or she pays the entry fee and submits the film under the festival's rules. Anyone can win, too!

Entering and Winning Secrets

The secret to entering film festivals is what I call *entry etiquette*. Winning is beyond your control, but following the basic rules I describe in this section brings you closer to that win.

Don't take it personally if your film doesn't make it into a festival. With many festivals receiving thousands of submissions annually, a film can easily be overlooked.

Submitting a work-in-progress — Don't!

Even though some festivals accept works-in-progress, you're just donating your entry fee to the festival when your film doesn't get selected because it isn't finished. I've made this mistake before and want to warn you to avoid it. Wait until your film is completed — including music and sound mix — before you submit it for consideration. Many filmmakers eager to make the deadline for the big festivals like Sundance and Toronto end up sending a work-in-progress. But the festival selection committee rarely gives an uncompleted film the benefit of the doubt. The unfinished film is viewed alongside completed films and usually loses out. Submitting a work-in-progress wastes your time and money — and the festival's time as well.

Entering the right festivals for your film

Your film is in the can, and you can't wait to send it out and start collecting invitations to all the great film festivals. But wait: You have to choose carefully which festival is best to enter. You can start by going to www.film festivals.com for up-to-the-minute information about film festivals, including entry details and deadlines. Going to a film festival's Web site enables you to get updated information and even download an entry form immediately. Note that most film festival Web sites have the extension .org, *not* .com; many festivals are nonprofit organizations. Withoutabox.com has become the norm for submitting to virtually any film festival (more on this later in the chapter).

So how do you decide which festival is right for your film? Think about your intended audience. If your film is a mainstream piece that *Star Wars* or *The Lord of the Rings* audiences would love, it isn't exactly Sundance Film Festival fare; Sundance often looks for off-beat or controversial films. If your film's about an escaped convict who kidnaps grandmothers, it isn't going to be accepted at a children's film festival — unless it's a comedy, and the heroes are an odd gang of misfits.

The following is a list of ten top film festivals, in order of popularity, to consider for your film. The list is a compilation of my favorites, including first-film and independent film-friendly festivals and a family festival dedicated to those rare independent family-produced films.

- ✔ **The Sundance Film Festival** takes place in Park City, Utah, in January, with an entry deadline in early October. This is the festival of festivals, established by actor Robert Redford and named after one of his favorite classic films, *Butch Cassidy and the Sundance Kid.* (That's why he's often still referred to as the *Kid.*) Sundance has become one of the toughest festivals to get a film accepted at. The festival is overloaded with submissions, and a film has to have a sophistication that Sundance audiences and judges have become accustomed to. The festival favors independent films. If your film gets accepted for screening, that's almost as good as winning — being accepted carries a lot of merit. But it's a tough one, so don't rely on Sundance to be your film's festival premiere. For information, go to www.sundance.org/festival.

- ✔ **The Toronto International Film Festival** takes place in Toronto, Ontario, Canada, in September, with an entry deadline in April/May. This festival has been around since 1976 and is considered the second most popular among the elite film festivals, after Sundance. Films are judged on artistic values and subject matter, similar to the Sundance Film Festival. Independent films are especially welcomed. Go to www.tiffg. ca or phone 416-967-7371.

- ✔ **Telluride Film Festival** takes place in August/September in the mountain village of Telluride, Colorado, with an entry deadline in April/July. The festival is for real movie lovers and accepts all types of films as well as experimental, first-film, and artsy styles. A lot of gems have been discovered at Telluride. Go to www.telluridefilmfestival.com or phone 603-643-1255.

- ✔ **Worldfest Houston** is in April, with an entry deadline in February. It accepts digitally finished films transferred to DVD for best image quality, as well as the traditional 16mm and 35mm film prints for projection. The festival accepts a wide array of styles, from wide commercial appeal to experimental short films. This is one of my favorite festivals, run by J. Hunter Todd. For information, go to www.worldfest.org or phone 713-965-9955.

- ✔ **Cannes Film Festival** takes place in May, in the breathtaking city of Cannes, France, with an entry deadline in March. The Cannes Film Festival is in the elite company of Sundance and Toronto. It carries a different sophistication and is run with the international elegance of a European gala event. The festival accepts higher-profile films, especially with an international flair. Go to www.festival-cannes.fr or e-mail festival@festival-cannes.fr.

- **American Film Institute Fest** takes place in November, in Los Angeles, California, with an entry deadline in June/July. The American Film Institute's fine reputation offers credibility to any film that is accepted into the festival. If you win, it doesn't hurt your credibility, either. The festival accepts most styles of films, especially independent. Go to www.afifest.com or phone 866-AFI Fest (866-234-3378).

- **Slamdance Film Festival** takes place in January, with an entry deadline in October. Slamdance was created in 1994 to catch the spillover of films that don't get accepted into Sundance. It's very much a festival for independent filmmakers and first-film entrants who find themselves left out in the cold — even though they have a film that an audience would appreciate and enjoy. Go to www.slamdance.com or phone 323-466-1786.

- **Palm Springs International Film Festival** is in January, with an entry deadline in November. Established by the late Sonny Bono, it has fast become a festival favorite. In the quaint city of Palm Springs, the festival enjoys the closeness of Hollywood but is just far enough away to find its independence. It accepts independent and mainstream films. Go to www.psfilmfest.org or phone 760-322-2930.

- **The International Family Film Festival** takes place in February, in Hollywood, California, with an entry deadline in January. Organized by the people who ran the former Santa Clarita International Film Festival and the Burbank Festival, the International Family Film Festival is a great festival that recognizes films for families and children. Most other festivals don't screen many family films. Go to www.iffilmfest.org or phone 661-257-3131.

- **Dances with Films** takes place in July, in Los Angeles, California, with an entry deadline in April/May. Also known as the "Festival of the Unknowns," this festival boasts that it features films with no-name directors, actors, and producers. It was originally established to get away from the politics of other film festivals. It's very first-film friendly and welcomes independent films with great stories. Go to www.danceswithfilms.com or phone 323-850-2929.

A program called Gorilla, by Jungle Software (www.junglesoftware.com), is a complete production-management software package for independent filmmakers that includes a database of film festivals. The program lists addresses and contact information for more than 1,200 film festivals.

Deadlines and entry fees are subject to change, so always visit the festival's Web site or call ahead. Questions are usually answered quickly via e-mail.

FAB-ulous recognition

The Film Advisory Board (FAB) is an organization dedicated to recognizing quality films for children and family. FAB has acknowledged many studio pictures, including *E.T.: The Extra-Terrestrial* on its reissue. Films do not compete against each other; rather they are recognized on their own merits and, if worthy of a FAB award, receive recognition. There is no deadline date — films are looked at year-round. You can find information about FAB at www. filmadvisoryboard.org.

The Telly Awards, founded in 1980, are similar to FAB in that entries do not compete against each other. TV commercials, films, and TV programs are judged on individual merit and receive an award if the judges feel that the film or program has a high standard of excellence. All genres are accepted as long as they have not been broadcast on a major network. For more information about the Tellys, check out www.telly.com.

Choosing the appropriate genre and category

After you've selected the right film festival, you have the dilemma of entering in the correct genre and category (explained in detail in Chapter 2). If you choose incorrectly, you could blow your film's chances of winning or placing. Some festivals allow you to enter several genres for this reason — very helpful if you can't decide exactly which genre your film fits into. Is it a comedy, drama, science-fiction, or fantasy? A combination of several genres? If you don't know your film's genre, who does?

Usually, the judging committee won't correct your mistake if you enter under the wrong category. It has too many entries to weed through. If you're undecided, call the festival and ask its opinion. You can also screen your film for friends and ask what category they feel your film falls into.

Along with knowing the genre your film falls under, you have to choose the correct category, which is usually one of the following:

- **Animation:** Utilizing traditional drawings, stop motion (like Gumby and Pokey), or digital computer-generated images.

- **Commercial:** A 30-second to 1-minute commercial that's purpose is to sell a product or idea.

- **Documentary:** A behind-the-scenes nonfiction (sometimes controversial) production that shows the real side of a person or event.

- **First feature:** Your first attempt at a feature-length film (at least 90 minutes) with a cohesive story.

- ✔ **Independent film (low-budget):** A feature-film length production produced with limited funds and independent of a major studio or distributor.

- ✔ **Public Service Announcement (PSA):** A 30-second to 1-minute commercial making a statement about health issues, environmental issues, or any subject matter that promotes a better society.

- ✔ **Short film:** Usually under 30 minutes. Encapsulates a complete story with developed characters within a shorter running time.

- ✔ **TV movie:** Usually slotted within a two-hour time period on a TV network. Produced specifically for the small screen (TV) keeping in mind the TV censors with regard to subject material.

- ✔ **TV program:** Usually runs within a one-hour time slot. Can be a variety program (such as *America's Funniest Home Videos*), a reality show (like *Survivor*), or a one-hour drama show.

Some festivals accept screenplay submissions as well. So if you have an unproduced screenplay that you're proud of, submit it to the appropriate festival. I entered my original screenplay *Undercover Angel* in the Santa Clarita International Film Festival (now called the International Family Film Festival), and it received an award certificate. I then put the award logo on the screenplay to show that it was an award-winning script, which gave the screenplay credibility and raised interest in the project. (The film was produced and released successfully a year later!)

Writing a great synopsis of your film

Just like when you had a carefully prepared pitch to sell your movie idea to an investor or distributor (Chapter 3), you need to pitch an intriguing synopsis of your movie that will convince the festival screeners to consider your film for their festival. If you write a boring synopsis, they will anticipate a boring film.

Picture perfect: Selecting the best photos from your film

Photos from your film are an important marketing tool. Film festivals request still photos from your movie to use in their brochures and marketing materials — should your film be accepted. A picture always draws the reader's attention to an article and helps the reader to understand and remember the material more than with no photograph.

Make sure that you have photos taken on the set. Submit photos that best represent your film, such as an interesting confrontation between your actors, or something that causes an emotion in the viewer. If you have any name stars, then make sure they're in the photos.

When you send photos from your film to a film festival, be sure to label each photo with the name of the film. Identify the scene and the actors in the photo. If the festival people decide to publish the photo in their publicity ads or festival program, they need to have this information clearly marked.

Sending the best format

Only a few years ago, if you completed your film on videotape (as opposed to cutting on film for release in theaters), you were out of luck when it came to having a festival show your film. If a festival accepted your film for screening, you had to provide a 16mm or 35mm film print. Many independent filmmakers were knocked out of the game because their finished projects were on tape only. You can always transfer your finished video product to film, but that process is lengthy and expensive. Because you're taking a smaller video image and enlarging it for the big screen, the picture quality may suffer by magnifying grain and imperfections, depending on the quality of the original footage.

Now that digital filmmaking has come into its own, most film festivals have video projectors that can project virtually any form of video, digital files, DVD (including high definition formats) on which you submit your film. New filmmakers can now receive equal consideration regardless of whether their project is finished on videotape or digital files and then burned to DVD or submitted on videotape or traditional 16mm or 35mm film stock.

DVD is the favored format when using a video projector. A DVD can be as good as your original in picture quality if it's transferred digitally (especially if you burn it to a *Blu-ray* HD disc). Burning your projects onto DVDs with most computers is easy and inexpensive. Shipping a DVD also costs much less than shipping other formats. Check out www.Primera.com for an affordable Primera Disc Publisher SE DVD burner that also prints artwork onto your DVDs.

Entering without a box

The traditional way of entering a film festival consists of filling out an entry form and mailing it in with your film submission (usually in the form of a DVD screener) along with your entry fee and supporting materials (still photos, synopsis, and so on). A revolutionary company, Withoutabox, has simplified the film festival submission process for the filmmaker.

Withoutabox (www.withoutabox.com) is a unique service that creates a direct link between the filmmaker and the film-festival circuit by allowing you to submit your film entry online to hundreds of film festivals of your choice worldwide. Under their service DVDelivery, Withoutabox will even submit a DVD screener (you supply the master) directly to each film festival you enter. Online submission is especially invaluable when you're submitting to more than one festival. Most film festivals accept, and encourage, filmmakers to use Withoutabox. It's becoming the traditional way to enter film festivals.

Withoutabox collects all the necessary information from you online and then inputs it into the entry forms of all the festivals you want to enter. Your information is customized to each festival's distinct entry form. This saves you from entering the information on individual entry forms for each festival you want to enter.

Withoutabox enables you to do a vast search on the site to find the most suitable festival for your film, enter multiple festivals, upload scanned publicity photos from your movie, and track your entry submissions. Using Withoutabox is free; you only pay each festival entry fee and the cost of a DVD screener of your film.

Getting an entry-fee discount

Pretty much every film festival in the United States charges an entry or submission fee, which can range from $20 to $200. Then, if you win, some festivals charge you extra to purchase the award statuette or certificate! Some film festivals offer entry discounts to students and independent filmmakers. Calling and asking about available discounts is a good idea.

Some festivals reward you with an entry discount if you submit your film early. The discount is usually mentioned on the entry forms or festival Web site and on Withoutabox.com.

Part VI
The Part of Tens

"You know—this would make a great movie!"

In this part . . .

You find helpful tips, secrets, and priceless advice that can save you a lot of time and trouble and help make your film a success. You're given tips for discovering new talent, ways to avoid Murphy's Law, and ideas for publicizing your film to gain recognition and maybe even attract a distributor. You also find out how to stay up-to-date with the best entertainment magazines and trade papers.

Chapter 21

Ten Tips for Discovering New Talent

Discovering new talent can be a fun position to be in. You could be the catalyst that launches someone's acting career. Marilyn Monroe, Sandra Bullock, Dustin Hoffman, and Meryl Streep were all discovered — and you can bet that someone is taking the credit for discovering them. This chapter shows you how to root out unknown talent.

Studios often conduct casting calls, looking for that special someone to play a leading role. Daniel Radcliffe was discovered after an extensive worldwide search for the perfect Harry Potter. Emily Mae Young, the little girl featured in the Welch's Juice commercials, had never starred in a feature film until my mother saw her on the commercials. I hired Emily for my film *Undercover Angel,* and she went on to win several best-actor awards (which weighed more than she did!). After my film, she was called in for auditions with big-time directors, including Ron Howard and Martin Scorsese.

Viewing Independent Films

Watch independent films for actors whose performances you admire. Contact the production company that produced the film and tell them you enjoyed the actor's performance and want to find out how to contact his or her agent. If the actor is a member of the Screen Actors Guild (SAG), the actor's union that represents over 120,000 performers, you can call the guild for the actor's contact number (usually the agent or manager). The SAG phone number to locate an actor is 323-954-1600.

One way to track down an actor is to first get his correct name from the film's credits, and then try searching on the Internet. Many actors nowadays have their own personal Web sites and can be found by typing in their name with the .com extension or by locating them with an Internet search engine, like Yahoo! or Google. The Internet database www.IMDBpro.com lists virtually every actor who has ever performed a professional acting job, along with contact info.

Watching Local Theater

No matter what city you're in, you can go to the local stage show and discover great talent. Just make sure the actor is able to tone his acting performance down for your film because stage actors tend to *project* bigger (speak loud and over-enunciate so the theater audience can hear them) than trained film and television actors do. One of the many reasons actors do stage plays is to attract film-industry people (someone like you) who may hire them to act in a film.

Attending Actors' Showcases

Showcases are different from stage plays, in that it *showcases* actors' talents specifically for industry people, such as casting directors, directors, producers, or independent filmmakers like yourself. The performances are usually short monologues by an individual actor, or two actors performing a dramatic scene. Go down and see a showcase at a local theatre (almost every city has one) — you're bound to find some natural talent. The magazine *Backstage* (www.backstage.com) lists showcases and actors' events. Or check with local stage theaters in your area, where they often post upcoming showcases and performances.

Many actors now showcase their work on the World Wide Web by uploading samples of their work onto www.youtube.com or www.myspace.com.

Visiting Acting Schools

Almost every city or small town has an acting school or at least a drama department at the local schools or colleges. If you're in a big city like Los Angeles, New York, or Toronto, you'll have no problem finding actors through the educational system.

Talking to Agents and Managers

Agents and managers have done the hard work for you by finding and representing talented actors, many of whom may be new to television or film. I've worked with agents who are eager to get their new clients out working, gaining experience, and getting performances on DVD to show off the actors' talents.

Searching the Academy Players Directory

The Academy of Television Arts and Sciences publishes *The Academy Players Directory* every six months. The directories consist of two books divided into actor types:

- Leading men, younger leading men
- Leading women, ingénues (supporting women)

Each book includes the categories for character actors, stunt performers, and children. These directories are usually purchased by casting departments, directors, studio executives, and independent filmmakers looking to cast their own films. The set costs $75 and can be ordered by calling 310-247-3058 or going to the Web site at www.playersdirectory.com. *The Academy Players Directory* is also available online with membership.

Schmoozing at Film Festivals and Markets

Film festivals are often attended by actors whose films are being showcased (see Chapter 20). Film markets (see Chapter 19) offer an informal environment to catch people relaxed and in a schmoozing mood.

Many actors attend the various film markets and festivals for the sole purpose of meeting filmmakers who can use them in their next films.

Walking Down the Street

I'm not talking literally finding someone "on the street," unless you hit them with your car or bump into them on the sidewalk. But you can often find actors in common everyday places. A great place to meet actors is at a photocopy place — actors are always photocopying their résumés. A photo retouching store or printer that does headshots (especially in Los Angeles, New York, or Toronto) is a great place to find actors, too.

I found my leading lady for my film *Undercover Angel* while dining in a local neighborhood restaurant. I found a purse at my table and a few minutes later saw a woman looking around like she'd lost something. It turned out this was her purse — and she turned out to be Yasmine Bleeth (of *Baywatch* and *Nash Bridges*). I sent my script to her agent explaining how we met, and the rest is history: She starred in my film!

Holding Talent Contests

Clubs, theaters, and TV programs sometimes hold talent contests. Find out where these contests are being held and go down to meet people waiting in line. If you have a comedy club in your town, go down on amateur night, and you're sure to discover some great comedians. That's how Steve Martin, Jim Carrey and Howie Mandel were discovered (I put Howie Mandel in his first film *Just Joking* when I was a director student at The American Film Institute in the early eighties).

Starring Your Family

Maybe your star is right in your own family. I put my mom in my film *Undercover Angel* as the landlady (besides, if I didn't, I was afraid she'd send me to my room). She did such a great job I hired her again to play the cleaning lady in my film *Light Years Away*. How about your brother, sister, or dog? I cast my dog, Little Bear, to star in my feature film, *Teddy: First Dog*, where he plays the canine companion to the President of the United States.

Maybe *you* have that star quality — so why not cast yourself? Director Kevin Smith cast himself in his films *Clerks, Dogma, Chasing Amy,* and *Jay and Silent Bob Strike Back*. Mel Brooks starred in a lot of the films he produced and directed, like *Young Frankenstein, Blazing Saddles,* and *High Anxiety*. Plus, if you star in your film, you can give yourself top billing!

Chapter 22

Ten Ways to Get Publicity for Your Film

In This Chapter

▶ Publicizing your film

▶ Creating attention for your film

You made a film and now you want people to know about it. Some people think publicity is to stroke a filmmaker's ego, but the real purpose is to get your name and film out there — to create awareness through repetition. When you see a commercial for a soft drink, suddenly you're thirsty. You see a pizza commercial and consider ordering one. In this same way, you want to create awareness for your film so that distributors and audiences will flock to it. Publicity can also give you credibility as a filmmaker and get you more work. It's amazing how people accept you when they see your name in print.

 Generate publicity only when the timing is right. Usually the best time is when you've scheduled a *screening* (projecting your film in a theater) for your film, whether it's for a general audience or one specifically for entertainment industry guests, such as distributors and home-entertainment and TV buyers.

Submitting a Press Release

A *press release* is a one-page announcement of a publicity event for your film that you can fax or e-mail to your local newspapers and TV stations. Use a clever heading to catch a reporter's attention. The release should also have the words "For immediate release, please" (it never hurts to be polite) so they know it's timely and important. It should state what, where, when, and why. This way, your press release for a screening or other publicity stunt allows the press and the rest of the population to show up at the proper time and place.

Doing a TV or Radio Interview

Promoting your film on a local radio station or on a cable-access program is a great way to create exposure. You can even run a short clip from your film on a local TV show or news program. The opportune time to do interviews is when you have a screening of your film planned.

Getting a Review from Movie Critics

When you're planning a screening of your film, contact local movie critics in your town and invite them to the show.

If you can't afford a screening, you can also mail DVD screeners to the local critics and ask them if they'd consider reviewing your film (see the following section). I've had favorable reviews of my films on www.movieweb.com and www.einsiders.com. If you get a great quote from one of the reviews, you can use it on the DVD box cover, posters, or newspaper advertisements for your film. As a courtesy you may want to ask permission to use a particular quote.

Mailing Out DVD Screeners

After you've completed your film, you need to make DVD screeners to send to distributors and potential TV buyers. Even if you plan a screening, you still need to send DVDs because many distributors or buyers won't attend and will ask for a viewing copy instead. (I use the Primera Disc Publisher SE that burns and prints labels of my DVD screeners that I send out. To get the Primera Disc Publisher SE, go to www.primera.com.) I've used PIP printing to print my color DVD insert jackets and other film marketing artwork (www.pip.com/burbank). Tell them I sent you, and they'll give you a deal!

Attending Film Festivals

Enter festivals to start creating awareness of your film. If your film places at a festival, you can then contact your local newspapers and TV news programs and notify them of your award-winning film.

Here's a crazy idea: Organize your own film festival. Enter your film (don't let anyone else enter) and award yourself first prize for best film. Then send a press release to newspapers and local TV news. Even if people find out it's your own private film festival, it still makes for a funny news story.

E-Mailing and Setting Up a Web Site

Set up a Web site for your film. You can purchase software programs, like Freeway (www.softpress.com), that guide you easily through the process, or you can hire a professional to set up your site. A Web site can be a promotional site letting people know the details of your film (storyline, cast, fun details, movie trailer, and so on). You can direct distributors to your site if they're considering picking your film up for distribution. If you set up the Web site before you make your film, the site can provide information for potential investors and also for actors you're considering. For an example, check out the Web sites for two of my films: www.misscastaway.com and www.lightyearsawaymovie.com. It's also a good idea to put your trailer up on YouTube (www.youtube.com) and e-mail everyone you can with a link directing them to the site.

You can also send e-mail messages to a select group of people, telling them about your new film and any publicity events you're planning. Send messages to potential distributors, studio acquisition people, including DVD distribution companies and TV network executives. Be sure to target your mailing list — you don't want to be considered a *spammer* (someone who solicits over the Internet to people who don't request mailings from them).

Designing T-Shirts and Other Premiums

Promotional products, called *premiums* or *giveaways,* such as buttons, T-shirts, mugs, pens, key chains, and hats with your film's logo, create great publicity for your film. (People rarely throw away something that has any type of value to it.) You can give these away at shopping malls, at your premiere screening, or at film markets and film festivals. Most cities have promotional product and apparel companies; check out your local Yellow Pages or search the internet under "Advertising — Promotional Products."

For my film *Undercover Angel,* I created Mr. Dodo stuffed animals and sent one with each screener of the film (see Mr. Dodo at www.mrdodo.com).

Planning a Publicity Stunt

A *publicity stunt* is anything that draws attention to you or your film. Choose a publicity stunt that isn't dangerous or illegal (you don't want to get arrested — that's the wrong kind of publicity!). A costumed character giving out flyers or delivering a DVD copy of your film to a studio executive or distributor is okay. Sending a singing telegram with a copy of your film to a potential distributor might work, too.

A more expensive publicity stunt is having a prop plane fly a banner advertising your film. A cheaper way to go is to hire some beautiful models to give out flyers on your film or sell tickets to a screening.

When I was a teenager, I shot a film when the circus came to town and wanted to create some publicity for the screening. My friend Gary Bosloy volunteered to dress up in a gorilla suit and run around the neighborhood. Someone called the local radio station and reported that a gorilla was loose, and everyone assumed it escaped from the circus that was in town. I then called into the radio stations and local news programs and told them it was a publicity stunt to promote our film. This stunt got us free publicity!

Organizing a Screening Party or Charity Event

If you can afford to rent a screening room or theater, consider setting up a premiere to introduce your film to an audience. The audience should consist of potential buyers for your film, including distributors and TV and home-entertainment acquisition people.

Your screening can also be a charity event where all proceeds go to a specific charity. A charity screening creates positive exposure for your film and helps a good cause at the same time.

Placing an Ad

Consider placing an ad in the newspaper to announce a screening of your film. If you want to see the response to your film with a paying audience, this is a way to go. However, advertising in a newspaper costs considerable money, so you may only want to run a small ad so you have a better chance of making a profit on your screening.

Chapter 23

Ten Ways to Avoid Murphy's Law

In This Chapter

▶ Anticipating problems

▶ Planning a smooth shoot

"*E*verything that can go wrong will go wrong." Welcome to Murphy's Law — the curse of any project. But you don't have to be a victim of Murphy's Law if you plan ahead. If you anticipate disruptions and know how to problem-solve, you'll be prepared to handle Murphy or even keep him away.

In regards to planning, my dad used to say, "You can't go right doing wrong, you can't go wrong doing right." I always have a plan A and a plan B and even a plan C. Think through all the possibilities that could hold up your production and then plan for them. It's like puppy-proofing your house — you have to think of everything the puppy could get into and lock those things out of reach. Every time I forget to take my lunch off my desk, the dog always remembers. Avoiding Murphy's Law is like buying insurance. Ensure your production by planning ahead for those things that will go wrong.

Testing the Camera

Before you begin shooting your movie, test the camera. If you're shooting with film stock, shoot some test footage and send it to the lab to check for scratches and steadiness of picture and to make sure you don't have fogging on the film from a light leak in the camera. Testing your camera is really easy if you're shooting with a camcorder (analog or digital). Just record some footage and then play it back to make sure the image looks okay.

Make a checklist of all the items and equipment you'll need, along with any important reminders (like giving your Aunt Sally a credit for letting you shoot in her apartment for one scene). You can start the list way ahead of schedule and continue to add things until the day of shooting. Don't rely on your memory — no matter how good you may be at remembering things, you'll always end up forgetting something. It's like going to the grocery store. You make a grocery list so you know exactly what you need and don't end up forgetting something.

Scouting Locations for Noise

Planes, trains, and automobiles — not good news for your sound takes. Make sure the location is quiet enough to record sound on your shoot. If you're shooting a scene that's supposed to be taking place on the shores of a desert island, you don't want to find out the first day of shooting that you're in the fly-zone of a major airport. The roar of planes taking off and coming in every few minutes can make it extremely difficult to get a clean audio take (see Chapter 12). Same with train tracks. If you must shoot near train tracks, find out the train schedules so you can be forewarned when recording dialogue.

Watching the Weather Channel

If you have an outdoor shoot scheduled, watch the Weather Channel (or go to www.weather.com). If torrential rain is predicted, you'll know to plan for your indoor cover set ahead of time. (A *cover set* is an indoor scene that you're prepared to shoot in the event that your outdoor scenes are rained out.)

Backing Up Locations and Actors

Take nothing for granted. You could lose a location because of the owner changing his or her mind, charging you more than what was agreed upon, or for disturbing the neighborhood. If you don't have a backup arranged, you could waste a lot of time trying to find a new location.

Have a backup for actors, too. In Los Angeles, I've had my share of flaky actors who were late or forgot to show up on set.

Using a Stunt Double

Don't take a chance with your actors. Always use a stunt double for any type of action that could potentially disable your actor. Even if a stunt seems pretty simple, you don't want your lead actor spraining an ankle and hobbling around the rest of the shoot. Very few actors in Hollywood do their own stunts. Jackie Chan is one of the few who does, but he's broken almost every bone in his body in the process!

Standing by with First-Aid Kit or Medic on Set

Be prepared for injuries — whether a simple knee bruise, a cut finger, or something more serious — by having a first-aid kit on set. Even better, have a medic on set if you can afford one (especially if your film has stunts or pyro-technics). And always make sure you have the phone number and directions to the closest hospital.

Anticipating that Cellphones and Internet Don't Work Everywhere

Check out your locations beforehand to make sure that cellphones and Internet access work in the area. If it's a remote area and you don't pick up a signal (unless you have satellite service), make sure you have access to a land phone and have dial-up internet access. You always need communication to and from the location.

Mapping Out Directions

Always have maps drawn up and distributed to cast and crew so no one can say he or she didn't know where the location was. In addition to the visual map, have the directions spelled out from all directions.

Some people are visual and can read maps just fine; others are better at following written directions. You can get maps or step-by-step directions from Web sites like www.maps.google.com or www.mapquest.com. You can also e-mail these maps to cast and crew. Many people have portable GPS (Global Positioning System) devices in their cars which give them no excuse for getting lost.

Providing Plenty of Parking

You don't want your cast and crew driving around the block for 20 minutes on the first day of your shoot. Plan ahead and find a parking lot that your team can use while at this location. If everyone has to park a distance from the set location, arrange to have a mini-bus shuttle everyone from the parking lot to the set.

Securing Security Overnight

Pay a few extra dollars to have someone stay with the equipment at your location if you're shooting there the next day. Maybe someone on your crew, like a production assistant, would be willing to sleep on a couch or in a tent. Don't ever leave your equipment like your lights and camera in an unlocked vehicle. (Try not to leave them in a vehicle, period!) Someone will be sure to steal something if it's left unattended — Murphy's Law, you know. I've even had a trampoline, clapboard, and director's chair stolen off my set.

Powering Up Ahead of Time

Here's a bonus tip to guard against Murphy's Law. When you scout your locations, make sure they have places to plug in your lights and equipment. Otherwise, you'll need to budget for a generator to run all your electrical devices.

Even if the location has power, the location owner may request that you bring your own power and not tap into his or hers.

Chapter 24

Ten Best Filmmaking Periodicals

*I*f you want to be a successful filmmaker, you need to tap into the entertainment industry, and the best way to do that is to subscribe to some of the following trade papers and magazines. You can't hope to pick up all of your knowledge just from hearing it through the grapevine. (Be sure to double-check subscription rates listed here before sending in your payment!)

While it's not really a filmmaking periodical, don't neglect your local newspapers for unique stories and events that may not reach a national readership (there's less chance of a Hollywood producer seeing the same story) that you could turn into a commercial screenplay. (Always check with an attorney on whether you need to obtain rights to a story you read in the paper.)

The Hollywood Reporter

The Hollywood Reporter is one of the two top trade papers in Hollywood. Subscription prices are $175 for 52 weekly issues and $229 for 255 daily issues. The *Reporter* keeps you up to date on anything and everything happening in Hollywood — from the latest studio deal to the current deals of the movers and shakers you need to know about.

> 5055 Wilshire Blvd.
> Los Angeles, CA 90036
> Phone: 323-525-2150
> Web site: www.thehollywoodreporter.com
> E-mail: subscriptions@hollywoodreporter.com

Daily Variety

Daily Variety, along with *Weekly Variety* (which comes out once a week and recaps the news from *Daily Variety* for the prior week), is considered the top periodical next to *The Hollywood Reporter.* This paper contains news stories and current events including weekly box-office grosses. A yearly subscription to *Daily Variety* is $329.99. *Weekly Variety* is $299.99 for a yearly subscription.

> 5700 Wilshire Blvd., Ste.120
> Los Angeles, CA 90036
> Phone: 323-857-6600
> Web site: www.variety.com

Backstage

Backstage is for actors, filmmakers, and film and stage crews. This paper comes out once a week, and features classified ads, casting notices, and related articles of interest to actors and filmmakers. A one-year subscription (51 issues) costs $99 ($145 if you're up there in Canada, eh).

> 5055 Wilshire Blvd. Los Angeles, CA 90036
> Phone: 800-562-2706
> Web site: www.backstage.com
> E-mail: backstage@espcomp.com

Videomaker

Videomaker is a magazine that covers everything from camcorders, editing, audio, and video tips to everything else you need to know about making digital movies. Twenty-four issues cost $21.97.

> P.O. Box 3780
> Chico, CA 95927
> Phone: 1-800-284-3226
> Web site: www.videomaker.com/subscribe

Entertainment Weekly

Entertainment Weekly has entertainment news and stories and lots of gossip, with entertaining and informative reviews on all the new movies.

Interesting stories on your favorite movies and movie stars and what new films the studios and stars are working on. A one-year subscription starts as low as $15.

> Phone: 800-828-6882
> Web site: www.ew.com

People Magazine

People Magazine is full of fascinating stories that could inspire a screenplay, whether by triggering an original story in your mind or by helping you track down someone written about in the magazine so you can write that person's life story. Promotional rates are around $1.99 an issue for 52 issues. You do the math (okay, I'll do it — that comes to $103.48).

> Phone: 800-541-9000
> Web site: www.people.com

American Cinematographer

Find out more about camera techniques and secrets with *American Cinematographer* magazine. Each issue unravels the mystery of how photography and effects were done in popular films. A one-year subscription runs $29.95.

> 1782 North Orange Dr.
> Hollywood, CA 90028
> Phone: 800-448-0145
> Web site: www.theasc.com
> E-mail: circulation@theasc.com

DV Magazine

DV Magazine is a technical magazine that keeps up to date on digital technology. This magazine (or online edition) includes equipment reviews and great articles offering technical tips and essential information for the digital-video enthusiast. A one-year subscription is free to qualifying U.S. residents (determined by the publisher).

> P.O. Box 221
> Lowell, MA 01853
> Phone: 888-266-5828
> Web site: www.mydvmag.com

MovieMaker Magazine

MovieMaker Magazine, geared toward the independent filmmaker, has articles and up-to-date information on lab deals, insurance, shooting techniques, and new equipment. The magazine also keeps you informed on film festivals and includes interviews with top moviemakers. Sign up online for subscription rates starting at $18 for one year (6 issues a year). Canada is $28 for 6 issues.

174 Fifth Avenue, Ste.300
New York, NY 10010
Phone: 212-766-4100
Web site: www.moviemaker.com

StudentFilmmakers Magazine

StudentFilmmakers Magazine is a great resource for film and video makers. An annual subscription — hardcopy or online — costs $19.37.

Phone: 888-222-0652
Web site: www.studentfilmmakers.com

Index

The Old Chicago Neighborhood
Remembering Life in the 1940s

By Neal Samors and Michael Williams

Introduction by Edward M. Burke Essays by Fr. Andrew Greeley, Leon Despres,
Jon Hahn, Bill Gleason, Bill Jauss and Sandra Pesmen

Edited by Neal Samors, Michael Williams, and Marcee Williams.

Produced by James B. Kirkpatrick of Kirk's Computer Service.

Book designed by Michael Williams.

Printed in Canada by Friesens Corporation.

ISBN: 0-9725456-0-3 (Softcover)
ISBN: 0-9725456-1-1 (Case)

Front Cover: *Irving Park and Seeley, 1944*. North Center (Courtesy of the CTA.)

Back Cover: Top Left: *Tug-of-War, Roosevelt Road Beach, 1947*. Near South Side (Courtesy of the Chicago Park District.)
Top Right: *Mrs. Harry Riley and Children, ca. 1944*. Near North Side (Courtesy of the CTA.)
Bottom Left: *Children Cheer for the Cubs Victory over Harry "The Cat" Brecheen 3-1, 1948*. Lakeview (Courtesy of the Chicago Sun-Times.)
Bottom Right: *Service Guard, Marquette and Maryland, 1943*. Greater Grand Crossing (Courtesy of the Chicago Park District.)

Frontispieces:
Regal Theater, 47th and South Parkway, 1941. Grand Boulevard Photograph by Russell Lee. (Library of Congress)
Chicago Public Library, George M. Pullman Branch, 1944. Roseland (Courtesy of Special Collections and Preservation Division, Chicago Public Library.)
Jackson Park, ca. 1946. Woodlawn (Courtesy of the Chicago Park District.)
Service Guard, Marquette and Maryland, 1943. Greater Grand Crossing (Courtesy of the Chicago Park District.)

Page 8: Chicago Bungalow Neighborhood, Southwest Side, ca. 1940. (Private Collection)

For more information on this book as well as the authors' other works contact us at:

Neal Samors
E-mail: NSamors@aol.com
Website: www.chicagosneighborhoods.com

Michael Williams
E-mail: kkbmfw@earthlink.net

For my late parents, Joe and Bernette Samors, your love of Chicago and its neighborhoods motivates me to write about the city. The memory of both of you remains as my inspiration.

For my wife, Freddi, and my daughter, Jennifer, your support and encouragement keeps me going and has allowed me to pursue my "second career."

N.S.

For my mother, Sheila, a born storyteller...

M.W.

Table of Contents

Acknowledgments

The authors wish to gratefully acknowledge the support and contributions from many individuals who assisted in the completion of this book. More than 125 current and former residents of Chicago who lived in or near the city during the 1940s agreed to be interviewed for the project and their memories provide the basis for the book.

Among the many people who took time from their busy schedules to recall life in their Chicago neighborhoods during the '40s, some deserve special recognition because they wrote essays for the book, and others provided us with access to the photographs and memorabilia found in this publication

We deeply thank Chicago City Council Alderman Edward M. Burke, novelist and social scientist Fr. Andrew Greeley, former Alderman and attorney Leon Despres, sports writers Bill Gleason and Bill Jauss, and journalists Jon Hahn and Sandy Zuckerman Pesmen for providing stimulating and insightful essays about Chicago neighborhoods and parishes during the 1940s. Their essays capture the vibrancy and special nature of the decade in Chicago. Also special thanks to Dan Miller of the Chicago Sun-Times, Thomas O'Gorman, Phil Holdman, Cook County Circuit Court Judge Richard Elrod, Julia Bachrach and Robert Middaugh of the Chicago Park District, Jeff Stern of the Chicago Transit Authority, the staff of the Harold Washington Branch of the Chicago Public Library, Richard Bitterman, Deborah Mieko Burns of the Japanese American Service Committee, Bill Watson, Anthony Reibel, Mary Brace, Bill Swislow (for more information on Joe "40,000" Murphy go to interestingideas.com) and Keith Sadler for providing access to photographs and memorabilia that were used in the book.

A second group of individuals were both interviewees and referrals to the many other people interviewed in this book. They include: U.S. Magistrate Judge Ian Levin (who provided access to members of Chicago's legal community), Cook County Circuit Court Judges Richard Elrod and William Phelan, Illinois Appellate Court Judge Neil Hartigan, Playboy Magazine founder Hugh Hefner, Illinois Secretary of State Jesse White, former U.S. Congressman Morgan Murphy, Jr., former Superintendent Chicago Park District Edward Kelly, former Illinois State Senator Arthur Berman, attorneys Leonard Amari, James Casey, Joseph Lamendella, and Jerry Petacque,

attorney and journalist Joel Weisman, businessmen Sam Carl, Frank Considine, Richard Jaffee, James McDonough, Andrew McKenna, Ron Michaels, Ron Newman, Jim O'Connor, Jack Sandner, and Lee Stern, sports agent Steve Zucker, journalists Ann Gerber, Rick Kogan, and Norman Mark, former Chicago Cardinal Donald Stonesifer, administrator Jim DeLisa, legal researcher Harriet Ellis, medical records administrator Nancy Bild Wolf, and jazz musicians Joe Levinson and Ted Saunders.

And, finally, our deepest thanks to all the other individuals who participated as interviewees, and whose recollections about Chicago neighborhood life in the 1940s made this book possible. They include, in alphabetical order: Dorothy Ash, U.S. District Judge Marvin Aspen, Jim Bachman, Bruce Bachmann, Dolores "Champ" Mueller Bajda, Sandy Bank, Estelle Gordon Baron, Irv Bemoras, Gerald Bender, Dr. Ira Bernstein, Charles Bidwill, Jr., Edward Brennan, Margaret Burroughs, Earl Calloway, Howard Carl, Dr. James P. Carter, David Cerda, Chuck Chapman, John Creighton, Bob Cunniff, Ron Davis, Raymond DeGroote, Anna Marie DiBuono, James Dowdle, Tom Doyle, George Dunne, Joesph Epstein, Alice Fink, Rick Fizdale, Johnny Frigo, and Truman Gibson.

Jack Hogan, Edie Phillips Horwitz, Dave Hussman, Tom Hynes, Bernie Judge, Penny Juhlan, Wayne Juhlan, Dorothy and Hiroshi Kaneko, Bob Kennedy, U.S. District Judge Charles Kocoras, Otho Kortz, Kay Kuwahara, Margaret Short Lamb, Marvin Levin, Ramsey Lewis, Hal Lichterman, Richard Lukin, Jack Mabley, Ed McElroy, Henry McGee, Jr., Blanche Majkowski, Ray Meyer, Hank Mitchell, George Mitsos, Joe Molitor, James Mowry, Bill Nellis, Ray Nordstrand, Mary McCarthy O'Donnell, Chiyoko Omachi, Andy Pafko, Mel Pearl, Mike Perlow, Billy Pierce, Lawrence Pucci, Frank Rago, Anthony Reibel, Lou Roskin, Howard Rosen, Sheldon Rosing, Dan Rostenkowski, Chuck Schaden, Arnold Scholl, Burt Sherman, Seymour Simon, Shirley Ochs Simon, Charles Simpson, Father Gene Smith, James Thommes, Dempsey Travis, Sheila Morris Williams, Adelaide Gredys Winston, Nancy Bild Wolf, and U.S. District Judge James Zagel.

Authors' Notes

This book is not meant to be a history of Chicago's neighborhoods in the 1940s. Instead, this book is a collection of memories about the experience of growing up and living in Chicago during that time. The stories are not told by us, but by the interviewees, in their own words. Our goal at the outset of this project was to find a diverse group of Chicagoans who could speak openly about their experiences in the '40s, be they positive or negative. The response was overwhelming. We are truly grateful to the interviewees for the rich body of experiences they related to us. Their honest and straightforward answers to our questions were, at times, nothing short of courageous.

Readers of this book may find neighborhood names that are unfamiliar to them. The issue of defining specific neighborhoods, parishes and community areas is a complex one. By the 1940s, the City of Chicago had already delineated 75 community areas, based on the work of the University of Chicago's Social Science Research Committee in cooperation with the United States Bureau of the Census. Community areas, unlike the 176 neighborhoods presently in Chicago, are based on census tracts and often have names that are, and were, unfamiliar to city residents. We have included neighborhood names that are cited by individual interviewees in their stories, but also refer to the larger community areas that match those on the map provided on page 15 in this book. The key issue is that neighborhood boundaries were more often psychological than specific.

Introduction
Edward M. Burke

Neighborhoods and parishes have been the essential building blocks of Chicago's growth and development from its earliest days. Chicago is first and foremost a city of neighborhoods. Its first neighborhood, the stockade-fenced Fort Dearborn, was probably America's western-most neighborhood when it was constructed in 1803. During the late 1820s, neighborhood life picked up at Wolf Point, a strategic small stretch of land at the juncture where the Chicago River forks to the north and south. This was home to one of the city's earliest settlements, the neighborhood containing the well-known Wolf Point Tavern, an important meeting place during fur-trapping days and the town's first genuine public house. Not far away, at Lake and Market Streets (now Wacker Drive), the true social center of Chicago was to be found, the Sauganash Tavern. Owned by the ubiquitous pioneer Mark Beaubien, no visitor or resident of this inn came away without being entertained by him on his fiddle. These proto-neighborhoods were places of refuge and shelter, community celebration and nourishment. This has remained Chicago's unique formula for neighborhood life for more than a century and three-quarters.

Since the beginning of Old St. Mary's, Chicago's first Roman Catholic parish in 1833, the same year Chicago incorporated as a town, all the ingredients for social and religious reinforcement were set in place. The establishment of St. Mary's school for girls and St. Joseph's school for boys by the Religious Sisters of Mercy provided the early population of Chicago with a primitive road map to heaven. Under the leadership of such devoted communities of religious men and women, the growing metropolis of Chicago would share with the burgeoning diocese of Chicago a remarkable capacity for helping to civilize the prairie. As the population of the city grew with teeming numbers of Irish immigrants, later

followed by swelling numbers of Poles and Germans, the grid of ecclesiastical development expanded, forging a unique hybrid American urban religious institution, the city parish. Often, the boundaries of parish demarcation followed the characteristics of language, custom and culture. Within two decades of the city's incorporation in 1837, the grid of parishes across the flatland of urban Chicago kept pace with the arrival of each new ethnic resident. By 1848, Chicago had become its own diocese. And within little more than thirty years, by 1880, its exponential growth transformed it into one of the nation's fastest developing archdioceses. In the years before the American Civil War the skyline of Chicago was shaped by steeples, not skyscrapers. As the city was transformed into the capital of the American heartland by its marriage of commerce and industry, the masses fleeing European poverty and oppression found the landscape of Chicago far less forbidding and strange because of the softening touch and familiar signposts that the parishes of the city provided. Parishes would remain a tether of the old world, refreshed in the new.

The true significance of Chicago neighborhoods can be seen in their remarkable development in the decades that followed the Great Fire of 1871. With three-fifths of the central city in ruins, stretching from Roosevelt Road to Fullerton Avenue, the rebuilding of the urban grid and infrastructure became a singular priority. Out of the disaster came a host of new neighborhoods, and a flood of new residents to assist with the rebuilding. Many of the people coming to the city were Americans from New England who saw a singular opportunity for success in a fresh part of the country. Others came from across the length and breadth of Europe. This great mix of origins and cultures became an essential element in the expansion of Chicago neighborhoods and imbued them with their unique variety. Immigrants, too, were attracted to the expansive opportunities for employment here, especially in rough and tumble industries like the meat packing empires of the Chicago Stock Yards and the railroads that turned the city into the nation's rail hub.

In the decades that followed the fire, the population of the city doubled every ten years. From more than 250,000 residents in 1870, the dramatic waves of newcomers swelled the numbers to more than 500,000 by 1880. That number doubled once again to 1,000,000 by 1890 and 1,600,00 by 1900. The city was undergoing a tremendous boom as it began to lose the patina of its cow town identity. By the time the famed World's Colombian Exposition of 1893 took place in Chicago, the city was exhibiting a braggadocio and swagger that brimmed in its success and modernity. The city was awash in expanding neighborhoods, each developing its own peculiar character and identity. The city boasted more Poles than any other city in the world outside of Poland, more Germans than any city outside of Germany and more Irish than lived in Dublin. Customs and languages were carried to Chicago like treasure. They could be seen with bold variety and a peculiar confluence of traditions along the streets and roadways of neighborhood life.

Life in some immigrant neighborhoods could be exceedingly dangerous. Long before the Levee, a neighborhood of cheap rooming houses, brothels and thief dens, became famous for tourist muggings and wallet -liftings, one group of the early Chicago Irish settled along the Chicago River near Erie Street, in a placed called Kilglubbin. So serious were the grudge matches or faction fights there among the Irish from rival counties in Ireland that Chicago Police declared it a "no go zone" more than 150 years ago. Some neighborhoods took longer to civilize than others.

Nothing helped to civilize the variety of life across Chicago's neighborhoods than the Roman Catholic Church. Famous for its skills at organization and institution building, the growth of the Catholic Church in Chicago kept up a breakneck pace in meeting the needs and movements of its voluminous population of co-religionists in the city. Irish parishes were the first to ring out around the old parts of Chicago. The establishment of Old St. Patrick's in 1846 was quickly followed in 1848 by that of St. Bridget's on Archer Avenue, a parish established to meet the needs of the Irish who dug the Illinois and Michigan Canal. Back on Roosevelt Road, the Society of Jesus began Holy Family Parish in 1857, counting Mrs. O'Leary of fire fame among their members. The parish, miraculously, was spared by the flames due to ferocious winds blowing from the south. The pattern continued. As communities of Roman Catholics fanned out across the city, the trusted accouterments of Catholic life were quick to follow. This familiar pattern continued for other ethnic groups as well. With the arrival of large numbers of Polish and German immigrants in the post-fire decades, parishes meeting their special language and culture needs were also established by the Archdiocese of Chicago. Often, these parishes were staffed by fellow immigrant clergy who became the guardians of both language and customs. Frequently, the churches erected by such immigrant communities resembled the great cathedrals found in their old countries. Today, their domes and spires still reach heavenward and display artistry and faith that is timeless.

The ever-growing network of parishes across the city became a powerful force for both the civilizing and educating of new immigrant groups. Schools were often more important to the newcomers than elaborate church buildings. The structure of parish life was not complete without a parish school in which young people were educated, often through the high school level. The bishops of the United States established the policy that every Catholic had the moral obligation of attending a parish school. Such parish schools also permitted the children of non-English speaking immigrants the opportunity to learn the language of American commerce and industry.

For many Chicagoans, neighborhoods and parishes were indistinguishable, identities that went beyond their secular and religious nature. For generations, if you asked a Chicagoan where they were from, they would most likely respond with the name of their parish. Parishes were shorthand identifications that quickly provided a host of social, cultural and economic statistics. Stories abound of Jewish and Protestant Chicagoans who found it saved them lots of time to just give the name of the local Catholic parish when asked where they lived. Parishes provided quick reference to location (South Side, West Side, North Side or suburb), or ethnic make-up (Irish from Visitation, Polish from St. Hedwig, German from St. Benedict, Bohemian from St. Paul or Italian from Our Lady of Pompeii). It also provided a ready reference for economic detail (working class folk at Nativity of Our Lord in Bridgeport, more advantaged, lace-curtain Irish at St. Mel on the West Side, or the well to do at St. Philip Neri in South Shore).

Parishes have been the true glue and identity of Chicago life for generations of Chicagoans. The most intricate and intimate of life's comings and goings took place amid the rigors, rules and regimes of parish life. The story of parishes is the story of schools, gymnasiums, religious pageants and countless weddings, funerals and Sunday Masses. But it is also more. Woven into the life cycle and heartbeat of parish life is the sustaining power of belonging and being home. In a less mobile age, when families lived in the same community for generations, parishes evoked a dominant sense of allegiance and loyalty transcending the realities and boundaries of common life. Experiences were shared and convoked a mutuality that lasted a lifetime. Parish ties were familiar and familial, providing a sense of turf and sacred space.

It is important to remember that Chicago was not just a city of Roman Catholic parishes. Many thousands of German and Scandinavian Lutherans, African-American Baptists, Scotch Presbyterians and many varieties of Eastern Orthodox Christians brought vigor, dignity and great success to the urban life of the city. Large numbers of Ukrainians and Russians populated the Near

Northwest Side. Andersonville, a community with a strong Swedish heritage, developed in the Edgewater community. The Greek Orthodox population, centered just west of the Loop in Greek Town along Halsted Street, became one of the city's oldest ethnic enclaves. Many residents of Greek Town were uprooted in the 1960s when the University of Illinois at Chicago campus was constructed on top of them. African-Americans settled in large numbers on Chicago's South Side, the Bronzeville neighborhood being a historic and cultural center for generations. Strong Jewish communities developed, first in the old Maxwell Street neighborhood, and then expanded west to Douglas Park, north to Humboldt Park, Albany Park, and Rogers Park, and south to South Shore. More affluent members of the Jewish community settled in Hyde Park along the lakefront environs near the University of Chicago. Each of these non-Catholic neighborhoods created rich and textured cultural communities that generated political and commercial leadership enriching Chicago.

The growth and development of Chicago neighborhoods and parishes reached a high point in the 1940s. Chicago was a vibrant, brawny survivor not only of the great Depression, but of the crime-filled era of Prohibition. The city's national political influence became significant and local residents took pride in the fact that Franklin Delano Roosevelt was nominated for his unprecedented third term as President in Chicago in 1940, and his fourth in 1944. Chicago's larger-than-life political leaders like Mayor Edward J. Kelly and his successor, Mayor Martin H. Kennelly, prided themselves on being "neighborhood" men. Each came from the city's Irish working class Bridgeport enclave that would go on to provide three more Chicago mayors in the 1950s, 1970s and 1990s. As World War II began, neighborhoods and parishes took on a particular role in supporting those tens of thousand of local GIs who were fighting half a world away. Neighborhoods and parishes took on deepened emotional significance as home and family, neighborhood and parish became symbols of American identity worth both fighting for and dying for.

However, in the decade that followed World War II, neighborhoods and parishes in Chicago underwent massive transition. Returning GIs found city housing a vanishing commodity and in the great population boom that ensued began a push out to perimeter suburbs. Also, the influx of new populations of African-Americans to older neighborhoods on the city's South Side, stimulated a further movement of families to outer city neighborhoods and the suburbs. This pattern continued through the 1960s and 1970s, which saw more than 500,000 white residents leave old neighborhoods and parishes and a growth of more than 300,000 African-American residents. Parishes underwent an equal change as the majority of African-Americans were not Roman Catholic. Parishes saw a drastic shift in their numbers of parishioners. Urban change was significant. Neighborhoods and parishes underwent massive transitions.

Chicago has always been a geography-focused city, due in no small part to its obsession with its own strategic location at the juncture of the prairie and Lake Michigan along the banks of the Chicago River. Location means everything. As Chicago's fortunes and geography expanded, neighborhoods and parishes became manageable everyday expressions of the local life of the big city, whether you are a newcomer or an old-timer in Chicago. This is where you learn to navigate the geographies and politics of local living. Chicagoans have always understood that the strength and stability of the city is dependent upon the quality of understanding and hope that exists within each local neighborhood. The vitality of any local community can never just be the result of urban government or municipal legislation. Rather, it is intricately dependent upon the goodwill and leadership that rises up among neighbors and local residents whose roots go deep into the prairie soil of Chicago.

Neighborhoods define our urban terrain and make livable the magnitude of our metropolis. The health of our city has always been measured by the fitness of our neighborhoods. Here, people are at home. People take charge. And the great challenges emerge within the rhythms and contours of daily life. Neighborhoods remain both a distinctive and enduring resource of everyday Chicago life. Bonded with the parishes of the past and present, they have helped the immigrant and newcomer fit in, and old-timers feel a sense of pride and ownership.

The true textures of Chicago life are to be discovered in the neat rows of bungalows, three-flats and six-flats that have been the timeless backbone of neighborhood life. They form a special expression of Chicago identity, together with the cottages, lakefront high-rises and apartments over countless shops, taverns, grocery stores and undertakers.

It is no accident that Chicago has become known as "The City of Neighborhoods." Neighborhoods have been our most vibrant resource and our most imaginative treasure. Gilded by the faith and history of religious loyalty, the parishes of the Archdiocese of Chicago brought an internal catalyst to Chicago's prairie success and human drama. Neighborhoods and parishes have been a winning combination in Chicago life, the twin pillars of allegiance and identity that have softened the harsh terrain of the nation's center and helped to make Chicago America's most American city.

Alderman Edward M. Burke is the Dean of the Chicago City Council. He has served as Alderman of Chicago's 14th Ward for more than three decades and he is a recognized expert on city budget matters. Alderman Burke is the Chairman of the City Council Committee on Finance. He entered politics in the footsteps of his father, Joseph, and became Democratic Committeeman of the 14th Ward in 1968 and alderman in 1969. Like his father, he was a Chicago Police Officer. Alderman Burke is also partner in the law firm of Klafter and Burke, as well as co-author of the book *Inside the Wigwam: Chicago Presidential Conventions, 1860-1996*. He lives with his wife on the city's Southwest Side.

Community Areas
City of Chicago
1940

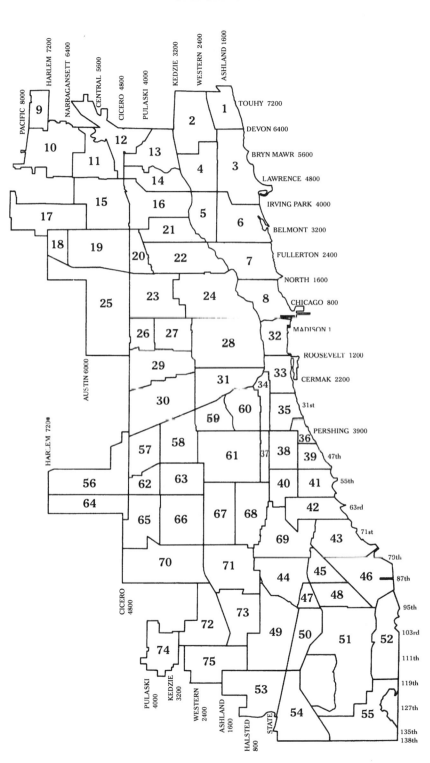

Legend

1. Rogers Park
2. West Ridge
3. Uptown
4. Lincoln Square
5. North Center
6. Lakeview
7. Lincoln Park
8. Near North Side
9. Edison Park
10. Norwood Park
11. Jefferson Park
12. Forest Glen
13. North Park
14. Albany Park
15. Portage Park
16. Irving Park
17. Dunning
18. Montclare
19. Belmont Cragin
20. Hermosa
21. Avondale
22. Logan Square
23. Humboldt Park
24. West Town
25. Austin

26. West Garfield Park
27. East Garfield Park
28. Near West Side
29. North Lawndale
30. South Lawndale
31. Lower West Side
32. Loop
33. Near South Side
34. Armour Square
35. Douglas
36. Oakland
37. Fuller Park
38. Grand Boulevard
39. Kenwood
40. Washington Park
41. Hyde Park
42. Woodlawn
43. South Shore
44. Chatham
45. Avalon Park
46. South Chicago
47. Burnside
48. Calumet Heights
49. Roseland
50. Pullman

51. South Deering
52. East Side
53. West Pullman
54. Riverdale
55. Hegewisch
56. Garfield Ridge
57. Archer Heights
58. Brighton Park
59. McKinley Park
60. Bridgeport
61. New City
62. West Elsdon
63. Gage Park
64. Clearing
65. West Lawn
66. Chicago Lawn
67. West Englewood
68. Englewood
69. Greater Grand Cr.
70. Ashburn
71. Auburn Gresham
72. Beverly
73. Washington Heights
74. Mount Greenwood
75. Morgan Park

1947 — The Axial Year
Fr. Andrew Greeley

Much of the popular history of the last century and some of the serious history assumes that America changed dramatically in the 1960s. The assumption is made by those who matured in the 1960s and is despicably self-serving. The years before their advent, the time between the end of the Second World War — their parents' era — is dismissed as a time of rigidity, conformity, and "togetherness;" a time when women gave up the jobs they had during the war and settled for domesticity; a time of the emergence of suburban culture (still viciously attacked in such films as *American Beauty*).

In this assumption of moral and cultural superiority, the sixties generation ignores many obvious facts. All generations have their own form of conformity (such as the current political dogmas). A culture based on sex, drugs, and rock n' roll is not necessarily any less rigid in its demands. There is no evidence that this generation has produced any more great works of art and literature than its predecessors (where are their Fitzgeralds and Hemingways?) or more impressive political leadership. The proportion of women in the workforce increased since 1947. The goal of universal higher education meant that women and blacks had a chance to attend college, a necessary prerequisite for the development of the civil rights movement and feminism. Sexual liberation does not seem to have enhanced the levels of sexual satisfaction in society, nor is there any evidence on measures of happiness that there has been an increase in happiness. Nor, as far as we can tell, has mental health improved (though various chemicals such as Prozac may have made emotional stress easier to bear).

The real change in America came after the end of the war, especially in the late 1940s. This was the axial age of American history, the real turning point that shaped everything which has happened since. It was the time when permanent prosperity became a given in American life. The war was over indeed, but more was happening than just the end of the war. Slowly but surely Americans began to realize that the Great Depression was not coming back. Many of my family and friends were convinced that it would return. The Depression had always been with us. Eventually it would be with us again. Yet by the late 1940s, the young men with whom I had graduated from grammar school and who had not attended college were going back to school so that they could compete with the returning vets who were flooding onto college campuses. Slowly but surely it dawned on us that if the Depression did appear again, it would be a long way into the future. Now a half century later, it appears that, barring a catastrophe, we will never again have unemployment levels around 25%. The periodically recurring economic crises of the 19th and early 20th centuries had become a thing of the past.

Those TV commentators who compare any of the various recessions of the last 50 years with the Great Depression were either not around at the time or have read no economic history.

The reasons for the prosperity which has marked American history since 1940 and European history since 1960 are beyond the scope of this essay. My point is only that such prosperity, the "revolution of rising expectations," did not exist in our imagination in my neighborhood even as a remote possibility in 1945. By 1947, my generation of young people began to take the risk of betting on such a promise. By the time I was ordained and sent to a parish of successful professional-class Catholics, prosperity was taken for granted and everyone was eager to forget the memories of the Great Depression. Many of the people in this parish assumed that their success was a proof of their own worth (just as a somewhat older group my father's age thought that their failure and unemployment was proof of their own lack of worth). Both groups were caught up in the economic processes of their own era. My parishioners were not successful because they were men approved. They were successful because they were lucky. It would have been hard in that time and that place not to be a success. Only the drink could destroy you.

When my class graduated from high school in 1946, college choice was for the very few. Eight years later in my new parish, composed essentially of the same kind of people, it was assumed that everyone would go to college. The whole world had changed. All the other changes which would happen in the next half century, for weal or woe, were locked in by a flourishing economy which has never ceased to expand. Prosperity makes possible all kinds of other things — drugs, promiscuity, trophy wives, trips to Europe, postponement of work and marriage, voting Republican, movements, protests and all other luxuries which were not available on the West Side of Chicago in 1942. I rejoice in the expanded possibilities of life "beyond our dreams in 1942" and I accept the abuses that seem to be inherent in this expansion. I deplore and despise the failure of those who matured after 1960 to realize that it was not ever thus. Our generation didn't have senior trips. The next one went to Springfield, the one after that to DC, the one after that to Paris and on their junior trip! Good for them. Only don't think that these are inalienable rights that Americans have always had.

It may be that a half century is not enough time for people to learn how to live with prosperity. I'm not sure the rigid ideologies of the environmental movement point in that direction. But that argument is beyond the scope of this essay.

The standard of living has doubled three, perhaps four times since then. We were there when the first doubling was taking place. I have never seen any serious historiography that records what it was like, the excitement, the exhilaration, the hope of those very special times. I have tried in two of my novels, *A Midwinter's Tale* and *Younger Than Springtime*, to describe it narratively. Perhaps, however, it will take only a long time, a couple more decades for people to begin to understand what it was like to grow up in a depression and a war and then suddenly see the limits of our lives wiped away and the outer horizons of our hopes disappear. Now suddenly much was possible, not quite everything perhaps, but almost everything.

The men coming home from the service could go to college, obtain degrees (the visas to suburbia as David Riesman would later call them), marry and start families, purchase new cars, buy homes of their own, join country clubs and, God forgive them for it, vote Republican. To a generation which wants to start marriage with a home, like that in which they were raised, this may not seem like much. It did in 1935 and 1945 and indeed in the whole past history of the human condition.

It took our breath away in the bungalow belt around Division and Austin in those days. When I think about it, it still takes my breath away.

Fr. Andrew M. Greeley is a priest, distinguished sociologist and best-selling author. He is a professor of social sciences and research associate at the National Opinion Research Center at the University of Chicago. He has written many books and articles on issues in sociology, education and religion and his column on political, church and social issues is carried by the New York Times News Service. Fr. Greeley is the author of more than 30 best-selling novels and the autobiography *Confessions of a Parish Priest*.

Returning Servicemen Usher in 1947, New Years Eve at the Keymen's Club, Madison and Cicero, 1946. Austin (Courtesy of Charles F. Simpson.)

Hyde Park Politics in the 1940s
Leon Despres

The 1940s was an interesting decade in Hyde Park politics. Following the national trend, the Democratic Party grew to a majority and the Republican Party declined. The radical third parties, which found Hyde Park a hospitable resting place during the 1930s, withered. By the end of the decade there were definite signs of the independence in liberal politics which have characterized Hyde Park for decades afterwards.

Hyde Park had not always been predominantly Democratic but, on the contrary, had historically been Republican and the site of rivalries between branches of the Republican Party, between the grafters and the honest people, between the moderates and the extremists. It was a Republican battleground, and the winner of the Republican primary usually won the election. By the beginning of the 1940s, however, Roosevelt had become a great vote-getter in Hyde Park, as elsewhere.

During the early 1930s, when the nation was in economic turmoil, radical third parties found a welcome in Hyde Park. They never amassed huge votes but they gave promise of growing into a significant influence. In 1935, for example, the Socialist Party ran Maynard Krueger for alderman and garnered 600 votes. This was a small total but the Socialist Party members thought it was the beginning of a swelling influence. The Communist Party did not engage in open vote campaigns but it maintained a branch in Hyde Park and its adherents thought it would grow. By the beginning of the 1940s it was apparent that these parties were going nowhere.

At the beginning of the 1940s, Paul Douglas was in office as alderman of the 5th Ward. He was Professor of Economics at the University of Chicago and one of Hyde Park's most distinguished citizens. Before the 1940s he had engaged in genuinely independent and anti-Machine politics. In 1935 when Maynard Krueger was the Socialist candidate for alderman, Paul Douglas recruited Divinity Professor Joseph Artman to run, and substantially managed an energetic campaign which won several thousand votes. In 1939, to the astonishment of Hyde Parkers, Douglas became the Regular Democratic candidate for alderman. Hyde Park's peerless independent was running with the support of the Machine! This occurred for several reasons. The Machine was able to buy respectability by slating him. And, in addition, there was a contest inside the Democratic Machine between the Thomas Courtney wing and the Edward Kelly wing. Kelly, who was party Chairman and Mayor, knew that by supporting Douglas he would gain the margin he needed for victory.

Although elected by the Machine, Douglas was a splendid alderman. He dramatized the great social issues of the day. He was a star on issues of racial discrimination and relief of poverty. In 1942, however, he ran in the Democratic primary for Mayor against Kelly, lost, and resigned from the City Council to enter the Marines. Hyde Park was left without a strong Democratic candidate and without a functioning independent movement.

In 1943, the independent torch was grasped by University of Chicago History Professor Walter Johnson, who waged a praiseworthy anti-Machine campaign for alderman as a liberal Democrat, kept the movement alive, and gained a respectable total, but lost.

The last gasp of the radical movement occurred in 1948 when University of Chicago Economics Professor, and still Socialist, Maynard Krueger ran for Congress. To his supporters' enthusiasm, at a political rally for him, all 1,090 seats in the University of Chicago's Mandel Hall Auditorium were filled. Unfortunately the spectators were attracted less by Krueger than by the presence of Norman Thomas as speaker, and Krueger did poorly in the election. That was the end of radical third parties in Hyde Park, but not the end of independent liberal politics.

In 1947, Hyde Park was shaken to its political roots by an aldermanic campaign which was mixed independent and Machine. The 5th Ward Democratic Committeeman was Barnet Hodes, who relied on the money and the patronage army which the Machine furnished him. Without difficulty he elected his choice, Bertram Moss. In office, however, Moss realized he could win re-election on his own only if he showed signs of independence. He took a strong stand against the corruption of the Board of Education and the decline of the Chicago Public Schools. Refusing to kowtow to his Ward Committeeman who had elected him, Moss was marked for defeat. To win the election, however, Committeeman Barnet Hodes had to select a candidate who would attract the independent vote as Douglas had done in 1939. His choice was Robert Merriam, a University employee and the son of Charles E. Merriam, who had been one of Chicago's best aldermen years before. The name was magical. Charles Merriam was then Chairman of the University of Chicago Political Science Department. Robert Merriam was a war veteran and had written a book about the Battle of the Bulge. He was articulate, liberal, and intelligent. In the tightly contested 1947 election, he won. Just a few days before the election, Moss, fighting for his political life, flooded Hyde Park with an expensive, color-printed booklet filled with photographs and slogans intended to carry the day for him. It backfired. It was just too expensive. Merriam, the independent-Machine candidate, won in 1947 and won again for a second term.

The significance of these aldermanic elections was that they showed the stirrings and beginnings of an independent liberal Democratic movement in Hyde Park.

Other factors also foreshadowed a new political future for Hyde Park. After the war ended, Hyde Park was flooded with new residents, war veterans taking advantage of the GI Bill of Rights, and men and women who entered Hyde Park with a desire for a better world and a willingness to work for it.

In 1948 an event occurred, which, while not directly political, nevertheless greatly influenced the political texture of Hyde Park. The United States Supreme Court declared racially restrictive covenants illegal. This changed the quality of Hyde Park's population. It stimulated a flight of residents afraid of African-American penetration and also stimulated the determination of other residents to preserve and protect Hyde Park as "an inter-racial community of high standards." Thanks to leadership from the First Unitarian Society, the 57th Street Meeting of Friends, and Congregation KAM, the Hyde Park-Kenwood Community Conference was formed. It created an atmosphere of freedom and independence which contributed strongly to incubation of

independent liberal political movements. In 1949, the Independent Voters of Illinois was formed, with its strongest base in Hyde Park. By 1955, Hyde Park elected an independent alderman, and in 1956 a state representative. The die was cast.

Leon Despres has lived in the Hyde Park neighborhood for all except two years since he was born in 1908. He still practices as an attorney and was the Alderman from the 5th Ward for twenty years where he was known as "the conscience of the Chicago City Council." Leon was a key figure in civic improvements, education, ethics and good government. He and his wife still live in Hyde Park.

The "Nortwes" Side
Jon Hahn

I never knew I had a Chicago accent until we moved to Seattle, where there are no discernible accents, hardly any snow and ice storms, and absolutely no good Italian beef sandwiches.

My Chicago, in the 1940s, was pretty much bounded by Irving Park, Addison, Cicero and Central and latticed with elm-lined streets and alleys busy with junk men and fruit peddlers. This was the "new" neighborhood, where we lived on the just-above-ground floor in a red brick two-flat with our grandparents, great-aunt and uncle and great-grandparents. Downstairs we spoke Chicago; upstairs they spoke German. Sometimes we communicated by a series of code knocks on the radiator pipes. Or just plain yelling. People yelled a lot more then. And there was a wine cellar below the full concrete basement that smelled of homemade wine and sauerkraut.

No one in the neighborhood seemed to move away, even if only to those almost foreign suburbs with strange names like Arlington Heights or Mount Prospect. Places like Evanston and Winnetka seemed as distant and unattainable as, say, paradise, or New Jersey. Most people like us in the 1940s were living in the same bungalows or two-flats, or not far from, where their parents lived in the Depression. And we were the third generation ascendancy, inheriting all the prejudices and tastes and trappings that could be squeezed into an 800-square-foot-per-family lifestyle. Bowling leagues and occasional Cubs games at Wrigley Field were our Vegas. O'Hare Field was just a fenced-in, mostly military air strip that couldn't begin to match Midway Airport, but no one you knew actually flew anywhere.

Our neighborhood was referenced variously, sometimes as the Six Corners, where Irving Park, Cicero and Milwaukee came together. That configuration failed to impress our great-grandfather, who as family story goes once had a chance to buy part of that intersection for $1 per foot(!). Sometimes you said you lived in Portage Park, which was a quarter-mile-square park with indoor and outdoor swimming pools, athletic fields, playgrounds, tennis courts and horseshoe pits. And sometimes, even if you weren't Catholic, you told people you were from "St. Bart's" because St. Bartholomew Roman Catholic Church was an indirect but significant link to the Irish-Catholic political power structure downtown and through much of the city. Being Catholic *and* Democrat with a good voting record and a few connections was a big help in lining up one of the thousands of patronage jobs everyone seemed to want after World War II.

The 1940s were pre-Dutch Elm Disease, and cathedral elms created gothic corridors along the side streets. Old-style street lamp posts had open, screw-in bulbs that sent out little haloes of light as people sat on the front stoops or porches of their bungalows and two-flats. It was unthinkable to make a $.05 phone call when you could shout to, or walk to wherever or whomever you wanted to speak. There was plenty of room for kids to play red rover or spin tops in the street because not everyone had cars and those who did mostly parked them in one-car garages by the alley.

I was about twelve before I had met and mingled with enough South Siders – as foreign from our perspective as were the Polish aunts and uncles in Milwaukee – and discovered that *Dey talk diff'rent*. Even today,

I can hear *Sout'Side* on some tongues when we make the occasional pilgrimage back to the Old/New Neighborhood. We don't have any relatives left in the old, Old Neighborhood, where my Grosspa (actually, great-grandfather) Kuehner ran a blacksmith shop at about North Ave. and Larabee. Much of his business was shoeing horses for what then were about a dozen breweries.

Grandpa Hahn, who died before my twin sister and I were born in 1940, was a fireman in the small firehouse on Tripp, just north of Irving Park Rd. Our father recalled that if he or his brothers took too long in rushing the growler (covered tin beer pot) home from the tavern on Cicero Avenue, Grandpa Hahn would give them a thwacking with the razor strap that hung behind the bathroom door.

We didn't have a car – that had been sold when the war started and Dad went to work behind a punch press. So, we walked pretty much everywhere — to William P. Gray School, where our parents and older siblings had many of the same teachers we inherited; to the little three-checker Jewel Tea store with wooden floors, on Irving Park; to Schmidts' Bakery; Stanley's Drug Store; and to Tabor Evangelical & Reformed Church. And sometimes to Portage Park, although oftentimes Grandpa Kuhrt or Dad would stop the old wooden wagon behind Ole's Tavern at Irving Park and Laramie and take us into the long, dark establishment and take a little refreshment. "Now if Grandma or Mommy ask how was the park, you hafta tell them you had fun on the swings and playing in the sand, or we can't come back here again for free Coke and pretzels!"

We grew up knowing about the red-white-and-blue pennants hanging in front windows, signifying a son in the armed service. We also knew the significance of a Gold Star, memorializing a son who would never return from Europe or the Pacific. Europe seemed not so distant or foreign because every other house in the neighborhood had vestigial trappings of the old country, whether it was the kitchen table language or the music or the decor.

Probably because ethnicity and prejudices seemed as permanent then as the WPA sidewalks, there was a sort of cultural isolation from other neighborhoods. But it was all right to play with the Italian and Polish kids across the street or the Scotch-Irish ones next door. The only black we ever saw was the coal man, who was dropped off along with a couple tons of coal at the curb and spent most of a summer's day shoveling and pushing a wheelbarrow between the curb and our coal chute.

The more rigid line between people or neighborhoods was religion. Our family was very anti-Catholic – something about Grandma Hahn's having been sexually assaulted when she was a novitiate in the old country – and it was a big buzz if a Protestant family discovered one of their own

was dating a Catholic. I suppose the Catholics felt the same way in this Capulet and Montague thing. It came to rest on my head years later when I fell in love with a Polish-Catholic girl (Gasp!) in Schurz High and my mother went off the deep end. Ironically, she later converted to Catholicism, even though my big brother was an ordained Protestant minister.

We could play in the street or alleys together; we could swim at Portage Park or skitch behind cars in the winter together. But the Catholics, mostly Polish or Italian, held, or were held by, a doctrine that they were better-different. I remember my older sister coming home in tears because her best school and play friend down the block told my sister that she could never get to heaven because she wasn't Catholic. I knew that kids at St. Bart's School had some kind of lock on the good life because they got out of school for more religious holidays, and they were out of school and riding their bikes by William P. Gray Elementary, rattling sticks against the long iron fence while we languished in the June heat inside.

Summer vacation in the 1940s was a hot flash and a long simmer. Sometimes your mother would pack you off to a local Vacation Bible School. The YMCA on Irving Park and Kildare offered summer programs with field trips to the Borden Dairy, the Schwinn Bicycle plant, the Rosenwald (Sorry, Museum of Science & Industry) Museum, and, most memorable, the Stock Yards.

The Sears store at the Six Corners offered a wonderful year-round playground, where you could play Saturday morning hide-and-seek ("No fair going in bathrooms or dressing rooms") and filch hot cashews as you rode down the escalator. Or you could sneak over to ("Don't you kids ever go near there!") the "hobo jungle" alongside the railroad tracks east of Sears. The men who slept under pieces of Kenmore refrigerator boxes and built campfires there were always pleasant, and showed us how to catch "land crabs" with pieces of hot dog on a string. Like uncles, they warned us when we went onto the tracks to place pennies that would later be squashed by the Hiawatha as it made its 80 mph run to Milwaukee (most of those pennies vanished).

Further east, the Chicago & North Western Rwy. still was running steam engines, and you could lie in bed with the windows open on summer nights and visualize the locomotives as their laboring chug-chug-chugga-chugga-chugga blotted out the sound of the cicadas and locust.

That Sears store parking lot was not only the starting point for the annual Memorial Day and July 4th parades, but also the venue for a week-long summer carnival with special appearances by Roy Rogers and Trigger the Umpteenth.

Carnivals and Roy Rogers were tame, however, compared to Riverview Amusement Park. For years, our family went there for ethnic

Six Corners Shopping Area, Irving Park, Cicero, and Milwaukee, ca. 1938. Portage Park (Courtesy of the CTA.)

picnics, when whole pergola-centered picnic groves were reserved for German Day or Lithuanian Day. But the most special day was 5-Cent Day, when most – but not the very best – rides cost only a nickel. Admission cost about the same as a double-bill showing at the Portage Theatre, but it got you a whole day of high rides, sick-to-your-stomach thrills and a chance to maybe sneak around the side of a building to search for a peep of the bearded lady or the snake charmer. From atop some of the half-dozen or so roller coaster rides you could see the wood-hull mine-sweepers still being built for the Navy in the boatyard below on the North Branch of the Chicago River.

From the parachute ride tower – a feature transplanted from the original Colombian Exposition – you could see well out into Lake Michigan and far beyond the city boundaries to the north and west (the South Side seemed always hazy, perhaps from the steel mills near the south end of the lake). My older brother (remember, the minister?) once caused me to pee in my pants when our porch swing-type ride seat became stuck at the top of the parachute tower and stranded us for a small eternity. He gleefully swung the seat back and forth, side to side, telling me that I'd surely fall and make a big splat.

It was a time of innocence, when a 10-year-old boy was allowed to take the bus or streetcar and subway or "L" downtown. Although a certain percentage of weekly allowances went into Postal Savings or a Christmas Club account at the local S&L, spending money could be stretched farther by sneaking onto the streetcar behind a fat lady and transferring umpteen times, sometimes even the reverse direction. If you had lots of time, you could ride all the way to the south end of Western Avenue, back to the northern terminus, and then back to Irving Park and thence home. About the same cost and time could get you down to the Lincoln Park Zoo (Free Admission) on the Chicago Motor Coach double-decker bus.

The Irving Park streetcar went west only a bit past Narragansett, beyond which point was a string of cemeteries. Redoing the family graves there was occasion for a picnic that was schlepped out on the streetcar along with garden tools, stopping once we were afoot for some pansies, marigolds and other annuals. Redoing the graves was why the last weekend in May was then called Decoration Day. But the picnic lunch brought along made the cemeteries more like big rock gardens.

More ominous was the old Dunning Mental Hospital on the north side of Irving Park at the end of the streetcar line, with its foreboding brick dormitories and clinic buildings set back from the high brick-and-iron fence in a landscape of huge elms and wide lawns. Disheveled older people in pajamas and robes or overcoats stared blankly through the iron fence into a world of streetcars and parachute rides and Italian beef sandwiches and

Decoration Days they would never again enjoy. And insensitive adults would threaten youngsters: "That's where we're gonna put you if you don't behave!"

Not even the Catholics would say a thing like that.

Jon Hahn, currently a columnist for the *Seattle Post-Intelligencer*, was born and raised on Chicago's Northwest Side in the neighborhood that was called variably Portage Park, Six Corners or St. Bart's Parish. After graduating from Schurz High School, he attended several local colleges before receiving his B.A. in English from the University of Illinois at Urbana-Champaign. He worked as a reporter at the *Evanston Review* before going downtown to the *Chicago Daily News* as a labor and features writer. When the *Daily News* closed he moved to Seattle and lives there with his wife in Woodlinville, WA.

Let's All Go to the Park
Bill Gleason

Before I was old enough to go to school, I went to "The Park." The first few times I was holding the hand of my father. "Let's go over to the park and take a shower bath," he would say early on a Saturday afternoon. It was never a shower. It always was "a shower bath."

Why he wanted to leave the apartment when we had a perfectly good bathtub I couldn't understand. Maybe it was because he had been a baseball player and baseball players always took shower baths after games. Or maybe, as I realized years later, he wanted me to get used to male bodies without clothes.

As usual he didn't explain. And I didn't care, because we were in the most beautiful place I had ever seen. The park, Palmer, was filled with large trees that provided shade in summer, shadows in winter.

Our first time over there together I said, "This is a big park, Dad. Is it the biggest park in Chicago?" Looking down at me, he moved an arm and chuckled. "This is just a medium-size park," he said. "The city has parks that are at least ten times this size. On the South Side, about five miles from here, the city has Washington Park and Jackson Park. On the West Side there is Garfield Park where people can go to look at flowers. And up north there is a place so big that it has a zoo, Lincoln Park. They're all named for our presidents."

"Was Palmer a president?" I asked. After another chuckle Joseph Walter said, "Nope. He was a very rich gink."

During our early shower bath trips, when I was four years old, a man behind a counter would hand a towel and small bar of soap to my father and me. "On the house, kid," the man always said. When I was eight years old my dad had to pay twenty cents for our towel and soap. A year later there were no towels, no soap. Dad had to bring towels and a bar of soap wrapped in pages from the *Herald-Examiner*. "It's this damn Depression," he told me. "It better end before all the parks go to hell."

I was sure Palmer would last forever. It had to. It was my park. Just a half block west of Grandma O'Brien's two flat at 11251 S. Vernon Avenue. Before I was six years old I was allowed to go to the Park by myself. That was my training for Holy Rosary School just across 113th Street.

Sundays in The Park meant watching the Pullman Panthers and the Bauer Bonnies play football. I also saw a game new to me, soccer. "Our alderman, Shel Govier, was a star soccer player," my dad told me. I was beginning to understand that to succeed in Pullman a man had to have been an excellent athlete.

On weekdays in The Park I sat on the top slat of a bench and watched Irv Gorney, Frankie Moran and my other heroes play baseball. I dreamed of the day when I would be playing with them, instead of watching them.

It was not to be. Grandma O'Brien, a lively and glorious lady, surprised us. She died. Because my mother and her two brothers needed money during the most terrible year of the Depression, Grandma's two-flat was sold. We had to move.

My dad knew how I felt about my park. He knew because he felt the same way. "We'll find another park, Bill," he told me. "One thing Chicago knew how to do was to build parks."

But there was no park awaiting me after we moved into our new apartment at 7218 South Park Avenue. Instead of another Palmer Park I had to settle for a playground called Meyering. It was much too small for "hardball," as we called baseball. I was sure that there would not be another Palmer Park in my future.

Just when I was certain that my dream park would be nothing more than a joyous memory, my mother fooled me. She moved again. This was move number two in what would be a long series.

Helen Genevieve had found a lavish apartment just south of the intersection of 71st Street and Lowe Avenue. Across the street was the "Lily Park," which had real lilies growing in small ponds. But that wasn't it. The real park was a block to the east.

When I walked in through a south gate on 72nd Street, glories were everywhere. There was an outdoor gym with a running track. Just ahead was a library. Off to the left I found a large field house. I read the cornerstone. The park was pretty new. The field house had been dedicated in 1904. It was named for Alexander Hamilton. Hamilton Park was no more beautiful than the park of my childhood, Palmer Park. But I had been too young to appreciate Palmer.

After three years of tiny Meyering Playground, Hamilton Park left me breathless. Walking south from the field house, I saw a vast athletic field, larger than four Meyerings. There were four baseball fields, each with a backstop, and eight softball fields. I was twelve years old that afternoon in August of 1935 and now I could play baseball (hardball) forever. And I would.

Hamilton's playing fields were situated in a bowl between two railroad embankments. The Rock Island Railroad's trains shared the tracks on the eastern embankment with the Twentieth Century. The Wabash, the Chicago & Western Indiana and other railroads ran on the western embankment. Every engineer sounded his whistle as he drove his train past my park.

When late summer shadows were coming down and the Rock Island's new streamliner, the Rocket, came speeding southbound, I felt a strong sense of a past era — Hamilton Park's past, the railroads' past, Chicago's past.

This was my park, or so I thought, until a kid said, "You're new around here. You'll find out that the park belongs to 'John the Cop'." The kid was right. John, large and wide, was a park policeman, employed by the Chicago Park District, not by the city of Chicago. Every park of any size had its own policeman. Palmer Park's cop was known as Mr. Adams. Nobody called him "Adams the Cop." He was tall and slender and looked like a movie actor.

John the Cop looked like a bartender or a butcher or a flat janitor. He was the supreme authority at Hamilton Park. His authority was questioned from time to time but a questioner never won the verdict. If a kid was goofy enough to tell his father that he was in trouble with John the Cop, the kid then was in trouble with his father.

We didn't know John's last name and we didn't dare ask him to tell us.

He talked with my father and other fathers. He even talked with young men, but the only words kids heard from him were "Walk the bike!" and "You're banned from the park for two weeks."

There always are kids who think of themselves as risk-takers. They would jump off a third-story porch if somebody said, "double-dare ya." A few risk-takers were nuts enough to test John the Cop by riding their bikes down the asphalt walkway behind baseball diamond no. 1. They came wheeling, north to south, pedaling furiously. They were so proud of themselves as they waved to their friends.

They were daredevils in their own minds. They had defied John the Cop. Then, they went flying over the handlebars of the bikes. Their bikes careened behind them, rear wheels frozen.

There was a billy club in the wheel of one bike. John's billy club. John was a gifted man. He never lined his club at a kid. He never aimed for the front wheel. He skipped the club along the asphalt as though he were sending a stone across water. When the daring cyclists landed in a heap of contusions, John would say, ever so softly, "Next time, walk the bike." There was no smile. I never saw John smile.

Why "they" instead of "he?" Because foolish kids would try to elude John by roaring up the walk in pairs and sometimes in threes. He foiled that tactic by bringing down the bike in the lead. The other ones wound up in a pile of spokes, wheels, tires and handlebars. And if the cyclists tried to elude John more than once, they would hear his other order: "You're barred from the park for two weeks." He didn't mean ten days.

John the Cop was a five foot nine, two hundred and forty pound legend in his own park.

Bill Gleason is a print and media journalist who was born and raised on Chicago's Southwest Side. He has been a sportswriter for the *Chicago Herald-American*, *Chicago Sun-Times*, and the *Southtown Economist* for over 50 years, as well as a member of the "Sports Writers" program on radio and television. Born in the Depression in the Pullman neighborhood, he became an avid 16-inch softball player at a young age, and was the founder/coordinator for the Chicago 16-Inch Softball Hall of Fame. He served his country in World War II in Europe and earned a Silver Star for his gallantry in action. He lives with his wife in Oak Brook.

Parks in the Neighborhood
Bill Jauss

People my age, who grew up in Chicago in the 1940s, spent the first part of that decade going to grammar school, the middle of it in high school and the final years in college. Regardless of where we were in school, we spent huge chunks of that time in our neighborhood park.

For many of us, two forces dominated those years: World War II and our park. Mine was Sauganash Park, bounded on the north by Peterson Avenue, on the west by Kostner, on the south by Rogers and on the east by the tracks of the Chicago & North Western Railroad line.

We were too young to serve in World War II. Most of us were in uniform for the Korean Conflict. Many of our dads, brothers, uncles and cousins were overseas when we played in the park.

In fact, in spite of V-E Day and V-J Day celebrations, it didn't dawn on me that the war was really over until the summer of 1946. That's when the ex-GIs returned to the 'hood' — guys such as Jack McNamara, Pete Wilson and Bud and Bobby Osgood. Each evening that summer, a score of them would choose up sides and play 16-inch softball doubleheaders in the park. We younger guys would hang around, hoping to be picked on a team.

The returning GIs came home different people from those who had left. Their agendas called for more than 16-inch ball, and things like jobs, wives, kids, rent or house payments. When those responsibilities claimed their time, the park became "ours" again as it had been while they were away.

People have asked, "What was it like growing up in the parks in the 1940s?" It was like this — I'd leave the house on a summer morning, and my mother would ask, "Where are you going?"

"To the park," I'd reply.

"Be home in time for dinner," she'd remind me.

And that was that. Parents didn't have to worry much in those days about their kids' involvement with gangs, crime, perverts or drugs (except for beers we'd coax from the older guys). Oh, we got into trouble, but rarely in the parks. There, we exercised our own form of justice system.

Parents realized in those days that when their kids were in their neighborhood parks they would play games, make friends, have fights and make up with those they fought. Their kids would manage to scrounge up lunch on most days and manage just fine on lunchless days. They would progress in life by following the widely accepted rule of give and take. All of this was achieved with little or no adult supervision in the park.

I know. The 40s are a bygone age. The Park District runs worthwhile supervised programs these days.

But today everything is so structured. Kids rarely get to choose up sides, hire an ump, draw up a schedule, organize their own league, take care of their own field or devise wonderfully resourceful ground rules to take advantage of their park's own individual "personality."

We park kids in the 1940s quickly learned when we biked to other parks that each park is different. So, it was up to our own creativity to utilize our home field advantage.

At Gompers Park, for example, our center fielder Bob McClure had to learn to run up a sloped embankment to catch "Clinchers" that had been soundly struck. Green Briar Park, like our own, had some very short foul lines.

On both softball diamonds in Sauganash Park, the distance from home plate to the right field fence was extremely short. On the south diamond, one could clear the steel mesh fence that separated the park from the railroad track if he lofted a medium length fly ball down the line. All it had to do to clear the fence was carry the 160-foot width of the football field plus a dozen feet or so of bushes.

Thus, resourceful right-handed hitters such as Hector Andreos, Osgood twins Mickey and Sonny, and especially Richard "Dynamite" Enberg, concocted a scheme to achieve cheap home runs.

Dynamite was the master of this scheme. First, using his spikes as Carlton Fisk would do decades later in Comiskey Park, he would obliterate all traces of the chalked or drawn-in-the-dirt right-handed batters' box. Next, Dynamite would plant his right foot deep in the "bucket," swing late and loft weak fly balls down the line and over the fence.

This technique produced some of the cheapest home runs west of the Polo Grounds in New York.

Visiting players squawked so much that we finally enacted an unusual ground rule. Any ball that sailed over the fence from the foul line well over into right-center was ruled a ground rule single.

Hector, Mickey, Sonny and Dynamite didn't complain. Each was still able to pad his batting average with cheap singles, even on nights when his girlfriend did not keep the scorebook.

Now it was time for our left-handed hitters to complain. Jim Fegen, Vern Funk and McClure beefed that they were being limited to singles on some tape measure drives they socked atop the railroad tracks.

The configurations of baseball and softball parks always favor certain types of hitters. But football fields are all 100 yards long, and baskets always hang ten feet above the floor or ground. So, these standards should provide an even chance to all. Right?

In most places, yes. But Sauganash Park had its own personality in football and basketball too.

There was not enough room in the park to have 10-yard end zones behind the goal lines. So, late every August when the College All-Star Game approached, and goal posts were erected in our park, they went up on the goal lines like they were for the Bears in Wrigley Field, not at the back of the end zone as they were in college ball.

As a result, there was much more emphasis on place-kicking and drop-kicking in Sauganash Park. Kids practiced kicking at the invitingly close goal posts. Pete Wilton was one of the best. He and the parks' band of kickers may have been forerunners of foreign soccer players who would come to our shores saying, "I'll keeek a touchdown!"

Of all the sports played in our park, basketball benefited most from local rules.

Guys played hoops on one of the outdoor tennis courts that was rarely used for tennis. Half-court three-on-three games. First team to make 10 baskets wins. Winners remain on court. Losers wait their turn to play again. Call your own fouls — if the bleeding exceeded one pint.

Outstanding high school and college players from around the North Side took park in these three-on-three games. The local guys who hung out on the courts lacked the reputations of the outsiders, but the "chemistry" among them was good. And they had a few rules in their favor too.

Hector Andreos and Steve "Buddy" Rebora would shovel snow from the court to work on their games. Before and after military service, John Anderson made any three-man team he joined a good bet to remain on the court. Eddie "the Mailman" Wiloff could neither shoot nor dribble, but when he put his mail sack on the park bench and took the court wearing those Lil' Abner shoes with their steel-tipped toes, he was a painful rebounding force.

Finally, there was Dynamite Enberg and his patented "water fountain shot."

Dynamite was a pretty good player for the Land Juniors. He became unstoppable when he deftly hopped atop the water fountain in the corner of the court, thus improving his effective height from 5-feet 8-inches to something close to 8-feet 5-inches.

Then, Dynamite would accept passes from us and fire set shots down at the basket.

The hotshots from around the North Side would protest that the shot was illegal. I would point out that the area all around the bubbler was in bounds, so the fountain had to be in bounds too. It was located about eighteen feet from the basket between what would have been 3 o'clock and 4 o'clock in a game of H-O-R-S-E.

We never lost an argument about the legality of the water fountain shot. All we had to say to close the case was, "You're playin' in our park — so you follow the rules!!!!!"

Bill Jauss spent twenty years with three papers, *Neenah-Menasha, Wisconsin Twin City News Record*, the *Chicago Daily News*, and *Chicago Today* before joining the *Chicago Tribune* in 1974, and where he is still a sportswriter. Born in Chicago in 1931, Jauss grew up in Sauganash before graduating from Northwestern University in 1952, serving in the US Army, and then becoming a sports writer. He was an original member of the "Sports Writers" show that ran for 20 years on WGN Radio. He and his wife live in Wilmette, Illinois.

Parallels Between the 1940s and Today
Sandra Pesmen

The more things change, the more they stay the same. Accept that premise and you see many parallels between two time periods: The 1941 attack on Pearl Harbor followed by World War II, and the 9/11 attacks followed by the War against Terror in 2001. You also will be in a better position to understand that those traumatic events brought many similar changes to the lives and attitudes of ordinary people.

In both cases, Americans felt shocked, grieved, frightened and insecure. In both cases, the US presidents made stirring speeches reassuring the public not to be all of the above. Flags began flying, people rushed to join the armed forces, and patriotism ran high. In both cases, people made extreme efforts to remain calm and live their lives as normally as possible as they soldiered on.

As children did on September 12, 2001, children also reported to Chicago Public Schools the day after Pearl Harbor. We too felt confused, sad, afraid and unsure about what would happen next. We too had a sense that America was no longer the safe place we knew. We too thought bombs might fall on us.

But there were some obvious differences between that time and today. No therapists were brought in to comfort us or give us group therapy, and none of us was taken to a private counselor. Nobody I knew ever heard of such a thing. Instead we lived that golden rule President Richard Nixon quoted many years later: "When the going gets tough, the tough get going."

Our principal at De Witt Clinton School on Chicago's North Side was a feisty lady named Anna L. Cronin. She turned on the loudspeaker in her office and barked into the mike, "Attention, children! This is a practice air raid drill! Line up in single file behind your teacher. Walk to your designated place in the hall. Face the wall and sit down, lower your face, and cross your arms above your head. When you hear the all-clear bell, you will return safely to your classrooms!" You can't imagine how comforting that was. As we marched down the hall behind our fifth grade teacher, Mabel E. Twitty, we all were greatly relieved to know for a fact that this war was being handled very efficiently by Miss Cronin and Miss Twitty. We didn't have to worry about it anymore. We were probably more calm than today's kids are after their grief therapy sessions.

As people did in 2001, our families put forth an effort to win the war. Instead of giving millions of dollars to relief funds for 9/11 victims and others around the world as people did in 2001, we threw ourselves into different kinds of activities. One dad on each block became a Civil Defense Warden. He paid a visit to every home, and sat down to smoke a cigarette while he warned us to buy dark window shades and pull them down for a "blackout" when we heard a siren. Only dads smoked, of course. It was a macho thing. Also, cigarettes became very scarce because, as ads on billboards and in streetcars told us, "Lucky Strike Green Has Gone to War!" Our Hershey bars went too, disappearing from candy store shelves. Both were sent from the factories directly to servicemen overseas.

The purpose of the blackouts was to fool the enemy, so he couldn't see where to drop bombs. We also were supposed to go into the basement while the brave Air Raid Warden remained on a rooftop with binoculars, searching the sky for trouble, and ready to blare his siren when all was clear. Fortunately, we never had to do that. Instead of sending children to expensive overnight camps in summer as parents do today, our parents sent us outside with our little red American Flyer wagons to fight the war. We trekked up and down the neighborhood sidewalks collecting old newspapers and magazines. We took them to used paper centers. I still don't know what they did with them. We also collected tin cans that housewives filled with fat rendered from everything they cooked. We turned those tin cans in to the local butcher, who in turn was supposed to hand them over to the War Department to make bullets and bombs. Recently we learned that never happened, and we realized that then, as now, our government didn't always tell us the whole truth.

One big difference between the 1940s and 2001 is that today there is plenty of everything for everyone, with or without a war. During the 1940 war years several necessities were rationed. Wealthy friends and relatives continued to have everything they needed or wanted by buying it through the "black market." We didn't know exactly who or what that was. Regardless of how much money our parents did or didn't have, they considered such actions to be "un-American!" They used that example in lectures about honesty, morality, civic duty and/or patriotism for many years.

Our parents also sold our car when they couldn't get gasoline, and we all rode public transportation. When our mothers and aunts couldn't buy silk stockings because silk came from Japan, they drew brown lines with eyebrow pencil on the backs of their legs to look like seams and went barelegged. Occasionally the word went out that the Florsheim Shoe Store on Devon Avenue had received a small shipment of silk stockings, and every woman in the neighborhood ran to join the line that wound around the block in hopes of getting her hands on a pair. Meat was carefully rationed. Each member of the family qualified for stamps in a ration book that was replenished every month. There were different colors for adults and for children. The families with the most people in them had the most stamps and probably ate better than our small family of four.

As we moved on to high school, the effects of WW II continued. Our skirts became shorter because manufacturers used all their time and fabric to make uniforms. In 1948, after the war had ended, I went off to college. Factories got back to making women's clothes and our hemlines dropped dramatically. My older brother used to joke that you could tell incoming freshmen girls because they wore new college clothes with long skirts. Upperclass women still wore their old, short ones.

Both short and long skirts were worn with pastel sweaters, a single strand of pearls, brown and white saddle shoes, and "bobby sox". (In those days we didn't mind being called girls instead of women.) We wore our hair as long as it would grow, cut bangs in front and made curls around the edges with perms or curlers if it didn't do that by itself.

All the boys wore slacks and sweaters or plaid cotton or wool shirts to public school. They wore Levi's with T-shirts and sweatshirts after school, and most of them had one dark suit, or a sport jacket with slacks, to wear to church, synagogue or for special occasions. Girls in most Catholic schools wore black, navy or plaid jumper uniforms with white blouses from first grade through high school. In winter they added thick, long, tan, lisle stockings to keep warm. Catholic schoolboys wore dark pants and dress shirts. In contrast, today's girls of all ages go to school wearing low-rise jeans and midriff tees, baring their navels. They add jewelry to several pierced body parts, expensive makeup and straightened hair of many colors. Boys of all ages do all that too, with the latest addition being short, spiky, bleached blond hair.

But the one thing that remains constant in every era is the love and loyalty all of us feel for our country. During all our tragic times, our eyes fill with tears and our voices tremble as we watch our flag wave and place our hands over our hearts. We all feel the same resolve to keep America safe as we say the Pledge of Allegiance and sing *The Star Spangled Banner.*

Sandra Pesmen, a former reporter for Lerner Newspapers and the *Chicago Daily News,* was also features editor of *Crain's Chicago Business.* She now syndicates the weekly Career News Service, and in 1997 was inducted into the Chicago Journalism Hall of Fame. She and her husband live in Northbrook, Illinois.

The Old Chicago Neighborhood

During the 1940s, life in Chicago's neighborhoods was very different than it is today. Each neighborhood was self-contained, and all the necessities of daily life were within walking distance or a quick streetcar ride. Municipal, social, and religious services were close by, including churches and synagogues, public and parochial schools, libraries, police and fire stations and post offices. For shopping, there was a combination of small and large business districts nearby, including groceries, department stores, dime stores, delicatessens, butcher shops, bakeries, drugstores, and restaurants. For recreation, there were numerous parks, beaches, playgrounds or school yards. There were also many entertainment options, including first- and second-run movie theaters, nightclubs, and ballrooms. Other opportunities for socializing were always nearby, at the local tavern, coffee shop, delicatessen, or at activities sponsored by local fraternal or religious organizations. And when needed, all city residents had easy access in and out of their neighborhoods by various means, including diesel and electric commuter trains, elevated trains, buses, trolleys and streetcars.

Chicago neighborhoods were so self-contained they could almost be considered as small towns within the limits of the city. Except for a few trips downtown for shopping, movies, or museums, most Chicago residents found everything they wanted in their own neighborhoods. South Shore

Opposite: *Roosevelt and Halsted, 1944.* Near West Side
(Courtesy of the CTA.)

resident Andrew McKenna could be speaking for all of Chicago when he says, "We didn't wander very far away because everything was nearby. The stores were there, the movie theaters were there, your friends were close, and you did mostly everything on foot or by bicycle."

Many residents remember the '40s as a great time to have been living in Chicago, and have a strong sense of nostalgia about the "good old days." These are strong statements, given the struggles they had to endure during the Great Depression and World War II. The geographic changes that were yet to come, like the movement to suburbia and the introduction of larger centralized shopping areas, would not happen until the '50s. With those shifts, the feeling of community would begin to suffer due to the breakdown of neighborhood boundaries and the increased sense of mobility. To many, the '40s were more than just another decade. It was the time of World War II, of post-war change, and of "the old Chicago neighborhood."

Ethnic Enclaves and Religious Institutions

While many of Chicago's neighborhoods included a diverse combination of residents, some were ethnic, racial or religious enclaves with distinct "boundaries" that provided shelter for those living within. These enclaves date to nineteenth century Chicago, when immigrants and newcomers settled in neighborhoods comprised of people from their own backgrounds. In these enclaves they found the freedom to practice their own religious and cultural customs, as well as make a smoother transition into their new surroundings. From Irish immigrants settling in Bridgeport to Swedes settling in Andersonville, the pattern could be found across the city. This tradition was the foundation for many of Chicago's neighborhoods in the 1940s.

Leonard Amari grew up in the Cabrini neighborhood, an Italian enclave on the Near North Side. "The Italians who settled in Chicago were not unlike other immigrant groups. Many of them came between 1900 and 1920. Why then? It was mostly because of economics. And when they arrived the concept of *quintadina* applied. This meant that when you moved to a foreign land you moved to the neighborhood of somebody from your town. In Chicago, there were historically five Italian neighborhoods, including the Taylor Street area and down at 24th and Oakley. The neighborhood that I am from is on the Near North Side; it's now called the Cabrini-Green projects. It was predominantly Sicilian when I lived there. The actor Dennis Farina was from the Cabrini projects, and his father was the first pharmacist/doctor who had an office in the Cabrini projects. There were a lot of prominent people who came out of my neighborhood."

On the Northwest Side, Polish immigrants settled near St. Stanislaus Kostka Church at Noble and Bradley. Former U.S. Representative Dan Rostenkowski grew up in this Polish enclave right across the street from the church. "This was a Polish section of the city, and Noble Street was the Polish "Broadway" for a while. You have to remember that at one time St. Stanislaus Kostka was the largest Catholic Polish church in the United States. I went to that school, my sisters went to that school and my children went there. In those days, they would have a procession on Palm Sunday and you would have 10,000 people. There were 2,300 children in the school at one time. It was an all-Polish community."

Ethnic culture could dominate a neighborhood, and Bernie Judge remembers how it could even determine status in Our Lady of Peace Parish in South Chicago. "The marvelous thing about the neighborhood was that it was the complete reverse of a class system. My father was born in Ireland — the old country — so I had more status. It was a point of pride to have immigrant parents, because that really tied you to Ireland and its ways. It meant you really knew more about your history and were more inside the real Irish culture. It wasn't an intellectual exercise, but it was a perceptual thing. So, the fact that I had an Irish father who had the gift of gab and a real Irish brogue was a real plus when I was growing up. It gave me a lot of cache in the neighborhood, especially since we both had the same first name. It was important. Judge is an Irish name, a county Mayo name, from western Ireland."

The experience of growing up black in Chicago was very different from that of whites. Most were segregated to a small area on the South Side because restrictive covenants prevented homeowners from selling or renting to blacks. As a result of the waves of black migrations from the south, there was a large population of blacks in a narrow belt on the South Side that came to be known as the "Black Belt." Also known as Bronzeville, the Black Belt was a city unto itself. Except for a small area around Harrison Street on the West Side and in the Cabrini-Green section on the Near North Side, nearly all of the black population of Chicago was concentrated within Bronzeville's borders during the 1940s.

Author Dempsey Travis grew up in the Black Belt and remembers, "In the '40s, the safe boundaries for us were as far north as 22nd Street and as far south as 60th Street, but south of Washington Park was a dangerous area. Although we lived at 59th and Prairie, we didn't go to that end of Washington Park. We stayed closer to the area from 55th to 51st Streets. The boundary on the west was the Rock Island railroad, and on the east it was Cottage Grove. It was a narrow strip that stayed that way until the 1950s and the end of restrictive covenants. We knew that we couldn't cross Cottage Grove, or you were subject to being picked up by the police strictly because you were African-American. I learned early in my life not to cross Cottage Grove. So, we did everything on the west side of Cottage Grove and nothing on the east side."

DuSable Museum founder Margaret Burroughs recalls living in the Black Belt after moving to Chicago in the '20s. "I lived in a thriving neighborhood and there were many black businesses at 35th Street, 43rd Street, and 47th Street, including grocery stores, drug stores, tailor shops and shoe shops. All those streets were thriving areas, and black folks traded with each other. For entertainment, there were places like the Regal Theater, the Vendrome, Forum Hall, the Savoy Ballroom, and the Club DeLisa." Dr. James Carter describes his South Side neighborhood as, "a combination of middle-class and working-class people. We were near 63rd Street and Stony Island — that was the end of the line of the elevated. My neighborhood was mostly brick bungalows with some wooden houses, and although there was a slight mixture of racial groups, it was almost all African-American. Although the area was both middle- and working-class, it wasn't a blighted neighborhood by any means. In those days, people were still migrating out of the south and coming up north looking for jobs with the Post Office and various industries. People had decent jobs in those days and there were some professional people like my dad who was a doctor."

Religious institutions in Chicago, including Catholic and Protestant churches and Jewish synagogues, were powerful forces in the lives of

63rd and Loomis, ca. 1948. West Englewood   (Courtesy of the CTA.)

24th Ward Alderman Louis London, ca. 1942. Lawndale   (Courtesy of Richard Elrod.)

Edward M. Burke
New City

I grew up in Visitation Parish, which if you want to talk about a village, it was a village. Visitation was the largest Catholic parish in America in those days with some 2,400 kids in the grammar school, 1,200 girls in the all-girl's high school, and 400 kids in the kindergarten. The boundaries of the parish were 59th Street on the south, 52nd Street on the north, the railroad tracks on the east, and about Union Avenue to the west, which would have been the border with St. Basil.

The neighborhood was basically single-family, although we lived in a courtyard apartment building at 5240 S. Peoria Street. It was known as the Holly Oaks Building, which probably had 36 apartments. We lived on the second floor, and the Houlihans lived on the floor below us. There was no air conditioning, only one bathroom and one telephone. At that point, a five-person family lived in that one bedroom apartment. My two younger brothers slept in the bedroom where my mother and father slept, and I slept on a pull-out sofa bed in the dining room. We would move the dining room table and chairs over and pull out the sofa bed and that's where I slept. Back then we didn't think that we were entitled to our own bedroom, bathroom and car at sixteen years of age.

All my relatives lived in the neighborhood, including my grandmother and two aunts, who lived at 745 W. Garfield. Everything revolved around the church and the school. There was the Holy Name Society, the Catholic Daughters, and the Society of the Blessed Sacrament. The rectory basement had meeting rooms and there was a meeting going on every night of the week. I can remember that the Holy Name Society put on a show for which I played the piano. People "joined-in" in those days. Our local Knights of Columbus was Leo XIII. It had its own clubhouse on Garfield Boulevard with a bar and meeting rooms. People actually joined things — nobody joins anything anymore. I belonged to the Cub Scouts and the Boy Scouts, and Mrs. Houlihan was our den mother. I could stand in front of church on Sunday and say hello to 2,500 people whom I knew. If I didn't know them personally, I knew their sister or their brother or their mother or their father. In those days, there was no television, so people sat out on their porches and socialized. Future historians will determine whether television was our great boon or our biggest bust.

As to neighborhood parks, Sherman Park was our country club. We did everything in Sherman Park. That's where I took my first dog for training and obedience, where we learned to swim and where we played 16-inch softball. It had a beautiful lagoon where I probably fished for the very first time. During winter, the lagoon would freeze over and we would go ice skating and sledding in the park.

For movies, we would go to the Halfield Theater and the Radio Theater, and then you could go to 63rd and Halsted, which was the largest shopping area outside the Loop in those days. Sears, Wieboldt's, and Hillmans were there. Hillmans was in the Wieboldt's building and you would have to walk downstairs to get to Hillmans. Halsted Street had a string of little businesses all the way from our neighborhood to Morris B. Sachs at 67th and Halsted. There was also Bond's Men's Store, and if my recollection is correct, my father took me there to buy my first suit.

As for the White Sox, we could hop on the Halsted Street bus and get off at 35th, and either walk over or take the 35th Street bus to Comiskey Park. I was young when I went to my first Sox game, and it seemed as if we were allowed to travel on public transportation at a very early age. Our parents didn't have to worry about our safety. We used to take the Western Avenue streetcar straight down Western, all the way to Riverview.

My fondest memory of growing up in the neighborhood in the 1940s was the real sense of security. I don't think that anybody felt at risk. We didn't feel like we were poor — everybody was in the same "boat." Not everybody had a car. In fact, in those days it was rare if somebody had a car. People walked. I walked to school in the morning, and I walked home for lunch and my mother was there. She fixed lunch and we listened to radio serials. At one o'clock I walked back to school until three, and then walked home again. We lived at 52nd and the school was at 54th Place, so it was an easy walk down Peoria Street. Mother was at home during the day, and very few of our friends' mothers worked. It was rare. I can remember that Mrs. Houlihan worked because Mr. Houlihan died and there was nobody else to support the family.

Dan Rostenkowski
West Town

I will tell you about my youth. I was born in 1928 in an all-Polish community. Everyone here was either a saloonkeeper, tailor or a grocer, and they all used to meet at the tavern to discuss the politics of the day. My grandfather had a savings and loan here. It was a "home" savings and loan because it was in part of our home. He used to loan money from the commercial part of the building and customers would pay $.25 or $.30 cents a week, like on an insurance policy. Mind you, he would put receipts in all the cubbyholes for the people who were his clients, and if he wasn't there, they would come in and put their $.25 in. He knew who was paying by the receipts that were gone. Can you imagine leaving a store all day long and having people come in and deposit money and take their receipts? There was a high level of closeness and trust in the community — nobody would steal.

I remember once going to St. Stanislaus Kostka, and Sister DeClana, my teacher, told me to bring my mother to school. I knew I was in deep trouble. I came home and told my mother that she had to come to the school. She said, "You embarrass me! What did you do?" My mother whacked me around, although she couldn't hurt me because I was such a big kid. So, I went to the school with her — and both the sister and my mother beat me! It was discipline, but you would never think of striking a nun. I remember my mother chasing me until she laughed when she was so mad at me. The rule was that everybody's kid better behave, and everybody knew everybody. They built St. Stans' in 1847. My grandmother was young enough to have watched the Chicago Fire from the steeple of that church. The church didn't burn down in the fire, although the fire did go to Fullerton Avenue, but on the east side of the Chicago River.

The neighborhood is called East Humboldt because Bucktown is north of North Avenue. You might even call it the Pulaski Park Area. There was such community spirit. There were more activities in that park — the park district used to come here and put a wooden sidewalk over the cement so that you could walk with your ice skates on the wood to go into the park to warm up or walk to the ice. They used to flood that park. I remember my mother bringing big urns of hot chocolate for all the kids when we were outside all day. You are talking about community spirit, and it was fantastic.

As for entertainment in the summertime, there was none organized by parents. We were out there organizing ourselves. Across the highway, Morton's Salt off Elston Avenue used to be a ball field. Everybody played 16-inch softball in those days, and we played ball in fields. There were ten men on a team — the ball cost $1.20 for a Clincher or a Harwood, so it was $.06 a man and we played for the ball. So, the best teams were the ones that had all the softballs.

This community was very, very active in the war. Every kid in the neighborhood was gone because they all volunteered to go at the beginning of the war. You would've been amazed at all the blue and gold stars that were in the windows. Because of the rationing, you didn't get butter and sugar, and everybody felt the conflict. In those days, if a neighbor was sick, everybody was over there with chicken soup. Nobody went to the hospital, so neighbors took care of each other.

I remember my father, who was the alderman, and Ed Kelly, who was then the mayor of Chicago, going into the park across the street and taking things my mother had baked. The ward headquarters was at our house, and the precinct captains would bring in bread, biscuits and bakery goods to take down to the Servicemen's Center. Ed Kelly had one of the best Servicemen's Center in the world. Whenever a kid came through Chicago, and nearly every train came through here, they would go to that Servicemen's Center. They were treated like royalty there.

I went into the service from 1946 to 1948 after graduating from St. John's Military Academy in Wisconsin. Then, I came back to Chicago in 1948 and went to Loyola University. The neighborhood began to change by the end of the decade when the Polish displaced persons came in. There was a tremendous shortage of housing and many families had to live together. All the mansions in Wicker Park became rooming houses. The kids would come home from St. Stanislaus and teach their parents how to speak English. If you wanted to make a living, you better speak English — you learned how to speak English in order to communicate. I remember that if an Irish cop came out here to arrest a neighbor, my father, the alderman, would be screaming at the cop to get away. If necessary, he would then go down and bail out his constituents. That was what the alderman did in those days. It was a combination of neighborhoods and fraternal organizations that helped foster the new citizen.

When my dad, Joe Rostenkowski, was the alderman, he used to have a citizens' class in ward headquarters. When they were asked who the President of the United States was they would say, "Joe Rostenkowski." He was everything to them.

Irving Park and Seeley, 1944. North Center   (Courtesy of the CTA.)

Angel Guardian Orphanage, Devon and Ridge, ca. 1940. West Ridge (Courtesy of the Rogers Park/West Ridge Historical Society.)

Lee Stern
Uptown

I was born in 1926 at Michael Reese Hospital. I first lived in Lake View on Roscoe, then we moved north to Thorndale and Winthrop, and then we moved to the Grandeur Hotel on the southeast corner of Granville and Winthrop. My mother was a millinery buyer at the Fair Store, and my dad was with a company called Ross Federal Service, a theater-checking agency, so he traveled a great deal.

The neighborhood really centered around Swift School and the playgrounds. If there is anything to write about Chicago and its neighborhoods, it is that the playgrounds were where we "lived." The little asthma I had was caused by what we called the "dust bowl" at Swift School, at Thorndale and Winthrop, right along the "L" tracks. They had a big playground at the south end of the school, and a small one at the north end. In those days, the playgrounds had a male and a female instructor. There was a field house there, and they had wrestling, tug-of-war, and softball games. It was just an exciting time in the 1930s and 1940s.

We saw movies at the Devon Theater on Broadway, the Granada, the Uptown, and the Bryn Mawr Theater. We didn't go to the Riviera because that was where you might end up getting in fights. Once in a while, we would go to the Nortown Theater on Western, south of Devon. We also had a great spot called the Glenlake Bowl on Broadway, between Glenlake and Granville. In those days, you had pin boys, usually drunkards, who we were paying $.10 a line. Every once in a while, if they didn't have pin boys, a couple of guys from our group would go and set pins and we would see how quickly we could roll the balls down the lanes. You always had some guys who threw the bowling ball 100 mph. We spent a lot of time there before and after World War II.

We went shopping on Granville and Bryn Mawr, and there was also shopping on Broadway. The local hangout for high school kids, even after we got out of high school, was Al's Tic Tock. Al's was about three or four stores north of Thorndale on the east side of Broadway. It was a place with about half a dozen booths and counters. This was the hangout. We would go there after we left the Swift School playground. That was our place. We would go to the movies and then go to Al's Tic Tock.

South of there was the Edgewater Beach Hotel. The pier at the hotel extended into the lake, like a small Navy Pier, and they would have speedboats out there. The beach walk was a place to walk along the lake and go dancing. I remember hearing Xavier Cugat and all the big stars of the day there. As a kid, I would creep around the fence and sneak in — I remember drinking mint juleps at the Edgewater Beach. There was a tennis club next to the hotel and Bobby Riggs was there.

I started at Senn High School before the war began. You could eat in the lunchroom there, but there were also a lot of stores around the area. One of them was called Nagle's, and that was where all the athletes hung out. I had $.25 a day for lunch and that paid for three ham sandwiches, a bottle of Coke, and an ice cream. There was also Harry's, but the bad kids hung out there. We always heard about all the terrible things that happened there, including smoking pot. We formed a club at Senn called the "Green and White" that focused on the betterment of the school and of the community. I was never in a fraternity at Senn, but I played center on the football team for four years. We started dancing on the stage at Senn during the lunch period, and I was the DJ. I loved high school, and I think that my high school days were the greatest days I ever had.

Life in the 1940s was special because you could go out as a kid and never worry about whether somebody was going to beat you up, shoot you, or anything else. You could go downtown, to the park, or hang around the beaches until 11 o'clock in the evening. You could take your date to the park and you could stay until whatever hour you wanted. It was a wonderful time in my life. I remember getting on the bus as a little kid, I think about it now and it amazes me. I remember when they opened the new bridge over the Chicago River on the Outer Drive and President Roosevelt was there. I think that I was thirteen or fourteen years old, and I got on the bus by myself and went there to see him. You could do all of those things and not really worry. The best thing about the early '40s was the ability to get around and not worry about things. All you had to worry about was a local bully.

neighborhood and parish residents. These institutions, through a variety of religious services, educational opportunities, and fraternal groups, influenced the daily lives of the residents by setting the standards of behavior, morality, and ethics. In addition, they provided a sense of unity and camaraderie during the many national and international challenges of the 1940s.

Those Chicagoans who grew up in Catholic parishes often went to parochial elementary and high schools, attended masses daily, participated in social events at their churches on a regular basis, and were encouraged to live their lives according to the rules of the Roman Catholic Church. They felt a strong sense of community and neighborhood because of their parish lives.

Bernie Judge recalls that, "As a Catholic, other than your family, the church was the center of your life. That was where you did everything. It dictated your conduct and everything revolved around the school and the church. The celebration of young life was tied to your religious institution. It was the dominating influence of your early years and your pastor was more the emperor than the prince because he tended to rule with a strong hand. You were expected to support the parish financially, and to follow its dictates to the letter. Our church, Our Lady of Peace Church, was magnificent. We had ten masses each Sunday and three masses every other day of the week. It was a large parish and the school had about 700 students."

Mary McCarthy O'Donnell was raised at 5158 S. Morgan near her church, St. John the Baptist. "You could walk to seven churches in the neighborhood. St. John the Baptist Church had Irish Catholic parishioners, while St. John of God Church, further west, was predominantly Polish. At St. John the Baptist we had St. Anne's Novena. At the end of the Novena, there was a parade, and the marchers would go by our house all the way from 50th Place and Peoria to 55th and Morgan. All along the way, most every house would put out some kind of lovely statue. As they were going by, everyone was singing, '*Oh, good St. Anne, we call on thy name.*' It was just beautiful."

Beverly was Jim Casey's neighborhood during the 1940s. "Beverly was a very tightly knit neighborhood. It was primarily Irish and Italian, but mostly Irish Catholic. This kind of closeness in the neighborhood was not that unusual across the South Side. Christ the King Church was the dominant force in the community, and everything revolved around it." Morgan Murphy also grew up in Beverly. "In the 1940s, the neighborhoods and parishes meant close and caring neighbors. Your life revolved around your home, your school, and your church."

Dick Jaffee remembers life in South Shore and the importance of religious groupings. "I think that South Shore was roughly one-third Jews, one-third Irish Catholic and one-third Anglo-Saxon Protestants. I didn't know until I was fifteen years old that you could be Catholic and not be Irish. I really thought that all Catholics were Irish because the only Catholics I knew were Irish. Of course, the question about where you went to school was always whether you were 'Catholic' or 'public.' That was the way we thought of the neighborhood."

Irving Park resident Sheila Morris Williams remembers how a Catholic education could dominate one's life. "I went to both Catholic grammar and high school during the '40s. It was an excellent education, and very demanding. A typical school day was highly structured, and would always begin with a 30 minute mass. Of course, the school was filled with nuns. If we ever did anything wrong — like spoke out of turn — we got a rap across the hand with a steel-tipped ruler. If we did it again, we had to 'pay a dime for the missions.' Now, students in those days would never think about speaking out of turn, it just didn't happen. We were always perfectly behaved. We just lived in fear of the nuns — Sister Trinita in particular — she would hit the hardest and was as mean as could be! But we did learn discipline. Our world back then was dominated by the discipline of the church during the school day, and then reinforced at night by our parents, relatives and the community. We didn't have TV or any negative influences in our lives."

Those residents who grew up in the Jewish faith during the 1940s were influenced by the leaders of their synagogues and the teachings of their religion. Most Jewish children attended public elementary and high schools, but often attended after-school religious instruction, including Saturday Hebrew school and Sunday school classes. Most Jewish families wanted their sons to be bar mitzvah as a sign of manhood at thirteen. The tradition of bat mitzvahs for girls had not yet been established in the 1940s. Except for Jewish enclaves on the city's West Side, most Chicago Jewish families lived in mixed neighborhoods on the North, Northwest and South Side where they were a minority group.

For Art Berman, his religious education was an important part of life on the Far North Side. "I went to Ner Tamid Synagogue on California Avenue in the North Town neighborhood and attended Hebrew School there, which meant that when I was done at public school in the afternoon I would be at Ner Tamid four days a week. I even went to Hebrew High School for a couple of years, and that was the synagogue where I was bar mitzvah on the day of Israel's independence. It was the biggest synagogue in the area. The neighborhood was substantially Jewish, and it had evolved

North and Pulaski, ca. 1948. Humboldt Park (Courtesy of the CTA.)

Jim O'Connor
Gresham

I was born in 1937 and grew up in the Gresham neighborhood at 79th and Ashland, but it was really known as Little Flower Parish. Back then, pre-television and pre-mobility, your life was pretty much determined by the parish, particularly on Chicago's South Side. The parish you were in told volumes about you. You knew where people hung out, what they did, and where they played softball. Our neighborhood was defined by the railroad tracks at 75th Street, Ashland Boulevard west to Damen, and up to about 83rd Street.

Our parish dominated most everything. We had a tremendously powerful pastor, Monsignor McMahon. He walked through the neighborhood with two St. Bernard dogs wearing a silk suit with a homburg and cane, not because he needed a cane, but a walking cane. Every now and then, it was like God was coming down the street. He was a dominant character. He took a little basement church back in the '40s and built it into something that came as close to a cathedral as you could find on the South Side. It was a magnificent church, and so much activity revolved around it. They had the Sodality, the Altar and Roses Society, the Knights of Columbus, and McMahon must have had at least five associate pastors. It gives you an idea how large the community was. I would imagine it was probably 80% Irish Catholic — just a huge Irish Catholic population.

Being an altar boy was a major assignment when I grew up in the parish. Where you stood in the pecking order — at midnight mass, or the big weddings — determined how you were regarded by the pastor and the other priests in the parish. Almost all the boys were altar boys because there were so many masses. That was important. I had nothing but nuns as teachers, and I don't think there was a lay person in the school.

It was required that everyone pay something for school. Every month, my father would give me a dollar to give to the principal as payment for tuition. The tuition was $10.00 a year. Of course, you had nuns who were probably getting paid $30.00 or less a month, so you had very inexpensive labor. Every month I got this same lecture: "This represents a sacrifice and you owe something back. For this dollar we expect that you are going to do your homework on time and not goof off." Every kid got the same lecture. I've always felt that in life you don't get something for nothing. There was really built-in discipline.

During the drive to build the church, the pastor determined how much each family should give and what was expected from them. He would say to my father, "Okay, I expect $100.00 from you." The pastor ran the numbers and figured out what everybody was expected to give — and everybody did. He also put a list in the back of the church showing what everybody had committed. He got you to contribute because of your conscience and notoriety, not because of your good faith. Everybody's name and how much they had contributed or pledged was up there. It was phenomenally successful, and the new church was magnificent. Ceremonies around church activities were major, whether it was Good Friday, Easter or Christmas. Midnight Mass was spectacular — that was a large part of life in the '40s.

I was eight years old when the war ended, so barely in second or third grade, and during that time my life didn't change a lot. I remember things like the Texaco man, and how he would race to the car, wash the windows and check the air and oil. The biggest store in the neighborhood was the Hi-Lo Store at 79th and Paulina. That's where everybody shopped for groceries. I was their delivery boy. I would get a dime for carrying the groceries three blocks. It was the first job I had, and I was very, very young.

Milk was delivered on wagons drawn by horses in the '40s, and even up to the time we left the neighborhood in the middle '50s. We lived in an apartment that had an alley behind the building, and I remember the ragman shouting, "Rags a lyin!" Our back door was always open during the years we lived there. We had landings or back porches, and during the winter we would always pile the snow up and jump off the second floor landing. We did not have an iceman there, but we had an old GE refrigerator with the circular top. I never remember having an appliance changed in the eighteen years we lived in that apartment. The washing machine was the crank-type, and it was in a little room off the kitchen. Then they would put the clothes out on the lines to dry. In the basement, we had tubs where the heavier laundry was done.

The thing I also remember about the '40s was that most Christmas gifts were war surplus, such as large target kites, pill boxes, little ammunition cases, small hatchets, or Army-issue shovels. That was very common. There was a big war surplus store on 79th Street near Halsted. I remember a lot of the parents going shopping there in '45 and '46 — that was Christmas. There was not a lot of wealth during that period, and so much of the fun was do-it-yourself.

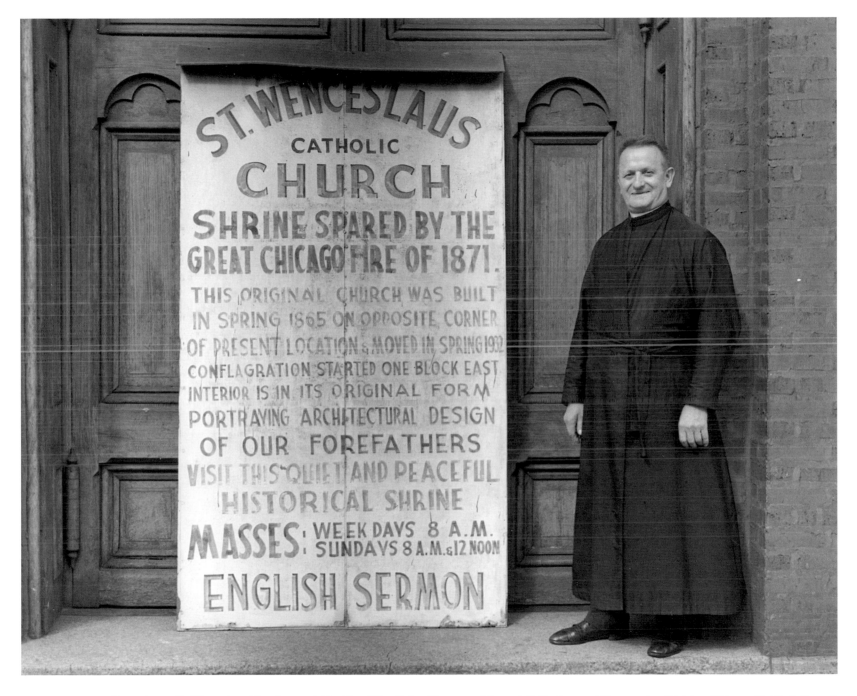

Rev. Thomas M. Sampelinski, St. Wenceslaus Church, ca. 1948. Near West Side (Courtesy of Special Collections and Preservation Division, Chicago Public Library.)

Chicago Home for Jewish Orphans, 62nd and Drexel, ca. 1940. Woodlawn (Courtesy of the Jewish United Federation.)

Mel Pearl
Lawndale

I was born in 1936 at Norwegian American Hospital and lived in an apartment building at 1537 S. Kolin, at the south end of Franklin Park. I had never been in a single-family home until we built our house in West Rogers Park. On the West Side, we lived in a courtyard apartment building with four entranceways. There were many kids in our building. When the weather was bad we used to go into the vestibule of the building and play all day long. You could have made a life out of that apartment building.

We went shopping and to movies on 16th Street, that was the big commercial street. All the stores were operated by old-world merchants, including Galler's Drugstore with a soda fountain and D&W Delicatessen at 16th and Kolin. There were all kinds of kosher stores, and it was a neighborhood that was a true ghetto. It was an old world ghetto. When my folks moved to the North Side, I stayed back on the West Side to graduate grammar school. During that time, I lived with my grandmother who also lived in our building. She had been in this country for 30 years, but spoke very little English. She spoke Yiddish and Russian, but mostly Yiddish. So, the year that I lived with her, I had to learn to understand and speak Yiddish. All the merchants on the street in our area, maybe eight to ten square blocks at that time, were Jewish and spoke Yiddish. Surrounding us was a Bohemian area, a Polish area, an Italian area, and there was no real trouble. You knew what streets to stay on and where not to go. There were Catholic schools around us, and, of course, the Hebrew schools and all the synagogues. My parents spoke fluent Yiddish because they were born in Europe, but they also spoke English. I would go to the store with my grandmother and my mother, and they'd converse in Yiddish. My grandmother had no real reason to learn English because everybody spoke Yiddish. It truly was a ghetto and there were all tenements. I remember so succinctly that every night in the warmer weather, all the kids would congregate on the corner. The mothers would open the window and yell, "Come on home, dinner's ready. It's time to come home and go to sleep!" Your whole life was on the streets. Franklin Park was a key for us, but it was just as important to hang out on the street corners.

We had a lot of little synagogues in our neighborhood, but the big, fancy synagogues were on Douglas Boulevard, including KINS. The little synagogues were connected to European shtetls, and they were named after little towns that the Jews came from. They were Orthodox, of course, and they would seat 100 people with the women sitting upstairs. I went to Hebrew school and cheder in a guy's kitchen. He was an old world rabbi on Kolin Avenue. He used to sit there with a ruler and give me a whack if I missed something. When I was bar mitzvah, I gave my speech in Yiddish. That was the environment — a little community of old world Jews. If you missed Hebrew school, it was like a crime against mankind, but I used to ditch all the time. On the West Side, we stayed in our own ghetto. When we moved and I went to Evanston Township High School, my first year was really tough.

At fourteen I moved to West Rogers Park. You talk about culture shock! We had built our house on Francisco and Estes. At that time, on our block, there were only four houses and prairie all the way to the clay pits. I had just come from a tenement where there were 700 kids in the yard to this prairie with four houses and you can't see a soul. I'm ready to kill myself and my parents. It was horrible. I went to Evanston because the kids across the street were going there. I only knew three kids, and there weren't any other kids around. You couldn't find a soul. So, I went to Evanston. They had never seen a Jew in Evanston at this time. You talk about culture shock! I had come from a strong Semitic neighborhood to Evanston Township High School. It took me about a year to deal with it. Anti-Semitism was very strong there. In a class of 1200 kids, there were seven Jewish kids. It was a very tough time for me — the Jews and blacks hung out together.

I'm telling you that it was great growing up on the West Side. Nobody had better growing up years than I did on the West Side. It was fantastic, and I loved every minute of it. What made the '40s unique was all the first-generation Americans, and the strong camaraderie in the neighborhood. You didn't get out of the neighborhood because you didn't have your own cars. You were circumscribed by the lack of transportation. You didn't get out of your eight square blocks because you were going into foreign territory after that. There was a very strong sense of closeness, of congregation of people, and everything was out on the street. I really cannot think of any negatives from the perspective of a kid.

Jerry Petacque
Humboldt Park

I was born in Chicago in 1930. We lived in Humboldt Park on Crystal Street, near Division. I have an older brother, Art, and we lived in that area until I was about five. Humboldt Park (the park) was kind of the dividing line. If you lived east of the park, you were considered lower in the social stratification. If you lived west of the park, you were in the higher stratification. We moved from the east side of the park to the west side of the park on Cortez near Kedzie, around 1935.

In the late '30s, the neighborhood was basically Polish, Italian and Jewish. There were probably four or five grocery stores and a kosher butcher shop in the neighborhood, all located on Division Street. We had local barbers who competed with each other — Hymie the barber on Division and Louie the barber on Spaulding. There were competing delicatessens, including Itzkovitz and another across the street, kiddy-corner to it. There was Brown and Koppel on Division and Damen. Many of the area luminaries would go there, including Mike Todd and the Pantzko brothers. The restaurant was in front, but if you walked through a door you would be in a gambling casino where people played cards.

Division Street itself was profoundly interesting. Beginning at Kimball Avenue there were the delicatessens and grocery stores. Then you would go through Humboldt Park and on the corner was Stelzer's Restaurant — that's another vignette. We had Levinson's Bakery, and Levinson was related to the Banowitz family. The Banowitz bakery was on Division near California. Louie's Poolroom and Nate the barber were on Division Street. You had a bunch of Hungarian card places as you worked your way further east. A little further down you had the famous Turkish baths — the schvitz.

I can think of 50 friends I had growing up in Humboldt Park. We knew each other's families, and the families knew each other. They played cards, played Mah Jongg, shopped together, and those connections continued all the way to Damen Avenue (Robey Street). Everybody knew each other. The corner of Spaulding and Division was the meeting place for the people I knew. For the adults, it would be Brown and Koppel or maybe Stelzer's Restaurant, and everybody knew each other. It was a warm, friendly atmosphere, and there was no stratification. You could be a police captain or work in the Turkish bath. They knew each other and they talked. There were no walls that separated them.

I think that the '40s were special because of the interactions between people and the lack of stratification. It was a warm, friendly and fuzzy kind of place to live and grow up. The camaraderie of family, friends, and neighbors made it an open community. My peer group of guys were from Jewish, Polish and Italian families and all got along well — it didn't matter their ethnic or religious heritage. We probably did identify ourselves psychologically, as being from Humboldt Park. We were a little sensitive about being from a community that was different than the affluent, lakefront neighborhoods along Lake Shore Drive.

My earliest negative experience in the neighborhood happened at the schul on Spaulding and Division. The German-American Bund had come to our neighborhood and threw bricks with swastikas through the windows of the synagogue and the delicatessen. My father, Dave, was the second Jewish police captain in Chicago. He was very active in his Jewish orientation and had his own group of vigilantes. There was a pool hall on Division near California and my father would get his group together, including some Jewish policemen, and they would reciprocate to the Bund. Instead of throwing bricks, they would throw fists. That was my earliest memory of negativism in the neighborhood.

In one other situation, there was Gerald K. Smith, a rabid anti-Semite. He gave a speech in Chicago in the early '40s, and when it was over my father and his vigilantes picked him up and took him to the police station for the weekend. Mr. Smith didn't sleep for a few days because my father poured cold water on him to expiate him out of his anti-Semitism. Whether it was successful or not, I don't know.

As for anti-Semitism on the police force, the way it worked was kind of circular. My brother worked at the Sun-Times and he was a Pulitzer-prize winning reporter. The anti-Semitic letters would come to him, not directly to my father. They would say things like, "How did that Jew become a captain?" Most of the people in the police department were Irish, so the anti-Semitism was unspoken. Occasionally, I would go to the morning lineup of policemen at my father's station. He would say, "Gentlemen, good morning. Do you have any complaints this morning? If you do, see your monsignor and don't bother me." They all burst out laughing, because the power in the police department was based on your connections to the parish.

Once my brother Art took me for lunch to a restaurant. Of course, he was a leading authority on crime and the Syndicate in Chicago. We walk into the restaurant — of course, all the hoodlums in Chicago would sit at the back of the restaurant because they were concerned that someone was going to come in and assassinate them. As we walked into the restaurant, these hoodlum-types in their shiny suits waved at my brother and said, "Hey, Art, come here and sit down with us!" So, Art introduced me to these people. Then someone asked, "Hey, Art can we drive you home?" He said, "No, your trunk is not big enough for me and my brother!"

in the '40s from a mixture of Swedish and Luxembourgers. In the '30s, most Jewish people were living in the old 24th Ward on the West Side. Since Ner Tamid was a conservative synagogue, it addressed the middle-class in the neighborhood, and they found comfort there, as well as great leadership. It was a very important institution in our community."

Like many kids, Sheldon Rosing had mixed feelings about attending after-school religious programs. "I was bar mitzvah behind a store next to the Ray Theater on 75th Street in South Shore. My folks were fairly conservative Jews and we had to go to Hebrew School several days a week from 3:30 p.m. to 5:00 p.m. right after grammar school, as well as on Saturday morning. I wanted to be out with my friends who were playing ball." Arnold Scholl echoes that experience. "I went to the Austrian Galician Congregation in Humboldt Park from the time I was seven or eight years old until I was bar mitzvah. It was an Orthodox congregation and it was not that enjoyable going there five days a week. We would have our recess each day and sometimes a couple of us would go into Humboldt Park and play ball. The teacher or the rabbi would come looking for us in the park and guide us back to class." U.S. District Judge Marvin Aspen remembers his Jewish education in Albany Park. "Most of the Jewish boys would go to Hebrew School several afternoons a week in addition to public school. We didn't really enjoy it because the rabbi ran the school the same way he would have taught the children in a European shtetl. We had some problems relating to it and many of us just wanted to finish our bar mitzvah and be done with it. Going to Hebrew School on all those afternoons didn't threaten our Jewish faith or identity. Yet, by the time that we became adults, most of my friends and I became members of Reform or Conservative synagogues, thus failing to emulate the Orthodox practice of Judaism that many of our parents had practiced. That was more a reflection of a new generation of Jewish children in a more modern world than a comment on our parents or on our religion."

Bruce Bachmann recalls the influence of the religious leaders in his Austin neighborhood. "I remember the time three of us stole punch outs from the dime store, and we got caught. In those days, who did you call? They called the rabbi! I got a visit from two older members of the synagogue who scared the heck out of me — all for $.40. I didn't need the money. We just swiped things because it was something to do. I can remember the two men coming up the stairs. I thought it was the police! I never stole again."

U.S. Magistrate Judge Ian Levin remembers growing up in Rogers Park. "The neighborhood was very interesting, and it seemed to be half-Irish-Catholic and half-Jewish. The two religious groups seemed to live separate lives and be in their own special worlds — and not bother each other. There were two different islands of people. We did have interactions when I played at Touhy Beach — a lot of the Catholic kids came to play there or be lifeguards for Sam Leone. But, on the whole, each group went their own way."

Neighborhood Ethnic, Religious and Racial Mixtures

In the 1940s, a broad mix of ethnic groups were represented in neighborhoods throughout Chicago. In some areas, there were enclaves of residents who desired to live close to others of similar backgrounds, but in most neighborhoods a mixture of ethnicities lived together. Some experienced occasional conflicts with other groups, but most discovered that they could live together with a relatively high degree of harmony even if their backgrounds were quite dissimilar.

In sportswriter Bill Jauss' Sauganash neighborhood, two community religious leaders worked hard to avoid divisions between Protestants and Catholics. "Reverend Richard and Father Dolan had similar backgrounds since they both started their churches in the community when it was new. In the 1930s, they were young men just out of ministerial studies, and they didn't have permanent church structures yet. Diversity was something they stressed and they abhorred divisions within the community. They worked together and the young families just getting established in Sauganash saw Father Dolan and Reverend Richard as role models and tried to emulate the standard being set. So we had minimal public vs. parochial divisions as compared with other neighborhoods in the '40s."

Jim Dowdle grew up in South Shore. "In the 1940s, South Shore was a very comfortable neighborhood. The dominant groups were Irish Catholics and Jews. We played softball at O'Keeffe Elementary School, and it was always the Irish against the Jews. It seemed like everybody south of 71st Street was Jewish. Everyone north was pretty much Irish Catholic, but I think that South Shore was a very cohesive neighborhood. There weren't any fights, or anything like that. I think softball is what really brought the two groups together. It was a great neighborhood to be raised in."

Shirley Ochs Simon grew up in Humboldt Park and doesn't recall major conflicts between ethnic and religious groups in her neighborhood. "I don't remember any conflicts in the neighborhood. I had Polish girlfriends and it didn't matter that I was Jewish. In fact, we had one or two black families in our neighborhood. Although we were aware of differences between ethnic groups, it was really the older kids who were involved in struggles and it had nothing to do with us."

Sandy Bank remembers the diversity of Hyde Park in the '40s. "The

Service Guard, 1948. West Town (Courtesy of the Chicago Park District.)

Henry McGee, Jr.
Douglas

I was born in 1932 on the site where Lake Meadows Housing Development is now situated, but I grew up in a two-story apartment building near Garfield Boulevard and State Street. My earliest memories are of my playmates, and attending Sherwood Elementary School. Like many people, I remember my kindergarten teacher, Mrs. Goodman. She, like all of my school teachers from kindergarten through graduate law school, was white. To this day, I have never had the privilege of having an African-American teacher except for my first violin teacher, Mrs. Lucille Davis, who lived in Woodlawn.

I did very well in school and received the American Legion Award for being the best student in my grade school graduating class. Of course, I have many childhood memories of playing with my friends, but I also remember having to pass through the white neighborhood near us to reach both my elementary school and my high school. My black neighborhood ended abruptly at the Rock Island railroad tracks, a half block west of my house. At that time, Negroes did not live west of the tracks, but that was where my grade school was located. There was a sense of great danger in walking beyond the tracks, but I don't remember ever having been beat up. However, I do remember instances of dodging stones being thrown as I walked or ran to school. The school was at 57th and Princeton, which was some four blocks west of the tracks, deep within white-held territory. There was less trouble and danger walking to Englewood High School, but we always came and went to school as much as we could through the black sections of the area.

We were able to journey downtown, to the center of Chicago, but throughout most of my school years we could not comfortably go north of the Chicago River. As late as 1958, an attempt was made to run me off the road after I returned from dropping a friend off near Amundsen High School. There were some black settlements near and about downtown, like Old Town, where there was a small enclave which is now the site of Cabrini Green Public Housing projects. But most of the North Side was off limits to blacks, and on the West Side, there was only a very small black enclave which formed a "L" with the South Side black neighborhoods. Later, I married a woman from that enclave whose family lived at 2037 Warren Boulevard, which paralleled Washington Boulevard. She went to Marshall High School in a formerly Jewish area. Earlier, my mother and father attended a West Side junior college, Crane, which is now called Malcolm X. Today, as it

has come to pass, the West Side is now exclusively black. But at the time I lived there, blacks did not go to any of Chicago's West Side. All through the time I was in high school and college, those white areas were completely off-limits.

My parents were deeply involved in the struggle against segregation and racism, but I was sheltered by them in ways that precluded much consciousness on my part about such restrictions as these. We lived in an entirely black world for most of the period I was growing up. My family moved to Hyde Park/Kenwood in the mid-fifties after I left home, and I believe that we were one of the first families to move east of Cottage Grove. Before that, blacks were subject to arrest if spotted east of Cottage Grove after dark. Our world was defined by Washington Park, where they had the Bud Billikin Day Parade on South Parkway.

My father was a postal clerk at the time I was in high school, and he ended his career as the Chicago Postmaster, appointed by President Johnson as the first black Postmaster of a major facility in the United States. He was also Chairman of the Board of Education and President of the NAACP. I remember that after the war, my dad and some of the NAACP people owned firearms because there was a lot of trouble in Chicago between 1946 and 1950. My dad was head of the NAACP during that exact period. We came from a middle-class family where we were able to avoid some of the horrors of segregation and discrimination, and we escaped some stuff that other blacks had to endure. My dad and sisters looked white, and at one point my sister had to pass for white to get a job at Marshall Field's. I looked like my mother, discernibly brown and African-American, what we called "colored" in those days.

I grew up with a consciousness that Chicago was not safe outside of black areas, but I really didn't think about coming into contact with whites. I was not conscious of racial prejudice until I went to college in the 1950s at Northwestern. I was among the first blacks in 1952 permitted to live in an integrated dormitory on the main campus of the university. Previously, blacks had to live off-campus. I remember a white guy from Kentucky trying to talk my Jewish roommate from New Jersey out of being my roommate. That, and other events, made racism personal for me, and I became more and more conscious of racial conflict and what it meant to be black or white. Today, when I go to visit my sister and walk around the North Side, there is an air of unreality for me. It still seems amazing to me that blacks can walk freely about the streets of the North Side of Chicago. I guess that Chicago is so changed now that people don't remember that.

Maxwell Street Market, 1941. Near West Side Photograph by Russell Lee. (Library of Congress)

Phil Holdman
Near South Side

My first recollection of Maxwell Street was going to the Irving Theater with my mother when I was five years old. The Irving was located about four houses north of Maxwell on Halsted. It cost only $.05 and that's why it was called the "Nickel Show." My mother never paid for me, telling the ticket-taker that I'd sit on her lap so as not to take up another seat. I would read the captions for her from those great silent movies of the '20s.

My family was very poor. We lived in the rear of my Uncle Jake's house on 13th near Blue Island Avenue. The heart of Maxwell Street was only two blocks away and we did all our shopping there, with the meager salary of my mother's "dollar-a-day" job. My father, Philip Holdman Sr., died two months before I was born.

Shopping with mom on Maxwell Street was really an experience. She knew all the stores and where one could get the best bargains. "Kingfish" Levinsky's fish store was on the south side of the 700 block. The live chicken store was on the same block. The shochet next door slaughtered your fowl for $.10, and an old man "robbed your chrane" (pulverized your horseradish) for your Friday night gefilte fish. I don't think that English was spoken on this block, only Yiddish. My mother was a live chicken maven and she always picked out the one with the most schmaltz.

In later years, when we moved to the more modern West Side, we would take streetcars back to Maxwell to do the weekly shopping. Mom didn't trust those fancy new stores on Roosevelt Road, with their cash registers. Coming home after buying her usual Thursday shopping specialties (a live chicken and a live carp or buffalo fish for gefilte fish), her linoleum shopping bags would wander to and fro because the live beings in them were getting frisky. Passengers in the streetcars eyes popped out wondering what was in those bags. Mom and I always laughed about those incidents. The only thing I didn't like about the live carp was that I'd lose my sleeping place for one night. I slept in the bathtub when it wasn't in use.

Another remembrance in later years was buying my first suit, at the age of twelve, for my forthcoming bar mitzvah. It was back to Maxwell Street to Shloimes Clothing Store with his bargains galore. I wound up with a $4.00 purple suit with one sleeve shorter than the other. If I bent over to one side, like the actor Henry Armetta, the suit would fit perfectly. Anyway, the price was right and my bar mitzvah was a huge success.

dominant groups in the area were older German-Jews, German refugees who moved into the area after the war, Eastern European Jews, and lace-curtain Irish Catholics who sent their kids to parochial schools. There were also Protestants in Hyde Park, but they were really a minority. For Jewish residents, there were a couple of Orthodox temples in the neighborhood, as well as a couple of Conservative temples, but the dominant ones were the Reform temples. When I went to Kenwood grammar school, the entire economic spectrum was represented at the school. There were people on relief as well as kids who were picked up each day by chauffeurs."

Occasionally, there were conflicts between Jews and Catholics, especially those who attended public and parochial schools. Ron Michaels grew up in Austin on the West Side. "My neighborhood was very diverse, but it was predominantly Irish Catholic along with some Jewish, Greek and Polish families. There were unwritten boundaries, and my problem was that my route to public school went past Resurrection Parish. Some of the older Catholic kids would stop me on a regular basis. They threatened me, hit me, and charged me protection money in order to get back on my way to school. I complained to my father about the treatment and I didn't want to go to school because it was such a terrible experience. I remember that he said to me, 'Good for you. When you get beat up enough maybe then you will learn to defend yourself. I'm not giving you money to pay those kids.' Sure enough, I decided to fight back and it became almost a vendetta for me. In the following years, I managed to fight every single one of those tough guys who had given me such a hard time. I also remember that one time I was playing basketball at Resurrection with my shirt off because it was a very hot day. Two nuns came over and told me that I had to put my shirt on. I recall saying to the Sister, 'If I put my shirt on, I will only keep the heat in and that would be detrimental to my health.' She said, 'My son, you should be a lawyer someday.' They let me keep my shirt off."

Harriet Wilson Ellis lived in Logan Square. "The neighborhood was a combination of different kinds of ethnic groups, but there were very few Jewish families in our part of Logan Square. Up around where we lived there were mostly German and Polish families. Although I experienced some anti-Semitism in the '40s, I did have many non-Jewish friends. However, some kids would actually let you know that you weren't invited to come to their parties because you were Jewish. They would say that the Jews had killed Christ and that topic was very common in many neighborhoods and all over the country and the world. My parents also encountered problems when they wanted to rent an apartment. Our last name was Wilson, but it had been Anglicized from the original Russian name when my great-grandfather had come to America from Vilna. Most people didn't know that I was Jewish, and when they found out they thought that I was trying to hide my true heritage. That was not the case since my family was very proud to be Jewish."

Howard Rosen had similar experiences in his Humboldt Park neighborhood. "My earliest brush with anti-Semitism was when we used to hear about the fights between the Jews and the Polish kids. There was a big Polish population on the east side of Humboldt Park — that was the Tuley High School side. The side where we lived was the Lowell grammar school side — it was more Jewish. We would hear about fights where they used fists and clubs, but never guns and knives. The first significant anti-Semitism that I ran into was when I was living in Albany Park. A friend and I were living about a quarter block from a small neighborhood church, right on the corner of Sunnyside and Spaulding. My friend and I were probably two of the only Jewish guys in our neighborhood. I remember being told that I had killed Christ, and I used to be called the 'Yid' and stuff like that. But I would never back down or anything like that. My father infused me with the idea that you stand up for your rights, and I did stand tough."

Lou Roskin also grew up in Humboldt Park. "I was born in St. Louis, and when I came to Chicago we moved to Humboldt Boulevard and Armitage. I was a tough kid and when my new friends told me that Jewish kids weren't allowed to go past Bloomingdale Street, I resolved to change that. During the 1940s, anti-Semitism was very prevalent in the neighborhood. I remember one time when we got news that a group of Polish lads was going to come over and do damage to our temple. We waited in hiding for them and when their car pulled up we jumped out. I grabbed somebody and one of my friend's father yelled, 'Louie — hold them.' While I was holding the fellow, my friend's father accidentally punched me right in the face."

During the 1940s, blacks found it uncomfortable and even dangerous to travel out of the Black Belt into bordering neighborhoods. Taunting, rock-throwing, and physical violence were all real threats that had to be dealt with. Ted Saunders recalls, "As a black man, there were neighborhoods where we didn't go. Usually we never went on the other side of Halsted, and we only went to South Shore every so often. As for downtown, middle-class blacks could go there. It was a matter of whether you were known or came from a prominent family, then you could mix and go anyplace."

Henry McGee grew up in the Douglas neighborhood on the South Side. "There were things you could and couldn't do, but I don't remember

---

David Cerda
Near West Side

I *was born on Damen (Robey) at Roosevelt in June 1927. A midwife came to the house and I was born there. That was the popular thing to do at that time, so it was nothing out of the ordinary. My father was a laborer. He started coming across the border during the Mexican Revolution in 1915. At that time some revolutionaries came into his small village and took the young men, and they killed his older brother. Later, all the men came across the border and worked on the railroad, fixing the tracks, while the women stayed behind. My father arrived in Chicago in 1922, just to work, and he stayed with his brother.*

My mother was always at home and never worked. There were only two kids in my family, including my brother who is four years younger. That is in contrast to my grandfather on my father's side, who had twenty-five children and outlived three wives. I never met him because he died before they came up here.

I attended kindergarten in that area around Polk Street and was baptized at Our Lady of Pompeii. We didn't stay there too long, because my mother thought that the schools would be better elsewhere — but the Mexicans were really being chased out of that area. So, we moved to about 1800 S. Kedzie, where some of my other family members were living — like my uncle Manuel, my grandmother and her two children. It wasn't a Mexican community. It was a Jewish area, and there were Jewish precinct captains. There were also some Irish, Polish, German, one black family and another Mexican family in the area. There used to be a Greek ice cream parlor on the northeast corner of Kedzie and Ogden, and across the street was the famous Douglas Park Yiddish Playhouse where Paul Muni performed. That was where I really grew up.

There were problems being Mexican in that neighborhood. They would call us derogatory names and make statements about my heritage, but the neighborhood was really a mixture of people and we were on the border of a variety of ethnic and religious groups.

We would go to Douglas Park on Sundays for family picnics. We would load up the cars with family and friends and go out to the Cantigny Woods around Route 66, where the McCormick estate was located. The kids would play baseball and everybody would bring food. The men would sing songs and my father played the guitar. When it would get dark, we would burn some logs and sing more songs. The families stayed close, and it seemed that we had picnics every Sunday.

Chicago Stockyards, ca. 1940. New City (Courtesy of the CTA.)

Hugh Hefner
Montclare

I was born in 1926 at a hospital at the University of Chicago. The hospital was located on the South Side, but I actually grew up on the Northwest Side of Chicago. The neighborhood was called Montclare. It was adjacent to Oak Park, and bordered by Harlem Avenue to the west, Oak Park Avenue to the east, and Grand Avenue on the north.

When I was four years old we moved into a house at 1922 N. New England. I went to Sayre Grammar School, which was just a block from where I grew up. The major business center for that area was Grand Avenue, and the Grand Avenue streetcar ran from Harlem Avenue all the way to Navy Pier. That was our major transportation downtown, but there was also the Lake Street "L." The streetcar was vastly superior in my mind. There was something quite romantic about those streetcars.

Grand Avenue was our main shopping street. The Montclare Theater was on Grand, just one block east of Harlem. There was a park located about two blocks immediately to the north of us called Sayre Park, and the railroad ran through it. A lot of my memories are related to those trains, which were both freight and passenger. You had to pass the tracks to get to the movies, and we went to the movies two or three times a week. That was the major center of my dreams and fantasies.

I grew up in a very typically midwestern, middle-class, Methodist home. My folks were farm people from Nebraska. They both were college educated and both were teachers at one point in their lives. But there was also a lot of repression, in the sense of the inability to really show emotion. It was very typical of the time. The movies were for me the escape into another magic world where dreams, fantasies and the romantic possibilities were all there.

As for shopping, the drugstore was right across the street from the Montclare Theater. There was a soda fountain that was kind of a hangout, a place where my folks would take my younger brother and me. It was on Harlem, half a block to the north of Grand. Sabbath's Department Store was on Grand, and the first girl who I went steady with worked in the electric department of that store. We bought our Big Little Books when we were kids at Woolworth's and Kresge's, across the street on Grand.

As for the ethnic mix in the Montclare neighborhood — I wasn't particularly aware of any, except that it was totally white. I don't think that there was any particularly dominant racial or ethnic group, as far as I was concerned or aware. The Montclare neighborhood was very homogenous. I was not aware of any bigotry during the 1940s, and was raised in a family that was very liberal.

The Second World War began at the very time I was about to graduate from grade school in 1939. I was at Steinmetz High School in December 1941 when America got into the war. The Depression and the war were, in many respects, an intensely romantic time. I grew up during the time of the World's Fair in 1933 and 1934, and we went there. I'm a kid who developed all kinds of creative games that we used to play, and a lot of them came from movies and things of that kind. I created a game called "Clay," which is actually an improvisational game that we played with modeling clay on a tabletop in which we would create murder mysteries, haunted houses, cowboy towns, and a lot of things inspired by movies. Then, I started drawing comic books and creating mystery stories and things, and a lot of what I did was, in a real sense, a rehearsal for what came later. I started a club and a magazine connected to it called the "Shudder Club," which was related to my fascination with murder and horror movies and radio shows. The magazine contained reviews and short stories that I wrote. It was part of a very inventive and imaginative childhood.

One of the major impacts from the war, particularly during high school, was the fact that I didn't have a car. One connects the teen years with a time when you become very mobile with an automobile, but during the war everybody had gas limitations. I only used the family car on special occasions, but most of the time I couldn't. I wrote a song called "The A Car Blues" that reflected the fact that I was wearing out the leather of my ration shoes. You had to go without certain things because of the war, but at the same time, it was a period in which America really was very homogenous and believed in what it was about. There was a strong sense of neighborhood. People knew their neighbors and tended to hang out with people who lived in their neighborhood. People tended to become romantically involved and to marry people in their own neighborhood. I think that was very much the way of things in the '40s, and I grew up with the same group of young people from kindergarten all the way through high school. I didn't interact too much with kids from other high schools.

It really was a small town community in Montclare. Growing up on the Northwest Side was almost suburban. In the '20s and '30s, it was almost rural. There was a tremendous amount of prairie, and as a boy, I loved that. As I said, my parents were originally farm people in Nebraska. There was a forest preserve just a few blocks west of us that was almost a woods. And, growing up in the late '30s, there were still horse-drawn milk wagons, coal wagons and rags and old iron peddlers roaming the alleys. I didn't play many sports in the alleys or the streets because I wasn't a big sports-person. I was much more interested in games of imagination.

I think that the '30s and the first half of the '40s, particularly during the Depression and war years, was a very romantic time. The popular music of the era was very romantic, and the most popular music of that time was Big Band Swing. It's a music that I still relate to and still play at the Playboy mansion when friends gather here on the weekends. I grew up on jazz, and one of the things that I loved about the music was that it spoke to me in a special way. It was black music, and very American, and for me there was something quite special about that. I had strong feelings about integration. The jazz clubs on the South Side were the only place where you really saw mixed audiences. I was a very liberal kid, and it was the beginning of the Civil Rights movement. Even when I was in the Army, the men whom I served with were all white. There was no bigotry in the neighborhood when I grew up, but I became aware of it when I was in the Army.

The late 1930s and early 1940s were a special time for me. Once I began Playboy, I began living in a world all my own that I created. For me, it is connected to the dreams that came directly out of childhood. It is the '30s and early '40s that are the most intensely romantic times for me, and a time that I remember with the greatest fondness.

Lincoln, Belmont, and Ashland, ca. 1940. North Center
(Courtesy of the CTA.)

any mistreatment — as long as you lived within your normal Negro existence. I wasn't aware about the status of blacks in the military, even though my father tried to join the Navy and they wouldn't let him do it. They had what was called the 'Negro Navy' and he refused to join it, but he didn't tell us that. So, my parents kept a lot of things from us, which I guess is how black, middle-class parents did things with their children. So, my biggest memory of the white world was the danger of going through a white neighborhood, or the fear of getting attacked because we might go through a white neighborhood to get to or from high school."

Former Alderman Leon Despres recalls the integration efforts in his Hyde Park neighborhood during the '40s. "I have lived in Hyde Park ever since 1908, except for two years from 1922 to 1924. I remember that in the '40s housing was very difficult to find in the neighborhood and there were rent controls during those years. As for integration, black families did start moving in, but there was no radical change. A lot of people moved out of Hyde Park, including German refugees, and there were some very distinguished people moving in, including many distinguished African-Americans. The remarkable action of the Hyde Park/Kenwood Community Conference was to welcome African-Americans into the neighborhood and to say that we wanted to have an interracial neighborhood of high standards. Hyde Park had a wonderful atmosphere in the '40s and '50s. It still has a great atmosphere of tolerance and there is a much greater sharing of social values than in most other communities."

The Sense of Community

Today, Chicago neighborhood life in the 1940s is remembered as a special time. Many aspects of life just seemed to be better — the clothes, music, movies — the list could go on and on. But for most who grew up then, the overall sense of community found in the neighborhoods is missed most of all. This sense of community unified the neighborhood, which was very important during the Depression and the war years, when people needed to work together, and depended not just on their families, but their neighbors, too. This helps explain why there is so much nostalgia for the "happier times" of the '40s, despite the fact that so many suffered hardships during the decade.

During the '40s, there were rules of behavior that governed neighborhood life, and neighbors worked together for the betterment of the community. Residents were expected to behave in a way that reflected positively on their families, and for children in particular, there would be consequences if they disobeyed. Montclare resident Chuck Chapman remembers, "I think that the '40s were unique because of the moral code

Hiroshi and Dorothy Kaneko
Near North Side

Hiroshi: *Until the time of the Pearl Harbor attack in 1941 we were farming in Oregon near Salem. After being sent to a temporary camp, we were moved to the Tule Lake Internment Camp in northern California in May of 1942. We couldn't get out unless we could find a job and a place to live, which could be very difficult. The best situation for us would be to find a domestic job where we could live and work together. In July of 1943 we found a domestic job working in Barrington, but after Dorothy got pregnant we had to move on. So we moved to the South Side of Chicago to 6404 S. Ellis Avenue.*

Dorothy: *I'll never forget that place. It was so hard to find a place to live. We would see a vacancy sign and they would always say, "We don't want any Japanese here." We would always tell them that we are not Japanese, we are American.*

Hiroshi: *Because it was so hard to find a place to live we decided to find an apartment building and rent to people coming out of the camps. In 1944 we leased a large, 150 room building at 1039 North LaSalle, it's called the LaSalle Mansion. It quickly became a gathering place, almost a community center for Japanese-Americans. People would come from all over to meet their friends and stay. Eventually we leased two other buildings, as well.*

Dorothy: *I had to cook for them all because there weren't any Japanese restaurants around back then. But soon other Japanese stores started opening there and that's how the Japanese neighborhood started at Clark and Division.*

Hiroshi: *It was a real rough neighborhood when we got there, and one of our buildings had a prostitute living in it — the police arrested me for prostitution and took me to the Chicago Avenue Police Station! My precinct captain, "Dinger" Maloney, heard about my arrest and came to the station. He talked to the officer who arrested me, "Hunchback" Kelly, and told him, "Don't ever bother that man again!" Maloney was a powerful man in the neighborhood and he got me released right away. He knew that there were a lot of votes in our buildings and he treated us well.*

Dorothy: *He brought us twenty-five pairs of nylon stockings one election year to give to the ladies. They were very scarce back then. Another year, he gave free breakfast "passes" to everyone that voted. That's the way it worked in those days.*

Hiroshi: *There were strip clubs and lots of taverns in the area back then. There even was gambling in the barber shop next door. Of course, the barber shop was just a front, with gambling going on in back. It was raided so many times! You would hear "bang-bang" and know it was being raided again.*

Rainbow Market, 218 W. North, 1949. Lincoln Park (Courtesy of the Japanese American Service Committee Legacy Center, Mary and James Numata Collection.)

99th and Halsted, ca. 1940. Washington Heights (Courtesy of the CTA.)

Lake Shore Drive Access, Foster and Sheridan, ca. 1945. Uptown (Courtesy of the CTA.)

Anna Marie DiBuono
Near South Side

I was born in 1938 and I still live on the same block where I was born, Vernon Park Place and Aberdeen. In 1946, we moved across the street. The boundaries of the neighborhood are Racine, Morgan, Harrison and Polk Streets — the neighborhood is called Little Italy.

It was a very united neighborhood. Different regions of Italy settled in different sections of Chicago, and most of the people from my father and mother's town settled in this section. It was called Accerra, and it is a province of Naples. They all settled in this section from Ryland to Loomis Street, from Harrison to Taylor Street. I think that it was the biggest or second biggest Italian section in the city. The Sicilians settled around Oak Street in the Cabrini area. The Tuscany and Venice regions settled around 24th and Oakley. The Neapolitans all settled around where I am located. It was a wonderful era, and it was wonderful growing up here because everybody was so close. There were strong bonds between families, and the majority of families all sponsored one another at baptism and confirmation. It seemed like all the families chose godparents who were close friends.

As for shopping, in the old days we went to Roosevelt Road. There was a variety store called the 12th Street Store that sold groceries, served root beer from the barrel, and they had hot waffle sandwiches with vanilla ice cream. Everybody still talks about the vanilla ice cream and hot waffles.

We had two movie theaters — the Villa Theater on south Halsted Street was a small theater where Greek Town is now — the Garden Theater was on Taylor off Racine. Everybody went to the Garden. It was a small show and it was loads of fun because the whole neighborhood would be there.

There weren't many Italian restaurants in those days. There was Granata's Restaurant on Taylor and Newberry, and Tommy Granata owned that restaurant. Mrs. Ferrara had Ferrara Bakery on Taylor and Halsted. We had all the stores on Halsted Street, including Conta di Savoy, which originally started out on Halsted near Taylor. In those days you had the baskets of snails and the snails would be walking all over. You had all the cheeses and the beautiful prosciutto and capicola and buffalo mozzarella. There weren't many restaurants in the old days, so people ate at home. There were a few other little restaurants near Halsted Street, but for me that would have been a little too far to walk.

My grandmother and grandfather had one of the first Italian bakeries in the city. Because people in the neighborhood didn't have much money they mixed their bread at home and would bring it to the bakery — and for a penny my grandmother would bake the bread for them. Everybody put their initials in the dough so they knew whose bread it was.

I can remember when my parents opened their restaurant — Tufano's. In those days, kids would take pizza from the bakery and walk a half a block to the restaurant. I remember all the celebrities who would come to the restaurant — Frank Sinatra, Tony Bennett, Dean Martin, Jerry Lewis, Jerry Vale, the Crosby Brothers, and the McGuire Sisters. People still talk about the crowds that formed outside to see the McGuire Sisters because they were in their prime. In the old days, it was the Italian restaurant for the Italian stars to visit.

We used to have the feasts on Morgan Street. The people from my parent's town would have a procession, and you would donate money by pinning it on the saint. If you made a nice donation, they would shoot a firecracker in front of your house. The bands would play happy music, and all the Italian men and women would be singing. It was just a different time. It was just a safe, happy time. Our parents wouldn't have to worry because they knew we were in the neighborhood.

We didn't get into trouble like kids do today. Our time was much happier. We didn't have things like children have today, but we were happy as larks. We played volleyball and the boys played basketball. It was such a happy time, and I cannot remember violence like there is today. We had everything at our fingertips. We had a tightly-knit neighborhood and we could go to all of the places we wanted to go. We always felt safe and we never locked our doors. We were never afraid, because nobody would harm us. You slept with your windows open. But, before you knew it, the University of Illinois came and the neighborhood went. We were fortunate because we lived on the right side of the street, but everything else went down.

Reading Time, Chicago Public Library, Austin Branch, ca. 1940. Austin (Courtesy of Special Collections and Preservation Division, Chicago Public Library.)

that applied at that time. By and large, there was a sense of community, of neighborhood, and a feeling that it was important to look out for each other. There was such a feeling of safety that when I was a little kid, I could stay out until late at night and my mother didn't have to worry about me. The condition of the neighborhood was such that all the kids were obliged to behave in a certain way so that if you saw another parent they were allowed to correct you if you did something wrong. It was just like having your own parent stop you if you misbehaved. In that way we sort of had a greater regard and an acknowledgment that this was a larger community family."

According to former Chicago Park District Superintendent Ed Kelly, there was also a strong sense of trust in his Cabrini neighborhood. "When I would go down to the Cipolla Grocery for milk or food, Mr. Cipolla would always write the cost on a brown paper bag. Then, I would go back on a Saturday and pay him. They trusted the families in those days. We would help each other and support each other, and that was going on through the whole neighborhood."

Marvin Aspen also remembers the closeness of his Albany Park neighborhood. "Most of the people in the neighborhood were first-generation Americans, and the second biggest group were immigrants. There were a few families who were fairly well off, but most were middle-to lower middle-class, although I'm sure I didn't know it at the time. You had no sense of lacking anything of substance, and there was a tremendous closeness. You knew everyone who lived there, and not only did you know them, you interacted with them. In those days, relationships were geographically-oriented to the neighborhood and within walking distance. You just knew, socialized and grew with everyone."

The lack of affluence during the era kept family life simple and focused on what was important — perseverance. According to Jim McDonough, "I think that life in the 1940s was a simple life and people learned to endure hardships. As a young kid, I never went hungry, but we certainly never had any luxuries. I think that you learned principles of life and an appreciation of the simpler things. I never felt any fear during those years, but I did learn 'street smarts.'" Mike Perlow would agree, " In our generation, most of us came from 'poverty,' although I hate to use the term because it really wasn't poverty as we think of that term today. Apartment living, especially for those of us who grew up on the West Side, was typical, and most of the kids came from first- and second-generation immigrant families. Coming through the Depression, jobs were valuable, although I never really felt that uncomfortable about money. I think that everyone had about the same standard of living through the 1940s."

In spite of all the challenges of the times, neighborhoods were special places to live in the 1940s. As Burt Sherman remembers, "I had a wonderful childhood, and even though I didn't realize it, we were going through very tumultuous times during the '40s and World War II. Life was so different than it is now. It was much simpler and less competitive. People were very nationalistic and families were very close. And the concept of neighborhood was very strong at that time. When I look back, I feel I would prefer it that way, but then I am looking at it from a biased viewpoint. There were inequities at the time that I wasn't aware of, and I feel bad about it now. But I had a good time during those years. I was fortunate enough to have wonderful parents, a good family, and we were close. It was a much more family-oriented time."

Finally, Jack Hogan recalls, "I think that camaraderie was the unifying force that kept the neighborhood so strong. The people got along so well, and we relied on that social interchange. I think that everybody believes that their neighborhood was the greatest neighborhood in Chicago, because we were all feeding off the same experiences. Everybody got along with everybody.

"Whenever I think back to what I enjoyed most about life, I look back on the '40s. In spite of the war and the struggles that came from it, it was the greatest time in the world."

Chicago Park District's "Save the Lawn" Contest, 8318 S. Rhodes, ca. 1940. Chatham (Courtesy of the Chicago Park District.)

LET'S SHARE OUR CARS
AND SPARE OUR TIRES
How about it, neighbor?
General Outdoor Adv Co

The War Years in the Neighborhood

America entered World War II following the attack on Pearl Harbor by the Empire of Japan on December 7, 1941. For the next four and one-half years residents of Chicago, like the rest of the country, had to deal with many changes in their daily lives. Life on the home front required citizens to adapt to new necessities that included paper and scrap drives, food rationing, Civil Defense preparations and air raid drills. Chicagoans participated in each of these efforts with an unmatched patriotic fervor and learned how to unite to meet the challenges. In addition to new governmental requirements, citizens became involved in the war effort by creating Victory Gardens on empty lots and prairies, purchasing War Bonds to support their country and help finance the war, and hanging flags in their windows to recognize family members serving in the Armed Forces. The Great Depression was over and World War II had begun.

Pearl Harbor Day

War in Europe and Asia had already begun by 1939, but most Americans hoped to avoid becoming an armed participant in the growing war fronts. Then, on Sunday, December 7, 1941, in a surprise attack, the naval and air forces of the Empire of Japan hit the American military on the island of Oahu in Hawaii and decimated the US fleet in Pearl Harbor.

Opposite: *Mrs. Harry Riley and Children, ca. 1944.* Near North Side (Courtesy of the CTA.)

World War II had begun for America. Many Chicagoans first learned of the attack while tuned to their radios on that early Sunday afternoon.

After the attack on Pearl Harbor, West Ridge resident Sandy Zuckerman Pesmen had concerns about what that event really meant to herself, her family, and America. "I was ten years old in 1941 when the war started and I remember saying to my aunt, 'What is this? Is this scary?' And, she said, 'Oh, no. There's nothing to be afraid of. We had the other war in 1918 and your dad was in the reserve. We knitted socks and afghans for the soldiers and that's what we'll do now. There's nothing to be concerned about. We'll all have to help America.' She just dismissed it. That was calming until we got to school the next morning. Anna L. Cronin, our principal at Clinton, said over the loudspeaker, 'Do not be afraid children. We are going to have an air raid drill, and you will be safe. Now, we will all go single file into the hallway. This will be our air raid shelter and you will all sit down next to the wall and you must not make any noise. Now sit down in the corner and your teacher will be in front of you.' We were doing this as her voice was bravely coming over the loudspeaker system from the office. We sat down along the wall, and felt that we were perfectly safe. We felt we would be safe throughout the war, no matter what happened."

On the Northwest Side, Bill Jauss felt the same impact. "I was ten years old when Pearl Harbor happened, and my first thought was 'Gosh, I guess my dad has to go.' But my dad didn't go into service because he was too old and had two kids. He was very fortunate because he escaped both World War I and World War II, just by the accident of when he was born."

Marvin Aspen, who grew up in Albany Park, recalls the limited understanding he had about the war. "I had three uncles who were in military service, two in Europe and one in the Pacific. My mother had one of those flags with three stars in the window. I was seven years old when the war began, and, to be honest with you, the impact on my life during the war years was very little because I was at an age when I was just becoming aware of the larger world around me. The war itself was somewhere out there in Europe, Africa and Asia. At my young age I didn't understand the consequences and certainly not the meaning that it had when I became a little older."

Home Front Efforts: Rationing, Scrap Drives, and War Bonds

One of the responses to the war on the home front was an effort to save and conserve materials that were in limited supply, including scrap metals such as aluminum, tin and brass, and raw materials such as silk and rubber. The city's response was huge, and eventually residents recycled materials ranging from newspapers to kitchen grease. As it turned out, the scrap metal that was saved would have a limited impact on the building of armaments. It would, however, be valuable in the making of consumer goods and allowed critical materials such as "virgin" aluminum to be used for the construction of aircraft.

Although there was some uncertainty by citizens about how newspapers and kitchen grease were actually used for the war effort, the evidence is clear that both materials were used to help the military. In the case of kitchen grease, homemakers would take the waste cooking fats to their butchers and receive a cash payment for the cans of fat. The fat was then turned into glycerin that became dynamite. As for the newspapers, they were used by the military to make waterproof supply cartons. Rationing of meat, sugar, butter, eggs, shoes, nylons, tires, and gasoline was necessary to preserve the supplies and redirect them to the military during the war.

The rationing of daily necessities was difficult for many, and often seemed to be administered unfairly. West Ridge resident Sandy Zuckerman Pesmen recalls, "There was meat rationing, but rich people somehow had as much meat as they wanted because they had more red ration stamps than we did. I don't know how they got them, but they would go to butchers and get steak. We didn't have a whole lot of steak, but lamb was available, so we had a lot of lamb chops and fish. We managed okay, and nobody was ever thin or hungry in our house. I do remember the limited availability of silk stockings. My aunts were upset because they didn't have silk stockings

and they would paint lines on their legs with make-up that was available."

Dick Jaffee also remembers the effects of rationing in his South Shore neighborhood. "When rationing started, meat and gasoline became scarce. There were A, B, and C stamps that were used for rationing. My father needed to get around because of his business, so he got a C stamp for gas rationing. One of the things about shopping that I remember was that my mother would take me to the store because of the meat rationing. She would put me in line to get a pound of ground beef, the allocation for the week. I would stand there and wait until I got to the front of the line and use the coupons to get the meat for the week."

For children, the lack of bubble gum was a problem during the war. Lawndale resident Mel Pearl recalls, "I remember that we could never get any bubble gum. I do recall that once my father somehow got a box of bubble gum. We treated that gum like it was gold. I went out and gave my friends a piece of it and told them that they had to chew it very slowly because they would never see it again."

Jerry Petacque's father was a Chicago Police Captain who had to deal with people who "lost" their ration books. "In the '40s, after the war had started, a lot of people fictionalized that they had lost their ration books. They had to report the loss to the local police station. My father, who had a fantastic sense of humor, would roll up a piece of paper and put it to his ear to make believe that he had a loss of hearing. So, the word was you didn't go to Captain Petacque if you lost your ration books."

Children were particularly valuable in the effort to collect scrap metal and paper. From roaming the alleys to going door-to-door, their enthusiasm and competitive nature could yield large amounts of material. U.S. District Judge Charles Kocoras recalls, "We were always having paper drives at school. Because my father had a truck, somehow, we had access to more paper than anybody else. We would go around collecting it and bring the paper to school, and I distinctly remember that with my dad's help we always had the most paper. There was always some kind of recognition for that good deed." Gerald Bender was also actively involved in helping the war effort in the Lawndale neighborhood. " I remember picking up all the newspapers from peoples' back porches, dragging them to school, and looking through the pile to see if there were any comic books. We had these giant paper drives at Bryant School, and I can remember carrying paper off the back porch and almost dying because it was so heavy. I remember that we were also collecting old pots and pans.

Competition was also a factor in the selling of War Bonds. Grand Crossing resident Frank Rago recalls, "Every Friday we would buy War Stamps or War Bonds at school. We didn't have much money, but when

Pearl Harbor Day

Fr. Andrew Greeley

Pearl Harbor is as fresh in my mind as September 11, 2001. I remember it very clearly. I was sitting by my family's Philco radio listening to the Bears playing the Cardinals. I remember the Bears were losing when they interrupted the broadcast — the Japanese had bombed Pearl Harbor and the battleship Oklahoma had caught fire — then they switched it back to the football game and the Bears were winning. My reaction was one of astonishment. I knew where Pearl Harbor was because I was a geography freak. I thought that our world was in a state of collapse and that we were at war, but I had no idea what that would mean.

Dan Rostenkowski

I was playing ball in the alley alongside of our building that had a tavern on the corner. Somebody came out and said, "The Japs are attacking Pearl Harbor!" I didn't know what that meant. I went upstairs and told my mother, "The Japs are attacking Pearl Harbor!" "Where is Pearl Harbor?" she asked. It happened on a Sunday afternoon, and my dad came home that night. He was the alderman at that time, and I'll never forget that he had a white hat on. He said, "We'll kick their asses in three weeks! Those sons of bitches, we'll kick their asses in three weeks!"

Bob Kennedy

I was sitting in the upper deck right below the announcer's box on December 7, 1941, during the Cardinal/Bear game. Bob Elson saw me sitting there, opened the window and hollered down to me, just before the half, "Hey, Bob, the Japs just bombed Pearl Harbor!" I said to my buddy, "Where the heck is Pearl Harbor?" I had no idea where it was located. So, some of the fans around me said, "What did they say Bob?" "We're going to war," I said. Then the fans started leaving and it got real quiet in the ballpark. It was amazing because the players stopped on the field and looked around and didn't know what was going on. People were driving away. No horns were blowing. There was no noise, and we were all aware that we're going to war.

Estelle Gordon Baron

On December 7, 1941, I slept in. We were living with my folks in an apartment on Paxton, and I got up late. It must have been around 11:00 am when I woke up. I walked into the front of the apartment and my husband said to me, "Would you believe the Japs bombed Pearl Harbor?" I had never heard of Pearl Harbor. Hawaii seemed so far away and so foreign to us. We weren't really on top of the news the way we are now. We have breaking news now, and can see events as they are happening. So, we were dependent upon the radio and the news commentators, like Edward R. Morrow. We hung onto their words because it was current and what was happening.

Ray Meyer

I'll always remember when Pearl Harbor was attacked. We were living with my wife's parents because I was out of work. Her sister and brother-in-law lived upstairs in the two-flat. We were eating lunch that Sunday, and, all of a sudden, they came running down to tell us the news — Pearl Harbor was bombed. We were shocked, and we listened to the radio all day, and heard Roosevelt's speech the next day. The war affected all of our lives in so many ways. The military started calling up people to join the war effort. I was about 25 at that time, so I went down with "Moose" Krause, who was going to join the Marine Corps. I was planning to join the Marines with him, but at the recruiting station they asked me if I had ever had an operation, and I had had one on my knee. They told me good-bye. I got a letter from Dr. Danny Leventhal indicating that I was in perfect shape, but too much cartilage was taken out, so I never served in WW II.

Howard Rosen

I was listening to the Bear football game on the radio with my dad. They interrupted to say that Pearl Harbor had been bombed. The next morning I went to school and my 5th grade teacher, Mrs. Evelyn Carlson, brought a radio to class and we listened to the Roosevelt speech. I felt afraid about the war. I remember my father putting his arm around me and saying, "There's nothing to worry about. They don't know who they're messing with!"

Jack Hogan

Everybody thinks about where they were on December 7, 1941, but I don't remember where I was on that Sunday, although I do remember the next day very vividly. I remember hearing Roosevelt deliver his Declaration of War speech to Congress on the radio. My mother cried during the speech because she knew what was going to happen. I was totally oblivious to it. I was in high school, and it was too remote for me. I didn't understand that I would be in the service in a couple of years. My mother knew. Her brother had come from Ireland and served in World War I, and he was gassed and it ruined his life. So, she immediately saw the possible consequences.

Wayne Juhlan
Portage Park

I grew up at 5527 West Irving Park Road, right across the street from Portage Park. I was four to fourteen during the 1940s, and the biggest thing during this time was the war. Everything seemed to be geared around the war effort, like the rationing. There was no bubble gum! If you were a kid this was a tragedy! We chewed it once or twice, but we couldn't get it. The other big thing I remember were the stars that hung in the front windows of homes. If you had a son who was in the war you'd proudly hang this blue star, and we were very aware of them around the neighborhood. Every now and then we'd see a gold star, which meant someone had been killed.

My dad was handy with wood and he built a large display case that he placed at the southwest corner of Irving Park and Long Avenue. It had the names of all the people in the neighborhood who were serving and what branches of the military they belonged to. He was very proud of it. It was for the whole neighborhood. And us kids did things that made us feel like we were doing our part for the war effort too, even though we were only six or seven years old. I had a Victory Garden where I grew tomatoes and beans. It really made me feel like I was doing my part.

Of course, all the games we played would be war games. Instead of cops and robbers we were GIs. One of the things we did was take cans filled with saw dust and play war. We'd hurl these cans and when they'd hit the target sawdust would scatter like a hand grenade. We would wear plastic helmet liners so the kids would never get hurt, but everything had to be about the war. Even trading cards were war cards. They were just like baseball cards except they had actual battle scenes on them, and kids would collect them like baseball cards. Kids collected War Stamps, too. We would keep them in a little book and when you filled the entire thing you could turn it in for a War Bond. It was about $17.00 for a bond, and the stamps were about $.10 apiece, so it took us awhile to save. We were so proud while we were doing it, comparing notes with the other kids, and asking, "How many stamps do you have?" This stuff kept us kids involved, and made us feel like we made a real contribution.

The funny thing about being a kid, you know, is that your imagination runs away with you. For example, we never saw many commercial planes flying during the war. When an airplane did fly over we would be kind of nervous, even though we knew the war was thousands of miles away. For a minute, we didn't know. And listening to the newscasts at the time could be funny because kids take things literally and don't know the language. We'd hear about a battle between us and "guerrillas with small arms" and imagine a bunch of apes fighting with little hands.

American Legion Scrap Drive, Devon and Ashland, ca. 1942. Rogers Park
(Courtesy of the Rogers Park/West Ridge Historical Society.)

Waste Paper Drive, Sherman Park, 1945. New City (Courtesy of the Chicago Park District.)

CITIZENS OF CHICAGO!

This harmless piece of paper was dropped from an airplane. It COULD have been an enemy's bomb bringing death and destruction, or a propaganda leaflet spreading disunity and bewilderment among us. That it is neither, is due to the skill, courage, and sacrifice of our fighting men now invading Europe.

When the War Bond Warden in your block calls, during the Fifth War Loan Drive, welcome him in. Then dig into your savings and buy EXTRA war bonds! Your block has a quota. Watch the thermometer on your corner. Put it over the 100% mark! If you have bought war bonds since June 1st where you work or anywhere else, fill out the Red, White and Blue Credit Slip which the War Bond Warden will have. Then your block will receive full credit for all bonds you buy, wherever you buy them!

Chicago and Cook County War Finance Committee. 5th War Loan Philip R. Clarke, Chairman

National Printing & Pub. Co. '31 2150 Blue Island Avenue

Handbill Dropped From Airplane Over Chicago, ca. 1944.
(Private Collection.)

the teacher called your name you would say how many War Stamps you wanted. The stamps were $.10 apiece. One day my dad gave me a dollar and I felt so important because I would be able to buy ten War Stamps at school. The teacher called out my name and she asked me how many stamps I wanted. I called out ten, and it made me feel great until the girl behind me bought a $25 War Bond. That upset me for a while."

Victory Gardens

Many empty lots, prairies, and Park District grounds in Chicago's neighborhoods became sites for Victory Gardens. Millions of pounds of fresh vegetables made their way to Chicagoans' tables from these gardens, allowing farmers to focus their efforts on growing fresh foodstuffs for the men and women of the military serving around the world.

Fr. Gene Smith recalls the Victory Garden in his South Side neighborhood. "I remember Victory Gardens at a place called the 'cornfield' that was a vacant lot between Dorchester and Blackstone on 72nd Street. On one side of the street, people grew corn, and on the other side, people grew tomatoes and other vegetables. I remember coming home with a lot of tomatoes one day, and my mom asked me where I had got all of those. I told her that they were free and you just go to this vacant lot over there and help yourself. Well, my mom told me that the vegetables weren't free and belonged to somebody else."

Radio historian Chuck Schaden remembers the Victory Gardens in his Norridge neighborhood. "My family had a Victory Garden north of Montrose Avenue on some vacant land. It must have been farmland at one time. They probably were going to develop the area before the Depression because they had put in sidewalks, but the 1930s changed everything. I guess there was a source for water, but there weren't any buildings under construction there in the early '40s. People just took over that land to build Victory Gardens during the war."

On the South Side, Dick Jaffee remembers the Victory Gardens in his South Shore neighborhood. "We had a Victory Garden that was a plot of ground on a Jeffrey Avenue empty lot, on the east side of the street. We would go there and cultivate the land, plant seeds and harvest some of our own food. I guess that we got some corn and other vegetables from that garden during the war."

Civil Defense

Immediately after December 7, there was fear that the Japanese and Germans might launch an invasion of the United States. This led to the creation of a Civil Defense effort that would impact every American. In

Chicago neighborhoods, thousands of citizens volunteered to serve as Civil Defense Wardens whose responsibility it was to be certain that Chicagoans were prepared for any eventuality. Residents were expected to learn a variety of activities, including how to survive an air raid, make sure that apartment and house windows were light-tight, and how to spot and identify the various types of enemy aircraft.

Frank Rago was active in the home front efforts in his Grand Crossing neighborhood. "I remember being a Junior Air Raid Captain — I assisted an air raid warden. Those were intriguing and eerie times because we would have to go around at night and check that people had covered their windows during the mock air raids. We would have to report people who had light showing from their windows. And planes would drop bags of white flour. If they hit anywhere on your block, then your area was considered destroyed because they had the so-called 'block-buster' bomb at the time. People took it very seriously."

Ron Davis has clear memories of Civil Defense and air raid drills in West Rogers Park. "On every block was a bulletin board that listed all of those who were in the service, and those injured and killed. And there was a Civil Defense warden for each block. He would wear a helmet and armband that had a CD on it. We would have blackouts, and on certain nights we were told that everybody had to turn off all the lights in their home, unless they had light-proof shades. The blackout would usually last half an hour. All the lights were out in the whole neighborhood except for the gas tank near Kedzie and the canal. Nobody ever questioned how airplanes could fly to Chicago from Germany or Japan."

Rick Fizdale recalls how the father of his friend and neighbor, Steve Zucker, was an Air Raid Warden in the North Town neighborhood. "Sometimes during the war Steve and I would go with him when he made his rounds. Everybody had to pull their curtains and make sure that no light was getting out to the incoming planes. Steve's dad would walk through the alley and look into stairwells and basements. It seemed frightening that this could happen so close to where I lived and played. How absurd that we were looking for enemy soldiers in what was the center of my universe! At some level I understood, because the news was so global at that point. Every time, throughout the entire war and deep into my adolescence, if I heard an airplane overhead at night I assumed it meant that there might be bombs. On one hand, I knew it wasn't so, but on the other, I couldn't stop my pulse from beating faster. So, I was conditioned by the air raid warden, by the blackouts, by the radio, and by the movies I saw at the Nortown Theater to believe that war kills people."

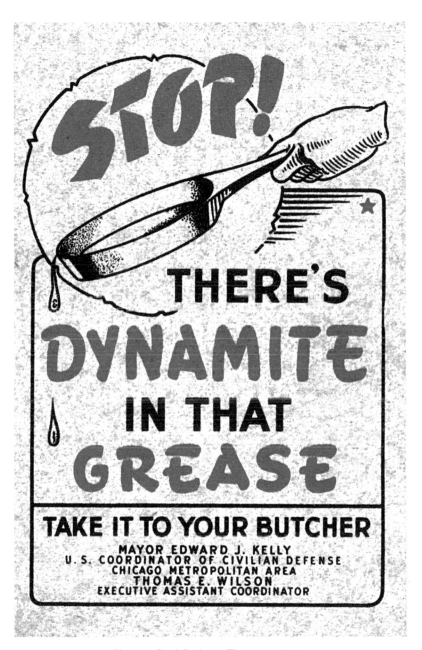

Chicago Civil Defense Flyer, ca. 1944.
(Private Collection.)

Children's War Games

Patriotism came in many forms during the war years. For children, one way of demonstrating support for the war effort was through games that they played. At the extreme, these games led to harsh stereotyping of Japanese- and German-Americans. But to most children, these games were just another variation of the "good guys versus the bad guys."

Burt Sherman remembers the patriotic games that he used to play during his childhood on the Far North Side. "I was born in 1936 and was only five years old when the war began, so I remember those years from the perspective of a kid. The main thing that kids played was 'war.' That was very common. At that time, we were either playing the good guys or the bad guys. The bad guys, of course, were Hitler and Mussolini. We used to make fun of them, and we had songs about Hirohito and Tojo. We sang popular songs that poked fun at them. All the children knew and sang the songs. At the same time, we would imitate the American soldiers — the good guys against the bad guys. We also played cowboys and Indians, and it was the same kind of thing. The lines were clearly drawn between the good guys and the bad guys. I didn't have a sense of fear during the war years. Even though we saw the newsreels, it probably didn't sink in the way it should have. As far as we were concerned, we were far enough away from the war. When you were a kid, the only thing that touched you was when you lost a relative."

Window Flags

"Son in Service" flags were first hung in windows to commemorate those Americans serving in World War I. The tradition continued during World War II, when each family who had a member in active service was entitled to hang a white flag with a blue star in their window. The blue star would be replaced with a gold star if the service member was killed. Often companies or organizations would fly multi-star flags in factories or meeting halls to support large groups of service people.

Author Fr. Andrew Greeley remembers the impact of the flags in his Austin neighborhood. "When the war began, my father was in his middle-40s, so there was no chance of him going into the service. I had cousins on my mother's side who did go into the service. I remember seeing the service stars in people's windows, including the blue stars and the gold stars. There were twenty-two young people from the parish who were killed during the war, so our parish flag had hundreds of blue stars and twenty-two gold ones. I remember being an acolyte at the funeral mass for one of the deceased."

The issues on the Southwest Side were the same for Tom Doyle.

"My father was about 35, so he missed serving in the military. But a lot of our neighbors served during the war, and some got killed. So, they would put flags in the front windows with gold stars on them. I also remember the memorial signs at the end of every block with the lists of neighborhood people who served in the military. Our neighbors were close, and we knew each other well."

For Belmont Cragin resident Chuck Chapman, patriotism had many meanings. "Some of the guys in my neighborhood were killed, so I remember seeing the gold stars in the windows. There were also a lot of blue stars, for those who were in the service. There was an optimistic view of everything at that time, and a high level of patriotism and American spirit. There was the strong belief that if we just put our minds to it we could do anything."

USO Shows

Chicagoans from every neighborhood served in the military. Many of those who couldn't serve supported the armed forces by participating in the USO (United Service Organizations). When servicemen could get a furlough to visit Chicago, or be in the city on layovers as troop trains came through, they would visit the USO Servicemen's Centers. The Chicago centers were very successful in providing the servicemen with a wide range of entertainment and recreational activities throughout the war.

Morgan Murphy, Jr. remembers gathering pies and cakes in his Southwest Side neighborhood that were brought to the USO. "Daniel Flaherty was head of the Chicago Park District at the time, and with that designation he became head of the USO. My job was to use my Red Flyer wagon and pick up all the pies and cakes in the neighborhood and take them to Mr. Flaherty's house. He would put them in his car and take them downtown. The USO Servicemen's Center at Union Station had 5,000 model planes hanging from the ceiling. I used to wish that Mr. Flaherty would take me with him so I could see them, but I was too young to go, although I always begged my parents to let me go with him."

Dan Rostenkowski's Northwest Side neighborhood put forth a similar effort. "I remember my father, who was the Alderman, and Ed Kelly, who was then the mayor of Chicago, going into the park across the street and taking things my mother had baked. The ward headquarters was at our house, and the precinct captains would bring in bread, biscuits and bakery goods to take down to the Servicemen's Center. Ed Kelly had one of the best Servicemen's Center in the world. Whenever a kid came through Chicago, and nearly every train came through here, they would go to that Servicemen's Center. They were treated like royalty there."

"Save Your Tires" Display Panel, ca. 1944. Loop (Courtesy of the CTA.)

School Children's Victory Garden, Jackson Park, ca. 1945. Woodlawn (Courtesy of the Chicago Park District.)

Victory Garden, 32nd and Keeler, 1942. South Lawndale (Courtesy of Special Collections and Preservation Division, Chicago Public Library.)

Office of Civilian Defense Drill, ca. 1942. Near West Side (Courtesy of Special Collections and Preservation Division, Chicago Public Library.)

Division 4 Christmas Party, 1942. Near West Side (Courtesy of Special Collections and Preservation Division, Chicago Public Library.)

Working for the War Effort

The demand for workers during the war opened up new opportunities for many neighborhood residents. For those who suffered through the Depression without employment, this was a welcome opportunity. As factories switched to the production of defense materiel in Chicago, women, teenagers, and even children could find a wide variety of work if they wanted it.

Richard Lukin of Kenwood remembers working for the war effort at a very early age. "During the war, a friend and I had a sub-sub-contract doing defense work. Here we were in grammar school, twelve- or thirteen-year-old kids, doing steel production and defense work. There was nobody else to do these things. Somebody had a defense contract and needed some hot bodies to do these simple mechanical things. So we set up a workshop in a friend's basement with vices, milling machines and drill presses. We threaded bolts — cases and cases and cases of bolts."

Bill Phelan had a job selling newspapers in the Englwood neighborhood during the war. "I worked at a newspaper stand at the railroad station at 63rd and Wallace. I worked there for long hours, from 4 o'clock in the afternoon until all the trains were out of there at midnight. I was still in school, so I was a pretty tired young man on some of those days. I remember one time when a troop train came through. For some reason, there must have been a problem down the line. They stopped the train at 63rd and Wallace, and there must have been 1,000 troops on that train! They let them off the train and they swarmed into the depot and bought out almost everything there — all the candy, cigarettes, and magazines. They cleaned us out!"

Margaret Short Lamb grew up in a little coal-mining town in Southern Illinois, but after graduating from high school in June 1942, she came to Chicago to work in a defense plant. Like many women of the time, she relished her "Rosie the Riveter" role. "My first job was at Harry Davies Plastic Factory on the North Side, where I learned how to operate drill presses, tapping machines and lathes. I was only making $.42 an hour without any benefits, so I left that company and went to work at the big Chrysler plant on South Cicero Avenue around 79th Street. I got a job there working on a lathe and cutting steel off of rocker arms that went into engines for airplanes. It was a huge, noisy place, and in the summertime it was a really hot place to work. In fact, some people would faint. They even had to bring ambulances to the plant. We were supposed to wear a safety hat while we worked, but one girl who had a pompadour wouldn't wear the hat. She got her hair caught in a machine and it scalped her. I worked nine hours a day on the swing shift, from late in the afternoon to 1:30 a.m., six days a week, even on holidays. I earned about $53 a week and thought that I was rich! So, I started sending money to my parents because my father had been disabled in the coal mines. While I was working in the plants, I lived on the North Side near 2800 N. Halsted with my sister's family. It was a long ride back and forth to the plant and sometimes I would have to take a couple buses and the "L" to get there and back home. Since I came from a small town, it was wonderful to live in the big city of Chicago."

Getting News About the War

Most Chicagoans got their news about the war from listening to the radio, watching newsreels at the movie theaters, or reading one of Chicago's several daily newspapers. War-related stories dominated both the airwaves and newsprint, but many residents grew to depend on the comforting voices of their favorite radio newsmen for their information.

Fr. Andrew Greeley recalls hearing famous broadcasters of the day. "I remember Gabriel Heatter saying, 'There's bad news tonight. There's bad news tonight.' And, then occasionally, as time wore on, he would say, 'There's good news tonight.' I remember H. V. Kaltenborn, Edward R. Murrow, Eric Sevareid and Elmer Davis. I also remember John Charles Daly, who went on to be one of the moderators on "What's My Line." Then, there was Charles Collingwood, reporting from London when Edward Murrow wasn't there. The 5:30 p.m. radio news somehow seemed more vibrant than the television news does today, perhaps because so much was left to your imagination. I remember Ed Murrow saying, 'This is London,' with all the portent of doom. Radio was very powerful because you were envisioning what they were talking about. And my memories about the war years are very powerful. I thought that our world was in a state of collapse and I had no idea what that would mean."

Charles Kocoras' father would listen to the war news on the radio in their Englewood home. "My father would listen religiously to the evening news to learn about the progress of the war. The name Gabriel Heatter sticks in my mind, and my father would always listen to him. My father kept up with the events, and Greece, his home country, was very much a participant and was actually subjugated by the Germans. First, the Italians controlled Greece, and then, because they weren't happy with the Italians, the Germans came in and basically took over. We had family back there during the war. Of course, I do remember an enormous sense of relief when the war was over and that exultation was present in all of Chicago."

Fr. Gene Smith was also an avid radio listener. "We listened to radio to hear news about the war. The radio was on the kitchen table and it was

Parade Float, 1942. Woodlawn (Courtesy of Special Collections and Preservation Division, Chicago Public Library.)

Blood Donor Honor Roll, Mundelein College, 1944. Rogers Park (Courtesy of the Rogers Park/West Ridge Historical Society.)

the center of our life while we were studying, ironing, eating or having family discussions."

Mel Pearl relied on the daily newspapers for the latest on the war. "Every day there was a headline about another battle in Europe or the Pacific. As the war came to an end, my first reaction as a kid was that I guess we will never have newspapers again because all I ever saw in the newspaper were war stories. I thought that there would be nothing else to report."

Serving in the War

Over 12 million Americans served in the military during World War II. They all had their own stories of where they were trained, stationed, and served in the states or overseas. For those serving in the country, much of their time was spent moving from camp to camp, occupied by mundane, often monotonous work. For those in combat, the goal was survival, and hopefully a return home to life in a safer world.

After the attack on Pearl Harbor, former Illinois Supreme Court Justice Seymour Simon closed his office in the US Department of Justice and was soon in the Navy. "I went to San Diego for training and shipped off to Pearl Harbor. I spent a year and a half at Pearl Harbor, which wasn't very difficult duty and I ended up becoming the assistant to the Flag Lieutenant, Commander, Service Force, Pacific Fleet. That was a good assignment. Then, I was assigned to the staff of the commander of a force that was organized to go forward with the fleet as they started across the central Pacific. The long-developed plan to fight a war against Japan called for having all the services on ships — flotillas — which they called 'the train.' The train would move forward with the fleet. But when Pearl Harbor happened they couldn't do it, because they no longer had control of the air. They had these slow moving supply ships and the Japanese would have bombed the hell out of them.

"So, they built these big naval bases in the South Pacific instead. Ironically, by the time most of them were built they were obsolete, because the fleet was operating 1,000 miles ahead. So, they decided in the Central Pacific they'd go back to the 'train' that would go with the fleet. When US forces took the Gilbert Islands they discovered that there were no Japanese aircraft closer than Saipan or Guam. So, they decided to leave the whole fleet of big carriers, cruisers and maybe one battleship out there. Overnight, we became the biggest supply base in the Pacific fleet. I was there until May 1945, when we went to Eniwetok and Ulithi, and the Pacific fleet mounted the invasion of the Philippines. It was a sight that I will never forget. We would stand on the deck of the ship and all you saw

was steel mass for twenty miles around you. What a sight that was, maybe the greatest collection of naval power ever assembled anywhere."

The Army put West Sider Phil Holdman's musical talent to work when he enlisted on April 8, 1942. "I went from Camp Blanding to Camp Stewart, Georgia, which was a real hellhole with swamps. They put me in a band because I was a drummer, and I made a lot of money. They used to pay me for dance jobs and for playing at the Officer's Club. My friend Miltie, who was in the South Pacific, got upset at me because I complained that I hated Camp Stewart because they didn't even have ketchup on the table, and he was reading my letter from a foxhole in the Pacific! I never went overseas because I was in the band. I used to play for the troops. One time I played on a program called "Parade Rest," which we did every Sunday night, outdoors, in a big band shell. There would be 10,000 troops on the hills, and they would listen to our band. We had guest stars like Bob Hope and Harpo Marx, and I even participated in skits with Harpo and Jackie Leonard. I was in the Army for four years, and I played in a band the entire time. I got out in December of 1945."

Lakeview resident James Thommes served in both Alaska and Europe during the war. "I got drafted in February 1942, and went into mechanics school in the Air Force. I was sent to the Aleutian Islands and got on a crew that was involved in bombing Kiska and Attu, where the Japanese were located. When I finished that tour, I came back to the States and went to pilot school but I 'washed out' like most of the other guys. Then, I was sent to gunnery school and got on a B-24 heavy bomber. I took overseas training in Mountain Home, Idaho, and was sent to Italy. While I was there, I was on fifty bombing missions that included Germany, Yugoslavia and Romania. As a result, I received three Air Medals and a Distinguished Flying Cross. I was lucky because I did not sustain any serious injuries, although on one mission my plane came back with 147 holes in it! When I finished my 50th mission, the Air Force sent me back to the States as a war casualty. At that time, the war in Europe had just ended. I went to Ft. Sheridan on a 30 day furlough, but then they said that anybody with over 85 points could get released. Since I had accumulated 120 points and fought on two fronts, I certainly didn't want to end up in the South Pacific or in Japan. So, I figured that it was time to end my service."

Jack Hogan left his Auburn/Gresham neighborhood for Europe after going into the military in June 1943. "I served with the 755th Field Artillery Battalion. We saw combat from October right up to May 1945, and our big distinction was that we were at Bastogne at the Battle of the Bulge. Our unit was with the 101st Airborne and we were part of the

Lincoln Park Servicemen's Center, 1942. Lincoln Park (Courtesy of the Chicago Park District.)

Lincoln Park Servicemen's Center, 1942. Lincoln Park (Courtesy of the Chicago Park District.)

Display Window, Chicago Public Library, Hild Branch, ca. 1944. Lincoln Square (Courtesy of Special Collections and Preservation Division, Chicago Public Library.)

Recruiting Center, 1942. South Lawndale   (Courtesy of Special Collections and Preservation Division, Chicago Public Library.)

Book Drive for Servicemen, Chicago Public Library, South Shore Branch, 1942. South Shore (Courtesy of Special Collections and Preservation Division, Chicago Public Library.)

Chiyo Omachi
Humboldt Park

I *was born on Terminal Island in California. It's a man-made island in Los Angeles harbor and my father was a ship builder there. Terminal Island was the first place that the government evacuated all Japanese-Americans after the bombing of Pearl Harbor. Well, they didn't exactly evacuate it. They told us to get off in forty-eight hours! Can you imagine? And the night before we were to leave the FBI came and took all the men off the island. So, the island was filled with hundreds of women and little kids and no one to help them. We had to get rid of everything, absolutely everything, from our refrigerator to our car. My mother had beautiful things from Japan, which we had to give away. We even gave away our pet cat. It was terrible.*

We were moved to an old, abandoned school and lived there while the government built the internment camps. The men and boys stayed in a large gymnasium and the women and girls were in these little classrooms. In May of 1942, there were signs posted that said all Japanese were to go down to the train station with two bags each. That was all we could take. All we knew was that we would be transported to another location, we didn't know where. Soon, we were moved to the first of the camps to be completed in Poston, Arizona.

Poston was one of ten internment camps built, and eventually it was expanded with the additions of Poston II and III. Conditions were bad. People got typhoid and died. We didn't have good medical care, or any medical care really. It was terrible, and it was so barren. We just marched into the camp quietly. We were Americans, and we kept shouting this, " We are Americans!" People wore patriotic badges and things, but that didn't make any difference.

Eventually, a time came when we could leave camp and go to school. I had to fill out a lot of paperwork and get the approval of the local police, the FBI, the Army, the Eastern Command —all sorts of people! I did this and went on to finish high school in Pennsylvania, where my uncle was living. I began college there, but came to Chicago to finish. I graduated from Roosevelt University in 1948. I came to Chicago because this is where my parents came after they were released. At that time, even after the war, Japanese-Americans still weren't allowed to return to California. It wasn't until a few years later that the okay was given.

We lived on Whipple Avenue on the West Side, near the Lake Street "L". I started working for the Japanese Resettlement Committee on LaSalle Street, which was helping to find jobs and homes for those coming out of the camps and starting a new life in Chicago.

Recruiting Center, 1942. South Lawndale   (Courtesy of Special Collections and Preservation Division, Chicago Public Library.)

Bill Gleason
Greater Grand Crossing

On November 16, 1944, which was my birthday, we went into attack for the first time. I was the second of two scouts. We were up in the attic of this French farmhouse overlooking a field — and I had never read The Red Badge of Courage.

The 442nd Regimental Combat Team was in our area, most of them Japanese-Americans from Hawaii, and many with parents who were in the Internment Camps. It was the most vicious outfit in the United States Army and they just frightened the Germans to death. This short sergeant, about 5'6", is standing there listening to our preparation. He tugs on my jacket and pulls me over. "Are you sons of bitches going to go across that field at 9 o'clock in the morning? Is that what I heard?" "That seems to be right," I said. "They'll shoot the crap out of you!" So I asked him, "What would you guys do?" "Well," he said, "we'd go over there at night and kill them in their foxholes."

Oh, God, was he right! That day, the two of us scouts got out there and made a very interesting discovery — they didn't fire on us. They let us proceed because they wanted all of the other guys too. So, I'm on one side of this field, and this town that we were supposed to take is about 3/4 of a mile away. The first scout is on the other side. I'm under this sapling, and it was mid-November, so there were dead buds on the tree. And I suddenly became aware that somebody was shooting these buds off the tree over my head.

"Holy Christ," I thought, "how am I going to shoot back at this son of a bitch even if I can find him?" You see, I made a discovery when I was about 12 or 13 years old, when I began playing kissing games. I realized then that I was the only person who could not wink his or her left eye. So, now I'm in the Infantry, and I can't wink my left eye. They tried to turn me into a left-handed rifleman but that didn't work. We would go down to the firing range, luckily I had a number of sympathetic guys who were down in the pits, and I would miss the target. Not only miss the bulls-eye, but miss the whole target! But they'd ring up that I had hit something, so I got to be a rifleman.

Well, after awhile I decided that I would go over to where the first runner was located. We were talking back and forth across the field and then some of the guys from our platoon came up. There was a clearing to cross, and our lieutenant was there. He was a big guy, he played football at Minnesota, and was the biggest man on the field. He had a lot of courage, too, because he was such a big target. So, he was up, and with about five other guys, two scouts joined them.

Oh, the other thing, I was wearing a white patch that I had cut from something and was using it over my useless left eye. One of the guys came to me and said, "Gleason, what in the hell are you doing with that white patch." So, I explained to him, and he replied, "Oh, my God, you're in combat and you can't fire. You better take that thing off because some Kraut is going to shoot you right in that eye." I cut a new patch from my gray gas mask container, and I used it instead.

As we were crossing this clearing, there was a big guy from North Carolina with us, a real rascal whose name was John L. Wilson. He saw too many WW I movies. So, he gets out in this clearing and he wheels around to fire and he is hit in his big thigh. He needed a medic, and the first scout said, "I'll go find him." So, I'm working on this big ass, and the first scout forgot one of the basic rules — babies creep and snakes crawl. Well, he was creeping and he got one right in his ass. So, now I've got these two guys. I go over to the first scout, and they're firing merrily at him. I said, "Just stay down!" So, I'm sort of on my side and ministering to him. I opened his pack of sulfa — and it was empty! After I cursed for about a minute and a half, I decided to give him my sulfa. He was so considerate that he said, "What are you going to do if you get hit?" I said, "Look, we're going to worry about that later." So, I poured the sulfa in and the medic, who was a tremendously brave guy, came to pull him off the field. I went back, and we got across the clearing and we went on from there.

After these first two days, we finally were taken off the line and were drinking great quantities of wine. The whole thing seemed so romantic. I realized quickly that I was a "war-lover." I just enjoyed the whole damn thing. While we were resting there I heard, "Gleason, you've got to fall out." "What the hell is this for?" I asked. "You're going to get a medal. You've got to be out there now." It was our captain calling. Joe Bell from Pittsburgh, Kansas, said, "If you're not out there, Captain Bell will get your ass." So, we scrambled out on a slope and there was Major Yao, who was second in command of the battalion. He was a guy who knew how to treat the men. I remember one time when we were coming down a road and Yao was there passing out apples to the men. He was in charge of this decoration. So, I figured, I'll probably get the Bronze Star.

But, it's funny, because the Silver Star kind of appealed to me. When I came up the first time, me and this other guy had been on a special assignment on a little trail in the Voge Mountains. This valley that *we had to cross was at the foot of the mountain. It was a narrow pass, and a GI came by and said, "Do not sit on the ledge. Do not sit down. Just go where you were going, and you'll soon see what I mean." Well, we soon learned what he meant, because two guys sat down on this little ledge, and one sat on a mine and killed them both. In other words, it was covered with mines — and we knew that war was earnest and real. Later, guys were talking about decorations, and some said that they didn't want any medals. I'm listening to this, and I figured that as long as I was over there, I might as well get a decoration. I thought that a Silver Star would be nice because it was for gallantry in action. I loved that. So, I said to myself, "I'll get the Silver Star."*

So, I walked up to the major, and it was so simplistic. He thrust this little thing into my hand and he gave me a little ribbon. I said, "What is this?" He said, "How the hell do I know what it is?" So, I opened it, and it was the Silver Star. And, it went on from there.

Thank God, we didn't have many days like that. We only had one other day like that first day. If we had more we would never have had any reunions — there would have been nobody left. We wound up in Austria on V-E Day, then they moved us back into France. We were in a tent camp near Rheims being staged for the Pacific until little old Harry dropped the bomb. I was discharged by September 1945, and then I was back in the neighborhood.

group that was surrounded. When I reflect on it now, I didn't think that I would be here today. We knew that we were encircled and were being attacked on an almost hourly basis, but our friend, General Patton, broke through and we survived. That was a very, very trying time. We stayed in combat until the American soldiers broke through and across the Elbe River. Some of our unit did meet some Russian soldiers up near the Elbe River."

When John W. Creighton graduated from Tilden High School in 1943 he went directly into the Army. "I went through basic at Camp Wallace, Texas, and from there we went to New York City and on a boat to England. We were in England for a while as part of the 480th Anti-Aircraft Division, and we were using 40 mm guns to shoot down Nazi planes. Then, on June 9, 1944, three days after D-Day, we landed at Normandy Beach. In Europe, we went in as a strafing unit and went across the Cherbourg Peninsula and all the way up the French coast until we finally got to Paris, just after it was liberated. The French gave us wine and liquor and were so happy to see us. I came home in January of 1946."

Ed McElroy was an accomplished athlete throughout high school. He was a White Sox bullpen catcher in 1943 until he entered the service. "I went from the Sox to the Army Air Corps in 1944. I enlisted in the Air Corps when I was just eighteen years old. First, I went up to Ft. Sheridan. They kept me there six weeks playing basketball. Then, I went down to Shepard Field in Texas, where I had basic training. I played on the baseball team there until I hurt my knee and I couldn't play ball. So, they shipped me out to Air Corps Intelligence at Chanute Field in Rantoul, Illinois, near Champaign. Next, I went to B-29 school in Patterson, New Jersey, and they kept me there until they sent me to Randolph Field, where I was a catcher on the baseball all-star team."

Playboy Magazine founder Hugh Hefner was also transferred multiple times during the war. "I enlisted in the Army in early 1944, right after graduation from Steinmetz High School. I was in service from the spring of 1944 until the spring of 1946. I went in when I was just turning eighteen, and I did basic training at Camp Hood in Texas. I went to a couple of other camps and ended up at Camp Meade in Maryland, between Baltimore and Washington, DC. I was going to be shipped overseas to the European Theater, but I had done some typing, so I was stationed in the Replacement Depot Headquarters at Camp Meade. When the war in Europe ended, I was shipped to the West Coast and had a similar job at Camp Adair in Oregon, just outside Eugene. Later, I wound up at Camp Pickett in Virginia and finally went back to Camp Meade for discharge."

Many Chicagoans have memories of family members serving in the military. West Ridge resident Ron Davis recalls, "I had a cousin who was

Alice Fink
Hyde Park

I was born in Berlin, Germany, but I had a side trip before I came to America. You see, Hitler came to power in Germany in 1933. With him came new restrictions on Jewish people every few months, little by little. I was still able to go to school until September 15, 1935, the day the Nuremberg Laws were passed, which among other things, meant I could not go to public school. These kind of things went on and on. You could only go shopping certain hours. Then you couldn't go to the theater. Then you couldn't go to the park and sit on the benches. When the Nazis went into Poland it was one big sweep. We, on the other hand, went through this process step by step.

My father, like many others, thought Hitler would not last. And like many of his friends who were soldiers in World War I, thought nothing would happen to them. These men would say, "I have the Iron Cross, they are never going to touch me." Unfortunately, a lot of people felt this way.

By 1938, everybody was trying to get out, but it was very difficult to leave. A cousin of mine in England made arrangements for me to go to nursing school there before the war started, and luckily I got my papers to leave. I was fortunate to get there, because the rest of my family did not get out. In the early 1940s, when the deportations began, many in my family were picked-up. My father, mother, and brother all died in the camps. You see, many of the things that happened during that time, we did not know about until much later.

So, I lived in England during the war. I did my training and then I worked. Sometime around 1943 the Jewish organizations in England formed a group to help Holocaust victims at the end of the war. In May of 1945 the first relief teams were able to begin their work. I did not go until September of 1946.

My husband, John, had been sent to Aushwitz, and a number of other places, and he ended up in Bergen-Belsen. That's where he was liberated from on May 15, 1945. When I returned to Germany in 1946 with the Jewish Relief Unit, I was sent to the Displaced Persons Camp at Bergen-Belsen, and that's where we met. We got married there in 1948. John did not want to stay in Germany. Many DPs went back to the towns and places they lived before, but some went back and found that there was nothing left to return to. A great many people just wanted to leave, one way or another. I was ready to go back to England, but my husband did not want to do that. I had distant relatives living in Chicago who would give us the papers needed to come here. We also applied to Australia and South Africa, but those did not come through. So this is what we did, we came to Chicago, and we came with nothing. Because we had a private affidavit, we were not eligible for assistance, so we started from scratch. We literally had to buy one piece of dinnerware at a time, having only two cups on the table, because that is all we could afford. Not like it is today.

My relatives lived in Hyde Park, and many of the German-Jews who had come before and after the war settled in that area. All we got was a small basement apartment — you just could not find a place to live in those days. It was pretty awful. There were thirteen different families living in the basement of that building. We had one small room, the smallest you could think of, and a bathroom down the hall that we all shared. My daughter was born four weeks after we arrived. It was very difficult. John would have a very long day at work and a bus ride, and in such a small room if the baby cries you do not get much sleep. We really did not do too much back then. We had enough to do just to make it day by day.

It was not easy. We did know a couple who had come to America a few months earlier, and there were other people we knew. But Americans, and even some Jewish people, questioned our past — Why did you survive? How come you did and everybody else didn't? You must have done something crooked. You did not necessarily get a friendly reception.

The Holocaust was not a subject that was talked about. It was something that you wanted to leave behind. Immigrants today get a lot of support and assistance. We were looked at very differently, especially if you were German. People just didn't realize that there were German-Jews who survived. The picture seemed to be that nobody was left. So if you somehow managed to survive people would ask, "How come?" It was very difficult.

After moving to Andersonville and living there for a few years we moved to Rogers Park in 1958. In those days this was a Jewish neighborhood (the Devon Avenue area). We moved here because we wanted our kids to go to Hebrew school and live in a nice neighborhood.

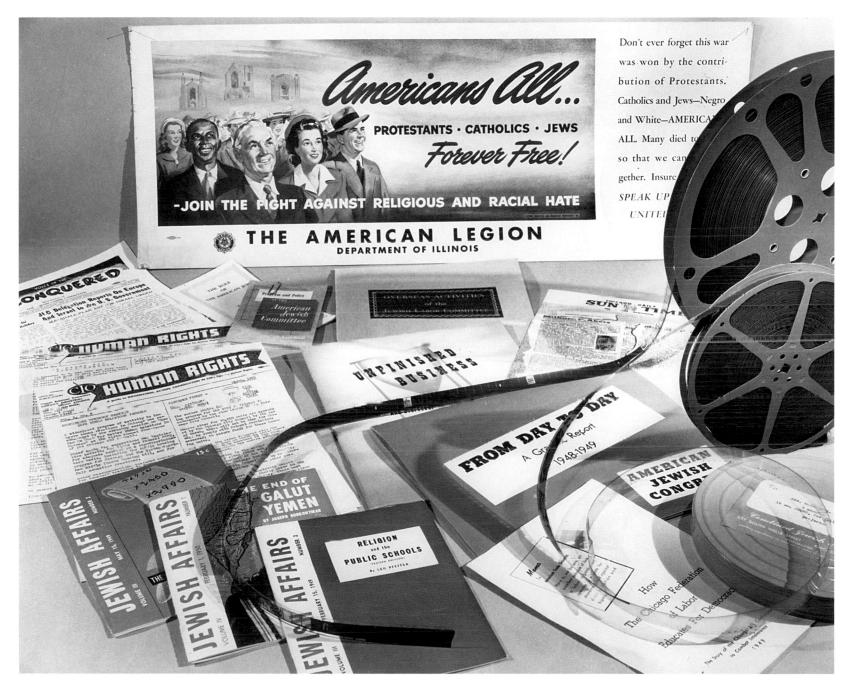

Anti-Defamation League Advertisement, ca. 1949. Loop (Courtesy of the Jewish United Fund.)

Flag Dedication Ceremony, 1942. Uptown Photograph by Jack Delano. (Library of Congress)

Sheila Morris Williams
Irving Park

World War II started when I was six years old. I remember my parents sitting hunched over a radio listening to reports of the attack on Pearl Harbor and worrying out loud. I felt the fear in their voices, even though I didn't understand what was happening.

Soon, children were involved in the war effort in our own little ways. We saved tin foil, rolling it into giant balls and competed for who had the biggest one. We saved newspapers and string, and pulled a red wagon around the neighborhood asking people for their donations of paper. We also helped by covering all the windows of the house in dark, heavy blankets to keep all light from shining through during the blackouts. Every block had an air raid warden who checked each house. If any light shone through, they would be fined.

Entire families worked in Victory Gardens. We grew seasonal foods we could eat right away, and canned foods for later in the winter. Mom stretched every dollar during the war by making her own bread and rolls twice a week and by canning the tomatoes she bought from the fruit man, who came through the alley with his horse and cart. We lived on ground meat and vegetables. I hated ground meat after the war.

When President Roosevelt died, I again sensed the profound sadness of the adults and remember sitting on the curb in front of my house, crying for our loss.

The end of the war is still clear in my memory — everyone outside cheering and dancing in the street, and throwing toilet paper over all the trees. We kids stayed up very late those nights. We all talked to everyone, even people we were not friends with.

The boy next door, who was about eighteen, joined the army and was gone for the entire war. I worried so much about him. I had a crush on him. When he came home, walking down the shady street in his uniform, I ran to meet him and jumped into his arms with joy and cried with relief.

My Aunt Pat was my hero of the war. Even though she was 40 years old when the war broke out, she joined the newly formed WAVES, for women in the service. She served in Hawaii and sent me a grass skirt and a funny top with two gigantic flowers on it. I thought it was great. But the most special thing of all was the WAVES navy blue trench coat that she let me have after the war was over. It was huge on me, but I wrapped it around me a couple of times and I became "Wonder Woman." It wrapped me in courage.

killed in the Pacific, and everyone had relatives who served in the war. My uncle, who was a doctor and almost 40 years old, had to go in as a Captain. He was in the South Pacific and served in the battles at Leyte and Guadalcanal — he operated on both American and Japanese soldiers. I remember that he sent my mother a bracelet made from a piece of a Japanese Zero airplane. He even put her name on it." Lawndale resident Mike Perlow's father also served in the Pacific Theater. "I remember missing my father, and it was tough on my mother. My father was overseas for a couple of years, so he wasn't around. He was in the South Pacific on Guam, Eniwetok, the Philippines, the Marshall Islands, and Japan. He didn't get injured during the war, but he was right there — because he was a surgeon and he was going into battle with them. My father, his brothers and cousins, and one of my uncles, many of whom were overage, all enlisted in the service. They couldn't get in there fast enough. I think that was very typical and they were very patriotic."

Many young men entered the service just as the war was ending. For them, life in the military meant helping the transition to a post-war world. David Cerda went into the military after graduating from high school in June 1945. "I volunteered when I was seventeen, right around the time that Germany surrendered. They were going to take me right after graduation, and soon we were on the train to Great Lakes. They were training us to go to Japan. We were learning how to identify Japanese airplanes and ships, but during boot camp they announced that the war was over. I knew how to type, so they decided to send me out to California and I spent time typing discharge papers. I would add up the points to see how fast they could get discharged. I was in the military from June 1945 to August 22, 1946. I got one check for $52.20 and that was my unemployment check."

George Mitsos' service in the Army also occurred toward the end of the war. "After I graduated from Amundsen High School, we went on vacation in northern Wisconsin and I registered for the draft up there. When I came back all my friends were getting drafted, but I wasn't called. So, I went to the draft board on Montrose at Damen and asked why I hadn't been called. A lady, who was a customer of my father, told me that since my father had lost one son already, she was delaying it. I told her I wanted to go, so they drafted me. I went up to Camp McCoy, Wisconsin, and helped to discharge the veterans who were returning home. After the first month, I only had one point — I figured that I would have to be in the Army for twelve years before I would be discharged! From there, I ended up coming to Ft. Sheridan, and I worked discharge there, too. I got out December 26, 1946. I had one year, twenty-six days of service."

As servicemen returned from the war, many found that cultural changes had taken place while they were away. Writer Jack Mabley returned to Chicago in the fall of 1945. "I walked into the offices of the *Chicago Daily News* to get my old job back and their attitude was, 'Oh, you've been away?' I had been replaced at the paper by a woman, which was unique at the time because before the war women had been confined to the society and cooking sections of the paper. There were only one or two women reporters on the news side then. But when we came back, they were holding most of the positions for us. There was a lot of shuffling, and I hoped to get my old job back. I had been getting $42.50 a week when I left, and four years later when I came back they offered me $65, although they were paying the women $75 a week. I leaned on my bosses and I managed to get $75 a week and my old chair. After the war, the city was really upbeat. The guys who came back were so glad to be alive and to be home. While I was overseas, I told myself that if I ever got home I was never going to leave again. There was a pretty good feeling in the air. The war had cured the Depression and there was a rush for college enrollment under the GI Bill, since the government picked up most of the cost. There were jobs and spirits were high because we'd survived that damn war. It was good times and they got better."

As African-American servicemen returned home, there was hope that the small movement towards integration in the military would be rewarded in American society. Grand Boulevard resident Truman Gibson recalls, "Everything changed after the war. You see, when the war began and the draft was instituted, southerners protested that blacks would be included in the draft at all. The Army had a big problem. We went from strict segregation to integration. President Truman was the one who integrated the military. In fact, I was on two presidential commissions and helped draft the desegregation order."

For many African-Americans, however, change did not come fast enough on Chicago's South Side. Dempsey Travis recalls, "The neighborhood didn't change at all as a result of the black soldiers coming back from World War II. The neighborhoods were just like the Army — Jim Crow. If I listened to my father — he had expectations that things were going to get better because we had served in the war. He and my uncles would say, 'You fought in the war and now you are entitled to more things.' But, if it was an entitlement, then the government was never forthcoming. That was something in my father's and my uncles' heads, but not in my head. The neighborhood didn't change a great deal after the war because there were restrictive covenants in 1948 and title policies

Remembering the End of the War

Howard Rosen

I remember that it was a mob scene downtown. On Madison at State they set up a huge platform from the north to the south side of the street. They were giving speeches and playing music. Thousands of people were just milling around cheering and dancing. Servicemen were hugging and kissing the people in the street.

Bernie Judge

I remember the end of the war in 1945. We climbed onto the roof of Jeffrey Food and Liquors that overlooked 79th Street. We went up with buckets of paper and we threw the paper to celebrate the end of the war on V-J Day. It was a big celebration and everybody was in a terrific mood. I was only five years old, so I shouldn't have been up on the roof. I had an older brother and sister, and we had a lot of freedom and could do a lot of things that kids can't do now. But it was okay, my parents knew what we were doing that day because it was a celebration. I remember that it was a very important event.

Chuck Schaden

When the war ended, we were living across the street from the fire chief, Walter Schoenfeld, of the Norwood Park Township Volunteer Fire Department. On V-E Day, he came out of his house with a gun and shot into the air a couple of times in celebration. I remember that kids on their bikes were riding up and down the street of our block ringing their bells and blowing their horns. People who had automobiles would drive up and down the streets blowing their horns. It was a totally unorganized expression of joy that was repeated on V-J Day, which was a little better organized and a little more solemn.

Steve Zucker

I remember my mom yelling out the window, "The war is over!" My friend Rick Fizdale and I went to the mailbox at Western and Rosemont and we sat on top of the green, metal mailbox waiting for the troops to come home. We waited for hours and hours because we thought that the troops were going to come marching down Western Avenue.

Joesph Lamendella

All the neighbors came out on the street and were banging pots and pans on V-J Day in 1945. I was eight and my brother was five at the time. We each got a bottle of white wine and a cigar and got drunk and disgustingly sick in the middle of the street. I have not had white wine, with rare exception, to this day, and I don't think that my brother has ever had another cigar.

Mayor Edward J. Kelly Reads News of President Roosevelt's Death, 1945. Loop (Courtesy of the Chicago Sun-Times.)

required a signature. There were 'no blacks allowed.' If you violated the law, you voided your deed."

The Aftermath

The impact of the war on the Chicago home front was complex. Passions raised during the conflict often encouraged bigotry and racism, perhaps most harmfully to the small but growing Japanese-American community. While only a small number of Japanese-Americans lived in Chicago before the war, many were relocated here from the West Coast both during and after the war. While violence was rare, war-time propaganda had created an atmosphere of fear and mistrust, leaving many Chicagoans unwilling to give jobs or rent apartments to the newcomers.

The Jewish-American population in Chicago was particularly impacted by the death and destruction caused by World War II. During the war, there was very little information coming out of Europe about the persecution of Jews. For many, it was only after the war that families learned of the Holocaust and the fate of their loved ones abroad.

Lawndale resident Gerald Bender had family living in Poland during the war. "The most important impact of World War II on my family was when we learned that my grandmother, aunts, uncles, and cousins were all murdered in Poland. They were put in a pit and buried alive in Lomza, Poland, near Bialystock. They were among 7,000 Jews murdered in that town. So, the war had a profound effect on my life because it let me know what a Jew was." Bruce Bachmann's Austin family was also touched by the Holocaust. "The most traumatic experience concerning the war was that a cousin of mine was in a concentration camp in Europe — he didn't escape Europe in time. He did survive, and he showed me the numbers on his arm, but he didn't talk much about his experience. His wife also survived, and my uncles sponsored them when they came to America."

Arthur X. Elrod, President Harry Truman, and Mayor Martin Kennelly at Union Station, 1948. Near West Side (Courtesy of Richard Elrod.)

Daily Life in the Neighborhood

In the 1940s, the routine of daily life in Chicago was similar to that in other major American cities. It centered around going to school or work, shopping for daily necessities, listening to the radio, reading the newspaper, getting together with friends and family, and relaxing or playing in parks. Once in a while, people would eat out at a restaurant or go downtown to see a show, but with limited funds available to most families, these luxuries were saved for special occasions.

Most families were close, both geographically and emotionally, during the '40s. Members of extended families, including parents, children, and grandparents often lived in the same buildings, or within a few blocks of each other. As a rule, families ate dinner together and children were expected to be at the supper table at a specified time each night. If a mother wanted the children to come home, she could open the window and her voice brought a quick reaction. Children rarely disobeyed their parents, and if they did something to break the rules, there was swift punishment "as soon as dad gets home."

There were also the continual issues of dealing with the Great Depression and the impact of World War II, as well as the changes that occurred after the war. By the early '40s, however, jobs were easier to find and that meant money for more than the bare necessities. The shortage of adequate and affordable housing was always an issue throughout the decade. Across the city, residents commonly lived in two and three flats, apartment buildings, working man's cottages, or if they were lucky, "modern" brick bungalows. Often, extended families lived together in apartments, two-flats and single family homes. Chicago Mayor Richard M. Daley tells of how he shared his Bridgeport bungalow with members of his extended family during the '40s.

As for shopping, there were few full-service grocery stores available during the decade. Thus, residents of Chicago neighborhoods bought their daily necessities at local neighborhood stores that were no more than a few blocks away. It was an era of small, independent shops that were often owned by first- and second-generation immigrants. In many of these shops, ethnic specialties were the focus, including meat, poultry, fish and baked goods. Daily shopping was also necessitated by the lack of reliable refrigeration to preserve food, the overall lack of storage space for large supplies of food, and the lack of funds available to families to purchase groceries for the entire week.

Many modern conveniences had yet to arrive. Air conditioning was available in movie theaters, but not yet in homes, so during the summer many residents would sleep outside on porches, grassy sections of boulevards and parks, or at the beaches along Lake Michigan. Transportation was also vastly different. With few people being able to afford automobiles and a limited supply of new cars available during the war years, neighborhood residents walked or rode buses, streetcars, trolleys, or the elevated trains.

Opposite: *Chicago Park District's "Save the Lawn" Program, 6342 S. Greenwood, ca. 1940.* Woodlawn (Courtesy of the Chicago Park District.)

For most people, life in the 1940s is remembered as a safer and happier time, despite the tremendous negative impact on lives caused by the Depression, World War II and its aftermath. It was also the last decade to still have nostalgic links to the nineteenth century — an era of ice men, waffle vendors, and value still counted by the penny.

The Depression

The Depression was still in effect at the beginning of the 1940s, and there was a constant struggle to find jobs, affordable housing and enough money for daily necessities. Adults and children adjusted to the severe economic hardships and tried to make the best of the difficult times. Interestingly, many Chicagoans do not remember themselves as "poor" because it seemed that everyone was in the same economic situation. Then, at the beginning of World War II, there was the sense that economically, things had begun to take a turn for the better.

Writer Bill Gleason grew up in on the Southwest Side of Chicago. "The '40s — that was my decade. I graduated from Parker High School in 1940, and, in September of 1940, I got lucky and found a full-time job. So, I finally had some money to spend. Everybody says, 'We weren't poor.' Well, we weren't, because my father worked everyday during the Depression. He was a blacksmith in the post office garage. But we still had to scramble, like so many other families. I got a job and I no longer had to go to the dime store and buy new soles that you put over the old soles of your shoes. I had money to spend. It was a glamorous job — I worked for the ticket broker in the Hotel Sherman."

Northwest Sider Bill Jauss has similar memories of the Depression and its effect on his family. "During the Depression, my dad worked at the Fulton Market in a meat packing plant, so we always had plenty of food and meat. I really thought that there was a barter system going on and that meat was money. I remember one time my mom took me to Klee Brothers down on Cicero Avenue at Six Corners to buy me a new suit of clothes and a pair of high-top boots — with a little crevice to put a knife in. My mom gave the clothier a bacon in exchange. You know, doctors made house calls in those days, and I remember my mom giving the doctor a ham for coming to take care of us kids. I think there must have been a barter system going on. I guess nobody had any money during those years, but we never missed any meals and we always had a roof over our heads. I never felt deprived and we always had everything that we wanted. It was an interesting time to grow up, and I think that families were closer."

Nancy Bild Wolf remembers the impact of the Depression on her family in West Rogers Park. "My mother worked as a stenographer, mostly because my father only worked on and off during the 1930s. She also worked as a salesperson at the Wieboldt's store in downtown Chicago. So, I would come home from grammar school and open the front door with the key that we left under the mat. Since my mother was willing to feed anybody in need of a meal, I would sometimes open the door and find a stranger eating lunch at my house. She would provide food in exchange for doing work around the house. During one period, we had a handyman named Hunt and he would come every summer and do carpentry work and painting. One day, a man came to our door who was an itinerant photographer and offered to take pictures of my family. My mother told him that she didn't have any money to pay him, but when he smelled food cooking he offered to take the pictures in exchange for a meal. He had all of his photographic equipment with him and he set it up and took family pictures. I was only seven years old when that happened, and because of his photographic skills we have many lovely pictures of my family taken during those years. It was obvious that during the Depression people did almost anything as a way to survive."

The Depression had a dramatic impact on real estate development. Land values dropped, foreclosures jumped, and many open lots and even some unfinished buildings could be found throughout the neighborhoods. Sandy Zuckerman Pesmen grew up in North Town. "There were many empty lots between houses because of the big Depression. We first lived in Albany Park in an apartment and then moved to North Town in 1940, when my father had enough money to put down on a little bungalow. Next to us was an empty foundation where somebody had started to build another bungalow, and the Depression had come along and they stopped. During the winter the foundation would fill with snow, and my friends and I would go out with a little sled and just jump in. Nobody watched us, and when we got cold we'd go inside. It was a safe place to play and it was a good neighborhood, with families all around us."

Apartments, Bungalows and Houses

It was a challenge to find housing throughout the 1940s due to the lack of new construction during the Depression. In the more densely populated neighborhoods, the dominant form of housing was apartment buildings, many of which were in a courtyard configuration. Although families lived close together in those arrangements, many Chicagoans have fond memories of living in apartments because of the camaraderie and community feeling among neighbors. Those lucky enough to afford their own houses, whether wood frame or brick bungalow, also have strong positive recollections about their living conditions.

Shirley Ochs Simon
Humboldt Park

I was born in 1927 and I lived in Humboldt Park at 1438 N. Maplewood Avenue, two blocks south of North Avenue. The neighborhood boundaries were Division, North, California and Western. My earliest memories are of playing in the street in front of our house. The house was a strange building because a tailor shop fronted it, with a big window, and we were in the attic above the tailor shop. The tailor's family lived in back of the store. Our entrance was at the back of the house and we had to go through a cinder path and then up some stairs. It was a rickety, unpainted, rat-infested cottage. It was terrible.

My parents met and married in Fall River, Massachusetts, and came here for work. My aunt lived next door, and she said that there was work in Chicago. My father was in poor health, and that affected his ability to have steady employment, so it was very hard for us. He struggled during the Depression. My mother worked at a hospital supply shop where they made doctors' and nurses' uniforms. It was a low-skilled, piecework job where they did sewing, and she worked very slowly. It was a very bad period in her life. There were just two kids in the family, my brother and myself.

My memories of those years are only partially positive. When I look back, I wonder how we survived it. We were always cold and always hungry. It was really bad. For example, we would play outside in front at night, but we knew that we could not walk back to the house through the passageway without mother because she would take her shoe off and hit the sides of the building to scare the rats away. And I'd hear rat's scratching in the wall. It didn't seem to bother me much, but she used to cry. It was rough for her, but I was a happy kid. I played all the time. We rarely saw an automobile on our street. When they came by, it was a big deal, and everybody had to watch it. I remember just hanging out a lot. My mother worked and I was on my own, even before school.

I went to the movies all the time, and the park was very important to me. Since my mother worked, I was at the mercy of older children to take me places, but they were willing. My brother was two years older, but I had very little to do with him in those years. He'd run the alleys and steal potatoes from our neighbors, making little fires with his friends to roast the potatoes. We would put tin cans on our shoes and run around. We would make our own toys, like scooters from boxes and skates.

I remember the milkman allowing me to hold the reins of the horses on his wagon. He'd stop and we would go half a block while I'd hold the reins. We had to stand up because there were no seats. Then I would get off at the corner because I wasn't allowed to cross the street.

The special thing about life in the '40s was the freedom. Oh, the freedom! Anything was possible, even during the war. I could go anywhere and do anything and be out as long as I wanted and see anyone. I never felt unsafe. In fact, when my husband and I courted, I remember sitting at the lagoon in Humboldt Park at 2 a.m. on a summer evening without a thought of fear. People slept in the park. Sometimes we slept in the grass on the boulevard on a very hot night on a blanket. Automobile traffic wasn't too bad. We always felt safe, and we walked everywhere and anywhere. At night, at the age of fifteen, I would be on Division Street and would have to walk six blocks to visit a friend. It was nighttime and it was dark, but I never thought twice about it.

I remember the time when we were living on Division and we had to move. They were tearing the building down to build a new dime store, so we had to go. My mother worked, so she said, "Okay, Shirley, find a flat with at least four rooms," and she gave me a rental price. I would look for signs as I went to school and on my way home after school. I would inquire and even look at the apartments, and I was only thirteen or fourteen years old! That was a feeling of freedom! I was working at that time, as well as going to school. There were jobs for kids, and we could go anywhere. I worked downtown at the Boston Store, and I went on my own.

We had our first telephone in our apartment on Hirsch Street, but that wasn't until I was fourteen years old. So, we would have to use my aunt's phone on Maplewood. The doorbells didn't ring, and when my girlfriends would come to visit they would have to yell for me. It would echo through the hall! One could live very easily without these services that we take for granted today.

Old Brace Shop, Michael Reese Hospital, ca. 1940. Douglas (Courtesy of the Jewish United Fund.)

String Instrumentalists, Jackson Park Field House, ca. 1940. Woodlawn (Courtesy of the Chicago Park District.)

Fr. Gene Smith
South Shore

I was born in 1936 and raised at 72nd and Dorchester, referred to as St. Laurence Parish. My neighborhood was blue-collar. We were, for the most part, children of immigrants. My parents were born in Ireland. People around me were, for the most part, born in Ireland, and a few from Sweden, Poland, Germany, and Japan. So, blue-collar workers would get up early to go to work and come back tired. Some people would head for the steel mills, others would go downtown where they had professional jobs.

The day before I began kindergarten, I was in the kitchen with my parents. My dad looked down at me and said, "Well, tomorrow is the first day of school. Bejesus boy, your playing days are over!" I said, "I'm only five years old, and all my playing days are over?"

Life was fine during grammar school. I remember in first grade I was supposed to buy cookies for the class for Halloween because it was my turn to bring them. I asked my dad for some money so I could buy cookies at the store that was next to the school. He reached into his pocket and pulled out a handful of change. As I mentioned, my father was from Ireland and had been a farmer there. He was a big, strong man with really large hands. He said, "Help yourself." So, I took a few coins out of his hand. I thought that with the size of this man's hands he would have been wonderful on Mary Hartline's show "Super Circus."

During the 1940s, most everything was within walking distance. Hardly anybody had automobiles and we could play in the street and not worry about running into a parked car. Everything was ambulatory. If we went someplace, we got on a bus or streetcar to get there or to visit relatives. So everything was pretty "medieval." You didn't get outside of your little community. My friend George Scales and I used to go to the railroad trestle that had tracks that ran from the Loop out to everywhere and anywhere. We would sit and watch the I.C. go downtown and wonder what kinds of jobs people had and what they did there. Then, the I.C. going out to the University of Notre Dame in South Bend would go hurtling by and we would wonder what it would be like to see them play football there. Other trains, like the Broadway Limited, the City of Miami and City of New Orleans would pass by. We would wonder — what it would be like to be outside this community and go to some of those places? We would sit and speculate about that for a long time. What will move us beyond 72nd and Dorchester into the next phase of our lives?

In South Shore, Estelle Gordon Baron and her family lived in an apartment building. "We all lived in six-flat apartments in my neighborhood and we were very close with our neighbors, particularly growing up. We would play in our backyards and in front of the building. The six-flats formed a 'U' shape in the courtyard. There were three apartments on either side of the entrances, and then a central staircase in the middle. We would play cat-in-the-corner and things like that out front. It was a small town life in a big city."

Dick Jaffee remembers living in several different apartments in South Shore before moving into a house. "When I was born in 1936, we lived at 8020 Dobson, west of Stony Island Avenue. I also lived in an apartment at 8227 Clyde. My mother enjoyed having arched doorways and canvassed walls, and they paid about $35 a month rent back then. They were very proud of it, and it was a great place to live. When I was about five years old, in May 1941, we moved to a first floor apartment at 7949 Jeffrey near the corner of 80th and Jeffrey. My first memories of apartment life were the notices on the doors about vacancies, but when World War II began, apartments were very hard to find. My memory is that our neighborhoods were like little towns — a place where I could ride my bike, use my roller skates on the sidewalks, and pretty much do whatever I wanted as long as I stayed within the boundaries of the neighborhood. Later in the '40s, we were able to buy a house. We decided to remove the fence separating our yard from our neighbors, the McCarthys. My dad and Mr. McCarthy built an outdoor cooking area as well as a screened-in summerhouse and the two families would frequently eat dinner together during the summer."

Marvin Levin spent most of his early years in Albany Park on the Northwest Side. "We moved to Albany Park in 1940, when my mother and father rented a one-bedroom apartment with a balcony on Monticello, between Wilson and Leland. It was a big courtyard building, and the landlord lived in the building. He seemed to cut the grass with scissors to keep it trim all the time and he kept the building in beautiful condition. Albany Park was a neighborhood completely filled with apartment buildings, so people were very close together. In fact, my childhood friends became my friends for life. We knew all kinds of people, and we were always hanging out together. We walked to school together, came home together, worked together and played together."

Steve Zucker remembers the special kinship that was established around his West Rogers Park apartment building. "Our building at the corner of Rosemont and Western must have been constructed in the early '30s. It went from the Nortown Theater all the way to Western, and then it turned the corner and went down Rosemont to the alley. There were three entrances in the rear of the building and it backed up onto the Nortown so that you had a huge wall to play around and against — we used to throw balls against it. I remember that there were many kids under the age of eight running around our backyard. We played every game known to kids, and developed friendships that have lasted a lifetime."

Howard Rosen's apartment building in Humboldt Park was a microcosm of neighborhood life. "In those days, everybody would sit on their back porches. In fact, the highlight of a summer day was to sit out there with a pitcher of lemonade. All the parents would be out there, and the older people, and they would be drinking lemonade, playing cards, and listening to the radio." Ron Newman remembers life in his Austin neighborhood in the same way. "I loved the West Side, and our building was like a little community where everybody took care of each other. There were two courtyards in our building. If my parents weren't home, I knew that I could go to dinner at a friend's house. My father, mother, brother and myself lived in a one-bedroom apartment with an inner door bed."

Although he was born in Albany Park, Journalist Joel Weisman moved to West Rogers Park toward the end of the '40s. "I was born in 1942, and grew up during the '40s in Albany Park, at Albany and Montrose. I lived in a three-flat building that was owned jointly by my mother and her family. The big question at that time was where we were going to move — Skokie, Lincolnwood, or Rogers Park. Those seemed to be the main choices, but I could never understand why we wanted to move. My mother used to bring me on walks with my sister who was a baby. She would take us over to Ravenswood Manor, which was just a lovely area, and only a couple of blocks from our house. It started at Sacramento, near Albany, and east to about California. I always thought that we were going to have our own house and I would have my own bedroom. My vision of a home was one of the places in the Manor, an older house with beautiful foliage around it. There was one place that had statues and an iron fence around it. I remember envisioning us living near there, but we ended up moving to a new house in West Rogers Park."

Austin was home for Fr. Andrew Greeley. " I lived in what we called North Austin, near Division Street and Austin Boulevard. My very early memories are of two-flat living, backyards, and playing with other kids in the alley. There was a house down the street that had been moved back toward the alley so that a second house could be built in front of it. I lived in an apartment until 4th grade and went to St. Angela grammar school, located a block north of Division and two blocks west of Central. We eventually moved into our own home, a Chicago-style bungalow, at 1301 N. Mayfield."

Leonard Amari
Near North Side

I was born on the Near North Side. I am from what is now called the Cabrini-Green projects. One of the corners in the neighborhood was called "murder corner" because every so often they would find bodies on that corner. But it was also a neighborhood where I would walk safely down the street as a little boy. All my aunts and uncles lived there. All the people on the block were relatives or seemed like relatives.

In my Italian neighborhood, most of the men of that generation didn't work — they were Damon Runyan characters. My mother was one of six sisters, and only one of the husbands worked. All my uncles lived in my grandfather's apartments for free and hung out at a poolroom at Maple and Clark.

We moved out of the neighborhood to the Lathrop Homes on Diversey. It was mostly non-Italian-American. We lived in three different apartments there, including two high-rises and one low-rise. Our place was at Diversey and Damen, and it was subsidized housing. I can't tell you if the people who lived there felt disenfranchised — I know I certainly didn't. I didn't realize that it was subsidized housing until much later. I remember the sense of community living there, and that people left their doors open. I remember that on Halloween we would be out trick-or-treating until midnight and never felt unsafe.

In the summer, they would show a movie on the side of the building in the main courtyard and we would all bring out our chairs and blankets. The movie was always The Man in the Iron Mask. *I also remember they had community showers along the Chicago River, just under the bridge at Diversey Street, and I remember the snapping turtles, the swing sets and baseball. It was a wonderful place to live.*

My father's parents, and my mother's as well, came from Sicily, where there historically has been less respect for the rule of law, so there was an attitude against authority. I don't remember anybody in my family having a vehicle sticker, let alone insurance. That was just part of the culture. To their credit, all of those parents insisted that the only way to get their children into the mainstream of American society was by going to school. I could steal or fight and it didn't matter, but if I got a bad report card my father beat the heck out of me.

Chuck Schaden
Norridge

I was born in 1934 in Chicago, but my family moved to Norridge in 1939, just west of Harlem, the city's western border. At that time, Norridge wasn't much and almost everything that we did, except for living and sleeping, was done in Chicago. Irving Park Road was the lifeline to the city. Just about everything that we did was either on Irving Park or an easy connection from Irving Park. We lived in a five-room brick bungalow with a living room, dining room, two bedrooms separated by a bathroom, a kitchen and an unenclosed back porch, that later on, was enclosed. The neighborhood was almost all single-family homes. Many of the people were there when the first homes were built, just before the Depression in the 1920s. A lot of people lost their homes in the '30s and I think that the home we moved into had been vacant for some time. I have a vivid memory of a backyard that was way overgrown with weeds. The grass was high and there were hollyhocks everywhere, so it took some time to clear all that stuff.

We had a lot of community activities during the war years. Before there was television, all the neighbors would sit on their front porches in the summer evenings after dinner. Down the street, a family with teenage sons would play music on the big open porch in front of their house. The kids would play music and the whole neighborhood would enjoy it. They played contemporary songs from 1942, 1943 and 1944, which were songs accepted by everyone, young and old. We had block parties and block picnics and everybody knew everybody. This was very important. You knew everybody on the block — up and down. If a new family moved in, you got to know them right away. Everybody looked out for everybody else. In most cases, the women did not work outside the home. Although, as the war years progressed, I know that some of the women were starting to work in defense factories and plants. My mother never worked outside of the home, but had a volunteer job where she was assembling service ribbons that would be awarded to people in the Army, Navy, Marines and the Air Corp. She was also involved in Red Cross bandage rolling projects, as most of the women during the war years were.

The '40s were special because it was a time when everybody had the same interests and concerns, and everybody looked out for one another. We were in the war together, and even post-war, we were still together. We did things for each other. It was a different time. It was an unsophisticated world, but a caring one. If a kid on our block was walking down the street and a neighbor saw the kid doing something wrong, the neighbor would say, "Stop doing that. Quit monkeying around. Don't throw that thing over there or I'm going to tell your mother!" If she did get to the point where she would tell your mother, your mother would not be irate, or tell her to mind her own business. She would very grateful that she told you, and be embarrassed that her kid was doing something wrong.

Do you remember the candy cigarettes with a little red thing on the end? They were called names that were take-offs of Chesterfields or Lucky Strikes. Kids used to eat those things. They loved to play with them, because everybody smoked in the '40s. We weren't smoking, but we were eating these candy cigarettes. In the winter, you could walk down the street with one of these candy cigarettes and pretend you were smoking, and your breath would be visible in the winter. I was walking down the alley one time with another kid. We were doing this, and one of the neighbors called my mother and said, "Charles is smoking in the alley." Boy, I got grabbed by the collar faster than you could say Jack Robinson. I had to prove to my mother that I had the candy cigarettes in my jeans.

I think that was a pretty good time to grow up. We had finally come out of the Depression. The families who had grown up in the Depression, like my parents, were doing better. It didn't affect me at all, and I didn't know that we barely had enough money for an ice cream cone. But the families in the '40s were beginning to be a little more prosperous because of the war. A lot of people who were in wartime industries were making more money than they had ever made before because they were working extra hours.

After World War II, Phil Holdman finally had enough money for he and his wife to move to their own apartment. "In 1947 or 1948, Alberta and I finally found our own place on Augusta Boulevard, across from Humboldt Park. It was a four-room apartment, but in those days it was tough to get an apartment. Part of the deal was that we had to buy the furniture from the people who lived there — it cost me $1,000 for the furniture! We were desperate to have our own place, so I gave them the money and then threw it all out. We then bought our own furniture. We lived in that apartment for several years."

After living in apartment buildings for most of the 1930s and early '40s, Sheldon Rosing's family bought a bungalow in South Shore. "We finally had enough money to buy a bungalow at 7637 S. Ridgeland, two blocks west of South Shore Boulevard. It was the best thing that we ever did. It was ideal because I could walk to school and come home for lunch. The house was a brick Chicago-style bungalow with an underground sprinkling system, and I think that my parents paid around $8,000 for the place. My dad had some money saved and borrowed the rest from a relative, who he paid back in a couple of years. The real estate taxes for the place then were something like $300 a year. It was great for my family to finally get into their own place and out of an apartment."

Transportation

During the 1940s, most Chicago residents relied on walking to get around their neighborhood. Automobile traffic was limited during the war years, due to gasoline rationing and the limited construction of new cars, so public transportation was generally used to get downtown and to other sections of the city. The "L," streetcars, trolleys, and buses were the most common means of transportation, and are remembered fondly for their fun, if perhaps, bumpy rides. For a small number of people, trains like the Chicago & Northwestern, the Milwaukee Road, the Burlington Northern and the Illinois Central were also options. These trains would have cost almost double the $.07 streetcar fare, so for most residents it wasn't a first choice.

On the South Side, Charles Kocoras remembers the "Green Hornet" streetcars. "When I was growing up trolley cars were on their way out. Then we got the Green Hornets, before they changed totally to buses. The Green Hornets were terrific. They were electric, moved on rails and they would zip right along. They ran on the main streets like State Street and they replaced the old red streetcars. I never took the Illinois Central, and only rarely did we take the "L" if we were going downtown. Going downtown was like going to another city, since we had all the shopping we needed in the neighborhood at 63rd and Halsted."

It was not uncommon for children to ride alone on public transportation in the 1940s. Whether traveling to school, downtown, or attractions like Riverview Amusement Park, kids enjoyed an unusual level of freedom. Joe Lamendella lived in the Lake View neighborhood during the '40s. "When I was just ten years old I would take the subway downtown. I used to take the Belmont bus to the "L" and then ride to the Museum of Science and Industry. It was safe and nobody gave a second thought about it."

Ian Levin grew up in Rogers Park and lived near the Morse Avenue Elevated Station. "We didn't have a car until the late '40s, so we would take the train to visit our relatives on the West Side and in Albany Park. Occasionally, my parents would take us downtown for dinner and a movie, but our neighborhood offered everything we wanted, so we remained there most of the time."

In 1943, the State Street Subway was completed. Howard Rosen was lucky enough to get a ride on the one of the first trains. "I remember the day they opened up the subway — not to the public, but for a trial run that would go from State Street to North and Clybourn. In order to get on you had to buy a War Bond. You see, they were offering a pass on one of the first trains as an incentive for the war effort. A lady who had just bought four bonds turned to me and asked, 'Would you like to go for a ride on the subway?' So I took a ride on the new subway. I was really fascinated with it."

On the South Side, Andrew McKenna remembers the transportation that was available in his South Shore neighborhood. "The Illinois Central was the dominant form of transportation and ran down 71st Street near where I lived at 72nd and Crandon. One of the attractions of my neighborhood, particularly for people who worked downtown, was the fact that the I.C. was there. In the 1940s, most people took the train into the city, unlike today where most use automobiles."

Morgan Murphy, Jr. spent his early years in Visitation Parish on the city's Southwest Side. In the 1940s, his father built a new house in Beverly in St. Cajetan Parish. "Beverly was in the city then, but the area was not heavily developed. In fact, the streetcar line only went to 112th Street. I remember that we still had gas streetlights back then, and there used to be an old lamplighter who would come around every night. He had a little ladder and he lit the streetlights. It was pretty far out and there was a lot of prairie in the '40s. The area did not really develop until after the war. My father would go downtown to work each day by taking the Rock Island Railroad from Beverly/Morgan Park at 111th Street. While I was waiting for him at the station I used to watch the big steam engines go by. I got to know the engineers and they used to wave at me."

Bill Phelan
Englewood

I was born in 1932 at 74th and Racine. It was a very interesting neighborhood, called Englewood. I went to St. Brendan's grammar school, at 67th Street, which was a full mile from 74th Street. In those days, they sent us home for lunch, so I would be walking back and forth twice a day, about four miles. We had two other parishes near us, including St. Sabina, which was only four blocks from my house, but I was not within their boundaries. Anything north of the railroad overpass at 75th Place was in St. Brendan's, south of there was St. Sabina. I am the oldest of seven children, and all of us went to St. Brendan's.

On my way to school, I used to go by a German church called Sacred Heart, which is kind of an interesting church. They had no boundaries and anybody of German descent, or anybody who was Catholic could go to that church. They had masses in German in those days, too. The other interesting place that I passed by was the Chicago Christian High School at 71st and Racine, which was all Dutch. So, there were a lot of Dutch, Germans, Irish and a lot of Italians in the neighborhood. I passed through the league of nations on my way to school every day! Many days I would have to fight my way back and forth, with my brothers and my sister. I had to take care of them, too. It was quite a job on some days.

During the war everybody was working. Even though I was young, I always had jobs that included delivering newspapers and working at a ballpark that was two or three blocks from our house. It was called Shewbridge Field, and all the public and Catholic leagues played their games there. On Saturdays there would be times when six to eight football games were played there. They would start at 8 o'clock in the morning and go all day. As for baseball, the women's baseball league used to play there. I know they had a lot of big manufacturing companies that had teams playing there, like the Ft. Wayne Zolmer Pistons, who later became the Detroit Pistons, the Seal Masters from Aurora, the Joliet Seven-Up and other companies that sponsored teams. The Chicago team was called the Chicago Matchmakers, and they were involved with a company that manufactured matches. They had some pretty good games there.

I started working at Shewbridge when I was ten or eleven years old, and it happened like this: one night, the lights were on at the field, and we had nothing to do, so we snuck into the ballpark. We got caught by a policeman. He yelled at us to stop and I stopped, but my friends kept on running. He brought me up to the priest who was running Shewbridge for the monsignor, Fr. Sweeney. He said, "What's your phone number so I can call your parents and let them know what you did." I said, "I'm sorry Father, we don't have a telephone." He said, "You be here tomorrow morning at 8 o'clock because your punishment will be to clean up these stands." So, I was there at 8 o'clock the next morning, and I cleaned up the stands. At 10 o'clock he came out and said, "You're doing a terrific job. You're hired." That was my first job at Shewbridge Field, and all my brothers and my sister followed me there. All of us worked there doing different things over the years. I hung the scoreboard, did the balls and strikes for the baseball games, and cleaned the stands. Then I got promoted to a big job: I was in charge of filling-up the concession stands with beer, pop, hot dogs and candy. I had total access to the commissary where they kept it all, and I had to fill everything up and ice down all the beer before the games. The ice used to come in 50 pound canvas bags, and I only weighed about 110 pounds, so I had a tough time engineering those bags and dumping them into the bins where the pop and the beer was kept. I'll never forget the day when I was about twelve years old, one of the beer bottles exploded and part of it was lodged in my thumb. I still have the scar to this day. I had a handkerchief and I just wrapped it around my hand and kept on going. There was a little blood in the beer and the ice, but I got the job done.

St. Rita High School, 63rd and Western, ca. 1946. Chicago Lawn (Courtesy of the CTA.)

Dempsey Travis
Washington Park

I was born in 1920 and grew up in the Black Belt. By the 1940s, my neighborhood had graduated to Bronzeville. Anthony Ogleton received a proposition about changing the name from Black Belt to Bronzeville. The Chicago Defender picked the name Bronzeville, and it sold newspapers. I say that Bronzeville is wherever black people live.

In the '40s, the safe boundaries for us were as far north as 22nd Street and as far south as 60th Street, but south of Washington Park was a dangerous area. Although we lived at 59th and Prairie, we didn't go to that end of Washington Park. We stayed closer to the area from 55th to 51st Streets. The boundary on the west was the Rock Island railroad, and on the east it was Cottage Grove. It was a narrow strip that stayed that way until the 1950s and the end of "restrictive covenants." We knew that we couldn't cross Cottage Grove, or you were subject to being picked up by the police strictly because you were African-American. I learned early in my life not to cross Cottage Grove. So, we did everything on the west side of Cottage Grove and nothing on the east side.

For me, life was interesting in the neighborhood and there were always people who were making it and were successful. Famous people lived close by, and that meant there was hope. My father was a laborer until he died. He probably never made more than $50 or $75 a week, and that had to be during wartime. I knew that there was a life beyond that, and he convinced me. That was how I got into the music business. He and my mother kidded me and said, "You're going to be the next Duke Ellington," and I believed them. My mother would take me downtown to all the shows, and there weren't a lot of black people going downtown to see shows then. The first time I saw Duke Ellington was in 1931 at the Oriental Theater. I said, "Ooh, that's him!" That experience made the case that he was a big image. He was bigger than God, he was so huge an image to me. He was handsome, articulate, and suave — just a good image for me. It was these kinds of things that kept me awake — they were my role models. It's my opinion that failure is a learned process, and I never hooked into people that I thought were failing.

When we lived on 36th Street, people at 48th Street and Evans were another class. There was Dorothy Donegan, and she lived right across the street, but never spoke to me. I was a little boy, and she was very attractive. I did silly things like playing ball by myself in front of her house with the hope that she would come out and say, "Look at that guy, isn't he wonderful."

Being an only child, you imagine and create your own games, and I think that was an advantage. I could always entertain myself — you become self-sufficient.

I would play at Ellis Park when I was growing up. It was between 36th and 37th, just west of Cottage Grove and east of Vincennes. It was a beautiful park. The West Point Baptist Church was at 36th and Cottage Grove. In the early evening, I could see black people dressed up in gowns and tuxedos, so I knew that there was something other than overalls around. Some people never noticed that there were other kinds of dress. We considered ourselves blue-collar, but with upper middle-class aspirations.

I started playing piano at five years of age, but I became interested in jazz at an even earlier age because my father was a piano player. He couldn't read, but he could play piano. Many black musicians couldn't read, but could play music because they were so talented. There were people like myself who could read, but were not very talented. I didn't realize how inadequate I was in that area until I got to DuSable High School, which was then called Wendell Phillips High School, then Wendell Phillips-DuSable. That too, was based on a newspaper contest like the naming of Bronzeville.

DuSable High School was interesting, because they had an economic mix of people who went there. There would be a doctor's son, a lawyer's son, and a post office worker's son. Back then, post office workers were prominent. In fact, many doctors worked in the post office because the medical profession was slow during the '30s. I also remember when people had difficulty getting an apartment, but it was different for my father because he had a piano. If you had a piano there was stability, because you couldn't move out in the middle of the night. That made you a good tenant.

At DuSable, I ran into the color thing and the shades of black. I hadn't really been aware of that issue when I was younger. My uncles' girlfriends looked as if they could have been white. People played this game of color, and it became an issue of who was the "blackest." When you start fighting with yourself about that kind of stuff, you are really in serious trouble. What damned difference does it make what color you are? There was more status, in your mind, if you were a lighter color. I thought that it was a lot of nonsense! The light girls got the better guys, and they had an advantage in the professions. They got the goodies.

Grocery Store in the Black Belt, 1941.   Near South Side   Photograph by Russell Lee.   (Library of Congress)

Earl Calloway
Near South Side

I came to Chicago from Buffalo, New York, with my mother and sister. I was about seventeen years old when I came here back in 1943. I arrived on the train at the 12th Street Station. We took an old streetcar, the one where you enter at the back door and exit by the front door, to 2020 Roosevelt Road. All along the way, I remember seeing the juke joints, where they danced and drank whiskey and beer. These places didn't have sophisticated entertainment. They jammed all night and sometimes during the day. If they didn't have live entertainment, they would play music on jukeboxes or Rockolas. They had many juke joints on Roosevelt Road.

We lived with this lady by the name of Mrs. Taggert. Her husband was known as "Old Blind" Taggert. He played the guitar, and he traveled all over. He was quite famous. We stayed with him and his family. He was the one who encouraged my mother to come to Chicago. I stayed upstairs in a room, and they stayed downstairs. At first, I slept on the floor and my sister and mother slept in a bed. Then, I got sense to move upstairs to a room with a bed. That was my introduction to Chicago.

I got a job quickly working as a bus boy because I had to make money so that I could get back to school. When I started I didn't know what a busboy was. I thought it was working with a bus, or transportation, or something like that. Finally, someone told me, but it didn't make any difference to me. So, I started working at the Harding Restaurant. Then, I went to the Congress Hotel at Congress and Michigan, and I worked there for about a month. In the meantime, I was looking for a better job. I came here to this building (now the offices of the Chicago Defender), and upstairs on the second floor, was the office of the Urban League. I went up there and told the gentleman what I wanted, and they gave me a job washing fluorescent lights. I had a bucket and rags and went all over the city washing those lights. I went to one of the most fascinating places out in Cicero. It was in the back of the storefront, and man, I spent the entire day washing fluorescent lights where they were gambling, and doing all those kinds of things. I did two or three of those kinds of places out in Cicero. I did that all summer, but you know, it never occurred to me the historical importance of what I was doing.

Shopping

Shopping was an important part of daily life throughout the 1940s. Larger shopping areas, usually clustered around primary intersections and transportation hubs, would include major department stores, appliance stores, men's and women's clothing and apparel stores, confectionery stores as well as first-run movie houses. Each neighborhood had its own local shopping area as well, including a combination of small grocery stores, drugstores, shoe repair stores, dry cleaners, meat and fish markets, bakeries, candy stores, hardware stores, taverns and small restaurants. Many neighborhoods also had small "Mom and Pop" grocery stores, usually located on the corner of the block or on the first floor of apartment buildings.

Estelle Gordon Baron has vivid memories of the sweet shops in her South Shore neighborhood. "I remember that at 71st and Merrill, going east, there was a Fannie May candy shop, and it was the prettiest little place you ever saw. When you walked in, the wallpaper was covered with roses and it had white wrought iron along the walls. The whole store was white and pink with little green leaves all over. On top of the glass counter where the candy was located, they always had a little dish with a paper doily and little samples of Fannie May cream-filled chocolates. They were so delicious, and I remember them so clearly. In those days, the candy wasn't prepackaged so that you could select exactly what you wanted. You had the option of taking the candy in a bag or a box. Also nearby, was another place that brings back strong memories — Newman's Bakery had the most marvelous pastries! They were very fancy, and I can still taste them. There was one shaped like a horn, made of very flaky dough, filled with sweetened whipped cream, and powdered sugar on top."

Andrew McKenna remembers the shopping around 71st and Jeffrey in South Shore. "Shopping was on 71st Street between Stony Island on the west and Yates or South Shore Drive on the east. In a half-mile area between Jeffrey and Yates or South Shore Drive, there were three Walgreen Drugstores: one at 71st and Jeffrey, one at 71st and Paxton, and one at 71st and Yates. Shopping included a drugstore, florist, candy store, shoe repair, and a men's store/haberdasher. There were also a few restaurants, the Hitching Post and the Shore Post. These were not white tablecloth restaurants, and very often the dinner or luncheon menus were much the same."

A few blocks away, on 79th Street, Bernie Judge recalls the places where his family used to do their daily shopping. "For day-to-day shopping, we went to 79th Street, which included a meat market, fish store, a liquor store, drugstore, cleaners and the shoe repair. There was also a Kroger store that opened on 79th and Euclid on the north side of the street, and people shopped for everyday items there. Most of the stores were owned and operated by Jewish people who were primarily first generation. Years after Kroger opened, a Jewel opened in 1953. I also remember a Dressel's bakery and Hackelman's bakery on that street, so we always ate fresh bread."

It seems every neighborhood had a small corner store that stocked the essentials of daily life. Sheila Morris Williams remembers the store at Montrose and Central Park in her Irving Park neighborhood. "Our corner store was the 7-11 of the 1940s. The owners were immigrants who worked very hard, keeping the store clean and open long hours. They lived right upstairs, which made going to work very easy for them. My mother would send me to the store to buy milk or bread. If I had a couple of cents extra I would buy some candy, like the little candy cigarettes you could get in a cardboard box. I would sashay around with one hanging out my mouth, pretending to be cool. The store had plenty of penny candies, which were very tempting for us kids. The store was really a gathering place for kids, and the owners never seemed to complain about all the kids lounging around."

David Cerda lived in East Garfield Park and remembers, "My mother would shop at Goldblatt's Department Store a lot. For grocery shopping, there was a place in the middle of Kedzie, between 19th Street and Ogden Avenue. We would go there or down the street to A&P. There were also some stores on 22nd Street that were predominantly Polish and Bohemian. As for Mexican food, there was a store called Casa Estados on Halsted Street, north of Roosevelt Road, and that was where my family would get Mexican food."

Joseph Lamendella and his family did their shopping on Lincoln Avenue at Belmont. "That was the number one retail center on the North Side, outside of the Loop. My mother would also go to the local grocery and butcher. Kresge's and Woolworth were up the street from us at School and Lincoln, and they used to sell live turtles as pets for a dime. Wieboldt's was also at School and Lincoln, and it had a record store on the ground floor with individual booths to listen to the records. Of course, there seemed to be a tavern on every corner back then."

In the North Town neighborhood, Joesph Epstein remembers the Devon Avenue shopping area. "Devon was one of my favorite streets because it was very grand. During the '40s, it was the 'Jewish renaissance' on Devon, with stores like Seymour Paisin's Dress Shop and Hillman's Stop-and-Shop, an elegant place with the supermarket downstairs and the delicatessen and restaurant upstairs. I also remember Neissner's, Kresge's, Abram's and the Crawford Department Store. My favorite Chinese

Jesse White
Near North Side

I was born in Alton, Illinois in 1934. When I was seven, my family moved to Chicago. We lived on the Near North Side in an area that is now called Cabrini Green. We lived at 536 W. Division in a four-story walkup where we used coal for cooking and heating.

When I was a kid, the area was integrated and cosmopolitan, and was really inhabited primarily by Italians. I worked at an Italian grocery store, Sam Aiello's, where I was a stock boy. I was also responsible for the chickens. I would clean them, take them out of the coop, lock their wings behind them, weigh them, dip them in hot water, and then use the chicken picker to pluck their feathers off. Then I would cut them up and gut them if they needed that done. Of course, I lost a love for chicken because of my close involvement with them.

We got along well in the neighborhood, and we acquired an appreciation for the other person's culture. We had a religious festival, known as the Feast, where they would line the streets with booths and people would sell food. Then they would bring the angel through and parade each day of the three-day festival. The band would play, and they would put dollar bills on the angel. They would have Ferris Wheels and other rides. We would always look forward to the Feast, just like the city today where blacks look forward to the Bud Billikin parade.

We were very poor, so us kids would have to work. My brother shined shoes and I worked in a grocery store. My other brother delivered papers. We were determined to be survivors and to bring money into the house for the family. We were on public aid, so we would get butter, but we would have to mix yellow coloring in it for it to look and taste like butter. We probably ate beans seven days a week. My mother knew how to cook them, and she would take potatoes and mix them with onions and smother them so that we could make a meal out of that. She would also make chili, doing what she could to stretch a meal a long way. She would somehow make nutritious and enjoyable meals with limited amounts of food on a very limited budget.

The neighborhood had a very positive impact on me. One of the first things I learned from growing up in an integrated environment was that you do not have prejudice in your heart. But, when I went off to college, I went to a segregated environment where I would hear black people saying that we should hate white people. I wasn't raised like that. I grew up to believe that we should love each other, work together, and do all we can to live in peace and harmony with one another.

Sheila Morris Williams
Irving Park

Our neighborhood was on the Northwest Side of Chicago. I lived at 4314 North Central Park Avenue, near Montrose. There was a tavern on the corner, of course, all neighborhoods had one. Ours was Goodman's Tavern, and all of the men in the neighborhood hung out there after a day's work. Women never went in, but sometimes children did, if their father sent them out for cigarettes. Imagine that today! I can still remember the smell of stale beer and heavy cigarette smoke. It was like walking into a smelly fog. I never spent more that two minutes in there. Two doors down was the Lincoln Bottling Company, and if you asked the right way on the right day, the manager would give you a free bottle of cola. That really made our day.

The Drake Theatre was only a block away from our house, on Montrose Avenue. At least once a week we went to the movies and saw a double bill, with a newsreel, cartoon, and an action short for the boys. I think it only cost a dime. I remember the bill changed twice a week, but we couldn't afford to go twice. Next door was the local ice cream shop, like on "Happy Days." That was where I had my very first date, at about age twelve.

My brother Bill and I delivered the Chicago Daily News and the German paper, the Abenpost. We were about nine and ten years old at the time and it was really difficult for us to push the huge newspaper cart down the street. We took turns walking up to the second and third floors of apartment buildings and laying the paper nicely on the back porch doorstep. We would be reported to the newspaper agency if we did not deliver the papers perfectly.

The neighborhood was alive with service and delivery men, most of them driving a horse-drawn wagon — the ice man, rag man and produce man. The ice man had a truck with a back that folded down and the kids would scramble up on the truck looking for ice chips on a hot day. There was no air conditioning back then. In the winter we would hitch a ride on the back of the truck and skid on the ice.

We played games in the alley behind our workingman's cottage. Hide and seek and kick the can were our favorites. We even put ash piles from furnaces to good use in the winter. The ashes were usually dumped into a large pile along the fence. We dug into these frozen ashes, which were covered with snow, and made a fort or house out of them. Pretty risky, since we also shared the alley with rats. I remember one year when giant rats ruled the alleys, there was an epidemic of them. They were really scary.

The neighborhood kids were Jewish, Swedish, Polish, and German. We were the only Irish people on my block. I loved to pick up my friends at their homes for a day's play because of the wonderful smells that wafted from their homes. I never found out what exotic foods were cooking, but it kicked off my interest in cooking later in life.

We did all kinds of things for amusement. Our local grammar school, Patrick Henry, had a great playground and gigantic sand pit, which I really loved. We would work together, all ages, to build a giant sand castle. We called it a "ball castle," because we made tunnels and balconies in it and dropped a tennis ball in the top and watched it whiz through the building. I loved ice skating at the local school yard, which was flooded all winter. I never felt the cold. Sometimes we would even put our ice skates on at home and skate down the side street to the ice rink.

My brothers and I also devised a "roller coaster ride" starting in our back yard and ending in our basement. We charged $.02 and put kids in a sturdy wagon near our basement stairs. We put a large piece of stiff wood, twice the width of the wagon and about six feet long, over the cement stairs. We whizzed those kids into our dark basement where we had ghouls and ghosts set-up to scare them. The speed of the ride and the darkness scared those kids to death. It was a popular ride. No lemonade stands for us — we were city kids.

Judges, Chicago Park District's "Save the Lawn" Contest, 1633 N. Mason, 1940. Humboldt Park (Courtesy of the Chicago Park District.)

Raymond DeGroote
West Ridge

I was born in 1930 in the North Town neighborhood, and have lived on Claremont ever since. When I was growing up this was a brand new neighborhood, having been laid out in 1926. This was a typical two-flat neighborhood in that owners lived in one apartment and rented out the other. Many of the corner lots around here were not built on right away, so they were just vacant lots. During the winter, the fire department would clean them out a bit and flood them, and we would go ice skating on these corner lots.

My neighborhood was nice, with good schools, and of course, good transportation. I've always had an interest in transportation. In fact, my parents told me that as early as seven years old I noticed there were different streetcars running in the city. Some had round roofs and some had squared-off roofs. My father insisted that they were all the same, except for "the funny blue cars" running on Madison Street. Those funny blue cars turned out to be the first of the new "Green Hornet"-type streetcars, the PCC car. They were an attempt by the transit companies nationwide to improve the image of public transit, making them more streamlined. Chicago had one of the largest fleets of these cars. They were blue before the war and painted green after. They got the name Green Hornet because they were quiet, fast and because the Green Hornet was a popular character at the time.

I remember going downtown, alone, at seven years of age. A seven year old kid going downtown by himself! That was pretty good stuff! My father made me a map — take the Western Avenue streetcar to the Ravenswood "L" line, get on and go to Quincy and Wells, then walk a couple of blocks west to the Marquette Building. It wasn't scary at all, it was an adventure! I liked riding up front on the streetcar with the motorman. We kids always stood up front and rode with him. It was a grand adventure!

Streetcar fare at that time would have been around $.07, compared to $.15 or $.20 on the Chicago & North Western line. This would have been a staggering difference in those days! The North Western wasn't off-limits, but it wasn't practical. Occasionally, I would ride the Illinois Central trains for special occasions, which were also higher fare. We would ride them to the Museum of Science Industry and get off at 57th Street, which was within walking distance.

Riding the streetcars of the 1940s was not very different than riding the buses of today, except that the ride back then would have been smoother. If the tracks were good at all, it was a smooth ride. The older "Red Rocket" streetcars could be noisy, as they growled along, especially when they stopped. If the tracks were not maintained properly, which was the case during the war, the car would rock back and forth. The Green Hornet style streetcar was smoother and faster, and it could pick up speed rather quickly. These new streetcars performed well, which was one of the objectives when they began production in the mid-thirties — to make a high performance car. These were good pieces of machinery, and they served for years and years.

A critical transportation addition came in October 1943, when the State Street Subway opened. It was pushed through because it was considered essential to the war effort. The congestion in the Loop was pretty bad, because all the trains had to run on the elevated tracks back then, including the North Shore Interurban trains. While they could manage it, service was slow. The subway relieved that congestion. It allowed people to get downtown quicker, which was something that was deemed critical to the war effort.

Kids had a role in this success as well, because if we bought a War Bond, we got a free ride on the subway the day it opened. And I did! Believe me, I was down there! I think I was in eighth grade at the time and I was the Transportation Coordinator at my school. My job was to tell the kids how to ride the subway, and I even gave a class one day! I showed pictures and used a map. I told how to buy a fare and use a transfer, and talked about how not to be afraid of the dark and all the noise.

The other important transportation event of the decade was the forming of the CTA (Chicago Transit Authority) in 1947. It was created to take over the various transportation properties that were near bankruptcy. Public transportation rarely makes money, and this was the case here. The CTA was set-up to buy Chicago's two major transportation systems — the Chicago Surface Line, which was the streetcars and buses, and the Chicago Rapid Transit Company, which was the "L" and subway. Eventually it bought the Motor Coach Company as well, which included the double-deck buses that ran on Sheridan Road. The goal was to merge all these lines together and improve the transportation system in the city. Many of the CTA's changes did help. They cut down the number of local stops, which helped speed-up service. They eventually got rid of all the streetcars, and parts of most of the PCC cars became parts of the 6000 series elevated cars — the green cars.

But the automobile was always the greatest threat to public transportation. Everybody wanted their own means of transportation. It began as early as the 1930s. After the Depression, as more and more people began to get some income, they wanted a car. My father was a good example of this, he had to have his Buick! Public transportation ridership dropped tremendously after the war, for two reasons — they all bought automobiles and they all started moving to the suburbs.

"Green Hornet" Streetcar, Garfield Park, 1947. East Garfield Park (Courtesy of the CTA.)

Clark and Balmoral, ca. 1940. Edgewater (Courtesy of the CTA.)

Ann Gerber
Edgewater

My world really revolved around Clark Street in Edgewater. In the 1940s, I was living at 5705 North Clark Street, in a third floor walk-up. It was a Swedish and German neighborhood back then. My father had a grocery store at 5555 North Clark on the corner of Clark and Bryn Mawr. I remember during the war my father thought there was going to be a shortage of sugar. He put all the money he had, about $5,000, into Domino sugar. The back of the grocery store was filled with little yellow boxes. But the sugar crisis never came, and the sugar got harder, and harder, and harder. My mother used to upbraid him, "Why did you do that?" Because of that, I've never nagged any of my three husbands.

Down the street from the grocery, across from the Calo Theater, there was a big church on Clark. The minister used to stride through the neighborhood wearing a long black coat and hat. I think he was very tortured. He never looked happy, and we were all very terrified of him. His manner was very scary to us. He was probably a very nice man, but I only saw him as a specter walking through the neighborhood.

I also remember the peddlers on Clark, especially the one who made ice cream fudge. It was not cold to the touch and it was not frozen, but when you ate it, it was cold. I don't know if it had menthol in it, but it was delicious. I remember some of the women in the neighborhood would ask, "How do you make this?" And he would say, "I'm never going tell you, because I'm going to make a fortune off of this!" I don't think he ever did.

As a Jewish girl living in Edgewater I remember feeling very left out. There were only a few Jewish families in the neighborhood. I went to Pierce School, and one day after classes I went over to a girlfriend's house and her mother answered the door. She said, "You can't come in. The girl's have formed a club called 'IHS,' that means 'In His Steps,' and we don't want any little Jewish girls coming in." It just broke my heart.

In the summer, on really hot nights, my mother would take two sheets and we would sleep at the Bryn Mawr beach. At that time there was a very big beach at Bryn Mawr. It was very safe, and you would see your neighbors sleeping there, too. And I do remember going to Riverview in the summer. My girlfriend, Dorothy, had a big, heavy father who was a motorman and he took a group of us to Riverview for the rides. I was the skinniest and the littlest, so I got to sit next to him. When we went on the roller coaster I was the only one who wasn't afraid because I was so wedged-in! He was so big there was no possible way I could fall out!

One of my first jobs was working at a dime store on Clark near Foster. I started working at Miesner's when I was around fourteen years old. I was a really scrawny little kid, but I told him I was seventeen. I loved working there! My first job was in the basement making Easter baskets. They had a formula: she would give you a basket, and you would put in twelve jelly beans, three marshmallow eggs, two little rabbits, and then you would wrap it in cellophane with a bow. But they never looked full enough for me. So I would put in extra jelly beans and extra eggs, and things like that. I remember he came down and said, "Our baskets have never sold as well since you have been making them!"

I was very conscious of being poor as a kid. I wanted to be on Sheridan Road in the better section! I always had hand-me-down clothes. My mother had a son and three daughters, and I was the last. I didn't have a dress of my own until I was about twelve. I was very much aware of being deprived, but everyone around me was deprived. I didn't like it. I remember seeing girls at Senn High School with angora sweaters and matching ankle socks, and they could buy French fries at lunch, too. I saved my money.

Back then, it seemed everyone who had money went to Sullivan High School. "Good girls go to Heaven, bad girls go to Senn." That was the saying. Senn was just okay, but we were always in awe of the girls who went to Sullivan. They were better dressed, and people picked them up in cars! I remember one boyfriend who rode me home on his bike everyday. That was as good as it got!

restaurant was the Pekin House, whose owner began to look more Jewish as he grew older. For a while I worked at Pekin House for $.70 an hour, and I could eat anything I wanted for free except the shrimp dishes because they were more expensive."

Rogers Park resident Dr. Ira Bernstein moved to the neighborhood in 1943 after living in Virginia. "We lived at the corner of Columbia and Lakewood, and I went to grammar school, Hebrew School and high school all within a block of my apartment. Since my mother was ill, my sister and I did the shopping. There was a grocery store on Sheridan Road between Columbia and Pratt on the west side of the street. Abe's Delicatessen was on the southeast corner of Columbia and Sheridan, and I also remember Mesirow's Drugstore on the northwest corner of Pratt and Sheridan."

Former Cook County Sheriff Dick Elrod remembers shopping as part of his daily life on the West Side. "Roosevelt Road had many little grocery stores and dress shops and it was like a long shopping mall. The Jewish people tended to stay in the neighborhood for their shopping. In fact, I remember a grocery store on Roosevelt that delivered, and they used to bring our groceries to our third floor apartment at 1323 Independence."

Next to State Street, Maxwell Street might be Chicago's most famous shopping experience. Mel Pearl grew up on the West Side, and when he was just ten years old began working at his grandfather's shoe store near Maxwell Street. "It was on Halsted, just north of Maxwell Street and it was called Brusman's. I used to go there and help by pulling the shoe boxes for the salesmen. The Maxwell Street area was a bustling place, almost like a movie set. Around the corner from my grandfather's store was a little delicatessen in the basement and they used to send me there to get sandwiches for the staff at the shoe store. I remember that there was such a wonderful smell of hot corned beef that permeated the neighborhood. Mexican vendors had come to the area by the late '40s and they used pushcarts to sell their wares. However, during the '40s, Jewish merchants were still the predominant group on Maxwell Street. I remember the street was a hubbub of excitement and it was an incredible experience to be there. It was a great, great time!"

Working Life

From working in the steel mills of the Southeast Side to department stores in the Loop, Chicagoans have always been known for their strong work ethics. And during the 1940s, residents of Chicago neighborhoods found a wide variety of jobs to provide income for themselves and their families. The war provided a big boost to the economy, and many residents who had gone without jobs could now find employment. Children and young adults were also encouraged to work too, ranging from delivering and selling newspapers to setting pins in bowling alleys. It became a family affair to find enough income to cover monthly expenses and still have extra funds for entertainment.

Howard Rosen commuted from his Albany Park home to his job in the Loop during the '40s. "The first job I had was one I got through some friends of mine who were working at Kitty Kelly's Shoe Store on State Street near Monroe. I wasn't allowed to sell shoes on that job, but they had me wrap packages during the Christmas season. When Christmas ended, I didn't have a job. So, I went back downtown to find a new job. I walked into a store off State and Madison called Berland's, another ladies' shoe store. I remember walking up to some guy and saying, 'You don't need anybody to work here, do you?' I was so sure that he wasn't going to hire me. The man's name was Mr. Spiwak, and he said, 'Yeah, I do need someone, as a matter of fact.' So, my first official job was selling shoes at Berland's. They had a downstairs area where they sold the more expensive dress shoes, and an upstairs where they sold the 'play' shoes. I was hired to work upstairs, and although I was a very shy, laid-back kid, somehow I developed a whole new personality and turned into a terrific salesman with a strong personality. I would still be shy when I left the store, but when I was selling shoes it was a new me."

Jim O'Connor's father bought a farm in northwest suburban Woodstock in the 1930s, and the family would go there on weekends. "We would spend our summers there. It started as a dairy farm and then became a beef cattle farm in the late '40s. We also had a lot of chickens. So, the deal was that on Sunday we would collect the eggs, wash them, put them in large cartons, and then bring them back to Chicago. My sisters and I would go door-to-door and sell the eggs to our neighbors. We did this during the '40s, and the three of us would go to all the apartments in our Gresham neighborhood around 79th and Ashland and sell the eggs for $.15 or $.20 a dozen. Our parents let us keep the money. We tried to sell 30 dozen eggs every Sunday night."

Edie Phillips Horowitz lived in Edgewater and remembers, "One of the best jobs I ever had was working for the Chicago Bears and George Halas. I was a receptionist and secretary for Rudy Custer, one of the top people in the Bears organization. They were located at 37 S. Wabash, and Mr. Custer gave me a nice desk in his huge office. It was a very easy job and a lot of fun because it didn't involve a lot of typing. Clark Shaughnessy was the head coach of the Bears at the time. In fact, I had to be bonded for the job because I was asked to sit down with him while he drew the plays on the blackboard — I then copied them down in the play

Chicago Public Library Bookmobile, 115 S. Crawford, 1944. West Garfield Park (Special Collections and Preservation Division, Chicago Public Library.)

Looking North on Clark, South Loop, ca. 1944. Loop (Courtesy of the CTA.)

Charles Kocoras
Woodlawn

I was born in 1938 at 6614 S. State Street. That was an odd structure. I lived on the second floor, and there had to be at least twenty rooms on that floor. The first floor of the building was a huge, barn-like warehouse. My father, who was a wholesale dealer in fruits and vegetables, would sell his produce to horse-and-buggy fruit peddlers. Peddlers kept their horses and wagons on the first floor and lived on the second. Most of these people were Greeks from the old country who came here as young men because the economy in Greece wasn't so good. America was the land of opportunity! So, they came here and lived with my father and mother.

The Greek community concentrated around 67th, 69th, and 71st and State. Like all of Chicago, when immigrants first came, they tended to stay to themselves. There were some a little further west, and there was a big Greek community in Greek Town west of the Loop. There were Greeks up north, but we never crossed Madison Street other than when I went to my first Cubs game in 1948. As people became more successful and more mobile, they felt less of a need to stay among their own kind, so they started disbursing. At one point, compared to Athens, we had the second or third highest concentration of Greeks in the world. There are more than 250,000 Greeks in the Chicago area.

My father came to America around the turn of the century. He was about seventeen years old when he came in 1901 or 1902. Then, as immigrants often did, he worked for the railroad for a while. The railroads were the big employers then, and he was just a water boy. He wound up in Utah someplace, but somehow made his way back to Chicago and got into the produce business at the wholesale end. Once upon a time, he was the premier guy in the south markets around 71st and State.

A very fond and vivid memory of mine was going down to the markets with my father. The daily routine was for him to get up at 2 o'clock in the morning. You have to understand that these were the days before the interstate highways were developed and built. In those days at 2 a.m. there was no street traffic. None. For me, it was fun to be with my dad. For him, it was the beginning of an eighteen hour workday. When you're a kid, you don't understand what these people went through. So, we would get in our empty truck and drive to the market, around 15th and Morgan. I learned to drive about the age of fifteen. When I got behind the wheel of the truck I couldn't hit a car or a building even if I wanted to, because

there was nobody on the street. We would come most of the way down State — there was no traffic at all. The street was quiet and the city was quiet.

When we got to South Water Street, my dad would purchase his merchandise and by 6 a.m. the truck would be loaded. We then would drive back down south to his store and unload the truck. All the grocers from "ma and pa" grocery stores would come and buy their morning goods. Then, in the afternoon, my dad would spend time delivering the merchandise to these stores. He would begin his workday at 2 a.m. and wouldn't get home until 6 or 7 o'clock in the evening. Even when he was in his 60s, he kept that schedule.

One of the stores I delivered to is still in business, and the owner is still a friend of mine. In those days it was on Commercial Avenue, and it was called Gayety Candy Company. When I was a kid, Gayety Candy made their own ice cream and chocolates. They would buy bananas from my dad for banana splits, and they would always buy the best bananas. When I was twelve or thirteen years old I always made that trip to Gayety Candy because they would give me homemade ice cream.

I think that the '40s was a time of expansion of ability. The early immigrants worked with their backs and they sweated. Suddenly, the schools were being attended by them and by their children. So, there was an expansion of learning by immigrants at that time. All the Greek parents, even though they weren't formally educated in their own countries, insisted on everybody going to school and excelling in school. We had to bring our report cards home every time, and while some parents couldn't read English, they knew what the grades were. If you brought home a grade that wasn't good, you had to explain it. There was this emphasis on education that is characteristic in Greek culture. There was an understanding that you were Greek ethnically, but you lived in America. So, it was exploring not only your own culture, and being proud of it, but being exposed to different cultures and different races.

It was a marvelous time living in the city and growing up during the 1940s. Crime was much less in those years, and murder was a rare event. There wasn't the sense of insecurity that would come later. There wasn't a sense of fear if you were in a strange neighborhood, but there was little reason to go anyplace else.

book for the team. The funny thing was, I never really understood football, or had much of an interest in the sport."

Hal Lichterman grew up in the Albany Park neighborhood. "To many people, Albany Park was centered around Lawrence Avenue. On Lawrence and Central Park was a very famous delicatessen called Rudich's. People hung out there, and at Lawndale Pool Hall. However, my stomping grounds were on Kedzie Avenue, where there was a bowling alley called Leland Bowl with a pool hall upstairs. I would swing around to Montrose and I'd set pins at Monte Cristo Bowl and Drake Bowl. They had leagues at that bowl, and I was probably one of the only Jewish kids who set pins there."

Otho Kortz grew up in Englewood and has memories of the nearby stockyards. "Englewood was a fantastic neighborhood, and in those days almost every family had someone working in the Union Stockyards. I worked there, so did my dad and my grandfather. My dad worked in the stockyard business from the time he was fourteen — and he died in the stockyards in Joliet. He was weighing some cows, and he had a stroke. He was happy to die there." Another resident of Englewood, Bill Phelan, remembers the work ethic in his neighborhood. "It was a great, interesting neighborhood, and I wouldn't even call it middle-class. They were all hard-working people — blue-collar people. My father was a Chicago streetcar man for many years, and later became a policeman during World War II. He was born in Canada, and when he was eighteen years old he came to Chicago with some of his other brothers and sisters and got a job at the Rock Island Railroad. He also worked for the Chicago Surface Line, and then the Chicago Police Department, from where he retired. My mother worked a good part of her life as a housewife, and she also worked outside the home a great deal to help the family, because it had to be done."

Sheldon Rosing's life changed when his father had a heart attack at age 38. "My dad had been a life insurance salesman for Metropolitan Life and worked in South Chicago. We lived in South Shore, and when he couldn't work, my parents opened a grocery store downtown near State and Van Buren. They sold fruits, vegetables, candies, nuts and stuff like that in their little store that near the Dearborn Street Station. When people traveled on the trains, they would stop in for cold cuts and other food. Our rent was about $140 a month in 1941 because of rent controls, but when the war ended, the rent skyrocketed to $900 a month and we just had to close the store."

Young people had to be versatile when it came to finding a summer job. Mike Perlow, who grew up in Garfield Park, recalls, "I have always had a very strong work ethic, and when I was a freshman in high school my father suggested that it was time for me to get a summer job. I had come

Kay Kuwahara
Near North Side

My beauty shop was at 111 W. Division, inside the Mark Twain Hotel. When we got here in 1945, the neighborhood was pretty rough. Many of my customers were waitresses, strippers, showgirls, prostitutes, and "26" girls. Back then, all the taverns had "26" girls. The girls had to be very attractive and dress provocatively, and run the dice game called "26."

The hairstyle back then was "the more the merrier" and the "bigger the better." That was our specialty, making hair larger. And back then women would come in once a week to get their hair done. They didn't wash their hair everyday like they do now. They would come and get a shampoo and set, and then maintain it during the week. The hair wouldn't get dirty because the dirt couldn't penetrate all that lacquer!

At first, people would come to the beauty shop, but after they saw that I was Japanese, they would never come back. But the nightclub girls and waitresses didn't care, and kept coming back. They liked my specialty — blondes. I loved blondes and could make their hair a platinum blonde, which was very popular back then. We got really good word of mouth and pretty soon all the waitresses would come in. Then, because their hair looked so good, all the strippers started coming in. Then the prostitutes started coming in! It was a real wide-open place back then!

When we got to the Mark Twain we didn't know of its bad reputation, but we soon learned. I was told the prostitution was run this way — you gave a tip to the porter and he would get you a girl. These were our clients! Not all of them, but a lot of them were.

We also had all of the big-time syndicate and mobster's girlfriends coming in. At the time I didn't know who they were, but they all talked the "Sopranos"-talk! They were all very nice to us. In fact, they were protective of us. If anybody came along that bothered us, they would say, "Move on. She's a good girl!" These guys dated a lot of the showgirls working in the neighborhood, on Rush Street and on Clark.

All these sweet girls were just being used by these men. I prayed for these girls, but they were just willing victims. I told my minister, "I feel so bad. I do these girls' hair and they go right out and do their business with the men." He said, "Kay, you must do this, because you are one of the few graces in their lives. You treat them like human beings."

These guys were just so clever, giving them money and furs. They gave them their dreams.

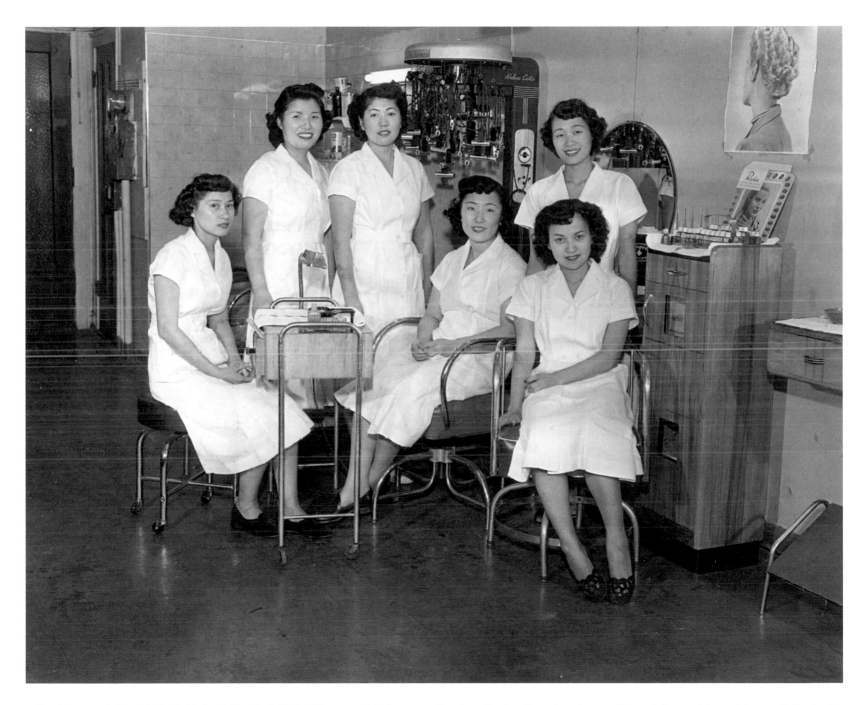

Co-ed Beauty Salon, 1305 E. 53rd, 1949. Hyde Park (Courtesy of the Japanese American Service Committee Legacy Center, Mary and James Numata Collection.)

West Side Historical Society Meeting, 1947. West Garfield Park (Courtesy of Special Collections and Preservation Division, Chicago Public Library.)

Adelaide Gredys Winston
Logan Square

I was born in 1919 and moved to Chicago in 1930. We lived in Logan Square in the attic apartment of a bungalow on Richmond near Diversey. I went to Roosevelt High School and graduated in 1936, during the depths of the Depression. I was pretty high in my class and was invited to attend the University of Chicago, but my family couldn't afford to let me go there. So, a girlfriend of mine whose uncle was the head telegrapher at the Chicago & Eastern Illinois Railroad told me about an opening in the telegraph office for a messenger girl. So, I went to work as a messenger girl at the C&EI Railroad. I was always a friendly, outgoing kid, not fresh or anything, but never a shrinking violet. Soon the railroad needed an additional reservation clerk during the winter season. So, I worked two winters in the reservation bureau. It was a different time and world.

The head of the passenger reservations would always walk around and listen to us to see what kind of job we were doing. One day in 1943, I was asked to go to his office. I wasn't worried because I knew I was doing a good job. When I got to his office, he said, "Ms. Gredys, the boys are being drafted too rapidly for us to train another man on the ticket counter. Would you be interested in learning to be a ticket seller?" Well, I was very interested, and that's how I became a ticket seller. And I was paid on the same scale as the men when I was hired. I was moved to the 175 West Jackson Boulevard Consolidated Ticket Office, a lively place during the war. I became Chicago's first female railroad ticket seller when I was hired to sell tickets for the B&O, the Nickel Plate and the Alton Railroad. It's hard for young people today to imagine what railroad travel was at the height of the war. In the days when servicemen were moving from unheard of hometowns to unlikely sounding bases, the job was very stimulating.

One of the trains which I sold tickets for was the Capitol Limited. This line carried many important wartime figures to and from Washington. One such person was Silliman Evans, who was brought from Nashville, Tennessee, by Marshall Field to launch the Chicago Sun. When he returned south after the paper was established, I received what in those days was an unheard-of generous gift — a check for $100 for the help I provided in ticketing his trip. In addition, that Christmas I received a jar of Tennessee Mountain Honey and a crate of Texas citrus with his compliments.

I thoroughly enjoyed my job and I would have been there until the railroad collapsed, but I got sick in 1945. In fact, on April 12, 1945, when Roosevelt died, I was so sick that my mother came downtown in a taxicab and took me home. That was the end of my railroad career.

Speech Class, Mundelein College, ca. 1944. Rogers Park (Courtesy of the Rogers Park/West Ridge Historical Society.)

Wayne Juhlan
Portage Park

In Portage Park the Six Corners shopping area — Irving, Cicero, and Milwaukee — was the big deal. I remember the Sears Department Store, which was the flagship store in the neighborhood, had this giant window they would put displays in. We would all wait with great anticipation for the unveiling of the next big display in the window. During the war they had patriotic stuff in the window, but at Christmas they always had a giant Santa Claus in the window.

Down the street was the Portage Theatre, and going there was a big deal. They had something called the "Fifteen Cartoon Show," where they played all cartoons with no features. Other stores in the area included Klee Brothers and Abraham's Department Store. To get you into the store, Abraham's offered cheap hair cuts, which were popular for mothers who wanted to save a quarter. I remember a delicatessen around there that had this big barrel filled with herring. There were smells in this place that I never smelled before! Big vats of pickles and fish! Then there were the dime stores, like Woolworth's. These stores had a wonderful combination of smells because they sold so many different things. Live fish and turtles would be sold alongside fabric and candy. Oh, the sweet smell of candy!

Not far from there, at Cullom and Montrose, was Rock-Ola Stadium. They had a women's fast-pitch softball league there, and my dad and I would go every night to see them play. The team was called the Rock-Ola Music Maids, sponsored by the jukebox company, and they would play teams like the Queens and the Bloomer Girls. Our ritual was this: my dad would pay for a ticket, and I would crawl through a hole in the fence out in left field! I would crawl through and then meet my dad in the stands. We actually got to know the players pretty well. In fact, I set-up a date for one of the girls. I introduced Josephine Kaybeck to one of the Chicago Cubs who used to come out there. We followed that league for years, and they had some great players. Wilda Mae Turner was the best pitcher. She wasn't a bad looking girl either, real blonde and statuesque. Then, these two massive woman came into the league — Frida and Olympia Savona. A lot of guys thought they were men, because they were so muscular and stocky. They broke all the records! Just shattered them!

After the game we'd walk back home and stop at the hot dog stand. You know, there used to be stands and vendors all over the city before the Board of Health put limitations on them, saying you couldn't serve food without a washroom. And there used to be guys who would come to your door selling all kinds of household items, like needles and thread, and other things that ladies bought. Today, people would be much more nervous about opening their doors. Then, there was the "rags-old-iron-man," the junk man, the knife sharpener, and the ice man. The ice man would deliver ice in a horse-drawn truck. I remember one of the thrills as a kid was to try to run under these big horses without getting kicked!

Radio was a very big deal back then. I knew the daily schedule so well that I would have people test me on the times the shows were on. At night, with my family or alone, I listened. One of my favorites was the "Lux Radio Theater," where they would take a movie and condense it down to a hour-long radio version. On Saturday mornings, they had kid shows like "Let's Pretend," which would have great actors doing fairy tales, and "Grand Central Station," where the actors would come out and announce themselves. Then there were goofy shows like "It Pays to be Ignorant," which asked simple questions and a panel would give unbelievably dumb answers. A question might be, "What Indian tribe weaves Navaho blankets?" Then the panel would give stupid responses like, "Duhh, now dese' blankets you got, are dey thick blankets?"

Another of my favorites was "Steve Wilson of the Illustrated Press." He was a crime-fighting reporter who ended his show the same way every week! It would go like this — he would chase down and corner a criminal with a gun, and then his cab-driving partner would say, "Let me hit him with my noggin-knocking monkey wrench!" "No, that's not necessary," Steve would say, "I'll talk him out of it!" He would then deliver some moral message, and the criminal would always end up saying, "You win Wilson!" Week after week, it would always end the same way!

The 1940s was a special time in Chicago, and this could not happen again. It just couldn't happen again.

Lincoln Park, 1942. Lincoln Park (Courtesy of the Chicago Park District.)

home from a long summer vacation and went over to Lake Street and began walking down the street looking for some work. I didn't find a job until I got to Clinton Street, at a machine tool shop. It was a hard job cleaning up the place, running jigsaws and lathes, and that began my work experience. During those following summers, I worked in a lumberyard, as an electrician's apprentice, at the Chicago Board of Trade, and at the real estate office of Arthur Rubloff and Company."

Street and Alley Vendors

By the end of the 1940s, the era of street and alley vendors was coming to a close. Dating back to the nineteenth century, these enterprising vendors were fixtures in Chicago's neighborhoods providing many valuable services. Knife-sharpeners, junk men, Fuller Brushmen, icemen, fruit and vegetable peddlers and milk men, many in horse drawn wagons, saved customers a trip to their local stores.

Kenwood resident Richard Lukin recalls, "In the '40s, you still had the horse and wagon vendors working in the neighborhoods. Bryman and Wanzer delivered milk every day in a wagon. That was the way customers got their milk. You had a cardboard form stapled to the back of your door and the delivery man would mark off what you ordered. Then, at the end of the month, you would get an invoice. And there were still a few apartments in the '40s that didn't have an electric refrigerator, so they had iceboxes. You would see the iceman trudging up the stairs with a heavy load of ice. In those days, you had to put a delivery card in your back window or door indicating how much weight you wanted — 25, 50, 75 or 100 pounds. The guy could see from the alley what you needed, and he would chop a piece off of a big 300-pound block. It was also very common to see fruit and vegetable peddlers. These guys would get a beat-up old truck or horse and wagon and load it up at the South Water Market, then work the neighborhoods. I remember so many of these vendors in the neighborhoods. By my grandmother's house over on North Avenue there was a guy who sold penny waffles with powdered sugar from a little wagon. When I was in grammar school, there was a guy who parked by the school who sold hot dogs, ice cream, and something I had never seen before — sugar cane — little four or five inch pieces of real live sugar cane."

Peanut Vendor, Sheridan Road, ca. 1948. Rogers Park (Courtesy of the Rogers Park/West Ridge Historical Society.)

Sports and Recreation in the Neighborhood

If you grew up in a Chicago neighborhood in the 1940s you needed to be creative, both in finding places to play and filling up your time. Most children created their own fun, without any adult supervision, in the streets, alleys, courtyards, gangways or one of the many empty lots or "prairies" that dotted the neighborhoods. If they were lucky enough to live near a park, and old enough to cross streets to get there, the parks would be gathering places for activity. Public and parochial school grounds were also used regularly, with baseball and softball played on gravel school yards, and fast-pitch against school yard walls. Other popular neighborhood games including line ball, football, pinners, hide and seek (also known as rolevio), kick the can, street hockey, and red rover. The key element for many children's activities during the 1940s was the almost complete lack of adult supervision — something very different from neighborhood life today.

As children got older, there were many adult-organized activities in the neighborhoods: at parks, beaches and field houses, as well as in public and parochial school yards. In the spring, as the temperature would begin to warm, it was time for playing ball, whether 12- or 16-inch softball or baseball. In the summer, kids would leave home at an early hour and spend the entire day playing sports and games, swimming at the larger parks, and if they could find transportation to Lake Michigan, having fun at the city's beaches. Then, in the fall and winter, the sports changed to football, basketball, ice-skating and hockey.

For kids and adults there were also ample opportunities to attend and participate in the many high school, college, semi-pro, and professional sports in the neighborhoods. Pro games by the Cubs, White Sox, Bears, Cardinals, Stags, and Blackhawks were highly attended, as well as college games by DePaul, Loyola, University of Chicago and the neighboring Northwestern University. High school sports were also significant events in the lives of city residents, and many great public and parochial school teams played in the 1940s. In addition, there were numerous semi-pro leagues, including men and women's hardball and softball leagues, that played at ballparks including Mills, Thillens, Parichy, Shewbridge and Bidwill.

Street and Alley Games

Children of all ethnic, racial and religious groups played street and alley games in the 1940s. Due to limited space in the urban environment, parental admonition against crossing major streets, and the general lack of automobile traffic, streets and alleys were popular locations for boys and girls to play. Invariably, if they played in the alleys, someone would be assigned the task of climbing on top of garages or going into backyards to retrieve the balls. If games were played on the street, manhole covers, street lamps and parked cars became bases and boundaries for baseball and football games. Empty lots or "prairies" that had not been developed for

Opposite: *Lifeguards, Jackson Park, 1940.* Woodlawn
(Courtesy of the Chicago Park District.)

housing or businesses could be found in most Chicago neighborhoods in the '40s. Children, sometimes with their parents, would clear the undeveloped land of bushes, trees, weeds and garbage to transform them into usable places to play. Creativity ruled the day, and children did not have to venture too far from their apartments, bungalows or houses to have fun.

Ian Levin and his friends spent many hours playing in front of their apartment buildings on Estes Avenue, west of Sheridan Road, as well as in the alleys behind the buildings in his Far North Side neighborhood. "During the '40s, there was no Loyola Park on Sheridan Road, so we played on Estes. We used to play pinners, and we liked playing on the street so much that even after the park was finished in the early '50s, we just continued to play our games on the street. The games included field hockey, touch football, bounce the balls off the buildings, and spud. However, the big game for us was pinners. For pinners we used a pink, Spaulding high bounce ball and threw it against a curb or the side of a building. The goal was to make the ball bounce over the opponent's head and land in the area designated for single, double, triple or home run. Pinners was meant to be played in limited spaces. We used a ledge on a building, and we had a batters box by the alley. Interestingly, some of us actually used to slide on the concrete street into second base when we played pinners, but at least I had the sense not to slide head-first. Many times I would come home with torn pants and cuts on my hands and legs. We spent our entire summers playing those games around our apartment buildings."

In Albany Park, Marvin Aspen and his friends also played street and alley games. "As we got older, our recreation included line ball in the alleys and in the streets. Line ball was a variation of baseball and only required two players on each team. The teams would agree on specific fair and foul territories. There would be a pitcher and one fielder on each team and the goal was to hit the ball into safe territory without it being caught. Just like a baseball game there were balls, strikes, and outs. When we got a little bigger space, we played bounce and fly. If you caught the ball either on a bounce or a fly, you were out. We played pinners, and the biggest pinners site was in front of the Albany Park Hebrew Congregation against its facade. The congregation was kitty-corner of the Max Strauss Center, on the southeast corner of Lawndale and Wilson. One of the greatest forms of entertainment was playing in empty lots. It wasn't a prairie to us, it was an empty lot, and our favorite empty lot was one with tall weeds located on Lawrence Avenue, about two or three stores from the southwest corner of Lawndale and Lawrence.

To a kid of three, four, or five years of age, it felt like a forest because the weeds were taller than we were."

A nearby "prairie" became the center of activity for Tom Hynes and his friends in the Gresham neighborhood. "The parks were far away from us, so we basically made our own parks and created a baseball field from a prairie, a vacant block that was actually a half a block wide and a block long. With the assistance of many of the fathers in the neighborhood, we cut down the weeds and small wild saplings and filled-in many of the holes. We had a blast, but it was not exactly up to modern Little League standards. We played mostly 16-inch softball, but we played hardball and 12-inch softball too."

Alderman Edward Burke grew up in Visitation Parish on the Southwest Side. "We played in the streets and the alleys all the time. The games included tag, rolevio, red rover — where you ran to see if you could break through the line — cops and robbers, and of course, cowboys and Indians. We would play touch football, but not baseball in the street. When we wanted to play baseball we would go over to the park."

Ed Brennan grew up in Austin and enjoyed playing softball in the street. "We always played 16-inch softball in the streets, and home plate was in the middle of the street. There wasn't that much traffic back then, although you had to move aside for cars all the time. Living two doors off of Madison Street meant there would always be a certain amount of traffic on the street. But the side streets were a good place to play, and most of the stuff we did was by ourselves."

In Lake View, across from Belmont Harbor, U.S. District Judge James Zagel recalls, "During the 1940s, we played in a vacant lot that someone landscaped nicely — it was our playing field. We used to play softball there, and we would play pitcher's hands out because we usually didn't have enough people. Then, in the winter, we would play football there. I distinctly remember the billboard for Butternut bread that was on the property. The bottom of the picture of the blue-checked loaf was about ten feet above the ground, and it was fairly wide. So, for the first time, we were able to kick field goals. If we place-kicked a field goal and it hit the bread, or went directly above it, we scored three points."

Joseph Lamendella grew up on Lill Avenue near Diversey and Racine. "Lill Avenue was a very homogeneous street that included people of many nationalities. Our play consisted of street games like kick the can, tag, hide and go seek, red rover, and rolevio. In rolevio, there were two teams of children. While one team was hiding around the neighborhood, it was the goal of the other team to find the hidden kids.

The street games were coed, by and large, although some of the hide and seek games were played primarily by boys because they were rougher games. We also played stick ball in the streets, and a game called 'bounce out' where we would take a soft rubber ball and hit it against the steps of an apartment building or a house and depending on where the ball landed, it was a single, double, triple or home run. Other people called this game pinners."

In West Rogers Park, Ron Davis remembers playing football in front of his house. "In the '40s we would play touch football on the street. There weren't many cars in those days, and maybe only one or two would be parked on our street. In the huddle of our touch football game, we would instruct the receiver to go down to the blue car and turn left, and I would pass the ball to him. The games would always be from sewer to sewer and they would become the goal lines. The sewers were 42' apart, and that was how we would play touch football. The cable at the alley became the crossbar to kick extra points and field goals. It was terrific."

Bernie Judge remembers the alley basketball games in his South Shore neighborhood. "Alley basketball was a full-time job during the basketball season. We would play behind Dr. Wall's house. There was a basketball hoop on the garage, and you just showed up. Nolan's Shoe Store was right at the corner of 79th and Bennett, next to the Red Keg, and he used to say that alley basketball was the shoe man's best friend because we wrecked our shoes playing. We played every day. To start a game, you would shoot from the free throw line, and if you sank your shot, you were on the team. The first eight or ten guys who sank their shot, they were on the team. The rule was that you called the fouls — nobody who played alley basketball would last five minutes in a real game. Occasionally fights would break out, but the game was among friends so it didn't last long."

Public and Parochial School Gyms and Playgrounds

In the 1940s, kids and adults often played their favorite sports on gravel school yards and in school gymnasiums. Children used the facilities for activities during the school day, and after school, children and adults used the facilities, playing sports such as softball, line ball, football, and fast-pitch.

Norman Mark remembers playing softball and fast-pitch in his school yard at Dixon Elementary School in Chatham. "The school was only a block and a half from my home. So, I would go over there and we would play 16-inch softball. It was a gravel lot and you were always slipping

Line Ball, 4500 Block of West Congress, ca. 1940. West Garfield Park (Courtesy of Charles F. Simpson.)

Lifeguard Tests, Washington Park, 1940. Washington Park (Courtesy of the Chicago Park District.)

Tug-of-War, Roosevelt Road Beach, 1947. Near South Side (Courtesy of the Chicago Park District.)

Recreation Demonstration at Portage Park, 1942. Portage Park (Courtesy of the Chicago Park District.)

1st Tee, Jackson Park, 1947. Woodlawn (Courtesy of the Chicago Park District.)

and falling on the gravel. I think that I still have some gravel in my knee! We also had a game that we called 'fast pitch' where you would draw a batter's box on the wall and somebody would throw a tennis ball as fast as he could at the person who was batting. If you hit it over the fence into someone's living room, it was a home run. There was one guy, Jim Mann, who was the best fast-pitch pitcher ever. If they ever created a fast-pitch league, this guy would be incredible!"

Bob Cunniff grew up in Edgewater and recalls neighborhood basketball games inside nearby churches. "We lived right next door to the Church of the Atonement on Ardmore and Kenmore, where we used to play basketball. We had one friend who was an Episcopalian so we could use his resources to play in their gym. We had another friend who was a Presbyterian, and he belonged to the Presbyterian Church on Bryn Mawr and Kenmore. Their gym was a much better gym, and he actually switched from being an Episcopalian to being a Presbyterian in order to use the gym."

Bill Nellis recalls the weekly softball games held at Sullivan High School's gravel field in Rogers Park. "After World War II, around 1946, the big activity after Sunday church services at St. Ignatius was a doubleheader of 16-inch softball. They would use a new Clincher softball for each game. I would describe it as an 'ethnic' or 'religious' game because it was usually between teams of Catholic guys versus Jewish guys. The games would be played on the gravel field at the south end of Sullivan High School and they would usually begin at noon on Sunday. Both teams had some great players ranging in age from nineteen years old at the youngest, to guys in their late 30s, many who were war veterans. They were great games and the teams were a good reflection of the religious makeup of the neighborhood around Loyola University."

Bernie Judge remembers the softball games that used to be played on the gravel school yard at Horace Mann Elementary School in the South Shore neighborhood. "It was very difficult to play hardball at Mann because the ball would take crazy bounces, plus it would ruin the ball. There were big softball money games played there, and sometimes they would have three umpires. They were playing $100-a-man games in the late '40s and early '50s and then a keg of beer afterward. There were also lesser, $10-a-man games every Sunday. There were no leagues, they were all neighborhood games."

The Lake and the Beaches

In the 1940s, many Chicagoans used the beaches that stretched from Juneway Beach on the north to Calumet Beach on the south. Lake Michigan and the waterfront were popular spots for sunbathing and swimming by day, but they also provided important relief from the summer heat at night. In fact, it was not unusual for families to sleep overnight on the beach during summer's hottest nights, mingling with neighbors and enjoying the effects of the cool lake breezes.

Estelle Gordon Baron grew up in South Shore only a few blocks from Lake Michigan. "We lived down the street from Lake Michigan. None of us knew how to swim, so we couldn't go to the lake unless our mothers went with us. We would just splash around in the water. That lake was wonderful, though. In the summer, we would make sand castles on the beach. We went to the lake during the winter, too. I remember how the water would splash up on the boulders and would freeze over until it was smooth. My dad used to bring some cardboard boxes from the grocery store and we would climb up to the top, sit on the boxes, and go down the side of the frozen boulders. So, in the summer we had the lake for fun, and in the winter, when it was snowing and the schools would close down, we had the lake, too."

Irving Park resident Sheila Morris Williams remembers going to the beaches throughout her childhood. "I have many good memories of going to the beach, but most of my neighbors didn't go to the beaches, it was just too far away. In fact, only one family had a car in my neighborhood, and that was quite a novelty. My introduction to Lake Michigan was when my father, an Irish immigrant, threw me into the lake to 'teach me' how to swim. 'This is the way we do it in Ireland!' he screamed. During the last two summers of World War II, I would go to the beach with the wife of a soldier who was away. She was a boarder at my grandmother's house, and she would take me to the beach after she got off work. She was lonely for her husband, and just wanted to talk about him. The evenings were pleasant, but sad for her."

Fr. Gene Smith grew up on the South Side. "Rainbow Beach was important to us. It was a beautiful beach that ran from 75th to 79th Streets. The streetcar went right up 75th Street and made a circle by the beach. I remember that by 11 a.m. on Sunday mornings there were no more parking spots available at Rainbow Beach, and you couldn't see the sand because the people went there in droves."

Touhy Beach was an important part of the Rogers Park neighborhood. Shecky Greene remembers the beach, the field house, and Sam Leone. "When I was a lifeguard at Sam Leone's Touhy Beach in the 1940s, I would spend a lot of time at the lifeguard station with the other guys. During the winter we would ice-skate there, and, in the summer, we would play softball. Many years after I had moved out of Rogers Park, I came

Swimmers at Garfield Park, 1948. East Garfield Park (Courtesy of the Chicago Park District.)

back to honor Sam at a party for him at the American Legion hall on Devon. I was singing to him when I remembered that Sam couldn't hear a thing. He was almost deaf! But I loved being there and seeing everyone and honoring Sam. There was a man who really loved his job, and he loved the kids. I think that if they didn't pay him at all, he still would have done that job."

The Parks

As early as the 1860s, Chicago began to build a comprehensive park system. In 1864, an ordinance was passed to build Lake Park on the North Side. It would be renamed Lincoln Park in honor of the assassinated 16th President of the United States. By 1869, Chicago would begin to develop a city-wide park system that included Humboldt, Garfield, Jackson, South, Washington and Douglas Parks. Each of the parks would have a wide range of facilities available to Chicagoans, including baseball, tennis, boating, swimming, horseback riding, ice-skating, dancing and band concerts. By the 1940s, there were hundreds of large and small parks and play lots across the city.

During World War II, the Park District played an active role in Civil Defense activities, utilizing field houses and other facilities to aid in the home front effort. In addition, many residents planted Victory Gardens in their neighborhood parks, allowing farmers to focus their efforts on growing food for the men and women of the armed services.

To South Shore residents, Jackson Park provided just about every recreational activity one could ask for. Dick Jaffee recalls, "It had been the site of the Columbian Exposition and there were still things left in the park when I was a kid, including the Japanese Gardens. We used to go over there on many summer nights, before air conditioning, and rent a rowboat or fish in the lagoon. I also used to play hooky from Sunday school with my brother, and we would play ball in the park and then tell our mother that we had learned a lot in school that day."

Andrew McKenna's favorite park was also Jackson Park. "Jackson Park was near us, and later on I worked there during the summer when I was in high school and in college. The park was a little bit north of where I grew up, but it was still our park. We could walk down any of the streets we lived on to get there. I lived on Crandon, and it dead-ended at the park. You would just walk through the golf course there. Jackson Park might be the biggest park in the city. It had an 18-hole golf course, a number of different beaches, and a lot of recreational facilities. Jackson Park played a role for all of us growing up in South Shore."

On the Far North Side, Steve Zucker's favorite park was Green Briar. "We would spend every day, from the time we woke up until we went to sleep, at Green Briar Park on Peterson Avenue, between Washtenaw and Talman. I must have started going there when I was seven or eight years old, as soon as I could ride my bike. Ed Kelly, who would later on become Superintendent of the Chicago Park District, was the supervisor at Green Briar and he was always organizing things at the park. There was always something happening at Green Briar, and if they weren't organized games, it would be pick-up games. You usually had 100 guys to choose from, and we would just sit there and wait for our turn to come. It would be one pick-up game after another, and there would be sports questions in-between. My friends would quiz me on sports while we waited for the next game. They didn't have lights at Green Briar, so we played until it was dark and then, unfortunately, we had to stop and go home. In the wintertime, they would freeze part of the park for ice-skating, and we also played basketball inside the field house."

Howard Carl grew up in Albany Park and spent most of his time at Eugene Field Park. "We lived at Ridgeway and Argyle, so we were only a couple of blocks from the park. Every possible day, from the age of eight or nine, I was at the park and on the basketball court. We only played half-court games in those days, and on a Sunday when the place was packed we played three-man team games. If your team lost, you might have to wait as much as 30 minutes to get back on the court. In the winter we played basketball inside the field house at the park. When I attended Volta Elementary School at Argyle and Avers, as soon as school was let out for the day, we would race the seven or eight blocks to get to the park and shoot baskets before the regular park activities would begin. By the time I was twelve or thirteen, I would go to the park and serve as a scorekeeper or timekeeper for the older guys' basketball games. At the end of each quarter, at half-time and in between the games, I would shoot baskets. That way, I could get in more shooting. I was just obsessed with basketball!"

Humboldt Park was the key place for Arnold Scholl when he grew up in the '40s. "We moved to the Humboldt Park neighborhood around 1943. I lived a half block east of the park, between California and Fairfield, and one block south of North Avenue. I did everything at Humboldt Park, including baseball. They had tennis courts, but nobody seemed to play tennis at that time. So, we played baseball on the tennis court since it was on a hard surface and there were no nets on the courts. If we felt like walking, we would go over to the softball field which was a little bit further into the park. At that time, nobody seemed to play hardball, just softball. There was also a lagoon in the park and a boathouse, and in winter, we could ice-skate on the lagoon when it froze. There was also a field house

Chicago Park District Baseball Championships at Wrigley Field, Clark and Addison, 1942. Lakeview   (Courtesy of the Chicago Park District.)

Portage Park Juniors, Champion Baseball Team, Wrigley Field, 1942. Lakeview (Courtesy of the Chicago Park District.)

Ed Kelly
Near North Side

I grew up in a neighborhood called, at various times, Smoky Hollow and Hell's Kitchen. It is presently called Cabrini-Green. On Elm Street, there is a park called Seward Park. We were born and raised at Seward. We lived at 340 Elm Street, right across the street from the park, and of course, that was where I played — softball, basketball, and boxing. We did everything over there. It was a great neighborhood, and growing up, we never walked two blocks out of the area.

I went into the Marine Corps during the war, and was in the South Pacific in the Marshall Islands on an island called Majero, where I spent about a year. When the war ended, I went to Tsingtao, China. We were stationed there because of the problems with the Chinese Communists at that time. After I was discharged, I went to DePaul University and I played basketball until I got hurt.

When I returned from the war there was tremendous change in my neighborhood. Many African-Americans had moved into the neighborhood, and a lot of the Italian and Irish families were moving out. This was happening while the war was going on. We had a rapid disbursement of families in the neighborhood. We moved out of the area and into the 47th Ward at 4510 N. Ashland Avenue. The separation from the neighborhood was very drastic. A lot of the people who were born and raised there were moving into different areas of Chicago, including some of the suburban areas.

So, it was difficult to come back and see people you were raised with, your buddies, had moved. We started an American Legion post, and we called it a C.M.C. Post. We started it down at Seward Park and it stayed in the neighborhood. The American Legion post kept us together. I think that is what held us together, along with playing softball and basketball. I went away when I was eighteen years old. When I came back, I was an adult. It was a tough time. The neighborhood was breaking up and people were moving out.

The parks had a key role in holding neighborhoods together, and even though there were changes taking place when I came back, we would still play in the parks. We had our softball games there, and we played basketball, cards and dice. So, basically, the park was what kept us together. And the older guys, who were not playing ball, were over at the American Legion post at the park. That was where you hung out. The park was important because that was where all the different age groups and religious groups could hang out.

where I played basketball when I was older. I was in the park all the time during the summer. If I wasn't in the park, we were playing on the street."

Former Cook County Assessor Tom Hynes grew up in Brainerd, on the borderline with Gresham, and remembers, "The closest big parks to us during the '40s were Brainerd Park at 91st and Racine, and Foster Park at 85th and Loomis. We used to go to both parks, but they did not have the kind of facilities that you see in parks today. They had small field houses, but neither one had a gym, swimming pool, big baseball fields or tennis courts. While they were good parks, they were nothing compared to facilities that existed in later years."

Bill Gleason remembers the popularity of tennis in his Park Manor neighborhood. "When we moved to the neighborhood around 72nd and Normal, near Eggleston, we were near Hamilton Park, and it was an adventure to be there. It was a paradise for me because there were four baseball fields, eight softball fields and action all the time. Hamilton Park was a tremendous producer of tennis players, although I was not one of them. The man who was the supervisor was a tennis enthusiast, and they not only had clay courts but lighted clay courts. This was during the Depression, and for a dime you could turn the lights on. Out of that park came nationally famous tennis players — John Jorgensen won the state tournament two years in a row. These tennis players from the park would get on the streetcars and would travel all around the city — they would beat everybody! I remember a Sunday morning in Hamilton Park when the number one and number two tennis players in the world played an exhibition — Fred Perry and Ellsworth Vines. That's how important this park was. The Rock Island Railroad tracks were the eastern boundary of the park, and the Wabash Railroad tracks were on the western boundary. It was like a little valley between these two embankments. So we sat on the slope coming down from the Rock Island tracks watching these two great players. Looking back on it now, it seems so unlikely."

Softball

When Chicago-style 16-inch softball first developed it was an indoor sport played in gymnasiums with eleven players on a team. By the 1940s, it was primarily an outdoor sport with teams playing in every park, gravel school yard, empty lot and prairie across the city. For kids, it was one of the many sports and activities played throughout the spring and summer. For adults, it could be a passion, with some players competing in as many ten softball games a day, and traveling across the city just to play in another game or two.

James Casey grew up in Beverly and played at Ridge Park. "When I grew up in Beverly, softball was one of the big sports for me. We would play softball in the prairie. There were also a couple of parks in the neighborhood, including Ridge Park at 95th and Longwood Drive, and another one at 91st Street. Softball was totally unorganized, and teams were made up of those kids who just showed up to play. There was no Little League and little, if any, parental involvement. We played 16-inch softball, but no hardball."

Tom Doyle played softball while living in the Back of the Yards neighborhood. "I had my own softball team. Before there was a Clincher, there was the Wilson Top Notch softball, and it was a great softball because it was soft and light. We would play for the ball and a dollar-a-man, and we would play in the empty lots. There was also a ball field at 49th and Troop and we might go over there, or we would play in the park."

Jim O'Connor remembers playing softball in his Gresham neighborhood. "We played 16-inch softball, and Windy City Softball was the main sport. We'd play in the empty lots if they were big enough or in the street and use sewer covers as bases. The closest park was O'Halloran Park at 79th and Wood. That was the neighborhood softball park and left field was south of the alley. There was an apartment building on one side of the park, and only the most athletic people in the neighborhood could hit the ball to that building located a half block away. It was a real distance to hit it there. A guy by the name of Bob Smith from Leo High School could hit the ball that far, and he was a hero in the neighborhood because nobody else could hit the wall."

Charles Bidwill, Jr. grew up in Austin. His father owned the Chicago Cardinals as well as a professional women's softball team. "My father was very active in women's softball, the 12-inch ball thrown underhand. He had a team on the South Side and I used to go to games with him. The team played at Bidwill Stadium on 75th and Euclid. My dad's team was called the Bluebirds. There was also a team from the West Side called the Perishey Bloomer Girls, and a North Side team called the Brachs."

In South Shore, where Jim Dowdle lived in the 1940s, softball was a major sport. "We used to play for some pretty good money and one time we were playing a team from the Southwest Side for $500. While we played the game, there were two guys sitting in a bar with the money. Then, after the game, somebody would call the bar and say, 'The Irish won,' and they would exchange the money. If you brought the money into the neighborhood we were afraid that a fight would break out. So, softball was like a conduit that brought people together."

Bill Jauss grew up in Sauganash on the Northwest Side. During the post-war years, there would be high stakes softball games that could involved large amounts of money. "When the war ended and the veterans would start coming back, there were some pretty serious money games — as much

Tony Reibel
North Center

Softball was a big part of my life when I was young. And it was softball all the time when I lived next to Bell School on the Northwest Side. There were two diamonds there, as was the case in most schoolyards. A softball was very cheap — we kicked in $.10 apiece, bought a ball, and the winning team won the ball. Softball only took a bat and a ball, and with twenty young boys you could go out and play.

Sixteen-inch softball started in Chicago in 1887 at the Farragut Boat Club. George Hancock was the man who came up with the game. The story is this: while watching the results of the Yale-Brown game on ticker tape, attendees took a broom handle and a tied-up old boxing glove and batted it around the gym. That was where it got the name "indoor" softball. It was called that well into the 1940s. They played it in gyms, playgrounds and, obviously, in the parks. One of the big advantages was that you didn't need a lot of space to play the game, like you did with a baseball diamond. I played it at Paul Revere Park where we had an indoor softball league. We played it in the winter before the basketball season would start. They would have eleven players on a side, including two positions that they called "upshort." It was fast pitch and the ball was very soft, not like the Clincher softball that we used later on. The two upshorts were positioned on either side of the pitcher, and they would run at the batter. Sometimes it would be one upshort, sometimes two, sometimes none of them, as the pitch was being thrown at the batter — just to distract him. You played the ball off the wall, and if you caught it off the wall before it hit the floor it was an out. It was a very fast-paced game.

Once spring came, you played softball outside. Softball was being played all summer long, including the grammar school leagues and CYO leagues. Plus, all the parks had their own leagues. During the summer we were using the Clincher, the George Young ball, or the Harwood ball — that ball was like a rock!

The Windy City League began in the '30s. It was very big. Harry Hannin formed the Windy City League — he was Abe Saperstein's right-hand man. Saperstein founded the Harlem Globetrotters. Big crowds watched games played at Parichy Stadium on the South Side, Hilburn Stadium on the North Side, St. Philip Stadium on the West Side, and North Town Stadium on the Far North Side.

The Queens, Welles Park League Softball Champions, ca. 1948. Lincoln Square (Courtesy of Tony Reibel.)

Ray Meyer with 1944-45 DePaul Blue Demons, 1944. Lincoln Park
(Courtesy of the Chicagoland Sports Hall of Fame.)

Ray Meyer
Austin

I was born on the West Side of Chicago near 13th and Central Park, right off Douglas Boulevard, in 1913. In the 1940s, I lived at 925 S. Austin Boulevard, right off Columbus Park, by the "L" tracks.

At that time, I was working at the LaSalle Hotel in the catering department and as a room clerk. We had a basketball team there that I coached, too. All of the players lived at the LaSalle Hotel. When the hotel was sold, I was out of work.

Jim Kelly was head of Columbus Park, and since I was out of work, I was refereeing basketball games at the park for $3 a game, or something like that. Then something odd happened in 1941. I was scouting for a number of schools — Notre Dame, Illinois, University of Chicago, Northwestern, Wisconsin and Iowa — and Kelly kept telling me that I had a good mind for basketball, but I didn't want to coach. He made an appointment for me anyway to go to Joliet Catholic High School, but I told him that I didn't want to interview for a job there. Kelly said that I had to since he had promised that I would be there. So, I went, and with my wife out in the car, I interviewed for the job. I was offered the coaching position. They told me that I would be paid $1,700 a year, but I told them that I couldn't live on that amount of money since I was married. I needed $1,800 a year. They wouldn't give me $1,800, so I went home.

That night, I got a call from the president of the University of Notre Dame. He asked me if I would come to South Bend to coach the basketball team. Their coach, George Keegan, had just had a heart attack that afternoon. They asked the Notre Dame players who they wanted as their coach, and they wanted me. So, on Sunday I was out of work, and by Monday, I was the coach of Notre Dame! I was supposed to referee some games on Monday night, and I was embarrassed about the new situation. So I asked my wife to call and say that I couldn't make it. Well, she told Jim Kelly that I couldn't make it and she told him why.

When I went to Notre Dame on Monday, they told me they would announce it, and that I shouldn't say anything. On Tuesday, when I was taking the team to play Marquette in Milwaukee, I passed through Chicago. Irv Kupcinet had a big headline announcing "Ray Meyer is coaching at Notre Dame." So, when I got back to Notre

Dame, the president called me and asked me why it was announced in the Chicago papers. I said that I didn't know what had happened. I didn't know until I went home about a week later and found out who let the cat out of the bag. Kelly was a friend of Kup, and when my wife, Marge, called Kelly, he told Kup and he had a scoop.

In 1942, I came to coach at DePaul after two years at Notre Dame. Then a big thing happened. I had about 24 players, but then the Selective Service draft came along and all of them were called except George Mikan, who was too tall, and Dick Tripto, who was 4-F. All the rest were gone. They were going to cancel the schedule, so I called Bill Shea, who was coaching at St. Phillips High School. Well, Bill said that he had a lot of 4-F's over there, so we got about four of them and played the schedule. We had about eight players, and when we practiced, the team manager and I played so that we would have ten players. We were successful because we had Mikan.

Actually, it was really tough to deal with the situation at that time. Travel was rough because we had to take the train all night to get to New York to play games there. We had nothing like it is today. We couldn't afford individual compartments on the train, so the players sat up all night or slept in their seats. It was very difficult at that time to even get a schedule of games, especially with Mikan, because the schools didn't want to lose to us.

When George left in 1946, we got Ed Mikan, and he was the second best center I ever had. We didn't know it because every place we went, he was compared to his brother, George. I remember playing in New York City — Ed played there in a tournament — and coaches there asked me, "Where has this guy been all year?" I said that he had been with us, but he was always being compared to George. Ed was about 6'8", a little shorter than George, but he never got the recognition he richly deserved.

All of our kids were from Chicago because I didn't have a recruiting budget. In the late '40s, we started to put kids in rooming houses around the school because we didn't have dormitories. The black players lived at Lawson YMCA. We were recruiting against schools that gave their players tuition, room and board, and books. DePaul only gave them tuition and books. I didn't have a budget at DePaul for 29 years, so I would have to find housing and convince them to play at the college.

At that time, if you had black players on your team, the other teams wouldn't play against you. When we had our first black player and we would play games in the south, we had to call ahead of time and let them know that we had black ballplayers. When we wanted to have dinner, they would tell us that the blacks had to eat in their rooms. I remember in St.

Louis, when they brought us our dinner, they said that the black ballplayers couldn't eat with us. Our first black player was in the late 1940s, and we began to get more black ballplayers in the 1950s. Even in the neighborhoods, it was an unfortunate situation for us to play around the city.

When I first started, we played some of the Big Ten schools. We had to play there twice and only once at home. We played our home games at Chicago Stadium because all we had was something that we called "The Barn" that only seated about 2,000 people. So, you couldn't play the big teams there, but you could play the Division II or III teams, and maybe a few lesser teams. So, we played all the big teams at the Chicago Stadium, and the others at DePaul. We played fifteen or sixteen games at Chicago Stadium, and we always played doubleheaders with Northwestern and Loyola. We drew very well at the Stadium.

When we started, the NIT was bigger than the NCAA, so we went to the NIT because we got more money. If you were a conference school, you would share the money with all the other schools. But, being an Independent, all the money came to us. When we were invited to play in the NCAA, I said no, we are going to the NIT. But the NCAA said that we were going to play, and then they put in a ruling saying that the NIT couldn't take teams until the NCAA had chosen all their teams for their tournament. Then the NCAA put in a "crumb" saying that the NIT could have a pre-season tournament, and eventually allowed them to have a post-season tournament. When DePaul played in the NIT, all the games were played in New York at Madison Square Garden. It was great for the kids to go New York, and from 1945-1950, they had the NCAA and the NIT tournaments in New York at Madison Square Garden.

Wrestling Advertisement, ca. 1940. Uptown (Courtesy of Joe Molitor.)

Joe Molitor
Lincoln Square

I was born in 1922 in the Ravenswood Manor neighborhood, and we lived at 4443 North Richmond. My father worked at City National Bank, where he organized special promotions. One that stands out the most was when he set up a wrestling ring in the lobby of the bank. They moved all the tables and desks out of the way and wrestled right there. "Strangler" Lewis and all the big wrestlers were there.

Eventually, my father became a promoter and manager of wrestlers. I would go to a lot of these matches as a kid, always in the best seats that my father would get me. The Chicago Stadium was the big time, but I also went to the Rainbow Fronton at Clark and Lawrence. I used to go up to the edge of the ring and pound on the canvas yelling, "Come on, throw him over here and let me at 'em!" One time the guy did just that! Back then, they used to get a guy over their head and twirl him around. Well, the wrestler threw him right at me — boom! Right in front of me. You have to be in that situation to appreciate it.

Now, these wrestlers would put their opponents into these holds, like the "Boston Crab." If you got stuck in that, you were dead. "Strangler" Lewis had a headlock that was impossible to get out of. He would lock his opponent's head between the big muscles on his arms and then flex so hard they would pass out — that's where the "strangle" comes from. Sometimes, the sport back then could get a little boring — a guy could get trapped in a headlock and head scissors and they would sit there for five minutes or longer. Nothing would happen. "Are you gonna give up?" he'd ask. "Nope!" his opponent would say. So he'd squeeze a little harder. It kills me to watch wrestling today. The wrestlers practice their matches today. Sometimes a guy is supposed to be getting killed and he doesn't even know he's being touched!

My father used to hang out with a lot of athletes. When I was a kid, a lot of these wrestlers used to come over to my house. They would pick me up by the scruff of my pants and lift me up like a barbell. Then, they would pass me around like a football back and forth.

My father also played baseball in the Banker's League. In those days, they had what was called the Industrial Leagues — the Banker's League, the Fireman's League, and the Policeman's League. All these little teams played around the city. A lot of second and third string pro players used to moonlight in these leagues to pick up extra money. Back then, the pros didn't get paid much at all. A lot of former big-leaguers played in the industrials — guys that were just too wore-out, and dumped by the big-leagues. Some of these games could get rough. I remember an Industrial League football game that was played with policemen stationed every ten feet along the field. It wasn't because of the teams fighting, it was because of the fans fighting! The fans could be terrible!

My father used to take me to games all the time. At the Logan Square Ballpark, at Kimball, Addison, and Elston, a lot of kids used to sneak under the grandstands during the game to look for money that had been dropped. If the peanut vendor fumbled the money that had been tossed to him from a four or five rows away there would be kids down there to find it. You'd sift through a few feet of peanut shells to search for change. It was a good ball park, and all the big draws would play there — the House of David team, the guys with the beards, and the Negro Leagues. They tore it down a long time ago.

We'd go to games at Wrigley Field, too. I remember a great triple-header in 1940s — the Major League old-timers played five innings, then the city high school championship was played, and this particular year the Hollywood All-Stars played, with Marilyn Monroe and Ward Bond. Hopalong Cassidy was the umpire and some of the "sweater girls" were cheerleaders.

In 1940, when I was in high school, my father put me to work collecting dues for the Old Timers Baseball Association dinner. The association was started to commemorate the 50th anniversary of baseball in Chicago, so the old-timers went back to players from the 1800s. Many guests would come, like Mayor Kelly, Fire Chief Bill Hughes, broadcaster Leo Fisher, and Charlie Grimm would play the ukulele. They had a lot of talent in those days, and would sing songs and give toasts. It's a wonder any of them could stand up when it was over because they gave so many toasts, sometimes as many as twenty! This guy would toast to the White Stockings, then somebody would toast to the Cubs, and back and forth.

We didn't have women in the organization back then, so people would get up and tell stories from their playing days. Stories about the long train rides from New York where they'd sneak woman into their bunks, play cards, and drink. The baseball writers would travel with the players, and they could be just as bad! It's not like that anymore, you know.

Dolores "Champ" Mueller Bajda
Belmont Cragin

I grew up around Fullerton and Pulaski on the Far Northwest Side. There were a lot of German, Norwegian, Swedes, and Polish there — a real mix of people. I spent most of my time at Mozart Playground, that's 2200 North Hamlin. We lived at 2148 North Hamlin, so it was just a hop, skip, and a jump to the playground and the school. I lived in that playground from morning until night. I was there everyday. That was it.

One Saturday, when I was about eight years old, I went over to the playground. Before I left, I pinned my father's athletic award medals to my blouse. When I got there a teacher asked, "Are those yours?" I said, "Yes, they are!" She said, "Well, you must be a pretty good athlete. We'll have to call you 'Champ'." That nickname stuck with me the rest of my life.

We played many sports and games there. We had "batball," which we played with a volleyball. It had the same rules as baseball, but you hit the ball with your hand, and the other team threw the ball at you to get you out. We had "fieldball," which was a combination of football and soccer. You couldn't run with the ball, you had to throw it and pass it off, and get it though the goal. That was a tough game, because we played against the boys. We also played softball at Milwaukee and Tripp in the Chicagoland Girls Softball League. We traveled all over the city to play games — at Shewbridge Field at 74th and Aberdeen on the South Side and at 51st and State against the girls there. The games weren't always played on ball fields, but sometimes in big empty lots.

In 1948, when I was seventeen, my gym teacher at Mozart, Mr. Jacobson, started coaching girl's baseball. He asked me if I wanted to play pro baseball. So I went out and bought a glove and he taught me how to pitch over-hand. He'd make me throw about two hours a day! He taught me how to throw the knuckle ball and the curve ball, and that's when I started to play at Thillens Stadium. I played pitcher and third base. This wasn't the All-American Girls League, but it was a farm league with four teams — North Town Co-eds, North Town Debs, Blue Island Stars, and the Blue Island Dianas. The girls on the South Side were good, and there was a lot of competition. If it wasn't for the Thillens family and this league, the girls from Chicago who wanted to play pro ball wouldn't have made it to the All-American Girls League.

Girl's baseball had the same rules as the men's Major Leagues, but the bases and the mound were shorter. We played every night at nine, right after the men played 16-inch softball, and we had good crowds watch us. A season would be about 50 or 60 games, and we got $5.00 a game. Like the All-American Girls, we played in skirts, and each team had their own chaperon. She had to make sure the girls were on time, dressed perfectly for the games, and went right home.

We had fun and played hard. It was great playing under those lights. We girls could hit the ball over the fence, and even beyond the fence into the river. What we did try to do was hit the ball over the center field wall and hit the sign with the armored car. We would aim for that to get the cash prize.

At the end of the season they had a tryout for the All-American Girls League at the field house on Lawndale at 18th Street. We had to practice, play and slide on a wooden floor! All the scouts were there, and they chose from the best girls. I got picked by South Bend to play for the Blue Sox in Indiana, and other girls went to different teams. The league had teams in Peoria, Rockford, Kenosha, Racine, Muskegon, Grand Rapids, Fort Wayne and later, the Chicago Colleens. It was great, and it was the first time I really went someplace. We made good money. When girls first came up they got about $50.00 a game, but some got up to a $100.00 a game. That was a lot of money back then.

When I played home games in South Bend I lived with a private family in town, not at a hotel. When we were on the road we stayed in hotels. We traveled around in those old buses. There were no interstates back then so we took the old country roads. Some girls played cards, some would sing, and some would sleep. It was just like in the movie A League of Their Own.

Even after I was done playing for the All-American Girls I went back and played at the Mozart playground — softball, table tennis, volleyball, horse shoes, or any sport. I loved to play them all.

Dolores "Champ" Mueller Bajda (left) at Thillens Stadium, 1949. West Ridge
(Courtesy of Dolores Mueller Bajda)

as $1,000. It wasn't our money, but it was the backers who would put up the cash. It worked out to $50 a man, a lot of money back then. Those games were played at a park at Crawford (Pulaski) and Touhy. I remember one time we were playing a game and were comfortably ahead with a couple of innings to go, when it started to rain. There was all this money and we had to decide what to do with it while we were waiting through the rain delay. So, it was amicably decided that the fiancees of two of the guys would sit alone in a car and hold the money. So, here were all of these guys on both teams hovering around and wondering if these broads were going to take off with the money. Finally, the umpires decided to call the game and declare that my team had won. We took the money down to Bob Wolf's Village Inn at the corner of Crawford and Devon and dumped it out on the table. I had never seen so much money in my life. As I recall it, there were only one or two $20 bills, maybe a $10 or $5, and the rest were $1 bills."

High School and College Sports

In the 1940s, high school and college sports were very popular across all religious, ethnic and racial lines. Rivalries were played out in both the public and parochial school leagues, drawing large crowds for football, basketball, and a wide range of other sports. For many participants, the games were about more than the final score, as neighborhoods competed against other neighborhoods for bragging rights. DePaul, Loyola, and the University of Chicago often played in front of large crowds in their home gyms and at the Chicago Stadium. In particular, the DePaul Blue Demons saw great success in the 1940s, with Ray Meyer coaching the team to the NIT and NCAA tournaments.

Bruce Bachmann went to Austin High School and remembers great basketball and football teams in the '40s. "The Austin football team was a powerhouse during those years, but not the basketball team because all the great basketball players went to Marshall High School. During the '20s, '30s and most of the '40s, basketball seemed to be a Jewish sport, a ghetto sport. Of course, you didn't need a lot of money to play basketball. When I was growing up, the powerhouses in public high school sports were Von Steuben, Roosevelt and Marshall."

Irv Bemoras was a star basketball player at Marshall High School, the University of Illinois, and in the pros with the St. Louis Hawks. "On the West Side, I grew up around the American Boys Commonwealth (ABC), a Jewish boys club near Lawson grammar school. They had quite a few programs there. They had music, a band, a glee club, and all kinds of sport activities and workshops. There were two important people there:

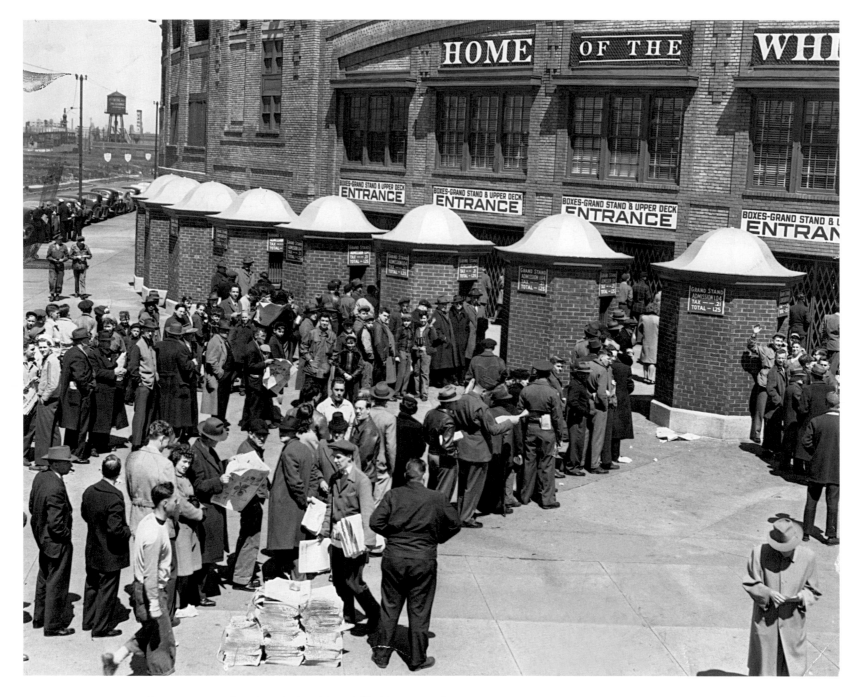

Opening Day at Comiskey Park, 35th and Shields, 1946. Armour Square (Courtesy of the Chicago Sun-Times.)

Ed McElroy
New City

I was born in 1925 on the South Side, at 55th and Morgan, in Visitation Parish. I used to play basketball at Visitation and we won a championship there. Across the street is the church and I used to be in the band and the choir. Visitation Parish was the key to my upbringing.

We used to play football in the middle of Sherman Park, and I probably played baseball there for two million hours, sometimes nine or ten hours a day. I was good at baseball and was batting champ and most valuable player. During the 1940s, at a very young age, I was with the White Sox as the batting practice/bullpen catcher. I was exposed to something that 99.9% of kids were never exposed to. At that time, the ball games were at 3:00PM each day. Don Kolloway, who played second base, would pick up Bob Kennedy, who lived at 9755 Charles, and then they would pick me up at 55th Street. A lot of times we'd stop at a drugstore where they had milkshakes with vanilla wafers for $.15. It was out of this world! Then, we would go down to the ballpark really early.

My name wasn't on the team roster, but I got to meet a lot of people I never would have met otherwise. I was a very young kid, but I was exposed to a lot of things because of this opportunity. It was extremely interesting meeting all these people, most of which I never would have met otherwise. At that time, the clubhouse at Comiskey Park was on the second floor, and you would come down through the runway and dugout and onto the field. So, I'd be coming up and down and people would want my autograph. I felt a little uncomfortable with this, so I went to Mr. Dykes, the manager, one day and said, "Mr. Dykes, I have a question." He said, "Yes, Edward?" He always called me Edward. So, I told him about people wanting my autograph. He said, "Edward, as long as you are in a White Sox uniform, you are somebody." So, from then on, I signed the autographs.

Jackie Friedman, the director, and Bosco Levin, who ran the gym — he was also a gym teacher at Marshall. Those were the days when they had excellent basketball players. That was where I learned all my fundamentals."

Morgan Murphy, Jr. recalls high school sports in the parochial schools. "I remember during my freshman year at Leo High School, Leo won the Catholic League football championship. I played a lot of sports in school, including basketball and football, and my life seemed to be centered around sports at Leo. We used to start our spring practice at the beach when Joe Gleason was our coach. I was the quarterback and captain of the team in my senior year at Leo and I got a football scholarship to Northwestern University where I played for two years."

Jack Hogan also went to Leo High School and remembers intramural basketball in the 1940s. "In 1943, right before I went into the service, even though I lived in St. Sabina Parish, I played basketball with the Leo CYO team. In those days, it was customary for the CYO (Catholic Youth Organization) champs to play the BBYO (B'nai B'rith Youth Organization) champs. The champs that year were Marshall High School's lightweight team. At that point they had won 82 straight games, but we beat them in the game played at Lane Tech on April 1, 1943."

George Mitsos had great success in high school sports. "I was into sports in high school and played basketball for three years at Amundsen. I was also a co-captain of the swimming team. I went to grammar school and high school with Bob Fosse, the dancer and movie producer. He lived on the other side of Montrose, and we were on the swimming team together. In high school, I broke the rules because I swam and played basketball in the same season. But, we had a real good swimming team and they were short on basketball players. Then, my third and fourth years, I ended up playing with two fellows who would lead the Big Ten in scoring for three years. Our high school was the second smallest high school in the city, and Sullivan was the smallest. In my third year, we won North Section in baseball, football, and basketball."

Illinois Secretary of State Jesse White was both a high school and college star athlete, and went on to play in the minor leagues for the Cubs. "At Waller High School, I became an all-city baseball and basketball player. I scored 68 points in a high school game, and then I won a scholarship to Alabama State College in Montgomery. I was a forward and I could jump high. I became an all-conference baseball and basketball player in college. After I graduated from college I signed a contract to play baseball for the Cubs. In March of 1957, I was scheduled to go to spring training, but I was called up for military service. After I was formally discharged from

Bob Kennedy
Washington Heights

I was born and raised on the South Side of Chicago, and baptized at Visitation Church at 55th and Halsted. We lived in the parish until I was about seven years old, and then we moved out to 7146 S. Morgan. The next move was to 9722 S. Loomis, then 10220 Charles, 10041 Charles, and 9755 Charles. Can you imagine? I haven't thought about those street addresses in years! I went to St. Margaret's grammar school, and then to De La Salle High School.

I signed my first baseball contract on June 22, 1937, at Comiskey Park, the same place I sold Blue Valley popcorn for the Louis-Braddock fight when Joe Louis won the title. The boxing ring was at second base for that fight. I went away to play ball the next day.

The White Sox didn't have a minor league system, but they had a couple of players planted here and there. I went to Dallas for a while and then went to Vicksburg, Mississippi, and then back to Dallas and finished the season. A funny thing happened in 1938 when I went to spring training in Dallas. We were playing an exhibition game — I was just seventeen years old — and I'm warming up before the ball game. I threw the ball and Lou Gehrig walked right between us and I almost hit him in the head. I hollered to him and he ducked and the ball just missed him. I apologized and he said, "Don't worry about it kid, don't worry about it." That was when he was starting to get sick.

So, I went to the plate, and Bill Dickey is catching and "Bump" Hadley is pitching. Dickey looked at me and could see that I hadn't begun to shave yet. He said, "Can you hit the fast ball?" "Yeah," I said. He threw a fast ball. Strike one. He said, "You didn't believe me, did you?" I said, "No, I didn't." He replied, "Okay, be ready, here's another fast ball." And, I hit a line drive base hit. The next time up, he said, "Can you hit the curve ball?" I said, "Yes, sir." So, Bump Hadley, who had a real good curve ball, threw the curve and I hit a line drive base hit. He looked at me like, " What the hell was going on!" The next time I came up there were a couple of men on base, and Bill says, "Okay, kid, you're on your own."

I got to the majors on September 1, 1939, with the White Sox. I came up for the month of September to finish the season, and I was paid $235. I was a third baseman, mostly, then I moved to the outfield. When I was with the Sox I lived at home in Chicago at 95th and Ashland Avenue. I would travel to the games by streetcar because my dad wouldn't let me have a car. I did the same thing when I went to high school, and took the same streetcar to get there. When I got off at 35th Street, instead of taking the 35th Street streetcar east, I would get off and walk from the corner where Bob's Tavern was located at 35th and Wentworth. It was tough getting home after we lost because there wouldn't be any seats on the streetcar, and you'd be standing there holding onto one of the straps and the guys who were sitting in front of you would say, "Why the hell did they get that third baseman? That guy can't play ball!" I would have to listen to that jazz all the way home.

A trivia question — what team played nine innings in the big leagues and no averages changed? The Sox were the only team in history where that happened. Bob Feller no-hit the White Sox to begin the season on Opening Day of 1940. We started with zero and we ended with zero. That was the only no-hitter ever pitched on Opening Day.

In 1940, I played 154 games for the White Sox, and, in fact, I batted more than 600 times as lead-off hitter. I was paid $400 a month. That year, the White Sox had a pretty good season. Of course, the war was coming and everybody thought about that. I was in the military from 1942 to 1945, and was stationed in the Pacific toward the end of the war. I was a fighter instructor in Pensacola, Florida. In fact, I was one of Ted Williams' first instructors down there. We became great friends.

When I returned from the war, I immediately came back to the White Sox. In 1946, everyone was damn glad that we were back. Those were tough times. Owners were trying to get organized and get back to the way baseball had been before the war.

I went to Cleveland in 1948, then Baltimore, and I finished my playing career with Brooklyn in 1957. I came back to Chicago to manage the Cubs in 1963, 1964 and 1965, and I became general manager of the Cubs on November 1, 1976. I was with the Cubs organization until the Wrigleys sold the club to the Chicago Tribune in 1981.

I don't have a squawk in the world about anything. I had just about the most wonderful life that a man can have.

Children Cheer for the Cubs Victory over Harry "The Cat" Brechcen 3-1, 1948. Lakeview (Courtesy of the Chicago Sun-Times.)

Andy Pafko
Kelvyn Park

I was born in 1921 and grew up in a little town by the name of Boyceville, Wisconsin, about 25 miles out of Eau Claire. I didn't get to Chicago until the tail end of the Pacific Coast League season of 1943. When our season was over, the Cubs had about thirteen games left, so they brought four of us up from the club. Of course, I had never been to Chicago before and I had never seen Wrigley Field. That was quite a thrill for me, and I'll never forget my first time at bat. I had an extra base hit and drove in a couple of runs. The next time up I got another hit and drove in a couple of more runs. I broke in kind of good, and it was a great feeling. I will never forget the feeling of walking into Wrigley Field for the first time. I opened the clubhouse door, and the first guy I ran into was Stan Hack, the Cub's third baseman. He said, "Andy Pafko, welcome to the big leagues. Welcome to Chicago!" That was the greatest moment of my life. I mean, just getting into a big league clubhouse, and then playing in Chicago for as long as I did. The Cubs radio announcer, Bert Wilson, used to call me "the kid from Boyceville."

I played outfield, and primarily I was a center fielder. I also played right and left field, and eventually I even played third base for the Cubs, when Stan Hack retired. They had no third baseman at the time, so I filled in and had a good year. I made the all-star team as a third baseman.

When I first came to the Cubs, I didn't move to Chicago. I always lived back home, but after I played with the Cubs for a couple of years I met a girl in Chicago and we got married. Then, of course, I made my home here in Chicago. We lived on the Northwest Side, at Grand Avenue and Camerling. We later moved to the Kelvyn Park neighborhood, and I lived there for about 20 years, until we moved to Mt. Prospect.

When I was living in Chicago, I used to drive to the baseball games at Wrigley Field. I drove my car the same route everyday, but if I had a bad day, I would skip a couple of streets in order to change my luck. I was kind of superstitious, and I don't know if it helped. I think that a lot of ballplayers have their own pet superstitions. When I drove from Kelvyn Park, it was Diversey to Southport, then Southport up to Addison, and then right to the ballpark where I would park my car. They had a special place for the ballplayers to park their cars, along the railroad tracks just south of the fire station.

Wrigley Field was a beautiful place to play baseball. A lot of players complained about the wind blowing in — of course it blows in. People said it was a pitcher's park, but it's a fair park, and the distances are fair for the pitcher and hitter. If you hit a home run at Wrigley Field, you deserve it. It was not like a lot of other ballparks where I played, like the old Polo Grounds. It was so close, you could drop kick the ball over the left field fence there. It was only about 280' down the line. So, Wrigley Field was a fair park for both pitchers and hitters.

The year the Cubs were in the World Series was a great year. In 1945, we were battling the Cardinals for the championship and I drove in the winning run to clinch it for the Cubs. I hit a fly ball into right field and that put us in the World Series. Of course, playing in the series was a tremendous, tremendous feeling. There is nothing else like it. Ultimately, when you get to the big leagues, your number one thing is to get into the World Series. I was very fortunate in my career, because I played on three different clubs and they all went to the World Series. I'll never forget the first one in 1945 — that was thrilling.

I used to room with Bob Rush, a great pitcher, and when I was traded to the Dodgers, I roomed with Johnny Schmidt, a former Wisconsin resident. But, with the Cubs, Bob Rush was my roommate most of the time. I was with the Cubs until 1951, just about the time Hank Sauer came to the Cubs. Do you know how the trade happened? We were playing the Dodgers in a three-game series in the middle of the 1951 season at Wrigley Field. I came out on the field before the second game of the series, and we were standing around the batting cage during batting practice. Big Don Newcombe came out of the Dodger dugout and he yells to me, "Hey, Pafko, you're going to be a Dodger tomorrow!" My God, did my ears perk up. I hadn't heard any rumors around Chicago about me being traded, but I guess the Dodgers were looking for a left fielder. So, we played that second game and I showered, went home and my wife made dinner. The phone rang, and it was the Cub's front office calling to tell me that the Cubs had just made an eight-player trade, four Dodgers for four Cubs. I was one of the eight. My poor wife started to cry because I had to go out to the ballpark the next day and pack my bags because the Dodgers were leaving for St. Louis. So, I went to the ballpark and into the Cub clubhouse to get all my personal gear. After I got my stuff together, I walked across the infield and went into the Dodger clubhouse on the first base side — I was a Cub one day and a Dodger the next. It was a strange feeling. In those days you got traded, so you didn't mind that issue, but the way it happened right in the middle of the season. If you get traded in the off-season, you have time to adjust. But, *here I'm a Cub one day and I'm a Dodger the next day. The trade was very unpopular among Cub fans. I had many good seasons with the Cubs, and I appreciated that the fans of Chicago were loyal to me. But no matter what, I always gave it 100%.*

Now, that was the same year that Bobby Thompson hit the "shot heard around the world." I was the left fielder in that game and the ball went over my head. Everybody knows that Ralph Branca threw the pitch and that Bobby Thompson hit the homer, but very few people know that I was the left fielder who watched the ball go over his head. Yours truly.

People tell me now, "Andy, don't you wish you were playing today with all the big money?" I always say, "No." And I have no regrets. I played during the greatest era of all, the '40s and the '50s. I played against Joe Dimaggio, Ted Williams, Bob Feller and all those guys. You can't replace those guys. It was a great, great era.

To me, it was just a thrill to be in the big leagues. I played with the Dodgers and the Milwaukee Braves, but I think that the greatest fans are here in Chicago. They have to be — they've been so loyal all these years. It's been since 1945 that the Cubs were in their last World Series. It's hard to believe that they haven't won one since 1908, or been in the World Series since 1945. I think that the Cub fans are the best fans in the country.

Andy Pafko at Wrigley Field, ca. 1948. Lakeview
Photograph by George Brace.

Billy Pierce at Comiskey Park, 1949. Armour Square
Photograph by George Brace.

Billy Pierce
Hyde Park

I was born in 1927 in Detroit, Michigan. During my playing days I lived in Detroit in the off-season, but when I played in Chicago, I lived in an apartment hotel in Hyde Park. I stayed at the Flamingo, the Piccadilly, the Shoreland — they all had furnished apartments and I would bring my family along.

I got into professional baseball when I signed my first contract in the fall of 1944 with Detroit. My first season was 1945, and I was with the Detroit Tigers about 3/5 of the year, while the other 2/5 of the year was spent at Buffalo. I was eligible for the World Series against the Cubs. I didn't pitch in the games, except for during batting practice. It was a tremendous thrill to be in the World Series. The year before I was still in high school, and here I was a year later in the World Series. It was quite a thrill, I tell you. I don't think that a young person really realizes what is going on, but it was a tremendous thrill. There is no doubt that the World Series is the top thing of all. The Tigers played in Briggs Stadium, and it changed to Tiger Stadium after that. Wrigley Field was the same that it is now, and it hasn't changed much over the years. We were playing in the fall, so the vines weren't very green. I had never been in a National League ballpark before, and it was very exciting. The ballpark was jammed, and there was bunting all over. The Tigers won the series 4-3.

In fall of 1948, I was traded to the White Sox. So, from 1949 to 1961, I was in Chicago with the Sox. I had 211 victories in baseball, 186 with the White Sox. I was traded for Aaron Robinson, who was a catcher, and with the short porch in right field, Detroit wanted to get a catcher to hit that porch out there. They had Trout, Newhouser, Trucks, and a big group of young pitchers. I was so bad that they threw $10,000 into the deal. As for salaries around that time, I was fortunate. I received a bonus when I signed my original contract, but I was signed to a major league contract at minimum salary of $600 a month for seven months. It was a little different than it is now. Back then, for a young fellow only eighteen years old, that wasn't bad.

My first full season with the Sox was in 1949 and my record was 7-15. At that time Frank Lane was making trade after trade because in 1948 they had lost a hundred or so games. They were getting rid of all the older veterans on the ball club and going with youth. We had trades with every team in the American League, and probably with the National League. Teams were changing all the time, and things didn't really develop in Chicago until 1951. Attendance wasn't too strong at Comiskey Park when I got here, but we would draw a little better when we played the Yankees. In later years, we drew fantastic crowds when they came to town.

One of the worst things about the White Sox in the 1940s — and it changed after a while — was the aroma from the Stock Yards during the night games. When I was with Detroit, I made up my mind that there were two towns I hoped that I would never go to — one was Philadelphia, and the other was Chicago — just because of the aroma from the Stock Yards. But, after a while, maybe the winds changed and slowly the odor started dwindling. We would get the breezes at Comiskey Park first, and then the odor would move toward downtown Chicago.

When I got to the Sox, I had a good opportunity to pitch. Jack Onslow was our manager and we had a lot of young fellows on the 1949 team. One of the key things that year was that we had veteran Luke Appling, and we had a young man by the name of Gus Zernial, who was just starting out and hitting home runs for us. But then he dove for a ball and broke his collarbone, and that hurt us. Later, Gus went to Philadelphia.

If I remember correctly, in spring training in 1949 we had seven left-handed pitchers who were trying out for the club. The Sox were thinking about signing kids for bonuses or making trades. In those days, there were two different trade deadlines — May 15 and June 15. You never knew who was going to be traded. We went out for a picnic one time to our pitching coach Ray Berry's cottage. When we got back, two of the fellows had been traded. We were always thinking that it could happen.

Comiskey Park changed from when I first arrived there. It was 440' feet to center field and the wind blew in most of the time. I remember once when Vern Stephens, a pretty good hitter, hit a ball off me. I turned around and saw the outfielder go out a couple of steps, but then he came in a couple of steps and caught it. It was a big park for pitchers. But soon they moved center field in, and actually after my first three or four years there Comiskey was not what you would call a "pitcher's ballpark" anymore, because the balls carried and more balls were hit out of the park. In fact, one year they put in a temporary fence about 10'-15' feet closer to the plate. There were about fifteen home runs hit, and the Sox hit two of them. So, they took the fence down. It was 352' feet down the right and left field lines, and that was a pretty fair distance. Now all the ballparks are smaller, meaning more home runs.

Things began to change for the Sox by the early 1950s. In 1950, Nellie Fox came to Chicago and that helped. Slowly, he became a different kind of a hitter and he began using a bottle bat and spraying the ball around. He became a very tough hitter to get out. In 1951, Minnie Minoso came to the Sox, and we had Chico Carrasquel at shortstop, who came over from the Dodger organization. Even in 1950, we had a pretty good defensive ball club. By 1951, the team really started developing. In fact, we were in first place at the All-Star Game. But, we were all young fellows and although some of the guys were hitting .330 by mid-year, they ended up dropping off to .290 in the second half of the season. Then, by 1952, we had much of the team that would be successful in the 1950s, including Jim Rivera, Minoso, Fox, Sherman Lollar, and me. That team stayed around a long time. Minnie, Nellie, Sherman and myself were each with the White Sox for ten years or longer.

The White Sox fans were tremendous and they were rooting for us all the time. Whenever we went into the local taverns after a game, the fans were always good to us and they enjoyed the game and the players. In those years, we had fan clubs. Nellie had one, I had one, Rivera had one, Lollar had one, and Minnie had one. They were little clubs with boys and girls and we were invited over to their houses with their parents and, one time, even had dinner with them. In fact, when we had our first child in 1953, they brought my mother over so they could have a shower for my wife. It was a very close-knit situation here on the South Side. Fans were very dedicated and loyal. It is always remarkable to me how many families are split on their loyalties — one is a Cub fan, one a Sox fan. But, it is a good thing because it gives them something to argue about.

the military in March of 1959, I began my baseball career. I went to Mesa, Arizona, and then, after spring training, they shipped me off to Carlsbad, New Mexico. That was class D Ball, the lowest classification. I led the team in hitting and stolen bases, and I played center field."

College basketball was of interest to Otho Kortz when he was growing up on the South Side. "In the 1940s, I went down to the old Chicago Stadium where they had great college basketball doubleheaders. I could take my little brother to the Stadium and it only cost $.07 for me on the streetcar and $.03 for him. We would watch great basketball games, as well as hockey games with the Blackhawks. I would even go down there to see prizefights with some of the big names in boxing. I loved going there."

Professional Sports

Chicago had some very successful professional teams throughout the 1940s. The Cubs won their last National League pennant in 1945, only to lose in seven games to the Detroit Tigers in the World Series that year. The White Sox, while popular on the South Side, continued to rebuild their franchise during the '40s and struggled to attract fans to Comiskey Park. Despite this, they did finish as high as 3rd place in the American League standings in 1941.

Like professional baseball, Chicago also had two professional football teams — the Bears and the Cardinals. The Bears were champions of the National Football League in 1940, 1941, 1943 and 1946, and after going 11-0 during the 1942 season, lost the championship to the Washington Redskins. Their cross-town rivals, the Chicago Cardinals, won the title in 1947 and lost the championship in 1948 to the Philadelphia Eagles.

The Blackhawks also did well during the '40s, competing in the Stanley Cup finals in 1944, but losing to the Montreal Canadiens. The National Basketball Association had its first year in 1947, and the Chicago Stags lost the championship series 4-1 to the Philadelphia Warriors.

Growing up in Chicago has always meant choosing a favorite team. You were either a Cubs or Sox fan. Although neighborhood location often influenced choice of teams, many South and West Siders became Cub fans during the '40s because the Cubs had more success during the decade. Bill Jauss became a big Cub fan in the 1940s. "I would get on the Peterson bus in Sauganash, take it to Clark Street and then take the Clark Street trolley to Wrigley Field. I went to Cub games with my dad the first few times, and then he said that since I knew how to transfer buses, I could go with my friends. I would get by with $1.00 to pay for admission, food and drink, but I was at least twelve or thirteen years old before I started drinking beer at the games! My reaction when I went to my first Cub game was,

'Oh my gosh!' Wrigley Field was like a cathedral. Although I usually sat in the bleachers, I really loved to sit in the grandstands because the seats were so close to the field. In those days, the Cubs were all over the radio band on five or six stations — WGN Radio didn't have exclusive rights. I can remember announcers like Charlie Grimm, Hal Totten, and Harry Creighton."

Harriet Wilson Ellis was a Cub fan when she grew up in the '40s. "We could almost walk to Wrigley Field, and I went there a lot. My mother would let my brother take me when he was ten or eleven years old and I was just seven. He would drop me off in the bleachers and then he would go sit in the grandstands. There was a fabulous vendor there called 'Gravel Gertie,' a man with a gravely-sounding voice, and he would kind of look out for me. Then, after the game, my brother would pick me up and we would go back home. I first started going to Wrigley Field in 1944 or 1945. My father only had two tickets for the 1945 World Series, so he took my brother. We grew up idolizing Phil Cavaretta, Andy Pafko, and Charlie Grimm."

Joseph Lamendella remembers going to Wrigley Field in the '40s. "I started going to the Cub games at Wrigley Field when I was around ten years old, and I would sit in the bleachers. I brought my lunch one day and it fell onto the center field warning track, and Andy Pafko, the Cub center fielder, picked up my lunch and threw it back up to me. I probably still have the bag somewhere. I can remember going to the Cub games during the war when Dominic Delassandro and Bill Nicholson played for the Cubs. I enjoyed being out there in the open with the guys."

Albany Park resident Joel Weisman has gone to Cub games since childhood. "My mother would take us. We would get on the Montrose bus and take it to Clark, then take the Clark streetcar to Addison. We would just walk up to the window and buy tickets. I went to my first game with the Cub Scouts. My father used to take me on Sundays because he had to work all week, and I always would talk him into going to doubleheaders. It was quite a long day. I was a big fan and I really liked baseball. By the time we moved to West Rogers Park, I would come home from school and turn the sound off the television and announce the game myself. I actually was allowed to go to some of those Cub games by myself — sometimes for free — if you collected the cushions from the seats after the game, you would get a free pass to another game. I later worked at Wrigley Field and Comiskey Park as a vendor."

Dan Rostenkowski remembers getting into the games for free as well. "If you cleaned up the place a little — wiped off the seats — you could come back and watch the next game for nothing. They would give you a little ticket to return the next day. The games started at 3 p.m. each day, and sometimes the nuns would let us out of school at 2:30 p.m. if we had a ticket to the game. I remember being at the park with my dad the day in 1938 when the Cubs played the Pittsburgh Pirates and Gabby Hartnett hit the 'homer in the gloaming.' They were going to call the game because it was dark and foggy, but they continued playing and Gabby hit the decisive home run. I was ten years old and my dad put me on his shoulders, turned me around and said, 'Danny, look at all these people. You'll never see happier people in your life.'"

West Sider Mike Perlow has similar memories of the Cubs in the 1940s. "I used to go to Wrigley Field a lot. When I was eight or nine years old, I'd go with my friends. After the game, we would clean up the park and they would give us free tickets for the next game. About 40 or 50 of us kids would clean up the ballpark and pick up the seat cushions. I went to 30-40 games in 1945, but not the World Series. I remember Andy Pafko, Hank Sauer, Stan Hack, Hank Borowy, and Lenny Murillo. I happened to have been there when Andy Pafko lost the ball in the vines and someone got an inside-the-park home run. Very rarely did I go to White Sox games. It was much easier to get to Wrigley Field. I would take the Madison streetcar to Clark Street and then the Clark streetcar or the "L" to Wrigley Field."

During the 1940s, many of the Cub and Sox ballplayers lived in Chicago's neighborhoods. Marvin Aspen recalls, "Bill Nicholson of the Cubs lived in our Albany Park neighborhood. They used to call him 'Swoosh.' He hit a lot of home runs, but he also struck out a lot — that's why he got the name 'Swoosh.' He was an outfielder who had some great years during the war, but when the 'real' ballplayers came home, he wasn't as good. One of the things the kids in the neighborhood would do, and these were innocent kids, believe me, was after school they would ring the doorbell and ask for Mr. Nicholson's autograph. The only reason they did that was to get Mrs. Nicholson to answer the door. She stayed at home in the afternoon, and she always answered the door wearing a slip. That, of course, in terms of dress today, means absolutely nothing. But to some young pre-teens, that was the big thrill!"

Ed Brennan also grew up on the West Side and became a Cub fan. "We were mostly Cub fans out there in Austin, but there were some kids who were White Sox fans. Since there were all kinds of taverns near us and we could get a deposit if we brought beer bottles back, I would fill my wagon up and take it down Madison Street and get the money to go to Cub games. We would get on the Madison streetcar and go to Central, then take the Central bus to Addison and the Addison bus to Wrigley Field. I went to Wrigley Field in 1945 when they won the pennant, and I knew all the players. I remember that some of my friends were White Sox fans because they liked to listen to Bob Elson when he announced the games by reading it off the ticker tape."

As Bill Gleason remembers it, "I became a White Sox fan at birth. My grandfather, who came from Tipperary, Ireland, was the family's first Sox fan. Then came my dad who saw his first game at the old White Sox Park at 39th and Wentworth in 1904. Now, me and my sons and grandsons are Sox fans. For variety, one of my sisters is an ardent Cub fan, and my dad says that's worse than if she left the church."

Fr. Gene Smith was also a White Sox fan. "I saw my first White Sox game when I was ten years old — a Labor Day double header against the Detroit Tigers. When I was a little older my mom would make a couple of sandwiches for me, and a couple of the other kids would do the same thing, and we would take the Green Hornet down Wentworth Avenue to Comiskey Park. We would spend Sunday there, right after mass. We would get autographs and talk to the players."

Jim Dowdle has been a Sox fan since growing up in South Shore. "I grew up on the South Side and have always been a die-hard White Sox fan. My first job was as an Andy Frain turnstile operator at Comiskey for a dollar a game. I wouldn't be caught dead at Wrigley Field! Ironically, in 1981, I made the presentation to the *Chicago Tribune* board and convinced them to buy the Chicago Cubs. One of the members of the board said to me, 'Well, you've got to be proud of this deal.' And, I responded, 'Well, I am. But there is a tombstone in Calvary Cemetery that has just moved — my father would be very upset with me for what I just did. He was a die-hard White Sox fan.'"

Sandy Bank grew up in Hyde Park/Kenwood. "My father was a grain broker at the Chicago Board of Trade. After the Board of Trade would close at 1:15 p.m., my father would leave work, get on the streetcar, and during baseball season, he would often go to White Sox games, since they started in those days at 3:00 p.m. Occasionally, when there was no school or I got out of school early, I would meet him at Comiskey Park. During the summer, I would go to the White Sox games quite a bit, and I remember one year I saw 75 games."

The 1940s were a great decade for Chicago football. Both the Bears and Cardinals were champions during the era, but after 1959, there was only one football team remaining here. Charles Bidwill's father owned the Chicago Cardinals, and he has strong memories about professional football during the war years. "At the time of Pearl Harbor, my father owned the Chicago Cardinals. He had bought the team in 1932, and they played all

Neighborhood Kids at the Home of Phil Cavaretta, ca. 1940. Photograph by George Brace.

their games at Comiskey Park. The impact of the war on the Cardinals was great. I remember that in 1944 the team merged with the Pittsburgh Steelers and became the Pitt-Cards for one year because they couldn't get enough players and my father and Mr. Rooney couldn't afford the payrolls at that time. I remember my dad talking about how hard it was to keep the team going. Attendance was light during those years, and the situation didn't change until the war was over."

Don Stonesifer was raised in Logan Square in the '40s and became an All-American football player at Northwestern University and a star for the Chicago Cardinals. "I started high school in 1941, graduated in 1945, and then I went into the service from 1945 to 1946. I came back from Germany in 1946, and 1947 was my first year at Northwestern. That helped me with football because I was two years older and forty pounds heavier. Otherwise, I would probably not have made the football team. My dad was a big Bears fan, and when George Halas told me that he was going to draft me in the upcoming NFL draft, my father was very happy about that. But instead, the Chicago Cardinals drafted me because they were higher in the draft. My father said to me, 'I hope that you play well, but I will always pull for the Bears.' I played six years with the Cardinals, from 1951 to 1956. I signed my first contract for $7,000, with a $500 bonus. When the Cardinals decided to move to St. Louis, I chose to stay in Chicago."

Entertainment in the Neighborhood

In the 1940s, residents of Chicago's neighborhoods had a wide variety of entertainment options to choose from. In addition to first- and second-run movie theaters in each neighborhood, residents could also listen to music at jazz and night clubs, dance in one of the many ballrooms or dance halls, and thrill to the rides at Riverview Amusement Park.

Of course, radio was in its heyday, and Chicagoans listened to the many popular entertainment programs, news broadcasts and soap operas that filled the airwaves. Listeners were devoted to their favorite radio programs and the stars that performed in them: "The Jack Benny Show," "The Lone Ranger," "Fibber McGee and Molly," and "Jack Armstrong, All-American Boy" — as well as the music programs that featured big bands and popular orchestras.

Many special events would take place at one of the city's two main arenas. The International Amphitheater, at 42nd and Halsted, would host trade and farming shows, the circus and special exhibits, and the Chicago Stadium, at Madison and Wood, would have boxing and wrestling matches, bicycle races, roller derbies and concerts.

During the war, socializing and morale-boosting were critical elements of the home front effort. In addition to the USO Centers downtown, servicemen and women, war workers, and residents alike found a release from the stresses of daily life in the many neighborhood-based entertainment venues. It was during this time of global conflict that many residents made the most of their nights, uncertain of what the future might hold.

In this last decade before the automobile would draw residents further away from the city, Chicago residents didn't need to travel far to have fun. It was all there in their own community — close to home.

Movie Theaters

Movie theaters provided the least expensive and most accessible form of entertainment in the neighborhoods. Residents could spend hours "at the show," viewing full-length films, shorts, serial adventures, cartoons and newsreels. Some of the neighborhood movie palaces were as lavish as the big shows downtown, especially those operated by the Balaban and Katz movie chain. Moreover, the ornate theaters could be attractions in themselves, capturing the imagination of the public with their elaborate furnishings and exotic motifs. Somehow, life was more bearable during the '40s because of the availability of neighborhood movie theaters and the opportunity to escape, even if briefly, from the concerns about the war.

One of the most beautiful movie palaces on the South Side was the Avalon Theater. The Persian-inspired theater still exists today as the New Regal Theater. Dick Jaffee grew up in South Shore and recalls the Avalon experience. "We went to movies at the Avalon Theater on 79th Street, just a block east of Stony Island Avenue. The movie routine was something we did every Saturday at the Avalon. We would walk to the movie and my first memory was that it was $.11 to get in, and a nickel for the candy. My

Opposite: *Century Theater, Clark and Diversey, ca. 1940.* Lakeview (Courtesy of the CTA.)

friend's mother would make us take his younger brother with us. Because he was little, we would sneak him in and then we used his admission and candy money to buy more candy. We would go there on a Saturday morning for a double feature and we would come out hours later. Our eyes would be so sensitive to the daylight! We first became aware of the war in the newsreels we saw at the movies. The war seemed unreal because it was so far away, but real because we could see pictures of it. Once in a while, we would go down to South Chicago to the Cheltenham Theater at 92nd and Commercial because they had triple features for about a dime. When we went to South Chicago, we rode the bus or streetcar. When we left the movie we would go across the street to 91st and Commercial, where our friend's dad was a dentist in an old walkup. We would sit there and wait until he was done and he would drive us home."

Sheldon Rosing was also from the South Shore neighborhood. "In addition to the Avalon, we also went to the Shore Theater at 75th and Essex and the Ray Theater at 75th and Exchange, where they had triple features. My allowance was $.11 and we went to the movies every weekend. If I went to the Ray Theater at 1 p.m., the three movies were over at 5 p.m. I would stay for a second round and my mother would pull me out at around 7:30 p.m. Two other popular theaters in the neighborhood were the Hamilton Theater and the Jeffrey Theater and they were both located near 71st and Jeffrey."

Raised in nearby Chatham, Norman Mark recalls the rich history of movie theaters in his neighborhood. "First, there was the Rhodes Theater — it had a miniature Graumann's Chinese Theater in the lobby. There were about two-dozen footprints and hand prints of movie stars on display. The Rhodes was located at 79th and Rhodes and they would have cartoon Saturdays. You would show up at 10 a.m. and you would stagger out of there at 5 p.m. in the afternoon having seen a million cartoons. In the middle of the cartoons, if you remembered to hold your ticket, they would have a drawing. I remember that I won a Bugs Bunny sweatshirt. It was the only thing that I won as a kid and I was very proud of it. Another movie theater for us was the Avalon Theater. When you walked into the Avalon, on the left was a blank wall, and it was odd because everything was decorated except for this wall. But when the theater first opened, it had air-cooling, and that wall was really a window. So, if you were waiting in the lobby, you could see technicians dressed in white and wearing gloves, and they were keeping the air-cooling system going.

"Occasionally, we would go to the Capitol Theater, another B&K theater. It was famous because it had a capitol dome on it. A neighbor complained that the dome was 18 inches onto her property line and that she was going to sue them. Late one night, they got about 50 guys and jacked up the dome and moved it back a foot and a half. That solved the problem! When you were inside the Capitol Theater, it was like you were at the nation's capitol. They had a portico, and inside the portico there were columns — that was where the movie screen was located. They were so involved in building the theater that they didn't install a projection booth, so they had to take out 300 seats in order to put in the booth. It was the only theater with a main floor projection booth."

Raised on the South Side, Sandy Bank remembers the theaters in the Hyde Park neighborhood. "When I grew up in Hyde Park in the '40s we were always going to movies. The Piccadilly Theater, at 51st between Dorchester and Blackstone, was a major theater. We also went to the Harper Theater on Harper, between 52nd and 53rd, and the Hyde Park Theater on Lake Park, between 53rd and 54th. Those were the three main movie theaters in the neighborhood. There was also one on 55th between Maryland and Ingleside called the Frolic Theater. The Frolic was a minor movie house except for one amazing thing: the auditorium was the reverse of what you normally expect. When you entered the auditorium you didn't face the screen, you faced the back of the theater. There was another theater at 47th and Kenwood called the Ken Theater, and one on 47th between Drexel and Cottage Grove called the Pix Theater. The Pix was located on the borderline between the black and the white areas."

On the Southwest Side, Tom Hynes recalls the theaters in the Auburn Gresham neighborhood. "We would go to the Capitol Theater at 79th and Halsted. It was a big fancy theater, and across the street was the Cosmo Theater. The Capitol would have double features, while the Cosmo would frequently have triple features, plus cartoons. We often went there because we got to see three movies instead of two. The Cosmo didn't get the first-run movies, but the Capitol did. So, we kind of alternated, but that was our major source of entertainment. In fact, we would go to the show once a week. There was also another theater, the Beverly, at 95th and Ashland, that was about a mile and a half away. They had single features there and we could never understand why anybody would pay admission to only see one movie."

On the West Side, movie-goers had many beautiful theaters to choose from, including the 4,000 seat Marbro Theater and 3,600 seat Paradise Theater. Ed Brennan recalls his favorite movie theaters while living in Austin. "The primary one for us was the State Theater, located between Austin and Central. It was a very big movie theater, although not as big as the Marbro Theater on Crawford — that was a Balaban and Katz theater. There was also a small theater on the south side of the street, called the Austin Theater. In addition, we went to the Byrd Theater located near Larrabee, and the Paradise Theater on Cicero. Movie theaters were really

Regal Theater, 47th and South Parkway, ca. 1940. Grand Boulevard (Courtesy of the CTA.)

Ambassador Theater, Division and Waller, ca. 1935. Austin (Courtesy of the CTA.)

Southtown Theater, 63rd and Lowe, ca. 1935. Englewood (Courtesy of the CTA.)

Kedzie Theater Bike Contest Winners, ca. 1948. East Garfield Park (Courtesy of Special Collections and Preservation Division, Chicago Public Library.)

the social centers for the neighborhood, and during World War II Hollywood was turning out movies like crazy. There were double features that changed twice a week. They also had serials and cartoons, as well as newsreels about the war."

In North Lawndale, Irv Bemoras remembers movie theaters clustered along Roosevelt Road. "The Central Park Theater was the main one, between St. Louis and Central Park, on Roosevelt Road. Across the street was the 20th Century, and then further east, the Independence Theater. You could also go up to Madison, where they had the Marboro and the Paradise. Next to the Central Park Theater was Ye Olde Chocolate Shoppe, famous for their hot fudge sundaes, and a very popular place. In those days, we didn't eat out much, but when we did, we went to Fluky's — that was about three or four doors down from the Central Park Theater."

In the '40s, many movie-goers bought their candy and popcorn before they entered the theater. Dan Rostenkowski, who lived on the Northwest Side on Noble Street near Division, recalls, "I remember that if you took popcorn in a theater, you bought it at a confectionery next door. And you better not dirty up the theater! That was always the argument against selling food inside the theater. Of course, in those days, they would give you a plate at the movies on Fridays. In 52 weeks, you would have a set of dishes. Every once in a while a plate would fall and break and everybody would stand up and applaud. As for movie houses, there were tons of them. At the corner of Milwaukee, Ashland and Division, was the Chopin Theater. Across the street on Division Street, on the west side of Ashland Avenue, was the Crown Theater. Down Blackhawk Street, on Paulina near Milwaukee Avenue, was the Paulina Theater. Then, up Milwaukee Avenue, were the Banner Theater, the Royal Theater, and the Wicker Park Theater. The biggest theaters in the area were the Congress Theater and the Harding Theater.

"I remember when I was a kid there was something called 'late checks.' For example, if you went to the Crown Theater, you didn't have to wait for the movie to begin. You just went in during the middle of the picture. They would give you a blue check, and then you would sit down. I remember that there were often two of us in a seat, and it might be a kid you didn't even know. At the end of the movie, the house lights would go up and they would come around and collect the 'late checks.' If you had a 'late check' you could stay for the next movie, but if you didn't have one you had to leave. That was the way they handled all the kids. At that time, the movies cost about a nickel or $.06."

Howard Rosen recalls that movie theater give-aways and promotions could be just as important as the films he was seeing. "Movies were an important part of everyone's social life in my neighborhood. As a kid, one of my best memories was the time my family went to the Crystal Theater in Humboldt Park. On certain nights, the Crystal used to have a game called 'Screen-O.' When you bought a ticket you were given a card, and if they called the number on your card you went on the stage and chose a number. If you picked the winning number, you won the prize that was under the number. One time, my mother had the winning number and she won $10. In those days, that was a very big deal. I also recall that when we lived in Albany Park, there were two movie theaters that dominated our life. One was the Terminal and the other was the Metro. They were both on Lawrence Avenue, and every Saturday we spent our entire day at either one of those two shows. The Metro had triple features, and in order to get the kids to leave, they would give us comic books. Otherwise, we would stay there all day!"

Albany Park was also Marvin Aspen's neighborhood. "Our movie theaters included the Terminal Theater, a little bit east of Kimball, and across the street was the Metro Theater. The Terminal Theater had second- and third-run movies. The movie would play downtown first, then it would be at the Uptown or Gateway, and then it would be at the Terminal. At the Metro Theater, they had the old movies that had been everywhere else before. The Metro Theater was especially interesting because you walked in backwards. At the Terminal Theater, you walked in like you do at most theaters — the screen is in front of you. But at the Metro Theater, the screen was in front, so you would walk in past the screen. The Terminal Theater was special because it had a balcony, and on Friday nights you would go there to have a rendezvous with a young lady. You would find your place in the balcony and do 'your thing', which in those days was kissing and holding hands, or putting your arm around her and hoping it didn't fall asleep. The wonderful thing about both theaters was that they showed double features as well as cartoons, serials, short subjects, and documentaries. It meant that you could go into the theater on a Saturday afternoon and spend six hours, or if you wanted to see something again, even longer!"

Ed Kelly grew up on the Near North Side in the Cabrini neighborhood. "On Saturdays or Sundays, we would go to the movies. There was a show called the LaSalle Theater. One guy would pay and the rest of us would sneak in through the back door. We weren't too smart because we used to sit in the same seats every time, and the manager would just come and get us and throw us back out. The theater was on Division Street, between La Salle and Wells. When we wanted to go to a higher-class show, we would go to the Windsor Theater, over on Clark Street, north of Division. A famous movie theater that was open when I was really small was the Sittners Theater on Sedgwick and Division. I remember going there when I was very small.

The singer Frankie Laine came from that neighborhood, although his original name was Frankie Lavechio."

Chuck Schaden grew up in Norridge, just west of the city limits. Since Norridge had no theaters at the time, residents needed to travel to the Northwest Side of Chicago for entertainment. "There were many movie theaters that we went to in the '40s. One of them was the Patio Theater at Irving Park and Austin Avenue. No one ever called it the Patio — they called it the 'Pay-Show.' We used to think they called it the Pay-Show because you had to pay to go to the show. At Milwaukee, north of Irving Park, was the B&K Portage Theater. If you went further north on Milwaukee, to Lawrence, you were just a few steps away from three theaters: the Gateway Theater, the Times Theater, and a little storefront theater in Jefferson Park called the Jeff Theater. That was the theater where they would say that they were going to raffle a bicycle every Saturday for the matinee. You would go in there and they would supposedly have a drawing from the ticket stubs. So, you would hold onto your own half of the ticket to see if you were a winner. Well, they would come out with a bicycle on stage just before the movie started. They'd get everybody to be moderately quiet, because the kids were making a lot of noise, and then they'd read the number — once. As you were trying to read your ticket, the lights would go out — nobody ever had a chance to win the bike! They repeated this procedure every week, and I don't think that the bike was ever raffled off. There were second- and third-run features at the Jeff, while the Gateway had first-run features. The Times was always showing triple features, but never anything first-run. They would show three comedy shorts, such as Laurel and Hardy, Abbott and Costello, or Olsen and Johnson, and other cartoons and shorts. Occasionally, they would have an all-Western day or all-mystery or all-ghost story show."

The North Side was home to many of the city's best movie palaces. Bob Cunniff remembers that admission was sometimes optional at a few of these grand theaters. "When I was growing up in Rogers Park, we went to the 400 Theater, on Sheridan Road near Columbia, and when we moved to Edgewater, we went to the Bryn Mawr Theater at the "L," the Devon at Broadway and Granville, the Granada Theater on Sheridan and Devon, the Nortown Theater on Western and Devon, and the Uptown and the Riviera Theaters at Lawrence and Broadway. You could sneak in the Granada Theater by going up the marble steps on the side of the building. The ushers really didn't give a damn, although sometimes they had to pretend that they cared. One time, an usher grabbed my friend Tom O'Malley and me and told us they were going to call our school. He really scared us, so I went home and told my father, who told me to forget about it. At the Devon Theater, you could always sneak in through the bathroom window."

Lawrence Pucci
Uptown

I grew up on Sheridan Road in the shadow of the old Edgewater Beach Hotel. At that time the hotel was famous internationally, with guests coming from all over the country and the world. Remember, this was before the Outer Drive was built. The hotel had a boardwalk, restaurants, and shows. The boardwalk was on the threshold of the beach, and at night, the boats would float in to listen to the music. People would walk along the boardwalk, like a promenade, with lighted Chinese lanterns glowing.

The Meriel Abbott Dancers were one of the big acts there, and all the big orchestras played there — Wayne King, Len Gray, Jimmy Dorsey, and the Ted Weems Orchestra with Perry Como. Perry Como played in the band at the time, before he turned into a star. In the hotel, they had the Marine Dining Room and a very famous bar called the Captain's Quarters. As you came into the bar you had to cross a rolling gang-plank that felt like the sea, which, as you left, seemed to be rolling even more! They had a number of dining rooms, including one that was famous for its pancakes and waffles.

Many movie stars who came to town stayed at the hotel. I remember Cary Grant and Katherine Hepburn being there. There were these long corridors leading to the different rooms, like the Empire Room, and on the walls they had pictures of the actors and actresses who had stayed there.

The hotel had a quality, a feeling about it. It wasn't like the modern age, they had the traditions of the past. The service was magnificent, with the old-time waiters. At that time, men always dressed in a suit, or a sport coat and tie, and the women always dressed well. People don't understand today, but back then, if you had a position, you had to dress like you had a position. If you were a doctor, than you looked like a doctor. If you were a lawyer, than you looked like a lawyer. Today, you can't tell a doctor from an orderly! People don't have the pride they once had.

A good example of how things have changed were the Easter Parades. In the 40s, people would get dressed-up, go to church and have what they called an Easter Parade — and they would promenade. Then, they might go downtown to Michigan Avenue, all dressed-up, some even in top hats. You don't see Easter Parades like that anymore. There was an elegance to the past.

Edgewater Beach Hotel, Sheridan and Balmoral, ca. 1946. Uptown (Courtesy of the CTA.)

For many North Side residents, Rogers Park's Granada Theater had no equal. From 1942 through early 1945, John James was a head usher at the Granada Theater at Sheridan and Devon. "My job at the Granada was Chief of Service, or head usher. I told a fib about my age and got the job when I was a little younger than fifteen years old, instead of the required age of sixteen. The usher force consisted of some eighteen young men attending Sullivan, Senn, and Amundsen High Schools. I also had the additional assignment of preparing the payroll at the theater. As head usher, I made $.03 an hour more than the other ushers, which brought my hourly rate up to $.37 an hour. I remember that on the back door of the old usher supply room, near the elevator on the third floor, was a hand-written list of all the ushers who went into military service in World War II, including those who had been killed in action. I maintained this crude list on the closet door until I entered the Marine Corps in April 1945."

West Ridge resident Burt Sherman remembers the overall experience of going to the movies in the 1940s. "When you talk about the '40s, movies were the top form of entertainment for kids. From the earliest time I can remember, we used to go to theaters like the Nortown, the Granada, or the Adelphi. Most of the kids loved Abbott and Costello movies. They were very funny and we had a terrific time when we saw them. I don't think that it cost even a dime for a kid to get in to the movies. There were always double features, and, in addition, you often saw a half dozen cartoons, serials and newsreels. They really gave you your money's worth in those days. When you got to the theater, you went in even if it was the middle of the movie because it didn't seem to make any difference. You didn't check the time beforehand, you just went there. If the movie was already in progress, or almost half over, you just sat and saw it all over again."

Community Theater

During the 1940s, religion played a big part in the stability and unity of each Chicago neighborhood. Religious education provided a foundation for young men and women, and the religious institutions they attended also served as centers for social interaction and events. Community theaters, many housed in church basements and auditoriums, brought neighbors together and offered the chance to perform on stage.

On the Far North Side, many people remember the importance of the Loyola Community Theater at St. Ignatius Church. Former Lt. Governor Neil Hartigan grew up in the Rogers Park parish and his mother, Coletta Hogan Hartigan, was very active in the Loyola Community Theater. "The participants were called the 'Green Room Players' and they were part of a six or seven element program that was held annually at St. Ignatius Church's

Dorothy Ash
Near North Side

*I*n the early 1940s, I was living in apartment 1703 of the Seneca Hotel. The Seneca is on Chestnut about a block east of Michigan. It was truly elegant, and magic. It had the magic that some places just had. The Seneca was the hotel where all the entertainment stars stayed, like Sophie Tucker. After ten months of living there I gave birth, and our one-bedroom unit was no longer big enough. So, we opened a wall between apartments to make more room.

I remember that during the war our children's nurse, Grace, couldn't wait for Sundays. She would get dressed-up in her nurse's outfit and make herself pretty, and take the kids to Seneca Park to see all the servicemen. You see, the armory was right next to the park and would be filled with hundreds of navy boys in full uniform. They looked gorgeous! She had more dates — I'm telling you! And she married one of them!

Before I got married I worked as a dancer. I started in high school. During the summer we would do state fairs all across the country — vaudeville-type shows at race tracks and fairgrounds. I got my start performing at Navy Pier in the Children's Civic Theater. We lived at 3330 North Bell at the time, and I had to take three streetcars to get there — Roscoe, Damen, and then down to the pier. During the summer the theater ran from morning until night. And it was free — sponsored by the Chicago Drama League. We had dancing training for two hours, music for two hours, and then it was drama. We then performed twice a week. Thousands of people came to see us. It really was a training ground for kids in the arts. Some children went into radio, some into music and a lot of the girls went into dancing, and that's what I wanted to do.

I went on to be a dancer in two different lines — I was a Winnie Hoover girl and a Betty Coletts girl. We danced in Chicago at the Oriental Theater and at Harry's New Yorker, as well as big theaters all over the country. I was in a show called the Circus de Paris, and they had lions. One of the numbers had a girl dancing in a cage with the lions, about ten of them. The girl would go in and flick her veil at the lions. Well, the audience at one of the shows thought that the lions weren't scary enough, so the girl tried to agitate them a little. She put a bolt at the end of her veil so when she flicked it they would really roar. Well, one day, at a matinee, a lion came down and mauled her — and killed her. It was really terrible. They closed the show because of her death.

Loyola Community Theater, St. Ignatius Auditorium, ca. 1948. Rogers Park (Courtesy of the Rogers Park/West Ridge Historical Society.)

Jim DeLisa
South Shore

When my dad, Jim, came from Italy he first stopped in New York to visit relatives and friends. My uncle Mike was a tailor there, and my uncle Louis was a shoemaker. My dad came to Chicago and became a carpenter. After he got here he called my uncles and said, "You gotta come to Chicago because there are bushels of money being made here." This was in the 1920s, and it was moonshine that was making the money. So, they came and opened five places on the South Side — five stills. Then, when Prohibition ended, they opened up the Club DeLisa at 55th and State in 1933. When it first opened, they would give free pretzels and popcorn to draw the crowds. They kept getting bigger and bigger, but then the club burned down due to an electrical fire. So, they decided to open a bigger Club DeLisa. People said they wouldn't be able to open up another club quickly. Well, my dad said that you could put your finger through the plaster, but he was going to open it up, and they did, about a year later. The new one sat 1,000-1,500 people, and it had a stage with sets under the floor. First, you would hear "Red" Saunders beating on the drums, then the stage would rise, and there would be Red with Louis Armstrong or whoever was performing there. There wasn't a bad seat in the house with that raised stage.

At the old club, John Barrymore would arrive from the Blackstone Hotel wearing his robe, and he would be eating salami, drinking and admiring the women. The Blackstone would always call and ask if my dad was stealing John Barrymore. He would say, "You can ask Mr. Barrymore yourself." Bob Hope would come and stop in, as well as John Wayne, who wasn't too good of a tipper. All of the top jazz people came to Club DeLisa, and Monday was the breakfast show at 6 o'clock in the morning. Everybody who was appearing in Chicago would come to the club and do their thing on stage and then watch the other performers. The Kirby's, the Eckstine's, Joe Williams, La Verne Baker, and Moms Mabley all started there. Even Sammy Davis Jr. appeared, along with his dad, when they came through Chicago. My dad and his brothers fed them because they didn't have enough money to eat. Sammy acknowledged that later in his career.

"Blind" John Davis at the Boulevard Hotel, California and Warren, 1944. East Garfield Park (Courtesy of Special Collections and Preservation Division, Chicago Public Library.)

Patrons, Ritz Lounge, Oakwood and South Parkway, 1943. Grand Boulevard (Courtesy of Special Collections and Preservation Division, Chicago Public Library.)

Joe Levinson
Hyde Park

There were many places to hear jazz across Chicago from the late 1930s to the early 1950s. On the South Side, there was Jump Town at 47th and Western Avenue. This joint always had stars playing there, including Louis Jordan's Tympany Five. In those days, they cordially welcomed the white listener and you could have a great time. There was also the famous Regal Theater on South Parkway around 47th Street. It was a large, well-appointed theater that featured movies followed by a stage show. I saw Pearl Bailey's stage show there, and whites and blacks always were at that theater. The Sutherland Lounge, located at Drexel Parkway and 47th Street, was near the Regal. That lounge was high-style and they had some of the greatest black jazz artists of the day, like Ahmad Jamal and Nat King Cole. You needed to have money to go there. On 63rd Street was the Crown Propeller Lounge, where I heard some fine local talent along with many traveling jazz artists.

One of the most famous nightclubs in Chicago was the Club DeLisa at 55th and State. That was the legendary black-and-tan club that was famous for running late, late shows known as "The Milkman's Matinee" beginning around 2 a.m. and ending after 6 o'clock in the morning, always with huge crowds. Everybody who was anybody got their start at the Club DeLisa, and all the movie celebrities made it a point to hit the club during their stays in Chicago. Many local musicians played long stretches there and developed their styles at the club. It wasn't a cheap place to go.

Also on the South Side was Robert's Show Lounge at 65th and South Parkway. It was a big hangout for black musicians and white audiences in the 1940s and was a very famous spot. A few other South Side places that I remember were the Emerald Lounge, where musicians would sit in with the bands; Gussie's Kentucky Lounge at 67th and South Ashland Avenue, where Ira Sullivan and Tommy Ponce worked; the famous Cotton Club at 63rd and Cottage Grove; the Bee Hive on 55th Street near Lake Park Avenue, where I heard Charlie Parker, Gene Ammons and Miles Davis; and Chimaqua's at 14th and Pulaski that featured Latin Jazz when it first emerged on the scene in the late '40s and early 50s, and where the late, great pianist Gene Esposito got his early training.

A big place for top name dance bands was the Trianon Ballroom on the South Side. It was jammed during the war years with people who came to listen and dance to the popular music of the day.

When you went downtown, there were several great jazz clubs. One was called the Downbeat, located in the basement of the Garrick Theater. It featured Henry "Red" Allen's band with J.C. Higginbotham on trombone and Cozy Cole on drums. Allen was a Dixieland trumpeter and he was a great entertainer and showman. Then, there was the Blue Note, often called Frank Holzfiend's Blue Note. It was a world famous place that began as a joint on the second level of a building on Madison, west of State Street. I saw many groups there including Dizzy Gillespie's and Duke Ellington's bands, as well as the giant Sauter-Finnegan Band. Even though I was a teenager of seventeen or eighteen, I could still get into the Blue Note to hear great jazz. There wasn't a famous jazz group that didn't play at that club in the 1940s.

Another popular location in the Loop for great music was the Panther Room, located in the College Inn of the Sherman Hotel. The Panther Room was elegant and featured most of the big traveling jazz and dance bands that were working during the 1940s. I saw Woody Herman's great First Herd there, although I was too young to do more than stand by the doorway and watch and listen as people went in and out. It was the place to take an important date if you were a college man and had money.

You can't talk about the scene in Chicago during those exciting days without recalling the city's most sophisticated Dixieland jazz nightclub, Jazz Ltd. It was located at the corner of Grand and State, right by the subway entrance. The club was owned and managed by Ruth and Bill Rheinhardt. It was long and narrow and could only seat about fifty patrons, with a tiny bar for a few more. On weekends, there always was a line outside waiting to get in and hear the band. Ruth ran the club with an iron hand while Bill played clarinet and led the band. The band was always a five-piece outfit — piano, drums, clarinet, trombone and trumpet. For many of the club's years the players besides Bill were Dave Remington, trombone; Norm Murphy, trumpet; Eddie Higgins, piano; and Bob Cousins, drums. Freddie Kohlman, a wonderful New Orleans drummer, worked there too for a long time, as did Waldron "Frog" Joseph, a trombonist also from New Orleans. Famed jazz pianist Art Hodes worked there often. Ralph Hutchinson, the best jazz trombonist in town in those years, often played there. Freddie Williamson played trumpet there, as did Sidney Bechet, the great soprano sax virtuoso. Doc Evans on cornet was there, too, as was Max Hook on piano and Fred Greenleaf on cornet, from Detroit. Trombonist Miff Mole played there a lot — he was a jazz legend. Often I would show up at the club around 1 a.m. with my bass, after I played at a society party in the Loop. Bill Reinhardt would ask me to sit in, because they had no bass player in the band. I'd close the joint with the rest of the guys early in the morning. It was a fine place to learn the Dixieland repertoire, and the guys were wonderful characters to hang out with.

When you reminisce about those days you have to describe the London House at Wacker and Michigan Boulevard. This was a world famous nightclub owned by George and Oscar Marienthall. The world's most famous jazz and pop artists performed there: George Shearing, Oscar Peterson, Lionel Hampton, Woody Herman, Errol Garner — a list that goes on and on! For a while, I worked there on Sunday and Monday nights with the Eddie Higgins Trio and I got to see and hear and meet many of the "name" artists who worked there. It was an advanced education in jazz performance and I absorbed it like a sponge. One Sunday night I was there, taking a break in a booth at the back of the room with Eddie Higgins and Jack Noren, our drummer, when Bob Hope came by and sat next to me in the booth. He just wanted to "chew the fat" with musicians, and had us in fits telling one-liners, none of which I can repeat here. It was that kind of room: movie stars, politicos, athletes, radio and TV entertainers all came to the London House. And the steaks and chops were divine. We had a rule of thumb: never get on the bandstand to play with an empty stomach! The waiters came by carrying those trays filled with stupendous dinners, and the odors wafted up to us as we were playing. It could drive you mad.

One of the most popular music venues in downtown Chicago was the Blackhawk on Wabash Avenue. It was a famous restaurant, featuring the "spinning salad bowl," and they had the top pop and jazz groups performing there. It was where my parents took me to hear my first live jazz performed by Fats Waller and his quintet. He was a sensational pianist, the king of the stride piano, and a fantastic entertainer and composer. His works include "Ain't Misbehavin'," "Your Feets Too Big," and "Honeysuckle Rose." Big name bands worked at the Blackhawk and they also aired radio broadcasts of the music around the country from the bandstand at the restaurant. Bob Crosby's band was often featured there.

At State and Van Buren was the Rialto Theater. Before World War II it was a burlesque house, but during the war years it changed formats to a movie and stage show venue. I heard Cab Calloway and Duke Ellington's bands there, as well as Andy Kirk and his 12 Clouds of Joy, a wonderful dance band that swung harder than any others. There also was the Cloister Inn at the Maryland Hotel on Rush Street. The lounge in the lower level of the hotel was where you could hear black vocalist Lurlean Hunter backed by pianist Dick Marx and bassist/violinist Johnny Frigo. It was a piano bar and you could sit close to the performers. Nearby was the Back Room on Rush Street, and you could only find it by walking down a tiny, narrow alley. A lot of jazz piano players worked there. There was also the Preview on Randolph, a second floor joint that featured Louis Prima, The Dukes of

Dixieland, Al Cohn, Zoot Sims and other well-known entertainers and jazz men.

Another downtown club was the Capitol Lounge, located one door south of the Chicago Theater and featuring small jazz groups in a loud, raucous and garish environment. Finally, I remember Lipp's Lower Level near South Water Street below Michigan Avenue. It was a small, inexpensive club that featured Roy Eldredge during the '40s.

On the North Side, the Aragon Ballroom on Lawrence next to the "L" stop, like the Trianon on the South Side, was a popular place for big band music. As a teenager, I went to the Aragon to hear Jimmy Dorsey's band with Helen O'Connell and Bob Eberle as the vocalists. I was part of the crowd that always gathered right in the front of the bandstand to get a close-up view.

Then, there were a group of small clubs on the North Side — Abstract Lounge on Fullerton Avenue which featured many local jazz players; the Key of C on Broadway near Wellington, a small and dark club; the Warm Friends in the Wilson Hotel in Uptown where jazz musicians used to jam; the Lei Aloha at Windsor and Sheridan where Johnny Frigo and Dick Marx made their reputations; and the Spotlight Lounge at 3113 N. Broadway where local jazz artists played.

I also remember dives like Mario's Lounge on North Milwaukee Avenue. On weekends, Mario featured a quintet that included trombonist Eddie Avis. I used to play some bass there on weekends in the late '40s when I was young and tough and smoked cigarettes. A jazz place still in operation is the Green Mill at Lawrence and Broadway. All the great jazz players eventually wound up at the Mill, either playing on the tiny stage or egging on the musicians who were performing. There was the Holiday Ballroom at Milwaukee and Lawrence, owned by Dan Bellock. Many big bands played there. I played there many times with the Bill Scott Orchestra which featured great sidemen like Joe Daley, Bill Porter, Eddie Avis and Tom Hilliard. Finally, there was the 1111 Club at Bryn Mawr and the "L" stop. This was a popular Dixieland jazz joint that, for many years, featured the band headed by George Brunies, the famous tailgate trombonist. The bar was very long and the legendary drummer "Hey Hey" Humphries played there. Hey Hey got married in the club. He and his bride walked down the length of the bar to the preacher who read the service. This has to be one of the world's most bizarre marriage ceremonies ever.

Jazz and big band music dominated the scene in the late '30s and throughout the 1940s, and this music had a tremendous influence on the development of my career.

1,000-seat theater. They had shows with all sorts of national acts involved, and in later years it was also the site of teenage shows that involved hundreds of kids and their parents." Bill Nellis, who also attended St. Ignatius, recalls the professionalism of the program. "The Loyola Community Theater was a big thing in the parish. When we attended St. Ignatius you were lucky if you were selected to participate in the show, which was done in a Broadway style. Professionals put the show together each year, and it was a real show with song and dance numbers. One year we did *South Pacific* and it was a really great show. It helped to reinforce the sense of community in the parish."

Ball Rooms, Jazz Clubs and Night Spots

Throughout Chicago's neighborhoods, there were numerous music halls, jazz clubs and night spots. Some were just tiny dives down an alley, while others were nationally-known clubs that were able to showcase the top musical talent of the decade. For dancing, many Chicagoans frequented the ballrooms around the city, including the Trianon Ballroom, at 62nd and Cottage Grove, and the Aragon Ballroom, at Lawrence and Broadway. Built by the Karzas brothers in the '20s, these grand ballrooms and the dance bands and orchestras that played in them were extremely popular during the '40s, particularly by the many servicemen and women stationed in the Chicago area.

For many young Chicagoans, a love of music began in high school during band practice and music classes. Hank Mitchell grew up on the West Side and became a musician in the '40s. "I didn't start playing a musical instrument until I got into high school. My parents decided that I should learn to play a musical instrument to keep me out of trouble. It was 1944 and I liked the trumpet because Harry James was popular at that time. So we went downtown to Wurlitzer on Wabash Avenue and we bought what we thought was a trumpet. It turned out to be a coronet. My parents bought it for me, on time, with lessons, and that was how I got into music. At Harrison High School, I got into the beginners band and studied with Captain Joseph Ewald who was a strict technician for classical music. He wasn't too hep to bebop music, but we convinced him that he should have a swing band. The war was going on and the big band thing was very popular. The big bands playing jazz included Cab Calloway, Duke Ellington, Count Basie and Harry James."

Bob Cunniff's love of jazz began at Senn High School in Edgewater. "Students would stay at school during lunch and dance to records on the auditorium stage. It was a fun thing to do. Tommy Dorsey and Glenn Miller were very popular during those years. Several friends and I were big jazz fans, and we would go to the Regal Theater at 35th and South Parkway — we saw Lionel Hampton and Duke Ellington there. I remember when we saw Duke Ellington — the curtain came up and there he was in a white suit, and I realized that I had seen my Zen master. He just owned us. I also went to the famous Club DeLisa during those years at 55th and State. There was also the Blue Note on Randolph Street, just west of State Street, where they claimed that the "World's Greatest Trombone Player" played — J.C. Higginbotham. On Argyle, there was the Tail Spin, and on Broadway there was the Green Mill, where Charlie Parker and Lester Young would sometimes play. On Bryn Mawr by the "L" there was the 1111 Club. We also went up to Howard Street after the war, and Art Tatum was performing at the Club Silhouette to an empty room. So, I got my own personal 'audience' with Art Tatum."

On the northern border of Rogers Park, there were several music and jazz clubs on Howard Street. Many servicemen, tourists, and suburbanites would fill these clubs, particularly those from neighboring Evanston and the North Shore. Comedian Shecky Greene got his start in entertainment on Howard Street during the '40s. "I remember Howard Street because I really started my career as a comedian at the Club Silhouette. I was going to college at the time, and I stopped by the club on amateur night. Sarah Vaughn was on the bill at the time. So, I got up and performed and won the amateur contest. Years later when I became friendly with Sarah I told her the story about my appearance, but she didn't remember it. I also remember places like the Club Detour and the Bar-O on Howard during those years."

Auburn Gresham resident Jack Hogan traveled all across the city to hear music. "The '40s were a very, very important part of my life because of the music. The Aragon Ballroom and the Trianon Ballroom were the places to go. Even though I was a South Sider, I didn't really frequent the Trianon as much as I did the Aragon, probably because of my desire to hear the Dick Jergen Orchestra. They would bring in different bands like Kay Kyser, Glenn Miller and Eddy Duchin. Another place for music was the Panther Room, down at the Hotel Sherman (also known as the College Inn). That was a great place for kids to go. The Walnut Room at the Bismarck Hotel, on Randolph near Wells, was also very popular. Back in those days, there was music everywhere, including the Blue Note, Helsing's Lounge, and many other places downtown. The '40s were just a great time for music.

"In 1942, there was a place that was going to open at Clark and Montrose, geared for young people. There wasn't going to be any hard liquor, just Cokes, sandwiches and ice cream. The night that it was supposed to open, it was going to feature the Charlie Spivak Orchestra and Dinah Shore. We went opening night, and everybody was mingling around waiting for it to open, but they never opened because they didn't have the proper licenses. We ended up over at the Aragon Ballroom, not too far away. It was customary in those days, if it was a big name band, to hang around the bandstand and

Johnny Frigo
Roseland

I was born in 1916. I grew up in Roseland on 116th Street at Kensington Avenue, just east of Michigan Avenue, across from St. Anthony's Church. We lived in a house when I was growing up, and at one point my mother had fourteen boarders who she cooked and washed for.

My musical career really started when I began playing violin with the son of the ragman to whom I sold junk. I used to do this when I was young after school: I would collect junk, and when the ragman would come by on Saturdays with his horse and wagon to collect rags and iron, and I would sell him my weekly collection and get a quarter. I can remember when copper was five cents a pound and it was like finding gold! He eventually talked my mother into having me take violin lessons with his son, Nathan Oberman. So, I started taking lessons when I was seven years old.

During my last year at Fenger High School, I was playing and singing at Club Citro on Taylor and Halsted. It was broadcast on WKYW radio. We weren't there for too long, maybe a month or so. When someone asked me for a request, they would give me a tip and put the money right into my bass. At the end of the night, I had to lift up my bass and shake it to get the money out. One time, a guy came up and dropped some money into my bass. I remember seeing a bill going in, and the next night someone told me that it was Al Capone. He had put in $5.00 or $10.00.

One night there my voice cracked on a high note, and the bouncer said, "Don't sing no more!" I thought he meant not to sing that song anymore. He meant don't sing at all. So, the next night I was singing and he rushed up on the stage and grabbed me by the back of my collar while I was on the radio. He dragged me off the bandstand and onto the dance floor on the back of my heels. All the kids wondered what had happened to me!

I started playing jazz because I didn't have enough formal training to be a concert violinist. So, I just started playing, and in 1940, I began playing bass with a group called the Four Californians. We played at the Morrison Hotel and at the Drake Hotel. I played bass because Curtis Junior High School on 115th didn't have an orchestra, they only had a band, and the only instrument that nobody wanted to play was a tuba. So, I got stuck with the tuba. When I got into high school, the obvious thing to play was the string bass. I made 95% of my living playing string bass for the 50 years because of that situation. If they had an orchestra, I would have probably stuck with the violin.

I remember playing in many clubs in Chicago's neighborhoods. There was Giovanni's on 111th and Michigan, and I used to play on the "National Barn Dance" on WLS-AM. After we finished with our broadcast at midnight I would rush over to Giovanni's and play there until 3:00 o'clock in the morning. I also played at the Embassy Club at 119th and Michigan, and Jay Berkhart played there, too. I played at a lot of clubs on 63rd Street. Mostly, I played bass at the Trianon Ballroom with Wayne King and at the Aragon Ballroom with Dick Jergen.

On the South Side, I would sit-in at the black jazz clubs after my gigs. I would park my car in an alley on a Saturday night at 2 a.m. and take my violin into some jazz club like Club DeLisa. On Monday mornings they had what was called a "Milkman's Matinee." They had eight dancing girls there — the sun was already up — and they had Albert Ammons and his band, the son of the great tenor player, Gene Ammons. They would let me sit-in. When you sit-in, you play one or two sets and then let somebody else play. I was so ignorant — once I kept playing the entire time. When I finished, the announcer said, "OK, Johnny, let Teddy Wilson play on piano."

In 1942, I played with Chico Marx at the Blackhawk Restaurant. They would broadcast live every night. Mel Torme would sing, and we had the quartet. He was from the Hyde Park area, and had just gotten out of high school. It was during the time with him that I signed up for World War II. I picked the Coast Guard because I thought I would be on some stormy shore looking for German submarines, but they heard that I played violin, so they sent me to Ellis Island. I played bass with the band, and I played tuba and trumpet with the military band from 1942 to 1945. I did concerts at Walter Reed Hospital and radio programs.

After I got out of the service in 1945, I came back to Chicago and began traveling with Chico Marx. I joined Chico at Tower Theater in Kansas City, and we did theaters all over the country. When he saw that I played violin, he asked me to bring it on stage one day — we sort of fell into a comedy routine. He had an Italian accent, and we would do stupid stuff and improvise routines like, "You noodle on the fiddle, and I'll spaghetti on the piano."

Roller skaters, Savoy Ballroom, 47th and South Parkway, 1941.   Grand Boulevard   Photograph by Russell Lee.   (Library of Congress)

Dancers, Rhumboogie Nightclub, 343 E. Garfield, 1941. Washington Park Photograph by Russell Lee. (Library of Congress)

"Red" Saunders and Band, Club DeLisa, 55th and State, 1941. Washington Park Photograph by Russell Lee. (Library of Congress)

Ramsey Lewis
Near North Side

I was born on the South Side of Chicago in 1935. We lived there for only a few years, then we moved to the North Side when I was five. We lived in a number of places — on Scott Street, and then we moved to the Cabrini Homes, a series of low rises. We didn't live there for a long time because you had to make a certain amount of money, both minimum and maximum. Once my dad passed the maximum, he didn't qualify any more, so we moved to 1142 N. Orleans Street. I went to Schiller and Edward Jenner grammar schools, and to Wells High School.

As for the neighborhood, life focused around the immediate blocks where I lived. There were about five of us — Tommy and Claude Kennard, Leroy Austin, Buddy Boyd, and a couple white guys who were a part of our group. We hung out together and played baseball, touch football, basketball or stood on the corner. We didn't do a lot of standing on the corner that I recall, unless we were planning how we were going to raise money to go to the movies. Until a certain age, you earned your money. In those days, you could collect pop bottles, loose paper, as well as old iron, and sell it at the junkyard. Of course, we couldn't go to the movies unless we had gotten all our housework done, practiced piano and done our homework.

During the years when I was five to fifteen, that would be 1940 to 1950, I had a regimented schedule. It was a pretty tight schedule although I didn't realize it at the time. I was taking piano lessons from the time I was four years old, and practicing, going to school, and going to church. This pretty much filled up my life. My parents were very religious, so they were conservative in nature. There were certain records we couldn't play at home because they were too racy, and certain movies we couldn't see. I started playing for our church when I was nine years old, so not only was I going to church regularly, I was playing at the church, and there were church choir rehearsals and concerts after church, and piano lessons.

When I was fifteen, one of our church musicians needed a piano player. He was a little older than me, and played on weekends for fashion shows or whatever was available. They asked me at church one Sunday, and my parents had a long talk with him about seeing that I got home and other stuff. So, I started playing with the Clefs. Wallace Burton was the leader, and had it not been for Wallace teaching me the ways of jazz music, I wouldn't have played jazz. He thought that I could play jazz because he heard me play gospel on Sunday mornings.

We didn't even rehearse that first night at this dance where we were playing. They just thought that I could play, and he said, "Let's play a Charlie Parker piece based on the blues in a medium tempo. Ramsey, you start." All I knew about the blues was from some records that my dad had brought home when I was eleven or twelve years old, and it was the boogie-woogie. So, that's what I started playing, but it didn't quite fit. So, he said, "Let's play a couple of standards. What do you know?" I didn't know any. So, he told me to sit out the rest of the night. I figured it was over, but he said I should come to his house the next day, and Wallace Burton took the time to introduce me to jazz music.

As for life in the '40s, I don't really have any other recollections about those years. If you can picture me getting up in the morning and going to school, coming home and doing homework and practicing the piano, that was my life. Dad was very, very strict on practicing, and when he would come home from work, the first thing he would ask my mother was, "Did Sonny practice?" As I got older, I had a job working after school, in addition to practicing and homework and going to church. That was pretty much it. I thank my lucky stars and I thank my parents for being conservative.

My father was a janitor and maintenance man at W. Hall Printing Company. He raised three kids and put all three of us through college. It was wonderful, and my structured life was good for me. It probably helped me with my jazz, too. The life that we lived taught us responsibility, sharing, to be sensitive to other people's needs, and commitment and follow-through. When my sisters and I are together, we often relate to each other how mom and dad were very, very tough, but we thank God that they were.

Bartender and Tavern Owner, South Side, 1941.
Photograph by Russell Lee. (Library of Congress)

Richard Lukin
Kenwood

I grew up in Kenwood, at 822 East 46th Street. It was a middle-class neighborhood. On my street, and really in that area, almost everybody lived in apartment buildings. There were some homes around 47th and 48th and Woodlawn, but almost everybody lived in apartments. I wouldn't say there was any particular ethnic group living there. It was a real mixture, we had everything. In fact, on my way to school, I passed a synagogue, St. James Episcopal Church, Woodlawn Community Church, St. Ambrose Church, and the Swedenborgian Church. So, we had a real mixture, and everybody was friendly with one another. We were just people. We never made any differentiation in those days. We were just people. It never occurred to me that anybody was different.

My dad owned a restaurant at 28th and Wabash called the Wabash Tavern and Grill. It was blue collar, and it catered to the local people. It was a "shot-and-a-beer" joint with good food. There were a lot of industries in the area so workmen would come in for their breakfast in the morning, lunch at noon and a shot and a beer in the afternoon. This kind of place was common, and it provided a couple of families a life. They're still around, like the Anchor Bar downtown, and Gianardo's on Taylor Street. These are shot-and-a-beer joints, and they serve good food in the back, too.

There were some interesting places around back in the 1940s. At 79th Street there was a liquor store called Twin Liquors. It was a regular store like you see today, with shelves and so forth, but in the back, behind a swinging door, it was set-up like a living room, with couches, cushioned chairs, tables, and a small service bar. They were Swedish, and they had a table with free pickled herring and cheese and crackers. You could sit there and talk to your neighbors. In those days a lot of guys would go suck on a beer for a few hours after work. Life back then was work, work, work.

We didn't go out much back then, but on Sundays we would occasionally eat out. If somebody you knew had a car, you could go to what we called "destination" restaurants. You know, let's get in a car and go there! Places like the Terminal Tap in Blue Island for Polish sausage. Of course, the big South Side restaurant was Phil Smidt's, at 1205 Calumet Avenue in Hammond, and it's still there today. They had lake perch and chicken, with big baskets of rolls, butter, cottage cheese, beets, and potato salad served family style.

The Morton family, of Arnie Morton's Steak House, had a place run by Arnie's father at 54th and Lake Park, and that was always a nice dining place. They moved to 56th and the lake after the city tore up Lake Park Avenue in the late 1940s.

One of the major hamburger chains in the city, and this was years before McDonald's, was Wimpy's at 51st Street and Dorchestor. They started in Chicago and eventually expanded. They even went to England.

Cafeterias were very big in the 1940s, and one of the best was Pixley-Ehlers. Like Krispy Kreme, they had a bakery with the oven in the window. They had great sweet rolls and raisin rolls. Another great cafeteria, which is still around today, is Valois on 53rd Street. Valois is an icon for American food. What a lot of people don't know is that Berghoff used to have a cafeteria line in the lower level until 1956. They always had brats, corned beef hash, roast beef, turkey wings and a daily special. You would get a choice of entree, mashed potatoes, and vegetable for $.45. I think the best restaurant in Chicago is Berghoff. I started eating there when I was four years old, and have been going ever since.

The first Mexican Restaurant I ever saw was at 95th and Ewing. This was back in the late 1940s. The steel mills at that time were among the first to hire Mexican laborers, who used to congregate on the east side around 95th Street.

For hot dogs on the South Side, everybody went to Carl's. It was in an old, dumpy garage converted into a hot dog stand. That's what a hot dog stand should be! It should be in a shack! Carl's was in a typical old Chicago wooden garage, with a window cut out, on the corner of 83rd and Jeffrey. I remember he would always buy his potatoes from the Jiffy Potato Spud Company, but he only bought the left-over chips. As you know, the potato is round, and after it goes through a square cutter there are these little chips left over — that's what Carl used. He would give you a tremendous handful of those and a hot dog for a quarter. People would go there and order ten or fifteen of those things.

And there were a lot of great barbecue places on the South Side, including the Tropical Hut. The Tropical Hut, for anyone living around Hyde Park, was the place to eat in the 1940s. It was by the University of Chicago. They had an unusual cooking device, a vertical medium, and the roast beef would twirl around on a chain in the window as you were waiting to come in. They had wonderful barbecue!

There were many destination spots — Rainbow Cone at 95th and Western, where you could get nineteen flavors on one cone; Horvath, for Bohemian style food on Harlem Avenue; Russell's Barbecue, at Thatcher and North; Gianetti's, the big Italian Restaurant on Roosevelt Road west of Harlem; or any of the Czech restaurants on West 22nd Street.

Now, if my mother wanted to cook a certain ethnic dish, we had to go to that particular neighborhood to shop. For instance, we would take the "L" over to the West Side to California and North Avenue to the Swedish neighborhood. We'd buy herring, pickled fish, sauerkraut, potato sausage, and cheeses and breads there because these things were never carried at the major grocery stores. It was the same with Italian food. If you needed Italian you would go to Taylor and Halsted — sausage, ham, pasta, or Italian cheeses — you had to go there to buy these. So much of this food is impossible to get today, like finan haddie, nobody eats this stuff today. It's smoked haddock — I love it. And blind robins, a north Atlantic herring that's been hard smoked like a beef jerky. These used to be sold in bulk to bars which would sell them for a dime. Now you can't find them or buy them! You don't see pickled eggs anymore or pickled pig's knuckles — absolutely delicious!

Everyday shopping was done in the neighborhood, at the smaller corner shops and at the independent stores. I can remember two different bakeries and three different butcher markets in my neighborhood, in addition to the larger Jewel. For sweets, there were many small Greek-owned confectionery stores. Cunag's, at 53rd and Ellis, was one my favorites. Generally, next to every movie theater was a Greek-owned candy store that offered popcorn, candy, ice cream, and all the confections. We would shop much more often than we do now — everyday or every other day. We did have electric refrigerators, but there were no freezers, so if you went to Walgreens to get ice cream, you only got a pint. As the population changed, and the older people died off, the independent places just melded in, and everybody became an American. You went to Jewel, National, Kroger, or A&P.

Now, if we really wanted to do something that was cheap, there was smelt fishing. People still do that now, but not to the extent that they did in the 1940s. Back then, the rocks along the lake at 31st Street, all the way to the point at 55th Street, would be packed with people. It was a rite of the season. To get a good spot you would get out there before it turned dark and set-up your line, but you couldn't put your net in before sunset, which was the state law. What you would do is this — you would throw out your line as far as you could, anchor it, attach your net to series of rollers that move up and down the line, and the smelt would get stuck in the net as they swam through. Between drinking cans of beer, you'd pull it in. It was cold, icy, usually around thirty-one degrees, but it was free, and it was a good source of protein. Sometimes you could get thirty, forty, or fifty pounds of smelt out there. The first of April everybody would be out there smelt fishing. You would freeze, but smelts are good. A smelt is a derivative of a freshwater herring, about eight or nine inches long. You whack the head off, dress them, and fry them up.

listen to the music and watch the musicians, as opposed to dancing. That's what I was doing that particular night, when Dick Jergen's Orchestra was playing. All of a sudden, the band vocalist, Harry Cool, came down off the bandstand and tried to make out with my date! I remember that so well! As for the Trianon Ballroom, when I came out of the military, I used to go to the Trianon quite a bit. Lawrence Welk played there, and he was one of the resident bands there. The entire time I went to listen to Lawrence Welk, I never knew he had an accent. He never talked, and if he did it was very brief. I didn't know he had an accent until I saw him on television."

Ted Saunders father, "Red," was the lead drummer at Club DeLisa beginning in 1936. " I was born in 1935, and we lived behind a famous place called the Rhumboogie Club at 343 E. Garfield Boulevard, but the most famous club in Chicago was Club DeLisa at 55th and State. It was the first place where blacks and whites could go in and mix and sit down and watch shows together. There were white acts and black acts in the show—they called them 'black and tan' shows. All the famous people came to Club DeLisa, including John Barrymore and Bob Hope.

"My dad's full name was Theodore Dudley 'Red' Saunders. He was a light-skinned black man and they called him 'Red.' After I was born, my parents went on the road with a show called 'Harlem Scandals' and my dad was the drummer in the show. When my dad was performing at Club DeLisa, I used to be there all the time. In fact, when I was four years old, they made me a miniature set of drums and I would play them at the club. My father came up to Chicago from Memphis, Tennessee, around 1917. Lil Armstrong, Louis' wife, had just come up from Memphis around that time. She and my auntie had gone to school together and they lived together in Chicago. Chicago was the key place for entertainment from the 1920s on, and the hottest recorders were the Red Hot Five and the Red Hot Seven. Lil Armstrong was the piano player for the group and also the one who wrote the music. Lil was a wonderful woman and that was how my dad got interested in music."

Phil Holdman was a musician and record salesman in the Chicago area during the '40s. From calling on juke box operators to playing in bands, he acquired a special knowledge of the Chicago music scene. "I remember going to Jump Town at 63rd and Western with a bunch of my friends from the West Side. One of the guys was able to get his father's car and take a load of us to hear good music. They featured Anita O'Day, as well as many of the great jazz singers and trios. It was a very hot spot. I went downtown to the Panther Room at the Sherman Hotel many times. I took my girl, Alberta, there and she later became my wife. There was no cover charge at the Panther Room and a beer was $.50 a bottle. We didn't drink, so we just sipped it like we were drinking beer, and most of the time we would go up on the

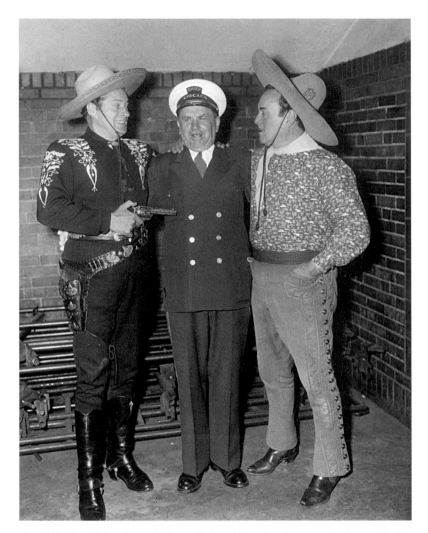

Joe "40,000" Murphy with Cisco Kid and Pancho, Chicago Stadium, 1949. Near West Side (Courtesy of Bill Swislow.)

Joe "40,000" Murphy was an Andy Frain usher who lived in Bridgeport. His passion was to be photographed with the famous people he met on the job — Frank Sinatra, Bob Hope, Milton Berle, Jimmy Durante, and Louis Armstrong — the list goes on and on. After he died, he left behind hundreds of photographs in his three-flat on 34th Street documenting his colorful career.

Joe "40,000" Murphy with Marilyn Monroe, Comiskey Park, 1949. Armour Square (Courtesy of Bill Swislow.)

Raymond DeGroote
West Ridge

We always went to Riverview on the Western Avenue streetcar. It was perfect for us, we rode right down Western Avenue. My mother knew the secretary to the owner there, so we got free passes and reduced rate tickets all the time. We would usually go on a Saturday after lunch and stay until about five o'clock, leaving enough time to get home for dinner.

We would go as a group of four or five kids, starting when I was eight or nine years old. There was no concern about harm coming to us back then, unless we did it to ourselves! There was just no thought about kidnappings or stuff like that.

We went there for the rides. We weren't really interested in the sideshows. We wanted the exciting stuff! You see, we didn't have that much money, so we saved our money for the rides. Most rides were $.05 or $.10, which in those days could be a lot. But they did have $.02 days, where everything was $.02, except for the more exotic rides, which might have been $.05. We would not eat much at Riverview, though there were plenty of places to eat, especially things like cotton candy. But these things cost money! We only had a certain amount we could spend — a couple of bucks. When it was gone it was gone.

The entrance was on Western, at the corner of Western and Roscoe. When we entered we would always follow the same circuit— go west, and head for the Greyhound. There were about five roller coasters at Riverview, the Bobs being the steepest, fastest, and most exciting. The initial drop was a really big fall, and then you came right up again. You could really feel that pull of gravity! I didn't get on the Bobs at first because it was too much for a youngster. I was confined to the Greyhound or the Silver Streak. They were tamer and had covered cars. They were not quite as fast, but thrilling enough for a ten- or eleven-year-old. The Silver Streak was a basic roller coaster covered with a streamlined shell, sort of an Art Deco design.

Aladdin's Castle was a fun house, where you could walk over rolling barrels, go through a house of mirrors, or watch the jets of wind blowing up the girl's dresses. Of course, there were dark passageways you could walk through where monsters would jump in front of you and then disappear. It was a $.02 ride, so everybody would go there. There would always be a tremendous crowd.

The Shoot the Chutes ride started in a big pond where you would board a large flat-bottomed boat, probably fitting almost twenty or so people.

Soon the boat floated to the back of a big tower where an elevator lifted you to the top and shwoosh — you came down at a twenty-five degree angle into the pond where, of course, everyone would scream. It was great on a hot summer day with the cool water spraying on you. I guess it seems kind of corny by today's entertainment standards.

The Caterpillar was a round, circular-shaped ride with small cars that were all connected together. It would roll around a track with small hills and gradually a covering would come over you, like a convertible car top. Eventually this shell totally covered the car and it looked like a caterpillar. Finally, it would slow down and the top would come off, and it was over. It was a pretty good ride. It was fun, and smelly, from all the grease, and made lots of noise from the clattering gears.

Then there was the Mill and the Floss, which was a ride through water on a slow moving boat, sort of like a love boat. These were long boats that weren't just for one or two people. It was a more relaxing ride through slow moving waters that you could go on with your parents or a date.

We always finished the circuit at the Pair-O-Chutes ride. Generally, by the time we got there it was getting late in the day, and we had probably spent most of our money. The Pair-O-Chutes was on a big, tall tower with arms that stuck out of the sides. There were two to a seat, and you'd get hauled up very slowly to the top of the tower. When you hit the top — bang! It was automatic — it would open up the chute and you'd come flying down really fast. It was a gorgeous ride, because on a clear day you could see all over the city, for miles and miles around. I wish I would have taken my camera with me, because it was a magnificent view. That was the thrill of the day, and it was the last ride of the day for us.

Riverview Scout, Riverview Amusement Park, 1948. North Center

dance floor. Charlie Barnet played and we would sway while we listened to the band. We had a great time! The entire night cost me a dollar, and then Alberta took me home in her mother's 1938 black Ford. It was a great date, a great time, and it was cheap!

"The Aragon and the Trianon were the most beautiful ballrooms in the city. I went to the Aragon more than the Trianon, which was on 62nd and Cottage Grove. The Aragon was on the North Side, at Lawrence and Broadway, and was closer to us. We liked Dick Jergen and he was featured a lot there with Eddie Howard. I think that the place opened in 1923, and the Paul Whiteman Orchestra was the first to perform there. At that time, only society people went there, sometimes in carriages drawn by horses. Another beautiful place was the Rialto Theater, at State and Van Buren. It was one of the most popular burlesque shows in Chicago, and for a while, the only one outside of New York. They had big name acts and some great comedians started at the Rialto, including Ada Leonard who led an all-girl orchestra. She was one of my favorites. We also saw famous strippers there, and they would have hawkers during intermission, including some who would walk down the aisles selling Cracker Jack. There were also smaller burlesque shows in that area, including the Gym — that only cost a dime to get in. It was a very sleazy place and they didn't have any good headliners. A lot of bums would go in there to sleep since it was so cheap to get in."

Riverview Park

By the 1940s, Riverview Amusement Park was the only one of its kind in Chicago. White City on the South Side burned down in the '30s, and except for the neighborhood carnivals and amusement fairs, Riverview was the only place to go for rides and attractions. Originally built as a gun club in 1904, the owners began adding rides and amusements to quiet the complaints of the shooters' wives and children. Eventually, it grew to include over 30 rides, a midway, and even the Riverview Ballroom, a popular spot for dancing during the war years. It was truly a memorable experience to go to Riverview.

Howard Rosen remembers going to Riverview to celebrate graduation from grammar school. "Riverview was a major part of the lives of kids growing up in my era. My father could afford to take us there because they used to have 'two cents day.' You could go on just about any ride for $.02. I remember that the big deal was the Bobs and the Blue Streak, but the Bobs was the favorite. I remember on the night of my graduation in '43, I did something that my father would never allow me to do — go on the parachute ride. You would sit down and get harnessed in, then it would go way up in the air until it hit a release — then you were free-falling. Apparently it was a very safe ride."

Sam Carl
Albany Park

I started working at Riverview Park in 1946 when I was fifteen years old. I started working there as an extra, and that meant that you would wait in front of the park and a guy would call out your name and then you would be assigned to a different ride each day. As an extra, you would get a uniform that you would put on over your street clothes. At the end of the week, you would go and collect your little envelope that had cash in it. I worked on various rides, and eventually worked on almost every ride in the park. I worked on the roller coasters, and would take tickets and help people off the rides. Some days there was no work. We would stay by the corner with a bunch of guys, and they would call out names and if you weren't called, you would go home.

Mondays, Wednesdays and Fridays at Riverview were two-cent days. So you could get into the park for $.02, and many of the rides cost $.02 during the daytime, and they were $.05 or $.10 at night. Tuesdays and Thursdays were nickel days. It was always a very busy place with big crowds.

One summer, when I was in high school, I worked there as a boatman and would take the boats down the Shoot the Chutes. I would steer the boats from the back by controlling the rudder, and leaned with my weight. The water would splash when the boat hit the water at the bottom of the ride. It was a great ride! On Thursdays, we used to test the rides for an hour, so they would give us $.50 extra. I did that for a whole summer.

I always liked basketball and I always played whenever I could. So, on my breaks, I would go over to the basketball concession and shoot baskets. I became very friendly with the guys who operated that concession. The following year, after working at the park for about three years on the rides, I worked the basketball concession and, eventually, in the early 1950s, I took over the concession. I didn't own it, but managed it. I went on to the University of Iowa for one year on a basketball scholarship, but I broke my foot, and then I came back to Chicago and went to Wright Junior College.

Riverview Chutes, Riverview Amusement Park, 1948. North Center

Joel Weisman grew up in Albany Park and remembers going to Riverview Park a lot. "My sister had tuberculosis and my mother used to take us on the streetcar to a public health clinic, and we had to take the Western Avenue streetcar. So, every time we would come back from the clinic, we would go to Riverview at Western and Belmont. I knew every single ride, including the roller coasters, the Bobs, the Silver Flash, the Blue Flash, the Greyhound, and the Comet. I remember the Shoot The Chutes, Aladdin's Castle, the Freak Show, the Caterpillar, the Whip, and the Tunnel of Love, as well as the Merry-Go-Round. I loved going there when I was growing up."

Joseph Lamendella lived in Ravenswood in the 1940s. "I started going to Riverview as a child. I went there on penny nights, free nights and nickel nights. I probably went to Riverview from the time I was eight until I was a teenager, when I would cut classes at Lane Tech to ogle the girls who were part of the "come-on" in the Freak Show. I never went into the Freak Show, I just looked at the pretty girls outside. Being a coward, and knowing the kid who was killed on the Bobs by standing up at the top, I rode the Greyhound, which was kind of the sissy roller coaster. Once, perhaps, in bravery, I think I rode the Silver Streak. I do remember that next to Aladdin's Castle, which was a popular place, there was a mentalist named Lady Nina. I would stand there and watch her very carefully with the audience. I was convinced that she had to be given some clues. I thought that her assistant might approach people beforehand and to get clues. I would stand for hours trying to figure out the angle, but I was never successful."

The Arrival of Television

Although television did not have its spectacular growth until the 1950s, there were some Chicagoans who owned televisions in the late 1940s. The new medium would have a tremendous impact on the daily lives and overall entertainment habits of neighborhood residents. Most importantly, television altered the way Chicagoans spent their evenings, causing a drastic reduction in attendance at movie theaters, restaurants and clubs, and reducing interactions among neighbors since they remained indoors.

When television sets were first arriving in the neighborhoods many residents were unsure if there would be long-term health risks. Norman Mark remembers the rules his parents established in the house when they bought their first television. "My parents didn't want television because they were sure that it was going to ruin our eyes. But, finally, they decided to get one because we had neighbors who had one. However, the deal was that you had to sit back one foot for every inch of the screen. I recall that we bought a 12" or 14" television, so according to the rules I was supposed to sit 12' to 14' away from the set. Of course, since we had a 12' living room I would have had to almost sit in another room."

Albany Park resident Marvin Aspen recalls the beginning of the television era in his neighborhood. "I remember that 1948 was a very important year because that was when television became available. My first memory of television was going to the home of Bobbi Terry, a girl in my class whose father owned the Terry Cigar Store on Kedzie, just south of Lawrence. Her father had done very well in the cigar business and they had the first television set in the neighborhood. It was a DuMont television with a small, round screen inside a big console. It looked like a window in a washing machine. A group of about twenty of us kids would go over to her house to watch television that, of course, was only black and white in those days. In the late 1940s, I recall watching Dave Garroway doing a program from the roof of the Merchandise Mart before he went to New York. I only remember seeing local programs back then. Television was a major change in our lives."

Finally, Tom Hynes recalls how the availability of television changed life in his Gresham neighborhood in the late 1940s. "There are so many conveniences that people now take for granted that didn't exist prior to 1945. Even if they had been invented, everything went to the war effort. After 1945, there was a boom in the production of consumer goods, including air conditioners and televisions. I remember the first television set that appeared on our block was a small DuMont with a 7" screen and a rabbit ears antenna that sat on top of the set. My buddy's parents bought it because they were the wealthiest people on the block, and it got to the point where everybody would be over there watching shows and old movies that they would never have gone to the theater to see. They would also watch Friday night wrestling with people like Chief Don Eagle and Gorgeous George. They would turn out all the lights because the screen was so small that it was the only way to see the picture. Everyone would sit there and watch those programs and appear to be enthralled by what was on television. Of course, within a few years, we got our own television set and soon watching television became the number one thing for everyone to do. Television totally became the center of family entertainment by the end of the 1940s. I think it was probably the worst thing that happened to the intellectual growth of America."

Index

Opposite: *Patron, Chicago Public Library, Legler Branch, ca. 1944.* West Garfield Park (Courtesy of Special Collections and Preservation Division, Chicago Public Library.)

Photograph Index

Interviewee Index

Page 208: *Pushball Contestants, Loyola University, 1946.* Rogers Park (Courtesy of the Rogers Park/West Ridge Historical Society.)

Poster Contest, 1945. South Chicago (Courtesy of Special Collections and Preservation Division, Chicago Public Library.)